Joe Rochefort's War

Courtesy Janet Rochefort Elerding

Joe Rochefort's War

The Odyssey of the Codebreaker
Who Outwitted Yamamoto at Midway

ELLIOT CARLSON

NAVAL INSTITUTE PRESS
Annapolis, Maryland

*This book has been brought to publication with the
generous assistance of Joyce I. and Edward S. Miller
and Marguerite and Gerry Lenfest.*

Naval Institute Press
291 Wood Road
Annapolis, MD 21402

First Naval Institute Press paperback edition published in 2013.
ISBN 978-1-59114-161-7

The Library of Congress has cataloged the hardcover edition as follows:
Carlson, Elliot,
  Joe Rochefort's war : the odyssey of the codebreaker who outwitted Yamamoto at
Midway / Elliot Carlson.
     p. cm.
  Includes bibliographical references and index.
  ISBN 978-1-61251-060-6 (hbk. : alk. paper) 1. Rochefort, Joe, 1900–1976. 2.
Midway, Battle of, 1942. 3. Cryptographers—United States—Biography. 4. United
States. Navy—Officers—Biography. 5. World War, 1939–1945—Cryptography.
6. World War, 1939–1945—Electronic intelligence. 7. World War, 1939–1945—
Military intelligence—United States. 8. World War, 1939–1945—Naval operations,
American. 9. World War, 1939–1945—Naval operations, Japanese. I. Title.
  D774.M5C28 2011
  940.54'8673092—dc23
  [B]
                                                        2011025666

♾ This paper meets the requirements of ANSI/NISO z39.48-1992
(Permanence of Paper).
Printed in the United States of America.

20 19 18 17 16 15 14 13   9 8 7 6 5 4 3 2 1
First printing

To the officers and men
who served in
Joe Rochefort's basement

"To Commander Joe Rochefort must forever go the acclaim for having made more difference, at a more important time, than any other naval officer in history."

—Captain Edward L. Beach, USN (Ret.)
The United States Navy: 200 Years

Contents

Foreword

This book is an account that is long overdue. Joseph J. Rochefort was a singular player on the world scene in the early months of the Second World War, but his major accomplishments at that time became buried in a cloak of security and unjustified criticism. Chief among his achievements was the crucial role he played in the stunning American victory in the Battle of Midway, although his contribution would remain unappreciated for decades, even after his death.

As a Naval Reserve ensign, I was an analyst assigned to Rochefort's Combat Intelligence Unit (CIU) at Pearl Harbor in February 1942, and I can attest to the validity of both his stellar successes then as well as his occasional questionable actions. Joe Rochefort was a complicated naval officer in a manner that can be properly understood only by looking at his entire life, now revealed for the first time in this book. From humble beginnings, he was attracted to the Navy in the immediate aftermath of World War I. He enlisted at the age of seventeen, thanks to a little imagination regarding his date of birth. His enlisted service demonstrated that he possessed latent intellect and capabilities that ultimately led to an officer's commission without the benefit of having graduated from the Naval Academy. As the reader will see, some of that background served to haunt him for much of his career despite his brilliant service to the Navy and the nation.

The highlight of Rochefort's career was his amazing thoroughness in identifying, interpreting, and reporting to Admiral Chester W. Nimitz the Japanese plans to assault and capture Midway Atoll. The enemy saw Midway as the first step in defeating the U.S. fleet and eventually removing the threat of the

U.S. naval base at Pearl Harbor. That Rochefort provided such critical intelligence accurately and in time for Admiral Nimitz to organize and deploy a credible defense made the difference between our forces participating in the Battle of Midway and not even knowing that the Japanese were headed there. Clearly Rochefort's work enabled the victory at Midway, but his contribution to the battle, as well as the impact on history of the battle itself, are still being debated today.

Rochefort's detractors outnumbered his supporters, and they held higher positions in the Navy's hierarchy, resulting in occasionally unjust treatment as the years and his career progressed. But he never displayed any sense of defeat or disappointment over the consequences of such treatment. His first loyalty was to the Navy, and he accepted his fate as it arose, continuing to carry out his duties with enthusiasm and distinction wherever he was assigned. In all respects he was a leader who was held in high regard by his subordinates. I'm honored to have been included among them.

My experiences during that early and critical period of the war are clearly the most memorable of my forty-two years of service to the intelligence arms of the Navy and the federal government. Although my personal contact with Commander Rochefort was limited at the time, I had an opportunity to observe him on a daily basis, plus I was able to learn more about him from his friend and former fleet intelligence officer Edwin Layton. I still regard Rochefort, Layton, and Jasper Holmes, one of Rochefort's top analysts at the CIU, as my primary mentors and the ones who most influenced my decision for a career in naval intelligence.

As you will read toward the end of this book, a great American president cited Rochefort for inclusion among a few who individually made a difference in the outcome of a history-changing battle. That puts him in lofty company, with men like Themistocles at Salamis, Admiral de Grasse in the Chesapeake Bay, and Colonel Joshua Chamberlain at Little Round Top. But Rochefort stands out even among that noble company, for he achieved his triumph without ever firing a shot or even coming within sight of the enemy.

With the long-suppressed facts of his life masterfully revealed on these pages by Elliot Carlson, the full and factual story of Joseph Rochefort can now be known.

REAR ADMIRAL DONALD "MAC" SHOWERS,
U.S. NAVY (RETIRED)

Acknowledgments

This is a reporter's book, and a reporter's work is only as good as his sources. For this work I was blessed with extraordinary sources—many individuals who provided invaluable assistance during the six years I needed to research and write Joe Rochefort's story. Without their knowledge, goodwill, and selfless aid, this book would never have materialized.

I am indebted first and foremost to Joe Rochefort's daughter, Janet Rochefort Elerding. She invited me into her lovely home in Newport Beach, California, consented to the first of what would be numerous interviews and phone conversations, provided access to Joe's service record and few remaining papers, loaned me never-before-seen photos of Joe, and, of incalculable importance, furnished crucial details about her father's life.

I also benefitted from an interview with another Rochefort family member, Karen Rochefort Ballew, the daughter of Joe's son, the late Colonel Joseph Rochefort Jr. and his wife Elinore Mae, of San Diego. Ms. Ballew provided many interesting vignettes about her grandfather.

Of all the individuals interviewed for this book, none was more generous with his time and more unstinting in his support than Rear Admiral Donald M. "Mac" Showers, one of probably no more than two officers from Rochefort's Station Hypo unit at Pearl Harbor known to be still living. From spring 2004 through summer 2010, Mac granted me more than forty interviews at his Arlington, Virginia, apartment. Our talks covered every conceivable Navy subject, from Joe's personality and character to the nitty-gritty of code-breaking.

If Mac transported me into Rochefort's basement hideaway at Pearl circa 1942, Daniel A. Martinez, National Park Service Historian, USS *Arizona* Memorial, showed me what that room looks like today. In two separate trips to Hawaii, Daniel accorded me grand tours of Pearl Harbor that culminated in Joe's basement, now an abandoned storeroom littered with debris. Daniel's recollections of meeting Rochefort years earlier as a teenager made an indelible impression on me.

In addition to Mac Showers, I located sixteen other survivors from Rochefort's decrypt and radio intercept units on Oahu and elsewhere in the Pacific during 1941–42. Captain Forrest R. "Tex" Biard, now deceased, is well known to many. Several of the enlisted men—Mike Palchefsky, Ferdinand Johnson, James B. Capron Jr., and Harold Joslin—provided rich portraits of Rochefort's secret space at Pearl and the Navy's intercept operations on Oahu and Guam. (A list of the names of these gentlemen can be found in the bibliography under the heading Author's Interviews.)

Philip H. Jacobsen, a onetime enlisted man, took special pains to instruct me in the finer points of codebreaking. Phil served as an intercept operator at Wahiawa in central Oahu (Station H) in the weeks leading up to the Battle of Midway. After retiring in 1969 as a lieutenant commander and an expert in communications intelligence, Phil went on to become one of the leading writers dedicated to rebutting the current crop of revisionist theories concerning Pearl Harbor. During spring 2006 he sent me no fewer than fifty emails explaining arcane aspects of comint. Our meeting at his home in San Diego in late summer 2006, shortly before his death, is a memorable one for me.

Invaluable assistance was rendered by the volunteer leaders of the Naval Cryptologic Veterans Association, a nonprofit group based in Pensacola, Florida, consisting of about 3,200 active and retired Navy radiomen and cryptologists. Led by executive director Robert H. Anderson III, these gentlemen welcomed me into their headquarters, gave me the run of their library, and submitted to interviews on the intricacies of radio intelligence. Among others, John Gustafson, Jay Browne, and William Lockert gave me a feel for radio intercept work that I could not have gotten anywhere else.

None of these meetings in Pensacola, Pearl Harbor, Arlington, San Diego, and elsewhere would have happened without pointers, tips and suggestions from a number of very well-informed individuals. Naval historian Paul Stillwell met with me as I was getting under way. Paul opened up his Rolodex and ticked off the names of many key individuals in the history community who proved indispensable.

I also received wise counsel from prominent naval historian Edward S. Miller, who provided a sharp-eyed critique, as well as encouragement, after reading four draft chapters. David Kahn, dean of historians of the art and science of cryptanalysis, provided good advice, as did Raymond P. Schmidt, former historian of the Naval Security Group, and Donald M. Goldstein, former professor of international affairs at the University of Pittsburgh.

I am especially grateful to three reviewers who read the final draft. Two of them, the aforementioned Paul Stillwell and Ronald W. Russell, author and moderator-webmaster of the Battle of Midway Roundtable, helped as historical analysts and technical advisers on a wide range of issues from Navy hardware to terminology. Robert J. Hanyok, former senior historian at the Center for Cryptologic History, National Security Agency, provided essential guidance on issues related to cryptanalysis and communications intelligence. He consented to many interviews and shared materials concerned with Pearl Harbor and Midway. I am indebted to all three individuals for their historical insights as well as the many improvements they made in the manuscript.

Numerous experts in cryptology deepened my knowledge of comint. They include David Hatch, historian and technical director of the Center for Cryptologic History, National Security Agency (NSA); Jack E. Ingram, former director of the National Cryptologic Museum, Fort Meade, Maryland; John Schindler; Henry Schorreck (now deceased); and Frederick D. Parker, author of two landmark monographs on the role of codebreaking during the Pearl Harbor and Midway campaigns.

In either face-to-face meetings or phone interviews, others gave generously of their time. Pacific War historian John Lundstrom furnished perspective and insights and pointed me toward files at the National Archives II facility in College Park, Maryland, that I might otherwise have missed. Robert W. Love Jr., professor of history at the U.S. Naval Academy, shared his legendary knowledge of Commander in Chief, U.S. Fleet, Admiral Ernest J. King. J. Michael Wenger provided transcripts of crucial interviews with Japanese intelligence officers from the voluminous files of Gordon W. Prange at the University of Maryland.

In his office at George Washington University's history department, Ronald H. Spector analyzed the problems faced by mustangs—the Navy's slang word for commissioned officers such as Rochefort who rose up through the ranks. While passing through the Washington area, John R. Ferris, professor of history at the University of Calgary and an authority on World War II intelligence, found time to discuss the impact of intelligence during the Battle of Midway.

Midway historian Jon Parshall put me in touch with Captain Noritaka Kitazawa of the National Institute for Defense Studies in Tokyo. Kitazawa shipped me Japanese navy documents describing Admiral Isoroku Yamamoto's use of radio deception during the weeks before the Pearl Harbor attack. Another Institute researcher, Ken Kotani, emailed information amplifying on that provided by Captain Kitazawa.

Close relatives of several cryptanalysts and linguists assigned to Rochefort contributed valuable information. Ann L. Dyer, daughter of Station Hypo cryptanalyst Tommy Dyer, consented to an interview and made available her father's personal papers. Gregory A. Finnegan, son of Hypo linguist Joe Finnegan, provided part of his father's oral history, the bulk of which years earlier had been classified by NSA. Through a request filed under the Freedom of Information Act, I received a larger portion of it. The family of another Hypo linguist, Alva B. "Red" Lasswell, also was generous. From her home in San Diego, Jennifer Lasswell Albers mailed a copy of her grandfather's World War II memoir and a trove of marvelous Hypo-era photos of Red and some of his fellow officers.

Local historians, church officials, and school administrators provided details of the Rochefort family and Joe's youth. Drawing on his huge collection of city directories of London, Ontario, Canada, Daniel Brock traced the early work history, and marriage of Joe's parents, Frank and Ellen Rochefort. Bill Markley of the Ohio Historical Society tracked the family in Dayton from 1891 to 1911. Lynne Davenport, parish secretary of St. Joseph's Church in Dayton, provided Joe's baptismal papers establishing his birth as 12 May 1900 (no birth certificate was ever filed). In California, Margaret Chirivella at the Archdiocese of Los Angeles helped me search for Joe's elementary school. Sheri J. Lopez at John H. Francis Polytechnic High School welcomed me and unearthed the school's newspapers and yearbooks for the years Joe attended.

Most of the documents used for this book reside at three sites of the National Archives. At the Archives II I benefitted from the assistance of Barry Zerby and Patrick Osborne. Rebecca A. Livingston solved my archival problems at Archives I in downtown Washington, D.C. Robert E. Glass did the same at the Archives' Pacific Region branch in San Bruno, California, setting before me more than forty boxes of material.

My home away from home for many years were the weathered buildings of the Naval History and Heritage Command (NHHC) at the Washington Navy Yard. There I received invaluable assistance from Rear Admiral Paul E. Tobin during his brief tenure as director of history. At NHHC's Operational Archives Branch, I was ably aided by branch head Curtis Utz; his predecessor, Kathleen M. Lloyd; and their exceedingly helpful archivists, Michael Walker, Timothy Pettit, and John Hodges. Two flights of stairs below them, at the Navy Department Library I found many of the cryptologic documents I needed, invariably receiving cheerful and uncomplaining help from library head Glenn E. Helm and his capable staff, J. Allen Knechtmann, Linda Edwards, and David Elliott.

At the Naval War College in Newport, Rhode Island, Evelyn Cherpak guided me to the papers of Edwin T. Layton. At the American Heritage Center at the University of Wyoming-Laramie, Carol L. Bowers and Shannon Bowen Maier helped me tap the papers of C. C. Hiles, Laurance Safford, Clay Blair, and Husband E. Kimmel. David M. Hays, archivist at the University of Colorado at Boulder, went out of his way to make available the papers of William J. Hudson and Roger Pineau. I also received timely assistance from librarians Rowena Clough and her successor, Rene Stein, at the National Cryptologic Museum at Fort Meade, Maryland; Helen B. McDonald, program director, National Museum of the Pacific War (Fredericksburg, Texas); James F. Cartwright, special collections archivist, University of Hawaii-Honolulu; and Jennie A. Levine, curator for historical manuscripts at the University of Maryland, College Park.

Other individuals assisted in various ways: Arthur David Baker III; Jeffrey G. Barlow (NHHC); John and Patricia Barry; Colin Burke; Richard Carlson (NCVA); Captain Frank L. DeLorenzo, U.S. Navy (recently deceased); Walt Duka; Gerry Fallon; Bill Ferguson; Dave Gaddy; Joe Glockner; Jack Green; Jon Houp; Daniel O. Jones (NHHC); Graydon Lewis (NCVA); Edward J. Marolda (NHHC); Captain George McGinnis, U.S. Navy (Retired); Doris Oliver (Stevens Institute of Technology); Robert R. Payne (editor of NCVA's *Cryptolog*); Norman Polmar; John Prados; William Price; John Reshoft; Rika Seya (translator, George Washington University); Sister Patricia Rose Shanahan; Richard Slonim; Skipper Steely; Robert G. Summers; Craig Symonds; Mark Wanamaker; and Thomas Wildenberg. Captain DeLorenzo was one of five pilots who flew Admiral Nimitz to Pearl Harbor on Christmas Day in 1941.

At the Naval Institute Press, I'm indebted to its director, Rick Russell, who recognized the importance of Joe Rochefort and encouraged me in writing this biography. I also want to thank members of Rick's staff who helped transform my text into a book. Susan Corrado, Emily Bakely, George Keating, and Judy Heise adroitly guided its pages from manuscript to print and into the marketplace. I'm especially grateful to my editor, Annie Rehill, who combined editorial prowess with extraordinary patience in helping me bring this project to a successful completion.

My wife, Norma, joined me as a co-researcher at the National Archives as well as on many trips I took around the country. She reviewed each of several drafts of the Rochefort manuscript and made many important criticisms and observations. She also gave me unsparing encouragement, realizing how important it was for me to write Joe Rochefort's story.

If I missed mentioning anyone, this does not lessen my appreciation for the help.

Introduction

The Riddle of Joe Rochefort

Rochefort is caustic, witty, unorthodox, tactless, intolerant,
blunt but quick, intimate and brilliant.[1]
—Walter Lord

In spring 1942, Commander Joe Rochefort, America's lead cryptanalyst
at Pearl Harbor, appeared to be one of the rising stars in the U.S. Navy.
Just about everybody who knew this bright, sharp-edged, competent officer
believed he was headed for the highest rungs on the Navy ladder, almost certainly flag rank. It was just a matter of time.

Rochefort himself had every reason to feel confident about the direction
of his Navy career. He had just earned the gratitude of Admiral Chester W.
Nimitz, commander in chief, U.S. Pacific Fleet, for his role in the Battle of
Midway, which lasted 4–7 June. Rochefort headed the unusual group of codebreakers that had cracked the Imperial Japanese Navy's operational code just
prior to the battle. That coup fixed the two small islands of the Midway Atoll
as the probable target of Admiral Isoroku Yamamoto's impending campaign
in the central Pacific.

Not all Navy leaders accepted Rochefort's forecast. Many in Washington,
along with some of the U.S. Army's top brass, flatly rejected it, doubting Yamamoto would amass so large a force to seize a mere atoll of dubious strategic
value. But Nimitz went along with Rochefort. He put his carriers in a place
where they could surprise the sizable Japanese armada bearing down on Midway. They did so and achieved a stunning naval victory—an outcome that,

some writers maintained, turned the tide of war against Japan in the Pacific. Nimitz credited Rochefort, in part, for that success, and recommended him for a Distinguished Service Medal (DSM).

But in the summer and fall of 1942, something happened to Rochefort's career. Late in June, for reasons that didn't seem clear, Admiral Ernest J. King, commander in chief, U.S. Fleet, denied Rochefort the DSM. Four months later, in October, King approved a plan shaped by Rochefort's Washington bosses— Rear Admiral Joseph Redman and his brother, Captain John Redman—to oust Rochefort from his job running the Navy's codebreaking unit at Pearl.

Suddenly Rochefort was gone. Many people wondered what had happened to him. Members of his decrypt team were especially puzzled. They couldn't square the news of his expulsion with the Joe Rochefort they had served for seventeen months in a dank basement at Pearl—the top secret hideaway where they carried out their codebreaking effort. In that stuffy and frequently chilly haunt, they had come to know Rochefort as an exceptional individual—a tall, slender, taciturn officer who spoke quietly but knowingly, radiating authority and his own distinct brand of bemused seriousness. People liked being around him to soak up his smarts.

True, he had his peculiarities, chief among them a capacity for irreverence, sarcasm, and blunt speech that astonished even his closest friends. Still, given his quick mind, obvious leadership abilities, and masterful performance during the weeks leading up to Midway, they regarded him as an officer on the way up, certainly not a candidate for misfortune. There did not seem to be an explanation for what had happened.

From what Rochefort's friends believed, and even Rochefort himself, Admiral King had been influenced by officers around him who were part of an anti-Rochefort cabal, led by the Redman brothers. They had clashed with Rochefort over Japan's target before the Battle of Midway and were said to be motivated by jealousy and revenge when Rochefort's prediction held up.

Adding another layer of interest to the drama was Rochefort's status as a mustang—Navy slang for an officer who rose up the Navy ladder from enlisted ranks, not the Naval Academy. He wasn't part of the Annapolis club. He didn't have friends in high places.

Rochefort's downfall had all the makings of a great saga. After the war, bits and pieces of the story started to make their way into print, albeit slowly. In one of the first detailed accounts of the Battle of Midway, appearing in the

26 March 1949 issue of the *Saturday Evening Post*, writer J. Bryan III called attention to the cryptanalytic prowess of "a smart young officer, Cmdr. Joseph J. Rochefort," who confirmed Midway as Yamamoto's target ("Never a Battle Like Midway"). More narratives were on the way.

A milestone in the story occurred in 1967, when Walter Lord published his lively, groundbreaking book on Midway, *Incredible Victory*. Lord captured Rochefort breaking codes in his Pearl Harbor basement work area—a shambles of a place cluttered by stacks of folders and papers. "Presiding over it all was a tall, thin, humorously caustic man in a red smoking jacket and carpet slippers—Commander Joseph J. Rochefort, Jr."[2] Lord's version served as a kind of template for future Rochefort accounts.

The saga evolved into a morality tale complete with good guys and bad guys, the bad being the people who engineered the commander's sudden banishment from Pearl Harbor. In his 1985 Pacific War memoir *And I Was There*, written by Rochefort's friend Rear Admiral Edwin T. Layton, with help from coauthors John Costello and Captain Roger Pineau, U.S. Naval Reserve (Retired), Rochefort is depicted as a gifted codebreaker martyred on the anvil of World War II Navy politics.[3] Rochefort now became a legend, very nearly a figure of myth.

As his story continued to unfold and accounts multiplied, Rochefort was invariably "brilliant," if not actually a "genius." He was "the dean of the Navy's cryptanalysts," blessed with "a superlative memory for detail and a deep intuitive knowledge built up over years of studying Japanese naval operations." Not only that, "His colleagues considered him the finest cryptanalyst in the entire Navy."[4]

Yes, he had blemishes, but they were really functions of his virtues. They were what you would expect of an eccentric genius. "He was quirky, touchy, a difficult customer," said one writer. He could be "arrogant and irascible," added another. And he was also an "idiosyncratic but scintillating cryptanalyst." To be sure, he had a weakness for "caustic speech." After all, he "was somewhat of a maverick."[5]

Separating myth from reality has never been easy with Rochefort. Too many people liked the legend. And Rochefort, for his part, complicated the search for reality by his own contrariness. He could be many things at once. Were they all real? Was he, for example, the dean of Navy cryptanalysts?

Rochefort certainly learned, and practiced, cryptanalysis in Washington from 1925 to 1927. But for the next fourteen years—from 1927 to 1941—he stayed as far away from cryptanalysis as he could get. He didn't look at another Japanese code until 1941 when, with war rapidly approaching, he agreed to head the Navy's codebreaking unit at Pearl Harbor. He hardly qualified as the dean of Navy cryptanalysts.

Was he a maverick—an independent officer who didn't go along with the group? Rochefort did indeed display intellectual independence. He was inclined to speak his mind even when it would have been to his advantage to shut up. But if a maverick is someone inclined to go his own way at whatever cost, the vast majority of captains and admirals under whom he served didn't think so. Fitness reports described him repeatedly as "an officer of excellent personal and military character."[6]

And when, after the war, he was asked why he hadn't written a book about his travails with his Washington bosses, the people who had derailed his career, Rochefort didn't hold back: "I [did] not see that this would be to the advantage of the Navy."[7] He may not have been an Annapolis man, but he was a Navy man. Some maverick.

The fantasizing got out of hand in 1976 when the actor Hal Holbrook, in the blockbuster movie *Midway*, portrayed Rochefort as a sort of clown—an officer who ambled about sloppily dressed in a red smock, spoke with a folksy twang and, when he wasn't puffing on a cigar and making wisecracks, rode around in a jeep with Admiral Nimitz.

What Rochefort thought of Holbrook's portrayal would never be known. He didn't live long enough to say. Having served as a consultant on the movie, Rochefort died 20 July 1976, in Torrance, California, shortly after *Midway* was released. His friends, however, were outraged. Yes, Rochefort wore a burgundy corduroy smoking jacket in his work area, but he did so for good reasons: a cold, clammy basement habitat. "Everyone who spent hours on end in that environment had to add clothing for comfort," declared Rear Admiral Donald "Mac" Showers, U.S. Navy (Retired), who served in Rochefort's unit in 1942. Holbrook's characterization "could not have been more completely opposite Rochefort's true personality. The mustachioed, cigar-smoking, loud-mouth, red-neck type portrayed by Hal Holbrook was totally out of character. Joe Rochefort was clean-shaven, occasionally smoked a pipe at his desk, was quiet-mannered and soft-spoken, a gentleman in all respects."[8]

Given the mythology surrounding his career, it would be easy to lose sight of the fact that Rochefort was a real officer who did real things at Pearl Harbor. True, he didn't do everything by himself. Or everything people said he did. The intelligence developed at Pearl Harbor was the work of many, not just Rochefort. And he didn't operate strictly as a cryptanalyst, or codebreaker, as portrayed in most accounts. Others did that work.

All that being said, it would be hard, if not impossible, to envision the Battle of Midway unfolding as it did without the involvement of Joe Rochefort. He was easily the most consequential shore-based actor in the Midway drama. As the head of Pearl's decrypt unit, he used his knowledge of the Japanese language and the tools of cryptology and radio intelligence to establish first, through consensus with his analysts, the target of the Japanese attack. Then he used the moral authority of his position to make that estimate stick with the officer who mattered most: Admiral Nimitz.

And when doubters in both the Army and Navy challenged his Midway theory, Rochefort, again with help from his team, contrived what still stands as the one of the supreme intelligence moments of World War II: an ingenious radio gimmick that tricked the Japanese into betraying Midway as the object of their impending campaign. Historian David M. Kennedy called this stroke "the single most valuable intelligence contribution of the entire Pacific War."[9]

Remarkable as his work might have seemed, it wasn't enough. Not only did Admiral King veto his medal, but he stymied his subsequent naval career as well. Questions arise. What was going on in Washington to bring about such decisions? Was Rochefort, in truth, a victim of scheming by the Redman brothers? Were they really all that jealous? Or did Rochefort exacerbate an already delicate situation? Did he use the word "clowns" once too often in dealing with his Washington adversaries? Was he an accomplice in his own downfall?

Rochefort was indeed "a difficult customer," as one writer aptly described him.[10] An exploration of his life and naval career reveals an officer as puzzling as the codes he tried to break. Intentionally or not, he didn't make the researcher's job easy. He left few footprints as he moved through life. Always the intelligence officer, he continued to cover his tracks in retirement. Late in life he destroyed his family letters, eliminating any record of his wartime correspondence with his wife, Fay, and other family members.

Much to the unhappiness of postwar writers who wanted to tap into his knowledge of Pearl Harbor and Midway, he did the same thing to nearly all of his Navy papers. "The great tragedy is that in a fit of something or other he destroyed all his papers some time back," the revisionist historian Harry Elmer Barnes wrote a colleague in 1962.[11] Rochefort left only a small box containing little more than his Navy personnel records and a few Navy memoranda of special interest to him.[12]

As a result, a certain amount of mystery has always surrounded the life and career of Joe Rochefort. Many questions persist about things that happened and things that Rochefort did or failed to do. With the help of Rochefort's few papers, the records of many archives and libraries, and interviews with historians, family members, and some Navy colleagues who survived him, I have done my best to solve as much of the Rochefort puzzle as possible. The questions with which I was obsessed are, by now, probably those engrossing the reader: What led Rochefort to the Navy? Did his mustang status hurt his career? What attracted him to, then turned him away from cryptanalysis? At Pearl Harbor, could Rochefort have done more to warn Kimmel? What part did he play in breaking the Japanese naval code, and in identifying Midway as Japan's target in spring 1942?

And, of course, the granddaddy of all questions: Did Rochefort deserve the DSM that he did not receive in 1942, but was awarded posthumously in 1986? Was Nimitz right about Rochefort, or was King? Did Rochefort's brusque, gloves-off style estrange his superiors in Washington? Just who was Joe Rochefort?

1

Trolley to San Pedro

I wanted to be an aviator, a naval aviator. I had a
very high regard for these people.

—Joe Rochefort

Joseph John Rochefort entered the world on 12 May 1900, the youngest
of seven children born to Irish parents, Francis John and Ellen Rochefort of
Dayton, Ohio. Francis, known as Frank, and Ellen were not stay-at-homes.
Nine years earlier they had moved their growing family from London, Ontario,
three hundred miles across the border in Canada, where, sometime in the early
1880s, the two had met.

Born in Dublin on 2 February 1852, Frank was something of a wanderer.
Why he decided to leave Ireland wasn't recorded in any family history. But
life was hard for many there and may have been so for Frank, the son of a
Catholic pawnbroker.[1] Sizable numbers emigrated to either the United States
or Canada. On 16 July 1875, at age twenty-three, Frank boarded a steamer
that took him to Halifax, Nova Scotia, a major port of entry for Irish im-
migrants.[2]

From there Frank made his way to London, a bustling city of about
30,000 that, while predominantly Protestant, had a sizable Irish Catholic community. He started at the bottom of the economic ladder, working first as a
miller at a grain mill, then tending bar in a hotel in downtown London. There
he met an attractive young woman, Ellen Spearman, an earnest Catholic girl

four years his junior, the daughter of working-class parents who many years earlier had also emigrated from Ireland.[3]

Frank and Ellen fell in love and were married 6 November 1883 at St. Peter's Cathedral in London. They started to raise a large family. Their first-born, Hamilton, arrived in 1884. He was followed by Frank Patrick in 1886, Harold in 1888, and William in 1889. The family moved around a bit, eventually moving to Dayton, Ohio, in 1891. They found themselves in a raw industrial city of 61,000, prospering from textile mills, a tobacco factory, and many small manufacturing firms. Now thirty-nine, Frank returned to one of his old trades: tending bar. He ran a saloon in downtown Dayton, with the whole family living one floor above it.

Always striving to better himself, Frank tried different jobs before finding a vocation at which he excelled, that he liked, and with which he would stick: department store salesman.[4] He moved the clan to a larger house, a modest row house on South Bainbridge Street, in a well-kept working class section of Dayton. The extra space was needed. Margaret, the only daughter in the family, came along in 1895, followed by Charles in 1898. Two years later, at home on Bainbridge Street, Ellen gave birth to Joseph John.[5]

Margaret, Charles, and Joe would make their way across the tracks of the old Dayton Railroad, through open fields to St. Joseph Parish School, where they got their introduction to a formal education. Margaret took hold at this school. Joe did not, later making clear that a parochial education was not for him.

One thing that did capture Joe's imagination had little to do with school or family. It was the presence in Dayton of Orville and Wilbur Wright, whose workshops were just a few miles from the Rochefort home. They had been making headlines since 1903, when, on a windy December day in Kitty Hawk, North Carolina, they had made the first sustained flight in a heavier-than-air machine. The Wrights became instant celebrities as Dayton found itself gripped by an aviation fever that touched young Joe.

Frank, however, was getting restless and again decided on a change of scene. Whether to escape Ohio's bland, sometimes dreary weather or to find better prospects in the West, in 1912 Frank and Ellen herded the children onto a train and took them to Los Angeles.[6]

Their timing was good. They arrived just as the city was starting to boom and fill up with easterners looking for opportunities. Still energetic and confident at fifty-eight, Frank found a job as a salesman in the rug department at Barker Brothers, a quality furniture store in downtown Los Angeles. He moved his wife and children—five sons (Hamilton had relocated to Boston) and a daughter, ranging in age from twelve to twenty-six—into a cheerful bungalow in a fast-growing, middle-class neighborhood in west Los Angeles.[7] Hamilton rejoined the family a few months later in the small stucco home at 2096 West Twenty-Seventh Street.

Everybody worked or went to school. Frank Patrick followed his father into sales. Harold worked as a plumber, William as a silver plater. Margaret found work as a telephone operator. A photographer, Hamilton opened his own studio in downtown Los Angeles.[8] Charles stayed in high school, and Joe neared graduation from St. Vincent's elementary school.[9]

Outwardly, the Rocheforts resembled a family out of a Currier and Ives print. Resolute, forceful, something of a taskmaster, Frank relished his role as patriarch. He joined his equally pleased wife in taking great pride in the family. A photograph of the group, taken about the time they moved into their new home, shows a mustachioed Frank looking a little like William Powell in *Life With Father*, amiable but very much in command. Ellen, determined and elegant, looks protective as she holds her youngest sons, Charles and Joe.

The Rocheforts had high hopes for their children. College was out of the question, with insufficient money, but Frank and Ellen had strong ideas, especially for Joe. They wanted him to become a priest. Joe may not have been as extroverted as his gregarious father, but he had inherited Frank's willfulness and independence. He had no desire to enter the priesthood, an intention he made clear after finishing grammar school, when he asked his parents to let him enter Polytechnic High. This was a nondenominational school in downtown Los Angeles; they agreed.

It was then that Joe started going his own way, leaving his parents wondering where his new path would lead. Even though he resembled his father in some respects, in others he differed profoundly. When he tried his hand at sales one summer, selling magazine subscriptions door to door, the line Joe used became a standing joke in the family: "You wouldn't want to buy a subscription to *The Saturday Evening Post*, would you?"[10] Joe was no salesman.

High school provided few clues as to what direction he would take. Joe was a good student, at times even outstanding, but "genius" or "brilliant" did not apply. He did show a gift for mathematics, getting A's in algebra and trigonometry. But in applied electricity, geometry, physics, and chemistry, he averaged B's. He was terrible in one subject, earning a D in the now rarely used category of deportment.

The reason for this does not appear in school records and is difficult to imagine, given his strict Catholic upbringing. He could be rambunctious; he liked to fire off what people referred to as verbal zingers. But he was never considered mean or unruly. No one who knew Joe Rochefort ever heard him use profanity. "Nerts" was about the worst thing that ever came out of his mouth, said one family member.

If Joe sometimes irritated his teachers with zingers, he also impressed them as a serious, hardworking young man. Yet he did not emerge as a leader, rousing little attention. He engaged in no sports and few activities, although as a junior he did join the Emergency Club, a group created to bring together students who were interested in first aid and nursing. That earned him a picture in the 1917 yearbook.[11]

But the following year, Joe's senior year, the period typically considered a high school student's defining moment, he vanished from the yearbook. He wasn't pictured with the Emergency Club or any other club. Joe was never a joiner, but a likelier explanation was that he had acquired new interests. One was Elma Fay Aery, a pretty brunette at Polytechnic one year behind him. They quietly got to know each other. Joe had one other new thing on his mind, as did the rest of the country. He got caught up in the "news from Europe"—a fascination that began shortly after April 1917, when the United States declared war on Germany.

His brother Frank Patrick, also engrossed by the European War, joined the Army as soon as war was declared. As anti-German feeling mounted and as military recruiters intensified their appeals to young people, a wave of patriotic feeling rippled through Polytechnic High. The school paper, *The Poly Optimist*, launched a war column entitled "From the Front and Elsewhere," filled with vignettes from recent graduates and even students who had quit school to go off to war. One ex-student writing from "Somewhere in Italy" reported: "At last I am what the Italians call a 'Pilota Militaire,'" a status that enabled him to "sport a gold eagle on my chest." As this grad proceeded with his story, it became clear that some of America's young people in Europe weren't only serving their country, they were also managing to have a darn good time.

The Poly Optimist editorialized proudly: "The example set for Polytechnic by those of her students who are offering their lives for the cause of Freedom in the army and navy can not fail to inspire the rest of us, if we are real

Americans, to do what we can, and we can do a lot." Students did a number of things. Some formed themselves into a school-sponsored military battalion that went off to Camp Arcadia on a weeklong bivouac. Others raised money in a "Liberty Loan" drive to help finance the war.[12] And some went further.

⸱⸱▮⸱⸱

The arrival of April 1918 marked twelve months since the United States had joined the Allied coalition in the war against Germany. America's interest in "war news" remained at a fever pitch. Sometimes a development would cheer the entire country, as when Baron A. Manfred von Richthofen, the famed "Red Baron" who had shot down eighty Allied planes during four years of war, was himself killed in a dogfight over France.

But most of the news was grim. In March, the German army launched the first of five major offenses that pushed back Allied forces all along the western front. The U.S. Army, at this stage, had not yet been able to make its presence felt in ground combat. The Navy, in the meantime, was doing what it could to convoy troops to Europe. A development that interested many in California was the Navy's new aviation station in San Diego, set up to train fliers.

Against this background of war-related activity, on 20 April 1918, Joe and a couple of his friends hopped one of Pacific Electric's Red Cars heading south. For a dime, they rode the trolley twenty miles straight into San Pedro, a small community located on San Pedro Bay, where the Navy had established a submarine base and, more recently, a recruiting station. "[With] some of my friends, we all went down and enlisted," Rochefort said later.[13]

The recruiters were no doubt happy to see them. "At a time when judges were still sentencing criminals to rehabilitation by service in the fleet," notes historian James D. Hornfischer, "the Navy would take whatever able-bodied, hardy-souled young men it could find."[14]

But getting into the Navy wasn't just a matter of showing up. A young man had to be eighteen or older; otherwise he needed written parental consent. Joe on 20 April was three weeks short of his eighteenth birthday and did not have parental consent. In all likelihood, the recruiters didn't worry much about the age issue. Joe Rochefort, after all, wasn't the first, nor would he be the last, young man to lie about his age to get into the Army or Navy. With or without the Navy's knowledge, he added an extra year to his age, putting it down as eighteen years and eleven months. He was, he said, born 12 May 1899.[15]

Nine days after enlisting, Joe was called up. He reported to the San Pedro Naval Station for active duty on 8 May, four days before turning eighteen and four weeks before receiving his high school diploma.

He joined "because of the spirit of the times," Joe said later. "Everybody was more or less patriotic." Moreover, he said, he was fascinated—virtually in awe—of fliers, especially naval fliers. "I wanted to be an aviator, a naval aviator," Rochefort recalled. "I had a very high regard for these people, which was, of course, a result of the newspapers, but I never pursued [it]. As I grew up, I forgot that."[16]

Patriotism may not have been the only factor in Joe's decision to sign up. Pressure was building at home. Even though Frank Patrick had joined the Army and Hamilton had returned to the East Coast, the Rocheforts' small stucco home was crowded. By 1918, it still accommodated seven people. "Going into a national war was, for many young men, a relief," observes historian John Lukacs.[17] It may have been so for Joe.

Joe's parents and siblings weren't the only people affected, and possibly troubled, by his sudden departure. There was also Elma Fay Aery, the classmate he had been dating. It is not known what she thought of Joe's enlistment, or what she told him about it. She finished her senior year; the attractive young woman is pictured in the Polytechnic's 1919 yearbook, smiling shyly, with these words next to her name: "There's nothing ill can dwell in such a temple."[18] Joe wouldn't forget Elma Fay.

Whatever his friends and parents thought of the fateful step he had just taken, it was done. Young Joe was going off on his own, maybe even to war. He might be a high school dropout, but he had a new title: Joe Rochefort, electrician 3rd class in the Naval Reserve, called to active duty.

⊹⊹⊹

Rochefort didn't think he would be an electrician for long. No sooner had he completed recruit training on 14 August 1918 than he applied for transfer to the Naval Reserve Flying Corps. His chances looked good. His commanding officer, Commander Guy Whitelock, endorsed his application, telling the Navy's Bureau of Navigation in Washington that Rochefort "appears to be well qualified mentally and physically and to have the required officer-like qualities."[19] High praise for a young man who had just turned eighteen and been on active duty only three months.

San Pedro suited Rochefort just fine. He took to Navy life and acquired basic naval skills. He was rated a qualified swimmer, made a favorable impression on his instructors, and was ready to go ahead with what he had joined the Navy to do: fly. Joe waited patiently to hear from BuNAV, as Navy people called the Bureau of Navigation. Despite its name, this department handled the service's personnel, issuing orders and shaping careers. Weeks slipped by.

By late summer 1918, the war in Europe was turning against Germany. The picture also darkened, in a way, for Joe Rochefort. As Allied troops pounded German lines, Rochefort heard back from BuNAV and the news wasn't good. Without any explanation, on 16 September Rochefort was notified "that it is not considered practicable at this time to approve your application for transfer to . . . flight instruction."[20] Developments in Europe had made his request irrelevant: the Navy's need for an increasing number of fliers ended with the imminent end of the war.

When the Allies and Germany signed an Armistice on 11 November, all fighting ceased in Europe. So did many naval careers. Thousands of Navy men, regulars and reservists alike, were deactivated. Rochefort wasn't among them. He may have felt that having left home under painful circumstances, he couldn't go back. Whatever his motives, he found a way to stay on active duty. His career was saved by the Navy's belated recognition, triggered by months of improvised convoy service, that it needed more engineers to run its ships. Rochefort wasn't an engineer, but his record at Polytechnic High suggested he might have the makings of one.

Rochefort didn't look back. He arranged to be transferred to the Naval Auxiliary Reserve in New York, reporting on 1 December 1918 to the Reserve's headquarters at the Municipal Ferry Terminal in downtown Manhattan.[21] Where this transfer would lead him remained to be seen.

The Naval Auxiliary Reserve, or NAR, as it was usually called, was established in 1917 to train deck officers and engineering officers for the Navy's merchant fleet, called the Naval Overseas Transportation Service, or NOTS. The Navy set up NOTS in January 1918 to transport the American Expeditionary Force to Europe.

NOTS had plenty of merchant-type vessels—more than 450 by the end of the war—but it lacked engineering officers. To alleviate that shortage, the Navy turned to the Stevens Institute of Technology, a fully accredited four-year college on the banks of the Hudson River in nearby Hoboken, New Jersey. In response, Stevens placed its campus—including its entire faculty—at the disposal of the Navy. Called the U.S. Navy Steam Engineering School at Stevens Institute, the program was essentially an officer-training course from which graduates could expect to be commissioned as ensigns in the Naval Auxiliary Reserve. Rochefort liked that prospect.

Happily for him and other would-be ensigns, the Stevens program didn't end with the signing of the Armistice. NAR continued to round up suitable candidates for its engineering school, and Stevens agreed to keep it operating through the first half of 1919. Rochefort was an obvious candidate. But was he eligible? The Navy had its standards. To qualify for enrollment, a candidate had to have completed high school or graduated from an engineering course at a recognized technical school. Another requirement was age. A candidate had to be at least twenty-one.[22] Rochefort fell short in both areas.

Yet he got in. In all likelihood he represented himself as a graduate of Polytechnic High in Los Angeles, a school with a strong curriculum in science and math. Navy people recruiting for the program probably didn't ask too many questions. That was one problem solved. Overcoming the second difficulty also was easily done. With or without the complicity of a senior officer, Rochefort simply added another year to his age. Filling out new paperwork in New York, he put down his year of birth as 1898—the year he would stick with throughout his naval career.[23] He was now close enough to twenty-one to be eligible.

Rochefort was on his way. He was reclassified a chief machinist's mate and, in January 1919, ordered to the U.S. Navy Steam Engineering School at Stevens, where he joined about three hundred other naval students. Designed to last four months, the program was rigorous, giving Rochefort a salty introduction to the world of steam engineering. He received intensive instruction in boilers, engines, and auxiliary equipment, followed by several weeks of practical work in the engine rooms of tugs, ferries, river steamers, and ocean steamers.[24]

At least initially, Rochefort did well. On 17 March, after completing all this coursework, he was promoted to machinist, a development that propelled him forward in the program and, not insignificantly, doubled his monthly pay to eighty-three dollars. Now he was ready for what the Steam Engineering School regarded as the pièce de résistance of its program: a four-week cruise intended to give the would-be ensigns their first sustained duty on board a naval vessel.

On 30 March Rochefort reported to the training ship *Koningin der Nederlanden*, a Dutch vessel that had been seized in San Francisco Bay at the outset of the war and incorporated into the NOTS fleet. Now anchored in Charleston, South Carolina, the ship was commanded by Captain W. P. Cronan, a seasoned, somewhat grizzled officer who had commanded an antisubmarine force during the European War. When hostilities ceased he was ordered to the *Koningin der Nederlanden*, which began ferrying American forces home from Europe. The vessel continued to do so, but it also was used to provide instruction for cadets in the NAR program.

Rochefort now got his first test as a potential officer under real-life conditions. The ship weighed anchor on 2 April and steamed out into the Atlantic bound for Brest, a thriving French seaport on western tip of Brittany. This was the first of many stops the ship would make along the French coast as it picked up the remnants of American forces awaiting transport home. The cruise would not be boring. After encountering more than its share of gales, rain squalls, and heavy seas, the *Nederlanden*, to everyone's great relief, set sail for home around 23 April.[25]

On 30 April she dropped anchor at Newport News, Virginia, ending a cruise that for young officer candidates had been a chance to impress their superiors and begin a Navy career. That wasn't how things worked out for Rochefort. What difficulties he may have experienced do not show up in the ship's logs. He certainly worked hard, primarily as a machinist in the ship's engine and boiler rooms, two of the hottest spots on any ship at that time. Whatever he did or didn't do on board that vessel, he failed to impress Captain Cronan.

On 5 May, shortly after the ship's return, Cronan prepared the first fitness report of Navy machinist 3rd class Joe Rochefort. This was no minor exercise; a bad fitness report, if it was bad enough, could doom a young officer's career. Assessing Rochefort's temperamental qualities, Cronan found him "calm, even tempered," but, alas, "not forceful." Cronan did see some strengths. Surprisingly, given Rochefort's later reputation as a contrarian, he rated "good" for his ability to cooperate with others. He was pleasant and mild-mannered. He even earned one 4.0 (the highest numerical grade available) for conduct, not a glamour category, but an appraisal showing that Rochefort remained on his best behavior.

That's where the good news ended. Turning critical, Cronan characterized Rochefort as unfit to be trusted with important independent duties and graded him "indifferent" in his specialty, engineering. The CO saved his most damning judgment for Rochefort's professional ability, assessing him "below average" in this key category. Then he delivered a verdict that could have squashed Rochefort's career. Cronan judged him "not qualified for promotion."[26]

Rochefort's Navy run seemed over. Yet, in the strange way the service worked, he moved up. His luck held. Shortly after Cronan's sobering appraisal, the Navy ignored the captain's remarks and promoted Rochefort to temporary ensign, effective 14 June 1919.[27] On that date he graduated from the Navy's Steam Engineering School at Stevens Institute.

ıı■ıı

The ceremony that conferred on Rochefort his commission meant a lot to the young reservist, as evidenced by his words years later. "Shortly after [being called to active duty], I was sent to New York where I was enrolled at the Stevens Institute of Technology in an engineering class," he said. "I graduated from that early in 1919."[28] Historians later misinterpreted Rochefort's words to mean that he had graduated from that prestigious Institute.[29]

In fact, as previously explained, the program he participated in was separate from the college's regular curriculum.[30] While not a Stevens graduate, Rochefort was now indisputably a commissioned ensign in the Naval Reserve. He was buoyed by this development—and deflated by the next one. Three weeks after making Rochefort an ensign, the Navy continued to do things in its own mysterious way: it relieved him from active duty and ordered him to return home. "You are hereby detached from such active duty as you may be performing," the commandant of the Third Naval District told Rochefort in a form letter. "The [BuNAV] takes this opportunity to thank you for the faithful and patriotic services you have rendered to your country in the war with Germany."[31]

ıı■ıı

Rochefort was no longer in the Navy. He was just another reservist on vacation. He bought a car and traveled 3,111 miles in eight days, reaching the family home on 5 July 1919.[32] One big change he found on arrival was that soon after Joe's enlistment, his father had moved the entire group into a larger house next door. Now they had a second story.

The Rochefort family needed it. Frank, now sixty-seven and still a salesman, continued to head the household with Ellen, now sixty-three. Joining them in the move were sons William, thirty and unemployed; Charles, twenty-one, holding down a job as a clerk; and Harold, thirty-one and still a plumber. Known as Uncle Harley, he was popular in the family, and he and Joe were on good terms. During Joe's first weeks at home, the reservist joined his brother in the plumbing business. The Los Angeles City Directory for 1920 lists Joe living at 2090 West Twenty-Seventh Street, his occupation, plumber.[33]

Other siblings had left home to pursue different interests; about the same time Joe had joined the Navy, Margaret had entered the Sisters of St. Joseph of Carondolet, a Catholic order in Los Angeles.[34] Joe took steps to mend fences with his parents, partly to smooth over his impetuosity a year earlier and partly to address a developing sore point. The elder Rocheforts were concerned about Joe's courtship of Elma Fay Aery. They had nothing against her; she came from a good family. Her father, William T. Aery, was a skilled carpenter and cabinetmaker who provided well for his family. But she wasn't Catholic. Elma Fay was a Southern Baptist.[35]

Frank wasn't a towering figure. He was short and wiry, not as tall as Joe, who now stood at nearly six feet. But Frank was a man of conviction with an Irish temper and superior skills in salesmanship. He expressed himself forcefully. And when he was joined by Ellen, equally strong in her beliefs, they were a formidable duo. They didn't want Joe to marry Elma Fay. Tension was mounting in the household.

⚓

Whether Joe was surprised by the letter he received from BuNAV on 19 September 1919 does not show up in family records, but it brought news he wanted. It was an offer. If he accepted it and took an oath of office, he was to report as an ensign for temporary service on board the *Cuyama*, an oil tanker now anchored off San Diego. Joe didn't pause. He signed the oath and reported on 7 October.[36] His real Navy career was about to begin.

2

Mustang

Joe Rochefort was part of a very tiny, tiny number.
—Ronald H. Spector

Arriving on board the *Cuyama* marked a turning point for Joe Rochefort. After joining this supply ship he would never again be detached
involuntarily from active duty. His career was now in the Navy, and in the
time-honored fashion of commissioned officers, he would work his way up.
"From there I just progressed in the normal way," Rochefort said later.[1]

His new home, the unspectacular *Cuyama*, at 475 feet, 7 inches long and
capable of just 14 knots, wasn't big or fast. But she had an importance. Commissioned in April 1917, the same month the United States declared war on
Germany, she was one of the Navy's newest ships and represented the drive
to modernize—to move away from a coal toward an oil-driven Navy. The
Cuyama was a good ship on which to start.

Rochefort's job on the tanker was demanding. As assistant engineering
officer, he was responsible, along with his immediate superior, for overseeing
the operation of the engine and boiler rooms. The two officers commanded the
so-called black gang, an old Navy slang term designating those who worked
belowdecks in the steam- and soot-filled chambers that drove the ship. Sailors
found the term descriptive—and a source of pride—even as ships switched to
oil.[2] The gang was not easy to impress or always to command.

The *Cuyama*'s missions weren't complicated—mostly picking up and dis-
pensing oil and gasoline cargoes, servicing ships, and transporting freight and

occasional passengers, nearly all of which was carried out on the West Coast. But they provided a good learning experience. Rochefort now came into his own as an engineer and officer.

ıı ▓ ıı

With his future looking brighter, early in 1921 Rochefort took a momentous step. During a brief leave home, on 29 March Joe married his high school sweetheart, Elma Fay, over the strong objections of Frank and Ellen. In the all-important area of religion, the couple compromised. They were married by a Catholic priest, but not in a traditional Catholic wedding. They would go to church together but alternate—Catholic one week, Baptist the next. The elder Rocheforts may not have been happy, but they weren't mean-spirited. Gradually they accepted Fay into the family.[3]

Back on board the *Cuyama*, Rochefort started to click. After a modest start, he eventually impressed his CO, Commander Isaac B. Smith. Unlike Captain Cronan, who had found Rochefort insufficiently forceful, Smith judged him "calm, even-tempered, forceful." He wrote: "In comparison in rank and grade to other officers of the Reserves [with] Temporary Duties, this officer is qualified for a commission in the Regular Navy."[4]

Smith's evaluation was timely. The same day he prepared Rochefort's fitness report (16 May), the reservist was on Mare Island in San Francisco Bay, taking an examination for transfer to the Regular Navy. That event was followed three days later by an unexpected development: BuNAV detached him from the *Cuyama*, now anchored in San Diego, and ordered him to report to the *Cardinal*, a minesweeper based at San Pedro.

Ordinarily transfer to a minesweeper wouldn't be considered a step up, but in this case it was. On board the *Cardinal* he served as the ship's chief engineer, no longer the assistant. The transfer had other positive aspects. The *Cardinal* was less than half the size of the *Cuyama* with a crew correspondingly smaller, meaning officers doubled up on some duties. In a small ship everybody did everything. Rochefort soon became the vessel's communications officer as well as its chief engineer.

He reported 11 June 1921 and awaited the results of the Mare Island exam, taken three weeks earlier. The verdict was a long time coming. At last, on 20 October, BuNAV informed Rochefort that he had been appointed an ensign in the Regular Navy.[5] This was no routine promotion.

Rochefort now entered sacred and unfamiliar ground for any reservist, especially one who had started out as an electrician 3rd class. "Until the 1930s, commissioned rank in the navy was virtually limited to Annapolis graduates," historian Ronald H. Spector observes in his 2001 study of American sailors in the twentieth century. And although the number of reserve officers surged during World War I, "the regular officers viewed them as a necessary evil and purged the service of most of them by 1921," he notes. "Those who remained were not promoted."[6]

Rochefort's experience shows that the Navy did provide examinations for reservists who wanted to transfer, but "they made sure almost nobody would pass it," Spector explained during an interview, adding that Rochefort's transition to the Regular Navy was "extremely unusual." Rochefort "was part of a very tiny, tiny number."[7]

Barriers blocking the way of reservists and enlisted men stemmed in large measure from the Navy's preoccupation with college graduates for its officer corps. Why the service insisted on a college education for its officers was never any mystery. The policy reflected, Spector suggests, the social preferences of career officers who, having gone to college, believed themselves part of the "favored few" of American society. The graduates-only standard helped maintain the "social distance" between officers and enlisted men.[8]

Somehow Rochefort managed to overcome these barriers. Presumably he had done extremely well on his 16 May exam. Also, he certainly made a favorable impression on the captains of the two ships in which he had served: the *Cuyama* and the *Cardinal*.[9] Despite the Navy's built-in bias toward Annapolis grads, merit still counted. Rochefort ascended the Navy ladder on the basis of sheer ability and performance.

He now took his place in the rarefied world of Regular Navy officers, which had its drawbacks. Besides his fellow officers being overwhelmingly Annapolis grads, most were from well-to-do families.[10] Rochefort, the son of a rug salesman, was an alien. And now, in Navy parlance, he was a mustang—a commissioned officer who had risen from enlisted ranks. Such officers often found themselves slighted in the Navy's social circles, and Rochefort was no exception.[11]

From time to time, he later recalled, he would run into a Navy breed that riled him—junior officers who were "gung ho for the Naval Academy." In his relations with these enthusiasts he found himself viewed as an inferior, in a situation "something like [what] the colored people have today," he said in a 1969 interview. "I would run across those instances occasionally but never from anybody a little senior."[12] Rochefort hated this part of the Navy but didn't let it affect his behavior. He was getting used to breaking Navy rules.

Rochefort wasted no time taking advantage of his new status. Believing he could learn more on a battleship than a minesweeper, on 16 November 1921 he requested a change of duty from BuNAV—specifically to the *Connecticut*, flagship of the Pacific Fleet.[13]

To Rochefort's delight, BuNAV approved his request. But in another display of the Navy's strange way of doing things, his duty in the *Connecticut* lasted only four days. Reporting on 31 December 1921, he was detached 4 January 1922, at which time he was transferred to a destroyer, the *Stansbury*. These moves were the first of a series that baffled Rochefort. He served as the engineer officer on board the *Stansbury* for five months, until she was decommissioned on 27 May 1922. BuNAV promptly ordered him to a cruiser, the *Charleston*, for duty that again lasted four days. There was no explaining these assignments or BuNAV's reasons for ordering him to his next duty: back to the *Cuyama*.

On 31 May, three years after joining the *Cuyama* as an ensign (temporary), Rochefort reported back to his old tanker.[14] He wasn't pleased, but took the development in stride. He did not resign himself to the *Cuyama*, however. Rochefort didn't quietly accept the fate to which BuNAV had consigned him, nor did he give up going after a battleship.

Shortly after returning to the tanker, hoping to build on his earlier momentum, Rochefort took another examination, this one in San Diego. He again was successful, learning on 21 December 1922 that he had been promoted to lieutenant junior grade, his second major advance in fourteen months.

But he remained on the *Cuyama*. At first all went well. By this time he knew the tanker backward and forward. He was given different duties this time around, becoming a division officer in the Engineering Department, then a watch officer with broader duties. He also supervised fueling and discharge of fuel oil, but wanted still more to do. Soon he was granted permission to act as assistant navigator. "[He] is rapidly learning the practical fundamentals of that subject," Commander John H. Blackburn, his new CO, wrote on 14 August 1922. "He performs his duties in a conspicuously earnest manner."[15]

Blackburn tried hard to keep Rochefort absorbed. He piled new duties on his restless subordinate. His successor, Commander C. C. Moses, gave Rochefort still more to do, making him the ship's communications and radio officer.[16] Acting on his own, taking a step that reflected his drive to escape what must have seemed like a treadmill, in 1922 Rochefort enrolled in a two-year correspondence course sponsored by the Naval War College in Newport, Rhode Island. The course provided instruction in everything from international law and world history to tactics, strategy, and the problems of warfare. Each month he took a written quiz.[17]

Still, Rochefort remained fidgety. In September 1923 he requested a transfer to the Construction Corps School in Annapolis, Maryland.[18] When that request came to nothing, he asked BuNAV to transfer him to the Mine Force based at Pearl Harbor. Again BuNAV said no, responding in language that by now was all too familiar: "It is impracticable to detach you from your present duty prior to the expiration of winter maneuvers," wrote the bureau's chief, Rear Admiral A. T. Long, on 8 December 1923. And since "you will be eligible for shore duty in September, 1924, you will not be transferred to the duty requested."[19]

One bright spot for Rochefort at this time was the birth of his son, Joseph Junior, on 27 September 1923 in Los Angeles, where Fay now lived with her parents. Joe was granted a month's leave early in 1924 to visit his family.

Once back on the *Cuyama*, Rochefort tried again to extricate himself from the tanker. He sent BuNAV another letter, this time seeking shore duty at Mare Island Navy Yard, in San Francisco Bay. "My reason for making this request is that I am taking an extension course at the University of California and wish to include a study of the Japanese language," he wrote on 23 June 1924. "This is only available at the University or one of its branches." He added plaintively: "I am now on my fifth year of service on this vessel."[20]

What BuNAV thought of this request isn't known. No trace of the agency's reply turned up in Navy personnel records or in Rochefort's personal files. His request was not approved. He wasn't transferred to Mare Island, a place that would have given him easy access to the University of California. Even though it was turned down, Rochefort's Mare Island bid turned out to be significant: it signaled his first documented interest in the Japanese language.

II ■ II

Months dragged by. As 1924 drew to a close, Rochefort was still on board the oil tanker, probably wondering if he would ever get off that ship. The low point in his *Cuyama* career came in the early morning hours of 27 September 1924, as the tanker lay anchored in San Francisco Bay, with Rochefort standing as officer of the deck. Something went terribly wrong. At first Rochefort didn't notice anything amiss. The night was clear; the Bay was calm.[21]

With sixty fathoms of chain on the port anchor, the *Cuyama* was positioned to fuel six destroyers—the *Sloat, Macdonough, Shirk, Hull, Wood,* and *Yarborough*—lined up alongside. Shortly after midnight the tanker swayed slightly in her berth. The *Cuyama's* anchor loosened, and the ship started dragging her anchor. She bumped into her neighbor, nudging it loose from its berth and causing a chain reaction. Soon the *Cuyama* and all six destroyers were drifting into San Francisco Bay, sometimes colliding, sometimes sideswiping other vessels in the Bay.[22]

Hours passed before crews finally regained control of their ships and anchored them properly. Miraculously, damage was modest. The battleship *Tennessee* sustained a few bruises. The *Wood* found herself with a broken strut and a damaged propeller. The *Hull,* the most damaged of the ships, ended up with a three-foot hole in her deck, a missing propeller guard, and a warped port shaft. The *Cuyama,* astonishingly, emerged unscathed.

Even more amazing, no one was injured. In effect, no real damage had been done in what could have been one of the most surreal collisions in peacetime Navy history. Navy brass, however, couldn't understand how such an accident could have occurred. They promptly convened a court of inquiry, with the focus initially on the conduct of Joe Rochefort, the young lieutenant (jg) who was, after all, the responsible officer in the ship that had triggered the incident.

Assembled on board the battleship *California,* the court—consisting of two captains and a commander—brought in nineteen witnesses to give testimony, Rochefort among them. His career was hanging by a thread. The court wasted no time deciding which officers should bear primary responsibility for the debacle. A commander on board the *Macdonough* was charged with "culpable inefficiency in the performance of duty," and a lieutenant in the *Hull* was accused of "neglect of duty." Both were ordered to face a trial by general court-martial.

Rochefort's boss, Commander Moses, was criticized. Not on board the *Cuyama* that night, Moses was "admonished for neglecting his duty" because he left the ship in the hands of young Rochefort. But Moses escaped a court-martial.

।। ■ ।।

Amazingly enough, so did Rochefort. He was spared the full wrath of the panel. But it did find him remiss. It held that the *Cuyama* indeed set in motion the strange chain of events that unfolded that September morning, because the tanker's "anchor was not holding normally." Rochefort had erred, the court said, by "not [taking] proper precautions to see whether or not the ship was dragging."[23] Then the court turned what could have been a career-ending disaster into what very nearly became a professional triumph for Rochefort.

After hearing all the testimony, the court found much to praise in Rochefort's actions taken during the crisis. After he became aware of the dragging, the panel declared, "[Rochefort's] judgment and handling of the *Cuyama* was excellent," probably keeping a bad situation from getting worse. His "excellent" seamanship during this episode saved him from a court-martial. Rochefort got off with a reprimand.[24]

He had had a narrow escape. A copy of the reprimand would be attached to his permanent record, but he had avoided a court-martial. Also, Rochefort's CO didn't blame him for the events of 27 September. Moses didn't even mention the episode in his next fitness report on Rochefort, rating the young officer "above average" in professional ability. "A well balanced officer, very proficient," Moses wrote.[25]

।। ■ ।।

If Rochefort took away any lessons from the episode, they don't show up in his personal records. No Rochefort surviving letters from this period hint at any hard-earned wisdom gained, or any sense of the fragility of careers and life's fickle fortunes. But the events of that weird and troubling day carried significance. They exemplified his previously unsuspected ability to show leadership in a desperate situation, and they displayed his recurring ability to bounce back from adversity, even to turn a bad situation positive. And they probably did nothing to diminish his already very strong sense of self-confidence.

Whatever Rochefort's mood following the September 1924 incident, he still faced one obstinate fact: he remained on board the *Cuyama*. For the better part of two years he had been trying to get off. But now his opinion of the tanker might have been more favorable. Not only had the colliding ships in some strange way worked to his advantage, but he had formed a friendship that would change his Navy career.

Rochefort's friend was a superior officer on the *Cuyama*, Lieutenant Commander Chester C. Jersey. "He and I had several things in common," Rochefort later explained. "One was bridge, the other being that I liked to work crossword puzzles, which were just coming into style. Jersey remembered this, and when he was ordered to the Navy Department, he asked me if I would care to come to the Navy Department on temporary duty in connection with preparing codes and ciphers. It was then that I was introduced to cryptanalysis."[26]

For now the two men went their separate ways, Jersey to the Navy Department and Rochefort, to his enormous relief, to his next ship. Without asking for it, without requesting any change of duty, finally he got his battleship. Early in December, shortly after the *Cuyama* had paused in San Pedro, BuNAV ordered him to the *Arizona*, now also anchored at San Pedro. He reported 9 December 1924 as assistant engineer.[27]

Rochefort should have been delighted. In 1921, shortly after getting his Regular Navy commission, he had formally requested a change of duty to a battleship. Now BuNAV put him on board one. It finally had given him something he had asked for. As engineering watch officer in the *Arizona*, he performed well. In the more demanding environment of that battleship, he showed "considerable engineering talent which, with more experience, will enable him to develop into an excellent engineer," commented his CO, Captain H. P. Perrill. "His work and performance of duty have been satisfactory."[28]

But Rochefort by this time had other ideas. His interests had changed. He was no longer thinking engineering or, for that matter, cruisers and battleships. As his immediate superior commented in one appraisal of the young lieutenant, Rochefort had "shown a keen interest in cryptanalysis." On 19 September 1925, ten months after reporting to the *Arizona*, he was detached. BuNAV ordered him to report in three weeks to the Chief of Naval Operations in Washington for temporary duty to receive instruction in advanced cryptanalysis.[29]

The mythology surrounding Rochefort was that his potential as a cryptanalyst was deduced through puzzles, believed at the time to be indicators of cryptologic skill. As part of an effort to build up its codebreaking capability, the Office of Naval Operations in the mid-1920s had inserted puzzles and cryptograms in various Navy publications, hoping to attract the attention of would-be codebreakers. According to legend, one of these turned out to be Joe Rochefort, who did so well on those exercises that the Navy plucked him off the *Arizona* and whisked him to Washington.

Given an opportunity years later to confirm the puzzle theory, Rochefort would go only so far. He agreed that puzzles may have been a modest factor in his selection for training, but he indicated they were less important than was his friend Chester Jersey. "I was probably ordered to the Navy Department for temporary duty because of Commander Jersey's recommendation," Rochefort said in 1969. Not ready to give up on the legend, the interviewer pressed: "Was that because you were good at crossword puzzles?"

"Probably," Rochefort replied, elusive as always, "and [Jersey] liked my way of playing bridge with him. Auction bridge was just disappearing then into contract bridge. Contract bridge came to the fore. It was probably because of that."[30]

The question of whether it was Rochefort's ability with puzzles or bridge or Commander Jersey's recommendation that propelled him into the codebreaking program would never be resolved, but Joe Rochefort reported to the Navy Department in Washington on 1 October 1925.[31] He was an apprentice codebreaker, about to enter the strange new world of cryptanalysis.

3

Odyssey of a Codebreaker

Breaking codes makes you feel pretty good. . . . It was always
somewhat of a pleasure to defeat them.

—Joe Rochefort

When Lieutenant (jg) Joseph J. Rochefort arrived in the nation's capital
in fall 1925, he might well have felt like a man of destiny. He had
every right. Twelve months earlier he had been facing a Navy court of inquiry,
fighting for his career. Now he was reporting for duty at Main Navy—the
service's term for its sprawling, brutish-looking headquarters that stretched
for blocks along Constitution Avenue, near Washington's famed mall. Uninviting as it might have been, the building remained a magnet for ambitious
Navy men: transfer to Main Navy could jump-start a career stuck in neutral,
a career like Rochefort's.

"Duty in the Navy Department was arduous and confining," observed
Admiral James O. Richardson, who ran BuNAV a couple of years before
assuming command of the U.S. Fleet in 1940. "Living was expensive and
recreation facilities were available to only a few, but there was opportunity to
become known to the officers and officials who were running the Navy."[1]

Rochefort had hit the jackpot. His luck had held. Given the intense competition for a Main Navy slot, he would have seemed an unlikely candidate
for such a posting. At age twenty-five he was young (two years younger than
the Navy thought). His Navy experience had been narrow. He had spent
five of his seven years in the Navy on board the oiler *Cuyama*. While he had

branched out into navigation and communications, most of his experience had been in engineering, keeping the *Cuyama*'s engines up and running. Not the stuff of brilliant careers.

Another factor might have worked against Rochefort's relocation to Washington: congressional budget cutting. Since the end of the European War in November 1918, lawmakers had slashed the Navy's budget by four-fifths and its personnel by three-fourths, greatly diminishing opportunities for ambitious officers in Washington.[2] Fewer officers were being ordered to Main Navy because there were fewer slots to fill.

But if some officers envied Rochefort for his Washington coup, they did not covet his particular billet. Rochefort was not, after all, going to Washington to sit at the right hand of the Chief of Naval Operations, or hold down a highly visible posting in a prestigious bureau where he could be seen by the Navy's movers and shakers. He had been ordered to report to the Code and Signal Section, a small, almost invisible activity founded in 1917, buried in a corner of the Communication Office, a forerunner of the highly regarded Office of Naval Communications (ONC), as it shall be called here.[3]

To the extent that savvy Navy people thought about that section at all, they regarded it as a graveyard for careers—a place to be avoided at all cost. The section's first leader, Lieutenant Commander Russell Willson, performed ably during his stint from 1917 to 1918. But when his term ended he moved his career in another direction, at times making clear his low opinion of those who showed an inclination for this type of work.[4] His successor, Lieutenant Commander Milo F. Draemel, was no more eager than Willson to make a career out of codes and signals.

One problem was that codes and signals seemed far removed from the main work of the Navy: forging powerful fleets that could thwart any sea-based enemy. Ignorant of codebreaking and related activities, many high-ranking officers rejected the entire field as a crackpot endeavor. As Rochefort soon discovered, those venturing into this esoteric realm tended to be written off as "odd characters" or, on bad days, "one of these nuts."[5]

In fact, many top brass associated codebreaking with an activity that, amazingly enough, was even lower on the Navy's totem pole of prestige: intelligence. A specialty centered in the much-maligned Office of Naval Intelligence (ONI), it was considered one of the lowest forms of activity in the peacetime Navy. "[Intelligence] was not at all accepted in the pre–World War II Navy," observed Vice Admiral George Dyer, who served during World War II as

Admiral King's personal intelligence officer. In gunnery or communications, "You had something that produced a favorable reaction, if it was done well," Dyer said. "In intelligence, that was not true. By and large it just didn't arouse people's interest."[6]

        ıı∎ıı

None of this bothered Rochefort in the fall of 1925. From his point of view, what mattered was that he had extricated himself from the *Cuyama*. He looked forward to learning a new discipline. He was especially pleased when Fay and Joe Junior arrived by train from Los Angeles. Assured of at least a two-year tour of duty, the family found a comfortable, two-story town-house far out on Reservoir Road, an attractive, tree-lined street in northwest Washington.

Joe Rochefort entered Main Navy for the first time on 1 October 1925. He found himself in a cavernous, mazelike structure with austere offices that stretched interminably along dreary hallways. Thrown up hurriedly after America's entry into the European War, the building already appeared old, with water-stained ceilings, creaking doors, and floors that shook whenever someone walked down a corridor. Yet it was only eight years old.[7]

Making his way around the huge edifice, Rochefort headed for Room 2621 on the second deck (as floors of Navy buildings are known) of Main Navy's sixth wing, home of ONC. There he met his new boss, Captain Ridley McLean, a much-traveled officer who had served in a battleship in the Atlantic during the European War. McLean had been named director of naval communications in 1924, and now, one year later at age fifty-two, presided over an empire that included the latest innovations in radio technology.

ONC had been set up in 1912 expressly to harness those breakthroughs. In doing so it found itself straddling two worlds, in effect, two centuries. Perhaps unavoidably, ONC retained some of the fetters of the old Navy, keeping alive just about every type of service activity that went under the name of communication. As late as 1925, ONC continued such quaint methods as carrier pigeons, maintaining lofts for nearly 800 birds.[8] But the agency also looked toward the future. It had put in place a dizzying variety of radio equipment, including, of particular importance, the latest developments in radio direction finders (DF)—ingenious devices used during the European War to fix the bearings of enemy submarines many miles away.[9]

Advanced as the Navy clearly was in DF technology, it had fallen behind in another critical area of radio activity: communications intelligence, or comint, as its practitioners called it. The term referred to information derived from the study of foreign communications; it covered the work of analysts who decrypted, translated, and evaluated the contents of intercepted radio transmissions. Some farsighted Navy officers believed such intelligence might someday influence, if not dramatically alter, the nature of warfare. Rochefort's arrival at Main Navy in fall 1925 coincided with the Navy's belated effort to catch up with the Army in this controversial, yet potentially transformative area.

The Navy wasn't a complete newcomer to codebreaking. It had first ventured into this realm in 1917 with the previously mentioned Code and Signal Section. But the section concentrated primarily on how best to encrypt U.S. naval codes, an activity known as cryptography. The idea was to make U.S. codes hard, if not impossible, to break if intercepted. That was important work, but it wasn't the same thing as cryptanalysis: the science of compromising the other side's codes and ciphers. Code and Signals attempted no cryptanalytic work during the European War, choosing to rely instead on the British admiralty for its "secret intelligence."[10]

The Navy's hesitation left the door open for the Army to seize the lead in cryptanalysis. In June 1917 the War Department set up America's first fully functioning codebreaking unit, handing that billet over to a persuasive, fast-talking twenty-seven-year-old named Herbert O. Yardley. Yardley had little experience as a codebreaker, but he did have an interest in cryptography, acquired during a brief stint as a code clerk at the State Department. When he asked the War Department to create a codebreaking unit with him in charge, it did so. Yardley later dubbed his operation "the black chamber."[11]

After the war, Yardley's black chamber, now partly funded by the State Department, pulled off one of the great intelligence coups of that era. During the Washington Naval Conference of 1921, convened to set limits on the tonnage of capital ships in the navies of Great Britain, the United States, France, Japan, and Italy, Yardley's chamber broke Japan's diplomatic code. So when Japan's foreign office cabled new instructions to its representatives in Washington directing them to soften their tonnage demands if necessary for an agreement, Yardley's team decrypted the message. Yardley informed U.S. Secretary of State Charles Evans Hughes.

"The intelligence provided by the code breakers had bolstered Hughes's toughness and helped win the day," historian David Kahn pointed out in his biography of Yardley.[12]

Pleased as the U.S. Navy was by the outcome of the 1921 conference, it also found reason to worry in the implications of Yardley's feat. Recognizing the vulnerability of codes in an age of communications intelligence, in 1922 the Navy started searching for new ways to secure its own codes.[13] As an outgrowth of that effort, the service also took baby steps into the world of cryptanalysis.

II ■ II

It was this world that Rochefort now entered. After meeting Captain McLean on Main Navy's second deck, Rochefort was escorted one deck below to Room 1621, where naval communications housed one of its newest and most secret activities: the research desk. This was a subunit of ONC's Code and Signal Section, which remained primarily concerned with cryptography to ensure the security of U.S. naval messages.

But the research desk recently had assumed a different mission. Its innocuous title disguised an activity that existed in many military organizations but was seldom advertised: cracking the codes and ciphers used in the communications of foreign countries and their navies. Running the desk was the officer who had founded it twenty-one months earlier, Lieutenant Laurance Safford. Eccentric, uncommonly bright, sometimes looking a little out of place, Safford had arrived at Main Navy in January 1924, knowing little about codes and even less about codebreaking.[14]

Only once, while serving as a communications officer on board a destroyer during the recent war, had he ever tried to break a code. "My first attempt at code solution occurred around July 1917 when my transport received a message in a British code which we had not been supplied," he commented later. "I tried to solve the message, but failed miserably."[15]

This faux pas aside, he was an extraordinarily gifted officer with many interests. Along with an enthusiasm for soccer, Safford was an avid chess player and expert marksman.[16] He radiated brilliance. He had graduated fifteenth in his class at Annapolis, where he had demonstrated a flair for mathematics and later a skill with mechanical devices. But those skills hadn't been put to good use. The Navy seemed not to know what to do with him. By 1923 he was commanding a minesweeper on the Yangtze River in China.

But when ONC decided in 1923 to strengthen its cryptographic capability and make U.S. naval codes as impenetrable as possible, someone remembered Safford and his fortuitous combination of skills. When his minesweeper duty ended late in 1923, he was rotated to Main Navy, where he was ordered, much to his delight, to the research desk. He became its founding officer, the leader of a group consisting of one officer (himself) and four civilians.

Safford had no trouble explaining his selection for this post. "They wanted somebody with an analytical mind who was slightly unusual," he said later, someone "who they thought could make good in this arcane subject and I was selected out of all others who were available to come ashore to start the thing off."[17]

Nicknamed Sappho by his Annapolis classmates for his eccentricity (referring to his creativity, not other characteristics of the lesbian Greek poet), Safford's staff regarded him as a "mad genius," a label reinforced by any number of peculiarities. Always a little disheveled, his uniform rumpled as if he'd slept in it, he didn't project the usual sleek image of a Navy officer. Sometimes the object of furtive smiles, Safford was an outsider among Main Navy's more conventional officers. His "most remarkable feature was his eyes, which were constantly darting back and forth, as if watching out for some danger," said one colleague. "He spoke in little bursts, unconnected phrases that unnerved his listeners."[18]

Out of the ordinary as he may have been, Safford had found his niche. The first thing he did was change the orientation of the research desk from defense to offense: he found he couldn't work to secure U.S. naval codes without first mastering cryptanalysis.

"I don't think it would be an exaggeration to say that when Safford was ordered to the Navy Department to establish this cryptographic section, it was initially for the purpose of improving our own systems," Rochefort later said. "It became very apparent to Safford that a knowledge of worldwide systems in use by, say, the British, the French or the Japanese or anyone else, would be very valuable. So he sort of drifted into a study of other systems while still making every effort to improve our own, which were not very good at that time."[19]

In his effort, Safford was aided by a talented civilian, Agnes Meyer Driscoll, a code clerk in the Code and Signal Section. Known as Miss Aggie, she had many abilities. At Ohio State University she had majored in mathematics with strong minors in physics, foreign languages, and music. When the U.S. entered the European War in 1917, she joined the U.S. Naval Reserve and wound up in the Code and Signal Section as a chief yeoman. After the war she left the Navy for a research job, then returned in the early 1920s. Valued for her uncanny knack for cracking codes, Miss Aggie tutored Safford and went on to instruct many of the Navy's future cryptanalysts, becoming a legend in the process.[20]

The research desk thrived under Safford. With his newly acquired cryptanalytic skills, he and his small team branched out in new directions. They began work on Japanese naval messages intercepted in real time. The inflow of new material stemmed from a 1924 decision by Safford and his bosses to set up a station at the U.S. consulate in Shanghai. This was the Navy's first unit aimed at Japanese traffic, and it was soon followed by others in Hawaii, Peiping, Guam, and the Philippines.[21]

The decision to focus on Japan flowed naturally out of U.S. naval planning that had begun shortly after 1905, the year the Japanese navy had destroyed a weary Russian fleet in the Battle of Tsushima—a campaign marking the emergence of Japan as a major naval power. Sizing up Japan as its likeliest adversary in any future war in the Pacific, the U.S. Navy initiated a planning process that spanned four decades, the object of which was the defeat of the Imperial Navy should such a conflict arise. In this planning, Japan was called Orange and the United States Blue. Later known as War Plan Orange, Navy planning was in full swing by the 1920s.[22]

To learn everything he could about the Imperial Navy and, if possible, fathom Japan's intentions, Safford instituted the first course to train naval officers in cryptanalysis. His classes would need students. Encouraged by like-minded officers in the Office of the Chief of Naval Operations (OPNAV), Safford put puzzles and problems in the monthly Communication Division bulletins to identify young officers with "any latent talent" for this abstruse activity and turn them into "a reserve of expert cryptanalysts."[23]

Safford never said what kind of response he got, but there wasn't a stampede of Navy men trying to enter his class. By the fall of 1925, only a handful had showed up. One was an earnest, mild-mannered young officer just off the *Arizona*, Lieutenant (jg) Joseph J. Rochefort.

11 ▮ 11

Rochefort and Safford hit it off, even though they might have seemed unlikely partners. Safford, after all, was an Annapolis grad while Rochefort was a mustang who had come up through the ranks. But they had much in common. They both were uncommonly smart, as well as being outsiders. Although Safford technically was a member of the Annapolis club, he never quite fit in.[24]

They also shared a zest for the fine points of cryptanalysis, taking pleasure in the game itself, the satisfaction of solving a puzzle. "These things just present a challenge, and a true cryptanalyst will never give up until he has solved this particular system," Rochefort explained. "He's what you call a technician who will solve a system for the sake of solving a system. He doesn't usually apply the results to any operation or need any purpose or anything else. This would be a true cryptanalyst. This would be Safford."[25]

At least for a time, it would also be Rochefort. Thanks to Safford, he was about to get caught up in the game. He was about to be tutored, with Safford doing the tutoring in his own offbeat style. Safford's approach was to throw cryptograms (communications in cipher or code) at Rochefort and his fellow learners to see what would happen. "There was no formal education process at all," Rochefort commented. "They would just turn over maybe several messages and see which one of us could solve them quickest."[26]

Rochefort and his classmates had one resource at their disposal, the book *Elements of Cryptanalysis*, a 176-page manual written by the chief cryptanalyst at the War Department, William F. Friedman. By the time Rochefort showed up at Main Navy, Friedman was a superstar. A dapper little man with a neatly trimmed mustache, reminding some of the actor Adolphe Menjou, Friedman bore little or no resemblance to the typical bureaucrat.[27] But he was held in awe by many as the premier cryptologist in the federal government.

Housed in the Munitions Building next door to Main Navy, Friedman was known to Safford and Rochefort, as well as to Miss Aggie. She took a more skeptical view of him. As his reputation grew, the two inevitably became rivals. But his book was "our bible," Rochefort commented. "We would study [it] and then attempt to solve these little cryptograms or ciphers that Safford would prepare for us. . . . It was very helpful. We got our principles from this book . . . then after that we were more or less on our own."[28]

Elements was, and remains, a mercilessly detailed how-to guide through the mind-boggling world of cryptanalysis. Arduous reading as it may been for a novice, *Elements*, from Rochefort's point of view, proved invaluable, laying out the key strategies to be employed in codebreaking. Beginning with the fundamentals, itemizing each of the building blocks, the book told the beginner the one thing he needed to know to get started: the difference between a cipher and a code.[29]

Through *Elements*, Rochefort learned that cipher systems could be broken by tools that enabled the cryptanalyst to identify the key in a cryptogram—the mathematical element that determined the steps to be followed to solve an encrypted message.

Perhaps the most valuable lesson Rochefort grasped was that solving a cryptogram involved trial and error and almost infinite patience. He certainly needed patience. For more than four months, from October 1925 into February 1926, Rochefort did little else but grapple with Friedman's cryptograms and whatever puzzles Safford chose to throw at him. Rochefort did well—well enough to impress both his superiors, Lieutenant Safford and Captain McLean.

Rochefort also pleased himself. Breaking a code "makes you feel pretty good," he said, "because you have defied these people who have attempted to use a system they thought was secure, that is, unreadable. It was always somewhat of a pleasure to defeat them."[30] Rochefort's delight in the game was fortunate, because if cracking codes was his idea of fun, his career was about to take a very pleasurable, if wholly unexpected turn.

⁙

Any officer who hoped to be promoted had to spend a lot of time at sea. Too much shore duty, even if it served a vital national interest, could doom a career. Two years were about as many an ambitious officer could spend on land without raising eyebrows, and Laurance Safford had almost used up his allotment. He may have been an "odd character," in Rochefort's view, but he wasn't a fool. Like most officers who had been to Annapolis and stayed in the service, he wanted to ascend the Navy ladder.[31]

While still tutoring the fast-learning Rochefort, Safford applied for sea duty and, in February 1926, was ordered to report to the *California*. This left Rochefort as the senior officer on the research desk. ONC director McLean soon made the appointment official. "During the period 1 October 1925 to 1 February 1926," McLean remarked in his 17 February appraisal of Rochefort, "this officer received instruction in Advanced Cryptanalysis. He is now qualified to take charge of a cryptographic staff in case of war. He has been detailed to succeed to the Cryptographic Desk in this office."[32]

Whether Rochefort, with little more than four months of training, was qualified to run a cryptologic operation in wartime might have been questioned. William Friedman, who soon would teach a course of his own, maintained that cryptographic proficiency required a minimum of two years' training.[33] But McLean had little choice. Other Navy men in Rochefort's class of instruction had either failed to impress or drifted away. The job was Rochefort's, even if by default.[34]

Rochefort didn't regard the appointment as anything unusual. "I was ordered to relieve the officer in charge," he commented dryly.[35] Along with a new job came a promotion: Rochefort on 6 February 1926 moved up to full lieutenant. It had been a good month.

Taking over the research desk—in effect, the entire cryptanalytic capability of the Navy—Rochefort now faced the same difficulties that had beset his predecessor: tight budgets and limited manpower. Aside from three young women who served as typists, the desk now consisted of three professionals: Rochefort, as officer in charge; one cryptanalyst, the formidable Miss Aggie Driscoll; and one assistant, Claus Bogel, an ex-actor who had briefly performed some cryptologic duties for Yardley. Recently transferred to Main Navy, he had, Rochefort recalled, "no particular abilities."[36] The bulk of the workload would fall on Rochefort and Driscoll.

Rochefort had no problem with that, being keenly aware of Driscoll's codebreaking acumen. At age thirty-five, a tall, thin lady with a patrician bearing, Miss Aggie seemed forbidding to many. She and her husband (Washington lawyer Michael B. Driscoll) seldom, if ever, socialized with Navy personnel. She could be warm and friendly but wouldn't tolerate anyone who patronized her, an attitude, friends said, reflecting her sensitivity to her role as a woman in a man's world.[37]

"Colleagues sometimes referred to her as Madame X, perhaps because she tended to keep to herself at work," remembered one officer. Wearing little if any makeup, "she usually had an air of severity which was heightened by plain dresses and school-marm spectacles," he recalled, adding in amazement, "It was surprising to hear her curse, which she frequently did—as fluently as any sailor I ever heard."[38]

Rochefort and Madame X clicked; indeed, she made an indelible impression on the young officer. "I used to refer to her either as Aggie or Mrs. Driscoll," he commented. "I would say she was a first class cryptanalyst. She was extremely capable, very quiet, and the thing I think of more and more was how she used to turn pages on the book or dictionary—she'd do it with the rubber end of a pencil, always flipping over the pages in the upper right-hand corner—that's what I always remember most about her. She was a very talented person—awfully good." Not only that, "I considered her sort of a teacher to me."[39]

Driscoll's presence on the scene was fortunate. Rochefort may have been the officer in charge, but his title couldn't erase the fact that he had no real-life cryptologic experience. He was still a student, but Miss Aggie was on hand to offer instruction.

Rochefort needed help to handle the first real-life project that dropped in his lap, a highly secret task that had occupied Safford and now would absorb him. This project wasn't physically centered at the research desk in Room 1621. It was one flight up. Rochefort climbed the stairs to Room 2646, at the end of a long corridor in ONC's sixth wing, hidden from the rest of the offices and requiring special permission for entry.[40]

"One of the best kept secrets in the U.S. Navy for more than twenty years concerned room number 2646 in the old Navy building on Constitution Avenue and what went on behind its locked doors," Safford observed later. Behind those locked doors Rochefort found a retired Japanese linguist, Emerson J. Haworth, and his wife, a stenographer, busily translating, as best they could, a photographic copy of the 1918 operational code of the Imperial Japanese Navy, dubbed the Red Code because it was kept in a red binder.[41]

11 ▮ 11

Obtaining the Red Code marked a milestone in the evolution of Navy cryptology. It also signaled the arrival in codebreaking circles of the Office of Naval Intelligence. Cryptanalysis had been the exclusive domain of naval communications, but ONI wanted a role in this exotic field. It seems to have earned a place at the table because it was naval intelligence that had secured the Red Code: ONI operatives had stolen it from the Japanese consulate in New York.[42]

For years ONI had been looking for ways to get a foothold in cryptology. It drew on a secret $100,000 slush fund set up in 1917 by Secretary of the Treasury William Gibbs McAdoo Jr. for the exclusive use of naval intelligence.[43] In spring 1920, ONI used the money to finance a series of break-ins— black-bag jobs, they would be called today—at the aforementioned Japanese consulate. A counterespionage squad picked the lock of the door, then the safe, of a high-level naval officer known to be based there. Inside his safe, Navy raiders found and photographed the voluminous codebook of the Imperial Japanese Navy (IJN) fleet.[44]

ONI then handed the book over to its rival, ONC, an apparent act of generosity in the highly competitive environment of Main Navy. The gesture seemed to make sense from several points of view. ONI had translators (the Haworths were bankrolled by ONI) but no cryptanalysts.[45] ONC had cryptanalysts but lacked translators. ONI's top officers expected ONC to share the information resulting from their new collaboration, and they thought their actions had demonstrated ONI's worthiness for equal billing in the Navy's codebreaking program.

An opportunity for ONI to gain a stronger presence in cryptology arose in 1926, when the Code and Signal Section was reorganized. The overhaul was engineered by ONC's Captain McLean. He had his own ideas about how the Navy's comint effort should be structured. As director of ONC, he carried an organizational designator, OP-20, signifying Division 20 within OPNAV. And, as director, he ran the Code and Signal Section. When that section was made part of the director's office in 1922, it became OP-20-G, the final letter denoting security.[46] Would there be a place in OP-20-G for ONI?

Yes, but not as envisioned by ONI, which remained on the outside looking in. Under the change, Code and Signals was transformed into three subordinate offices: OP-20-GC (the codes and ciphers desk); OP-20-GS (the visual signals desk); and OP-20-GX (the research desk), under Rochefort. Later the research desk would become OP-20-GY. Not until 1934 was a language section added to OP-20-G, designated OP-20-GZ and operating under ONC. Meanwhile, ONI continued to supply translators.

ıı ▆ ıı

By the time Rochefort took over the research desk, the Red Code project had reached an impasse. Attacking the text that accompanied the coded material, ONI's translators had taken the project about as far as they could. When Rochefort first met the Haworths, they had been on the job four years and still hadn't completed their work. They couldn't always find English equivalents for technical Japanese terms, leaving huge gaps in their translation.

Rochefort suggested that the research desk bring in a Navy language officer familiar with Japan's military and naval lexicon.[47] ONI's man assigned to the project, Lieutenant Commander Walter McClaran, agreed. He found an excellent Japanese linguist serving on a cruiser, the *Rochester*, based in the Panama Canal zone. The officer was a worldly, aggressive lieutenant commander named Ellis Mark Zacharias. Zacharias was ordered to Washington.

A career intelligence officer who projected an air of confidence, Zacharias was drawn to the work by his belief that "romance and glamour" surrounded the field, Rochefort later opined.[48] Whatever his motives, Zacharias knew Japan about as well as anyone in the Navy. Six years earlier he had served as an assistant naval attaché in the U.S. embassy in Tokyo, learning the language and getting acquainted with Japan. He had been one of the first beneficiaries of a new Navy program to send promising officers to Japan to master that country's complicated language.[49]

⊪

Reporting to Room 2646 early in 1926, Zacharias confessed to bewilderment about the world he now entered. It was a side of intelligence work he had never seen before and, he quickly discovered, there was nothing glamorous about it. "The few persons who were assigned to this section of the Navy Department were taciturn, secretive people who refused to discuss their jobs or to reveal details of their assignment," Zacharias wrote after the war. He couldn't have provided a better description of the Haworths, Driscoll, Bogel and, of course, Rochefort. Zacharias found the work mind-numbing but fascinating in its own way. "Hours went by without any of us saying a word," he wrote, "just sitting in front of piles of indexed sheets on which a mumbo-jumbo of figures or letters was displayed in chaotic disorder, trying to solve the puzzle bit by bit like fitting together the pieces of a jigsaw puzzle."[50] He succeeded in his assignment, filling in all the gaps in the Red Book, as the Red Code had come to be called.

Zacharias remained for a while in what he called "this phantom outfit," working seven months with Rochefort and Miss Aggie as they turned their attention to the code itself.

⊪

Rochefort now assumed responsibility for breaking the Red Code. The basics were known. The code had two parts, the first straightforward, consisting of some 100,000 code groups, each a cluster of numerals representing a Japanese word, sentence, or syllable. Matching up these groups with Japanese terms would have been hard enough. But the second part complicated matters by cloaking the underlying groups in another layer of digits.

This involved a second book consisting of thousands of additional numerals, called additives. A code clerk on the sending end would simply superimpose a set of randomly chosen numerals on the code groups. Another code clerk on the receiving end looked for a keyword in the message that told him what page to turn to in the additive book to find how the code had been enciphered, thereby enabling him to strip off the additives before looking up the meaning of each code group.

Rochefort and his team had the code book, but they didn't have the additive book. They couldn't get anywhere until they separated the superimposed numbers from the actual code group. As one writer explained, it was "like finding a way across a strange country without a map or a compass."[51]

To this task, Rochefort brought his own distinctive style. "It first off involves a process I call the staring process," he commented. "You look at all these messages that you have; you line them up in various ways; you write them one below the other; you write them in various forms and you stare at them. Pretty soon you'd notice a pattern; you'd notice a definite pattern between these messages. This is the first clue."[52]

In this instance, however, the "staring process" didn't yield results. Rochefort's team struggled months without making a breakthrough. Still on the scene, Zacharias was awed by the spectacle he witnessed, describing Rochefort and his crew as "the Trappist monks of Intelligence," people who said nothing but knew and saw all. They were "simple and unspectacular people, completely absorbed in their work," Zacharias wrote, without naming names. "They were hard workers keeping long hours, forgetting meals and Sundays when engaged in the solution of an enigma. Often they hit upon the solution after midnight while pondering the problem in bed. They would leave home as soon as possible, rush to their offices, and continue their work without interruption until assured of the solution or the fact that they were up a blind alley."[53]

Leaving aside Zacharias' odd notion that these were "simple people" interested only in their work, he provided a pretty good description of Joe Rochefort. Truth be told, the struggle to break the Red Code, the tension generated by the project, was weighing on Rochefort.

Sitting at his desk for hours, concentrating intensely on the papers piled in front of him, smoking constantly now, at least one cigar a day along with cigarettes and two or three pipes of tobacco, he was expending enormous amounts of nervous energy while working at least ten hours a day. Night after night he returned utterly worn out to the townhouse he and Fay rented in northwest Washington, often sick to his stomach.[54]

"Three evenings out of four, maybe more often, I would come home, say, at 5:00 or 5:30 or 6:00 in the evening from the Navy Department, and I would immediately have to lie down because I couldn't eat anything maybe until 8:00 or 9:00 at night," Rochefort said later.[55]

He tried everything he could think of to relax. He took up golf and took long walks. One day a week he walked the two and a half miles from his home on Reservoir Road to Washington's Dupont Circle and back. Nothing worked. He lost weight, dropping to around 155 pounds from his usual 175.[56]

Mercifully, after approximately a year, he and Miss Aggie finally reached a point where they could "read" the Red Code, the "bunch of messages" they couldn't make sense of earlier that had been driving Rochefort home in frustration night after night. He attributed this success to Miss Aggie. "I would say she was mostly responsible for the first one we solved while I was in charge," Rochefort commented. "She deserves all the credit for that."[57]

Strenuous as this labor may have been, the results justified the effort, Safford wrote later. Because of messages the research desk could now read, the Navy learned of various accidents on Japanese men-of-war, better understood the capability of Japanese torpedoes, and gained an "early knowledge" of their advances in naval aviation.[58]

11 ■ 11

Not all of the research desk's activities were grimly serious. One of the lighter moments occurred when Rochefort asked his class of junior officers learning cryptanalysis to solve one of the State Department's "unbreakable" codes. They did so easily, thereby incurring the wrath of State's top officials. "They got quite indignant over this whole thing," recalled an obviously pleased Rochefort. "They said it couldn't be [done], because never in history had they lost a copy of this [particular] code. Therefore, no one else could beat it . . . this was ridiculous."[59]

Such diversions were rare. Rochefort's grueling schedule continued. No sooner was the Red Code solved than new messages showed up, courtesy of the intercept sites Safford had set up in Shanghai, Hawaii, and elsewhere. Attacking new intercepts wasn't the only burden weighing on Rochefort. He was disturbed by the in-fighting and bureaucratic politics that marked relations between naval intelligence and naval communications. ONI had been unhappy for years. The problem centered in part around the Red Code. ONI had turned over this asset to ONC with the "expectation that [naval intelligence] would be furnished the information obtained by the use of this code."[60]

That didn't happen. Believing they had been double-crossed, ONI's top officers mounted a behind-the-scenes effort to take over the research desk. Rochefort found himself caught in the middle of a power struggle. "Several attempts [were] made to bring the section over to the Office of Naval

Intelligence," he wrote. "These attempts all failed because of strong opposition of the Director of Naval Communication"—Rochefort's boss, Captain McLean.[61]

It was hard to say whether ONI or ONC did the most sinning. There was no question that many top officers in each unit took a dim view of their brethren next door (ONI was in the seventh wing). "Naval intelligence was kind of a dumping ground for the misfits in the Navy for a long time," as Safford later put it.[62] Rochefort respected many of ONI's officers but shared Safford's essential view. Intelligence "was just a nice social job," Rochefort said. "You're invited to various parties at various embassies or legations or one thing and another, and you mix with nice people, but you don't do anything. This is intelligence."[63]

Rochefort seemed to support McLean in his effort to fend off ONI. But that wouldn't last. His views regarding the split would change markedly in the years ahead. Indeed, his assessment of the merits of the two offices would very nearly reverse. Always careful to exempt Safford from any criticism, Rochefort would find fault with many top officials in communications and, surprisingly for a research desk alumnus, incline toward the ONI side of the dispute. But not yet.

ıı■ıı

Rochefort never summed up his years at Main Navy, but he probably would have called them a mixed bag. On the plus side, he evolved into a full-fledged cryptanalyst and impressed his bosses. Captain McLean pronounced him "particularly well-fitted for this highly specialized work," and went on to remark that Rochefort "has much self assurance and shows promise of becoming one of the experts in cryptanalysis in the service." He found Rochefort "eminently qualified to organize a Radio Intelligence Unit in peace or war, and for the present his services would be of greater value to the Government in connection with this work, than any other." McLean's fitness report was dated 13 October 1926, just eight months after Rochefort had assumed charge of the research desk.[64] Rochefort seemed headed toward a career in cryptanalysis.

Besides winning over some seasoned senior officers, he forged strong friendships that would shape his naval career. His bond with Laurance Safford would work to the advantage of both men as they pursued paths that would ultimately intertwine. And Rochefort also made a favorable impression on Ellis Zacharias that, unbeknownst to him, would benefit the young lieutenant sooner rather than later.

Highly prized as he may have been by his Main Navy superiors, Rochefort, for his part, wasn't pleased by his two years in Washington. The totality of his experience there led him to make a fateful decision. Praised by Captain McLean as "eminently qualified" for a career in cryptanalysis, Rochefort now abandoned that field as a career goal. He thought he had good reasons.

He didn't like Main Navy politics. Appalled by the previously described power struggle, he believed the feud weakened the cryptanalytic effort—which, he believed, had the potential to become a vital program in time of war. Additionally, his health had suffered. "I had ulcers as a result of [cryptanalytic work done from] 1925 to '27," he said.[65] It wasn't until later that Rochefort would be diagnosed with the peptic ulcers that plagued him in middle age, but he traced the seeds of the ailment to his years running the research desk.[66]

Finally, he wanted to rise in the Navy. He didn't think that would happen if he remained in cryptanalysis. For two years he had observed the fate of officers who landed in codebreaking. "Every time he goes to Washington and goes to this particular division, nobody knows what he does or anything else," Rochefort commented, "so he becomes known as somewhat of a nut." Rochefort didn't want to become known as a nut. "I wanted to get in the fleet," he said. "I considered myself a naval officer, and I would much prefer to have gone through the normal tours of a ship or shore duty" than find himself channeled into the shadow world of codebreaking. "So I made every effort to stay away from cryptanalysis."[67]

On 24 September 1927, after nearly two years at Main Navy, he got his way. He was ordered to report to the destroyer *Macdonough* for duty as executive officer and navigator. Rochefort had four days to get to San Diego; he didn't waste any time. He and Fay left by train immediately. Rochefort couldn't wait to get back on board a ship.

4

Fleet Gadfly, Tokyo Whiz

I commenced to realize why they had sent this
individual out there.

—Arthur H. McCollum

Rochefort rediscovered his zest for sea duty on board the *Macdonough*. Launched in 1920, the vessel was now middle-aged by Navy standards— in 1930 she would be sold for scrap. But in 1927 the *Macdonough* was an integral part of the Battle Fleet—the U.S. Fleet's main offensive arm. Based in San Diego, the destroyer operated primarily along the West Coast, sometimes joining the Battle Fleet for maneuvers. Capable of a top speed exceeding thirty-three knots, the ship was fast and, along with other "four-pipers," as these old-style destroyers were known, brought some bite to naval combat. "We used to call them the 'light cavalry of the sea,'" Rochefort said.[1]

The young lieutenant liked his duty as the *Macdonough*'s executive officer. He relished the enlarged responsibility granted him as second in command to the ship's captain, Commander Arthur S. "Chips" Carpender. A stern, dour figure with a piercing gaze, Carpender was held in awe by many. Commanding the destroyer *Fanning* in 1917, he had gained fame for being first in the U.S. Navy to sink a German submarine in the European War. The deed earned him a Distinguished Service Medal, the Navy's second highest decoration at that time.

Carpender was a hard-nosed CO and "most competent," Rochefort recalled. "Unfortunately, his requirements reached nearly perfection. That was all. He merely required perfection." He didn't get it. "As far as I was concerned, he set a marvelous example," Rochefort said, but it was one "his officers just couldn't meet." And when they fell short, "he'd be very rough on his officers. Very rough."[2]

Rochefort survived Carpender. He enjoyed destroyer duty and, he admitted, found the rigorous drills imposed by his hard-to-please captain "valuable." Carpender seemed to think well enough of Rochefort, describing him first as "satisfactory" but later going further. "I consider him a very good officer," Carpender wrote of Rochefort in spring 1928.[3]

If Rochefort was now making a stronger impression, it was at least in part because of his two years on the research desk. Washington had done two things for him. Already cheekily self-assured, he was now imbued with even greater confidence in his ability to hold his own with the Navy's panjandrums, the crème de la crème of Annapolis. And Washington added another dimension to his naval skills. As the master of a strange and little-understood art, Rochefort now possessed a tool that might come in handy on a warship and prove useful to a ship's captain.

Cryptanalysis followed Rochefort to sea. As much as he wanted to get away from codebreaking, there was no escaping it; he was inextricably tangled up with the world of cryptology. In a switch from his mood at Main Navy, he now welcomed it. He made cryptanalysis a subspecialty. From his new perch, he scrutinized U.S. Fleet communication practices, particularly as they affected the handling of coded messages. He didn't like what he saw. Sloppy handling of sensitive material had disturbed him in Washington, and it bothered him now that he was at sea on board the *Macdonough*, steaming with the Battle Fleet. This time he started telling people.

On 25 November 1927, two months after joining his new ship, Rochefort dashed off a "confidential" memorandum to Lieutenant Ralph O. Myers. He was the radio officer on board the *Litchfield*, flagship of Destroyer Squadron Twelve, in which Rochefort served. "Since joining the Destroyer Squadrons," Rochefort began, "I have noted several instances of, in my opinion, serious misuses" of codes. This caused vessels to tell headquarters results of gunnery performances by radio through a code he believed had been "compromised."

As a result, Rochefort maintained, ships routinely "read" the secret messages of other ships. So every time the *Macdonough* or, for that matter, any other ship, fired her guns during practice and radioed home the results—information intended to be confidential—the ship's performance was instantly common knowledge. "Almost every officer and man in the ships knows how many hits were obtained and a little later the score," Rochefort pointed out.

He traced the security breach to communications officers, most of whom, he alleged, didn't know the difference between routine messages and important ones. He proposed to Myers that "steps be taken" to correct the situation, by either less frequent use of radio or better encryption of messages.[4]

Whether this memo produced any changes in Navy thinking about codes was never clear, but Rochefort wasn't through yet. Over the next sixteen months he continued to watch how ships in the Battle Fleet secured, or sometimes failed to secure, their codes. His ability to observe was aided by the fleet's periodic exercises, during which Rochefort and other officers with some background in cryptology were transferred as needed to set up codebreaking teams. Through these sessions, Rochefort hoped to demonstrate how easily U.S. Navy codes could be broken.

Early in 1929, he found himself in the right situation to do just that.[5] Transferred to the *California*, Rochefort joined forces with Lieutenant (jg) Thomas G. Dyer, earlier one of his students at the research desk and now assistant communications officer with the Battle Fleet. In this exercise, Rochefort and Dyer were to tackle codes emanating from a handful of Pacific Fleet ships—hypothetical enemies. "Rochefort and I were quite successful," Dyer remembered. "We solved every key change that they had and read every message that we were able to intercept."[6]

⸻ ■ ⸻

After observing the Battle Fleet's communications for nearly eighteen months, Rochefort judged its code-handling practices careless and slipshod. He said so in a 23 February 1929 memorandum to the commander in chief, U.S. Fleet, Admiral Henry A. Wiley, with copies to Captain Harold R. Stark (commander, Destroyer Squadrons, Battle Fleet); Captain Husband E. Kimmel (commander, Destroyer Squadron Twelve); Admiral William V. Pratt (commander in chief, Battle Fleet); and Lieutenant Commander Oliver L. "Pug" Downes, who had relieved Carpender as skipper of the *Macdonough*.[7]

The future Rochefort had just showed up—the one who spoke his mind and always told his superiors exactly what he thought. If he had any qualms about addressing so august a group, they weren't apparent in his memo, boldly titled "Suggestions for Improvement—Naval Communications." Suffused with sarcasm bordering on insult, Rochefort's memo asked if commanders who originated messages and the communications officers who encoded them took "the care of codes and ciphers which the investment of thousands of dollars" in their training would seem to demand. "It would seem not," Rochefort answered his own question.[8]

Drawing on his recent observations, he said he found commanders sending too many trivial and inconsequential messages in code—a practice that, he maintained, produced two unfortunate results. It clogged communication channels and provided a boon to eavesdroppers, who, with more raw material to work from, could more easily see patterns in the encrypted messages. In other words, the more messages sent, the more transparent they were.

Unable to resist a mocking tone, Rochefort recommended that "experienced communication officers" should write instructions and deliver lectures to officers dealing with communications to make sure they were "properly indoctrinated in (a) how to write despatches, (b) when to write despatches, (c) what means of communication to use, and most important (d) how to encipher a message."[9]

іı■ıı

What the Navy's top brass thought of Rochefort's advice, or whether they even read his memo, remained unclear. No reply ever showed up in his papers. But his critique probably didn't go entirely unnoticed. After all, he was an officer in good standing with an excellent background in cryptanalysis. His credentials conferred on his memorandum some measure of credibility.

Moreover, given the memo's many addressees, it was logical to expect that some copies were circulated throughout naval communications. And even if Admiral Wiley did not read the memo himself, the document probably was reviewed by an aide, who, to cover himself if for no other reason, would have passed it around for comments from some of the U.S. Fleet's communications officers. Among those who might have seen it was Lieutenant Commander Joseph R. Redman, radio officer assigned to the *Texas*, flagship of the U.S. Fleet. This is speculation. What isn't speculation is that the paths of Rochefort and Redman would cross again.

Whatever the ripple effects of Rochefort's memo, its candor clearly signaled the arrival of an unusual officer. Rochefort remained ambitious. He still did all the right things to get ahead. His superiors continued to rate him highly. Carpender's successor, Pug Downes, valued him. Shortly after Rochefort submitted his "suggestions" to Admiral Wiley, Downes described him as "an officer of excellent personal and military character—qualified for promotion."[10] But a few other traits now also appeared in his fitness reports.

Of the measures Downes had used to assess him earlier, in fall 1928—attributes ranging from leadership and judgment to tact and neatness—Rochefort now received his lowest grade in tact. He was still graded "reasonably tactful," avoiding the "unsatisfactory" category. It was not a bad grade, just the lowest of his grades.[11]

⠁⠁■⠁⠁

Whether Rochefort's combination of attributes would have advanced his fortunes with the U.S. Fleet or conspired to undermine them would never be known. It turned out the Navy had something else in mind for Joe Rochefort.

Three years earlier, while still running the research desk at Main Navy, he had sent a letter to BuNAV that would change his life. He had asked for duty in the Japanese language school in Tokyo. BuNAV's chief, Rear Admiral R. H. Leigh, had acknowledged the memo, telling Rochefort, "A note has been made of your request and it has been filed for future consideration."[12] Months went by and nothing more was heard of the matter. Rochefort joined the four-piper in September 1927. Tokyo seemed a long way away.

It got closer on 26 July 1929, when Rochefort got the news he had been hoping for. Since the early 1920s, the Navy had been sending two naval officers every year (and one Marine officer every third year) to Tokyo to study Japanese. Rochefort found he had been picked as one of the two for 1929. He was ordered detached from the *Macdonough*, told to proceed to San Francisco, and, on 6 September, to board the steamship *President Adams* for Kobe, Japan.[13] Even better, he was authorized to bring with him his wife, Fay, and the couple's six-year-old son, Joseph Junior.[14]

Rochefort would always insist that the order came as a complete surprise. "I had given no thought to it at all until I received a letter from the Navy Department asking me if I would be interested in going to Japan for the purpose of learning the language," Rochefort said later. "I hadn't considered the possibility because I was married, and in those days the Navy Department disliked to send anybody out there who was married."[15]

Why Rochefort professed to be astonished is baffling; he had been seeking the appointment for years.[16] But he was right about one thing: The Navy tried to avoid sending married officers overseas. Of the fifty-five officers who passed through the Japanese language course in Tokyo from 1910 through fall 1941, only three were married.

Rochefort attributed his good fortune to his Main Navy friend Ellis Zacharias, now serving with ONI in Washington. ONI ran the Japanese language program. "Zach told me he was responsible for this," Rochefort said.[17] Impressed with Rochefort's abilities, Zacharias might very well have pushed the young officer forward. Clearly Rochefort needed a strong advocate inside ONI to have pulled off the Tokyo coup, and Zacharias probably was that person.

⏸ ■ ⏸

The year 1929 turned out to be pivotal for millions, not only Joe Rochefort. The Great Crash that fall plunged the country into a deep depression from which it wouldn't recover until war-related spending started putting people back to work in the early 1940s.

The year was notable for another event. Although of lesser magnitude than the crash, it still had historic importance. It stemmed from the new man in the White House, Herbert Hoover, a high-minded Quaker who brought with him a new team of national leaders. One of the most distinguished was Henry L. Stimson, chosen by Hoover to be secretary of state. Stimson was a very proper gentleman—"gray suited, gray mustachioed, gray-haired," as historian David Kahn described him.[18]

When Stimson learned early in 1929 that State was underwriting the Cipher Bureau, the so-called black chamber headed by Herbert O. Yardley, he blew up, calling this work "highly unethical." He encapsulated his wrath in a phrase that seemed to epitomize the innocence of the era: "Gentlemen do not read each other's mail."[19] Stimson cut off Yardley's funding, ending a program that eight years earlier had broken Japan's diplomatic code and permitted a negotiating coup at the Washington Naval Conference.

Yardley and his team were out of work, but all was not lost. In a move that would prove visionary in just a few years, the U.S. Army snatched up the remnants of Yardley's Cipher Bureau. With no fuss or publicity, the bureau's records were turned over to Army's Signal Intelligence Service, under the leadership of its ace cryptanalyst, William Friedman. Soon Friedman and his team would lead the attack on Japan's most secret form of communication: its revised and substantially tougher diplomatic code.

While Yardley's black chamber was being shuttered, the Navy's crypt-analytic effort was running into troubles of its own. Hobbled by weak leadership, the research desk had failed to maintain the high level of activity it had demonstrated earlier, first under Safford and then Rochefort. A particular sore point was that the desk had made little progress in training new cryptanalysts.

A 1930 ONC memo reflected the disappointment of naval communications. "Six years after the establishment of a Research Section there are but six officers in the Navy who can be considered eligible and competent to perform special cryptanalytical duties," the memo noted. It pointed out that sixteen officers detailed to codebreaking instruction had washed out. In addition to Safford, the six who were successful included Lieutenants Bern Anderson and Joe Wenger and Lieutenants (jg) W. H. Leahy, Thomas Huckins, and Thomas Dyer, by now known to all as Tommy. Of these, four (Wenger, Dyer, Leahy, and Huckins) had no more than six months instruction in cryptanalysis.

Rochefort's name wasn't on the list. By entering into the Japanese language program run by ONC's archrival, ONI, he had moved out from under ONC's protective umbrella. This apparently had disqualified him for membership in the cryptanalytic community. The ONC memo referred to Rochefort only fleetingly, almost as though he had gone over to the enemy. "Rochefort has more or less divorced himself from [cryptanalytic] duty by becoming a Japanese language student," the memo said.[20] But if he had known about the ONC memo, Rochefort probably wouldn't have cared. He was now moving in a very different direction.

⠁⠿⠁

With San Francisco in the background and Fay and Joe Junior in tow, on 6 September 1929 Rochefort boarded the steamer that would take them to Japan. Awaiting him on board was one of the more pleasant surprises of his naval career, an encounter with Lieutenant (jg) Edwin T. Layton, the second officer picked that year to study Japanese in Tokyo. The two men liked each other immediately. "Our lifelong friendship began that [month] on board the steamer *President Adams* when the long Pacific crossing gave me a chance to get acquainted with him, his attractive wife, and their infant [*sic*] son," Layton wrote later.[21]

The Rochefort-Layton meeting would prove fateful. Their friendship would continue, but in a few years it would change, evolving into something resembling an alliance. Their accord during the weeks leading to the pivotal naval battle of the Pacific War would shape the outcome of that campaign. But that was thirteen years away.

Despite contrasting personalities—Rochefort quiet and soft-spoken, Layton brash and sometimes pushy—they had much in common. Both were young, Rochefort twenty-nine (thirty-one in Navy years), Layton three years younger. Rochefort, a lieutenant, outranked Layton, a lieutenant junior grade. Standing about six feet tall, they were both on the lean side and smart, very sure of themselves, and cocky.

And they wanted to learn Japanese. Rochefort's curiosity about Japan had been whetted by his years on the research desk grappling with IJN codes, his desire to study the language encouraged by Ellis Zacharias. Layton's interest in Japan had been piqued in 1925 when, as an ensign assigned to the battleship *West Virginia*, anchored in San Francisco, he had been chosen as one of six officers to escort around that city six Japanese midshipmen who were there on a cruise as part of their course of instruction. Three spoke perfect English, the other three perfect French.

"But here is the real kicker—there wasn't one single U.S. official—no naval officer, or anyone on our side, who could speak one word of Japanese!" Layton recalled. "For the first time I learned what 'losing face' was. I felt ashamed for the United States, feeling that we should have had someone there who could speak Japanese."[22]

On board the *President Adams*, Rochefort and Layton, both with their quirks and rough edges, enjoyed each other's capacity for sass and irreverence, especially when directed at superiors they deemed overrated or stuffed-shirts. Pugnaciously competitive, Layton could be intimidating, even abrasive. His classmates at Annapolis (class of 1924) had saddled him with the nickname "Brute," a moniker he hated and the mentioning of which he discouraged.[23]

Overbearing as he sometimes was, Layton didn't confine this personality trait to encounters with subordinates. Late in World War II while serving as the Pacific Fleet's intelligence officer on Guam, he mocked an admiral who asked him for details about Yokosuka, saying no such city existed when the older officer mispronounced it.[24] Layton didn't pull such stunts with Rochefort. They regarded each other as intellectual equals. Indeed, they enjoyed engaging in a certain amount of intellectual horseplay, kidding each other as "dunderheads" when one of them didn't know something. "It was all in good clean fun," said an officer who knew them both.[25]

If Layton had his foibles, so did Rochefort. One was his ceaseless preoccupation with security. There were things Rochefort wouldn't tell his new friend. "Throughout our three years of study in Japan, Rochefort never once mentioned his involvement with the Navy's secret codebreaking operations," Layton said later. "Not knowing of his experience with Japanese codes and communications, I was surprised by his apparent familiarity with the country."[26]

Rochefort was running true to form. Estranged as he may have been from the culture of Main Navy, he still observed the central ethic of a good intelligence officer: adherence to the principle of need-to-know.

ıı▉ıı

Three weeks after starting out, the *President Adams* arrived in Kobe, a thriving port city on the northern shore of Osaka Bay. A day later, on 28 September, Rochefort and Layton reported to the U.S. Embassy in Tokyo and met a naval attaché, Captain James Vance Ogan. A crusty, blunt-spoken man, Ogan kept his instructions brief: "You have only two duties to perform," he told them. "One, study and master the Japanese language; two, stay out of trouble. If you fail in either, I'll send you home on the next ship. You are not to engage in any spying or other espionage activity. Don't think of yourself as some Nathan Hale or anything like that. Keep your nose clean. Oh, yes, pay day is once a month. Other than that I don't want to see you."[27]

Admitting he didn't know the language, Ogan turned the pair over to someone who did, assistant naval attaché Lieutenant Commander Arthur H. McCollum. A stocky, affable man who spoke excellent Japanese, McCollum had been born in Nagaski in 1898, of missionary parents. He'd lived in Japan off and on during his childhood years, later attended the Naval Academy, then returned to Japan in 1922 for the same course that now brought Rochefort and Layton to Tokyo.[28]

McCollum gave Rochefort a scare. He greeted Layton but wasn't all that happy to see Rochefort, accompanied as he was by his wife and son. McCollum didn't see how anyone could learn this most daunting of languages and still manage a family and cope in a perplexing city like Tokyo. He thought the Rochefort clan should be returned to the United States at once. "I sent a dispatch to the Navy Department protesting the sending of a married naval officer out there because living conditions were most difficult," McCollum said later.[29]

McCollum heard back from Washington quickly. "I was told that they had special reasons for overlooking the normal encumbrance of a wife and a child," he said. "This fellow was going to stay anyway," the Washington cable added. Upon McCollum's return to Washington many months later, he explained: "I commenced to realize why they had sent this individual out there." Naval intelligence saw that Rochefort had unusual ability. That was that.

McCollum and Rochefort would eventually become friends, but not yet. There was much to be done. McCollum's first task was to assist the Rocheforts and Layton, to find suitable housing. They toured Tokyo. After finding one hotel after another out of their price range, they ended up at a place called the Bunka Apartments. The three Rocheforts moved into a twin-bedded room with a kitchen and dining area, while Layton took a single room down the hall.

Layton became a presence in the Rochefort household. They celebrated birthdays together and joined forces to escape Tokyo's stifling summer heat. Later Rochefort rented a house in Karizawa, a mountain retreat far from Tokyo, complete with cook and maid. By this time practically a member of the family, Layton joined them. He and Rochefort found the setting conducive to their work. "We studied from early morning until late at night," Layton recalled, "then we would always sit around and discuss things."[30] Studying Japanese with Rochefort also put Layton in a good position to study Rochefort.

He found his friend and colleague "not bookish, but he was one who wanted to know why things are done, what makes them tick," Layton said. "And with the language he kept asking questions as to why they do this and that. Like when the instructor explained to him that you had to read some things from the context; then he wanted to know how you recognize context, when you didn't know it. The instructor looked at him and said, 'you'll know it when it comes.'" Layton summed up their language tour: "In Japan his only hobby was learning Japanese. He spent all his time at that. That's all I did, too. All we did was study."[31]

⁍⁍◼⁍⁍

Ogan hadn't been kidding when he'd said the two men would be on their own. As language students they had no diplomatic status, meaning little protection if they got into scrapes with the Japanese government. They followed orders about staying away from the U.S. Embassy, dropping by only to collect their monthly paychecks and the fifty-dollar monthly bonus they received for education costs.[32]

Rochefort and Layton used the extra money to hire Naoe Naganuma, an excellent instructor who was, in effect, the principal of the U.S. language school in Japan. Each day Naganuma spent one hour in Rochefort's apartment and another in Layton's, employing a unique system of teaching that he had developed himself, tailored to meet individual needs of adult students.

Instead of starting with a Japanese primary-school text, as a Japanese youngster would use beginning his schooling, Naganuma introduced students to the complex language through hearing. "This was relatively painless, since Japanese is one of the easier languages to comprehend in simple spoken form," Layton later said. After his students could understand a little Japanese, Naganuma took them to movie houses showing American silent films. There they listened as an interpreter explained the action in colloquial Japanese.[33]

Once they were able to converse a bit—to make wants known, express feelings and ideas—they moved on to a more difficult task: reading and writing. They discovered that written Japanese was based on Chinese characters superimposed upon the independently developed spoken language. Each character, in effect a Chinese ideograph, had two or more pronunciations. Rochefort and Layton memorized thousands of ideographs and many times that number of pronunciations.

Rochefort thrived under Naganuma's system. Before his teacher's arrival each day, "I would study for a couple of hours memorizing all the characters," Rochefort said. "And then [an] instructor would come and then possibly I would take a walk and chat with people on the street." Through these meetings, Rochefort said he eventually learned some 3,500 Japanese characters. "I wouldn't call it too difficult," he said later, matter of factly.[34]

ıı■ıı

Rochefort and Layton joined a small community of Americans in Tokyo. Most were diplomats, attachés, or political officers attached to the U.S. Embassy, but some were Japanese language officers, or JLOs, who had arrived earlier. Rochefort and Layton raised their number to nine, seven Navy and two Marines.[35]

Many of the JLOs and embassy people Rochefort met during his three-year stint in Tokyo would become lifelong friends. Some, like Ogan, would ascend the promotion ladder at naval intelligence, and in the years ahead give Rochefort invaluable career advice. Others would occupy positions of influence in Washington's intelligence bureaucracy. McCollum, as chief of ONI's

Far Eastern Intelligence Section during 1941, would be among those responsible for keeping the Pacific Fleet commander in chief, Admiral Husband Kimmel, informed of Japan's military intentions.

One JLO, Lieutenant Alwin D. Kramer, who was in Tokyo from 1931 to 1934, would head OP-20-GZ, OP-20-G's translation desk, in 1941. That billet made him, in effect, the Navy's chief translator of Japan's diplomatic messages in Washington during the weeks leading to the Pearl Harbor attack. Kramer, in fact, was on duty at Main Navy when Japan's final fourteen-part message arrived the night and morning of 6–7 December.

Another JLO, Lieutenant Redfield "Rosey" Mason (in Tokyo 1930–33), after serving as a Japanese linguist in the Philippines in 1941, would relieve Kramer at OP-20-GZ. He and Rochefort in mid-1942 would lock horns over the destination of a massive IJN armada gathering in home waters, preparing to spread out and invade—somewhere.

ıı■ıı

New difficulties faced Americans living in Japan. They found their lives complicated by a series of ominous events that began in June 1931 with the publication there of a new book, *The American Black Chamber*, by Herbert O. Yardley, the U.S. cryptanalyst who had lost his job two years earlier when Secretary of State Stimson closed down the Cipher Bureau. An instant best seller in Japan, the book related how American codebreakers had compromised Japan's diplomatic messages during the Washington Naval Conference ten years earlier, enabling America to seemingly "trick" Japan into accepting a position of naval inferiority.[36]

"That [book] occasioned considerable discussion among the Japanese," Rochefort would later recall.[37] It did more than that; it "infuriated many Japanese and embittered relations between Japan and the United States," observed Yardley's biographer, David Kahn.[38] Japan's moderate government was humiliated by the disclosures and struck back. Japanese officialdom became more secretive than ever. The Japanese didn't change their codes, but they tweaked them to make them less vulnerable, and took steps to make their naval call signs harder for American eavesdroppers to capture. They also accelerated their attack on American codes.[39]

Deeply troubled as American officials were by the Yardley book, they were unable to do anything about the author or his juicy volume. The curious fact of the matter was that neither Yardley nor his publisher, the Bobbs-

Merrill Company, had broken any law in producing the *Black Chamber*. Rogue intelligence operatives could legally publish tell-all memoirs, but that would change.

‖∎‖

Americans in Japan weathered the Yardley storm, but disclosures from his book did nothing to lessen the nationalism that had been gathering steam in that country. Japan's brand of democratic government was being pushed to the breaking point as attacks on Western-style politicians increased in the Diet, Japan's bicameral legislature. These xenophobic impulses boiled over on 18 September 1931, when mutinous generals of Japan's Kwantung army in Manchuria fabricated an "incident" on the Japanese railway line at Mukden. The generals used the incident as a pretext to seize the whole of Manchuria, China's northernmost province.

The occupation of Manchuria triggered a chain of events that would destroy Japan's frail democratic government and bring the country into a confrontation with the international community. Ignoring protests lodged by other governments, in January 1932 Japan sent naval units to occupy the international port of Shanghai. That May ultra-nationalists assassinated Japan's moderate, Western-oriented premier, Tsuyoshi Inukai, seen as insufficiently supportive of the Manchuria takeover. Condemned for these actions by the League of Nations, Japan walked out of the world body in February 1933.

These and other developments intensified Japanese paranoia and feelings against foreigners. Rochefort got a taste of this fast-spreading attitude from a Japanese businessman who seemed to provide a rationale for—and preview of—what Japan might do if it felt boxed in. "I recall talking at some party with a fellow about my age, and he was with Mitsui Company," which was one of the two largest corporations in Japan, Mitsubishi being the other. "This is the time when the Japanese had become involved in Manchuria and had then gone down to Shanghai," Rochefort said. "I asked this fellow, 'Why did you do a thing like this, because you know you cannot defeat the Chinese.'"

"That's right," the executive responded. "But you're forgetting one thing. Our honor has become involved in this, and when honor becomes involved you should forget all the realistics [*sic*]. That is why we went down to Shanghai. Now Caucasians and you Americans, you don't understand this at all. . . . When honor is involved, we don't care about anything else."

At the time Rochefort thought "this was a little stupid," to start a war you know you can't win. "One simple reason—honor."[40] Years later he would remember this conversation and wish he had paid more attention to it. Rochefort seemed to feel that he and other Americans had a blind spot where Japan was concerned, failing to give sufficient weight to its cultural concept of honor.

⊩ ▌ ⊩

Rochefort's three years were just about up. On 18 June 1932, he received orders detaching him from the U.S. Embassy in Tokyo, effective 4 October. He had just completed his final examination on oral and written Japanese, one of twelve he had taken since arriving. His examiner rated him "excellent" in every phase of the oral language, from "conversation on any topic" to "interpretation of a short Japanese speech." His writing was nearly as good. "Lieutenant Rochefort . . . shows that he has used his three years admirably in acquiring a knowledge of the Japanese language," wrote the embassy's new naval attaché, Captain I. C. Johnson, who had relieved Ogan. "He is able to converse with ease and fluency on any subject. Likewise he can translate with freedom and precision articles of the most difficult character on technical, military, political and social subjects. Lieutenant Rochefort is considered one of the best students ever sent out."[41]

Layton, too, had excelled in his studies and, like Rochefort's, his Tokyo duty was about to end. In October he was ordered to Peiping, China, where he served four months as assistant naval attaché at the American Legation. Then the Navy returned him to Washington for an assignment at ONI that was followed by sea duty on board the battleship *Pennsylvania*. Layton relished his years in Japan. So did Rochefort. "That was a very, very pleasant interlude," he later said.[42] He cited the pageantry—the emperor's Chrysanthemum Party, the New Year's Gala at the Palace—and friends made among the Japanese. One other thing made the interlude especially pleasant for both Rocheforts: in November 1931 their second child, Janet, was born in Tokyo.

On 4 October 1932 the four Rocheforts traveled to Yokohoma, and there boarded the passenger liner *President Coolidge* that would take them back to the United States. But back to what? Having just finished three years on shore, Rochefort was now overdue for sea duty. That was fine with him. He wanted to return to the U.S. Fleet. He particularly wanted duty on a battleship.

But afterward, would he choose to remain with naval intelligence, under whose umbrella he had served in Tokyo? Or would he seek a reunion with naval communications, which maintained its hold over codebreaking through its continued jurisdiction over the research desk? Some thought he would want to rejoin the cryptanalytic world. But if the Navy thought that by sending Rochefort to Tokyo they would, in effect, make him a kind of double threat—a skilled Japanese linguist who could also break codes—it would be disappointed. He had other ideas.

II ■ II

Rochefort was not a man in a hurry in fall 1932. After arriving in San Francisco on 18 October, he didn't rush to Washington, where he had been ordered for temporary duty at ONI. He dreaded the idea of another spell at Main Navy. He recalled vividly the infighting five years earlier, but that wasn't all that slowed him down.

Rochefort had pressing family business. Six months after settling in Tokyo, he had received word that his mother had died at age seventy-four of a heart ailment. There was no way he could get to the funeral; he would just have to wait until his Japanese tour ended before he could look in on the family. He asked BuNAV for two months' leave and was given one.

Visiting his father for the first time in years, Joe found the elder Rochefort, now eighty-one, doing remarkably well, living in a small bungalow on West Twenty-Seventh Street, three miles from their old house. Ellen and Frank had moved out of the larger home a few years earlier, when many of their children had scattered. To Joe's relief, two of his brothers, Harold and Charles, had stayed home. They now shared the bungalow with their father and helped pay the bills, not always easy in the depths of the Depression.

Rochefort's other siblings all had jobs now. Hamilton, the oldest at forty-eight, pursued his career as a studio photographer "back East," first in Boston and later Detroit. The others remained in the Los Angeles area, William holding down a job as a waiter and Frank Patrick trying to start a career in sales. To many the superstar of the family was Margaret. As Sister Francis Mary with a distinguished Catholic order, she recently had been promoted to principal of Our Lady of Guadalupe School in Oxnard, California.

Caught up with family affairs, all that remained for Rochefort was to find a suitable home for Fay and the children. She decided against following him East, realizing he soon would be at sea. The best place for the threesome, they reasoned, was with Fay's parents. Fay, along with Joe Junior, now nine, and Janet, not yet two, moved into the modest two-story home in south Los Angeles. Rochefort had a train to catch.

By the time he reported to his ONI boss, Captain Hayne Ellis, on 18 November in Main Navy's seventh wing, Rochefort had made up his mind.

While he remained unsure about his ultimate goals in the Navy, he was very sure about what he *didn't* want to do: return to naval communications or resume his old career in cryptanalysis. "I had no intention of going back to it," Rochefort said later. Yes, he knew why the Navy wanted him to learn Japanese. "For possible use in cryptanalysis," he conceded. "But I was not about to ask for this sort of duty. I wasn't going to press the issue, no."[43]

If Rochefort retained any lingering doubts about his future course, they were dispelled by the situation he found at Main Navy. Once again intelligence and communications were feuding. The dispute couldn't have come at a worse time for intelligence. In the wake of Japan's occupation of Manchuria, Ellis had ordered his crew of eighteen officers and thirty-eight civilians to develop fresh strategic information with which to revise the Navy's basic contingency plan for war with Japan: War Plan Orange.[44]

From the standpoint of naval intelligence, naval communications had made this task virtually impossible. Still responsible for the research desk (now OP-20-GY), ONC quite simply had cut off the flow of all cryptanalytic findings to ONI. In an act of bare-knuckle bureaucratic aggression, ONC denied ONI any of its estimates about the Japanese fleet. ONI claimed ONC was reneging on an earlier deal to share information.[45] ONC said it was simply following the orders of the Chief of Naval Operations, Admiral William Veazie Pratt. ONC had a point.

Named CNO in 1930, Pratt inherited a Main Navy team that included Captain Harry A. Baldridge as director of naval intelligence. Pratt held Baldridge in low regard because he was sickly and generally viewed as a weak leader. Believing he couldn't be trusted to run ONI in a responsible way, Pratt put in place a bizarre, and what later proved to be destructively myopic, policy: he ordered ONC's director, Commander S. C. Hooper, to withhold all decrypted messages from ONI. Pratt "put a taboo on the whole office," Laurance Safford commented.[46]

Baldridge's tenure proved short; he was gone by May 1931. But Pratt's gag order remained in place. Without access to OP-20-GY's decrypts, ONI remained cut off from what it had come to regard as a crucial window into the inner sanctums of the Imperial Japanese Navy. Naval intelligence now operated very nearly blind.

By the time Rochefort arrived at Main Navy in fall 1932, Pratt's blackout was in full force.[47] When he learned of it, Rochefort fumed. He did what he often did when something bothered him: he wrote a memo. This one was directed to the officer who had been his superior in Tokyo, Captain Ogan, now serving as deputy to ONI Director Ellis.

Going further out on a limb than ever before, using language that was strong even by his standards, Rochefort fired off a scathing three-page memorandum in which he itemized what he regarded as the flaws and failings of naval communications. He cited the gag order. "I have been told that the officer in charge of the Cryptographic Section [OP-20-GY] has been ordered not to furnish this information," Rochefort stated. Insinuating that ONC's top officers were opportunists, he declared that "the biggest defect at present is the fact that the Cryptographic Section has been and is being used by the officers concerned to further their own ends."

To correct what he saw as ONC's fatal shortcomings, Rochefort dropped what would have been a mini-bombshell, one with grave consequences for his career if it had circulated at Main Navy. Quite simply, he "recommended that the Cryptographic Section be removed from the Office of Naval Communications and placed under the Office of Naval Intelligence."[48]

Whether Ogan passed Rochefort's screed over to Captain Ellis or anyone outside ONI, can be doubted. He probably buried the memo to protect Rochefort. In any case, nothing came of his sally against ONC. No reply from Ogan or anybody else ever turned up in Rochefort's papers. Given ONI's damaged reputation at this time, Rochefort's idea would have been firmly rejected by CNO Pratt and, to say the least, mocked by ONC's top officers.

Rochefort now looked ahead to his next duty. Captain Ogan may or may not have responded to Rochefort's memo, but he did give his outspoken subordinate some advice. "I asked him where I should go next," Rochefort recalled. "He told me to get on a battleship and the bigger the better."

Rochefort put in for just such duty.[49] The Navy acted fast. On 30 December 1932, he was detached from his temporary billet at ONI and ordered to Norfolk, Virginia. There he was to catch a destroyer, the *Leary*, that would take him down the Atlantic through the Panama Canal, then up the Pacific to San Pedro. Awaiting him there was the *Maryland*. Rochefort got his battleship.

5

The Admiral's Confidant

A general encyclopedia of information and usefulness . . . and one of the most outstanding officers of his rank.

—Joseph Mason Reeves

After a thirty-day detour on board the cruiser *Augusta*, conducting a codebreaking workshop keyed to U.S. Fleet maneuvers (Fleet Problem XIV), Rochefort finally caught up with the *Maryland* in Puget Sound. He was glad he did. The *Maryland*, which boasted a new type seaplane catapult and the first 16-inch guns to be mounted on any U.S. warship, was made to order for an ambitious young officer. One of the most advanced battleships in the fleet, the *Maryland* afforded Rochefort duty squarely in the mainstream of Navy life, just where he wanted to be. His new job: turret officer in the gunnery department.

Gunnery represented an opportunity. Hardly an officer could be found holding flag rank who had not, at one time or another, demonstrated prowess in the field of gunnery. Rochefort looked forward to his new duties. But the good fortune that had seemed to surround his career since his brush with disaster on board the *Cuyama* in 1924 appeared again. His luck, already good, suddenly got better. Before doing much in gunnery, he received a letter. It came from Captain William A. Glassford, an officer with fleet command who had been one of Rochefort's superiors at Main Navy during 1925–27.

Dubbed "Tubby" by his classmates at the Naval Academy (class of 1906), Glassford was a hard-driving, square-jawed officer who combined an engaging personality with a perfectionist streak and a solid Navy record. He had earned a Distinguished Service Medal in the European War while commanding a destroyer, then returned to Washington, where he assisted the director of naval communications. There he met Rochefort, then heading the research desk. Glassford was impressed with the young officer and kept track of him.

By spring 1933 Glassford was preparing for a round of sea duty as operations officer to Admiral William H. Standley, recently appointed commander of the U.S. Battle Fleet. "Captain Glassford asked me to be his assistant," Rochefort commented later. "I accepted this."[1]

On 20 May 1933 Rochefort reported to the *California*, flagship of the Battle Fleet, anchored in San Pedro Harbor. This battleship was smaller than the *Maryland* but similar in other respects, and Rochefort quickly fitted in. As assistant operations officer, his task was to aid Standley and Glassford in keeping the Battle Fleet moving: he set up fleet exercises, prepared anchorage charts, scheduled gunnery operations, and much more.

A billet so filled with administrative detail would not have appealed to all officers, but Rochefort liked it. It gave him a view of fleet operations from the bridge of a flagship—and a taste of just about everything involved in running a large naval force. He flourished in his new post. Standley liked him, describing Rochefort as "An excellent young officer [with] an unusually searching mind."[2] That was a good omen.

But Standley's tenure proved short. After just a few months commanding the Battle Fleet, he was ordered to Washington to relieve the controversial William V. Pratt as CNO. His departure turned out to be a blessing in disguise. Rochefort's duty under Standley's successor, Admiral Joseph Mason Reeves, would be one of the highlights of his career. Reeves pushed Rochefort forward in a way that was almost unheard-of in the Navy. He was not single-handedly responsible for Rochefort's accomplishments, but he gave the younger officer more running room than he had ever before enjoyed. Under Reeves, Rochefort blossomed into a top-flight naval officer.

But first Rochefort's new CO took some getting used to. Promoted to admiral as he assumed his new command, Reeves was demanding in every way. He was a strong-willed individualist who ran ships and fleets by his own rules, sometimes making them up as he went along. He disdained paper-pushers and nettlesome Navy routines. Navy men called him "Bull" for good reason.[3]

Tall, thin, spare, impeccable in his military bearing, Reeves looked every inch the admiral. With his caustic manner and icy stare, he could be jarring.

His appearance was softened, however, by a set of closely cropped sideburns and an out-of-fashion goatee, giving him a quaint air that also made him the object of a certain amount of shipboard mirth. One moniker that followed him around was "Billy-Goat." Some called him "the old man with the beard."[4]

But Reeves was no wild eccentric; he was essentially a fiercely independent officer who had his own vision of what the Navy should be doing. Eight years earlier, at age fifty-three, he had learned to fly at the Navy's Pensacola flight-training base, earning his wings and qualifying as a naval aviation observer. A few years later on board the carrier *Saratoga*, he had become the first American naval officer to command a carrier division, a perch from which he contributed substantially to the cause of U.S. naval air power and the development of aircraft carriers.

As defined by Washington, Reeves' job was to make aviation a stronger component of the U.S. Fleet. He delighted in the assignment. He retained many who had been on Standley's staff, including Glassford and Rochefort. That may have been good news, but Reeves was not by any means easy to work for. In public he was quiet, dignified, and courteous, but behind closed doors he could be a terror. "When his dander was up his eyes flashed and his words would crack like a whip!" Thomas Wildenberg observed in his colorful biography of Reeves.[5]

⸱⸱■⸱⸱

Rochefort had a history of impressing tough bosses. Not only had he survived the *Macdonough*'s perfectionist captain, Chips Carpender, he had won his praise in 1928. Rochefort fared even better under the hard-boiled Reeves, who very early accorded the young lieutenant just about the highest mark that could be given an officer on a fitness report: 3.9 out of 4.0. "An exceptional officer of excellent judgment," Reeves said of Rochefort in October 1933. Reeves marked him down in only one category, and then only slightly. This was for tact, not the first time Rochefort had been twitted by a superior about his shortcoming.[6]

But Rochefort proved his worth in areas that mattered far more to Reeves than tact. Shortly after taking over the Battle Force in mid-1933, Reeves confronted a major task: conducting a previously scheduled fleet problem set for 7–10 July. The problem involved locating and tracking mock combatants in the Pacific waters near San Pedro. The exercise sought to determine the usefulness of combat intelligence at sea: coding, decrypting, and evaluating information. Reeves called upon Rochefort, his resident cryptanalyst.

Rochefort headed the decrypt unit with the blue team, representing the U.S. Fleet. His job was to study call signs from participating ships, classify radio traffic, and decrypt codes and ciphers. Throughout the fleet other officers performed similar duties. The results were disappointing. Commander O. L. Wolford, the fleet officer charged with evaluating the exercise, found the fleet so lacking in trained personnel and organization that it could not be counted on to identify a potential enemy at sea. But Wolford singled out one officer for praise: Joe Rochefort.[7]

Rochefort, Wolford observed, "rendered invaluable service but without adequate assistance was seriously handicapped." He continued: "In addition to being short-handed in the decrypting unit, Lieutenant Rochefort on occasion relieved the Intelligence Officer and attempted to carry on the duties of both."[8] Reeves liked that. A hard worker doing double duty, Rochefort clearly was Reeves' kind of officer.

After a dust-up between the commander in chief of the U.S. Fleet, Admiral David F. Sellers, and CNO Standley, Sellers lost his job. Standley had a successor in mind. Early in 1934, BuNAV cut orders designating Reeves the next commander in chief of the U.S. Fleet, or CinCUS, as the post was inaptly dubbed. On board the fleet flagship *Pennsylvania* in New York Harbor, Reeves was sworn in on 15 June 1934. He now occupied the highest post in the seagoing Navy.

Perhaps because the ceremony was held in the New York spotlight, or because world events were making people more defense-minded, or simply because people liked his goatee, Reeves captured the imagination of the press and became an instant celebrity. His portrait appeared on the cover of *Time* magazine. The accompanying article summarized his career, treating favorably his unorthodox ways. Reeves, *Time* said, was sure to put his "stamp on the Navy."[9]

Navy people wondered what he would do with the U.S. Fleet. Also unknown was what would happen to his staff from the *California*. Lieutenant Rochefort, as it turned out, had nothing to worry about. As Wildenberg put it, he had "so impressed Reeves with his acumen for intelligence that Reeves kept the young officer with him when he moved his staff" to the *New Mexico*, the fleet's temporary flagship while the *Pennsylvania* was renovated.[10] Rochefort would retain his old position, assistant operations officer, but he would perform his duties at a higher level. No longer would he work for the Battle Force; he now served the U.S. Fleet.

Reeves didn't keep everyone. William Glassford, Rochefort's immediate superior, was ordered to Argentina for duty with the Argentine Navy Department. Rochefort was sorry to see him go but pleased to find several old research desk and Tokyo colleagues all coincidentally on board the *New Mexico*. Among them were Tommy Dyer, now serving in gunnery. Expected soon was another cryptanalyst, Lieutenant (jg) Wesley "Ham" Wright, still in training with OP-20-G in Washington.

Rochefort also was delighted to come across his old friend Eddie Layton, now a full lieutenant. Like Dyer, Layton was a holdover from Admiral Sellers' recent tenure as CinCUS. Layton had been busy since language school in Tokyo, serving briefly as a translator with the American legation in Peiping. He had then returned to Washington and divided his time between naval intelligence and naval communications, where he had met Agnes Driscoll and picked up some of the rudiments of cryptology. Layton had rotated back to sea in 1933, joining the *Pennsylvania* as a gunnery officer. Reeves would tap both his and Rochefort's intelligence talents.

For many months the fleet flagship seemed a genial habitat for codebreakers. But the atmosphere changed in April 1935, when Reeves shifted his flag to the now-renovated *Pennsylvania* and brought on board a new officer to command the flagship: Captain Russell Willson. As the first director of the Code and Signal Section in 1917, he was known to Rochefort, Dyer, and Wright. They knew that he had walked away from cryptology, calling the field a professional dead-end. He also tended to disparage those who remained in this activity.[11]

Rochefort and Willson were different Navy types. If Rochefort was straightforward and sometimes brusque, Willson was just the opposite—soft, genteel, careful in his speech. If Rochefort had rough edges, Willson was smooth, a trait that earned him the nickname "Fusser" at Annapolis. "Look at his picture," teased the Naval Academy's 1906 yearbook, "there you see depicted a noble character, famed throughout for his fussing capabilities."[12]

By 1935 he remained dignified in his bearing and always well-groomed. Tall, silver-haired, still boyish-looking, Willson fell into the category of naval officers some called show horses. An Army general referred to him as the best-looking man in the Navy.[13] Willson and Rochefort took an instant dislike to each other. Rochefort thought the captain pompous; he never tried to hide his low opinion of him.[14]

Happily for Rochefort, he was assigned to Reeves' staff and was insulated from Willson. So he could get away with a certain amount of insolence. Or at least he thought he could.

❙❙■❙❙

Reeves quickly asserted his authority as CinCUS. He didn't like the way his predecessor, Admiral Sellers, had done the job. He found the U.S. Fleet mired in red tape and paperwork. He canceled all of Sellers' standing orders and directed Rochefort and other members of his staff to rewrite the fleet's instructions "to bring the fleet 'up to snuff,'" as Reeves put it. By this he meant getting the fleet ready for war, should it suddenly be thrust upon the country. He believed the fleet to be ill-prepared for such an emergency, calling it "over-organized, over-educated, over-theorized, over-administered, and over-complicated."[15] Reeves envisioned a more streamlined and flexible fleet governed by certain fundamentals, one of which was simplicity, leading to fleet movements that would be easy to execute and to understand in a crisis.

All this required drastic changes throughout the fleet. Many flag officers and ships' captains from the Sellers era suddenly found that months and sometimes years of planning were now obsolete. Rochefort ended up in the middle of Reeves' reform program as his place on the admiral's team crystallized.

The younger officer variously described himself as "a general handyman" and "a utility man and confidant of Admiral Reeves." He might also have called himself Reeves' troubleshooter. Rochefort was among those charged with the thankless task of having to deliver unwelcome news to reluctant fleet officers, virtually all of whom outranked him. "A new broom sweeps clean" was the way Rochefort described Reeves' actions, suggesting that he was simply doing what new admirals always tended to do: change things. But, Rochefort admitted years later, not all officers liked being swept clean, or the young officers who did the sweeping.

Reeves conferred on Rochefort responsibilities that far exceeded the prerogatives inherent in his modest rank of lieutenant. This irked some of Rochefort's superiors. But Rochefort admired Reeves' way of doing things, even if it sometimes put him in an awkward spot. "Admiral Reeves was quite a person, and he did a lot of rather unorthodox things," Rochefort said. "He tried to bring the fleet up to efficiency, and in doing this he undoubtedly stepped on some people's toes and then they would, with some reasonableness, ascribe his actions to some of these younger people [such as Joe Rochefort] that Admiral

Reeves surrounded himself with." Unpopular as he may have been with some officers, Rochefort found his duty "fantastic, because . . . I was serving at the very top level of the fleet," he said. "It was a far cry from there down to, say, commanding a destroyer or something like that. Oh yes, this was remarkable duty, and I enjoyed it."[16]

⸱⸱ ■ ⸱⸱

Rochefort embarked on many adventures set in motion by the unstoppable Reeves—who seemed never to miss an opportunity to display his scorn for Navy rules, anything smacking of bureaucracy. When Reeves saw a problem that needed fixing, he wouldn't bother going through channels. He would simply devise a scheme to get things done and frequently bring in Rochefort to carry it out.

One of Reeves' more bizarre gambits showed the extraordinary confidence he placed in Rochefort. This ploy grew out of the admiral's effort to obtain a seaplane-repair shop for use by the U.S. Fleet in San Pedro Harbor. The fleet had no funds to build such a facility on its own, and thus it had no choice but to load seaplanes needing repairs on barges and ship them to San Diego.

Reeves thought Los Angeles should build a seaplane ramp and machine shop for the fleet. He got in touch with city officials, who said they would be happy to discuss the matter with a representative of the fleet. Reeves called in Rochefort and told him to go negotiate with the Los Angeles city fathers to see what could be worked out. Reeves said, "I told them that I'm sending Commander Rochefort up." Rochefort looked at Reeves a minute and said, "Admiral, I'm a lieutenant." Reeves snorted, "I don't care what the hell you are. Put on a commander's uniform and go on up there. You're the commander." Rochefort went.[17]

Reeves got his repair shop. In July 1935 Los Angeles transferred a site on Terminal Island, San Pedro Bay, to the Navy at no cost, with the proviso that its use be renewed annually. Whether this coup stemmed from Rochefort's negotiating prowess or other factors was never established, but Rochefort presumably performed his task well.[18]

Reeves didn't use Rochefort only as "a handyman" to do crazy jobs. Praising him as "a general encyclopedia of information and usefulness" and "one of the most outstanding officers of his rank," Reeves now took Rochefort under his wing and handed him tasks intended to round out his education as an intelligence officer.[19] One such assignment required him to think broadly—to see the big strategic picture as it involved Japan.

The project coincided with Reeves' critique of Washington's most recent version of War Plan Orange, this one developed by the Navy's War Plans Division. Reeves questioned the wisdom of the division's idea that the Navy, in a crisis, could rapidly establish advance bases in the western Pacific, bases that would supposedly allow the Navy to quickly achieve superior strength in that region. Such bases couldn't be created easily in time of war, Reeves argued, because of Japan's control of the mandated islands and its strides in air power.

The mandated islands, or mandates, as they were usually called, consisted of the Marshall, Caroline, and Mariana Islands, previously possessed by the German Empire. Located in the central and western Pacific, the islands were "mandated" to Japan in 1919 during the Paris peace talks as a reward for Japan's participation in the war against Germany. The terms called for Japan to keep the region peaceful and demilitarized—but the U.S. Navy doubted the terms were being observed.

Rather than plan on building forward bases quickly in the middle of a war, Reeves proposed that the Navy, well in advance of a crisis, create a secure base of operations. As he envisioned it, the base would have protected lines of communication, dry docks, machine shops, materiel, and other facilities to maintain ships in fighting condition.[20]

Simultaneously, Rochefort prepared a memorandum of his own, "Courses of Action Open to Orange." Considering the Pacific scene from Japan's point of view, he set forth what he believed to be the options available to the Imperial Japanese Navy. Rochefort listed five offensive actions Japan might take: (1) Proceed to the Philippines and occupy Manila; (2) Reconnoiter, occupy, and advance along the Aleutian Islands; (3) Raid the U.S. West Coast; (4) Raid the Panama Canal; (5) Project light forces to the mandates, keeping the main fleet at home.

Rochefort's memo, his first recorded foray into strategic thinking, probably aided the admiral only modestly in his jousting with Washington, if at all. But it did dovetail with Reeves' own thinking. Of particular importance, it provided an unusual glimpse into Rochefort's early assessment of the Japanese threat. He made short work of the first four options, doubting that Japan posed much of a threat to the Philippines and suggesting that in all likelihood that country would be left alone unless the United States showed signs of moving there first with a sizable force. The IJN fleet wouldn't move along the Aleutians because it would be subjected to "continual attacks" by air from Alaska. The fleet wouldn't raid the U.S. West Coast because it "would stand very little chance of returning [home]." The same applied to the Panama Canal.[21]

Rochefort visualized the mandated islands in the western Pacific as the likely theater of action. "It should be remembered that any war would undoubtedly be caused by some aggressive action of Orange in the Far East, probably China or the Philippines," he speculated. "Orange strategy would be simply one of defense. They have taken or occupied or conquered certain areas and if we object or try to take back these areas, the only way to do it would be to proceed to [the] Orange homeland." Japan's probable response to such a thrust, he went on, would be to establish a defensive perimeter that would run "from [its] Inland Sea to the Philippines, along the Caroline or Mandates to Truk and back along the Bonin Islands with strong reconnoitering forces in the Kurile Islands, extending as far as Dutch Harbor, for reconnaissance work only."[22] Japan did establish such a perimeter in the Pacific War.

While not the work of a strategic genius, the memo was a workmanlike effort that was notable for the temperate view it took of Japan's military ambitions: threatening, certainly, to China and its Far East neighbors, but defense-minded toward the United States. Rochefort's view that the Philippines might be left alone if the United States refrained from beefing up its defenses there was not shared by many naval strategists, then or later.

His analysis might seem naive in hindsight, considering Japan's 1941 attacks on Pearl Harbor and the Philippines. But those strikes, from Japan's point of view, were primarily defensive—intended to prevent the United States from interfering with conquests elsewhere. Still, if Rochefort underestimated Japan's capacity for military adventurism, it should be remembered that in 1934–35 that nation did not yet seem irrevocably committed to a policy of large-scale aggression. If there was a flaw in Rochefort's thinking, it was his assumption that in a crisis Japan would act rationally, as defined by the United States.

⊓⊓■⊓⊓

The Reeves-Rochefort relationship remained strong. Judging from the fitness reports Reeves prepared on the young officer, the admiral liked just about everything he did. By the fall of 1934, Reeves was grading his assistant operations officer at 4.0, the highest rating that could be handed out. "Lieutenant Rochefort is an outstanding officer of the highest type," Reeves assessed on 18 October 1934. "He is strongly qualified in every respect for promotion and selection for the next higher grade is urgently recommended."[23]

Reeves continued to do everything he could to advance Rochefort's career. Early in 1935 he sent him off in a new direction, having heard that Japanese agents were conducting espionage in the San Pedro and San Diego areas.[24] Earlier there hadn't been much he could do about the problem, but now, as CinCUS, he had not only new authority, but also a new tool with which to investigate any danger that might be posed by spies ashore: Joe Rochefort. He assigned him the role of fleet intelligence officer. In addition to his current duties as assistant operations officer, Rochefort was put in charge of key aspects of fleet security, a role that licensed him to probe the rumored menace.

Now Rochefort ventured into the cops-and-robbers side of naval intelligence, the side represented by the black-bag jobs ONI had pulled off in the early 1920s, and the multifarious techniques of internal security, counterespionage, and surveillance. His new duty raised tricky legal and moral issues involving civil liberties and other concerns he had never had to confront while sitting at the research desk breaking codes. He faced new risks.

But Rochefort tackled his new duties eagerly. He quickly fashioned a plan to safeguard the fleet from subversives, proceeding like any other intelligence officer, putting security ahead of legal niceties. Many people tried to influence his thinking. As word spread around the Navy about Rochefort's new duty, he began receiving unsolicited advice on ways to assure the fleet's safety—most of it harmless, some clearly outlandish.

One of the zaniest ideas came from his old friend Ellis Zacharias, now on shore duty with ONI in Washington. He advised Rochefort to place spies on Navy ships to report any signs of disloyalty. Rochefort casually mentioned the notion to Reeves. The admiral exploded: "You do that and I'll send you so far away your wife couldn't get in touch with you."[25]

Reeves needn't have worried. Rochefort had already delivered to his old colleague a firm no. Blessed with plenty of common sense, Rochefort cobbled together a two-pronged approach to counteract the alleged subversives. The first prong involved a new twist on a familiar idea: put in place a naval undercover officer in San Pedro to track spies. Rochefort wanted Arthur McCollum, his old friend from Tokyo, now on shore duty with ONI in Washington. Reeves agreed to the Rochefort plan.

As McCollum recalled it later, Rochefort "suggested to Reeves that if he could shake me loose from [ONI], I would be able to handle this stuff. So Admiral Reeves told the then-director of naval intelligence, [William] Puleston that he wanted McCollum. So McCollum went."[26] Reeves arranged for him to be quickly transferred to the Navy's base at San Pedro. On paper he was listed as an assistant to the intelligence officer of the Eleventh Naval District, based in San Diego, but with his own office at the Navy's hydrographic office in San Pedro. The office served as McCollum's cover: he was really on special assignment as liaison to Reeves.

McCollum brought a fresh viewpoint—and a welcome skepticism—to his new billet. "There was a great deal of confusion . . . over the so-called Japanese menace in southern California," he commented later. "There was a feeling of mistrust of these people, whether they were American citizens or not, some of it justified, most of it, of course, not." McCollum soon found there was at least *some* foundation to Reeves' worries. Working closely with Rochefort on board the *Pennsylvania*, McCollum tracked down a former Navy yeoman who was going down to San Pedro's dock dressed as a chief petty officer. Wearing this uniform, he would make his way on board whatever ship was convenient and proceed to the gunnery office, where he knew secret material to be kept.[27]

He took what he needed and passed it on to a Japanese agent, in this case a language student enrolled at Stanford University who in reality was a lieutenant commander in the Japanese navy. The spy ring was broken up. The "student" managed to depart the country, but the former yeoman was arrested and convicted under the Espionage Act of 1917.[28]

Rochefort seemed to have a knack for this sort of thing. But the second component of his attack on West Coast subversion didn't bear fruit. Rochefort's plan called for the creation of a fleet intelligence unit that would use radiomen for clandestine eavesdropping. Under the plan, they would monitor traffic from sending stations ashore that Rochefort deemed suspicious, in particular two amateur radio stations operating in the Long Beach area. Also, responding to concerns lodged by the U.S. Coast Guard, fleet radiomen would be authorized to monitor the traffic of California-based fishing vessels owned by individuals of Japanese descent, some American citizens. Coast Guard officials told Rochefort they feared the boats were really Japanese spy ships; presumably the new fleet intelligence unit would find out.[29]

Reeves liked the overall plan, as did ONI. Even OP-20-G's director, Commander Howard F. Kingman, endorsed it. Concentrating on the shore-based radio stations first, Rochefort's team prepared transcripts from their broadcasts and sent them off to Kingman. But they yielded nothing of interest, no hint of espionage.[30]

There remained the fishing boats and their mysterious transmissions. To investigate, Rochefort called on the newest member of his comint team on board the *Pennsylvania*, Lieutenant Wright, an exceedingly bright young officer fresh from cryptanalytic training in Washington. Wright now focused on the fishing boats. Getting radio traffic intercepts from the Coast Guard, he spent an entire Friday night picking apart the code, finally unraveling it around dawn. His discovery: The fishermen were using their radios to inform others about the whereabouts of fish.

Wright didn't get the applause he might have expected. Staying up all night caused him to miss Saturday morning inspection, angering the *Pennsylvania*'s captain, Russell Willson, who scolded him for tardiness. When Wright explained, Willson bawled him again, this time for "fooling around with this stuff," referring dismissively to codebreaking. Trying to wriggle off the hook, Wright gently reminded Willson that he too had once been engaged in cryptography, as commander of the Code and Signal Section during the European War. Willson replied, "Yes, but I had the good sense to get out of it."[31]

Whether Rochefort confronted Willson over the Wright episode was never clear. But he and Willson did have a heated exchange over something, said McCollum, who happened to be present at the time. "Rochefort thought he was a stuffed-shirt," McCollum said later, "and maybe so, but he was under no pains to hide that opinion, and that wouldn't help out." According to Rochefort's old Tokyo friend, he had always been that way. "I remonstrated with him several times unofficially," McCollum said. "I'd say, 'Joe, you can't do that to these people,' and he'd say, 'Well, the stupid so-and-so comes in here with this. Who does he think he is anyway?'"[32]

Russell Willson knew exactly who he was. He was a rising fifty-three-year-old captain headed for flag rank. Rochefort didn't care. If an officer, be he high or low, didn't measure up to his own exacting standards of what an officer should be, he "didn't exert himself too much to hide his, you might say, contempt for that person," McCollum said, "and that's not a good thing to do in the Navy or in business or anywhere else." Repeatedly, "somewhere up and down the line, Rochefort stepped on toes of a lot of people who later got to be pretty important guys," McCollum recalled.[33] One of those was Russell Willson, as Rochefort would discover soon enough.

Rochefort wasn't worried. He did important work and had gained recognition in Navy circles. He enjoyed the trust and confidence of the commander in chief of the U.S. Fleet. That commander, Admiral Reeves, never hesitated to sing his praises. Earlier in 1935, Rochefort had received a note from Reeves telling him he was "destined to advance to positions of high rank and great responsibility."[34]

If Rochefort wondered what that position might be, he received a glimpse of it in the waning months of 1935 from an old acquaintance, Commander J. W. McClaran, the new director of OP-20-G. McClaran offered Rochefort a job. He wanted him to fill a new billet that OP-20-G planned to create: officer in charge of the first decrypt unit to be set up in Pearl Harbor, Hawaii, under the Fourteenth Naval District. Until now no such unit had existed in Hawaii. As far as communications intelligence was concerned, the Navy had only a bare-bones intercept station in a small coastal town near Honolulu, where a handful of radiomen picked up Japanese traffic. Now that station was being relocated to a larger one on the northern coast of Oahu. The operation was modest. Intercepts collected by the radiomen there were shipped or air-mailed to Washington for analysis. The station had no cryptanalyst or officer in charge. That would be Rochefort, if he took the job.

As McClaran explained it, the assignment would involve "pioneer organizing work." There was only one other operation like it in the Navy, a small decrypt unit up and running in the Cavite Navy Yard near Manila, administered by the Sixteenth Naval District. Considered in the context of that time and place, the offer might have seemed like a rare opportunity. "I feel that next to Safford you are probably the best qualified officer due for shore duty to create this billet and get it started on a sound basis," McClaran told Rochefort. He acknowledged that Rochefort remained officially attached to ONI, recognizing that he might have other goals. ONI, McClaran noted, would have to agree to release Rochefort, but this could "be arranged," he said. The key thing was Rochefort's own desires. Before "going too far in this matter I should like first to hear from you," McClaran wrote to his old acquaintance.[35]

Rochefort probably was flabbergasted that OP-20-G and its parent entity, naval communications, was still interested in him. Past differences aside, apparently the security division and naval communications were willing to let bygones be bygones. Or maybe they simply had no one else qualified to turn to. Whatever their reasons for selecting Rochefort, they seemed to be calling his bluff. Did he want to confine his codebreaking activity to fleet exercises, involving Navy codes that even he regarded as child's play? Or did he want to return to mainstream cryptanalysis? If so, this would be his chance. He had a lot to think about.

Rochefort let more than four weeks pass before getting back to McClaran. He probably felt he had plenty of reasons to say no, but they weren't anything he was willing to commit to paper. So the explanation he offered—that he was too valuable where he was—might have struck McClaran as feeble. "I naturally could not expect to leave here until the Admiral leaves," Rochefort explained, adding that the date of Reeves' departure was uncertain. "Consequently I would not be able to go to any job until the rather indefinite date of the Commander-in-Chief's relief." Adding that he thought there were other officers "more fitted" than he to handle the organizational and cryptanalytic duties in Honolulu, Rochefort added, "I am thinking right now of Dyer."[36] Dyer was indeed selected; he was detached from the *Pennsylvania* in 1936 and ordered to Hawaii to start up the district's first decrypt unit.

⚬⚬∎⚬⚬

Contrary to what Rochefort told McClaran, Reeves' days as CinCUS were numbered. By the time of Rochefort's return letter to McClaran, 19 November 1935, Reeves had commanded the U.S. Fleet for nearly eighteen months. By long-standing Navy custom, fleet commanders rarely served longer than two years, so under almost any scenario, Reeves would be departing around the middle of 1936.

In short, time was running out for Rochefort as Reeves' "confidant." Whether he went to Hawaii or not, he soon would be contemplating a very different future in the Navy. Not just shore duty, for which he was overdue, but a career outside the warm embrace of Admiral Reeves. Rochefort would come to have second thoughts about the "remarkable" duty he logged with the admiral, but now he just hoped for a billet that would at least *approximate* the pleasure he had enjoyed working with Reeves.

Twenty-four June 1936 marked a changing of the guard of the U.S. Fleet. Reeves' four-star flag was hauled down from the *Pennsylvania* and replaced by that of his successor, Admiral Arthur J. Hepburn. Reeves finished out his career serving on the Navy's General Board, a top advisory group, before retiring later in the year. He and Rochefort parted as friends. In his final fitness report on Rochefort, the admiral described him as an officer "at the top of the outstanding younger officers of the service [with] a brilliant future."[37]

Headed for shore duty, Rochefort traded billets with McCollum, who succeeded him as fleet intelligence officer on board the *Pennsylvania*. Meanwhile, Rochefort relieved McCollum as fleet liaison officer in San Pedro. "Technically, my immediate superior was the district intelligence officer in San Diego," Rochefort said. "He was told not to bother me, and I was just more or less independent. I was . . . on shore duty, but I was really working for the commander in chief [of the U.S. Fleet]."[38]

Reporting for duty Rochefort became aware—to his delight as well as his chagrin—that his past tie-in with Reeves continued to affect his career. He felt he was being viewed, even deferred to, as the fleet commander's pet. "There was a memorandum [in San Diego] stating that . . . I was to report to the admiral in person," Rochefort said. The admiral was Rear Admiral Sinclair Gannon, commandant of the Eleventh Naval District. "I did so, and he proceeded to quiz me pretty thoroughly on why the commander in chief did this, that, and the other thing," Rochefort recalled. "So I could detect the feeling right there. There were quite a few instances of this nature . . . I just had the feeling that I was being treated a little easier than maybe I should have been treated as a lieutenant."[39]

But he wouldn't be a lieutenant much longer. Not long after his San Diego visit, Gannon sent Rochefort a one-word note: "Congratulations." After serving more than ten years as a lieutenant, he had ascended a grade higher to lieutenant commander. Such a long wait was not unusual for the 1930s. Tight budgets had reduced officer vacancies, causing many officers to find they had to spend more years "in grade" before becoming eligible for promotion.

In time Rochefort would wonder whether he had benefited as much as he had initially thought from his close connection with Admiral Reeves. He would trace some of his woes with superiors to the bitter resentments aroused by his special activities for the admiral. "I sometimes think if I hadn't been coddled or made a protégé of some people, it would have been better," he said. "Several times I would be what you might call the . . . fair-haired boy to some admiral."[40]

But the troubles he would encounter with some of the Navy's highest officers were still years away. Right now he had a job in San Pedro. Operating more or less independently, Rochefort enjoyed the freedom granted him by his arrangement with the Eleventh Naval District. There was little of substance to do. As liaison officer with the U.S. Fleet, he worked with local officials on functions that had some meaning for the Navy, or at least for CinCUS. Routine as they were, the activities had to be handled correctly; Rochefort did that.

After two years, he had had enough of San Pedro and anxiously awaited his next round of sea duty. He got his new orders in spring 1938. On 18 June, Rochefort boarded the cruiser *New Orleans* and reported to his new commanding officer, Captain Augustine Toutant Beauregard. A dignified, courtly gentleman, Beauregard was the grandnephew of Confederate Civil War General Pierre Gustave Toutant Beauregard. Rochefort liked him, and he liked the *New Orleans*, a speedy heavy cruiser commissioned just four years earlier.

As navigator, Rochefort thought he had the next-to-best job there was in a warship. "Of course, I couldn't command anything at that time but a minesweeper, maybe, so navigator was my best job," Rochefort would later elaborate. "Navigator of a heavy cruiser was particularly desirable in that they were somewhat similar to destroyers—a lot of speed and power, and so they were very comfortable. This was a lot of fun." The *New Orleans* suited an officer of Rochefort's extraordinary ambition. On board this heavy cruiser, "you were still in the Grand Fleet," he said, "traveling with the high class, not being around the dregs or the backwaters. I thoroughly enjoyed that."[41] But the full tour of duty he contemplated with the heavy cruiser didn't materialize. Rochefort had caught the eye of another admiral looking for a capable intelligence officer.

6

Assignment Pearl Harbor

There was a feeling—we all knew that the war was coming.
It was a question of getting ready for it.

—Joe Rochefort

Rochefort's enjoyable "high class" service on board the *New Orleans* ended abruptly on 29 September 1939. On that day—four weeks after Germany invaded Poland and ignited another European war—Rochefort received new orders from BuNAV. He was directed to report the next day to the cruiser *Indianapolis*, anchored nearby in San Pedro Bay, on board which he was to serve on the staff of Vice Admiral Adolphus Andrews.[1] When he reported, the admiral told him he had six days to prepare for the ship's hastily arranged run to its new base: Pearl Harbor.

Although the United States remained officially neutral in the war now raging in Europe, President Franklin Delano Roosevelt took a number of steps he characterized as strictly defensive. One concerned the U.S. Navy and the threat posed by Germany's Axis partner Japan. Since early 1938, British and American representatives had been meeting quietly in Washington. They agreed that in the event of a European war, the United States would relocate its main fleet from San Diego to Hawaii—a change they believed would have a restraining effect on Japanese aggression.[2]

With that war now a reality, the U.S. Navy took a step to meet the terms of the 1938 agreement. On 22 September 1939, Chief of Naval Operations Admiral Harold R. Stark handed down to Commander in Chief of the U.S.

Fleet Admiral Claude Bloch orders that were quickly relayed to the commander of the U.S. Scouting Force, Vice Admiral Andrews, on board his flagship, the *Indianapolis*. He was to transfer his force—including twelve heavy cruisers, two destroyer squadrons, and an aircraft carrier—to Pearl Harbor, departing no later than 5 October.[3]

Andrews couldn't get under way without first beefing up his staff. He needed an officer to assist in operations and intelligence, and he thought of Rochefort. Andrews had first met him in 1933, while serving as chief of staff to Admiral Reeves, then commanding the Battle Fleet on board the *California*. He had gained a high regard for Rochefort's abilities. Now, six years later, he arranged for the younger officer to be assigned to the *Indianapolis*.[4]

On 5 October the force steamed toward Hawaii, with Rochefort wearing the same two hats he had three years earlier: assistant operations and intelligence officer, only now he discharged those duties for Andrews rather than Reeves. He had reservations about this repeat performance, fearing he had been typecast, and possibly doomed to always be some admiral's "personal flunky," a label he had rather unhappily attached to himself.[5] But, as Rochefort already knew, staff jobs had compensations.

He had a ringside view of Scouting Force operations at the highest level. He could see the problems the U.S. Navy would face should America find itself drawn into a Pacific war. They involved basic issues of readiness. Upon arriving at Pearl Harbor in mid-October 1939, Rochefort and his colleagues found the base poorly equipped to handle so large a force. The Navy people already stationed there seemed to be on vacation. Rochefort and his fellow officers couldn't abide the languorous work pace.

"We found to our horror that Pearl Harbor and the navy yard would practically close up shop on Wednesday afternoon and on Friday afternoon," he recalled. "There was no activity on Saturday at all. Well, we immediately speeded these people up."[6]

Barging onto the Hawaiian scene, the Scouting Force ran into troubles of its own. A sizable number of officers and even many enlisted men resented the hurried way the transfer had been handled, separating them from their families with little or no warning. Many months would pass before Navy people were allowed to relocate families. In the meantime, they had to adjust to a locale with insufficient housing, exorbitant prices, and, amazingly enough in Hawaii, inadequate athletic and recreational facilities.[7]

"There was a little bit of tension among some of the more senior officers but certainly not among the crew," Rochefort said later. As always, he covered for the crew. In fact, enlisted men shared in the disquiet permeating Scouting Force ranks.[8] In time, however, officers and men came around and accepted the change of scene. In Rochefort's view, they eventually grasped the seriousness of the situation: "There was a feeling—we all knew that the war was coming. It was a question of getting ready for it."[9]

Rochefort settled into his new duties. He and Andrews got along well. At first glance they seemed an unlikely duo. Andrews displayed many of the traits Rochefort found annoying in superiors. Like Russell Willson, he was something of a show horse. Columnists Drew Pearson and Robert Allen once mocked Andrews as a handsome, theatrical-looking officer "famous in Washington for his beautifully tailored clothes."[10] Secretary of War Henry Stimson later referred to him as a "terrible old fusspocket."[11]

But Rochefort respected Andrews for his professionalism. Andrews was so taken by Rochefort that he admitted him to his war-planning team, giving him a seat at the table. There he joined other members of Andrews' inner circle fine-tuning the current version of Washington's Orange war plans, known in 1939 as Rainbow One. Approved by FDR in August 1939, two weeks before Germany invaded Poland, this plan assumed Britain and France would be either cowed or defeated, requiring the United States to assume a defensive posture in the Atlantic and Pacific.[12]

Under Rainbow One, Hawaii and Alaska would be protected by naval squadrons and Army reinforcements. Japanese conquests in the western Pacific would not be challenged, at least not at first. Later, when all vital areas were secure, there would ensue a "subsequent extension of United States' control into the Western Pacific as rapidly as possible."[13]

Andrews and his team were comfortable with Rainbow One. Every aspect of it was discussed. There would have been no way to detect any contribution from Rochefort, sitting in as an adviser on Japan. But the views of Andrews' planners cohered with Rochefort's 1934 analysis of Japan's strategic options that he had prepared for Admiral Reeves. All agreed that Japan would not attack the Philippines or Pearl Harbor or Guam, as it didn't want war with the United States, knowing full well it would lose. As Rochefort had six years earlier, the group assumed Japan would act rationally, as the United States defined that term.[14]

।। ■ ।।

Along with his participation in Andrews' war planning, Rochefort enjoyed another perquisite stemming from his new staff job: reunion with his family. Somehow he managed to get everyone but Joe Junior (who was in a Long Beach prep school, getting ready to enter West Point the following year) relocated to Hawaii early in 1940: Fay; daughter Janet, now eight; and Fay's mother, Cora Aery. She had joined the family in 1936 when her husband had died, soon becoming a permanent and welcome addition to the group. Cora brought a buoyant spirit of camaraderie to family affairs. "She was an old-fashioned grandmother," remembered Janet. "She made cookies, made all my clothing and very nearly raised me," because of the frequent absences of Joe and Fay.[15]

Rochefort promptly moved the family into a spacious bungalow he had rented in Honolulu's Manoa Valley, near the University of Hawaii. He also bought an old Buick and, when he wasn't carpooling, used it to commute the ten miles to Pearl. Because his duties with Andrews didn't require him to be constantly at sea, he carved out for the first time in years something resembling an ordinary family existence. Everybody settled in.

"I just had a wonderful childhood," Janet said years later. She described a father living a seemingly typical life, out the door by nine o'clock every morning, back around five in the evening, and a household marked by lots of good-natured kidding and joking around. Joe's humor, to be sure, sometimes had an edge. "He was very sarcastic—every now and then he would come out with these zingers," Janet recalled. But sarcasm aside, neither she nor anyone else could remember any real friction between the Rocheforts. Fay had long been used to Joe's caustic sense of humor and accepted it. "My mother and father were very close," recalled their daughter, who over time became accustomed to the one trait of her father's that irked her—his perfectionism. He was a real taskmaster when it came to school. "My father could be harsh about grades," she remembered.[16]

।। ■ ।।

By the late 1930s the Navy was expanding, building more ships and adding to its rolls of officers and enlisted men. With growth came opportunities for higher rank. Usually an officer had to wait a minimum of four years "in grade" before becoming eligible for promotion. Rochefort had been a lieutenant commander little more than three years by fall 1939, but the Navy needed more officers in higher grades. Andrews backed him for promotion, and on 9 November 1939, Rochefort was found physically qualified.

On 14 November 1939, Rear Admiral Chester W. Nimitz, administering personnel matters as BuNAV chief, formed a selection board to recommend officers for promotion to commander. He ordered it to meet on 6 December 1939, a full year ahead of when Rochefort's promotion would normally have come before any board.[17] There were plenty of slots for commander. In a 25 November 1939 memo to the judge advocate general, BuNAV chief Nimitz noted that "before the end of the next fiscal year there will be 132 vacancies in the commander grade in excess of the number of officers now in the promotion list for that grade."[18]

The board consisted of nine members, all picked by the secretary of the navy, all taking an oath to assess each candidate "without prejudice or partiality."[19] By long-standing Navy custom, selection boards met behind closed doors, and it was never possible to discover what members said during what was usually a weeklong ordeal of haggling and excruciatingly frank repartee about officers seeking promotion. Board members were sworn to secrecy, and as a way to encourage candor, no transcripts were kept.

Rochefort believed it was this 1939 board that weighed his promotion. All its members were rear admirals, most of whom Rochefort didn't know. One he did know was Leigh Noyes, whom he'd met in 1926 when Rochefort headed the research desk, while Noyes served in naval intelligence. The two men had seemed to dislike each other from the start. Rochefort also knew a second board member, Russell Willson, his old nemesis from the *Pennsylvania*, recently promoted to flag rank. A third member Rochefort did not know yet but would meet soon, early in 1941. He was Wilson Brown Jr.

Under Navy rules, an officer seeking promotion needed at least six of the nine board members to support his cause. No Navy record surfaced showing how many votes Rochefort received, but he didn't get six. In Navy jargon, the board adjudged him *not* "best fitted" for advancement to the next higher grade. It selected him only "fitted" for promotion, with a recommendation that he be retained.[20] The difference in terms might have seemed trivial, but the implications for an officer's career were momentous.

Officers selected as best fitted were "guaranteed an indefinite continuance of their naval careers."[21] Not so those adjudged merely fitted, even if also recommended for retention. Such officers could, of course, remain on active duty, but careers were no longer guaranteed. The most such an officer could hope for was that a future board would find him best fitted for advancement. But even if that happened, he would be ineligible for further promotion beyond that one upgrade.[22] In Rochefort's case, he could reach the rank of commander, but he would be barred from attaining captain.

The board's action surprised many, including Rochefort. On the basis of BuNAV's historical averages, showing that 60 percent of lieutenant commanders seeking to move up the ladder did so, Rochefort's chances had seemed good.[23] He also had strong endorsements from a long list of COs, recommendations that board members were told to "study" and give "careful and thorough" consideration. Aside from the now-retired Reeves, Rochefort's list was impressive: a captain (A. T. Beauregard), a rear admiral (Sinclair Gannon), and a vice admiral (Adolphus Andrews). Reeves wasn't Rochefort's only champion.

Andrews went all out for Rochefort. "I consider [Rochefort] one of the best officers of his grade I have known," the admiral told the board. "[He is] fully qualified for all the duties of commander, and I strongly recommend him for selection to that grade."[24] Given all this clout, how could Rochefort's candidacy have failed? His friend Arthur McCollum had no trouble explaining it: Rochefort had made too many enemies. As a cocky young lieutenant serving the commander in chief, U.S. Fleet, he had stepped on too many toes.[25] He had been too sharp-edged in expressing himself.

Certainly the antagonism of Noyes and Willson might have played a role in the selection board's vote, possibly accounting for the thumbs-down from Brown and others. Another major factor could have worked against Rochefort: he was a mustang. "The selection process was controlled by Naval Academy graduates," Rear Admiral Mac Showers said in a later interview. "They had far more power over promotions before the war than they were to have later. That would have put Rochefort at a tremendous disadvantage."[26] A reserve ensign in 1942, Showers would serve as an intelligence analyst under Rochefort during the critical months of that year.

Whoever the naysayers were, and whatever their reasons for voting as they did, they scuttled Rochefort's promotion sometime between 1 October 1940 and 1 February 1941—the three-month period covered in Adolphus Andrews' 13 February 1941 fitness report on Rochefort. Andrews was furious. "I regret that [Rochefort] was not selected as best fitted, but adjudged fitted, by the last board," he thundered. "I believe him capable of any duty appropriate to the commander's rank."[27]

The board's action jolted Rochefort. This was his first real setback in the Navy, and it caught him off-guard. He'd had every reason to believe he would just keep ascending the Navy ladder. Given the high praise bestowed on him by so many superiors ("an excellent officer," said Standley; "outstanding—an officer with a brilliant future," declared Reeves), Rochefort by this time had acquired "a very good opinion" of himself, he told a friend later.[28] Now he had taken a real tumble; his uncanny luck seemed to have run out.

The situation almost got worse. When he learned early in 1941 that Wilson Brown would relieve Andrews as commander of the Scouting Force, he very nearly resigned his Navy commission. "He was considering retirement when Andrews was replaced by Brown," interviewer Percy Greaves wrote later. "Rochefort considered [him] incompetent." Even when Brown asked him to stay Rochefort refused, believing, as Greaves put it, that "Brown had been on the selection board that had turned him down."[29]

But Rochefort changed his mind. He almost certainly was influenced by BuNAV's quick decision to reexamine him, a step probably taken at the behest of the once-skeptical Wilson Brown. "I have no objection to being examined on my record," a disappointed Rochefort wrote in his 23 April 1941 fitness report. That report was submitted by Brown just before Rochefort's fate was reconsidered by a different board. Brown wrote, "This report is submitted at the time of his reexamination for promotion to commander, for which rank he is strongly recommended." Brown didn't stop there. "It is further recommended that when this officer becomes due for promotion to the next higher rank—Captain—he is selected as 'best fitted.'"[30] In short, Brown asked the selection board and BuNAV to ignore the Navy rule that prevented an officer, once selected "fitted but retained," from rising more than one grade.

The board did what Brown wanted it to do, thereby in all likelihood saving Rochefort's career. Many months after being reexamined, on 13 October 1941 Rochefort would receive the news that he had been promoted to commander, retroactive to 1 April. Brown clearly had a change of heart; from a "no" voter he had turned into one of Rochefort's staunchest advocates. In so doing he joined a lengthening parade of flag rank officers won over by Rochefort. Why this officer seemed so compelling to superiors—most of whom had never heard of him before meeting him—might have been puzzling. He had neither an Academy network singing his praises nor a scintillating personality.

He was no glad-hander or hail-fellow-well-met. Rochefort was usually found "pleasant" and "mild mannered," on the quiet side.

One clue to the spell Rochefort cast over superiors was his seriousness about the Navy. He was driven. When he got into trouble with Russell Willson, it wasn't because he was some kind of rebel or maverick. It was because Willson didn't meet *his* exacting standards of what an naval officer should be, as McCollum put it.[31]

What energized Rochefort may have been overcompensation for not having gone to Annapolis. Perhaps he figured that if he was going to succeed in the Navy, he had to be better than the Academy grads. The result was that he often ended up more exacting—indeed, more Navy—than the Academy's most exalted alumni. Rochefort didn't just do his homework, he turned himself into "an encyclopedia of information," as Reeves put it.[32] He won over his superiors because of his conspicuous ability.

ıı▇ıı

Even before Rochefort's encounters with selection boards, the wheels of the Navy's rotation machine were churning to place him in a new billet. He had been on sea duty nearly three years—fifteen months with the *New Orleans* and nineteen on board the *Indianapolis*. He was overdue for shore duty. But what duty would that be? Rochefort had definite ideas about his next stop. In two fitness reports filled out in early 1941, he specified his preference for his next shore duty: the Eleventh Naval District in San Diego.[33]

But in 1941 the preferences of individual officers were being subordinated to the overriding demands of the times. The Navy was moving to a higher level of war readiness. The disposition of the U.S. Fleet was one barometer of change. Completing a move that had begun in fall 1939 with the transfer of the Scouting Force, the main body of the fleet arrived at Pearl Harbor in spring 1940, with orders to remain there "until further notice." The command rankled then-CinCUS Admiral J. O. Richardson. When Richardson asked CNO Stark for an explanation of the move, he was told the fleet was stationed at Pearl as a "deterrent" to Japan.[34]

Still other changes were on the drawing board. Late in 1940, the idea percolated through Navy channels that its decrypt unit at Pearl Harbor, a shore-based operation housed with the Fourteenth Naval District, needed to be bolstered. Many high-echelon officers lobbied for the buildup. Fleet Commander Richardson wanted it. So did Rear Admiral Claude Bloch, who in

January 1940 rotated from CinCUS to commandant of the Fourteenth Naval District.[35]

Another advocate was Commander Laurance Safford, Rochefort's mentor from the research desk, now heading OP-20-G. This bureau had founded Hawaii's decrypt unit in 1936, when Commander McClaran (Safford's predecessor) had directed Tommy Dyer to Pearl Harbor. Dyer's orders were to report to the district's then-commandant, Rear Admiral Harry E. Yarnell, set up shop at district headquarters at Pearl, coordinate with the radiomen at the Navy's intercept station, then, as best he could working alone, solve certain IJN naval codes for the benefit of OP-20-G.[36]

Now, more than four years later, OP-20-G still directed the Pearl Harbor decrypt unit, known inside Navy circles as the COM 14 unit, since it was attached to the Fourteenth Naval District. Dyer remained there as a cryptanalyst, but he had been joined by a small band of specialists: traffic analysts, language officers, and one officer who was a hybrid, Lieutenant Commander Thomas B. Birtley Jr., who in the 1920s had been an OP-20-G student in cryptanalysis and later a language student in Tokyo. Senior to Dyer, Birtley took over in 1939 as officer in charge. With Birtley returning to sea in mid-1941, the Navy needed a successor. Somebody thought of Rochefort.

Exactly when Safford started corresponding with Rochefort about the COM 14 billet is unclear, but it was probably early in 1941, around the time Rochefort was to be reexamined for promotion to commander.[37] Rochefort might have been uncertain about where his career was going, but he remained sure about where he *didn't* want to go. His attitude hadn't changed since 1935, when OP-20-G's McClaran had first broached the idea that he create a decrypt unit at Pearl. Rochefort still had doubts about the job.

Not only that, but Rochefort during the past thirteen years had avoided any billet that would have brought him back under the umbrella of naval communications or require him to do serious cryptanalysis. True, he did codebreaking during fleet exercises, and from time to time fussed with Washington about the security of fleet codes. But he did this as a sideline, not a career option. In fact, since returning to sea in 1933, he had been given the opportunity in ten fitness reports to list a preference for his next shore duty: not once did he mention cryptanalysis. Even in the early months of 1941, he still thought in terms of a quiet billet in San Diego.[38]

The Navy had no intention of sending Rochefort to San Diego. He had assets that couldn't be ignored. No other officer in the Navy possessed his combination of skills. Layton knew Japanese and had picked up some of the basics of codebreaking, but he wasn't a cryptanalyst. Birtley also knew Japanese and, as noted, had studied cryptanalysis at OP-20-G, but he wasn't at Rochefort's level in either of those departments. Rochefort brought even more to the table. In addition to his language and cryptanalytic skills, he had a background in fleet intelligence, operations, and communications. He was a gifted, many-faceted officer.

But could Rochefort be persuaded to take the COM 14 billet? Safford embarked on a selling campaign. Rochefort didn't come around easily. In letters that continued over a span of weeks, the OP-20-G head addressed each of his concerns. The two officers dickered over personnel, equipment, and Rochefort's still-to-be-worked-out autonomy as officer in charge of the unit.

"You can have anything you want," Rochefort quoted Safford telling him. What Rochefort wanted was considerable, and he was stubborn as well as undecided. Safford made compromises, some of which sounded pretty good to Rochefort. He noted later that the Navy "decided to build up [this unit], if necessary at the expense of the home station in Washington, and transfer many of the activities they were then doing in Washington to [Pearl Harbor]."

From their bargaining, something like a deal began to emerge. Rochefort got his "pick of the personnel," stipulating, "Now, if you want to go ahead and build yourself another outfit in Washington, this is fine and dandy. But I'll take this job providing I can keep Dyer"—now in his fifth year at Pearl—"and I can get first shot at anybody else whom I need and I can get all the language officers." Safford agreed.[39]

Rochefort wanted one more thing: unprecedented autonomy. He got that too. The agreement was that COM 14 no longer regarded OP-20-G as its primary client. The latter would, of course, remain COM 14's superior in the Navy hierarchy, continuing to exert operational control. This included directing COM 14's decrypt agenda, specifying what IJN naval codes should be tackled, providing personnel and machinery, and sharing relevant cryptologic research done in Washington. OP-20-G remained the main play caller.

But it was now a secondary client. It would still get COM 14 reports, but not first. The Safford-Rochefort deal formalized one issue that was close to Rochefort's heart: he could regard the commander in chief, U.S. Fleet, as his principal customer. Rochefort from now on would report COM 14's intelligence estimates—based primarily on analyses of Japanese fleet radio traffic—directly to CinCUS, now Admiral Husband E. Kimmel. On 1 February 1941 he had relieved Admiral Richardson, who apparently had protested too vigorously the U.S. Fleet's relocation to Pearl Harbor, leading FDR to dismiss him in early 1941.

In truth, Safford hadn't given away as much as might have seemed. Some COM 14 reports of IJN ship movements, though limited in scope, were already making their way to fleet headquarters through Bloch's office.[40] Moreover, given Rochefort's background, the growing sense of emergency in the Pacific, and COM 14's proximity to Kimmel, both Rochefort and Safford thought it made sense for Washington to grant Pearl greater independence.[41]

Safford had another reason for meeting Rochefort's request: he wanted to insulate COM 14's officer in charge as much as possible from the bitter infighting that continued to mark relations between intelligence and communications. Rochefort "had special orders . . . to report direct to Admiral Kimmel," Rochefort's friend Layton later wrote. This "was an attempt by his old colleague Commander Safford to give the fleet an independent access to radio intelligence, free of Navy Department feuding."[42]

Even after he and Safford had come to terms, Rochefort still didn't have a job. Before he could fill the COM 14 slot, somebody would have to order him to it. Who would that have been? So many officers were involved in the Rochefort appointment that the question cannot be satisfactorily answered, but one thing was clear: it wasn't Safford. He certainly wanted Rochefort in the job, but he lacked the authority to make the final decision.

The Navy's chain of command regarding COM 14 had changed since Lieutenant Dyer had been sent in 1936, bringing little more than a cover letter from OP-20-G. He really worked for Washington. Five years later, the decrypt unit was an integral part of COM 14. OP-20-G exerted operational control over the unit, but Rear Admiral Bloch had administrative control. Dyer and all COM 14 personnel were assigned to him, so he would have been involved in the selection process.

As top officials at ONI would have been. Rochefort was attached to ONI for shore duty, meaning that before joining any OP-20-G arm, controlled as it was by naval communications, he would have needed ONI release. That agency would have been happy to approve Rochefort's transfer, since it would have placed an ONI-connected officer in a critical position in an ONC billet. Which ONI official sanctioned the transfer is impossible to know, but one player claimed responsibility for Rochefort's selection: his old friend and benefactor Captain Zacharias. Just as Zacharias had taken credit for Rochefort's Tokyo selection, he did so again for his COM 14 job.

Zacharias liked to promote the interests of his colleagues in the intelligence community. He had just played a crucial role in getting Rochefort's friend Lieutenant Commander Eddie Layton named chief intelligence officer of the U.S. Fleet. After two years commanding the destroyer *Boggs*, Layton reported to Admiral Richardson on board the *Pennsylvania*, rather prophetically, on 7 December 1940. He and Rochefort would soon be working closely together at Pearl.

"Zacharias told Layton that he used his influence to get him the fleet intelligence job," Rear Admiral Showers said in a later interview. "He also told Layton that he was the one who arranged for Rochefort to fill the Fourteenth Naval District opening."[43]

But was this true? Because of his long and distinguished service in intelligence, he certainly remained persuasive inside ONI. Zacharias could have helped Layton, but did he have the sway to influence Safford when it came to filling a critical position in the OP-20-G network, or to influence Bloch at COM 14 headquarters?

He did not. Rochefort got his COM 14 job through a different scenario. The process involved not only his exchange with Safford, but consultation between the latter and Bloch. Safford needed Bloch's okay to seal the Rochefort deal. If ordered to the decrypt unit, Rochefort would serve under Bloch for administrative purposes. This gave Bloch leverage, and he appointed Rochefort with Safford signaling approval. Safford most likely didn't inform his own superior about the deal, since his boss was Rochefort's old foe Leigh Noyes, now director of naval communications. Noyes probably would have vetoed the arrangement had he known of it.

But Noyes, directing a fast-growing communications universe, had much on his mind besides codes and ciphers. OP-20-G existed on the far periphery of his world. He did what seemed to make sense: he turned it over to Safford, one of its founding fathers, who could now preside over OP-20-G with a free hand.

That didn't mean Noyes liked Safford's role in the Rochefort affair when he heard of it. "Noyes nearly took my head off when he learned that I had sent a letter of congratulations to Joe Rochefort," Safford wrote later. For years, he noted, Noyes nursed a "personal peeve against Bloch for putting Rochefort in command" of the decrypt unit.[44]

Bloch was delighted to name Rochefort to COM 14's decrypt post. The two officers were well acquainted. They had met during Bloch's 1938–39 tenure as commander in chief of the U.S. Fleet, when Rochefort, officially assigned to the Eleventh Naval District, actually served as intelligence liaison to CinCUS. Like so many other superiors who had worked closely with Rochefort, he was impressed, and said so to the district commandant, Rear Admiral Gannon.[45]

If Safford and Bloch were pleased with how things had worked out, so was Rochefort. From his point of view there were also benefits. He wouldn't have to relocate the family. He could still drive to work in the morning and head for Pearl Harbor, only instead of turning toward the *Indianapolis'* anchorage, he would head for the Navy's cavernous, recently constructed administration building, where the decrypt unit was housed. And, of course, he would have a major leadership position, his first as a naval officer. The deal was done.

॥■॥

Monday 2 June 1941, on what turned out to be an uncomfortably warm and humid Hawaiian day, Rochefort reported to Commandant Bloch for duty. Bloch's office was located upstairs in the admin building, as it was colloquially called. An ungainly, sand-colored structure occupying what amounted to a city block, the building was a rabbit warren of offices and cubbyholes covering just about every activity at the Pearl Harbor Navy Yard, from dredging and housing to roads and harbor security. The building was, in effect, Pearl's city hall. Bloch, for all practical purposes, was the mayor of Pearl Harbor.

From his perch in the admin building, he presided over a sizable domain, directing all shore-based Navy activity in the Hawaiian Islands. Bloch had overall responsibility for the naval base, a realm that included machine shops, the potentially lethal "farm" of oil-storage tanks, harbor defenses, and security. He also was charged with providing housing, as well as food and clothing, for both the men of the U.S. Fleet and those based at the navy yard.[46]

Rochefort found Bloch in his regulation-gray office occupying one corner of the second deck. The two were a study in contrasts. Yet another Annapolis man (class of 1899), Bloch presented a textbook picture of an admiral—tall, suave, almost regal in bearing. At sixty-three, he was in the twilight of his career and was contemplating retirement in about a year.

Rochefort was still on the way up. A lean six-footer, quiet-spoken but cocky, still young at forty-one, he had arrived to take a position that represented a leap forward in his career. Despite the dustup over his promotion earlier in the year and his own brush with retirement, Rochefort's good fortune continued. He could contemplate "a brilliant future," just as Admiral Reeves had predicted.

The two had much to talk about. The news that Monday was grim. Crete had just fallen to German forces, a disaster that followed Germany's conquest of Greece and Yugoslavia. Most Americans worried about the worsening situation in Europe, but Bloch and Rochefort also saw trouble brewing thousands of miles away in Asia. Japan was on the move. Now part of the Berlin-Rome Axis, Japan's army had already occupied northern Indochina and now threatened to move into the southern portion of the country. Japan demanded more petroleum from the Dutch East Indies than the Dutch wanted to sell. Events raised the danger of war in Southeast Asia.

Both officers feared that the United States would get drawn into whatever war finally erupted. Neither saw any immediate threat to Hawaii, but Bloch had been sobered by a 31 March report on Hawaii's vulnerability to surprise attack. It had been prepared by Kimmel's air expert, Rear Admiral Patrick Bellinger, commander of the Naval Base Defense Air Force; and his counterpart on the staff of Lieutenant General Walter C. Short, commanding general, Hawaiian Department: Major General Frederick L. Martin. Congressional investigators five years later would call their estimate "a startling harbinger" of what actually occurred.[47]

Pointing out that relations between the United States and Japan were increasingly strained, the officers suggested that Japan might, as it had in the past, begin hostilities without a declaration of war. "*It appears*," they wrote, "*that the most likely and dangerous form of attack on Oahu would be an air attack*," brought about by carriers approaching within three hundred miles of Oahu (italics in original). They feared that such a force might arrive in Hawaiian waters without prior warning from the Navy's intelligence service.[48]

Rochefort certainly would have wanted to know about any Army-Navy report raising the possibility of a Navy intelligence failure. Whether he did learn of it was never established. As assistant operation officer on board the *Indianapolis*, he hadn't been cleared for *all* top-secret material. That put a limit on what Bloch could tell him.

Regardless of what Rochefort knew, the Martin-Bellinger estimate was symptomatic of an anxiety that was beginning to permeate higher command levels at Pearl Harbor. The source of the disquiet was information, or, more precisely, the lack of it. Top officers felt they were not being told enough. They worried about the flow of vital updates from Main Navy to Pearl Harbor. Kimmel, in particular, wondered whether he was getting all the diplomatic intelligence available about Japanese intentions.[49]

Representing Kimmel's concerns, Fleet Intelligence Officer Layton in early March penned a personal letter to his old friend at Main Navy, Commander McCollum, head of the Far Eastern Section at ONI. Layton expressed his worry and Kimmel's that Pearl was being shortchanged on diplomatic intelligence. McCollum disagreed, replying unsympathetically that because Washington bore exclusive responsibility for delicate "matters of security," it would be impractical for ONI to pass on to Pearl Harbor diplomatic intercepts.[50]

Kimmel remained uneasy. In fact, when Rochefort reported to Bloch on 2 June, he was already in Washington conferring with Navy Secretary Frank Knox, CNO Stark, and, as it turned out, President Roosevelt himself. Kimmel had already dispatched a detailed letter to Stark itemizing his problems as CinCUS: insufficient ships, personnel, patrol planes, and antiaircraft defenses. And he repeated a previously stated desire that he receive "vital information" regarding developments in the international scene, diplomatic and military.[51] Knox and Stark tried to reassure the Pacific Fleet commander he was getting all the relevant information they possessed.

|| ■ ||

Bloch had every reason to be out of sorts during the first week of June 1941. Weeks had passed since he had asked Stark for planes for his district's nonexistent air force. He doubted whether he would get them. New equipment and additional personnel requested for COM 14's decrypt unit had been slow to arrive. Yet on Monday 2 June, the day Rochefort reported for duty, Bloch was in a buoyant mood. Some things were going right.

After the two officers finished chatting Bloch performed a task he had been looking forward to: he escorted Rochefort to his new billet. Rochefort's office wasn't exactly a luxury suite. Down the hall from Bloch's quarters on the second deck, the room was a drab, windowless haunt whose doors were kept constantly locked; its inhabitants were virtually anonymous, coming and going quietly. No outsider knew who they were or what they did. Set up five years earlier by Tommy Dyer, this was COM 14's decrypt unit, now filling up with exotic specialists derided by many naval people as "nuts" or "blue sky merchants," as Dyer characterized Navy thinking. These were people Rochefort admired, even if they inhabited a world he had tried to avoid. In that effort he had failed. He was now their boss: officer in charge of ten officers and thirteen enlisted men.[52]

In this capacity Rochefort would exercise more responsibility and operate on a higher level than he ever had before. He would lead a unit that represented one of the U.S. government's most closely guarded secrets: the Navy's quickening effort to break the codes and ciphers of an increasingly threatening Imperial Japanese Navy. The security of Pearl Harbor, and the fortunes of the U.S. Pacific Fleet stationed there, would depend heavily on the work done by him and his assortment of unusual and largely anonymous characters. Rochefort would have his hands full.

But his burdens might be eased by a change that had been contemplated for months. Very soon, Bloch informed a delighted Rochefort, his team would move into spacious new quarters built specifically for this COM 14 unit and customized to meet its needs. The place would have everything: privacy, convenience, security. Rochefort waited impatiently for moving day.

Shortly after Rochefort's visit, Bloch zipped off an upbeat note to Stark. "Not much news here," he wrote that afternoon. "There is lots of talk about spies, et cetera, but I can't find any! We are very happy and cheerful and hope that you are the same."[53] Whether Bloch was as bubbly as he led Stark to believe is doubtful, but he was certainly pleased by Rochefort's arrival. His presence solved a problem.

7

A Most Unusual Place

We . . . called it "The Dungeon."
—Forrest R. "Tex" Biard

When Rochefort in mid-August 1941 led his small band of "nuts" and "blue sky merchants" to their new quarters deep in the lower depths of the admin building, the men might well have doubted that they had come out ahead.[1] They might have wondered whether they had traded one dreary hangout for another. They wouldn't have needed much time to size up their new realm: with no windows and poor ventilation, it was chilly and, at first glance, dismal. It was a typical basement.

But it did have one amenity they valued: privacy. The basement was separate from the rest of the admin building. The men entered it from the outside, through a heavy door on a walkway that bordered the building. This opened into a stairwell that took them down to a five-inch-thick, vault-type door, the central entry point into their netherworld of cryptanalysis and codebreaking. No longer would they run into people casually in the hallway, nor be objects of idle curiosity.

And to make sure they could do their work in relative peace and quiet, the basement offered an additional feature: unprecedented security. The doors were equipped with time-locks. The stairwells were guarded. "We moved from the upstairs little office, no bigger than [a living] room, down into the cellar where we had much more room and a Marine guard for the first time," recalled one cryptanalyst.[2]

That didn't last. Perhaps the Navy decided that putting a Marine in front of an obscure stairwell was a waste of manpower. Or it could have concluded that sometimes the best place to hide was in plain sight. The notion made a certain amount of sense, since the entryway leading to the stairwell was nothing if not uninviting: it resembled the kind of warehouse door that might seal off a furnace room or a broom closet. Whatever the reasons, the Navy decided to go easy on the security part of the basement operation. The time-locks were never activated. The Marine was reassigned, as five language officers fresh from Japan found when they showed up in September. Lieutenant Allyn Cole and lieutenants (jg) Forrest "Tex" Biard, Gilven Slonim, and John Bromley; and Marine Captain Bankson Holcomb Jr. were met by no guards. They simply pulled open the door and, stepping carefully to avoid the burn bags stuffed with cryptologic worksheets that littered the stairwell, clambered down the sixteen steps to the bottom.[3]

"We reported to a most unusual place," Biard said later. "We entered it through an unmarked door, unguarded, down a dark passageway into a somewhat lighter space, but still not too light, and still a little bit on the murky side."[4] Resembling a small-town pool hall, the room was indeed perpetually murky. It could hardly have been otherwise. Everyone puffed on something, whether cigars (linguist Red Lasswell coveted "cheap Cuban cigars," said one colleague); pipes, as in Rochefort's case; or cigarettes, which nearly everyone smoked.[5] The atmosphere wasn't helped by a ventilation system that did little more than circulate the old air already in the room. It turned out that the fresh-air intake had mistakenly been closed. Many months passed before this blunder was correctly diagnosed and corrected. "The only fresh air that entered the basement was what we brought in in our pockets," said one analyst.[6]

The denizens of the basement used a time-honored technique to adapt to the room's oddities: satire. "We, in that small group, had a more descriptive term for that unventilated enclosure in which we worked," Biard remarked. "We, more appropriately, called it 'The Dungeon.'"[7] With its walls swathed in a kind of muddy sealant ("dun-colored," Rochefort called it), the basement would always be regarded by its inhabitants, through good times and bad, as the dungeon.

Rochefort did his best to make the dungeon livable. Cut off from the Navy in his underground enclave, he created "a unique military organization," COM 14 intelligence analyst Jasper Holmes wrote. Many formalities were ignored. Officers felt comfortable addressing each other by their first names regardless of rank. Enlisted men found they didn't always have to say "sir." Dress standards were relaxed, and enlisted men could wear dungarees. "Not much attention was paid to uniforms or to military punctilio of any kind," Holmes said.

Rochefort embodied the informal culture he had helped create, as seen in his own clothing choices. When the basement's balky air conditioner pushed down the temperature, the place felt "like the inside of a refrigerator," as Holmes put it.[8] The concrete slab floor made the room even chillier. Just so he could function, Rochefort took to wearing slippers and a maroon smoking jacket somebody had given him—attire that fueled the notion, in later years, that he was some kind of maverick or weird character. "It wasn't that I was eccentric or anything," Rochefort said. "It was a practical matter. I was cold."[9]

As for basement security, Rochefort took care of that too. He instituted his own distinct system, a guard sitting near the door. Quite often that individual was Rochefort's personal gatekeeper and right-hand man, Chief Petty Officer Durwood G. "Tex" Rorie. Husky, gruff, and very able-bodied, Rorie maintained a commanding presence at his desk by the door. He screened every visitor. No stranger, no unwanted person, regardless of rank, ever got past Rorie or one of his equally formidable assistants. "Nobody came in without our knowledge," Rochefort said.[10] In other words, the arriving Tex Biard and his party, or anyone entering the basement, would not have gotten very far before they were intercepted.

For all the basement's shortcomings, it had one huge asset: five thousand square feet of glorious space. Inside a room that stretched fifty feet in one direction and one hundred in another, the twenty-three officers and enlisted men no longer bumped into each other. They put up with minor irritations in return for elbow room. Their spacious hideaway wasn't just handed to them; it was the work of Tommy Dyer. It had started out as an underground adjunct to a new wing being added to the admin building, but in early 1940, Dyer convinced Admiral Bloch that the decrypt unit had to have it. "Somehow, I don't know yet how I managed to do it, I wangled it mostly," Dyer said.[11]

And now Rochefort owned it. As a first move, he divided the basement into four sectors, each representing a different comint activity. Against the far wall was a cluster of desks used by the Japanese language officers: the translators. To a visitor's left, against the southern wall, was space for a little-known specialty: traffic analysis. To the far left, in the rear of the room, was a tiny section for the unit's ship plotters. To a visitor's right, against the eastern wall, was space dedicated to what some regarded as the meat-and-potatoes portion of COM 14: a hive of desks for the unit's cryptanalysts. A door placed inconspicuously at this end of the room opened into yet another space, smaller but invaluable: it housed the noisy IBM machines. The machines were a godsend: They could quickly assemble huge amounts of data that gave clues to the codes analysts were trying to break.

Rochefort saw his cryptanalysts as a special breed. He believed they were unusual and a little strange. To do the work they did, to turn puzzles into obsessions, cryptanalysts unavoidably had to be "odd characters" in Rochefort's view. He resented it when Navy brass dismissed codebreakers as "nuts," as they often did to derogate people whose work they didn't understand. But Rochefort, too, regarded cryptanalysts as a little on the nutty side—which, when he said it himself, he meant as a compliment. "If you desire to be a real great cryptanalyst," Rochefort said, "being a little bit nuts helps."[12]

If this characteristic was the key to cryptanalytic genius, then there was no mystery as to why Lieutenant Commander Thomas H. Dyer was COM 14's number-one cryptanalyst. By this time he had far outdistanced Rochefort in the field. Short, dark-haired, wearing large glasses, and known to all as Tommy, Dyer was a consummate individualist. He set the tone for many in the basement, dressing informally, even carelessly, at times resembling more a mathematics professor than a naval officer.[13]

In Rochefort's opinion, he was a classic of the type—one of those "people who will not generally conform to accepted ideas," whether the issue was clothing or a more serious matter.[14] Dyer tended to go his own way. He didn't scare easily. Once he grew a full beard because he knew beards irritated one of his Washington superiors.[15]

Nonconforming as he may have been, Dyer was no clown. He was regarded by OP-20-G (and Rochefort) as among the Navy's two or three top cryptanalysts, a reputation he had earned by hard work in Washington collaborating with Laurance Safford and Agnes Meyer Driscoll and, during his five-year stint at Pearl, in a post he created from scratch in 1936. Dyer was the ultimate professional. When Lieutenant Commander Birtley arrived at COM 14 in 1939 to take over as officer in charge because he had greater seniority, Dyer accepted the development without complaint.

Similarly, he didn't gripe when the more senior Rochefort arrived in June 1941 to take over as officer in charge. The situation could have been awkward, but the two men knew and respected each other. "I might have resented some total stranger coming in and upsetting my apple cart," Dyer conceded. "But I was only interested in getting the job done."[16]

Now, as senior analyst in COM 14's code and cipher section, Dyer continued to cultivate the light touch—in part to break the ice and allay the tensions that could mount quickly under the stress of codebreaking. Dyer agreed with Rochefort that people had to be nutty to do this kind of work; he thought everyone should appreciate their own weirdness and, if possible, retain a sense of the ludicrous. A sign he posted on his desk captured the spirit of the basement: "You don't have to be crazy to work here, but it helps!"[17]

Dyer was aided in his work by two strong cryptanalysts. His chief assistant was Lieutenant Ham Wright, a beefy, heavy-set man with craggy features, a large nose, and a thin mustache. He brought to mind Wallace Beery, the scratchy-voiced actor of that era. Rambunctious, playful, known to enjoy an occasional off-duty party, "Ham could have served very nearly as a double for that boisterous actor," mused one denizen of the basement.[18]

Good-natured and relaxed as he may have seemed, Wright was an accomplished cryptanalyst. He had learned the craft during an eighteen-month hitch with OP-20-G at Main Navy in 1933–34. As already noted, he'd done some codebreaking under Rochefort on board the *Pennsylvania* in 1935–36; it was Wright who'd proved the Japanese-owned fishing boats off San Pedro were radioing about fish, not military secrets. Rochefort valued both Dyer and Wright, describing the two cryptanalysts as "just about as good as they come."[19]

He also respected a third member of his team, an unusually seasoned lieutenant commander, Jack S. Holtwick. Dapper, always natty and sporting a dashing mustache, Holtwick was well-traveled. He'd learned cryptanalysis serving first in ONC in 1935–36, then during a tour with the cryptanalytic staff of the Sixteenth Naval District in Manila.

When Holtwick reported to COM 14 in May 1940, he was given a job many officers would have resisted: supervising the yeomen running the unit's IBM equipment. Most analysts at Pearl did their work with paper and pencil, but Holtwick had a knack for gadgets. In 1936, while serving with OP-20-G in Washington, he had devised a machine that solved a Japanese diplomatic cipher. Americans dubbed his device the Red Machine.[20] It remained in use until 1939, when the Japanese switched most of their diplomatic traffic to a more complex machine system.

Given his background, Holtwick was the right person to run the "boiler factory," Dyer's term for COM 14's separate machine room, located just behind the cryptanalytic section. Jam-packed with a variety of buzzing IBM machines, cut off from the rest of the basement, and, mercifully, rendered soundproof by thick cinderblocks, the machine room would be Holtwick's domain. Used to discern patterns in encrypted messages transmitted by the Imperial Japanese Navy and speed the compromising of its codes and ciphers, the boiler factory in the months ahead would prove its worth.

‖ ■ ‖

Cryptanalysts weren't the only odd characters in Rochefort's basement. Grouped around a hodgepodge of desks against the southern wall were two officers and their special assistants, saddled with the ungainly label of traffic analysts, sometimes known simply as the TA guys. The most senior TA guy was Lieutenant Commander Thomas A. Huckins, a tall, fair-haired, well-built man who spoke with a slow southern drawl. Trained in the mysteries of codes and ciphers by OP-20-G in the early 1930s, Huckins had rotated to sea duty, served with the Asiatic Fleet, then joined the Pearl Harbor unit in July 1940. Huckins' partner was another lieutenant commander, John A. Williams, a short, tense, nervous man who had come on board in February 1941.[21]

"These people were very hard to beat for what we called radio intelligence," Rochefort said.[22] Defined loosely, RI covered a broad swatch of radio activity, everything from cryptanalysis and codebreaking to the work done by Huckins and Williams. To the uninitiated, and even to people who should have known better, traffic analysis seemed like the low end of the RI totem pole. The TA phrase didn't help, conjuring an image of something dry and clerical.

Nothing could have been further from the truth. Technical yes; dry and clerical not at all. A blending of science and art, traffic analysis constituted the core of radio intelligence. But it was different from cryptanalysis or codebreaking. TA work involved finding out everything possible about an IJN message short of decrypting it. As defined by the Navy, traffic analysis was a method of obtaining intelligence by studying the "externals" of the enemy's communication system: the outer trappings of a message.[23]

Instead of addressing the contents of an intercepted message, as codebreakers did, TAs tackled its heading. They wanted to know what ship or command had originated the message and who received it. What was the relationship between the two? To do this type of work, analysts had to master the hundreds of call signs that ships used to identify themselves. From these and other clues derived from radio traffic, TAs could very often track the movements of particular Japanese vessels or even major portions of the IJN fleet to and from their ports.[24]

Burdened by their rather prosaic label, the TA guys didn't have the cachet enjoyed in later years by the codebreakers, but what they did was just as crucial. Huckins and Williams weren't perfect; they made their share of mistakes. Traffic analysis wasn't a foolproof method of locating the enemy. But in the early stages of the Pacific War, before the cryptanalysts cracked Japan's main naval codes, traffic analysis was about all Rochefort and his fellow analysts had to go on. It "was part of communications intelligence," Rochefort commented, "because you cannot expect to be forever reading [the contents of] these messages. You've got to put yourself in a position where you can expect a lot of information just from the messages themselves"—the so-called externals—"without being able to read them."[25]

⸱⸱■■⸱⸱

Proceeding clockwise around the basement, against the far western wall in the rear of the room dwelled another Rochefort team, this one nearly invisible. This was the recently created Combat Intelligence Unit, or CIU. The CIU was small, consisting initially of one officer, Lieutenant Wilfred J. "Jasper" Holmes, and an assistant, Yeoman William Dunbar. The unit was something of an anomaly. Neither Holmes nor Dunbar was an intelligence professional. Neither had received training in codebreaking or Japanese. Holmes was a former submarine officer who had retired in 1936. He then joined the engineering faculty of the University of Hawaii and, for a time, wrote short stories for *The Saturday Evening Post* under the pen name Alec Hudson.

With a Pacific war looking increasingly likely, early in 1941 Commandant Bloch wanted an officer with knowledge of navigation who could write readable reports. He recruited Holmes to do ship plotting. Because there was nowhere else to put him, Bloch prevailed upon Rochefort to accept him into the comint unit. Holmes arrived in June, the same month as Rochefort and, along with everybody else, moved into the basement that August, bringing with him a chart desk, plotting equipment, and a portfolio of Pacific Ocean charts. Using coordinates provided by the traffic analysts and other COM 14 resources, Holmes plotted the movements of U.S. and foreign merchant ships in Hawaiian waters and, later, IJN warships throughout the Pacific.

At first, Holmes' situation was awkward. He and Dunbar weren't really part of the unit. As outsiders, they entered the basement through a little-used backdoor that opened into separate rooms behind the unit's quarters. "It was distinctly understood that we were with, but not of [the Rochefort unit]," Holmes wrote later. "We were not told anything about [it] and were cautioned not to be curious about its operation. Space was allotted to us near the back door . . . and we could approach our area without passing through [Rochefort's realm]. We were expected to remain in our own space."[26]

But gradually Rochefort came to recognize the value of Holmes' work and incorporated his team into the overall operation. "We absorbed Jasper sort of by a process of osmosis," Dyer recalled.[27] Holmes' desks were moved into the center of the basement. He filled up his new space, creating a nest of file boxes, all holding cards with data provided by the basement's various analysts. Near Holmes' desk was a makeshift plot table constructed out of planks and sawhorses. Soon steel backing was placed on the planks, permitting Holmes to indicate ship movements with small magnets.[28]

Holmes' operation expanded, eventually becoming one of the unit's most bounteous sources of information. As the whole unit grew, "so grew the demands of cryptanalysts for odd bits of information—place names; charts and maps; positions of our own forces, especially submarines; news reports; and other information whose relevance I could only conjecture," Holmes recalled.[29] He supplied what he could. Soon Holmes and Dunbar entered the basement by the front door, having become "of" the dungeon.

॥ ■ ॥

Dominating the greater portion of the basement's northern wall was the final component of Rochefort's decrypt unit: the Japanese language officers and their assistants. Modest in size at first, their cluster would grow. In time, the translators would rival the cryptanalysts for honors as the basement's superstars. Rochefort anticipated their greater prominence, granting them desks and space equal to about three pool tables.

Leading the group, always wearing his signature green eyeshades to veil the bright fluorescent fixture overhead, was Marine Captain Alva B. Lasswell. Tall and sandy-haired, known as Red, Lasswell was something of a loner.[30] But he also was a gifted linguist. Fabled for his precise work habits and alleged fondness for cheap Cuban cigars, Lasswell had many distinctions. Among them, he and Rochefort were the basement's only regular Navy officers who hadn't been to Annapolis.

Lasswell brought a rich background to his duties. He'd joined the Marines in 1925, done his basic training at Parris Island, South Carolina; graduated from officer's candidate school, studied Japanese in Tokyo from 1935 to 1938 under the same ONI program that had sponsored Rochefort; then served as a Japanese linguist in the Philippines and in Shanghai. He was ordered to COM 14 in May 1941, arriving just ahead of Rochefort.[31]

No sooner had Lasswell arrived than he found himself heading a two-man team: himself and a colleague, Lieutenant Ranson Fullinwider. "Fully" was a courtly, quiet-spoken man who also had studied Japanese in Tokyo from 1932 to 1935. He had arrived at COM 14 in June 1939, making him the unit's longest-serving member after Dyer. He and Lasswell weren't alone for long. As noted previously, they got a lot of company on 30 September 1941, with the arrival of linguists Biard, Slonim, Cole, Bromley, and Holcomb.

The only Marine in the basement besides Lasswell, Holcomb also was seasoned. As a thirteen-year-old in 1921, he had followed his businessman father to Peiping and ended up staying in China several years, learning the language.[32] In 1939, along with Biard, Slonim, Cole, and Bromley, he was ordered to Tokyo to learn Japanese.

Safford kept his word; he had promised Rochefort the best cryptanalysts and linguists available. With war looking likelier all the time in late summer 1941, the U.S. ambassador in Tokyo, Joseph Grew, recommended the five linguists be pulled out of Japan for their own safety. The Navy did so. They were among the last Americans to make it out of that country before the war. COM 14 got them.

Rochefort welcomed the five heartily, in his own unceremonious way. Their initial encounter with him was especially memorable for Biard. He would long remember Rochefort's laconic instructions as the officer in charge escorted the linguists to open space near Lasswell and Fullinwider: "Gentlemen, here are your desks. Start breaking Japanese codes."[33]

The new linguists had just gotten a taste of Rochefort's mischievous humor. No newcomer to the world of codebreaking could be expected to break codes that quickly. But Rochefort's playful order wasn't as outlandish as it might have seemed. Contrary to their job titles, linguists did most of the codebreaking in Rochefort's cellar. Officially, their job was to translate into

English codes that had been compromised. But getting to that step involved many previous ones, a process requiring the full participation of the Japanese language officers.

The way the system worked was that the cryptanalysts—Dyer, Wright, and Holtwick—handled the first phase: solving the puzzle that arrived on their desks in the form of a radio intercept. This was essentially a cryptogram concealing a coded message. Their job was to "break" the cryptogram and expose the unidentified code groups that constituted the message. Cryptanalysts didn't need to know Japanese to do this; they had to be wizards at math, as were Dyer and Wright. But to attach meanings to the code groups required facility in Japanese, which was where the linguists came in. Using their skills, linguists like Lasswell became accomplished codebreakers.

All this was new to Biard and his friends just in from Japan. They had a lot of catching up to do. "Fortunately," Biard said, "my desk was next to Rochefort's. People in the basement came to him with problems or just to discuss the day's developments. By eavesdropping on these discussions I learned much."[34]

Sitting at his gray, standard-issue desk, surrounded by Lasswell's translators on one side and Huckins' TA team on the other, and with Holmes' ship plotters nearby, Rochefort occupied a middle space in the basement. His desk was the focal point of most activity in the big open room. He presided over his pack in much the way a kindly city editor ran a newsroom full of prima donnas, free spirits, grizzled veterans, and eccentrics

Rochefort didn't try to change their ways. "But, by the same token," he said, "these people who have this ability require generally somebody over them to keep them on the right track."[35] In that regard, Rochefort did everything he could.

Tall and still trim at age forty-one, his close-cropped, light brown hair just beginning to gray, Rochefort was a forceful manager. He instituted policies that, in effect, converted COM 14's comint unit from a peacetime routine to a near-wartime operation. He inaugurated an "eight-day" week, dividing his officers and men into eight sections, each of which worked six days then had two off.[36] Somebody was on duty every day of the week. Theirs "was the only unit in Hawaii on a seven-day week," said Wright. Rochefort "put us to work This was a serious matter. He got us becoming very enthusiastic."[37]

Rochefort also took a page from Dyer's playbook: he employed the light touch. To foster a collegial atmosphere among his sometimes very competitive analysts, he put up a sign of his own, attaching it to a pillar near his desk: "We can accomplish *anything* . . . provided . . . no one cares who gets the credit."[38]

While Rochefort worked to create a new kind of military culture, there remained ciphers to solve and codes to break, translate, and read. The activity taking place in every nook and cranny of the basement raised questions about Rochefort: With his own background in cryptanalysis and the Japanese language, what would be his role other than being the boss? How would he fit in to the operation he now ran?

The questions were ticklish. Rochefort hadn't worked on an encrypted Japanese message for at least fourteen years, since he'd headed the research desk in the mid-1920s. He had spent most of the past nine years involved in ship duty, which he always called "my first choice."[39] Having tried to stay away from cryptanalysis during the 1930s, he was now back in it with both feet. Some wondered how he could have been away from this bewilderingly complex field for so many years, then pick up where he had left off without missing a beat.

Rochefort would downplay these questions in later years. "During this period of time—actually I'd say about a twelve-year period—you don't get any great developments," Rochefort said. "So when I got involved again it was essentially about the same—the same problems, the same difficulties and everything—[we] had, say, fifteen years before."[40]

Actually, many things had changed. There had been a number of "great developments" in Japanese naval codes since the 1920s, and in U.S. Navy codebreaking. In 1931, for example, Dyer, then attached to the research desk, had been struggling with an Imperial Navy message presumably encrypted in the Red Code—the same one that Rochefort, Driscoll, and Zacharias had solved years earlier—when Driscoll had come by his desk, looked over his shoulder, and paused. "This is a new code," she'd said.[41]

It turned out to be the Blue Code, so named because, following the Navy's color-coded practice, it was filed in a blue folder. Breaking the Imperial Japanese Navy's just-issued code turned out to be a real coup. It enabled U.S. Navy codebreakers to score important successes against IJN exercises in 1934–35.[42] Another major advance was the introduction of IBM "tabulating machines," the same hardware that Dyer in 1937–38 had managed to get transported to his small room at Pearl Harbor.

The Blue Code remained the Japanese navy's main operational code until 1938, when it was succeeded by the Black Code. One year later, that evolved into a five-digit enciphered general-purpose code known first as the AN code and later designated JN-25 (the numeral picked at random).[43] Yet another code augmented the JN-25 system. This was an administrative code designated AD, used primarily for communication between Tokyo and the Imperial Navy's premier admirals.

Renamed the Flag Officers' Code, it was assigned to COM 14 by Safford and, upon Rochefort's arrival in mid-1941, was the main focus of the Dyer-Wright-Holtwick effort, much to their frustration. Because the AD system was so little used, cryptanalysts didn't have enough raw material to work with to make headway.[44] Safford assigned JN-25 to COM 14's sister unit in the Philippines, where analysts did their work in the Malinta Tunnel on Corregidor.

Rochefort couldn't know everything. He probably was privy to some of the developments that had taken place in the 1930s; regardless, nothing could erase the fact that he hadn't been involved. While Navy cryptanalysts led by the redoubtable Miss Aggie struggled against Japanese codes, Rochefort had been doing what he enjoyed most and, given his druthers, would have preferred to continue: sea duty. Now, back in the brave new world of cryptanalysis, Rochefort was, unavoidably, rusty.[45]

But he had remained fluent in Japanese. On board the *Pennsylvania* and more recently the *Indianapolis*, "I just kept up with the language by studying and reading books and by translating books or documents." Also, as an intelligence officer in San Pedro from 1936 to 1938, "I would have some dealings with the Japanese to the extent of being asked occasionally the itinerary or location of some Japanese individual. This involved close relationship with the Japanese community up in Los Angeles."[46]

Given the way his interests had changed, Rochefort didn't try to be a cryptanalyst in the COM 14 unit. He had long since ceased to define himself as one. As much as he admired true cryptanalysts like Safford and Dyer, he saw them as technicians—people who didn't apply the results of what they did to a particular operation. As far as Rochefort was concerned, they would "solve a system for the sake of solving a system." He had a broader vision of what his job should be. "I fancied myself a translator," explained Rochefort, who saw that aspect of the comint unit's work as "the crux of the whole thing. You can assign values [to code groups] and all that sort of thing, but unless you do a good job of translating then the whole value is lost."[47]

If a label had to be attached to Rochefort, it would have been something like crypto-linguist-analyst, with heavy emphasis on the analytical part of the job. His hybrid role did nothing to detract from his credibility or stature. Indeed, he was held a bit in awe, regarded as adept in every aspect of communications intelligence. Because of his two years running the research desk, he grasped the problems confronting Dyer and Wright. They valued his counsel, as did just about everybody else in the basement, whatever the issue. "Subordinates flocked to his assistance and tried to learn from him and to try to exemplify his savvy," one officer said.[48]

Nor, for the first few months of his new duty, was Rochefort's status tainted by the fact that he hadn't been promoted, news that seemed widespread in the basement. Everyone seemed to know everything about everyone. The fact of the matter was that Rochefort wasn't alone in this situation. Dyer too had been passed over, the result of his commitment to cryptanalysis—duty that unavoidably kept him from logging necessary sea duty. Fullinwider and Huckins had had similar encounters with selection boards. They were later promoted, as was Dyer, who was given a special designation ("engineering duty only") that relieved him from sea duty but permitted him to be promoted.[49]

Rochefort's setback with the selection board was short-lived, as noted previously; he was promoted in October 1941, an advance made retroactive to April 1941. How he felt about his belated upgrading Rochefort never publicly said, but he must taken some satisfaction that he had one more time prevailed over his detractors. He still seemed to have what Reeves had termed "a brilliant future."

A hands-on boss, Rochefort's quirks included liking a quiet shop. He didn't mind being disturbed if the question involved a matter of substance, but he didn't approve of loud talk or idle chatter. He dealt personally with those he thought disruptive, and he did all the assigning. "Joe would pull out particular messages for various others to work on," remembered one linguist. "No one marked time; Joe saw to that."[50] No piece of paper left the basement without Rochefort seeing it. He checked all the translations and wrote most of the reports distributed to either fleet headquarters or his superiors in Washington.[51]

Even if he had wanted to function as true cryptanalyst, Rochefort wouldn't have been able to. He didn't have time to devote hour after frustrating hour to the solving of a particular cipher or code; he had too much else to do. First and foremost, Rochefort wanted to build up his basement unit. He was especially in need of linguists, but also wanted more cryptanalysts and traffic analysts.[52] And, of course, he planned to do everything he could to bring in better IBM equipment—collators and tabulating machines—for Holtwick's boiler factory.

Rochefort had an unusual resource to help him with his many tasks: Chief Petty Officer Rorie. Besides supervising all enlisted men in the basement, Rorie also handled many of Rochefort's external dealings with the Fourteenth Naval District. He was Rochefort's troubleshooter and exercised uncommon authority, which rested on their strong relationship of absolute trust. "I could get to [Rochefort] anytime with anything, talk to him, get anything signed that I put in front of him," Rorie said. "He never looked at it. He would just sign it. And I made sure that he never signed anything that he shouldn't have been signing."[53]

Rorie's abilities proved especially useful in assuring that Rochefort's treasured equipment got moved to the basement. Delivery wasn't guaranteed just because it arrived upstairs, the part of the building controlled by naval district personnel. There could still be complications. The problem was the equipment: punchers, sorters, collators, and machine printers, to name just a few of the exotic items Rochefort ordered. They aroused resentment or jealousy. A lot of people coveted those items. Rorie sometimes had to use all his persuasive powers to get the district's officers to sign off on the deliveries.

Of course Rochefort's old friend, Commandant Bloch, knew why the equipment was being brought in. But many of the district's top officers, lacking the military's need-to-know for security reasons, remained uninformed and resentful about the secret unit in the basement. They begrudged Rochefort his equipment and seeming privileges, even his "prime" real estate. Rochefort "wasn't liked and they didn't like the [unit]," Rorie said. "Everybody resented us. We had . . . part of the basement of the main building. They wanted us out of there."[54]

All this state-of-the-art equipment also excited suspicion and speculation. "There were even amused suggestions that Rochefort was trying to break the Japanese code," Holmes recalled. To the extent that the officers and men at Pearl Harbor harbored such suspicions, they were unimpressed. "Most officers working in the navy yard, busy with nuts and bolts and fuel and ammunition were inclined to view code breaking with amused tolerance," Holmes observed.[55]

Rochefort didn't want people thinking about his unit at all. Preoccupied with security as always, he wanted the basement's work to be more than secret; he wanted it to be invisible. That intention carried over into his search for a name to confer upon his underground unit. The operation didn't have an official designation. Rochefort was simply a COM 14 staff officer with a number of personnel working for him in an organization with no official name.

The only phrase that ever showed up in Navy paperwork was "Navy Communications Supplementary Activity."[56] Rochefort didn't like that, as it was ungainly and raised questions. He thought of another name. "When we all moved into the basement together, Rochefort took advantage of the secrecy associated with ship movements to hide what his group was doing behind my charts," Holmes commented. "He adopted Combat Intelligence Unit as a cover name for the whole outfit."[57]

Rochefort's CIU was the hub of the Navy's communications intelligence network in Hawaii, but it was just one part of that network. Different parts with different names did different jobs. There was "listening in," done by radio operators at intercept stations set up at various sites around the island of Oahu. They picked IJN radio transmissions out of the air. Since Rochefort and his CIU analysts had no receivers in the basement, they could do no listening in themselves.

Rochefort's analysts depended wholly on those widely scattered stations for their raw material. His cryptanalysts and TA guys got most of their intercepts from Heeia, a quiet, isolated community thirty miles north of Pearl Harbor, across the Pali Mountain of the Koolau Mountain Range, on the windward side of Oahu. The Navy had moved into the village in 1935. It installed a second facility in the small coastal town of Lualualei, some twenty-five miles west of Pearl Harbor. Lualualei was primarily a DF site, constantly scanning for Japanese ship signals and their source.

Together, Heeia and Lualualei constituted a loosely coordinated radio intelligence system codenamed Station H (possibly for "Heeia" or "Hawaii"). This coexisted with another codename used by OP-20-G to designate Rochefort's operation: Hypo, representing the phonetic-alphabet version of the letter "H," for use typically on the telephone or by voice radio. Hence, "Station H" became "Station Hypo" when it was verbalized. Hypo became OP-20-G's term for the basement unit.[58] Whereas CIU was used routinely in public, Hypo was strictly secret, used only among OP-20-G's brass in Washington and Rochefort's officers. No one said the word out loud publicly.

Even those officers and enlisted men in the basement privy to the code-name never used it to refer to their unit. It was between Washington and Pearl. Some never heard the word until after the war, when historians picked up on it as a colorful label for Rochefort's unit.[59]

Station Hypo wasn't alone. As mentioned previously, it was part of a larger global structure, a Navy comint network with listening posts and decrypt units around the world, each with its own codename. Hypo's sister unit in the Philippines was Station Cast, headquartered in the Malinta Tunnel on Corregidor. The codename derived from Cast's previous location at the Cavite Navy Yard near Manila. Under Cast's umbrella was yet another listening post, Station B, on the island of Guam in the Marianas Island chain.

OP-20-G's decrypt arm, OP-20-GY, had its own codename, Station Negat (for "Navy" or "national"), at Main Navy headquarters. Negat got its intercepts from, among other sites around the globe, a Navy radio station recently constructed in nearby Cheltenham, Maryland. In due course, Negat became the shorthand term for the whole of Washington's OP-20-G operation.

Separate from OP-20-G but closely linked with it by terms of an agreement with Great Britain was another important decrypt unit: the Far East Combined Bureau (FECB), a British codebreaking operation with units in Singapore and Hong Kong. Hypo and Negat didn't have a direct, ongoing relationship with the FECB, but Cast did.

From his years on the research desk, Rochefort would have known how all pieces were supposed to fit together. To stay in touch with OP-20-G and all its far-flung outposts (the FECB excepted), he had at his disposal a remarkable piece of technology: the Electric Cipher Machine (ECM) Mark II, developed by the Navy around 1937–38. Consisting of fifteen rotors placed in three rows, the machine scrambled encrypted messages beyond any potential eavesdropper's recognition. Rochefort handed the ECM's operator an unencrypted message, and he it entered into a keyboard that converted the plaintext characters into electrical currents.[60] Through a secret circuit known as COPEK, which tied together OP-20-G's three main units, Hypo, Cast, and Negat exchanged secret information about codes without fear of compromise. "We had our own cipher system so that nobody, not even [regular Navy] communication watch officers, could read [it]," Rochefort said. "This was our own particular private system which was not available to anybody else in the Navy."[61]

Attached to a post adjoining Rochefort's desk was another critical gadget. This was a secure telephone that, with a couple of turns of the crank, linked him instantly with his friend Fleet Intelligence Officer Layton, located a little over a mile away on the second deck of the submarine base headquarters. Admiral Kimmel had established his headquarters there in spring 1941, and Layton's office was down the hall from Kimmel's. The secure phone line symbolized Rochefort's attempt to turn Hypo into a fast-moving unit that could provide the commander in chief critical intelligence in wartime situations. Rochefort was putting his stamp on Hypo.

Shortly after reporting to Bloch on 2 June 1941, he began "reorganizing, or let's say I was expanding the station at Hypo from a small research unit into more of an operating unit," Rochefort said. The idea was to "furnish quicker and better information to the [Pacific] commander in chief than possibly Washington could."[62] Rochefort's ability to do just that would be tested sooner than he expected.

8

Rochefort's World

It's like having a million-dollar organization with a
ten-cent-store communication system.

—Joe Rochefort

Rochefort moved quickly to exploit his agreement with Safford that he report directly to the U.S. Fleet's commander in chief, Admiral Husband E. Kimmel. He got his first big chance to do so during the "war scare" of 22–29 July 1941, when Japan's military ignored warnings from the United States and occupied the southern portion of French Indochina. The move put Japan's forces within easy striking distance of America's friends to the south: Malaya, Singapore, and the oil-rich Dutch East Indies. In response, President Roosevelt on 25 July clamped a "freeze" on all Japanese assets in the United States.

The action delivered a severe blow to Japan. It led quickly to the end of all trade between the two countries, a development that squeezed Japan militarily and economically. It now lacked the funds required to purchase—in the United States or anywhere else—the oil needed to fuel its military.[1] But the action, "designed to bring Japan to its senses," as one writer put it, seemed to have the opposite effect.[2] Rather than subdued, Japan appeared more bellicose than ever.

Roosevelt doubted Japan would react violently.[3] The Army and Navy weren't so sure. Alerted by Washington about the possibility of some action by the Japanese, on 26 July Admiral Kimmel , instituted long-range air patrols at Pearl Harbor, simply as a matter of prudence. For days Kimmel's planes searched five hundred miles to the west-southwest, toward the Marshall Islands, to detect any attack from that direction.[4]

The crisis erupted shortly after Rochefort had taken a giant step to put Station Hypo on a wartime footing: on 16 July the unit started generating new intelligence for Kimmel. It was conveyed to him via a daily intelligence summary, a two- or three-page document showing the movements of IJN warships across the Pacific. The summary was based on traffic analysis: direction finding done by a Hawaii-based DF network set up around the Pacific, and IJN fleet messages picked up by the Navy's radio-intercept site at Heeia.

Rochefort's intelligence suggested that Kimmel had been wise to order precautionary defensive measures. Hypo's daily summaries for 26–29 July showed, for example, the Japanese high command bringing together portions of its First and Second Fleets, including the carriers *Soryu* and *Hiryu*, and concentrating them in the Inland Sea, possibly for a drive south into the South China Sea.[5] Hypo's summaries enabled Kimmel to track this force as it cruised two thousand miles into the waters of Indochina.

Also forewarned by Washington, Lieutenant General Short, commanding general of U.S. Army forces in Hawaii, reacted to the crisis by placing his troops on a "half alert against sabotage." Army and Navy forces maintained their heightened vigilance—including air reconnaissance—for several days until the absence of "untoward eventualities" led both Short and Kimmel to relax the safeguards they had put in place.[6] Kimmel might have felt comfortable standing down his alert, because he now had Hypo's new intelligence resource before him. The changing picture of the Japanese naval forces that emerged from these summaries justified Kimmel's canceling the alert.

On Tuesday 29 July, Kimmel would have been relieved to read Hypo's summary for the previous twenty-four hours. It noted that the Naval General Staff in Tokyo had originated a message to the chiefs of staff of the combined fleet. "This is an operations message and may be directing the units mentioned to return to their normal commands," Hypo's TA guys deduced.[7] The armada soon turned around and headed back toward Japan's Inland Sea.

Hypo's TA team delivered still more reassuring news. Besides informing Kimmel that the IJN task force had reversed course, it told him that Japan's Third Fleet would "not move south to Indochina," that there was "nothing to report" about the fleet's submarines, and that closer to Hawaii, there was

Oaha

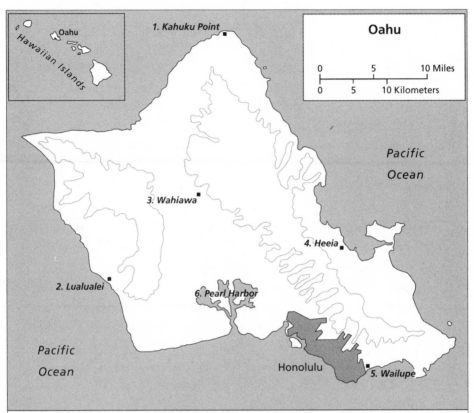

Oahu

0		5		10 Miles

0	5		10 Kilometers

1. Kahuku Point

3. Wahiawa

4. Heeia

2. Lualualei

6. Pearl Harbor

Pacific Ocean

Pacific Ocean

Honolulu

5. Wailupe

Oahu

Hawaiian Islands

1. Kahuku Point: Army radar site that tracked incoming Japanese planes on 7 December 1941 (technically, not part of Rochefort's area of operations).

2. Lualualei: Navy direction finding station through late December 1941, when moved to Wahiawa as part of the reorganization of the Station H intercept site.

3. Wahiawa: New intercept site to where Navy moved its main radio and DF listening posts in late December 1941.

4. Heeia: Navy's main radio intercept site until moved to Wahiawa in late December 1941 (after a brief interlude at Wailupe).

5. Wailupe: Navy's temporary radio intercept site for two weeks in December 1941 until moved back to Wahiawa.

6. Pearl Harbor: Home of Station Hypo.

"little activity" by Japanese warships in the mandated islands—the Carolines, Marianas, and Marshalls in the western and central Pacific.[8] Kimmel could relax.

Whether Kimmel actually used Hypo's summaries in his decision-making was never made known to Rochefort. The reports, after all, didn't answer all questions about the whereabouts of IJN warships; the submarines were silent, and some carriers were unaccounted for. Nor could they foretell everything these ships might do in the future. Still, Rochefort had put on display before the Pacific Fleet's senior officers the potential of radio intelligence to track, even if imperfectly, the movements of the Imperial Japanese Navy.

Rochefort accomplished one other thing. He established a working relationship with the fleet headquarters in which Kimmel was his primary client. As Rochefort intended, the daily reports fashioned by his analysts were delivered first to Kimmel, then to Rochefort's Washington superior, OP-20-G's Safford, usually by airmail but occasionally, when the news was hot, by radio dispatch. A third client was Hypo's counterpart unit in the Philippines, Station Cast; the two units exchanged information regularly through various channels, primarily COPEK.[9]

The daily summaries became a basement ritual. Each evening Rochefort's traffic analysts Huckins and Williams prepared the summary, based on transmissions intercepted at Heeia and Lualualei during the previous twenty-four hours. Rochefort reviewed the document early the following morning and then passed it to his designated liaison officer, Lieutenant Holmes, who delivered it by car to Fleet Intelligence Officer Layton at Kimmel's headquarters.[10]

Because Layton had few other intelligence resources, Hypo's summaries invariably served as the basis for his daily 8:15 a.m. briefing of Kimmel. After hearing Layton's interpretation of the events described, Kimmel perused the document and then put his initials, "HEK," at the bottom of the page on the right. Holmes, Layton, and Kimmel repeated this routine virtually every morning through 6 December 1941.[11]

Even though Rochefort was now reporting directly to fleet headquarters he didn't get his way about everything. He rarely met with Kimmel personally (the two would have one lengthy encounter late that November). "I had to go through Layton because he was the fleet intelligence officer," Rochefort said.[12] He would have preferred a closer tie with Kimmel, but he did have other points of contact with the fleet: copies of all Hypo dispatches conveyed to OP-20-G and Cast were also routed to Kimmel; and he and Layton kept in constant touch via their secure phone. "He and I talked possibly two or three times a day."[13]

॥ ▪ ॥

Rochefort had changed the character of Station Hypo. Originally the unit's mission had been limited. When OP-20-G had sent Dyer to Pearl in 1936 to start up a decrypt unit, the young lieutenant had been ordered to concentrate on research, and scanty research at that. His orders were to study the workings of a single Japanese cryptographic system. This was intended, primarily, to benefit Washington's hard-pressed comint staff, not the U.S. Fleet commander in chief.[14]

The research mission might have been appropriate for the mid-1930s, but with war now virtually inevitable, Rochefort altered Hypo's course in an overdue change. "One of the reasons for 'beefing up' Pearl, and assigning it responsibility for Navy traffic," Rochefort explained, "was that we had been in the dark for some time, and it was imperative that we get back in the business of reading the [Japanese] navy traffic again."[15]

Rochefort found reading Japanese navy traffic easier said than done. Many obstacles blocked his way. As he settled into his new job and became more familiar with the resources at his disposal, he realized that the change he envisioned—making Hypo a fast-moving unit that could deliver Kimmel vital intelligence in real time—would not come quickly. The immediate problem was the state of codebreaking inside the basement: it was somewhere between modest and nonexistent. The Japanese system that Hypo's cryptanalysts had been assigned to break, known as the Flag Officers' Code, was resisting solution. There was nothing Rochefort could do about that. His Washington superior, Laurance Safford, had exercised his prerogative as head of OP-20-G and assigned Hypo this rarely used but, Safford insisted, crucially important Imperial Navy code.

Unable to make a dent in the system, Rochefort's cryptanalysts found themselves relegated to the background of Hypo's world. With cryptanalysis coming up empty, the burden of "reading Japanese traffic" passed to the TAs. At their best, the traffic analysts could shadow at least some IJN warships, as they had during the 26–29 July war scare. But traffic analysis, for all its strengths, had limitations. Cryptanalysis, after all, held out the hope that a decrypted message would let U.S. Navy war planners look over the shoulders of Japanese commanders and, possibly, know some of what they knew. Under perfect conditions, they would know what was going to happen next. Crypt-analysis, therefore, was deductive and predictive.

Traffic analysis, on the other hand, was inferential; it looked backward. It required analysts to infer—in effect, guess—what was going to happen by drawing on the past, sometimes recent, sometimes distant. Its legitimacy rested on the premise that established patterns would continue, and thereby permit analysts to draw some conclusions about what might happen tomorrow or the next day. This was risky. The Japanese would have to do in the future what they had done before.

॥ ■ ॥

Rochefort's problems weren't confined to the vagaries of cryptanalysis and traffic analysis. His analysts depended for their raw material on Station H listening posts scattered around the island. Without radio signals from Lualualei and intercepts of Japanese messages from Heeia, Rochefort's analysts would have nothing to work on. In theory this wasn't supposed to happen. Station H and Hypo were supposed to work together seamlessly. But in practice, Hawaii's comint units were poorly coordinated and staffed, and much of the equipment was obsolete, unreliable, or both. The system was a mess.

To find a weak link in the Station H setup, Rochefort had to look no farther than Lualualei, the scruffy coastal town twenty-five miles away where the Station H direction-finding unit was based. Located unwisely on a small patch of land rimmed by high cliffs and, even more unwisely, near a naval ammunition depot, Lualualei's DF machine was the best the Navy had to offer. It reflected the great strides in that technology made since the European War.[16]

As they worked now, DF units involved radio receivers and directional antenna systems to determine the source of a signal. The antenna, usually a loop, rotated and pinpointed the direction from which a signal was strongest. Using the directions and positions of several DF units, a control station could use triangulation to fix the position of the ship.

But this required that DF units be able to communicate rapidly with their control station in central Oahu, or with other DF units. Making sure this happened was part of Rochefort's job. As officer in charge of Station Hypo, he inherited command of the Mid-Pacific Strategic Direction Finding Net, which included not only the Lualualei unit, but high-frequency radio direction finders on Samoa, Dutch Harbor, and Midway (where a DF unit was installed in September 1941). The net didn't operate as planned. Without their own communication system, the DFs could only communicate through the Navy's regular—or noncomint—channels. Thus, urgent DF information had to stand in line and wait its turn with other Navy traffic.[17]

Another problem was the DF machine itself. Known as the CXK model, it was incorporated in a structure (about the size of a small living room) that rotated along with the aerial on the roof. Radiomen had to get used to traveling in circles. Visually impressive, the CXK had shortcomings. Its major flaw was slowness in rotation to bear on a target: turning 180 degrees required 57½ seconds—an eternity under wartime conditions. "The CXK has been and is our 'crown of thorns,'" admitted one of Washington's top communications officers, Lieutenant Commander E. R. Gardner, in August 1940.[18]

By the fall of 1941, Rochefort was exasperated with the Navy's failure to upgrade Hypo's DF system. A replacement for the troubled CXK hadn't arrived. Not only did Rochefort dislike the CXK, but he was particularly unhappy with the fact that the cables powering the Lualualei unit ran through an Army installation. He wrote a memo, telling OP-20-G: "Strategic Direction Finder continues to be the weak point of Communications Intelligence set up.[19]

Vexed as he was by the DF situation, Rochefort was even more troubled by the setup at Heeia, the tiny settlement on the windward side of the island where the Navy had its main intercept site. At first glance the place seemed ideal. Perched on a bluff overlooking Oahu's northern coast and surrounded by luxuriant greenery, radiomen at the Station H facility enjoyed a sweeping view of Kaneohe Bay and the Kaneohe Naval Air Station, a few miles south. The unit's elevated site helped reception. Even on average days when weather conditions were only so-so, the station's twenty-one receivers could pick up signals across the entire Japanese communication system, from as nearby as Jaluit, 2,500 miles away in the Marshall Islands, or as distant as Kure, 3,500 miles away near Japan's Inland Sea.[20]

Consisting of little more than a gas station, a grocery store, and a couple of bars, Heeia met the Navy's needs for an intercept station: seclusion, privacy, and freedom from trespassers.[21] Visitors reached the site by negotiating the winding Pali Road that traversed the rugged Koolau Mountain Range, then taking a little-used highway to a rusty gate thirty miles from Pearl Harbor. At the site they found a ramshackle, one-story structure. "It was an old Pan American arc station which had been abandoned, shall we say, and picked up by the Navy," said Radioman Second Class James B. Capron Jr. "It was a little old stone building, high-ceilinged affair."[22]

Heeia's thirty-plus radio operators were a close-knit group. Nearly all had graduated from the Navy's legendary "on-the-roof-gang" school (and were known as OTRG'ers or roofers), so named because its classes were held in a concrete blockhouse atop the roof of the sixth wing of Main Navy. In that blockhouse the radiomen were trained in intercepting and taking down Japan's distinct version of Morse code.[23]

The Japanese had modified International Morse to accommodate their unique syllabary, known as katakana. Meaning "fragmentary kana," katakana compressed the two thousand ideograms of the Japanese language into forty-eight symbols, each of which represented a syllable with a Roman equivalent (usually one consonant, one vowel). Each also had a Morse equivalent that could be sent over international telegraph circuits by radio.[24]

The roofers had a daunting task. The International Morse code for the letter C (*dah dit dah dit*) was the same as the kana syllable "NI" in Japanese Morse; the letter A (*dit dah*) was the same as the kana "I"; and so on. They were aided by an innovation traceable to Laurance Safford, who years earlier had persuaded the Underwood Typewriter Company to develop a hybrid machine to convert kana to Roman letters. The result was the RIP-5 typewriter (for Radio Intelligence Publication, fifth in the series). It carried Romanized versions of the Japanese characters on the keyboard.[25] The kana characters were arranged ingeniously, in the same place as the corresponding International Morse letter would be on a regular typewriter. When a radioman heard *dah dit dah dit*, he simply hit the key where C would normally be for the lowercase character set, and the machine would print kana for "NI." This took care of twenty-six of the forty-eight characters constituting the katakana code and greatly eased the job of copying Japanese radio transmissions.[26]

In fall 1941 the OTRG'ers, were charged with one overriding task: copy as much Japanese naval traffic as possible. This was a tall order, since the Japanese generated far more radio traffic than could possibly be copied. There were other problems. Atmospheric conditions could play havoc with radio signals. Time of day mattered. Reception tended to be better at night when there was less interference from the sun.

Even when signals came in loud and clear, radiomen had their hands full. The work was exacting. Earphones in place, radiomen sat uninterrupted for as many as eight hours at a stretch attending one or sometimes two receivers, listening for dots and dashes on assigned frequencies. After long spells of relative inactivity, they suddenly could get very busy. Receivers started crackling, announcing the arrival of a coded message usually conveyed in Japan's forty-eight-character katakana syllabary. "You had to really concentrate," said OTRG'er Harold Joslin, a radioman on Guam. "We tried our best not to miss anything."[27]

The intercepts could be anything from routine to urgent messages. Information about the weather or a personnel change was transmitted in various lower-grade naval codes. Bulletins about ship movements were conveyed in very secret, highly complex codes including the Flag Code and a not-yet fully appreciated five-digit code called AN-1, soon to be renamed and gain fame as JN-25(b). Radiomen didn't try to intercept every message. They ignored diplomatic traffic, or dip, as operators called it. Dip was assigned to units at Bainbridge Island, Washington; Cheltenham, Maryland; Jupiter, Florida; Winter Harbor, Maine; and Amagansett, New York.[28]

Dip was also collected at Station Cast in the Philippines. Unknown to Rochefort, Kimmel, and everybody else at Pearl, Cast in April 1941 received a new machine delivered by a U.S. Navy supply ship. Perfected seven months earlier, it was an analog device for reading a cipher that Washington the previous year had dubbed Purple—Japan's highest-priority diplomatic cipher system. It was used by the Foreign Office in Tokyo for its most secret messages to ambassadors abroad. Solving it had been the greatest intelligence coup achieved by American cryptanalysts to that point. No one at Pearl knew anything about Purple.[29]

ııＩＩＩ

As the months passed, Heeia's radio operators found their lives getting more exciting. From "a quiet, restful duty station," as Radioman First Class Elliott E. Okins described Station H in 1940, it suddenly turned into "one of the most eventful of my naval career."[30] By the fall of 1941, "Japanese naval communications were showing signs of more sophistication. They introduced new types of coded messages. Their volume of message traffic increased steadily as the months went by," Okins said.[31]

All this was compelling to Rochefort and his codebreakers. But there was a near-fatal weakness in the Station H–Hypo relationship: the maddening lag between the time when IJN messages were picked up at Heeia and when Rochefort and his analysts saw them. Heeia's radiomen had no way of conveying their intercepts rapidly to Rochefort's basement. No teleprinter link or two-way radio tied in the two sites. There was a telephone connection between Hypo and Station H, but, astonishingly, it was a party line, used by many local citizens in the Heeia area.[32] The phone was useless for passing secret information.

Day after day the same routine was followed. A Station H operator, quite often Chief Radioman Homer Kisner, would take charge of the intercepts. Skilled as both a radioman and traffic analyst, he prioritized the messages gathered during the previous twenty-four hours. He then put together a chronology that highlighted the most noteworthy intercepts. "I would . . . write up a little script," as Kisner described it.[33]

His chronology finished, he wrapped it up in a package that also included all Station H intercepts. Then Kisner or another radioman got in a jeep or whatever vehicle was available, accompanied by an armed guard. Late in the afternoon, they drove the twisting Pali Road over the Koolau Range, descended sharply onto a roadway that became Nuuanu Avenue, and proceeded to Pearl, passing, ironically, the Japanese consulate on the way.

The thirty-mile trip took about forty minutes, sometimes longer, depending on traffic. The whole setup infuriated Rochefort. With Japan appearing more menacing every day, he believed Pearl Harbor should have been getting Heeia's raw intercepts in real time, not twenty-four hours after they had been copied. Rochefort wasn't angry at the radiomen. He knew they were doing their best; he was upset with the Navy's system. "We should have had numerous teletypes," he fumed. "We could have saved ourselves an hour each time, you see. Instead of that, we still had to [use] jeeps or bicycles or motorcycles, which was ridiculous. We had a lousy wire system, telephones and that sort of thing. This was just lousy. It's like having a million-dollar organization with a ten-cent-store communication system."[34]

Kisner's delivery set in motion Rochefort's business-like procedure for handling newly arrived intercepts. The bundle was handed over first to Hypo's two traffic analysts, Huckins and Williams. They examined the headings, using their knowledge of IJN call signs and ships' communications to identify the sending parties and determine who was talking to whom and, if possible, fix where vessels were headed. This done, the intercepts were carried to the other side of the basement, to the desks occupied by Hypo's cryptanalysts Dyer, Wright, and Holtwick. If they made sufficient progress cracking an encrypted message, the intercept then passed to the linguists, who moved the dispatch to its final stage: codebreaking and translation.[35]

In practice, of course, not all intercepts made their way from Huckins and Williams to Dyer and company. Transmissions encoded in AN-1 had another destination: OP-20-G's decrypt unit at Main Navy, Station Negat. AN-1 was relatively new. It had first appeared in IJN traffic on 1 June 1939. Initially Negat's cryptanalysts assumed sole responsibility for solving this system, then called JN-25(a). They made modest strides until 1 January 1941, when the Japanese navy scuttled it and introduced a stronger successor, JN-25(b).[36]

In their transition from JN-25(a) to JN-25(b) the Japanese made a mistake: they briefly left in place features of the old code (the so-called additives), which gave Negat's codebreakers a head start in recovering JN-25(b). But Negat wasn't able to fully exploit this advantage. Because its workload burgeoned in late 1940 and early 1941, thanks in part to the explosion in diplomatic decrypt work generated by the arrival of Purple, Negat lacked the manpower necessary for a full-scale attack on JN-25(b).[37]

By late January 1941, the window left open into the new Japanese code had closed—and also by this time Negat had decided to share the workload. Early that year, OP-20-G's Safford directed Station Cast on Corregidor to join Negat in the assault on JN-25(b).[38] The decision nettled COM 14's analysts. They remained stuck with the unyielding AD, or administrative code, more commonly known as the Flag Officers' Code. They couldn't get anywhere with it.

There was no mystery why. Not only had the Japanese revamped this code system, making it a good deal more complex, but early in 1941 they began using it less frequently, sometimes producing no more than three or four messages a day.[39] With the volume of traffic in AD falling off while that of JN-25(b) increased, Pearl's analysts were stymied. They didn't have the minimum number of intercepts coming in that would have allowed them to make headway. Dyer and Wright wanted COM 14 to take on JN-25(b). They made their wishes known early in 1941, well before Rochefort took over Hypo. "We had been begging for it," Wright said.[40]

For a while it appeared they might get their way. On 5 March 1941, Safford let it be known that responsibility for solving the code would be transferred to COM 14 that July. This time Cast protested, leading Safford to change his mind again. Agreeing with Cast that it was better positioned geographically to capture JN-25(b) transmissions, on 24 April Safford directed Cast to keep working on this code, stating that the "project will not be transferred to [COM 14] as previously planned."[41]

Safford's ruling would have far-reaching implications. It generated controversy later, as historians wondered how events might have been different if

Pearl's skilled cryptanalysts—considered by most a cut or two above Cast's—had been unleashed on this crucial code system as early as April or May 1941. But by the time Rochefort assumed charge of COM 14 in June 1941, the decision had been made, and he accepted the situation as he found it. In later years, some wondered why he hadn't mounted a campaign to get JN-25(b) for Hypo. Rochefort never said, but in all likelihood he wasn't troubled by the division of labor.

Because of the way Safford had characterized the two codes, Rochefort apparently believed the Flag Officers' Code was the more crucial. Safford certainly thought so; in 1945 he told Congress that it was "the most difficult as well as the most important system the Japanese Navy was using. If we could have solved the Flag Officer's System, Admiral Kimmel would probably have known of the Japanese plans and the Pacific Fleet would not have been surprised on December 7, 1941."[42]

Whether Safford was right remains a mystery. The Flag Officers' Code was never broken. Given Safford's credibility with Rochefort, Hypo's officer in charge probably shared his view. In any case, the fact remained that JN-25(b) was now outside Hypo's reach. The problem now wasn't how to break it. The issue was how best to transport the raw intercepts of messages encrypted in JN-25(b) to OP-20-G. Hypo did what it always did: it bundled up the intercepts and shipped them to Washington, sometimes by Pan American Clipper, sometimes by ship.

॥ ▌ ॥

Rochefort's cryptanalysts remained frustrated. "The amount of traffic in [the Flag Officer's Code] was wholly inadequate, but we were assigned that as a primary mission," Dyer said.[43] "I batted my head against a stone wall with very little to work on, I suppose, for about a year." Added Ham Wright, Dyer's equally unhappy partner: "Nobody ever got into this thing."[44] Hypo's linguists also were discouraged. With few decrypts surfacing from the cipher desk, they had many idle hours. "It was a boring job as we had little to work on," Red Lasswell said.[45]

Not all of Hypo's codebreaking efforts came to nothing. Dyer, Wright, and their colleagues notched victories against what Rochefort sardonically called "the nickel and dime stuff"—a variety of the Imperial Navy's lower-grade codes such as those for personnel, intelligence, merchant ships, and weather.[46] The Japanese navy's secondary codes yielded a steady flow of interesting information, but they didn't disclose where the ships were headed.

Months passed with meager results. "No [Flag Officer Code] values recovered," said Navy bookkeepers in Washington, auditing Hypo's results as of 1 October 1941. The story for JN-25(b) wasn't much better. In an effort to grasp the underlying structure of that code, Station Negat concentrated primarily on old JN-25(b) traffic, or back traffic. That work yielded little. Station Cast tried its best to read the code in real time, but by 1 October it had recovered no more than 2,400 of JN-25(b)'s 50,000 code groups.[47]

By early fall 1941, the Navy's most accomplished codebreakers—its expert cryptanalysts at Pearl Harbor, Washington, and Corregidor—weren't reading either of the Imperial Navy's two most important naval codes. But Rochefort did have a fallback resource. With no decrypts emerging from Hypo's attack against the Flag Code, he had no choice but to rely entirely on traffic analysis for the daily intelligence summaries he sent over to Layton and, ultimately, Kimmel. Imperfect as it was, the TA system now showed what it could do.

In late summer 1941, the picture of the Imperial Japanese Navy that had emerged from Hypo's traffic analysis turned suddenly ominous. Beginning in August and continuing through September, the activities of the Japanese navy assumed a different character. Hypo's summary for 5 September informed Kimmel that the navy was reorganizing: it was creating new task forces and tightening communications security. The intercepts suggested "a big shakeup in air activities," Hypo conjectured. Three days later, on 8 September, intercepts showed an increased "flow of traffic between carriers and the various air bases." This development, Rochefort told Kimmel, indicated the "the fitting out" of the IJN carriers with their plane complements.[48]

Another change occurred on 9 September, when Heeia picked up messages showing the carrier *Akagi* in Empire waters using secret, previously unused call signs when communicating with other IJN carrier units. That ominous trend continued through the next two weeks, leading Rochefort's daily summary for 24 September to sound a warning: "Normal peacetime operating or administrative frequencies or exercises are [being] replaced by entirely different frequencies in maneuvers or exercises and likewise secret calls [are replacing] the service calls."[49]

By early fall, the vast majority of IJN messages intercepted by Heeia were encrypted in JN-25(b), which was rapidly evolving into the main operational code. Rochefort and his traffic analysts started to draw some dire conclusions. Hypo cautioned on 28 September: "The general impression grows that preparations are increasing for either maneuvers on a large scale or possibly a hostile operation of some kind."[50]

What Kimmel and his superiors in Washington made of Hypo's reports remained unclear. There was never any question as to whether Kimmel read its daily summaries; his initials appeared on each document through 6 December 1941. But weeks would pass before he sought out Rochefort to explore more deeply his thinking on what Japan's moves might portend.

ıı ∎ ıı

The world wasn't waiting for Station Hypo to fix all its glitches. The war in Europe was spreading: After launching a massive invasion of the Soviet Union on 22 June 1941, German forces now menaced Leningrad and advanced toward Moscow. War with Germany neared on 4 September, when the U.S. destroyer *Greer* became the first American warship fired upon by a German U-boat. President Roosevelt ordered the U.S. Navy to "shoot on sight" if any American ship or ship under American escort was threatened.

Tensions also mounted in the Far East, as Japan consolidated its hold on Indochina and threatened Thailand. In Washington, Secretary of State Cordell Hull and Japanese Ambassador Kichisaburo Nomura continued their desultory talks aimed at averting war. But peace wasn't what Rochefort and his analysts saw coming in the Pacific. Increasingly IJN messages analyzed at Pearl Harbor revealed a Japanese navy reorganizing itself, almost certainly for military action.

Hypo's radio intelligence presented Kimmel with a remarkably accurate picture of Japanese moves in the Pacific, which were those of a nation preparing for war. For Kimmel, the main question was what these moves might mean for the forces under his command. The question wasn't only Kimmel's, it was also Rochefort's. What implications did he see for the U.S. Pacific Fleet and the security of Pearl Harbor? Rochefort had his own ideas. But were they on target?

9

Shadowing Yamamoto

> He was one of the . . . "firebrands," and might conceivably
> disobey any order from Tokyo.
>
> —Joe Rochefort

Rochefort was probably the only officer in the U.S. Navy who had met Isoroku Yamamoto and had come away unimpressed. Rochefort's closest friends, Ellis Zacharias and Eddie Layton, raved about the diminutive, five-foot-three admiral, now commanding the Combined Fleet, the central force in the Imperial Japanese Navy. They spoke admiringly of this complex, many-faceted man, noting his high intelligence, shrewdness, forcefulness, daring in card games, even his common sense. They found him fascinating.

Zacharias was especially dazzled. As a young officer in naval intelligence in Washington in 1926, he'd been invited to Yamamoto's comfortable apartment in northwest Washington. Then a naval attaché serving in Japan's embassy, Yamamoto made it a practice to invite his American counterparts to his place for occasional stag affairs that included moderate drinking and cards. "Poker was his favorite," Zacharias recalled, "and he played it with an unreserved and unconcealed determination, as if he must defeat us at this game before he could defeat us in war."[1]

From those games and other social encounters with Yamamoto, Zacharias sized up the Japanese navy leader as "restless and impatient" but also exceptionally able, assertive, and a man of quick thinking. Layton also had a soft spot for the admiral. The two had met once or twice between 1929 and

1932 when Layton was in Tokyo, probably at one of the social occasions—a theater party, duck hunt, or even a geisha party—that language students and embassy officials attended. Layton found him "a very human, a very real, and a very sincere man" who would make war on the United States only reluctantly. "I don't think his heart was really in it," Layton said later.[2]

Rightly or wrongly, Rochefort took a less charitable view of Yamamoto. He had met the Japanese navy leader at least twice, probably at the same functions attended by Layton, possibly on other occasions as well. Yet he saw a somewhat different Yamamoto. "Prior to December 7, 1941, I considered Admiral Yamamoto as not being particularly brilliant," Rochefort said. Rather than the wise, almost benign leader intuited by Layton, Rochefort viewed the admiral as "a strong character who might take violent action even without the knowledge or consent of his superiors in Tokyo." Rochefort thought he was a menace and a hothead, somebody who might do something dumb. "In reading the various statements attributed to him, and during the one or two occasions that I met him, my estimate was that he was one of the—what we called 'firebrands,' and might conceivably disobey any order from Tokyo under certain circumstances," he told a Navy investigating panel in 1944.[3]

Rochefort's hard-headed view of Yamamoto might appear to be the more realistic one in light of events to come. But his opinion of the Japanese admiral concealed a nagging contradiction in his own thinking. His feeling that Yamamoto was capable of anything, including rash action, conflicted with his long-held view of the Japanese Navy, one that preceded Yamamoto's 1939 appointment as commander in chief of the mighty Combined Fleet.

Rochefort saw Japan's strategic ambitions in the Pacific restrained by its navy's sense of its own limitations. Japan had been aggressive in its own neighborhood, seizing Manchuria and large parts of China, and threatening its Far East neighbors. But it would be defense-minded toward the United States, not doing anything crazy. Rochefort had thought that way in 1934, when he'd written his memo on IJN options for Admiral Reeves, and he'd continued to hold that outlook in 1939, when Admiral Andrews had added him to his Scouting Force war planning team.

Rochefort had now become more troubled by Japan, but he nevertheless remained comfortable with his central 1934 assumption. Whatever Japan did, it was likely to act in its own self-interest. It would be rational. If, against all reason and common sense, Japan were to militarily engage the United States at either Manila or Pearl Harbor, the result would be a foregone conclusion: war. Rochefort believed Japan knew how such a conflict would end.

"If we become involved in a war with Japan, the Japanese cannot possibly win," Rochefort said later, reconstructing his thinking at the time. "Therefore, the Japanese will not proceed against the United States directly but will rather reach their goals by, say, possibly [taking] Singapore, certainly Southeast Asia, maybe some of the islands but not the Philippines because this would probably bring them to war [with the U.S.]" Instead, he thought, the Japanese would "proceed along the Asiatic mainland . . . and might possibly move against the Malay Archipelago, but certainly not against the U.S." Rochefort wasn't alone in what he later called this "unfortunate attitude."[4]

This "attitude" was part of the intellectual baggage of many, perhaps most high-ranking officers at Pearl Harbor in fall 1941. True, they tended to think, as Rochefort did, that war with Japan was a likely outcome of events unfolding in the Far East. But they also thought that if war did come about, it would happen almost by accident. They speculated that Japan might attack an ally, the British or the Dutch, and that America would get dragged in. And if that happened, the United States would triumph during a climactic showdown far from Hawaii, in Empire waters. It would be the long-predicted decisive battle against the Imperial Navy.

Paradoxically, Yamamoto had reached the same conclusion. The Zacharias-Layton view of Yamamoto wasn't entirely wrong. In the context of Japanese military politics, he was seen as a moderate. He had opposed the invasion of Manchuria in 1931, the land war with China in 1937, and the Tripartite Pact with Nazi Germany and Fascist Italy signed in fall 1940. His stand on those issues made him a target of assassination by pro-war militarists. To keep him out of harm's way, in 1939 the Navy Ministry sent him to sea, giving him command of the Combined Fleet.

As Japan edged toward war in the closing months of 1941, Yamamoto was already a legend in naval circles and among the Japanese people. Every schoolboy knew the story of this fabled officer, who, serving on a cruiser during the Russo-Japanese war in 1904–5, was wounded at the Battle of Tsushima, losing the index and middle fingers of his left hand. In the years that followed, Yamamoto's career flourished.

As a high-ranking officer in the 1920s, he promoted innovations that advanced the cause of Japanese naval aviation.[5] He helped shape the development of the navy's medium-range bombers and planes that could carry long-range torpedoes. One outcome of Yamamoto's advocacy was the emergence of the A6M Zero, a long-range fighter noted for its speed and maneuverability. The Zero would be heard from shortly.

Yamamoto throughout 1941 worked to influence the Imperial Navy's strategic doctrine for fighting a war against the United States. He let it be known he opposed such a war. But if it turned out that war was inevitable, he urged the navy to reject what had been the centerpiece of Japanese naval planning: a decisive battle in which U.S. and IJN battleships squared off in Empire waters in a traditional exchange (a mirror image of America's War Plan Orange). Naturally, in the IJN version, the Imperial Japanese Navy vanquished the U.S. Navy.

But Yamamoto had traveled widely in the United States; he was aware of the country's productive potential. Given America's strategic advantages in military capacity, he didn't think the Japanese navy could prevail in a decisive battle by passively waiting for the enemy fleet to show up in Japan's home waters. If he was ordered to fight in spite of his better judgment, he wanted to deliver a preemptive strike so powerful that it would cripple America's ability to wage war in the Pacific, thus bringing a rapid end to the conflict.

If, on the other hand, the United States chose to fight, he feared the war would be long and that Japan could not win. "I shall run wild considerably for the first six months or a year but I have utterly no confidence for the second and third years," Yamamoto told Prince Fumimaro Konoye in early fall 1941.[6] Yamamoto was ready to throw the dice; he thought it was Japan's only chance.

What Rochefort didn't know, nor did anyone in the U.S. Navy, was that Yamamoto in the space of a few months had transformed IJN strategic thinking. From the wise philosopher that Layton had seen, he had become the firebrand that Rochefort had perceived. Although not out of the Imperial General Staff's control, Yamamoto nevertheless was preparing, as Rochefort probably would have put it, to do something dumb.

Rochefort's orders were to track the Imperial Japanese Navy. But he wasn't sure which one he was looking for—the restrained Japanese navy guided by self-interest, or a far more capricious one led by a firebrand. Unable to confirm either slant, he juggled his competing views while leaning toward his original notion—the "unfortunate attitude" he attributed to many of the U.S. Navy's highest-echelon officers. He thought the Imperial Japanese Navy would steer clear of the United States, and Rochefort didn't easily surrender a strong conviction.

"Now, he was an extremely brilliant man," said Tex Biard, who once tried to argue with Rochefort. "But he was also very, very opinionated."[7]

❙❙◾❙❙

But Rochefort wasn't foolhardy, and did not share the complacency of some at Pearl who doubted that the Imperial Navy would attack any Western power. He didn't underestimate the Japanese, and knew they were going to strike somewhere. War was coming; Rochefort just didn't know where. He doubted it would be U.S. territory, but that was an opinion for which he had scant evidence.

During fall 1941, Rochefort and his analysts searched for clues that would tell them one way or the other where the Japanese navy was headed. Their best hope to sniff out IJN movements was the steady stream of radio dispatches to and from warships intercepted at Heeia and delivered to Hypo daily by jeep. But Hypo's analysts operated under the handicap previously described: they couldn't evaluate messages encrypted in codes they couldn't break or, for that matter, were prevented by OP-20-G from attempting to break.

Still, more and more messages encrypted in the IJN's operational code, JN-25(b), reached the basement, were scanned by Rochefort's traffic analysts (taking down the call signs and other data from the externals), then shipped to Washington for decryption. Rochefort figured that JN-25(b) was in good hands at Stations Cast and Negat, assuming he would be informed of the fruits of those efforts if there were any.

While he waited for news relating to JN-25(b) and watched his cryptanalysts struggle with the stubborn Flag Officers' Code, Rochefort looked to traffic analysis for answers. Already radio intelligence had provided ONI analysts at Main Navy a remarkably accurate picture of Japanese naval forces: their numbers and general organization. That picture of the Japanese navy was available to Rochefort as officer in charge of Hypo. Thanks to radio intelligence, the U.S. Navy knew the Japanese had approximately 230 warships, the great majority of which were allocated to Yamamoto's powerful Combined Fleet.[8] Most of the remainder were assigned to the China theater.

From its RI outposts, including Station H, the U.S. Navy knew that Yamamoto's warships had been divided into separate fleets. They included a First Fleet, or Battle Force, comprising three battleship divisions of two ships per BatDiv, among other warships; a Second Fleet, or Scouting Force, constituted mainly of cruisers and destroyers; a Third Fleet used for blockade and transport purposes; a Fourth Fleet assigned for defense duties in the mandates; a Fifth Fleet that remained pretty much a blank; and a Sixth Fleet composed of six submarine squadrons.[9]

Spearheading the Combined Fleet were its ten carriers. Of these six were heavy carriers, so called because they were sizable, fast, and could carry a lot of planes. They included the older behemoths *Akagi* and *Kaga* (constituting Carrier Division 1), two smaller high-speed carriers built in the 1930s, the *Soryu* and *Hiryu* (CarDiv 2), and the recently built *Shokaku* and *Zuikaku* (CarDiv 5). The six were supported by four smaller carriers: *Ryujo, Hosho, Koryu,* and *Kasuga Maru* (later named *Taiyo*).[10]

For all its good information, the U.S. Navy never understood how Yamamoto's carriers were organized. Early in 1941, ONI placed CarDivs 1 and 2 with the Second Fleet, and CarDiv 5 with the First. Then in mid-1941, ONI saw the Imperial Japanese Navy reorganizing and arrived at a new conclusion: all ten carriers operated together in a single entity, the Carrier Fleet. ONI's configuration implied incorrectly that this was an operational unit. In fact, IJN carriers did operate in five divisions (two carriers per division), but they didn't belong to a single unit. The Carrier Fleet was an administrative entity, not an operational one.[11] IJN carriers might operate anywhere within the Combined Fleet.

Rochefort's TAs had their hands full tracking all those warships, which they accomplished primarily by drawing inferences. Under the Imperial Navy's scheme of organization, certain ships were always associated with certain others. Specific destroyers were assigned to specific carriers and battleships. Because there were more destroyers than carriers and battleships, it was often easier to obtain the call signs for those vessels. So when traffic analysis showed a certain destroyer moving—one associated with a particular carrier—analysts inferred that a carrier division was also moving. They were usually right.

Day after day Heeia's radiomen plucked messages from the air that, when analyzed by Huckins, Williams, and Rochefort, showed a steady buildup of Japan's naval and air forces, mostly in the South China Sea but also in the mandates in the western and central Pacific. Rochefort's summary for 21 October 1941 sounded a jarring note: "With nothing definite to point to, the impression grows that a large-scale screening maneuver or operation, at least, is in progress, involving mainly units in the Mandates, Takao-Hainan Indochina area [and] the Kuriles."[12]

The Imperial Navy had sizable bases at both Takao, in southern Taiwan; and Hainan, a large island off the southern coast of China, seized by Japan in 1939. Maneuvers in that sector weren't altogether surprising. The Kuriles were another matter. Administered by Japan, they comprised a deserted volcanic island archipelago hundreds of miles from the Imperial Japanese Navy's Inland Sea headquarters. They stretched 700 miles from the northernmost tip of Hokkaido, Japan's most northern province, to Russia's Kamchatka peninsula.

Given the Kuriles' proximity to the northern Pacific and their convenience as a jumping-off point to sea-lanes that led to the Hawaiian Islands and points east, maneuvers in those waters might have aroused curiosity. They didn't. No one at Hypo, neither Rochefort nor any of his analysts, questioned why the Japanese navy was holding exercises as far north as the Kurile Islands. No one suspected how they figured in Yamamoto's daring scheme that was now beginning to show itself and would hatch out in just a couple of months.

Just when Hypo's analysts seemed to be gaining a clearer picture of Japan's movements in the South China Sea and the mandates, the Imperial Japanese Navy suddenly threw up a roadblock. It changed the call signs for all fleet and air units, effective 1 November 1941 (31 October in Hawaii), a development that put U.S. Navy radiomen and analysts in the dark for a time. The move wasn't unexpected. The Japanese navy tended to change its call signs every six months or so. This wasn't alarming in itself, but it did mean that OP-20-G's traffic analysts scattered around the Pacific—at Pearl Harbor, Heeia, Corregidor, and Guam—had to work frantically for days to reestablish the call signs of the IJN forces they were tracking. At first the change seemed routine.

Astonishingly, Rochefort and his counterparts on Corregidor and Guam quickly identified at least some of call signs of each of the Japanese navy's major fleets.[13] In their recovery effort analysts were aided, ironically, by the Japanese themselves. "You could tell certain Japanese radio operators," said Guam radioman Joslin. "Some would have a certain swing," or personalized touch in the way they handled the radiotelegraph key. This gave them away, and thereby the identity of their ships. "We would get to know those guys."[14]

The call-sign change didn't prevent Rochefort and his Hypo analysts from making a major discovery, one that potentially could have changed Rochefort's whole conception of Yamamoto's strategy in the Pacific. Hypo's two chief traffic analysts, Huckins and Williams, aided by Lasswell's linguists, interpreted the addressee of an IJN dispatch—"Itikoukuu Kantai" in Romanized katakana—as First Air Fleet.[15]

This intercept indicated "an entirely new organization of the Naval Air Force," Rochefort informed Kimmel on 3 November. Hypo's daily summary also noted a curious association between shore-based air units and fleet air units. "Their association in a command sense . . . had never occurred before but under the concept of an *air fleet* can easily be accepted" (emphasis in original).[16] This was new, but what did it augur?

What Rochefort didn't know was that Hypo had chanced upon an unprecedented concentration of naval air power, one assembled in April 1941 by Yamamoto. He called this new group the First Air Fleet. It comprised six carriers: *Akagi* and *Kaga* (CarDiv 1), *Hiryu* and *Soryu* (CarDiv 2), and *Zuikaku* and *Shokaku* (CarDiv 5), carrying 464 aircraft: 137 fighters, 144 dive bombers, and 183 torpedo planes. It also included two battleships, three cruisers, eleven destroyers, three submarines, and eight tankers. It formed the most critical component of what the Japanese labeled the *kido butai*, or striking force.[17]

Rochefort thought Hypo's discovery was important, but he didn't know how important. Neither he nor his analysts nor Layton grasped that Hypo had come across the powerful fleet that would depart the Kuriles on 25 November 1941 (Hawaii time), proceed across the northern Pacific and, on 7 December, move to within 230 miles of Oahu's northern coast. Given the high volume of traffic directed to the First Air Fleet's carriers, Rochefort and Layton guessed that a major Combined Fleet exercise might be taking place. But the new fleet didn't seem to pose an immediate threat.[18]

Ferreting out more about this new fleet—and what was going on across the Pacific—suddenly got more difficult. Among the many things that Rochefort and his Hypo team didn't know was that the April creation of the First Air Fleet had scrambled the U.S. Navy's IJN organization chart. Unknown to ONI and all in the Navy, the First Air Fleet had been cobbled together out of elements of other Combined Fleet units and the purely administrative Carrier Fleet. The battleships *Hiei* and *Kirishima*, viewed by ONI as one section of BatDiv 3 with the First Fleet, and the cruisers *Tone* and *Chikuma*, seen earlier as CruDiv 8, Second Fleet, now belonged to the First Air Fleet.[19]

Yamamoto's First Air Fleet rendered obsolete much of what the U.S. Navy thought it knew about the Imperial Navy. As a result, Rochefort's analysts couldn't always be sure which ships belonged where. Call signs showed a pattern of shifting attachments among the warships, sowing confusion at

Hypo. From reading Hypo's daily summaries, Layton expressed his own bewilderment. "Various units no longer had their normal mothers," Layton said later. "In other words, each fleet commander, that we call mother, had certain chickens, and some of these chickens no longer belonged to the mother, but belonged to other mothers of other fleets."[20]

Disturbed by these and other developments, Rochefort drew a few conclusions. "Beginning about the first of November it became apparent to us in a study of the [radio] traffic that there was something afoot," he stated later. "We couldn't put our hands on it as to what it was to be or any direction . . . it became apparent that there was something building up."[21]

To sharpen Hypo's vigilance, Rochefort instituted a major change in the basement. In August he had established the seven-day work week; now he put all Hypo's officers and men on a twenty-four-hour schedule. The basement would now be manned around the clock. At least one officer, along with several clerks, would always be on duty. "Early in November 1941 the situation in the Pacific became alarming," Jasper Holmes wrote. "We realized that war was imminent, and the Combat Intelligence Unit began to maintain a continuous watch."[22]

⚬⚬▮⚬⚬

Hypo's analysts never again spotted the First Air Fleet in radio traffic. As far as Rochefort and his analysts were concerned, the new armada had dropped off the face of the earth. They had a pretty good idea why. They suspected that the 1 November call-sign change wasn't as routine as it at first had seemed, and they figured the Japanese had used the change as an opportunity to introduce more secure procedures for conveying messages. In this guess they were correct.

Much of the traffic radiomen now picked up at Heeia didn't make sense to analysts at Pearl. "General messages continue to emanate from Tokyo communications," Hypo observed on 3 November. "Such an amount is unprecedented and the import is not understood. A mere call change does not account for activities of this nature."[23]

Rochefort's traffic analysts were confounded because Japanese naval units receiving messages were now less likely to be addressed in the headings of dispatches, the externals. "Formerly Tokyo radio called the unit concerned when the dispatch was addressed to a member of that unit," Hypo noted in its daily summary for 6 November. "Beginning yesterday afternoon all broadcast messages are addressed to a single call without regard to the addressee of the message. The recovery of the radio organization will be hampered by this new advance in Communication Security."[24]

The Imperial Navy had changed its communication procedures in two critical ways. First, it now tended to avoid openly addressing fleet units it was contacting; messages intended for particular units were more frequently included in general traffic circulated throughout the fleet, making it harder for U.S. Navy eavesdroppers to identify addressees. Second, IJN call signs were more now likely to be buried in the text of the messages, which couldn't be read because they were encoded in the indecipherable JN-25(b). A hard job had just become harder.

The vanishing of the First Air Fleet and the tightening of IJN communications security coincided with another troubling development. On 5 November, CNO Stark informed Admiral Kimmel and Admiral Thomas Hart, commander in chief, U.S. Asiatic Fleet, based in Manila, that the Imperial Japanese Navy had ordered "the complete withdrawal" of all Japanese merchant vessels from Western Hemisphere waters. "No ships presently enroute from Japan," Stark stated in his radiogram, the essence of which Rochefort learned from Commandant Bloch.[25]

Rochefort regarded Japan's decision to pull from the Pacific its merchant ships (marus) as a "tip off" signaling fast-approaching warfare.[26] Whether he impressed upon Kimmel his heightened sense of danger was unclear. He was never asked. Kimmel allegedly was briefed about the significance of such a development by Rochefort's old friend Captain Zacharias, who said he had told Kimmel in March 1941: "Among the earliest indications [of imminent hostilities] . . . would be the withdrawal of merchant ships to Japan"—a warning that Kimmel denied ever hearing from Zacharias.[27]

The Zacharias-Kimmel hubbub haunted the Pearl Harbor debate for decades and raised questions about how thoroughly Kimmel had been briefed by his closest aides. Kimmel insisted he hadn't been clued in about the marus. What Layton said to Kimmel about their exodus from the Pacific was apparently not recorded. Although Rochefort never said so, this might have been one of those occasions when he would have liked easier access to the U.S. Fleet's commander in chief. He regarded Kimmel as his ultimate client, but they rarely met. As will be seen, they had only one notable meeting.

No matter how urgent the radio traffic intercepted, Rochefort followed his routine to keep Kimmel informed through Layton. This practice had worked most of the time, even though it kept Rochefort at one remove from the man he wanted most to serve. He didn't always know what Layton did or did not say to Kimmel. And Rochefort would never go around Layton, "being a close personal friend of mine." As he said later, "I could not bypass, or—as we used to say in the Navy—I couldn't 'bulkhead' him by going direct" to Kimmel. "I just couldn't do this sort of thing to Eddie."[28]

For weeks Rochefort and his traffic analysts squinted through the electronic fog for signs of Yamamoto's Combined Fleet. No sooner did they catch a glimpse of a new task force or a new pattern of fleet activity than they lost it, stymied by some stratagem employed by the Japanese navy's radiomen. They recognized the ploys, priding themselves on their ability to spot them, and to name and describe the amazing things they saw. They got to know all the different species of radio traffic. They weren't fooled.

So when Japan's sending stations filled the air with month-old orders, Rochefort's team labeled these intercepts with blunt precision: "Dummy traffic is again being sent on Tokyo broadcasts" (3 November). And when fleet units used irregular addresses in their communications, Rochefort's group noticed them: "A large amount of Combined Fleet traffic is now appearing with secret (tactical) calls" (6 November). And again: "Use of large number of alternate calls for major fleet forces . . . renders picture more confusing" (7 November).[29]

As the weeks, passed Rochefort, Huckins, and Williams found themselves extracting less and less information from Heeia's intercepts. They would get so far and then hit a snag. Rochefort and his analysts knew what was going on. Yamamoto's radiomen were using every trick in the book to hide the movements of IJN units. They were creating camouflage—an electronic smokescreen behind which the Imperial Navy could take cover. They weren't trying to deceive. Rochefort's team may have been baffled and at times blinded, but they were not deceived.

"Against a trained counter-communications intelligence organization like, say, [Hypo]," Rochefort said, "it is awfully difficult to deceive them, awfully difficult." He doubted the Imperial Navy even attempted systematically to use radio transmissions for falsifying location, movements, and direction of Combined Fleet units. To be sure, Rochefort's traffic analysts might misidentify ships or misread signals and, as a result, misplace ships. But that would be at least in part because of what the TAs did or didn't do, only secondarily because of anything the Japanese did. "No, I do not think radio deception in the Pacific would have been successful against our own operators in the field and against our own personnel such as Huckins and Williams," Rochefort said. "I do not think so."[30] But was Rochefort correct in this view?

⁞⁞ ■ ⁞⁞

On 1 November, Yamamoto yet again changed the rules. From his flagship *Nagato*, afloat in Saeki Bay in the waters of the Inland Sea, he issued Combined Fleet Order Number One. That and follow-up orders issued over the next few days instructed the First Air Fleet's communications unit, effective 23 November, to "send false messages to give the impression that the main strength of the fleet is in the western part of the Inland Sea."[31]

But the fleet didn't wait that long to start filling up the airwaves with phony messages and new kinds of dummy traffic. The Imperial Navy had put in place a concerted program of radio deception much earlier, said Lieutenant Commander Susumi Ishiguro, a communications and intelligence officer on the *Soryu* during its journey to Hawaii. One thing the Japanese hoped to do, Ishiguro said, was allay any suspicions that might be aroused among the Americans by the sudden rise in IJN radio traffic that necessarily would occur just before the attacks in December.[32]

The traffic the Japanese needed to disguise, Ishiguro explained, wasn't that from the First Air Fleet as it steamed toward Hawaii. No such traffic was expected. Under Yamamoto's plan, the *kido butai* would observe strict radio silence, emitting no signals. But the airwaves would be filled with signals as Imperial Navy headquarters in Tokyo dispatched messages to the *kido butai* sailing east, as well as to another IJN unit, the Southern Expeditionary Force, heading into the South China Sea. All had been ordered to begin hostilities on Sunday, 7 December 1941 (U.S. time). Of course, ships could receive signals without breaking radio silence; they only had to listen.[33]

It was this unavoidable explosion in shore-based traffic that Yamamoto worried about. So that U.S. Navy traffic analysts wouldn't notice any change in IJN radio patterns, the Imperial Navy had started sending out decoy messages early in November. The action was intended to keep the volume of traffic artificially high, as described by Ishiguro.

Yamamoto's deception plan had another objective: conceal the whereabouts of the *kido butai*. Since early November most of that fleet's thirty-three warships and support vessels had been scattered around the Inland Sea, receiving orders by a secret cable linking them with Tokyo. But in mid-November they were getting ready to redeploy to a new site; Yamamoto wanted the Americans to think they were still in the Inland Sea.[34]

⊩⊩■⊩⊩

Rochefort's window of observation continued to narrow. First Air Fleet carriers would not be detectable much longer. On 7 November the *Kaga* put in at Sasebo, on the western shores of Kyushu facing the East China Sea, followed two days later by the *Akagi*. "The flagship of Carrier Divisions is *Akagi* and is in Sasebo area," Hypo's daily summary reported accurately on 9 November. On the same day, the *Shokaku* and *Zuikaku* arrived in the port city of Kure, near Hiroshima, in the eastern waters of the Inland Sea. "Several units of the Carrier Division are in port at Kure and Sasebo," Hypo reported on 10 November. Hypo's daily summaries for 9 and 10 November would be its last accurate carrier reports—until 7 December.[35]

After 10 November, bogus radio messages emanated every day from five land-based air stations—Kagoshima, Izumi, Kanoya, Saeki, and Tomitaka—in Kyushu, Japan's southernmost province. Some messages were relayed from these bases to planes and from the planes back to shore. Messages were flashed at the same time on the First Air Fleet's familiar tactical frequency, 4963 kHz, which had been extensively used during a recent exercise. The effect was to suggest that the *kido butai* continued to train in the Inland Sea.[36]

Yamamoto also ordered deceptive messages to be transmitted from sea-based sources, one of which was the old battleship *Settsu*, now used as a training ship in maneuvers. In mid-November it assumed a new role. From 16 November through 27 November, the *Settsu* departed and entered no fewer than nine ports in the Inland Sea and the waters around Kyushu—among them Kure, Iwakuni Sea, Saeki, Aburatsu, Ariake Bay, and the Kohaku Sea—before returning to its base at Kure. "The large target ship *Settsu* transmitted false messages for American eavesdroppers from Japanese coastal waters," a Japanese naval source said in a letter to the author.[37]

With Kyushu's shore stations throwing out fake messages and *Settsu* doing the same as it circled around the Inland Sea, warships of the First Air Fleet during the second week of November started to slip out of the U.S. Navy's electronic grasp. Sometimes singly, sometimes in small clusters the vessels departed the Inland Sea, eased into the Pacific, then steamed north, undetected, to Hitokappu Bay, a deserted patch of water in the southern Kuriles, hundreds of miles from the fleet's headquarters in the Inland Sea. The ships moved north quietly, making little noise, while back in the Inland Sea the *Settsu* kept up a steady drumbeat of bogus traffic.

By 22 November, all thirty-three ships of the *kido butai* had reached the remote area where, on Yamamoto's orders, they followed a policy of strict radio silence. Communication to and from Hitokappu Bay was minimal. If messages needed to be delivered to either Tokyo or fleet headquarters in the Inland Sea, it was arranged in advance that a task force plane would fly the dispatch to Ominato, a port city in northern Japan, from where it would be routed to its intended recipient.[38]

Assembling in this desolate, almost unheard-of cove, the ships of the First Air Fleet awaited Yamamoto's final order to shove off into the wintry waters of the northern Pacific. "Now our Combined Fleet forces are deploying for war," wrote Admiral Matome Ugaki, Yamamoto's chief of staff, in his diary for 23 November. "Everything is advancing in profound secrecy, taking advantage of the poor preparations for war of the United States, England and Holland."[39]

The degree to which Yamamoto's elaborate program of radio deception misled traffic analysts at Stations Hypo and Cast remained a mystery. Hypo's analysts actually spotted many dubious IJN communications and either discarded them or discounted them. Possibly much of the electronic smoke generated by Yamamoto's radiomen wasn't even noticed by American snoops. "The Japanese dummy traffic in the Inland Sea before Pearl Harbor, sent in an attempt to trick the United States, was not intercepted by the U.S.," Tommy Dyer asserted years later.[40]

Whatever the reasons, U.S. Navy eavesdroppers in mid-November "lost" Yamamoto's six largest carriers along with the other warships making up the *kido butai*. They would have had a hard time trailing them even without Yamamoto's stratagems. Ships that do not emit signals cannot be tracked. As the ships steamed toward the Kuriles, radio traffic between the striking force and Tokyo practically ceased.[41] Having received their marching orders by secret cable to proceed to Hitokappu Bay, the ships didn't need to "talk." They knew where they were going.

॥ ■ ॥

As the *kido butai* moved from the Inland Sea to Hitokappu Bay, Rochefort's traffic analysts started to make mistakes, as did the radio intelligence officers on Corregidor. Still, on the major elements of the Combined Fleet, Stations

Cast and Hypo appeared to be in lockstep. Week after week the analysts of both stations placed the *kido butai*'s carriers in the Inland Sea and the waters around Kyushu. Hypo's daily summaries provided some assurance about that: "The Fleets remain relatively inactive in the Kure area" (12 November); "The Carriers remain in home waters with most of them in port" (14 November); "The carriers are mostly in the Kure-Sasebo area with the exception of a few which are operating in the Kyushu area" (17 November); "No movement from home waters has been detected" (18 November).[42]

But U.S. naval traffic analysts *did* see some things. Rochefort and company were not oblivious to all Combined Fleet movements. Not all fleet task forces were as tightly cloaked in secrecy as was the First Air Fleet, nor were all call signs lost, disguised, or so cleverly concealed they couldn't be identified. Through all the noise and electronic din, traffic analysts were able to follow many ships and discern some distinct patterns of IJN activity. What they saw was a hardening of trends first spotted in September and October—the massing of forces south of Japan in the South China Sea, and the continuing buildup of Combined Fleet elements in the mandated territories, especially the Marshalls.

The Marshalls were practically next door to Wake, and alarmingly close to Midway and Hawaii (Jaluit was 2,500 miles from Pearl Harbor). But the buildup there seemed clear. As that activity continued, Rochefort's team made a remarkable discovery. On 20–21 November, through the lucky pickup of a call sign, they confirmed the arrival of a submarine squadron in the Marshalls. Drawing on a wide range of indications and a strong dash of intuition, Hypo's analysts conjectured on 23 November: "With no means of substantiating the impression, it is believed that more submarines are operating in, or from, the Marshalls than it has been possible to definitely place from radio interceptions."[43]

Hypo's guesswork proved correct. Analysts had stumbled upon the advance guard of the submarine force that would be deployed in the waters around Pearl Harbor during the *kido butai*'s 7 December attack. But after that darkness descended: the subs were not heard from again until after the operation.

In the same 23 November summary, Hypo delivered a trenchant and disturbing assessment of the situation developing in the far Pacific: "Nothing [has been] seen to contradict impressions gathered during the past few days and summarized previously, that movement of forces is either imminent or actually under way, at least in part, to the southward, with covering forces operating from the Mandates, and possibility of a striking force assembled or gathering in the Palau area."[44] This referred to the Palau Islands in the Western Carolines, some 600 miles east of Mindanao in the Philippines.

Hypo's TAs followed up this estimate two days later, on 25 November, with an even more unsettling observation: "One or more of the Carrier Divisions are present in the Mandates."[45] The report concealed an ambiguity: The mandates stretched two thousand miles from the Carolines in the western Pacific to the Marshalls in the central Pacific. Hypo was fairly certain there was a carrier division in the Palau area. But was there also a carrier in the Marshalls? Four days earlier, on 19 November, Hypo picked up a call sign at Jaluit that it identified as the carrier *Zuikaku*, but analysts conceded this could be a communication error.[46] Hypo's TAs were getting jittery.

With Hypo's report of possibly two Japanese carrier divisions as nearby as the mandates—and the possibility that one might be in the Marshalls—Rochefort got Admiral Kimmel's full attention. Kimmel already had a lot on his mind. That same day, 25 November, he received the following alert from CNO Stark: "Chances of favorable outcome of negotiations with Japan very doubtful." The dispatch let him know that movements by Japan's navy and army indicated the possibility of "a surprise aggressive movement in any direction including an attack on the Philippines or Guam," vulnerably located in the southern Marianas.[47]

With Washington now actually visualizing a Japanese attack on U.S. territory, in this instance the Philippines and Guam, the idea that the United States could escape war with Japan got harder to sustain. On top of OPNAV's secret message, Kimmel also had to confront the possibility of an IJN carrier no more than twenty-five hundred miles away in the Marshalls. He called in his intelligence officer, Eddie Layton, and reviewed with him recent movements of the Combined Fleet as recorded by Station Hypo, notably the buildup of Japanese forces in the South China Sea, and now possibly even carriers in the mandates. Kimmel wondered if Hypo had received confirmation on these estimates.

"Admiral Kimmel asked what we had received from other units," Layton said. "I replied, 'nothing yet.' He then directed me to tell Commander Rochefort that he desired [him] to initiate a special message concerning the developments noted to OPNAV and [Station Cast]."[48]

The ball was now in Rochefort's court. Kimmel's instruction, delivered via Layton, was precisely the sort of order Rochefort believed Hypo had been established to handle: Tell the U.S. Fleet's commander in chief today what the Japanese were going to do tomorrow. He assembled top TAs Huckins and Willliams and solicited insights from his most seasoned analysts, Dyer, Wright, Holtwick, Lasswell, and Fullinwider.

Out of this brainstorming session emerged a 220-word dispatch in which Rochefort described the organization and probable movements of Imperial Navy forces coming together and beginning to move in the far Pacific.[49] They were moving south. For the past month, Rochefort said, the commander of the Japanese Second Fleet had been building a task force that comprised most of the Second and Third Fleets, plus Destroyer Squadron Three, Submarine Squadron Five, Cruiser Division Seven, the Combined Air Force, and elements of the Third Battle Division from the First Fleet.

Rochefort saw the greater part of the Combined Air Force, consisting of shore-based naval air squadrons, now assembling in Takao, on the western coast of Taiwan, and on the Island of Hainan off the coast of southern China. And he saw Third Fleet units moving toward Takao and Bako, a large naval base on the eastern coast of Taiwan. He said advance units of cruisers and destroyers were already moving toward South China.

Farther to the east, at least one-third of the Japanese submarine force, together with Air Squadron Twenty-four and at least one carrier division, were concentrating in the Marshalls, Rochefort surmised. From these rapidly deploying units, he concluded that "a strong force component" based in Hainan and Taiwan and complemented by units in Palau, the western Carolines, and the Marshalls, was poised to strike Southeast Asia and the Dutch East Indies. What Rochefort saw happening was the joining of two Japanese naval forces in a classic pincers movement against Malaya and the Dutch East Indies. "The stronger peg of the pincers would come down through the South China Sea, and the other leg would advance from Palau against the Borneo area," wrote Jasper Holmes, recalling Rochefort's thinking at the time. Under this scenario a large part of the Japanese submarine force, as well as the carriers already spotted, would take up defensive positions in the Caroline and Marshall Islands, to guard the eastern flank of the operation from any opposition that might be mounted by the U.S. Navy in Hawaii.[50]

Rochefort fired off his dispatch on 26 November, addressing it to CNO Stark, Asiatic Fleet Commander Thomas C. Hart, COM 16 in Manila (which administered Station Cast), with copies to Admirals Kimmel and Bloch. He didn't have long to wait for people to reply, although the responses weren't what he expected. Station Cast got back to him a day later, on 27 November, with an estimate of its own, taking issue, at least in part, with Rochefort's. In a dispatch routed to the same Navy brass Rochefort had addressed, Cast's radio-intelligence team questioned Hypo's view that submarines and carriers had arrived in the mandates.[51] There clearly was a difference of opinion between RI at Cast and at Hypo. There would be questions over which was correct.

Cast's report wasn't the only troubling dispatch to hit Pearl Harbor on 27 November, as Rochefort found out later in the day. He got a phone call from Commandant Bloch, who had just heard from Kimmel, who had received yet another secret message from Washington. Now Kimmel wanted to confer with Rochefort. Would he be available for a visit from the commander in chief of the U.S. Pacific Fleet? Rochefort would.

10

Encounter with Kimmel

It was something like two mountains coming to
Mohammed, but the basement was the most secure
place for a secret conference.

—Wilfred J. "Jasper" Holmes

Rochefort wasn't surprised that Admiral Kimmel wanted to see him. One
day after he reported IJN forces coalescing in the South China Sea and
even showing up in the Marshalls, Station Cast's response, though similar to
Rochefort's overall picture, differed in one important respect: Cast questioned
Hypo's finding that carriers and a large submarine force had arrived in the
Marshalls. Cast was especially emphatic about the carriers: "Our best indications are that all known First and Second Fleet carriers still in Sasebo-Kure
area." Cast closed its assessment with a kicker: "Evaluation is considered
reliable."[1] Cast copied Kimmel.

There were other areas of tension between the two decrypt units. Around
the time Stations Hypo and Cast filed their contradictory reports, OP-20-G's
Safford circulated a puzzling memo to CNO Stark, with copies to Rear Admiral Noyes, the director of naval communications; and Captain Theodore S.
"Ping" Wilkinson, the new director of naval intelligence. The memo troubled
Rochefort. Safford put down on paper that he considered Cast's estimates
"more reliable" than Hypo's.[2]

His memo seemed not to have been prompted by the Hypo-Cast clash
over the location of Yamamoto's carriers, although it had implications for that

dispute. Instead, it was based on an advisory that Safford had received from another of Rochefort's old friends, Commander McCollum, now heading ONI's Far Eastern Section. McCollum argued that Cast's estimates deserved greater weight than Hypo's because of its seeming superiority in three areas of radio intelligence: radio reception was better in the Philippines, Cast's analysts supposedly were "reading messages" in JN-25(b), and Cast was benefiting from the exchange of technical data with Britain's RI unit at Singapore, the Far East Combined Bureau.

Safford's memo contended that Hypo wasn't doing anywhere near as well with its own assignment of solving the Flag Officers' Code. Rochefort's unit was described as "being unable to read anything except the weather ciphers and other minor systems" of the Japanese navy.[3] Rochefort was dumbfounded. Granted, Cast's radio towers were more favorably located to pick up Imperial Navy traffic than were Hawaii's. Still, Hawaii was holding its own in this department, as Hypo's recent estimates of IJN movements in the South China Sea amply demonstrated.

Even more perplexing was Safford's invidious comparison between Hypo and Cast on codebreaking. Rochefort knew full well that neither Corregidor nor Pearl was basing its estimates of IJN activity on cryptanalysis. He knew both relied almost exclusively on traffic analysis for their estimates. This told him that neither Hypo nor Cast had progressed much in laying bare the codes each was charged with solving. He also doubted that the British were making that much of a difference in the JN-25(b) effort. The memo "hurt Joe," Layton said later. "He [was] a man who was quite passionate in what he believed. He didn't get these impressions, these things, without an awful lot of soul-searching and wrestling within himself intellectually. And [so] he was disappointed they didn't accept his finding."[4]

What Kimmel thought of the Hypo-Cast squabble can only be guessed, but he could hardly have been pleased. The last thing he needed was wrangling among the Navy's premier codebreakers. He needed clarity, not confusion. An offense-minded admiral little interested in defense, he needed to know which assessment to believe: Hypo's or Cast's. Where were Yamamoto's carriers? Were some relatively nearby—as close as 2,500 miles—or were they not? What was going on in the Marshalls? Did Japan's fast-growing force there constitute an immediate threat?

Kimmel's need for answers assumed greater urgency in light of yet another dispatch from Washington, this one received around midday on 27 November.

It was worded a little differently than the others, beginning with a short, punchy opening sentence: "This is a war warning." Prepared by Stark's director of war plans, Rear Admiral Richmond Kelly Turner, the message continued:

"Negotiations with Japan looking toward stabilization of conditions in the Pacific have ceased and an aggressive move by the Japanese is expected within the next few days. The number and equipment of Japanese troops and the organization of naval task forces indicate an amphibious expedition against either the Philippines, Thai or the Kra Peninsula or possibly Borneo. Execute an appropriate defensive deployment preparatory to carrying out the tasks assigned in WPL 46."[5]

The last sentence ordering the fleet commander to *execute an appropriate defensive deployment* would have jumped out at Kimmel. He had been briefed on the Navy's war plan, now known as Rainbow Five, of which WPL 46 was the most recent iteration. Under WPL 46, Kimmel was to follow a defensive strategy requiring him to protect U.S. possessions in the Pacific: Samoa, Dutch Harbor, Midway, Wake, Johnston Island, and, of course, Hawaii. This was the essence of the so-called Plan Dog strategy proposed by CNO Stark in 1940, and accepted by President Roosevelt and his military chiefs. Defeat Germany and Italy first, then turn to Japan.[6] Meanwhile, stay on the defensive in the Pacific.

But Kimmel was offense-minded. If war with Japan was to erupt, he wanted to act, to strike a blow against the Combined Fleet as best he could. OPNAV went along in a limited way, agreeing that in the event of war, WPL 46 might require him to mount a limited offensive in the central Pacific islands, but not right away. His primary mission remained defense, with the possibility of a diversion toward the Marshall and Caroline Islands later on to relieve Japan's pressure on Malaya and the Dutch East Indies.[7] Orders were orders, but Kimmel didn't like the idea of holding back. What he visualized was not a Pacific Fleet taking a defensive posture, but a fleet steaming toward the Marshalls.

Shortly after the OPNAV message arrived, Kimmel assembled his top aides in his Spartan quarters on the second deck of the old submarine command building, now fleet headquarters. The group included his chief of staff, Captain W. W. "Poco" Smith; his operations officer, Captain Walter DeLany; and his war plans officer, Captain C. H. "Soc" McMorris. The most important was the freewheeling, sharp-tongued McMorris, easily the most brilliant of those in Kimmel's entourage. His nickname, short for "Socrates," had been earned at Annapolis for his "well-ordered brain."[8] "We called him the Phantom of Notre Dame," Rochefort said. "For he was the ugliest man alive—a real mess, a pock-marked face, a big head on a dumpy body that set on spindly legs and a first-rate slouch as a dresser. But he was smart as hell and could curse with anyone."[9]

McMorris and Rochefort were well acquainted. Next to Layton, he was Rochefort's closest friend at Pearl. They had much in common, brains and a capacity for sarcasm being just two of the attributes they shared. McMorris routinely visited Rochefort in his basement quarters, where they sipped coffee and talked.[10] As fleet war plans officer, McMorris was familiar with Hypo's daily summaries, and as Rochefort's friend he would have been conversant with his thinking on the Japanese threat.

Before Kimmel and his staff got far into their discussion, they were interrupted. They learned that the Army had just dispatched a similar warning to the commanding general in Hawaii, Lieutenant General Short, who had the message paraphrased and delivered to Kimmel via Commandant Bloch. The Army's warning paralleled the Navy's, but it contained one different element, directing Short "to undertake such reconnaissance and other measures you deem necessary."[11]

This reconnaissance order may have gone to Short, but it related to Kimmel. Earlier in the year he, Short, and Bloch had agreed that while the Army was responsible for defending Pearl Harbor, the Navy would undertake any long-range air reconnaissance considered necessary. A question arose. With war seemingly imminent, should Kimmel put in the air some of the Navy's approximately fifty PBYs on Oahu, just as he had in July during the brief crisis following FDR's freezing of Japanese assets? None of Kimmel's top aides was particularly alarmed. Smith didn't think the new dispatch necessarily meant war.[12] Asked to estimate the chances of a surprise raid on Oahu, McMorris didn't hold back. He answered bluntly: "None."[13]

Kimmel couldn't have been surprised by what he heard. The improbability of a Japanese attack on Pearl Harbor was the accepted view at Pearl. It was also held by many of the Navy's senior officers in Washington. Five weeks earlier, on 17 October, CNO Stark had written Kimmel a nervous letter that still managed to reassure: "Personally I do not believe the Japs are going to sail into us and the message I sent you merely stated the 'possibility,'" adding that Washington was working to "maintain the status quo in the Pacific."[14]

Kimmel's own reaction to the 27 November message was restrained. He thought the expression "war warning" meant simply that Japan "was going to attack some place," but not Pearl Harbor.[15] Where, then? As a reader of Hypo's daily summaries, Kimmel had a pretty good idea, but he wanted to be sure. The questions swirling in his mind surely pointed toward Rochefort. Bloch set up a meeting in Hypo's space, a little more than a mile from Kimmel's headquarters. Late in the afternoon of 27 November, Kimmel and Bloch made their way into the dungeon. "It was something like two mountains coming to Mohammed, but the basement was the most secure place for a secret conference," commented Jasper Holmes.[16]

⸗⸗▪⸗⸗

Of his two visitors, Rochefort knew only Bloch well. They had met back in 1939, when Bloch had occupied the post now held by Kimmel: commander in chief, U.S. Fleet. They remained on good terms. But Rochefort and Kimmel were not well acquainted, since they communicated through Eddie Layton.

But Rochefort did know Kimmel well enough to have mixed feelings about him. Although he regarded him as competent, he also thought the admiral was pushing his men more than they could stand in peacetime.[17] Rochefort had a point, but Kimmel drove himself even harder. By the time he showed up in Rochefort's basement, he had been pushing himself almost to the breaking point. His tendency to immerse himself in work was not new.

Ever since graduating from the Naval Academy in 1904 (thirteenth in a class of sixty-two), Kimmel had been the epitome of a serious-minded Navy officer: crisp, energetic, exacting. Dreaming of one day commanding the U.S. Fleet, he kept driving himself. He moved closer to his goal in 1937, when he ascended to the rank of rear admiral. In 1939 he became commander, Cruisers, Battle Force and, simultaneously, commander, Cruiser Division Nine at Pearl. Yet Kimmel remained relatively unknown in the Navy. He had been noticed by one very important person: CNO Stark. So when President Roosevelt discharged Admiral Richardson as CinCUS early in 1941, Stark recommended Kimmel for the job and FDR agreed. Kimmel was elevated over thirty-one admirals who outranked him. He responded to the unexpected posting by plunging into his work. He involved himself in every aspect of the fleet's activities. The fleet became his consuming passion; he left himself little time for the relaxation and social life that often accompanied higher command in the Navy. He even declined to bring his wife to Hawaii because he feared she might be a distraction.

Kimmel's subordinates respected his capacity for work. They never said a word against him, remaining loyal through all the hard times. But there does not appear to have been deep affection. Kimmel was apparently a man easier to admire than to love. As historian Gordon W. Prange observed, he lacked personal magnetism and the ability to touch men's hearts, characteristics of his Combined Fleet adversary, Admiral Yamamoto, and even his Annapolis classmate Vice Admiral William F. "Bull" Halsey Jr.[18]

Kimmel's detractors saw what they thought was a deeper problem. They thought his dogged pursuit of work, even his refusal to bring his wife to Hawaii, betrayed a fatal character flaw: his own doubts about his abilities. They suspected that Kimmel's strong sense of dedication masked a basic insecurity, causing him to devote too much time to petty details that should have been left to others. They thought he lacked imagination.[19]

Kimmel's champions among his subordinates included Eddie Layton. A frequent visitor to his boss's bare-bones quarters, Layton found the admiral forthright, decisive, and human. When pleased by something, Kimmel was capable of a warm and infectious smile, Layton reported. But when displeased, the admiral could be difficult. "He could sometimes be a little starchy, but he was more starchy with senior officers who were lax, than with junior officers," Layton said. "He was demanding in devotion to duty, setting in his own performance an outstanding example. He had little tolerance for laziness or indecision."[20]

Decisive leader or quirky perfectionist, Kimmel cut a formidable figure. Even in the confines of the basement, nattily attired in his starched whites with one row of ribbons on his left chest and his shoulder boards shining with four stars proclaiming his full-admiral rank, Kimmel projected an air of authority. Grimly serious, imposing in manner, he squeezed into the cluttered and cramped space around Rochefort's desk, occupying one side while Bloch occupied the other.

Rochefort took over, holding court in his dress khakis (he shed his red smoking jacket when he had distinguished visitors) and puffing on his pipe. The threesome must have formed a bizarre tableau. Hypo's personnel in the basement probably relished the scene.[21]

Rochefort knew what was on his visitors' minds: the conflicting carrier reports and the war warning. He was aware of the messages, since Cast and Hypo always copied each other on dispatches to Washington and fleet commanders. Rochefort had also learned of the war warning. He believed his 26

November dispatch to Washington and the following day's warning were linked, confirming his view that Washington saw the situation in the Pacific as gravely as he did. "The war warning . . . was their reply," Rochefort said later.[22]

Uninterested in such questions, Kimmel wanted to know what it meant. "The commander-in-chief wished to know the basis for [Hypo's] estimate, why we placed certain units in certain areas, wished to know the distinction or difference between the estimates of [Hypo] and [Cast], and what our opinion was regarding the location and direction of movement of the various Japanese forces," Rochefort said. "[We] discussed the matter at great length, at least an hour and a half, I would say."[23]

By that time Kimmel was familiar with Rochefort's general assessment. He had been hearing about these views for weeks, delivered daily by Layton. Now he wanted a firsthand report from Rochefort. He probably felt he couldn't fully grasp the events unfolding without better understanding the man reporting them. He would get a better feel for the Japanese through a better feel for Rochefort. Kimmel also wanted a straight-up report from a man who was not afraid to speak his mind. He had no use for yes-men, Poco Smith recalled. "You had to be on your toes all the time with Kimmel," Smith said. "He never missed a thing."[24]

The admiral had come to the right place. As Rochefort had demonstrated on many occasions, he wasn't intimidated by anyone, not even four-star admirals, and he had long wanted to brief the commander in chief personally.[25] This was Rochefort's chance to make sure his message got delivered the way he intended it.

Observing the principles he usually followed in such meetings, Rochefort discussed matters only within limits, focusing strictly on the facts. He rendered his best judgment but did not feel free to give advice. In Rochefort's view, to do so would have compromised his objectivity. This tenet reflected his long-held belief that the intelligence function should be kept separate from operations. An intelligence officer, in Rochefort's ideal world, should do his job without reference to the policies of his superiors. Otherwise, he ran the risk of falling into the trap of advocacy or, worse, cheerleading. Rochefort didn't want to know what measures Kimmel had in mind, because he feared it might color his thinking.[26] He provided just the facts.

No one ever reported precisely what was said during the ninety-minute meeting. No log was kept by the participants. But Rochefort's thinking as of 27 November 1941 did become a matter of public record, thanks to his testimony before seven panels convened during and after the war to study the Pearl Harbor attack. From this testimony and other sources, the likely themes of his message to his eminent visitors have emerged.

What Was Going On?

If there was one thing on which Stations Cast and Hypo agreed, it was that the Imperial Japanese Navy was on the move into the South China Sea. Japan was going to attack, though Rochefort didn't use that terminology. He used the language of the intelligence officer: "We referred to it constantly as a strong offensive movement with major operations of the Japanese primarily toward Southeastern Asia," or, more simply, a massive aggression against British and Dutch possessions bordering the South China Sea: Malaya, Singapore, Borneo, the Dutch East Indies.[27]

When Would the Blow Fall?

Right now the bulk of the Japanese navy's Second and Third Fleets remained in the Kure-Sasebo region, Rochefort believed.[28] But already advance elements of those fleets were showing up in the Hainan-Taiwan region off the coast of southern China. It was a matter of days, not weeks, before the rest of the striking force followed. When "radio silence started you knew something was up."[29] At that point war would be hours away.

Had the Japanese Moved Subs and Carriers into the Marshalls?

Disputing Cast's contention that no such forces were in those islands, Rochefort reported that Hypo for weeks had tracked IJN submarines moving eastward toward the Marshalls.[30] He counted fifteen or twenty. He conceded the carrier estimate was less certain, but from all indications there could be two in the Marshalls. "The estimate was arrived at after mature consideration by the three or four officers best qualified in the Pearl Harbor unit," Rochefort said. "It was based entirely on radio intelligence."[31] In short, Rochefort was drawing an inference.

Through traffic analysis, Hypo had found early in the year that the Japanese tended to deploy so-called plane-guard destroyers with their carriers in the previously described system of particular destroyers with particular carriers. Now, in late November, Hypo picked up radio signals in the Marshalls associated with plane-guard destroyers. This "wouldn't prove that the carrier was there," Eddie Layton testified later, "but under normal circumstances it would be logical to assume it."[32] Rochefort assumed it and informed Kimmel and Washington that "at least one aircraft carrier" was in the Marshalls.

Did IJN Forces in the Marshalls Pose a Threat to U.S. Possessions?

Rochefort didn't think so. In his view, Japan's "objectives, insofar as [Hypo] was concerned, did not include areas to the eastward of the mandate islands," such as Wake and Midway.[33] Nor, by implication, would Hawaii have anything to fear. "No one thought in terms of Pearl Harbor at the time," Rochefort said.[34]

He believed he was justified in minimizing any threat from the Marshalls. The naval force there wasn't "the type of organization you would have for a striking force," Rochefort said. It lacked key elements of a dangerous and mobile force; cruisers, destroyers, and supply tankers. He didn't suggest that Yamamoto's forces in the Marshalls were harmless; their military role was to "cover the flanks" of the Combined Fleet's expected moves in the South China Sea. "It was our assumption at the time that that group of submarines there, with or without the carrier group, would be used to secure the flanks against any possible move on the part of the United States," Rochefort said.[35]

Where Were Yamamoto's Carriers?

Even if there were one or two carriers in the Marshalls, that would still leave eight or nine unaccounted for. The most worrisome, of course, were the heavy fleet carriers—the *Akagi* and *Kaga* (CarDiv 1), *Hiryu* and *Soryu* (CarDiv 2), and *Zuikaku* and *Shokaku* (CarDiv 5). A few days earlier, Hypo's traffic analysts had picked up indications pointing toward the *Zuikaku* in the Marshalls. Such a fast carrier would be of greater concern than one or two light ones, but that finding proved faulty, and analysts backed away from it. Presumably the carrier or carriers in the Marshalls were light, not heavy. Whether they were one or two, they remained elusive. "No further information on the presence of Carrier Division Five in the Mandates," Hypo's traffic analysts wrote in their 27 November summary.[36]

Where were the heavy carriers? Cast and Hypo now tended to agree. On 27 November Cast conjectured that CarDivs 1 and 2 were in the Sasebo-Kure area, that is, the Inland Sea and waters around Kyushu. Hypo concurred. However, both stations based their conclusions on radio traffic originating from other ships, not from the carriers themselves.

In fact, Yamamoto's heavy flattops had been quiet for weeks. They had transmitted no signals that radiomen could identify as coming from a carrier. The question was what to make of this inactivity. Was it the radio silence that usually preceded active operations? Or was it the silence that invariably followed after carriers had entered their home ports? There was no way to be sure. Rochefort repeated to Kimmel the conclusion reached on 27 November by his traffic analysts: "Carriers are still located in home waters."[37]

Was the United States Going to Get Dragged into War?

The steady buildup of Japanese forces in the South China Sea convinced Rochefort that Britain and the Dutch East Indies would soon be at war with Japan and, conceivably, the United States as well, depending on Washington's reaction. After the 27 November war warning citing the Philippines as a possible target, Rochefort came around to the view, albeit reluctantly, that a Pacific war involving the United States loomed ahead.

He did not, however, see Hawaii in Japanese crosshairs.[38] His thinking mirrored Layton's: "It was my personal opinion," Layton said later, "that the thought of attack on Pearl Harbor at that time was very far from most people's minds."[39]

ıı▬ıı

Many questions must have swirled through Kimmel's mind as he made his way out of Rochefort's basement. How could he use the information he had just heard? What were the implications for the Pacific Fleet? Sorting through all that material would not have been easy. In one sense he knew too much. He was now steeped in ship movements, call-sign reports, and all the oddities and subtleties of radio intelligence. Was there in this welter of facts a crowning lesson that could be applied to his situation at Pearl?

Kimmel could plausibly have departed Rochefort's basement feeling anxious. Four, possibly as many as six big carriers were unaccounted for. Most were believed to be in home waters, but they could be anywhere. The carriers were silent now, as they had been in July when most were held in reserve during Japan's occupation of southern Indochina. Maybe they were being held in reserve again, as their forces prepared to enter the South China Sea. There was no way to be sure. As Rochefort never tired of telling people, his estimates were really just "guesses."[40]

On the other hand, Kimmel might have come away relaxed. After all, Rochefort's appraisal of the Marshalls was reassuring. There was no attack coming from that quarter. Thanks to radio intelligence, Rochefort could say with virtual certainty that the forces in the Marshalls were not a striking force. They were defensive, assembled to block any interference with Japan's main operation: a massive drive into Southeastern Asia.

Was Kimmel more impressed with a view stressing the unpredictability of the threat, or did he give more weight to the reassuring scenario in which everything that was going to happen would be five thousand miles away? No one will ever know how Kimmel decided, but Rochefort's briefing might have unintentionally reinforced the fleet commander's attachment to the War Plan Orange model. Japan would strike—on the other side of the Pacific.

If the briefing failed to provide Kimmel with the certainty he sought, the fault wasn't entirely Rochefort's. He could only tell Kimmel what he knew. He had been ordered to pursue Yamamoto's Combined Fleet, to find out everything he could about it and make evaluations. But he couldn't make estimations on the basis of messages he didn't receive. Rochefort did not see large quantities of dispatches. He wasn't privy to crucial streams of information, potential intelligence, that passed through or around Hawaii day after day, but remained out of his reach.

The many types of diplomatic traffic fell into two basic categories: messages between Japan's foreign ministry in Tokyo and its embassies and consulates around the world, including its legation in Honolulu; and those between the ministry and Japan's ambassadors in Washington, Kichisaburo Nomura and Saburo Kurusu.[41] The Tokyo-Washington stream was deemed the most important and got most of the attention from U.S. Army and Navy codebreakers.

Unlike the Imperial Navy's main operational code, JN-25(b), most of Japan's diplomatic traffic could be read, even its preeminent diplomatic cipher. It was enciphered by a machine in Tokyo and deciphered by an analog in Washington, the so-called Purple machine the U.S. Army and Navy had built in 1940. Compromising the Purple cipher represented the U.S. government's greatest codebreaking coup up to this point of the war. The top-secret program devoted to that purpose was codenamed Magic.

To engage Magic traffic, Heeia's radiomen would have been ordered to collect diplomatic messages, and Rochefort's cryptanalysts would have needed a Purple machine. As noted, Cast's cryptanalysts had one, as did America's British allies at Bletchley Park, near London. Bletchley Park, in fact, received the machine that had originally been intended for Pearl Harbor, an outgrowth of an Anglo-American agreement early in 1941 to share intelligence.[42]

Without a Purple machine in Hawaii, Kimmel lacked one window that might have shed light on Japanese intentions. CNO Stark recognized Kimmel's need for news about the diplomatic situation, but his occasional letters were often contradictory and muddled, sometimes leaving Kimmel more confused than before he got them.

By the time Rochefort and Kimmel met in Hypo's basement, neither knew the extent to which American-Japanese relations, already bad, had worsened. Only readers of Purple machine decrypts would have known that Tokyo had given its Washington envoys a 25 November deadline for completing their negotiations with the United States. Nor would they have known that on 22 November Tokyo extended the deadline to 29 November, telling Nomura and Kurusu that date would not be changed and adding, "After that things are automatically going to happen."[43]

A glaring red flag by itself, that ominous sentence would have taken on even more meaning if Rochefort had been ordered to tap the other stream of diplomatic traffic—messages from Tokyo to Japan's consulate in Honolulu, located on Nuuanu Avenue, nine miles from Hypo's basement. Like the Purple messages, that traffic, arriving in Honolulu by either cable or radio, was unavailable to Rochefort and his analysts.

The Navy seemed to have good reasons for keeping Hypo away from that traffic. One was legal. Section 605 of the Federal Communications Act of 1934 banned the interception of messages between foreign countries and the United States and its territories. The law applied to both radio and cable traffic. U.S. intelligence observed that ban until around 1939, when the Army's chief of staff, George Marshall, encouraged a more relaxed attitude.[44]

U.S. eavesdroppers stepped up their collection of Japan's diplomatic traffic conveyed by radio. But cable traffic remained out of reach, since cable firms continued to follow the 1934 law and refused to hand over foreign communications. Radio traffic was another story. Targeting the transmissions of distant warships and sending stations, the radiomen at Heeia and Pearl paid no attention to the law. "All of us who intercepted, decrypted, disseminated, or used Japanese radio messages were in violation of the law," Hypo's Holmes wrote later.[45]

When it came to intercepting radio traffic intended for Japan's Honolulu consulate, though, the Navy let somebody else break the law: the Army. That traffic was collected at Monitoring Station-5, or MS-5, the Army's intercept site at Fort Shafter, near Honolulu. There the Army intercepted consular messages encrypted in a variety of codes, some fairly complex, others relatively simple. None was enciphered in Purple. Japan's failure to provide this consulate with a Purple machine may have led the U.S. Navy to mistakenly downgrade the importance of its consular traffic.

Rochefort paid little attention to activities at Fort Shafter. If the Army wanted to intercept Japanese diplomatic messages at MS-5, that was all right with him.[46] He understood there had to be a division of this labor between the Army and Navy, and he had his own orders. "We were not to do any work on the diplomatic systems," Rochefort said.[47] He was to stick to Navy business: tracking the Imperial Navy. That was all.

"Washington was undertaking the responsibility of taking care of the diplomatic systems," Rochefort said. "It was no concern of ours." If Washington saw anything in this diplomatic traffic that the fleet commander should read, Rochefort said, "I am sure that my feelings would have been, 'All right, they are going to furnish that to him.'" As a result: "I did not concern myself with this."[48]

He would have been more concerned had he known about the message nabbed by MS-5 on 24 September. It was from Foreign Minister Teijiro Toyoda to the Japanese consul general in Honolulu, Nagao Kita. Queries from Tokyo about the comings and goings of U.S. warships were nothing new. But this message contained a new wrinkle. It sought information not only on ship movements, but also on their precise anchorages. It wanted Kita to inform Tokyo of the exact location of U.S. vessels in five sub-areas of Pearl Harbor. The dispatch seemed to put an invisible grid over Pearl Harbor, an overlay that might have been intended to help bomber pilots pinpoint specific targets. It gained fame as the Bomb Plot message.[49]

Many future historians would doubt whether Tokyo's Bomb Plot request was actually intended to help its pilots in Pearl Harbor on 7 December.[50] They agreed, however, that this was the sort of message that should have been seen by the Pacific Fleet's commander in chief. Yet no codebreaker in Hawaii knew that the message existed. The Army-Navy intercept system had broken down. MS-5 didn't have codebreakers or translators. The Army in Hawaii could collect messages, but it couldn't read them.

Ironically, Rochefort had on his staff a cryptanalyst, Warrant Officer Farnsley C. Woodward, with expertise in consular traffic. Although rusty, he had some familiarity with the code in which the Bomb Plot message had been encrypted—a lower-level diplomatic cipher called J-19. He couldn't have cracked it rapidly; he would have needed supplies—keys and updated history on the code from OP-20-G—and a lot of time. But could Woodward have solved J-19? He wasn't asked to.[51] Hypo's focus remained narrow: the Imperial Navy.

Without the means to break J-19, the Army bundled up the dispatch along with other intercepts from that day's haul, placed it a secure pouch, and delivered it to a waiting Pan Am Clipper. Bad weather prevented the plane from flying right away. Twelve days passed before the pouch reached Washington. Processing of the message was slowed because J-19 was a low-priority code, taking second place to the highly valued Purple messages.[52] Finally translated on 9 October, the message was circulated to Army and Navy brass in Washington. Colonel Rufus S. Bratton, head of the Far Eastern Section of the Army's Intelligence Branch, thought the message might be important. In his view, "the Japanese were showing unusual interest in the port at Honolulu"—an opinion not shared by his boss, Brigadier General Sherman Miles, director of the Intelligence Division (G-2).[53] Miles saw the message as just another example of Japan's routine interest in U.S. ship movements. His Navy counterpart, Captain Wilkinson, concurred. The message was filed away.

Kimmel and Short weren't told of the Bomb Plot message. They never heard of it until years later. The discovery embittered both officers, who by then were retired and for all practical purposes living in disgrace. "No one had a greater right than I to know that Japan had carved up Pearl Harbor into subareas and was seeking and receiving reports as to the precise berthings in that harbor of the ships of the fleet," Kimmel told Congress in 1946. "Knowledge of these intercepted Japanese dispatches would have radically changed the estimate of the situation made by me and my staff."[54]

Rochefort essentially agreed, although he arrived at his conclusion by a different route. Like Kimmel, he didn't learn of the Bomb Plot message until the various Pearl Harbor inquiries. At first Rochefort thought the dispatch was no big deal. He admitted that even if he had known about it at the time, in fall 1941, it wouldn't have aroused his suspicions. He said the message reminded him of an incident in 1924, when a Japanese spy had mounted a "systematic investigation of the berthing of American naval ships at San Diego." In other words, it reflected the sort of extreme fact-gathering typical of the Japanese.[55]

But in time, Rochefort came to believe that Washington had erred by viewing the message in isolation from other intelligence. If examined alongside the diplomatic traffic between Washington and Tokyo as revealed by Purple, the Bomb Plot message would have been interpreted differently, Rochefort said later. In fact, Purple gave that message "a real sharp and current meaning," signaling, in his view, Pearl Harbor's emerging status as a potential target. If Pearl had had a Purple machine, he would have "jumped through a window, if necessary, to get to Short and Kimmel in a hurry."[56]

There is, of course, no telling what Rochefort would have done had he been able to read the Imperial Navy's traffic encrypted in JN-25(b), for months intercepted at Heeia, routinely examined by Hypo's traffic analysts, and transported to OP-20-G. As it turned out, nobody was reading that traffic. By 27 November 1941, Negat and Cast had recovered only a fraction of JN-25(b)'s 50,000 code groups. Neither had enough to read the traffic in any meaningful sense.[57]

If it had been readable, would it have made any difference? There would never be a definitive answer to that question. From the 2,413 JN-25(b) messages decrypted by Navy codebreakers after the war, one overwhelming fact emerged: Pearl Harbor was never mentioned by name.[58] There were hints, though. If those messages had been decrypted in a timely fashion, some might have rung alarm bells in Hypo's basement before Rochefort's 27 November meeting with Kimmel.

Any doubt about the identity of the country Japan intended to strike in the very near future would have been erased by a 1 November dispatch from the Combined Fleet's Submarine Fleet to fleet elements, directing that "At the beginning of the operation, KINU-CL and Y URA-CL [Japanese ship call signs] will ambush and completely destroy the U.S. enemy."[59]

Still other JN-25(b) messages disclosed the Combined Fleet's contemplated method of attack. In a 28 October dispatch, First Air Fleet Commander in Chief Nagumo ordered pilots to carry out exercises with torpedoes equipped with stabilizers—that is, modified to be effective in shallow water.[60] (Torpedoes typically spiraled downward seventy-five or ninety feet before returning to the surface, a pattern that would have doomed them in the waters of Pearl Harbor, with its average depth of about thirty feet.)[61]

From early September through October, the month of November was mentioned repeatedly as the time for the completion of key objectives: adjusting torpedoes, wrapping up pilot exercises with modified torpedoes, equipping tankers for long-distance refueling at sea. The last ten days of November were characterized as the period during which everything would come together, the when things would happen.[62] But what would happen?

Rochefort had no idea what secrets lay buried in Purple, J-19, and JN-25-(b) when he briefed Kimmel on 27 November, and, as detailed in this chapter, Kimmel also was not privy to critical pieces of information. Consequently, the defensive measures he instituted were minimal. He increased in-shore patrols and issued orders to the Pacific Fleet to depth-bomb all submarine contacts in the Oahu operating area. He decided against moving the fleet out to sea. Nor did he follow his own example in July, when he ordered aloft long-range air reconnaissance. This time he ordered no distant search for enemy forces.

General Short, meanwhile, put the Army on the lowest of three possible levels of alert: the one intended primarily to safeguard airfields against sabotage. Both Kimmel and Short believed they had taken every reasonable precaution against the aggression they had been warned about—an attack five thousand miles away.

Two days before Rochefort's basement meeting with Kimmel, around 10:30 in the morning of 25 November (Hawaii time), the thirty-three ships of Yamamoto's First Air Fleet slipped out of Hitokappu Bay and steamed into the icy waters of the north Pacific (see Appendix 4). Under the command of Vice Admiral Nagumo, they proceeded under strict radio silence on the first leg of a 3,500-mile voyage that would culminate 230 miles north of Pearl Harbor.

11

Ill Wind

Do you mean to say they could be rounding Diamond
Head and you wouldn't know it?
—Husband Kimmel

One day after his meeting with Kimmel, Rochefort received a top-priority
directive from OP-20-G. It concerned a diplomatic message that Tokyo
had radioed to its major embassies on 19 November. Because the dispatch was
encoded in a lower-priority system, the manual diplomatic cipher known as
J-19, nine days passed before Washington got around to making it readable.
When it finally did so, the decrypt touched off a flurry of activity throughout
Main Navy.

Tokyo's message told its Washington embassy and other legations around
the world that in case of an emergency—defined as the imminent severing of
diplomatic relations with their host countries—they would receive a coded
warning. It would show up in the middle of Japan's daily shortwave news
broadcast. The warning would tell them which of three possible adversaries—
the United States, Britain, or the Soviet Union—would soon be at war with
Japan. If the words "east wind rain" (*higashi no kazema*) were broadcast and
repeated twice, that would signal war with the United States. Upon hearing
the warning, Japan's diplomats in Washington, Honolulu, and elsewhere in
the United States were to destroy all their code manuals and secret papers at
once. On the other hand, the words "north wind cloudy" (*kitanokaze kumori*)
signaled war with the Soviet Union, while "west wind clear" (*nishi no kaze
hare*) indicated war with Britain. Hostilities would be just days away.[1]

158

The message generated more excitement in Washington than had any previous dispatch from Japan's foreign ministry. It was intriguing because it seemed to promise a shortcut way to determine which nation Japan was going to strike in the days ahead. Rochefort had long doubted Japan would level any blow at the United States or its possessions in the Pacific, but recent events had caused him to rethink his old opinion. This directive got his attention. He judged that Washington must have had good reasons to attach so much significance to the so-called "winds" message.

Indeed Washington did, because it knew something that neither Rochefort nor Kimmel knew. Unlike top officers in Hawaii, Main Navy's chieftains were reading Purple. They knew, as readers of Japanese diplomatic traffic deciphered by the Purple machine, that Japan's foreign ministry had given Ambassador Nomura a 29 November deadline for completing an acceptable agreement with the United States. As we have already seen, if no deal had been reached, things were automatically going to happen.[2] By coincidence, the winds message was decrypted in Washington just before the 29 November deadline. "That juxtaposition," Eddie Layton wrote later, "gave many senior staff officers the notion that the receipt of an 'east wind rain' broadcast would be tantamount to Japan's declaring war on the United States."[3]

Hoping to get a jump on the Japanese, Main Navy directed Hypo, Cast, and its radiomen at other U.S. Navy field stations around the world to listen for the coded warning (or execute message, as it was later called). Rochefort was unenthusiastic about losing four good linguists, but they had been complaining for weeks about not having enough to do. "We did not have a single Japanese language message to read," Tex Biard griped later.[4] Rochefort now gave him and his fellow JLOs an assignment. At least he would be spared their pestering.

On 29 November he ordered Lieutenant Cole and Lieutenants (junior grade) Biard, Slonim, and Bromley to proceed to the Navy's rustic outpost at Heeia, on the other side of the island. It wasn't a place they especially enjoyed, lacking many amenities. Biard likened the area to "a big banana patch."[5] But there they quickly settled into a routine. Standing four-hour watches, they took turns listening for the execute message on the voice frequencies provided by Rochefort. "[I put] four of my very best language officers on a twenty-four-hour watch," Rochefort said. "That is, a constant watch on the frequencies that were given us by Washington as well as at frequencies which we knew existed and which we had uncovered."[6]

:: ∎ ::

While his linguists listened for the winds message, Rochefort got ready for another Pearl Harbor weekend—Saturday and Sunday, 29–30 November. Rochefort was getting concerned. He was troubled by the drop-off in transmissions from Combined Fleet ships. There was plenty of radio traffic from shore stations, but few signals from actual ships. The small carriers of CarDiv 3 (*Ryujo* and *Hosho*), back in Empire waters after a trek to Taiwan, turned up in traffic on 19 November, but the big carriers remained quiet. "There was great unease in all of our minds because of the lack of traffic," Rochefort said.[7]

He stayed home over the weekend but was on edge both days, worrying that something might break at any time. He probably didn't feel any better after glancing at the banner atop the front page of Sunday's *Honolulu Advertiser*, blaring: "Japanese May Strike over Weekend!" (30 November 1941). The accompanying United Press article speculated that Japanese-American talks were "near collapse," a consequence of what appeared to be Japan's unhappiness with Secretary of State Hull's terms for further negotiations. These had been submitted to Japan's Washington envoys on 26 November.

Layton was equally unsettled. Both officers wondered why they hadn't gotten more news from Main Navy. It "was a source of concern both to Commander Rochefort and me," Layton said, "and we remained at our telephones throughout that weekend."[8]

But Japan didn't strike over the weekend. The *Advertiser* continued to see danger, running another front-page banner Monday morning declaring, "Hull, Kurusu in Crucial Meeting Today." The United Press reported that the U.S. secretary of state and Japan's two envoys were meeting in an atmosphere of "rising tension" (1 December 1941). Then Honolulu's afternoon paper, the equally bombastic *Star-Bulletin*, ran a headline of its own, "U.S. Army 'Alerted' in Manila" (1 December 1941). Both newspapers conveyed a feeling of events moving toward a climax.

News reports mattered less to Rochefort than information reaching him through his radio-intelligence network. Returning to the basement on Monday, 1 December, he scanned the daily traffic summaries prepared for the previous two days. Among findings that caught his eye were two concerning carriers. One stated: "The number of despatches originated on the 30th is very small. The only tactical circuit heard today was one with *Akagi* and several marus."[9] The *Akagi* seemed to have made a noise on a tactical circuit. That would indicate Empire waters.

There was also news about carriers in the mandates, a finding that Rochefort interpreted to mean the nearby Marshalls Islands. Hypo's traffic analysts said that the "presence of a unit of plane guard destroyers indicates the presence of at least one carrier in the mandates, although this has not been confirmed." The carrier mystery continued. Evidence for submarines in the Marshalls, however, had gotten stronger. "The continued association of Jaluit and Commander Submarine Force plus his known progress from the Empire to Chichijima to Saipan makes his destination obviously the Marshalls," Hypo stated on Sunday, 30 November.[10] The comforting news about the *Akagi* and the more troubling report about subs were circulated to Kimmel on Monday, 1 December.

Rochefort didn't know that the *Akagi* was nowhere near where his traffic analysts had put her. Instead, the ship was with the *kido butai* in the north Pacific, steaming eastward. In placing the *Akagi* in Empire waters, Hypo's analysts were misled by an IJN radio transmission that used the carrier's former drill call sign: 8YUNA. They didn't know that the Combined Fleet had changed the *Akagi*'s call sign shortly after the striking force had left Hitokappu Bay. What Heeia had heard and what Hypo's analysts interpreted as the *Akagi* was a radio deception signal from Sasebo naval base on Kyushu, bordering the East China Sea.[11]

Whatever tricks the Japanese were playing with their communications, the game got crazier on Monday: Yamamoto sprang another surprise. Effective midnight on 30 November (Hawaii time), for the second time in thirty days the Japanese navy changed the 15,000 identification call signs used by its ships at sea. The move caught everybody at Pearl off guard, including Rochefort. Ordinarily the Japanese navy changed its call signs every six months or so. To do so twice in thirty days was unprecedented. "It would have been the first time it had happened, to my knowledge," Rochefort said.[12]

His view was reflected in Hypo's summary covering traffic for 1 December: "The fact that service calls lasted only one month indicates an additional progressive step in preparing for active operations on a large scale."[13] Holmes delivered the summary to Layton on Tuesday 2 December; Layton took it over to Kimmel.

◆

Kimmel also was getting more concerned. His worries intensified on Saturday 29 November, when CNO Stark copied him on another war warning, this one stating that negotiations with Japan "appeared" to be terminated. "Japanese future action unpredictable but hostile action possible at any moment," Stark wrote. OPNAV directed Kimmel to undertake reconnaissance and other defensive measures but to do so quietly, without alarming the local population.[14]

With this new alert in hand, Kimmel on Sunday ordered Layton to drop everything and prepare a detailed report—due first thing Monday 1 December—itemizing the whereabouts of all Japanese warships. Drawing on Hypo's daily intelligence summaries and whatever additional material he could find from Cast and other sources, Layton worked all Sunday on his memo. He was struck by the lack of hard information on the disposition of Japanese carriers. "So I called Rochefort first thing on Monday to see if anything had come in overnight," Layton wrote later.[15]

Still believing in reports not yet discredited, Rochefort told him what had come in over the weekend: concrete news about the carrier *Akagi*, along with another agonizingly ambiguous indication of a carrier in the Marshalls. But the major event was the sudden change in call signs for Japanese forces afloat—a development Layton regarded as one more ominous portent of impending Japanese action.

Rochefort also let Layton know that traffic analysts Huckins and Williams believed many Combined Fleet units were changing their locations. "He suggested I postpone my disposition report one more day so that it would reflect the latest information," Layton wrote later. Kimmel approved a one-day delay, to Tuesday, 2 December. "I called Joe and told him I would work on it all night if necessary. But he had to get me his latest report first thing in the morning so that I could review my disposition chart before presenting it to the admiral." That "latest information" turned out to be trivial. "Even as I was reviewing my revised disposition report that morning, Joe called in a few changes," Layton said. "I made the alterations and additions in pencil, but there was still no hard information on the two carrier divisions we believed were still in Japan. There was no traffic—or traffic analysis—to or from these carriers or their commanders."

At 8:15 sharp Tuesday morning, Layton met with Kimmel in what became one of the Navy's most fabled intelligence briefings of the prewar period. He presented Hypo's daily summary reflecting Rochefort's view that the sudden change in IJN call signs indicated one more step toward a large operation, noting "no change" in the section dealing with Japan's carriers.[16]

Then Layton got into the meat of the meeting, handing Kimmel a five-page memorandum he had spent two days preparing, with the subject "Orange Fleet, Location Of." Drawing on what he described as the "best available information" as to where the Combined Fleet was *"thought* to be" (emphasis in Layton's original), Layton proceeded to walk Kimmel through Yamamoto's fleet, giving his sense of its strength levels throughout the Pacific and South China Sea. Aside from some forces in the mandates, including a possible carrier in the Marshalls (Rochefort's mystery carrier), Layton put all important IJN naval forces south of Shanghai. They included four aircraft carriers, CarDivs 3 and 4, in waters near Formosa, all pointing south.[17]

"Admiral Kimmel noted almost immediately that neither CarDiv 1 (*Akagi* and *Kaga*) nor CarDiv 2 (*Soryu* and *Hiryu*) were listed in this memorandum, and asked me where they were," Layton testified later. "I said that I had no good recent indications of their locations, but that if I had to guess, I would estimate them in the general Kure zone," a major IJN sea base on the Inland Sea.

"Admiral Kimmel said, 'What! You don't know where Carrier Division 1 and Carrier Division 2 are?'" Layton recalled. "I replied, 'No, sir, I do not. I think they are in home waters, but I do not know where they are.' Then Admiral Kimmel looked at me, as sometimes he would, with somewhat of a stern countenance and yet partially with a twinkle in his eye and said, 'Do you mean to say they could be rounding Diamond Head and you wouldn't know it?' or words to that effect. My reply was that, 'I hoped they would be sighted before now,' or words to that effect."[18]

The session probably left Kimmel with more questions than answers, as had the Rochefort briefing five days earlier. Did the buildup in the Marshalls portend greater danger than he thought? Or was Rochefort right that the force there was in all likelihood strictly defensive? What should he make of those missing carriers? Might they indeed be rounding Diamond Head? Not necessarily. Kimmel knew—and he so testified in later Pearl Harbor inquiries—that there was nothing unusual about the Japanese navy's carriers suddenly going silent. It had happened in the past.[19]

Kimmel's muted reaction to the missing carriers reflected the thinking of his top intelligence officers, Layton and Rochefort. Both were concerned—and becoming more so—about the lack of direct radio traffic from the flattops. But neither was alarmed at this stage. "The inability to locate more battleships and carriers was not considered in itself, as a bad sign," Rochefort testified.[20] A January 1942 study by Layton, for example, showed that the location of IJN carriers had been "uncertain" as many as eighty-four days during the previous six months.[21] They usually turned out to have been in port or in Empire waters.

❙❙■❙❙

If the Kimmel-Layton briefing accomplished nothing else, it marked a turn-ing point in Hypo's treatment of the missing carriers. Beginning with its 2 December report, Hypo ceased proposing that Yamamoto's flattops might be in Empire waters. "Almost a complete blank of information on the Carriers today," stated Hypo's summary for 2 December. A day later the report said simply, "No information on submarines or Carriers."[22] This new uncertainty did seem to indicate a greater respect for the unknown.

While most Hypo analysts continued to accept earlier assumptions about the carriers' whereabouts, some now had doubts. The absence of any calls to or from three of the four believed to be in the Inland Sea—the *Kaga*, *Soryu*, and *Hiryu*—touched off a debate inside the basement (they mistakenly thought they had heard from the *Akagi*). For a time, Huckins and Williams held the view that the blackout stemmed from the abrupt change in fleet call signs, noting that while some two hundred service calls had been partially identified during that time, not one carrier call had been recovered. It was "evident that carrier traffic is at a low ebb," they wrote in their 2 December summary.[23] But what did "low ebb" mean?

After 2 December, the two traffic analysts no longer agreed. Huckins thought, like Rochefort, Layton, and the majority of Hypo analysts, that the absence of carrier traffic probably reflected an old pattern: carriers tied up at their piers in Japan awaiting orders to sail. Williams suspected something was going on. He feared the absence of calls to or from the carriers meant Yamamoto's flattops had adopted radio silence and were on the move.[24]

Marine Captain Holcomb, one of Rochefort's newest language officers, shared Williams' worry. He had lived several years in China and Japan and had seen the Japanese gearing up for war. "I said they were getting ready and it wouldn't be a surprise to me if they attacked us," Holcomb recalled telling his Hypo colleagues. "They just laughed at me. They said 'Banks, you must be crazy, the Japs attack us? Never.'"[25]

Events the next day supported the worriers. On Wednesday 3 December, Stark's OPNAV radioed two messages to Kimmel and Hart, as well as to COM 14 and COM 16. Bloch briefed Rochefort. The first stated that Tokyo had ordered Japan's diplomatic outposts at Hong Kong, Singapore, Batavia, Manila, Washington, and London to destroy most of their codes and ciphers at once. The second message noted that Tokyo also ordered them to destroy their Purple machines, but to leave one cryptographic system in place.[26]

In Washington, War Plans director Richmond Kelly Turner considered the code-destruction order "a definite and sure indication" that Japan intended to make war on countries in which codes were being destroyed. He saw an attack coming "within two or three days."[27] In Hawaii, Rochefort reached a similar conclusion. Now thinking the Philippines would be targeted, and the United States drawn into the war just ahead, his "reaction at that time [was] that Admiral Hart [in Manila] is going to have himself quite a job very shortly," Rochefort recalled.[28]

Kimmel's first move after receiving the messages was to summon Layton. He wanted to know what a Purple machine was, but Layton didn't know either. He asked Lieutenant Herbert M. Coleman, fresh in from Washington. Coleman explained that Purple was a Japanese electrical coding machine that had been replicated in Washington, enabling top officials to read Japan's highest-grade diplomatic code. Destroying that machine was a sure sign the Japanese were preparing for any and all eventualities, Layton told Kimmel.[29]

Kimmel wasn't impressed. "I didn't consider that [information] of any vital importance when I received it," he told Congress in 1946.[30] The question raised then—and later—was why he minimized the code-burning news. And why didn't he notify his Army counterpart, General Short? The questions mattered. The Army and Navy in Hawaii had earlier signed a Joint Action Agreement to keep each other informed of important developments that might bear on the security of the Pacific Fleet. Under the agreement, the Army had responsibility for protecting the fleet when it was at Pearl.

News that the Japanese were burning their code books at many of their legations around the world ushered in a period of contradiction and confusion in the stories told by Kimmel, Layton, and Rochefort. A future Pearl Harbor investigator, Henry C. Clausen, later blamed Layton for failing to grasp the main implication of the 3 December code burning: war was imminent and unavoidable. "Layton failed to communicate this point to Kimmel," argued Clausen.[31] Layton had his own story.

In his 1985 memoir, *And I Was There*, he hoped to make Kimmel's actions understandable. He advanced two explanations for the admiral's failure to assign the code burning greater importance. One explanation involved Rochefort. First, Layton wrote, neither of Stark's two radiograms mentioned Japan's Honolulu consulate as a site affected by the Tokyo order. Kimmel apparently thought the omission significant. Because "most of the embassies, with the exception of London and Washington, were in the Far East, we believed the Magic decrypt was further evidence that Japan was preparing to launch operations in this area," Layton wrote.[32] Nor did Kimmel change his mind when he learned that Japan's local diplomats were indeed torching their codes and confidential papers. Layton said he promptly passed this news onto Kimmel who, once again, wasn't troubled.

Now Layton introduced a second explanation for Kimmel's disinterest: Rochefort had brought him the news of the Honolulu code burning on Thursday 4 December, one day after the arrival of Stark's original message. The "Purple information," Layton said, "did not appear to be 'vitally important' because it was not until the *next day* that Kimmel got news of the code burning in the local consulate"[33] (emphasis in original). If only he had gotten this news on Wednesday, Layton implied, Kimmel might well have granted it the significance it deserved.

Thus the timeline of events became crucial. Did Layton get his dates right? Was he correct that he and, therefore, Kimmel didn't hear of the local code burning until Thursday? If so, this might help Kimmel's case (Layton never explained why this one-day difference should be exculpatory for Kimmel). But if Kimmel, in Layton's opinion, is let off the hook, another officer is ensnared: Joe Rochefort. It was Rochefort, after all, who phoned Layton with the news about the Honolulu code burning. Was he late in calling Layton?

Rochefort wasn't at his best during this period, but no evidence ever surfaced that he failed to keep Layton informed. The problem more likely was with Layton's timeline. His 1985 book contradicted his Pearl Harbor testimony. In 1945, when he testified before the Hewitt panel, he wasn't sure when he had received Rochefort's call. "I don't recall which day I was informed that [Consul General Kita] was burning his codes," Layton said. While thinking the day was Thursday, he added, "It may have been the third."[34] Rochefort might have called Wednesday, after all.

In all likelihood, Rochefort called Layton on Wednesday. That was when he learned of the local code burning. He got the news that day from the naval district's intelligence officer, Captain Irving H. Mayfield, who had been tipped off by Robert L. Shivers, an FBI special agent stationed in Honolulu. The FBI had learned of the code burning around noon from a tap on Kita's phone.[35] Rochefort probably called Layton right away. He would have done what had become his practice over the past six months: keep Layton up to date. Layton then probably would have done what he usually did: convey this new fact to Kimmel. If so, did he also let Kimmel know the implications of the code burning? This remains a mystery.

Kimmel and Short were obligated to keep each other apprised of pertinent developments. So were the intelligence officers of the two services. That was the theory. Because of the culture of secrecy created by the two services, and because of their disjointed system for cooperation, real sharing of intelligence between the Army and Navy turned out to be slapdash and sporadic.

Once in possession of the 3 December code-burning information, Rochefort or Layton or both might have called their Army opposites. That wasn't as easy as it might seem. The way the two services were set up, neither officer had a designated counterpart in the other. The officer who came closest to filling the bill for Layton was Lieutenant Colonel Kendall J. Fielder, G-2 (Intelligence) on General Short's staff. But Layton, as fleet intelligence officer, didn't regard Fielder as his opposite, given that the Army had no structure resembling a fleet.

Layton didn't call Fielder. Instead, he called Lieutenant Colonel Edward W. Raley, the officer in charge of the Army's Hawaiian Air Force, with whom he sometimes met.[36] That call would later raise questions with Pearl Harbor investigators. One problem was that Raley couldn't remember getting it.[37] Another was that Raley lacked direct access to General Short, the one Army officer who needed the information more than any other. Fielder did have such access. Layton said he believed Rochefort had already phoned Fielder about the code burning.[38]

But if Rochefort made such a call it was lost on Fielder, who said he never heard from Rochefort.[39] He didn't rule out the possibility that Rochefort may have phoned his assistant, Lieutenant Colonel George W. Bicknell, who testified years later that he had indeed discussed the matter with Rochefort.[40] Rochefort disagreed with both Fielder and Bicknell. In an affidavit signed some three years later, on 20 February 1945, he swore that he informed Fielder of the ongoing code burning at the consulate on either Thursday or Friday.[41]

Fielder remained adamant he never heard from Rochefort or anybody in the Navy. Indeed, he insisted he didn't learn of the code burning until Saturday 6 December, when he was informed by Bicknell at a staff meeting. Fielder claimed he promptly notified Short, but Short, always seemingly the last to know, said he never heard of the code burning.[42]

The mixup over who called whom when called attention to fatal defects in the Army-Navy relationship. Not only did it reflect the military's inability to share information, it also underscored its obsession with secrecy, particularly the Navy's tight lid on any material connected with its RI and codebreaking effort.

The Fielder-Bicknell discrepancies also raised questions about Rochefort's fierce grip on Hypo's raw intelligence. Undoubtedly he was right to handle that material with care, but did he carry security considerations too far? Not as far as the Navy was concerned. If Rochefort was tight-fisted with crypt-analytic information, he simply exemplified the Navy's hard-nosed attitude, which he had acquired running the research desk in the 1920s. Now, heading the Navy's top-secret codebreaking unit at Pearl Harbor, Rochefort wasn't going to lightly divulge sensitive material to anyone, let alone an Army officer he hardly knew.

But he had recognized the need for some kind of relationship with Fielder. The two officers got together from time to time. They didn't have a formal ar-rangement for sharing information, but they met once or twice a week, maybe less often, to compare notes. They had an understanding that each would keep the other abreast of developments in their common interests, as Rochefort put it, describing their relationship as "cordial."[43]

And yet the arrangement proved faulty, at least for the Army. As Roche-fort structured the relationship, there was no way Fielder could have acquired any information at all related to radio intelligence or codebreaking. He could not have gotten around the catch-22 rules Rochefort had devised for access to that material. Fielder's problem began with a simple fact: He wasn't cleared to read material the Navy stamped Ultra. This sweeping term used by the Army, Navy, and U.S. allies referred to intelligence derived from decrypts of enciphered Axis army and navy radio communications.

As General Short's intelligence officer, Fielder might have seemed an appro-priate officer with whom at least some decrypts could have been shared. Rochefort ruled him out, because his name didn't appear on Hypo's list of high-echelon officers approved to read Ultra. But who had assembled that list? As questioning of Rochefort by lawmakers in 1946 ultimately determined, the list was prepared by Rochefort himself. In short, Fielder's exclusion was at Rochefort's discretion. Fielder couldn't get around Rochefort.

Almost certainly Rochefort denied Fielder access to Ultra for one over-riding reason: Fielder was Army. Whether this was a good or a bad reason, the fact remained that in the late months of 1941, the Army's G-2 at Pearl Harbor wasn't approved for Ultra. That put a limit on what Rochefort could tell him. "I could not communicate it to G-2 as Ultra," Rochefort said, "but I could communicate the sense of it, which I did."[44]

But Fielder maintained the information he got from Rochefort and other Navy intelligence officers concerned only local issues. "The passage of information between the Intelligence agencies of the Navy and myself had to do primarily with counter-subversive measures," Fielder said later. "No information was given to me by anyone in the Navy, which indicated in any way that aggression by the Japanese against Hawaii was imminent or contemplated."[45]

The Navy, of course, had no such information to impart. Fielder nevertheless grew bitter in later years: "I know now that had I asked for information obtained by the Navy from intercept sources it would not have been given me."[46] About that he was undoubtedly correct. Rochefort knew far more about the Japanese fleet than he ever told Fielder.[47]

Standoffish as Rochefort was, he came close to having one real meeting with Fielder, thanks to a bizarre plan hatched by two intelligence officers in Washington. The episode began in the Munitions Building on 3 December, when the Army's top intel officers first learned that Japan had ordered the destruction of its confidential papers around the world. The news particularly troubled Colonel Bratton, head of G-2's Far Eastern Section. Convinced this development signaled almost immediate war, he took his concerns to his boss, Brigadier General Miles, and the Army's head of the War Plans Division, Brigadier General Leonard T. Gerow.

Bratton argued that the code burning warranted another warning to General Short in Hawaii. Miles agreed but Gerow opposed such a message, maintaining that enough alerts had already been sent to overseas posts. Miles wouldn't go against Gerow, and that seemed to be that. But Bratton, rather than let the matter drop, walked next door to Main Navy and sought out Commander McCollum, running the Far Eastern Desk at ONI. McCollum agreed with Bratton about the need for another war warning to Short.[48] Rochefort's name came up in the conversation.

McCollum told Bratton that "Rochefort knew the situation between Japan and America practically as well as [Washington] did at that time."[49] Bratton had an idea. Maybe if G-2 in Hawaii (Colonel Fielder) could meet with the knowledgeable Rochefort, he would learn so much about the worsening situation with Japan that it would have the effect of a war warning, one that might be passed on to Short through the backdoor, so to speak.

Bratton clearly was desperate. "I was trying to get [Fielder] in close personal touch with [Rochefort], who was the ONI No. 1 man in Hawaii, who knew everything that we did in Washington at that time," Bratton said. "I felt if I could get Fielder to go and talk to this Naval officer under any pretext whatsoever, that I would be accomplishing my purpose, which was to bring them together for an exchange of intelligence."[50]

The pretext for this meeting was to be the "winds" execute message Rochefort's four language officers were listening for at Heeia. Bratton then prevailed upon his boss, General Miles, to cable Fielder in Hawaii the following message: "Contact Commander Rochefort immediately thru Commandant Fourteen Naval District regarding broadcasts from Tokyo reference weather. Miles."[51]

Miles' radiogram, message no. 519, went out on Friday 5 December. Not only did Fielder not contact Rochefort, he never got the order. Or that's what he said later. In truth, he *did* get the cable. His assistant, Lieutenant Colonel Bicknell, said he saw it on Fielder's desk that Friday and, like any good spook, read it, presumably upside down.[52] The enterprising Bicknell then took it upon himself to contact Rochefort. "On the day I saw this message I communicated with Commander Rochefort to ascertain the pertinent information," Bicknell testified, "and I was advised that he also was monitoring for the execution message of the 'winds' code."[53]

That's where matters ended. Bicknell didn't know the message on Fielder's desk was a Washington contrivance to bring Rochefort and Fielder together. The pretext for this breakthrough meeting, the winds message, had become an end in itself. Bicknell thought "winds" was the point and pursued it. Fielder, for whatever reason, never knew what the point was. He and Rochefort never got together. Message no. 519 was never found in Army files at Fort Shafter, and Fielder went on to become a general.

Whether Fielder could have extracted any useful information from Rochefort if they had met that Friday can be doubted. Even in the off-chance that Fielder might have asked the right question, Rochefort wasn't going to divulge anything he deemed inappropriate. He wasn't going to disclose, for example, that he and his analysts couldn't account for the whereabouts of four and possibly as many as six Japanese carriers. Rochefort was having a hard enough time admitting that to himself. Besides, the situation with the carriers wasn't really information. It would have been information only if he had known where the carriers were—if he had known they were bearing down on Hawaii. He didn't know that.

◼

While G-2 in Washington played games with the winds message, Rochefort at Pearl Harbor had questions of his own about the strange mission his linguists were engaged in at Heeia. Biard, Slonim, Bromley, and Cole had now been on duty at Station H a full week. They had been taking turns wearing earphones in a continuous twenty-four-hour watch, straining to hear the elusive weather message. At first the project seemed to make sense. If picked up, Japan's alert to its legations would tell the United States much of what it needed to know.

"East wind rain," as noted, was the signal that Japan and America would very soon be at war. Upon hearing the phrase, Japanese diplomats in Washington and in all U.S.-controlled sites around the world were to burn their code manuals. By Friday Rochefort's linguists had heard neither that nor the other two phrases they had been told to listen for: "north wind cloudy" (war with the Soviet Union) or "west wind clear" (Great Britain). The Heeia detour turned out to be a dead end. Hypo's four JLOs never heard any of the execute messages; in fact, powerful evidence surfaced later that no such message was sent before the Pearl Harbor attack.[54] But did this matter?

Given the events of the previous week, would the weather message have revealed very much? "That would not, in my opinion, [have been] an extremely important message," Rochefort said.[55] He minimized its importance for a very good reason: with the news that Japan's embassy in Washington and its consulate in Honolulu were destroying their code books, the Navy's chief decision makers knew everything that an "east wind rain" message could have told them. As Rear Admiral Turner put it, the code burning signaled war.

In other words, the winds execute would have added nothing to what top brass fully grasped—the United States was going to get hit in the very near future. It would not have disclosed what everybody wanted to know: the time and place of the strike. The Navy, surrounded by clues without realizing it, kept listening for the winds message because it was desperate for any clue it could get.

12

Comedy of Errors

We were uneasy. We thought that something might be under
way that we did not know about.

—Joe Rochefort

I f getting more information about Japanese intentions was the aim of U.S.
intelligence, then Rochefort should have jumped at the unexpected opportunity that now presented itself. It arrived in the basement on Tuesday 2 December, in the form of a note from Lieutenant (jg) Yale Maxon, assistant to COM
14's district intelligence officer, Captain Irving H. Mayfield. Maxon's note
advised Rochefort that the district office could provide him "through a very
confidential source known to you, rechecks on cables received from time to
time by the principal Orange establishment here."[1] Maxon was referring, as
Rochefort did indeed know, to the traffic between Japan's foreign ministry
and its Honolulu consul general, Nagao Kita.

Rochefort didn't jump at the opportunity. He never had been interested
in diplomatic traffic and didn't see how it related to what he regarded as his
main job: tracking the Imperial Japanese Navy. "We were directed to work
on naval systems only," he always said.[2] Given that priority, Rochefort felt
an overwhelming responsibility to protect his cryptanalysts from anything
that might distract them from the Flag Officers' code—which, Safford had
told him, and as he certainly believed himself, held the key to the movements
of Yamamoto's fleets.[3] He didn't see how reading consular traffic could help
him with that.

Another factor gave Rochefort pause. Hypo lacked the capability to easily read the cryptographic system used by Japan's Tokyo consulate, a manual cipher known as J-19. True, Hypo possessed some background on J-19, but Rochefort and his cryptanalysts didn't have the daily keys they would have needed to unlock it.[4] With luck the team could have exploited a J-19 message in a half-day, but, given their unfamiliarity with the system, they might have needed ten to fifteen days to decrypt such a message.[5] Consequently Rochefort hesitated. He didn't immediately accept Mayfield's offer.

Rochefort had no way of knowing, of course, what Tokyo and Consul General Kita had been talking about in their messages over the months. He might have been more receptive to Mayfield's offer had he been aware of the so-called Bomb Plot message, transmitted from Tokyo to Honolulu in September and translated in Washington in October.

Nor would Rochefort have had any way of knowing the contents of the cables that passed between Tokyo and Honolulu in succeeding months. Week after week the Japanese foreign ministry pressed Kita for more details about ship movements at Pearl Harbor. As previously noted, even if Rochefort had read such messages, he probably would have regarded them as routine. For the most part, Japan's Honolulu legation provided Tokyo with reports little different from those being sent in by its envoys at many American ports around the world, from Manila to Panama to Seattle.[6]

But Rochefort's curiosity might have been piqued by the 29 November cable in which Tokyo asked Kita to send reports not only when ships moved, but also when they didn't—in effect, when there were no ship movements. He almost certainly would have been troubled, possibly even alarmed, by the dispatch Kita received from Tokyo on 2 December, the same day he got Mayfield's offer, asking the consulate to report on whether there were any observation balloons above Pearl Harbor, and whether U.S. warships were protected by anti-torpedo nets.[7]

Rochefort could not have known about that message or the others. He knew the only way to collect cable traffic was to go to the cable company and ask for it. He knew that was illegal by order of the Communications Act of 1934, but Captain Mayfield had long been trying to circumvent the law. He had gotten nowhere; the cable companies always cited the law.

Their attitude changed in November, when David Sarnoff, president of the Radio Corporation of America, visited Honolulu. Commandant Bloch and Sarnoff were acquainted, and as the two chatted, Bloch persuaded the

RCA executive to authorize the delivery to Mayfield of company file copies of Japanese messages. This didn't happen right away, because the two cable companies serving Hawaii, Mackay Radio and RCA, took turns handling the consulate's traffic. RCA's turn didn't come until December 1941, but Sarnoff kept his word. Early in December, Mayfield received a bundle from RCA.[8] Mayfield instructed Maxon to drop Rochefort a note telling him about the trove.

Rochefort's reluctance to tackle the Kita messages proved short-lived. Two things caused him to change his mind. News received 3 December that Tokyo had ordered its legations in the United States—including its consular office in Honolulu—to destroy their code manuals told him that war with Japan was all but certain. Through his own contacts, he learned that Kita was now torching the unreadable J-19 system. With J-19 out of the way, Rochefort knew Kita would be required to encrypt all future cables in two simpler codes used for the consulate's more routine traffic—the PA-K2 system and the even lower-grade LA code.[9] As already noted, Rochefort had on his staff a cryptanalyst somewhat familiar with low-level diplomatic codes: Warrant Officer Woodward.

Less firmly established as a cryptanalyst than Dyer, Wright, and Holtwick, the relatively junior Woodward had experience that none of the others did. As a Navy cryptologist in Shanghai between 1938 and 1940, he had become familiar with Japan's J-19, PA-K2, and LA diplomatic systems. At the time, he'd learned to crack all three. When he'd been transferred to the COM 14 decrypt unit in August 1940—then directed by Rochefort's predecessor, Lieutenant Commander Birtley—he was ordered to work only on Japanese navy traffic. Sixteen months later, now out of touch with the more difficult J-19 (and lacking keys and an updated history), in December 1941 Woodward told Rochefort he believed he could compromise messages encrypted in the easier PA-K2 and LA systems.

ıı■ıı

Rochefort had no idea how Mayfield had obtained the Kita messages, or so he told Congress five years later. That probably was a stretch. In other forums Rochefort indicated he was fully aware that Commandant Bloch had approached Sarnoff about the cables.[10] He knew they could have come from only one place: the RCA cable office. Realizing that possession of them violated federal law, he took steps to minimize his, and the Navy's, legal risks.

Rochefort treated delivery of the Kita messages as a non-event, ordering that no paperwork be done in connection with them. Asked five years later by

Pearl Harbor investigators why he had failed to keep exact records of them, Rochefort answered bluntly. "I will put it this way," he said. "The reason we [did] not is that they [did] not exist. The document[s] in question, as far as we [were] concerned, up to the seventh of December, did not exist."[11]

Mayfield's bundle didn't show up in the dungeon right away. Possibly as many as three days passed between Yale Maxon's 2 December note and the arrival of the cables. Rochefort remembered only receiving "ten to fifteen messages" sometime between Wednesday and Friday. He gave different dates.[12] So did Mayfield, who first thought he had them delivered on Thursday, then changed his mind to Wednesday.[13] Mayfield's assistant, Lieutenant Donald Woodrum, testified he hand-delivered the package to Rochefort early Friday, 5 December.[14] Woodward had another memory: He said Rochefort asked to decrypt the messages "around possibly 1:30, 2 o'clock Friday afternoon."[15]

That was late. Even messages encrypted in simple codes like LA and PA-K2 required time to solve, and time was running out. Whenever he got the cables, Woodward got to work right away. The fifteen messages were encoded in three different codes. One was the indecipherable J-19 system used by Tokyo in its 2 December message to Honolulu; it was the last J-19 message exchanged by Kita and Tokyo. As noted, this explosive dispatch asked Kita to check on barrage balloons and the use of anti-torpedo nets at Pearl Harbor. Neither Woodward nor anybody else in the basement had the background needed to read that cable. Woodward set it aside. It wouldn't be decrypted until the Army did so on 30 December.[16]

Precisely how Woodward went about his task remains unclear. Did he tackle the LA messages first and then turn to the harder PA-K2 dispatches? Did he do all the work himself, or did he get help from another analyst in the basement? Did he make a fatal mistake in how he proceeded with the decoding? Questions percolated over the years because Woodward and Rochefort told somewhat different stories. Woodward's portrayal of his decrypt activity on 5 December was perplexing.

He denied wasting any time on the lowly regarded LA messages. Yet that work was somehow done. He admitted affixing a note to each of the LA dispatches stating when it was received (5 December), and that it had been decrypted and translated prior to the Pearl Harbor attack.[17] But he insisted that work wasn't done by him. Who did those decryptions? "That I can't say," Woodward said later, "because we were located in different parts of the building and the nature of my work at the time kept me at one end, where they just turned this stuff over to me and let me go to work on it where I was."[18]

Whoever did the work on the LA messages, the contents were "seen to be junk," Woodward said. When Rochefort saw the decrypts, he agreed. One dispatch reported the departure of a transport and another concerned the cost of sending families home to Japan.[19] Others had to do with wages, visas, and various personnel issues. Rochefort cranked up his secure phone and called Layton, who was standing by for some news. "I told Layton that we had some messages," Rochefort recalled, "but they were of absolutely no value."[20] LA may have been the simplest code; it was also the least important.

Woodward's account raises questions: Who else could have worked on that code but him? Dyer and Wright had no background in the LA system and, besides, were otherwise engaged, struggling with the still-intractable Flag Officers' system. Neither came to Woodward's aid. And, contrary to Woodward's testimony, there was no other part of the building where cryptanalytic work was being done. All such work was done in the basement, a large open area where everybody could see what everybody else was doing. Woodward's story is baffling. Did he work too long on the insignificant LA material and didn't want to say so? The contradictions in his story were never resolved before he died a relatively young man in 1946. Whether or not he worked on the LA system, at some point he turned to the more difficult PA-K2 code.

How many hours elapsed between the arrival of Kita's messages and the time Woodward tackled the PA-K2 cables would never be determined. Even for a cryptanalyst with Woodward's background, that would not have been child's play. Rusty in all these consular codes, he was essentially starting from scratch.[21]

Woodward moved ahead smoothly for a while, quickly solving a couple of routine messages encoded in PA-K2.[22] Then he ran into trouble. He encountered a PA-K2 message he couldn't break. He struggled for hours without making any headway. Other cryptanalysts were nearby but weren't called in to lend assistance. They could only look on helplessly. "I knew he was having difficulty," said Tommy Dyer. "He didn't ask me for any help."[23]

Woodward continued his solitary chore, working "pretty far into the night on that Friday evening," as he put it later.[24] Rochefort attested to the hours devoted to the project, describing it as "a matter of paramount importance." He testified that Woodward and Hypo linguist Red Lasswell devoted "approximately twelve to sixteen hours daily . . . to that work alone."[25]

Sometime late Friday, Rochefort realized Woodward was stymied. He didn't know quite what the problem was, but as best Rochefort could explain

The Rochefort family, circa 1912, grouped in front of their west Los Angeles bungalow approximately one year after their move from Dayton, OH. From left, twelve-year-old Joe, his mother Ellen, and the rest of the family to Ellen's left: Joe's brothers Charles, Harold, and William; his sister Margaret, his father Frank Sr, and brothers Frank Jr. and Hamilton. *Courtesy Janet Rochefort Elerding*

A young Joe Rochefort about the time of his senior year at Polytechnic High in Los Angeles. *Courtesy Janet Rochefort Elerding*

Japanese interlude: Rochefort looked for opportunities to meet civilians and members of Japan's military during his three years in Tokyo, 1929–32, studying the Japanese language. Rochefort (left) is pictured here with a Japanese army officer and two members of the U.S. diplomatic community, all unidentified. *Courtesy Janet Rochefort Elerding*

Tokyo traveler: During his three years
in Tokyo learning Japanese (1929–32),
Rochefort seized every chance that
came his way to see Japan close up. To
better understand the country's people
and culture, almost invariably joined by
Fay, he pedaled around parts of Japan
in the hope of making what discoveries
he could. He is also pictured next to a
Japanese shrine, unidentified, in Tokyo.
Courtesy Janet Rochefort Elerding

The four Rocheforts, circa 1933: Joe, nine-year-old Joe Jr., Fay, and young Janet, shown here shortly after their return to the United States from Japan. Janet was born in Tokyo in 1931. *Courtesy Janet Rochefort Elerding*

Gaming table: Gesturing emphatically, Rochefort demonstrates his prowess at dominoes on board USS *Indianapolis*, flagship of the U.S. Scouting Force, commanded by Vice Adm. Adolphus Andrews. As an intelligence officer, Rochefort served eighteen months on board the cruiser, 1939–41, impressing Andrews and paving the way for his next duty: officer in charge of Station Hypo. *Photo by Carl Mydans, @ Life Magazine. Courtesy of Getty Images*

Cdr. Joe Rochefort about the time of his duty at Pearl Harbor as OIC of Station Hypo. *Courtesy Janet Rochefort Elerding*

Friend at court: As a young language officer assigned to Main Navy's research desk, Lt. Cdr. Ellis Zacharias (shown here as a captain) joined forces with Rochefort's team in 1926–27 to break the Imperial Navy's Red Code. He later championed Rochefort and promoted his career at the Office of Naval Intelligence. *NARAII*

A friend and champion of Joe Rochefort, Rear Adm. Claude C. Bloch, as district commandant, put the younger officer in charge of the Navy's decrypt unit at Pearl Harbor in June 1941. *NARAII*

Known to all as Miss Aggie, Agnes Meyer Driscoll, the Navy's top civilian cryptanalyst, tutored apprentice codebreaker Joe Rochefort in 1926–27 on the fine points of his craft. *Naval Security Group*

Founding father: one of the pioneers of Navy cryptanalysis, Lt. Laurance Safford (shown here as a captain) introduced Rochefort to this arcane field in 1925 and later, as head of OP-20-G in Washington, granted Rochefort unusual independence when he took charge of Station Hypo. *Naval Security Group*

Teased by junior officers for his out-of-fashion goatee, Adm. Joseph M. Reeves was a strong leader as commander in chief, U.S. Fleet, 1935–36. He took Rochefort under his wing and introduced the younger officer to new aspects of naval intelligence. *NARAII*

Pearl Harbor's City Hall: Outwardly a bland edifice, the Navy's admin building at Pearl housed officials running every activity from harbor dredging to parks and recreation to base security. Virtually invisible was the activity in its basement, accessible by the sidewalk entrance (above), shielded by a heavy vault-type door (opposite, top), and reachable through a narrow and rather grim stairwell (opposite, bottom) that led to another vault-type door: It opened up into Joe Rochefort's Station Hypo decrypt unit. Unmarked, unidentified, unprotected by any guard, the Hypo entry was so uninviting that it stirred little curiosity; the time lock installed to keep the door closed and intruders out was never turned on. Unwanted visitors were never a problem. *Credit: Courtesy of Daniel Martinez*

Hawaii's Station Hypo was one of three codebreaking units managed by the Navy during World War II. Dubbed "the Dungeon" by its inhabitants, Hypo was located in the basement of the Navy Administration Building at Pearl Harbor. Presiding over this hideaway was Cdr. Joseph J. Rochefort, visualized here in the middle of the big room, surrounded by language officers on one side, traffic analysts on another, and his cryptanalysts against a wall on the far right. The bunk room at lower right was where Rochefort kept his cot for catnaps while working what were often twenty-hour days. *Created from memory by Rear Adm. Donald "Mac" Showers, USN (Ret.), who joined the Hypo team in February 1942 as an ensign*

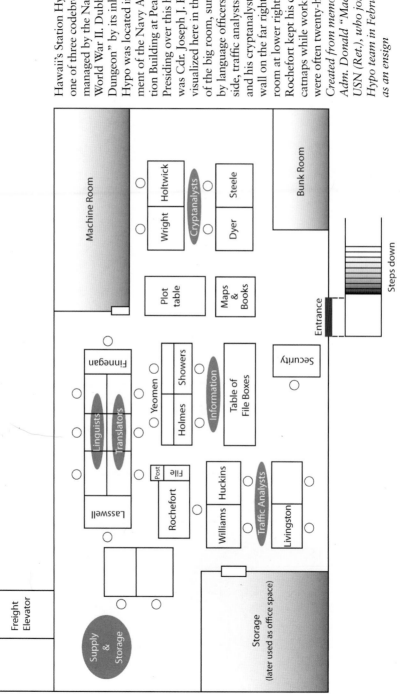

Machine Room

Holtwick

Wright

Cryptanalysts

Steele

Dyer

Plot table

Maps & Books

Bunk Room

Entrance

Steps down

Finnegan

Showers

Yeomen

Linguists

Translators

Holmes

Information

Table of File Boxes

Security

Lasswell

Rochefort

File

Post

Williams   Huckins

Traffic Analysts

Livingston

Supply & Storage

Freight Elevator

Steps down

Storage
(later used as office space)

LT Mac
Showers
1945

Rookie: lacking any background in codebreaking or intelligence, Ens. Donald "Mac" Showers nevertheless found himself ordered to Rochefort's Station Hypo basement in February 1942. He emerged as a full-fledged intelligence analyst. Showers called the assignment "dumb luck," launching as it did a thirty-one-year career that culminated in his later promotion to rear admiral. He thus became the only member of the Hypo team to achieve flag rank. *U.S. Navy*

Dueling codebreakers: Lt. Cdr. Wesley A. "Ham" Wright, Hypo cryptanalyst (left) and Maj. Alva B. "Red" Lasswell, Hypo linguist with signature cigar, play chess during an off-duty moment, circa 1941–42. Starved for recreation, Hypo's denizens often showed up at Wright's quarters to play chess and his classical records, and sometimes tap his bar. *Courtesy the Lasswell family*

Lt. Cdr. Joseph Finnegan was one of Rochefort's prized language officers and code-breakers. He collaborated with cryptanalyst Ham Wright to break the special cipher in the Imperial Navy's operational code that gave the U.S. Navy the date and time of Vice Admiral Chuichi Nagumo's attack on the Midway Atoll in June 1942. *Naval History & Heritage Command*

A former submariner, Lt. W. J. "Jasper" Holmes joined Station Hypo in June 1941 to plot ship movements, later evolving into one of Hypo's most valuable intelligence analysts. *Naval Security Group*

Dapper, always nattily dressed, Lt. Cdr. Jack S. Holtwick, one of Hypo's top cryptanalysts, ran the unit's famed machine room. He ended his career as a Navy historian.
Naval Security Group

Hypo linguist Lt. Forrest R. "Tex"
Biard (shown here as a commander)
was listening for the elusive "East
Wind Rain" message at Hypo's Heeia
listening post on 7 December 1942
when the Imperial Navy struck Pearl
Harbor. He and his fellow linguists
never picked up the message, which
Rochefort, contrary to his OP-20-G
boss Laurance Safford, believed had
never been sent. *Naval History &
Heritage Command*

Troubleshooter: CPO Durwood G. "Tex" Rorie was Hypo's senior enlisted man, in which capacity he served as Rochefort's right-hand man and all-around problem solver. Among his accomplishments: he persuaded the *California* band to join Hypo. *Naval War College*

"Odd character": Rochefort regarded Lt. Cdr. Tommy Dyer as Hypo's top cryptanalyst and resident genius, even if, like all cryptanalysts, he was "a little nutty." Dyer, to break the tension in the basement, cultivated the light touch, posting a sign near his desk reading, "You don't have to be crazy to work here, but it helps!" *Naval Security Group*

it, Woodward had set up the messages incorrectly, laying them out in a way that scrambled their order rather than clarifying it. "[That] fellow who did the job did it backwards," Rochefort told an investigating panel in January 1942. This "held us up three or four days. If he had done his job properly we would have had it Friday morning."[26]

Rochefort was wrong about that. Under no circumstances could Woodward have solved the PA-K2 message by Friday morning. He didn't start working on it until late in the afternoon on Friday after, from all accounts, he had finished the easier LA-encrypted dispatches. Still, the message might have aroused interest, had it been rendered readable in a timely fashion.

A long and detailed two-part message, it had been sent by Kita to Tokyo on Wednesday 3 December. Kita had drafted it at the behest of a Japanese agent, a German living in Oahu named Otto Kuehn. It described a set of signals to be flashed to nearby Japanese submarines indicating types of ships in the Hawaiian area. It also listed arrangements for various lights in houses, on beaches, and on boats; and signals from Maui Island, as well as want ads on Honolulu radio stations. All of these signals were to be picked up by Japanese spy ships. It wasn't until 11 December that Woodward and Lasswell, working together, managed to break the code and render it readable.[27]

In retrospect, the debacle over the Kita messages raises the issue of whether history would have been different if Rochefort had accepted Mayfield's offer right away. Would an earlier translation of the "lights" message, as it was called, have alerted Rochefort to the danger facing Hawaii? Or would Woodward simply have run into the same hurdles earlier?

Clearly the lights message was intriguing, and it could have raised eyebrows. But, like the Bomb Plot dispatch, it might very well have been sloughed off as a bizarre example of the extreme lengths to which the Japanese were willing to go to pass on information about the U.S. Navy. Also, there was nothing in the message that pointed to an air raid on Pearl Harbor. Yet many would regard Rochefort's handling of the Kita messages as a lost opportunity. Even his friend Eddie Layton thought the episode didn't show Hypo's officer in charge at his best. He saw the incident as one in a series of missteps by many at Pearl. Wrote Layton: "Rochefort's unwitting neglect of a source of potentially valuable intelligence in the final days before the Japanese attack was typical of the comedy of errors that bedeviled our operations."[28]

Admiral Kimmel changed his routine a bit on Saturday, 6 December. Usually he began his day at 8:15 a.m. sharp, with Layton's intelligence briefing. This morning Layton had to wait until Kimmel concluded an interview he had granted to a reporter passing through Honolulu, Joseph C. Harsch of the *Christian Science Monitor*. On his way to Japan, China, and Moscow, Harsch wanted to know Kimmel's assessment of the likelihood of war in the Pacific theater. Kimmel stated flatly that there would be no war in the Pacific, at least not one involving the United States.

The key to the situation, Kimmel believed, was that the Germans had just announced they were going into winter quarters in front of Moscow. "That means that Moscow is not going to fall this winter," Kimmel told Harsch. "That means that the Russians will still be in the war in the spring. That means the Japanese cannot attack us in the Pacific without running the risk of a two-front war. The Japanese are too smart to run that risk."[29]

What made Kimmel so confident can only be surmised. Nothing he said in the Harsch interview had ever been suggested by either Rochefort or Layton. Nor did such a scenario unfold at Layton's regular intelligence briefing later that morning, which probably got under way shortly after Harsch left Kimmel's office. Layton painted a picture of a Japan moving inexorably toward war in Southeast Asia and proceeding in a way that would certainly entangle the United States.

As always, Layton relied primarily on Hypo's daily intelligence summary for his sense of what the Combined Fleet was doing. It had been delivered earlier in the morning by the indefatigable Holmes. The summary covered radio traffic intercepted by Heeia during the twenty-four-hour period ending Friday afternoon. Drawing on Heeia's intercepts, traffic analysts Huckins and Williams had put together a one-page summary on Friday night. Rochefort had scanned it Saturday morning and passed it to Holmes, who'd driven it to Kimmel's headquarters.

Kimmel probably found the document unremarkable. It did note a high volume of radio traffic on Friday. "All circuits overloaded with Tokyo broadcast going over full 24 hours," the summary stated. The Tokyo-mandates circuit crackled with traffic. Ominato radio beamed broadcasts steadily to Sama at Hainan Island and Bako on the east coast of Formosa. Takao radio, on the west coast of Formosa, directed its broadcasts to the Second and Third Fleets, now steaming into the Gulf of Siam, just off the South China Sea. Some of the traffic seemed strange. "It is noted," Huckins and Williams wrote, "that some traffic being broadcast is several days old which indicates the uncertainty of delivery existing in the radio organization."[30] Apparently it didn't occur to either analyst to consider the possibility of radio deception.

Hypo's summary reported nothing else unusual. The Second and Third Fleets were quiet. In twenty-four hours, the air and ground forces of the two fleets would be arrayed against Singapore and exposed British positions along Malaya's coast, but now they weren't making any noise. The IJN fleets were getting traffic, but they weren't originating any. Nor were any of the Combined Fleet's carriers or submarines heard from. "No traffic from the Commander Carriers or Submarine Force has been seen either," the summary said.[31] As he always did, Kimmel scratched his HEK initials on the lower right of the page. It was the last time he would ever put his initials on a Hypo intelligence summary.

Aside from the more pointed movement of Japanese naval forces into the Gulf of Siam, Hypo's analysts had noticed little or no change in the Combined Fleet's alignment of forces. Indeed, there had been no apparent change since Tuesday, when Layton had confessed to Kimmel that he couldn't, with any reasonable certainty, account for the whereabouts of the Combined Fleet's Carrier Divisions 1 and 2, consisting of the *Kaga*, *Akagi*, *Soryu*, and *Hiryu*. "You mean to say they could be rounding Diamond Head?" Kimmel had asked.

It might have been the memory of his Tuesday conversation with Layton that stirred Kimmel to seek a second opinion. He ordered Layton to get the viewpoint of Vice Admiral William S. Pye, commander of the Pacific Fleet's Battle Force. Layton took a gig across the harbor to Pye's flagship, the *California*, moored off Ford Island at the head of Battleship Row. He found Pye and his acting chief of staff, Captain Russell Train, on the quarterdeck. Layton briefed them on the Japanese convoy moving into the Gulf of Siam, leading Pye to ask him what he thought. Layton's said Japan's objective was the Dutch East Indies—a move that would require Japan to engage the Philippines on its flank. In other words, the United States would soon be at war.

But Pye and Train doubted Layton's estimate. "Oh, no. The Japanese won't attack us," Pye said. "We're too strong and powerful."[32]

Layton reported this exchange back to Kimmel, who nevertheless discussed with his staff the possibility of sending the fleet to sea as a precautionary measure. The group included Kimmel's chief of staff, Poco Smith; his war plans officer, Soc McMorris; and his operations officer, W. S. DeLany. They questioned the advisability of moving the fleet out to sea without air cover (the carriers were away). They suggested that sending out the ships on a weekend would arouse the kind of alarm that Washington wanted to avoid. Plus they had other concerns. Why waste fuel when the fleet almost certainly would be steaming toward the Marshalls if, against all reason, hostilities broke out? In the end, Kimmel decided to leave the ships where they were.[33]

Kimmel and his top lieutenants may have seemed sure of themselves, but no doubt many factors diverted their attention away from the peril facing Pearl Harbor. To name just a few: the fixation with Japan's southward move into the South China Sea, the vast distances that separated the Empire from Hawaii's waters, the U.S. Navy's assumed potential to inflict devastating damage on any attacking force, and the long-held assumption that Japan wouldn't do anything foolish.

Another factor probably contributed to Kimmel's fateful decision: U.S. Navy doctrine held that carriers should be used only singly or, at most, in pairs as part of a larger battle group. If Kimmel made the common mistake of thinking the Japanese would behave in the same way as Americans, then he thought that an attacking force confronting Hawaii with just two carriers wouldn't pose much of a threat and could therefore be discounted. "What was going on here was a failure of imagination," Pacific war historian John Lundstrom said in a telephone interview. The possibility that the Japanese might build a task force around as many as six carriers was unthinkable. "It was unthinkable because that wasn't the way the [U.S.] Navy would do it," Lundstrom said.[34]

ıı ■ ıı

While Kimmel seemed more comfortable with the situation at Pearl, Rochefort was getting anxious. Now he questioned some of his most cherished assumptions, chief of which was that Japan could be trusted to act in its own best interests. Events of the past week had jarred his faith in that notion. Ten days earlier he'd thought he had a pretty good fix on the carriers. Four appeared to be in the Inland Sea, and on 26 November another carrier or two seemed to be in the Marshalls. Then on 1 December, the Imperial Navy changed its call signs, for the second time in thirty days. Three days later, on 4 December, the Japanese navy altered its main operational code, JN-25(b), a change that wouldn't have affected Hypo's analysts but would have confounded Cast's.

After that, silence. "About a day after [26 November] the carriers just completely dropped from sight," Rochefort said later. "[We] never heard another word from them." Equally disturbing was Tokyo's 3 December order to its legations around the world to burn their codes and Purple machines, an order that included the Honolulu consulate, which, while not possessing a Purple machine to destroy, was nevertheless incinerating all but two lower-grade code manuals. But Rochefort's growing edginess didn't extend to the possibility of a massive air raid on Pearl Harbor. That remained unfathomable. Why? "Probably it was due on my part at least to a feeling that the Japanese had more or less committed themselves in Southeast Asia [and] possibly the Philippines," Rochefort said later. That "would not leave them very much in the way of ships and planes for an attack on any other spot."[35]

But Rochefort had now come around to the view that the United States wouldn't be able to stay out of the war he saw looming in Southeast Asia. He no longer believed the Japanese would ignore the Philippines.

Rochefort began Saturday, 6 December, early as he always did, scanning the intelligence summary prepared the previous evening by his traffic analysts, then moving on to other business. He finally got around to cabling OPNAV in Washington that Consul General Kita was burning codes and papers. Rochefort fired off his message: "Believe local consul has destroyed all but one system."[36]

Strangely, the COM 14 communications office sent the message out "deferred status," the lowest possible priority. Layton, Rochefort's friend and defender, would later attribute the district's tardiness in moving out the message to a woefully ill-timed effort to keep costs down.[37] But the way things worked, it was the sending officer (Rochefort) who dictated priority; Rochefort could have sent the dispatch at a higher priority if he had wanted to.[38] In any case, his dispatch didn't reach Washington until after the Japanese attack.[39]

Even more curious was why Rochefort waited until Saturday to inform Washington of news he had acquired on Wednesday. The seeming lapse was never probed. Rochefort always insisted that his report to Washington was timely. "We are the one[s] that gave that [information] to Washington," he testified. "They told us that London and Washington were burning them, and then we told them also that these people here were."[40] Actually, Rochefort knew about London and Washington three days before he alerted Washington to the code burning in Honolulu.

He called Layton one more time to discuss developments. Layton wanted to hear about the carriers. Did Rochefort have anything new on Japan's flattops? He didn't. They hadn't been heard from for a week, possibly longer. "How in the hell did you lose them?" Layton asked. Rochefort answered: "I don't know but you can't expect the impossible."[41] The task was impossible because, Rochefort later testified, "they were not transmitting. They were on radio silence."[42]

A feeling of apprehension pervaded the basement. Williams and Holcomb had felt for several days that something was up. Dyer and Rochefort joined the band of worriers. "On 6 December we were restless," Rochefort said later, "for we did not know what was going on. We were uneasy. We thought that something might be under way that we did not know about. We had a big huddle about it in my outfit in the afternoon on Saturday."[43]

Exhausted after a trying week, Rochefort didn't put in his usual full day on Saturday. He planned to take the rest of the weekend off and returned around mid-afternoon to his home in Manoa Valley. He wasn't in the basement when, late in the afternoon, Heeia's driver delivered the daily package of intercepts from Station H.[44] This parcel included dozens of messages that had been intercepted during the previous twenty-four hours, along with a two-page chronology summarizing what Heeia regarded as the day's highlights.

As always, the intercepts covered a broad sweep of the Combined Fleet's activities, from ship movements in the mandates to the waters of Southeast Asia and the Inland Sea, all encrypted in a jumble of codes, some readable (such as the weather codes), most not (those in JN-25). The intercepts provided the raw material out of which traffic analysts Huckins and Williams wrote their daily intelligence summary for Admiral Kimmel. This one, dated 7 December 1941, wouldn't be delivered until 8 December. Kimmel would never see it.

But he didn't miss much. Like the summary he had seen Saturday morning, it was unremarkable, essentially a repetition of IJN fleet movements already established and previously reported. Heeia's chronology noted considerable radio activity in the south China and Indochina areas. But the report included no news about Yamamoto's carriers and little about his submarines. "No activity of importance was observed in the SubForce," the Station H document said. It noted that the commander of the fleet's submarine force was now believed to be in the mandates, in either Jaluit or Truk.[45] In fact, by now that force was taking up positions around Hawaii.

‖ ■ ‖

Shortly before Rochefort left for home Saturday afternoon, Japan's Honolulu consulate filed one last dispatch at the RCA cable office. The message was in reply to Tokyo's 2 December query about the possible use of barrage balloons at Pearl Harbor and torpedo nets by ships anchored in the harbor. "At the present time there are no signs of barrage balloon equipment," said the cable, written by Takao Yoshikawa, the spy Tokyo had sent to the consulate in March. "In my opinion the battleships do not have torpedo nets." He added, "I imagine that in all probability there is considerable opportunity left to take advantage for a surprise attack against these places."[46]

Hypo analysts didn't see that message on Saturday. Even if they had, the cable probably would not have yielded its contents easily, or in time to catch the attention of Rochefort or anybody else. But if it had been delivered to the basement Saturday afternoon, it at least would have been in an environment where there were codebreakers. As it turned out, Mayfield hadn't made arrangements with RCA for any of the consulate's dispatches to be picked up on Saturday—a monumental oversight if there ever was one, and another episode in the comedy of errors performed by America's actors at Pearl and in Washington, including Rochefort.

Another screaming *Advertiser* headline had greeted Hawaii's residents first thing Saturday morning. This one read: "America Expected to Reject Japan's Reply on Indo-China." The article reported "mounting suspense" in Washington over what answer Japan would give to President Roosevelt's inquiries concerning troop movements in French Indochina. But the United Press article made it clear that the real drama revolved around Japan's impending reply to Cordell Hull's 26 November message. "If press reports from Tokyo are borne out," UP reported gingerly, "Japan will not be able to accept the Hull document as a basis of negotiations on issues which have brought the United States and Japan to the brink of war."[47]

The extent to which Rochefort followed the course of these U.S.-Japanese conversations can only be conjectured. He might have been so caught up in the nagging problems swirling around the basement, and so dependent on radio intelligence for his information, that he paid scant attention to newspaper accounts. Asked by congressional interrogators during the 1946 hearings if he had been aware of Hull's note prior to 7 December, Rochefort pleaded ignorance. "I did not know that," he answered. "Other than what I read in newspapers, I did not know. . . . My information came from newspapers."[48]

Rochefort could be a puzzle. Contrary to the impression he gave lawmakers, Honolulu's two dailies did a credible job of reporting the key details of Hull's note. If Rochefort had only skimmed the front page of the 27 November *Star-Bulletin* he would have learned, among other things, that the United States was asking Japan to renounce the tripartite treaty with Germany and Italy and withdraw its troops from China and Indochina.[49] Rochefort would testify that if he had known America's terms earlier, he would have been even more worried on Saturday, since he thought those terms were humiliating, even provocative, to the Japanese.[50] Hull's terms had been fully reported in both local papers.

Whatever Rochefort knew or didn't know, there can be no question that neither he nor Kimmel were aware of the final diplomatic game being played out in Washington. Without a Purple machine, they would have had no way of knowing that Washington was waiting for a fourteen-part message from Japan—its answer to Hull's note—to be received Saturday evening and Sunday morning. Neither Kimmel nor Rochefort could have known that Nomura and Kurusu had asked Hull if they could deliver the message on Sunday at precisely one in the afternoon. But they would have known that one in the afternoon in Washington was seven-thirty in the morning in Honolulu.

What would Rochefort have told Kimmel had he known about those messages and been asked for his interpretation? "I would tell him it looked damn bad and we ought to take whatever steps we could," Rochefort told interrogators in January 1942.[51]

But, as noted, Rochefort didn't know any of this as he headed home Saturday. He had spent the previous Sunday on tenterhooks and expected to be just as jittery the coming Sunday. He could not have been comforted by other headlines in Saturday's papers. In addition to the UP story, the *Advertiser* reported that Japanese troops were massing on Thailand's border, presumably poised to strike into the heart of that country. And the afternoon *Star-Bulletin* unfurled an eight-column banner across the front-page: "Singapore on War Footing!" The paper hit the streets at about the same time Rochefort left the basement, bracing for a restless weekend.

13

Air Raid Pearl Harbor!

> This is the end of the Japanese Empire as we know it.
> —Joe Rochefort

Around 7:20 Sunday morning, just as Rochefort was packing the car for a family picnic, a single-engine Japanese reconnaissance plane entered the bright, cloud-streaked airspace over Pearl Harbor. Launched earlier that morning from the heavy cruiser *Chikuma*, the plane circled as the pilot studied the ground below. He must have been astonished at the tranquil scene. The only thing that would have bothered him was the absence of carriers—as luck would have it, all three with the Pacific Fleet were on duty elsewhere.[1]

Having seen all he needed to see, at precisely 7:35 the recon pilot radioed his report to the striking force, which quickly relayed the information to the Japanese planes now approaching Oahu from the north: "Enemy formation at anchor; nine battleships, one heavy cruiser, six light cruisers are in the harbor."[2]

The dispatch was a calculated risk, requiring the pilot to break radio silence. Hawaii's defenders might have gotten a jump on the *kido butai*'s rapidly nearing warplanes—now twenty minutes behind the *Chikuma* plane—if an alert or lucky radioman had picked up that transmission. The likeliest place where this could have happened was Rochefort's listening post at Heeia. His radiomen had their earphones on, but they were tuned to other frequencies. Hypo's Tex Biard, having just relieved fellow linguist Gilven Slonim, was still listening for the winds execute message, while Heeia's regular operators

185

searched for messages in Japan's version of Morse code. They weren't listening for airplanes over Pearl Harbor.

"The transmissions by the *Chikuma* plane were quite brief and it would have been nothing short of [a] miracle had they been intercepted," Hypo cryptanalyst Tommy Dyer said later. "They were no doubt in code and very little if any traffic in the appropriate air-surface code had been intercepted."[3]

There were other indications of trouble this morning. In the pre-dawn hours south of Oahu, officers on board the destroyer *Ward* noticed a peculiar object trailing the supply ship *Antares*, moving slowly toward the Pearl Harbor entrance. The *Ward*'s captain, Lieutenant William Outerbridge, recognized it as a submarine. At 6:40 a.m., he ordered his gunners to open fire. They did, causing the sub to heel over and sink. Outerbridge did his best to alert Pearl. He radioed in a message—which started making its laborious way up the Navy's chain of command to Admiral Kimmel.[4]

Twenty minutes later, Army privates Joseph L. Lockard and George E. Elliott were winding up their morning shift running the Opana mobile radar unit at Kahuku Point on the northern tip of Oahu, 230 feet above sea level. They were about to shut down when the two privates noticed a strange image on the oscilloscope. Lockard checked the machine and found nothing wrong with it. The blip was huge and closing fast on Oahu, leading the men to think "it must be a flight of some kind."

Bewildered by the spectacle, Elliott called the Army's Information Center at Fort Shafter. After negotiating his way through the switchboard, finally he reached Lieutenant Kermit Tyler, the pursuit officer and assistant to the controller on duty. Tyler knew something that Elliott and Lockard didn't: a flight of B-17 bombers was due in shortly from the U.S. mainland. Figuring they had picked up the B-17s, he told the two privates, "Well, don't worry about it."[5]

ıı■ıı

The Rocheforts were slow getting started Sunday morning. After several grueling weekends spent in the basement or near the phone at home, Rochefort had decided to give himself and his family a holiday. He thought he'd take everyone—Fay, Janet, and Cora—on an outing as far from the basement as they could get. Fay had already packed up the steaks, and Joe had loaded the cooler in their old 1937 Buick. But Joe lagged behind. "I had a premonition that something was wrong," he said later.[6]

Ten miles away at Pearl Harbor, the Navy yard was slowly coming to life. A day off for most military personnel, Sunday was a workday at Hypo. In the basement of the admin building, Tommy Dyer was finishing an unusually long twenty-four-hour stint, the result of rearranging his schedule so he could attend his son's piano recital Friday. Nearby were Captain Lasswell and Radioman First Class Tony Ethier. Scheduled for basement duty at 8 a.m. were Ham Wright and John Williams, now finishing breakfast at the submarine base wardroom, about a mile away.[7]

Across the harbor on Battleship Row—a gleaming spectacle of steel stretching along the southeastern bank of Ford Island—officers and men on board the huge warships awaited Sunday morning colors. Bands on each ship were poised to play the "Star Spangled Banner." On board the *California*, Seaman Second Class Mike Palchefsky, a trumpeter with the ship's twenty-member band, stood in formation. "We were getting ready to play," he recalled. "We were waiting for the signal which was a flag being hoisted on the *Pennsylvania*, way out in the dry dock."[8]

The flag was never hoisted. "As we were standing waiting for the signal, we heard this sound of many engines, sounds I hadn't heard before," Palchefsky said. "So, we're looking around and we look up and the noise gets louder and right out of the clouds comes this Japanese dive bomber." Moments later, "a bomb fell out of the plane and landed right on Ford Island," said Palchefsky, who had just witnessed the *kido butai*'s first strike against Pearl Harbor, officially timed at 7:55 a.m. "Everything happened in a matter of seconds," Palchefsky remembered. "I just took off."[9]

He headed for a point below deck where band members were supposed to gather in case of emergency, to assist in any way they could. Palchefsky stashed his horn in a toolbox and reported for duty. His help was needed. At 8:05 a bomb exploded belowdecks, igniting an ammunition magazine. A second bomb ruptured the ship's bow, dooming efforts to save the vessel. The *California* settled into the mud with only her superstructure jutting above the surface. In all, about one hundred men were lost, including one member of the *California*'s band. Muddied and exhausted, Palchefsky and his fellow bandsmen made their way to Ford Island.

California's band would be heard from again, though not as musicians. Palchefsky and his colleagues were destined for an unusual naval career. But not right away. It would be weeks before they met Joe Rochefort.

ıı▮ıı

In the submarine base wardroom, Williams and Wright were just finishing breakfast. Curious about the noises they were hearing, Williams wandered outside. But then "Johnny came back in and said, 'They're out there with the oranges on them,'" Wright would later recall. Wright headed for the door. "I dashed over to headquarters, dodging all the rifle fire," he said. "All the sailors were out from the submarine base, shooting rifles at these planes. Handguns and anything they could get hold of."[10]

The admin building wasn't a target, but bombs were falling a few hundred yards away. In the basement, Dyer awaited his relief. Below ground and windowless, the basement was relatively soundproof, "but I heard some explosions," Dyer said. "My first thought was that they were antiaircraft guns. I said, 'What's the Army shooting for today?'" Then Farnsley Woodward, the cryptanalyst who had struggled all weekend with Japanese codes, came down and reported, "There are planes flying around and they're dropping things."

Dyer had to see for himself. "I went up and looked around the corner of the building," he remembered. "About three hundred yards away, at an altitude of about two hundred feet, was a torpedo plane in a tight bank, a tight turn, and the rising suns were shining right at me. I caught on fast." He also acted fast. "I went down and called Rochefort and asked if he'd heard the news. He said, 'What news?' I said, 'We're at war.' He said, 'What do you mean?' I said, 'We're being bombed out here right now.' I never encountered anyone any calmer than he was. He said, 'All right, I'll be right out.'"[11]

Rochefort's radiomen at Station H learned of the war the same way he did—by phone. Biard and several operators were inside the old Pan Am building wearing earphones, impervious to sounds outside. A little after 8:00 they got a call from Jack Holtwick's wife, telling them that "planes with red balls on their wings were attacking the air station at Kaneohe," near which the Holtwicks lived. Biard and the others rushed outside. From their perch overlooking Kaneohe Bay, they watched as Japanese warplanes devastated the air base two miles to the south. Biard tried to call the basement. "The party line to the radio station was hopeless," he said later. "We could not get through to 'the dungeon' at all—could not call anywhere."[12]

ıı▮ıı

From the front yard of his home on Makalapa Heights, a hill behind the Navy yard that provided a perfect view of the harbor, Admiral Kimmel looked down at what was happening. He saw planes with rising suns on their wings destroying his fleet. His driver picked him up and sped toward Pearl.

Every Navy man on Oahu seemed to converge on Pearl Harbor. Jasper Holmes was in bed at his home near Diamond Head, fourteen miles east of Pearl, when his phone rang. "This is the District Intelligence Officer. General Quarters!" That meant show up immediately. Not sure whether he had been ordered to a practice drill or the real thing, Holmes took the family Studebaker. As he moved into the network of roads leading to Pearl, he noted the black bursts of antiaircraft fire over the Pacific near Honolulu.[13]

Living farther out, well beyond Diamond Head, Eddie Layton faced an even longer drive in, but he got lucky. He hitched a ride with a neighbor, Paul Crosley, Kimmel's flag secretary, whose wife drove them toward Pearl at high speed—until a highway patrolman stopped the car. Layton recalled, "I was in the 'rumble seat' and yelled out, 'The Japs are attacking Pearl Harbor. Please keep your light on and clear a path for us to Pearl Harbor.'"

The officer put on his siren and escorted them straight through Honolulu to Pearl, where Layton proceeded to his second deck office at Pacific Fleet headquarters, overlooking Battleship Row. He could see the *Arizona* burning, and shortly he would see two destroyers in dry dock, the *Cassin* and *Downes*, bombed. Layton remembered feeling "numb, but mostly sick."

By the time Layton arrived, Kimmel was already in his office conferring with aides. People rushed in and out of headquarters, but Kimmel, as Layton later recalled, "was calm, collected; shocked, yes; and he looked mad—mad at the Japs. He looked sad, too, because a lot of men had been killed." A little later Layton remembered seeing "a short, slightly heavy-set officer of the grade of vice admiral, still wearing a life jacket, his white uniform spotted with fuel oil, his face blackened by smoke or soot. His eyes were almost shut, he looked dazed as he stared into space, not saying a word."[14] That was Vice Admiral Pye, who had assured Layton the day before, on board the now-sinking *California*, that Japan wouldn't strike the United States.

⁙⁙

Taking the Buick's wheel, Rochefort wound through nearly deserted streets—until nearing Pearl Harbor. There, roaring traffic jammed in: fire trucks, emergency vehicles, cars filled with sailors trying to get back to their ships. All of it moved in one direction, squeezing through Pearl's main gate. It took Rochefort twenty minutes to drive ten miles from Manoa Valley to Pearl. He arrived during a lull, as the planes of the first wave began returning to their carriers.[15]

Not far behind was Jasper Holmes, who would always remember the strange feeling he had as he drove into the parking lot. A few hundred yards away, even though he couldn't see them because of the surrounding machine shops, thousands of men had died and thousands of others were manning guns, trying desperately to save their ships. "But the parking lot was as quiet and peaceful as on any other Sunday morning," he recalled.[16]

And yet the admin building was by no means out of harm's way. Located on the eastern, or Diamond Head side of the Navy yard, it was just a short distance from the Ten Ten Dock (so named because it was exactly 1,010 feet long) jutting into the harbor, now being pounded by Japanese planes. A block or two to the south and west of the admin building was a large tank farm for fuel-oil storage. If the Japanese bombed it, much of the surrounding area would be incinerated, probably including the admin building.

Holmes went about his business. "I parked my car and walked down into the basement where I belonged." The scene that greeted him there was anything but quiet or peaceful. Stunned and incredulous, puzzled by how such a catastrophe could have happened, officers and men milled about, wondering what they should do. Making matters worse, they had no way of knowing what was going on outside, with no live radio hookup with the fleet or even with fleet headquarters. They did their work—decrypting intercepts—from printed worksheets that were brought in by jeep from outlying listening posts. But right now jeeps weren't bringing in anything.

Rochefort was as shocked as everybody else, if not more so. Calm and collected as he seemed to Dyer and others, he was staggered by the Japanese attack. For months he had believed—and shared his belief—that Japan wouldn't be so foolish as to start a war it couldn't win. Now, against all military sense, it had done just that.

For long minutes he sat at his desk benumbed, saying nothing. What he thought at this time he never said, but his mind might have gone back to his 1932 conversation with the Mitsui businessman who'd defended Japan's thrust into Manchuria on grounds of honor: "When honor is involved, we don't care about anything else," the man had said. At the time Rochefort had thought that stupid. Now he knew what the man had meant.

Rochefort would never forgive himself for what he regarded as horrible lapses of judgment on his part. But he did immediately grasp the significance of what had happened. When Commandant Bloch phoned the basement during a lull, he heard Rochefort's bitter prophecy: "This is the end of the Japanese Empire as we know it."[17]

By now it was clear to all—cryptanalysts, linguists, and those who assisted them—that Pearl Harbor had been smashed in a raid executed by the Imperial Japanese Navy. It was the kind of action their unit had been created to anticipate. They all wanted to do something, anything, to strike back. Rochefort had a plan, but getting everyone to focus wasn't easy. The lull that began around 8:30 didn't last.

Around 8:45, the basement crew heard gunfire again. The sounds got louder. "Several heavy explosions rocked the solid earth, and our basement trembled," Holmes recalled. "Of course, none of us could see what went on above ground. The lights went out, plunging us into total darkness for a few minutes, then flickered briefly and came back on again. It was past ten o'clock before relative calm returned above us."[18]

Rochefort didn't wait until 10:00 a.m. to get everyone working. He thought there were two things he needed to know. One had to do with the Japanese fleet. From what direction did it attack? Could it be located? And where was it heading? The other issue had to do with resources. Did he have the means to find any of this out? The good news was that his best officers and men were present. Dyer, now on duty for twenty-five hours, was groggy but on hand. So were Wright, Lasswell, Ethier, Woodward, and Williams. Others were on the way. Holtwick, driving in over the Pali from Kaneohe, would show up soon. Rochefort would give them jobs.

That's where the good news ended. After a survey of the equipment available to him, Rochefort discovered to his horror that Hypo was essentially blind.[19] Due to a freakish chain of mishaps as well as missteps by various Army and Navy personnel, Hypo's main direction finder—the big CXK unit at Lualualei—was on the blink. Nor was the Lualualei station reachable by phone: the circuits had been disrupted. Rochefort could not call his man at that site, Radioman First Class Andrew Jackson "Andy" Cooper. He'd arrived on duty that morning to find the DF out of order and phones not working.

Cooper was stymied, but he didn't abandon the site, a makeshift structure that rotated slowly on rollers. He remained inside the ungainly contraption, thinking the power might resume at any time. He filled his time as productively as he could. When Japan's planes hit Pearl Harbor, Cooper was writing Christmas cards.[20]

For Rochefort, Lualualei was simply cut off. "We lost all communications with our direction finders right off the bat," he said. The problem didn't stem from sabotage or Japan's attacking warplanes. Rochefort blamed the U.S. Army. The lines powering the DF site ran through an Army area where construction was going on. "What with the Army yanking out all the wires and every conduit they could get their hands on, there was just general confusion all over," Rochefort said.[21] The phones were down, Layton explained later, because "the U.S. Army took over that telephone circuit—just pre-empted it without warning."[22]

With Lualualei unreachable, Rochefort did the only thing left: he sent one of Hypo's yeomen by jeep to the CXK site, twenty-five miles west of Pearl Harbor. Given the congestion around Pearl and confusion everywhere, he figured the trip would take a couple of hours, and it did.

Rochefort had one last option. He had another DF at his disposal, a relatively new unit recently installed at the Station H facility at Heeia. Technically known as a DY, the unit wasn't as accurate as the big CXK at Lualualei. It was used almost entirely for training, but it was all Rochefort had. The difficulty was that he had no easy way to contact Heeia. Even on the odd chance he got through, a party line couldn't be used to impart sensitive information of this nature. He had no choice but to put another yeoman in a jeep, this one to Heeia, with orders to the radiomen there to activate the DY.

As Rochefort's couriers sped west toward Lualualei and north over the Pali to Heeia, their task got a little easier. Admiral Nagumo's second wave tapered off around 9:30, and by 9:45 it was over. There were only a few stragglers in the air.

‖ ∎ ‖

Heeia's DY seemed to have come through. There's no way to know when Rochefort got the news, whether it was conveyed by jeep or telephone. The Mutual Telephone Company managed to provide a direct line from Pearl Harbor to Heeia shortly after the attack.[23] All we know is that at precisely 10:40, Heeia's DY picked up a call sign (YUNE 8) from the *Akagi*, flagship of the striking force, and plotted a set of bearings. There was just one problem. Unlike Lualualei's CXK, which could pinpoint the direction from which a signal emanated, Heeia's DY could not. It could provide only what operators called reciprocal, or bilateral, bearings—meaning signals could be on either of two bearings 180 degrees apart.[24]

According to Heeia's log, the *Akagi* was no more than two hundreds miles away, bearing either 357 degrees north or 178 degrees south.[25] To establish the *kido butai*'s location definitively, Rochefort would have needed cross-bearings that could only have come from another direction finder or two. He did have other units in his mid-Pacific DF net, with locations in Dutch Harbor, Samoa, and Midway. That didn't do him any good. Even in the best of times, communication with Hypo's far-flung DF units was laborious and unreliable. They couldn't be reached.[26]

Rochefort would have to make do with what he had. Fragmentary and disheartening as this information may have been, he thought it was better than nothing. He gave Ham Wright the dubious honor of calling in Heeia's flawed report to an anxiously awaiting Layton, whose superiors, Kimmel chief among them, had been pestering him all morning for the whereabouts of the attacking forces. After all, wasn't that what radio intelligence was supposed to figure out? Wasn't that what Hypo was for?

Kimmel wasn't pleased when told of Heeia's bilateral bearings. He wanted to strike back but he didn't know where to send his forces. "Goddamn the intelligence," Kimmel stormed at Layton. "We're under attack, everybody knows we're under attack, and here you don't know if they're north or south."[27]

Actually, there were people close by—or at least as close as Fort Shafter—who could have told Kimmel what he wanted to know. Army privates Elliott and Lockard knew the Imperial Navy's warplanes had originated from the north, and so informed Lieutenant Tyler at the Army Information Center. But the Army had no way of knowing that the Navy didn't know. Liaison between the two services had broken down. No one in the Army told anyone in the Navy where the planes had come from.

Kimmel suspected the planes had come from the north. War games conducted over the years were often premised on a surprise attack from that direction.[28] But on 7 December Kimmel was of two minds. He couldn't conceive that a Japanese force could traverse such an enormous distance—3,500 miles of ocean—undetected. Also, he felt prudence dictated that no one sector around Hawaii be deemed more dangerous than any other. He tended to believe they were all about equal. And yet, "I had on that morning what might be called a hunch and I did not know why," Kimmel told Congress in 1946, "but I felt the carriers were to the northward."[29]

Kimmel didn't act on that hunch.

Shortly after Wright phoned in the *kido butai*'s north-south bearings, evidence started piling up indicating that Japan's carriers were to the south. A report came in by radio that a carrier was bearing south of Pearl Harbor. The Pacific Fleet didn't have any carriers in that sector, leading Kimmel and his aides to conclude it must be Japanese. The sighting was incorrect. It was the cruiser *Minneapolis*, mistaken by an inexperienced scouting pilot for a carrier. But Kimmel and his team didn't know that.[30]

While Kimmel and his top officers—Chief of Staff Smith, War Plans Officer McMorris, and Operations Officer DeLany—discussed the report in the fleet commander's quarters, Layton came in. As Smith remembered the scene, Layton walked over to the plotting board and stated: "Here they are," pointing to the south, an area in a direct line with the Marshall Islands.[31] Layton had long been preoccupied with the Marshalls, believing Japan's illicit buildup there posed a threat to Hawaii. He now felt vindicated. He seized upon Hypo's bilateral bearings—indicating that the *kido butai* might be either north or south—as evidence it was south.

Layton thought he had good reason to do so. For days Rochefort's traffic analysts had been reporting carriers in the Marshall Islands. Rochefort thought they were there. He turned out to be wrong. His TA team had been tricked not by radio deception, but by the peculiarities of traffic analysis. They mistakenly inferred that flattops were there because of the presence of plane-guard destroyers. Weeks earlier, the destroyers had been cut loose from their carriers for other duty. No flattops were near the Marshalls.[32]

Neither Layton nor Kimmel knew that. Kimmel had shared Layton's concerns about the Marshalls, in June passing them on to CNO Stark. Now they appeared to have been well grounded. Everything pointed toward the Marshalls as the point of origin for the striking force. "For that reason the search was ordered to the south," Poco Smith said.[33]

Kimmel radioed Vice Admiral Halsey, on board the *Enterprise* 150 miles west of Pearl, to send aloft his scouting planes to cover a swath of ocean south and west of Hawaii.[34] Having just delivered a squadron of fighter planes to Wake Island, Halsey was returning to Pearl. He had been due back at 7:30 Sunday morning, but had been held up by bad weather and fueling difficulties.[35] Now, quite by accident, he seemed to be in a good position to search for Nagumo.

By what historians generally considered a stroke of even greater luck, Halsey was sent in the wrong direction. "Radio bearings indicate *Akagi* bearing 183 from Pearl [and] another unit bearing 167," Pearl Harbor radioed Halsey.[36] That was south, away from the *kido butai*. If the *Enterprise* had managed to find the invading ships, most historians believe it would have been no match for Nagumo's six carriers. The *Enterprise* was saved for another day.

As it turned out, all three carriers in Kimmel's fleet were out of Pearl Harbor on 7 December. Halsey, as noted, had just delivered planes to Wake. The *Lexington*, the centerpiece of a task force commanded by Rear Admiral John H. Newton, was making a similar delivery to Midway, a mission Newton aborted after hearing of the attack. The *Saratoga* was in San Diego.

Halsey's scout planes found no Japanese ships. They managed only to turn up a few suspicious sightings that, when reported back to Pearl, fueled an already frenzied rumor mill. Wild stories circulated all over Oahu. Some came from official sources. Fleet headquarters at 10:50 a.m. warned "all ships" that two enemy carriers, eight escorts, and three troop ships were approaching Barbers Point, on the southwestern tip of Oahu.

At 12:55 p.m., headquarters passed on to fleet units an even scarier development: "Men blue overhauls red marking landing around Barbers Point." This report was followed by news of a parachute landing at Nanakuli, a small coastal town not far from the Lualualei naval reservation.[37] The rumors all proved false, but people around the island, including those in the basement, could not know that at the time.

Rochefort, worried about his family, expressed his concern in a way that baffled them for years to come. Sometime in the afternoon, he ordered one of his yeomen to deliver a loaded pistol to his wife at their Manoa Valley home. "Joe wants you to have this," the sailor told Fay. "This is to protect yourself with," he added, referring to reports suggesting the possibility of a land invasion by the Japanese.

Fay was flabbergasted. "I don't think my mother had ever even seen a gun, much less fired one," Janet said years later. As she remembered the scene, "My mother thanked him profusely. Then, when he was gone, she took the bullets out of the gun and put it away in the closet. My father was kind of annoyed when he found that out."[38]

The wives and children of many military families were picked up during the day and relocated to quarters where it was believed they would be safer in the event of an invasion. Not the Rochefort family. They remained home this day, waiting for word from Joe. Fay could take some comfort in that she, unlike the wives of most men assigned to Hypo, had some notion what her husband did at Pearl Harbor. Security considerations kept Hypo's officers and men from discussing their work, even with their wives.[39] Rochefort was as tight-lipped as any of them, but Joe and Fay had been together so long that she had acquired a grasp of what he did. Understanding the importance of his work alleviated some of the anxiety about not knowing what was going on at Pearl.

For now, Fay and the family had to get along without Joe. "I don't think we saw him again for about three weeks," recalled Janet. "He just stayed out there at Pearl."[40]

⁘ ■ ⁘

As the day wore on, Heeia's radiomen redoubled their efforts to locate Nagumo's First Air Fleet. Now fully grasping what had happened that morning, they were as stunned and shocked and frustrated as were Rochefort's analysts at Pearl Harbor. "[All] of us felt the remorse of participating in a tremendous intelligence failure," Gilven Slonim wrote later. He had been relieved earlier in the morning by Tex Biard and was driving slowly along the narrow North Coast highway when the attack began. He pulled off the road to watch, then returned as fast as he could to Station H, arriving just in time to find nearly all of Heeia's thirty-plus radio operators crowding into the small station.

"Even with increased activity the atmosphere was oppressive: We were anxious," Slonim wrote. "More people listened intently for voice communications from the attacking aircraft. We could hardly believe the ominous Japanese silence on the air. Pulling out of their dives, Japanese aircraft flew overhead. Luckily they showed no interest in our station. We were not a target."[41]

The Station H men managed that morning to pick up only the bilateral bearing of the *Akagi*, identified by the familiar "fist" of its radio operator, who used "his transmitting key as if he is kicking it with his foot."[42] After that radio burst they hit a brick wall. Neither the DF operators nor the radiomen, by now surfing every relevant frequency on all the station's two dozen radios, picked up another signal they could be sure had emanated from the striking force.

By late afternoon the Navy started getting very strong evidence that the attacking planes had originated from the north, not the south. One intriguing report came from Hypo linguist Lasswell, who late in the day was on duty several blocks from the basement, near the eastern bank of the Pearl Harbor channel. A Japanese plane had crashed in that vicinity, and Lasswell was among those pulling the dead pilot out of his cockpit. Good intelligence officer that he was, he went through the man's clothing to see if there was anything of interest. There was.

"He was wearing heavy woolen clothing underneath his flight suit," Lasswell wrote. "I rushed back and called Layton," who, Lasswell knew, was wrestling with the north-south question. "I told him, 'This aviator came from the north. He was in heavy clothing, and I think you can feel very certain that his plane came from the north.'"[43]

What Layton did with this information isn't known. He never acknowledged receiving it. What may have happened was that he jumbled together Lasswell's report with a similar discovery that had just come to his attention. Late in the morning, a chart had been recovered from a Japanese bomber that had crashed. The chart consisted of navigation lines indicating that the plane had been launched from a point 250 miles north of Oahu.[44]

Now, late in the day, the chart had finally worked its way into the hands of an excited Layton. "This proved, for the first time, that the enemy was definitely to the north," Layton said. "With the 'plot board' was a temporary call sign card listing the call signs for the 'Carrier Task Force Commander,' the 'Task Force' (collectively), for the aircraft carriers *Akagi, Kaga, Hiryu, Soryu, Shokaku,* and *Zuikaku,*'" as well as the call signs used by other ships attached to the striking force. "Thus, by late afternoon we knew the composition of the enemy task force."[45]

What happened to this seemingly crucial information was never clear. Layton said he turned it over to Rochefort. Presumably he also took it down the hall to Kimmel's office. But Poco Smith, Kimmel's chief of staff, testified later that two days passed before he received information definitely establishing the direction from which the Japanese planes had attacked.[46] That would have been very late, but plausible given the confusion surrounding nearly all activity at fleet headquarters.

ıı▪ıı

As daylight faded on Sunday afternoon, 7 December, Rochefort's team—his radiomen at Heeia and his analysts at Pearl Harbor—continued to search for the striking force. True, Rochefort had received compelling evidence from Lasswell and Layton indicating that Nagumo's planes had come from the north. But even if that was correct, as Rochefort had every reason to believe, those morsels of information revealed nothing about where Nagumo was right now, late Sunday afternoon. Was he moving away from Hawaii? If so, by what route? Or, just as likely, was he approaching the island? Was the Sunday morning raid, as some Army people feared, a prelude to a land invasion?

Layton's plot board might have convinced Rochefort of the northerly origins of the striking force. But, like Poco Smith, he wasn't sure until Tuesday. That's when Hypo's direction finders, by then including Lualualei's reactivated CXK, picked up another set of bearings from Nagumo's striking force after nearly two days of radio silence. Rochefort's traffic analysts fixed the *kido butai*'s carriers as approximately six hundred miles northwest of Hawaii, moving in the direction of Midway.[47] The striking force by then was too far away for pursuit; Nagumo had successfully made his getaway.

But that knowledge was days away for Rochefort. Early in the evening of 7 December, with night approaching, the island's military chieftains struggled to calculate the danger ahead. Neither Kimmel's people at Pearl Harbor nor Short's staff at Fort Shafter had any idea what the Japanese might do next. Scouting planes couldn't fly at night, and patrol boats couldn't be everywhere. The job of locating the enemy fell primarily on Rochefort's group. There would be no going home this night. He ordered cots brought in for officers and men he particularly needed. Lasswell put a cot behind his desk. Rochefort put his in a closed-off space at one end of the basement. It would be his home away from home for weeks.

Even though they didn't find the Japanese that night, for Rochefort, as for millions of Americans, 7 December 1941 marked a turning point. It was his first major crisis in a leadership capacity. As the officer in charge of a top-secret unit in an emergency, he had demonstrated what he could do. He had rallied his officers and men and imposed a semblance of order on a chaotic situation. He made a strong impression on his colleagues, individuals who in the past had liked and respected him but regarded him as sometimes remote, even icy. Not now.

"Rochefort was marvelous," said Ham Wright. "He pulled everybody together beautifully. He got various people doing all kinds of things. He had one guy going out to bring in cots to sleep in at night; we were definitely on permanent watch. Water, bread and food coming in."[48]

The day never really ended. Virtually everything Rochefort and his co-mint team did on 8 December and the days that followed was somehow an extension of what they began on that fateful Sunday, triggered by the First Air Fleet's crippling raid on Pearl Harbor. Nagumo's warplanes pulverized the Pacific Fleet's striking power, sinking 4 battleships, 3 destroyers, 3 light cruisers, and 4 other vessels, as well as damaging numerous others. On the airfields, 164 planes were destroyed, against 29 Japanese aircraft lost. More than 3,500 U.S. servicemen and civilians were killed or wounded.

In Washington, President Roosevelt delivered his "day of infamy" address, leading Congress to immediately declare war against Japan. The president's top military advisers—Secretary of War Henry Stimson, Secretary of the Navy Frank Knox, Chief of Staff George Marshall, and Navy Operations Chief Harold "Betty" Stark—started work on a war plan intended to bring about the defeat of Japan. At Pearl Harbor, Admirals Kimmel and Bloch surveyed the wreckage and took first steps to salvage whatever they could and clean up the rest. In his basement, Rochefort had an agenda of his own.

One piece of unfinished business left from Sunday was the decryption and translation of recent diplomatic messages transmitted to Tokyo by the Japanese consulate. Woodward and Lasswell were still working on some that Captain Mayfield had sent the previous week. Now more such messages showed up in the basement, courtesy of the Honolulu police. Even before the bombing had stopped Sunday morning, local police, working in close cooperation with the FBI and Army and Navy intelligence, had raided the Japanese consulate on Nuuanu Avenue.

Upon entering the building, the officers spotted smoke coming from behind a door. "They asked [Consul General Kita] if there was a fire, and he said, 'No; there is just something in there,'" Colonel Bicknell, Short's assistant G-2, said later. Police opened the door and found a washtub filled with burning documents. "The room was full of smoke, and there was [this] bellows type envelope that was full of papers that had not been destroyed," Bicknell reported.[49] The papers were turned over to the FBI's Robert Shivers, who passed them on to Rochefort.

Among the papers rescued from Kita's flames was the consulate's tantalizing 6 December dispatch informing Tokyo that as of Saturday, there were no signs of barrage balloons over Pearl Harbor or indications that the U.S. Fleet's battleships were fitted with torpedo nets. Referring to Pearl Harbor, Hickam Field, Ford Island, and Ewa Field, the message closed with the legendary sentence noted earlier, that now would be a good time for a surprise attack on Hawaii's bases.[50]

Rochefort assigned the job of translating the cable to a newcomer, Lieutenant Joseph Finnegan, a burly, black-haired Irishman whose battleship, the *Tennessee*, had been slightly damaged in Sunday's attack.[51] Finnegan didn't want to wait around idly, so his boss, Rear Admiral David Bagley, loaned him to Rochefort. A trained Japanese linguist with cryptanalytic ability, he was a welcome addition to the basement. He already knew many in the room, having been for years part of the Navy's small band of cryptologic practitioners in which everybody knew one another.

Finnegan knew Fullinwider and Lasswell from Japan, where their paths had crossed in the mid- and late 1930s studying the language. After his Tokyo duty, he'd been assigned to the comint team at Station Cast at the Cavite Navy Yard near Manila, where he'd met, among other linguists and cryptanalysts, Jack Holtwick, now sharing Hypo's cryptanalytic desk with Dyer and Wright. (Cast had been relocated to the Island of Corregidor in Manila Bay in fall 1940.)

Finnegan, who now had his first meeting with Rochefort, later recalled the scene. "When I arrived Rochefort was under terrific pressure because of the attack the day before," he said. "At five o'clock on the morning of the Eighth, [Pearl Harbor] went to general quarters in a full red alert, standing by for another attack. It didn't take much imagination to know how tense things were." With few intelligence resources available, all that responsibility "was dumped willy nilly on Rochefort for lack of any other facility."[52]

Back in the basement, Woodward worked to clear up the pile of non-current items, one of which was the so-called lights message that had stymied him on Friday. As already noted, he and Lasswell finally produced a readable copy on Thursday, 11 December.[53] As for Finnegan, he rejoined the *Tennessee* on 20 December.[54] He would not be gone long. He liked the work in Rochefort's basement, and he had made a strong impression on Rochefort. Finnegan would return in February and join Lasswell to form one of the most effective partnerships in Rochefort's basement.

With Kita's messages out of the way, Rochefort resumed what he regarded as his overriding duty: tracking the Imperial Japanese Navy. That task would remain formidable, but he now received some welcome news. Because of an OP-20-G decision conveyed to him on 10 December, his job was about to get easier.

14

The Long Wait for JN-25(b)

If Hypo had set to work on JN-25 as originally intended in July, it is probable that the cipher could have been penetrated in time . . . for the course of history to have been changed.

—Edwin T. Layton

Rochefort didn't make the same mistake twice. Given an opportunity to attack Japanese consular traffic eight days earlier, he had hesitated, preferring instead to keep his cryptanalysts focused on the Flag Officers' Code. But now, with Washington flashing a green light, he didn't pause. Three days after the Pearl Harbor raid, he pulled his analysts off that unyielding code and put them on a different system. It would engross them—indeed, virtually consume them—for the next six months: the main operational code of the Imperial Japanese Navy, JN-25(b).

The world had turned upside down since the district's intelligence officer, Captain Mayfield, had told a skeptical Rochefort about the availability of diplomatic messages from Japan's Honolulu consulate on 2 December. Not only had Admiral Nagumo's *kido butai* smashed much of the Pacific Fleet at Pearl Harbor, but Japanese forces days later had seized Guam (eliminating the Navy's intercept station there), bombed Wake and the Philippines, and attacked Malaya, Shanghai, Thailand, and British Borneo. Japan's army and navy were on the move everywhere.

All at once, Navy war planners found themselves desperate for information about the Imperial Navy. Their concerns heightened when Japanese forces landed on Luzon and pounded Corregidor from the air, in the process wrecking some of Station Cast's antennae, halting its operations for a time, and raising questions about how long its comint team could hold out.[1]

Laurance Safford and his Main Navy bosses arrived at a decision that they probably should have made long before. On 10 December 1941 they pulled Station Hypo off the unshakable Flag Code and ordered Rochefort to tackle JN-25(b), an assignment cryptanalysts Dyer and Wright had wanted for months.[2]

Unknown to Rochefort and his cryptanalysts, in April Safford had reversed his earlier decision to keep JN-25(b) the exclusive preserve of Cast and Negat. Frustrated by their slow progress, he decided to tap Hypo's expertise. Safford's plan called for OP-20-G staff in July to prepare three detailed sets of JN-25(b) codebooks consisting of code and additive recoveries stockpiled over the months by Negat's analysts. A master copy was to be retained by Negat in Washington. A second was to be forwarded to Cast, given preference over Hypo, this time because Cast's cryptanalysts were sharing information with British codebreakers in Singapore and Safford wanted the U.S. team to have the most up-to-date material. The third package was intended for Pearl Harbor. From all indications Safford didn't notify Rochefort it was coming, but simply assumed his old friend would know what to do with it once it arrived. He apparently believed Rochefort would happily seize the chance to work on JN-25(b) and proceed discreetly, without a lot of fuss, without the analysts on Corregidor knowing their boss at OP-20-G had modified his decision to give Cast primacy in the drive to break the Japanese navy's main operational code.

After some bureaucratic delays, the package was finally shipped with delivery intended for 1 November. But the ship that was to transport the carefully wrapped parcel was unexpectedly detained at San Diego for three weeks. Then a shipping officer inadvertently placed the precious cargo in the rear of the vessel's already crowded vault, guaranteeing low-priority handling once the bundle arrived at Pearl. The top-secret material finally hit Rochefort's desk on 15 December.[3]

By that time he and his codebreakers had already received their orders to confront JN-25(b). What Rochefort thought or said when he opened Safford's package wasn't recorded. He seemed never to have been asked whether he thought the late arrival of the JN-25(b) material made any difference. But his best friend at Pearl, Eddie Layton, believed the delay had been unfortunate.

"If Hypo had received the latest recoveries of the JN-25 additives and code book recoveries as scheduled at the beginning of November," Layton wrote later, "Rochefort might have had a slim chance to get into the [Japanese] navy's operational cipher."[4]

Historian Frederick L. Parker surmised that if, by some miracle, Rochefort and his analysts had cracked the code quickly, they might have discovered the Imperial Japanese Navy's Hawaii operation. "Had [JN-25(b)] messages been exploitable at the time," Parker wrote, "their stunning contents would have revealed the missing carriers and the identity of other major elements of the Strike Force."[5]

Not all historians agree. After all, of those JN-25(b) dispatches decrypted and translated after the war, not one mentioned Pearl Harbor by name. Of course, under perfect conditions Rochefort and his analysts might have found clues suggesting a transpacific operation—for example, Tokyo's 27 November dispatch to the striking force alerting it to Russian ships traversing the ocean's northern sector. At a minimum, Layton speculated, they would have found "indications that an attack force of carriers was heading for an unknown target."[6]

But conditions weren't perfect, most critically the time Rochefort's group would have needed—far more than a few weeks to crack JN-25(b)'s stubborn defenses. As it turned out, Hypo required three months of concerted effort just to render some portions of the code partially readable. Safford's delayed shipment was a blunder, but the key error had occurred earlier, when Safford had decided against including Hypo in the endeavor. "If Hypo had set to work on JN-25 as originally intended in July," Layton wrote, "it is probable that the cipher could have been penetrated in time—especially with the cooperation of the cryptanalysts at Cavite and Singapore—for the course of history to have been changed."[7]

Safford's tardiness aside, unleashing Rochefort's codebreakers against JN-25(b) would stand as one of the milestones of World War II cryptology. In just a few short months, Hypo would demonstrate the power of communications intelligence to shape history. But in the days after Pearl Harbor, Rochefort, Dyer, Wright, and the other members of Hypo's team had no idea what awaited them.[8] They knew only that JN-25(b) would be hard.

They didn't find out how hard until they looked at the JN-25(b) code-group recoveries supplied by Washington and Corregidor. They learned that Negat and Cast had barely scratched the surface of the codebook. According to Navy records prepared after the Pearl Harbor attack, Station Negat, as of 1 December 1941, had recovered or assigned meanings to no more than 3,800 code groups out of some 50,000 in the JN-25(b) codebook.[9]

Negat's limited progress against JN-25(b) was reflected in the 1963 correspondence of Safford. OP-20-G's onetime director commented, "JN-25 had been solved to a readable extent by December 7," a sentence that, without the caveat that followed, might suggest that the Navy was deciphering and reading that difficult code. Not so. "Of course, we were not up to date, as the messages were a month old (on the average) when we got them."[10] In sum, Negat by 7 December was able to read, at least in part, some month-old JN-25(b) traffic.

Safford's portrayal of the state of codebreaking at OP-20-G was supported by Negat's monthly reports filed during 1941. The reports contained tables showing Japanese naval messages read during 1941; month after month the number was "none."[11] Some writers have suggested that Cast had outpaced Negat. "The reading of messages of the code before Pearl Harbor, however, must be understood as a qualified success," stated one postwar Navy history. "Current messages were read on Corregidor but they were few in number and invariably were ship movement reports: arrivals and departures, together with some fragmentary schedules."[12] This report probably exaggerated Cast's progress, since the information cited, supposedly from codebreaking, could have been obtained from traffic analysis.

Cast remained a long way from solving JN-25(b). As of 7 December 1941, "we were in the initial stages," the unit's officer in charge, Lieutenant Commander Rudolph J. Fabian, told Congress in 1946. "We had an established liaison with the British at Singapore. We were exchanging values, both code and cipher recoveries, but we had not developed either to the point where we could read enemy intercepts."[13]

Rochefort testified that before 7 December, U.S. Navy codebreakers could read no more than 10 or 15 percent of all Imperial Navy radio traffic, and not even that much of its main operational code.[14] That did not mean they could read anything approaching 10 percent of a given intercept. If a handful of recovered code groups turned up in a message, they might have been able to read 10 percent of it, but most messages would have been a total blank.[15]

⅂⅂■⅂⅂

Before Hypo's analysts could wholeheartedly engage JN-25(b), they had to settle an unresolved issue. Was it still the Imperial Navy's operational code?

The question arose because on 4 December, three days before the attack, the Japanese altered their cipher system, just as they had done on 1 August when they'd modified the cipher protecting the code groups but left the codes themselves intact. That change slowed progress but didn't prove fatal, since cryptanalysts didn't have to start from scratch. Now, four months later, they wondered again what the Japanese had done. Had they simply toughened the cipher system to make the overall code more secure or, this time, had they put in place an entirely new codebook?

A few weeks into December, Hypo's analysts got some good news. They learned from Cast, whose analysts were still well ahead of their counterparts at Pearl, that the Japanese navy had changed only the cipher that governed entry into the system. The basic codebook, with its approximately 50,000 code groups, remained unchanged.[16] Rochefort and company breathed a sigh of relief.

Now the Navy had all three of its codebreaking units—Negat, Cast, and Hypo—working against JN-25(b). But that was misleading. Negat functioned primarily as a research operation, concerned more with back traffic than current intercepts. Cast was besieged almost daily by attacks from the air, slowing down its work on JN-25(b). Unavoidably the lead in this effort passed to Rochefort's less-experienced team. Rochefort relished Hypo's new role.[17] "Washington and Cavite were to assist us," he said. "We were to take the lead and they were to assist us."[18] The JN-25(b) ball was in Rochefort's court.

They didn't have to start from zero. Not only did Cast and Negat provide Hypo with all code-group values already recovered, but Rochefort and his analysts fully grasped the architecture of the code. They knew it was a combination code and cipher system, similar in some respects to the four-digit Red Code that Rochefort and Agnes Driscoll had unraveled in 1926–27 and with which Dyer had grappled in the 1930s. But JN-25(b) was far more complicated.

The task of breaking through JN-25(b)'s outer defenses would fall primarily on Dyer, Wright, and Holtwick. Rochefort would lend his expertise, but he wouldn't work as a cryptanalyst, as he had in 1926–27. The all-absorbing work required hours of uninterrupted concentration, and, as described earlier, the officer in charge of this complex, multifaceted operation had too much else to do—especially after 7 December.

Rochefort continued to oversee the work of his traffic analysts, linguists, and cryptanalysts, reviewing every scrap of paper produced by Hypo for consumption by Pacific Fleet headquarters or OP-20-G. He also carved out an intelligence role distinctly his own. Drawing on his knowledge of Japanese and his earlier experiences as a cryptanalyst and U.S. Fleet intelligence officer, he fashioned himself into a combination translator-analyst, or a crypto-linguist, who could, within certain limitations, fill in the blanks of partially decrypted messages; intuit what the Japanese might do next; connect the dots.

The task Rochefort gave himself reflected his very strong sense of his own abilities. By this time he regarded himself as far more than a technician who could break codes. He believed he could also interpret the meaning of decrypted messages. "I considered that I was perhaps fairly [better] fitted to render a judgment on what the Japanese intended than [was] the average intelligence officer," Rochefort said.[19] But his definition of his role wasn't accepted everywhere. In time, Rochefort's perception of his job would clash with that held by some superiors. The feud wouldn't flare up just yet. Right now all Rochefort wanted to do was resume tracking the Japanese Imperial Navy. To do that he and his Hypo analysts had to crack JN-25(b).

I I ■ I I

Rochefort and his top analysts now tried to penetrate a codebook consisting of 33,333 five-digit code groups, each given a numeric value (e.g., 21936) and assigned a different meaning. This could be a phrase, word, letter, or number.[20] Some groups were assigned more than one meaning, a quirk that increased the number of valid code groups in JN-25(b) to more than 50,000.[21] A particular group could have 50,000 possible meanings, or values.

Breaking JN-25(b) would be like peeling back the layers of an onion; layer after layer would have to be sliced away and pulled apart before the code inside was revealed. Each code group was disguised by yet another five-digit group of a possible 50,000 random numbers, called additives, contained in a 300-page volume. Called the additive book, this consisted of many pages of five-numeral groups, each available to disguise a code group.

Hypo's analysts had their hands full. The journey of an intercept from its first stage as a worksheet consisting of row after row of five-digit numbers to final decryption and translation involved many complicated steps. Gazing at those rows ("a staring process," Rochefort called it), Dyer and Wright made the first moves. They looked for a pattern among the numbers that revealed the indicator group, or key holding the instructions that controlled the sequence of encryption. This provided a roadmap to the rest of the code.

Once the key was identified (a discovery that might require hours or days), Dyer or Wright turned the task over to another group of cryptanalysts who began the arduous task of "stripping," that is, subtracting the false five-digit groups (or additives) from the underlying code groups. Using additives supplied by Cast, Negat and Hypo's tabulating machines, the strippers (as some wags called them) proceeded to lay bare the actual code groups hidden underneath.

Then the job was handed off to the linguists, the Lasswell people, who were, in effect, Hypo's true codebreakers, or "book breakers," as they were also called.[22] Their job was to take the exposed code groups, now stripped of the additive numbers, and from them build a JN-25(b) codebook. The first thing they did was visit Holtwick's boiler factory, the machine room where many JN-25(b) code groups were indexed. Some were already assigned a meaning, in which case the group was considered "recovered." But most code groups in the messages intercepted by Station H were blank. Armed with whatever clues they could find in IBM printouts and using their knowledge of Japanese, the linguists then attempted to assign values to as many of the five-digit groups as they could. Then they attempted an initial translation.

Ironically, Hypo's analysts were aided by the war itself. The war brought with it a flareup in Japanese naval transmissions, a change that generated mountains of JN-25(b) intercepts. Hypo's cryppies, as Rochefort's cryptanalysts called themselves, would no longer be stymied by too little traffic. Help also arrived from the outside. Throughout December Cast's besieged analysts, still working in their much-pummeled tunnel, continued to supply Hypo newly recovered code groups and additives.[23] So did Negat, which radioed an additional 2,380 code recoveries.[24]

∎

The campaign against JN-25(b) held out promise for the future, but it provided no help for the immediate task facing Rochefort: locating and identifying the Japanese warships converging on America's seriously threatened outpost at Wake Island. Within hours of attacking Pearl Harbor, Japanese forces bombarded Wake. On 12 December the Marines' five-hundred-strong garrison, assisted by a Marine Fighter squadron, beat back a Japanese invasion force, raising hopes the island could be saved.

The Pacific Fleet, meantime, was having a hard time pulling itself together.[25] After many delays, on 16 December Admiral Kimmel set in motion a complicated rescue plan involving three separate carrier task forces. Task Force 14, commanded by Rear Admiral Frank Jack Fletcher on board the *Saratoga*, sailed toward Wake, 2,000 miles due west of Pearl Harbor. Task Force 11, under Vice Admiral Wilson Brown on board the *Lexington*, headed toward the Marshalls to raid Jaluit atoll, 2,500 miles southwest of Pearl. The planes attacking Wake were based on Jaluit. Task Force 8, commanded by Vice Admiral Halsey on board the *Enterprise*, would follow Fletcher later.

Kimmel hoped the operation would "retrieve our initial disaster," as he explained it to Washington.[26] But the effort seemed jinxed from the start. Shortly after his ships sailed, Kimmel received a dispatch relieving him of command "effective 3 p.m. on December 17." With Kimmel's successor, Rear Admiral Chester W. Nimitz, weeks away from reaching Hawaii, the Navy called on Vice Admiral Pye, commander of the fleet's Battle Force, to serve as interim Pacific Fleet commander.

An experienced seagoing officer and respected as an able strategist, Pye seemed qualified, but he found himself in a difficult spot. He had just inherited responsibility for an operation he hadn't ordered. Granted only two weeks to command what was left of the Pacific Fleet, he viewed his job cautiously. Pye believed his primary task was to hold the line against further Japanese encroachments, but did that include saving Wake? With the Imperial Navy on the move, he began to question Kimmel's highly ambitious operation. Was he putting the fleet's remaining carriers at excessive risk? For Pye, the operation looked increasingly dubious.[27]

But for Joe Rochefort, working virtually around the clock in the admin building's basement, the Wake situation looked different. He viewed it as his first real opportunity to bring into play Hypo's many eavesdropping tools in wartime. The only hitch was that he couldn't tap the contents of JN-25(b) dispatches, just now being accosted by Dyer, Wright, Holtwick, and the rest of Hypo's codebreaking team. The code wouldn't be readable for many weeks.

To keep the Navy's high command posted, Rochefort fell back on his old standby, traffic analysis. Benefiting from an inspired effort by Huckins and Williams, Hypo now provided a remarkably clear picture of what was happening in the waters around Wake. In a short time, using all the techniques of radio intelligence—direction finding, call-sign analysis, and traffic analysis—Rochefort was able to inform Admiral Pye about the composition, location, and likely future positions of the Japanese Wake Island assault force.[28]

Rochefort alerted Pye to IJN radio traffic for 20–23 December showing that Admiral Nagumo had detached two carriers—the *Soryu* and *Hiryu*—

from the *kido butai*, along with several cruisers and destroyers, to join the Wake invasion force.[29] As was his practice by now, Rochefort didn't presume to offer Pye advice, but in the confines of the basement he expressed the belief that the Navy's three task forces could potentially spring a surprise on the fast-charging Japanese. "I thought that it was an opportunity for fame and fortune for Willie Pye," Rochefort said later.[30] Assuming the role of a Monday-morning quarterback—a temptation he usually resisted—Rochefort conjectured, "There was very little risk involved in this, because the Japanese at that time had no knowledge of the location of any of our carriers, and I'm reasonably sure . . . that any hostile action on our part by way of our carriers would have been a tremendous surprise to them and probably would have been successful."

But he didn't pass these thoughts on to Admiral Pye. True to his creed, he continued to keep his distance from operations, setting a tone he would maintain in the months ahead. Even though convinced that Pye's forces could have caught the Japanese off guard, he believed the operation was none of his business, at least as an intelligence officer. "I did not know and I did not want to know and I didn't need to know what plans CINCPAC was developing [with regard to Wake]," Rochefort said.[31]

Whether Rochefort's intuition about Wake was right or wrong would remain conjecture. Looking at the same data as Rochefort, Pye reached a different conclusion. He considered Japan's heightened air activity in the Marshalls, and he weighed Japan's sizable force around Wake. He worried about the risk to his carriers. He was reinforced in his doubts by a message from CNO Stark telling him that he and Admiral Ernest J. King, soon to be sworn in as commander in chief of all U.S. naval forces, viewed Wake as more trouble than it was worth.[32] On 22 December, Pye halted the rescue effort. Wake fell to the Japanese on 23 December.

⁝ ▮ ⁝

In the days following Wake's surrender, a pall settled over the base. Still reeling from the 7 December attack and now infuriated by the failure of the Wake rescue mission, Navy people battled fatigue mixed with rage and bitterness. It didn't last. Slowly, the Navy shifted gears. Engineers mobilized work crews to salvage damaged ships piled in the harbor. But all was not well at fleet headquarters. Navy brass seemed confused about what to do next.[33]

The linguists and codebreakers in Rochefort's basement shared in the general feeling of disappointment, but eventually the gloom lifted. Hypo's crew worked around the clock, energized by Rochefort's example. In the weeks following the attack, "I spent all my time at the office," Rochefort said. "I'd come home every third or fourth or fifth day or something like that and get sort of cleaned up."[34] Everyone wanted to get back at the Japanese.

But Hypo's crew ran into roadblocks. Rochefort still had no teleprinter link with either Heeia or Lualualei. Intercepts picked up at Heeia and DF bearings collected at Lualualei still had to be transported to Hypo's basement by jeep or truck. Gasoline rationing didn't make things easier. "We were restricted to ten gallons a month," Ham Wright said, "so we had to put everybody's gasoline [allotment] into these trips back and forth to the intercept station to get the messages. Oh, it was quite a life."[35]

Nagging problems of one kind or another would persist. But the linguists and codebreakers at Hypo, along with everybody else at Pearl Harbor, were about to turn the page on what had been a bad month. Emblematic of that change was the four-engine Coronado PB2Y that circled low over Pearl Harbor on Christmas Day, before making a water landing near Pearl Harbor's East Loch. The plane carried Rear Admiral Nimitz, appointed two weeks earlier by President Roosevelt to revitalize the shattered and demoralized Pacific Fleet. Nimitz took hold immediately. He started learning everything he could about his new command.[36]

On 31 December 1941, on the deck of the submarine *Grayling*, moored alongside the submarine base, Nimitz was sworn in as commander in chief, Pacific Fleet (CINCPAC). He now wore the four stars of a full admiral. A day earlier, in another momentous event, Ernest J. King was sworn in as commander in chief, U.S. Fleet (CinCUS). King accepted the job but rejected the old title that went with it, believing the acronym sounded too much like "sink us."[37] In its place he adopted COMINCH, a punchier title that seemed to fit his temperament. The Navy would now be personified by two premier personalities: the COMINCH and the CINCPAC.

No sooner did Nimitz assume his new duties as CINCPAC than he wanted to meet individually with every Navy officer occupying a position of importance at Pearl Harbor. One officer he wanted to see right away was Joe Rochefort.

15

Pearl Harbor Aftermath

A whispering campaign has started through the Navy Department that the Japanese attack on Pearl Harbor was associated with some very clever radio deception.

—Laurance Safford

Admiral Nimitz caught Rochefort on a bad day, clearly fatigued. Even after the *kido butai* had slipped away and the threat of another Japanese attack had faded, he had continued to put in long hours. That wasn't all. Along with everybody else at Pearl, he had been badly shaken by the events of 7 December. But Rochefort felt especially chagrined because, as he put it, an intelligence officer's first job was to tell his superior today what the Japanese Imperial Navy was going to do tomorrow. "I feel that we failed in our job," Rochefort said later. "I personally felt very responsible for that."[1] Driven by a gnawing sense of guilt, he threw himself even more fervently into his work.

Perhaps because of Rochefort's sour mood, his first meeting with the Pacific Fleet's new commander didn't go well. Whatever Nimitz expected when Commandant Bloch led him down the basement's darkened staircase into the large, smoke-filled room, he probably didn't think he'd be brushed off by the officer in charge. Rochefort was busy. He was absorbed in a Japanese navy message, recently intercepted and partially decrypted. He was trying to translate it. He didn't have time for anyone, not even Admiral Nimitz. "[Nimitz] came down and made us a little inspection," Rochefort recalled, "and this was probably completely unsatisfactory from his point of view, because at that time I only had one object, which was to read Japanese traffic."[2]

211

Rochefort did say one thing of substance during his first encounter with the Pacific Fleet's new commander. He voiced what by now had become virtually his mantra, one his analysts had heard ad nauseam: Hypo's primary task was to make sure CINCPAC knew today what the enemy would do tomorrow. The idea seemed to resonate with Nimitz. But once he had imparted it, Rochefort lost interest in the conversation, which soon ended.

"I may have been a little abrupt, in that I wasn't paying too much attention to what he was saying to me or things like that," Rochefort admitted. "I couldn't recall any of that stuff at all, because I was interested at that stage of the game in what was in this message. That's all I'm interested in. I don't care about any commander in chief or anybody else."[3]

Nimitz had just met the quintessential Rochefort—obsessively focused, interested only in one thing, committed wholly to the task at hand, unbendable when he wanted to be, unimpressed with rank, impatient with small talk, even with the commander in chief of the Pacific Fleet. And willing to offend, if the occasion called for it. This wouldn't be the last time Nimitz would meet the quintessential Rochefort.

Nimitz didn't much like what he saw that day, a sentiment captured by his biographer. "Admiral Nimitz showed polite interest, asked a few questions, and departed," E. B. Potter wrote. "He was not impressed. If the radio intelligence units could do what they were set up to do and do it efficiently, why had they not warned of the impending attack on Pearl Harbor?"[4]

⠁⠁■⠁⠁

At Main Navy in Washington, a lot of people—some of them important—were raising the same question. Why hadn't Station Hypo sniffed out the movements of the *kido butai*? On 21 January 1942, three weeks after his forgettable first meeting with Nimitz, Rochefort received a troubling note from his OP-20-G superior, Laurance Safford.

"A whispering campaign has started through the Navy Department that the Japanese attack on Pearl Harbor was associated with some very clever radio deception," Safford told Rochefort. "The implication is that Combat Intelligence was sucked in by the deception and furnished misleading information to the Commander in Chief. We would like confirmation or denial of this, if not contrary to local policy, and preferably by official letter to the C.N.O."[5] Already in hot water with Nimitz, Rochefort now was under a cloud in Washington.

He didn't waste any time getting back to Safford. "The Japs did not even attempt deception," Rochefort declared. "There was plenty of deception out here, but it was all self deception. We furnished CINCPAC accurate information, and if we did not know we told him so." Taking umbrage at any suggestion his Hypo team had been "suckered," Rochefort concluded sharply, "The gang have been on their toes all the time and are in there slugging now. I repeat—it is all a damned lie."[6]

Did Rochefort really not know that the Imperial Navy had mounted an extensive radio deception effort in the weeks before Pearl Harbor? Such a notion would seem to strain credulity, given his RI savvy and years of experience. But Rochefort may not have been fully aware of every tactic Yamamoto employed. Because of shortcomings in radio intelligence that hadn't yet been ironed out, it would have been impossible for him to know everything the Japanese navy was doing. There remained yet another possibility.

Rochefort had his own rule about taking blame. He was willing to assume enormous responsibility for the 7 December debacle. But if anyone outside the basement suggested that he or his analysts might have been remiss, he resented it. Also, given his habitual skepticism regarding just about everything coming out of Washington, he might well have sensed a phony issue was being fabricated against him. His strong response to Safford's query didn't erase all doubts at Main Navy. Much to his annoyance, the deception rumor would surface again in the months ahead. But for the time being, there was only a whispering campaign.

Shortly after Safford warned Rochefort about the troubling rumors, he found himself fighting to save his own career. Just as it had for Rochefort, the Pearl Harbor disaster raised questions about Safford's leadership of OP-20-G, the entity charged with breaking Japan's naval codes. His superior, ONC director Noyes, ordered Safford and other department heads to suggest ways their operations could be improved. Safford's problems were brought to a head by a 23 January memo that he submitted to Noyes proposing a reorganization of OP-20-G.

Safford advocated streamlining OP-20-G by splitting it into two different operations—a front-line section (still called OP-20-G) that would direct the intercepting, decrypting, and analyzing of enemy communications; and a new section called OP-20-Q that would design safer codes for U.S. naval communications. Communications intelligence would be divorced from Communications security, a change that would permit OP-20-G to concentrate on essentials. OP-20-Q would be in the background.

The odd thing about Safford's plan was that he asked to be put in charge of OP-20-Q—a section that, while certainly relevant, would be of lesser importance in the war effort and in the Navy pecking order than the position he currently held. Under his scheme, he would be removed from the activity he had been associated with for seventeen years: radio interception, traffic analysis, codebreaking, and cryptanalysis.[7] In effect, he set himself up for a de facto demotion.

What led Safford to advance such a notion baffled many, then and later. The memo appeared "to be a spontaneous idea originating with Safford," observed Jack Holtwick, a Hypo cryptanalyst and later Navy historian. But as Holtwick quickly added, "doubt has been cast on this suggestion by some otherwise knowledgeable persons, who imply that the 23 January 1942 memo was written by Safford under some duress or compulsion."[8] Another possibility was that he sensed an overhaul of some kind was inevitable after Pearl Harbor, and this was his way of staving off a worse fate.

Safford's motivation aside, his memo failed to elicit any response from Noyes. Instead, either Noyes or his principal assistant, Captain Joseph Redman, passed the plan for review to an officer in another OPNAV section, Commander Joseph N. Wenger in War Plans. Age forty, brainy, lean, almost pencil-thin and dubbed Skinny by his friends, Wenger was known to most people in naval communications. Along with Rochefort, he had been one of Safford's earliest students in cryptanalysis in the 1920s.[9]

During the 1930s, Wenger had alternated sea duty with service at OP-20-G, where he briefly headed the research desk. After a tour as navigator on board the cruiser *Honolulu*, in June 1941 he had returned to Washington and been promptly assigned to the War Plans Division directed by Rear Admiral Turner.

After reviewing Safford's proposal, on 26 January Wenger submitted a sweeping reorganization plan of his own. It included Safford's central proposal—divorcing security from intelligence—but went further, calling for a reconfigured OP-20-G in which that organization would acquire "central coordinating authority for all communication intelligence activities." If implemented, this change would considerably dilute the autonomy of its far-flung units, such as Station Cast in the Philippines and Station Hypo at Pearl Harbor.[10] Clearly Rochefort's freedom to report directly to the fleet commander and only secondarily to OP-20-G in Washington, a freedom granted by Safford, would be imperiled by the Wenger plan.

For this or some other reason, Safford balked. He now withdrew his 23 January proposal and, on 10 February, submitted yet another plan to Noyes, this time retaining for himself leadership of OP-20-G. Given his long history in cryptanalysis, "I should be logically assigned to cryptanalytical duties so long as I am on active duty," he argued. After thinking things over, he now felt that his "knowledge and experience [would] be largely wasted" in communications security, the job he earlier had seemed to want.[11]

What possessed Safford to so awkwardly reverse himself can only be surmised. He probably wasn't pleased to see a former student, Joe Wenger, come out of nowhere with a restructuring plan that seemed to trump his own. He was likely troubled by the emergence of new personalities—people he didn't know well or respect—poised to run the OP-20-G world over which he had presided for so many years. And upon reflection, he surely didn't like the idea of moving from the center of action to a more peripheral realm. Safford didn't want to be marginalized.

His attempt to hang on to his old job failed. Noyes ignored his revised plan. On 12 February Noyes' deputy, Joseph Redman, announced a broad reorganization of OP-20-G with new officers at the top. To Safford's astonishment, and almost certainly to his dismay, Redman's memo named as new head of OP-20-G his own younger brother, Commander John Redman, with Joe Wenger designated his assistant. Safford was routed to the job he had first created for himself and then tried to avoid: designing new codes and ciphers for Navy communications, which he would do as head of OP-20-Q. He was out of OP-20-G.[12]

Safford's eventual eviction probably was inevitable, given the loose, slapdash way he'd run OP-20-G. Also, with the war now raging in both oceans, the prestige of this once obscure, frequently maligned unit suddenly increased. Rival Navy fiefdoms jockeyed for control of OP-20-G. Everybody now seemed to see the importance of radio intelligence, codebreaking, and cryptanalysis. All at once, communications intelligence became a magnet for ambitious officers on the rise.

ıı∎ıı

The OP-20-G shakeup didn't immediately touch Joe Rochefort, but it would have profound consequences for his Navy career. For starters, it marked the departure from codebreaking of his old friend Laurance Safford, the Navy cryptology pioneer who had launched OP-20-G's research desk and with whom Rochefort had a special relationship. It was Safford, after all, who ran cover for Rochefort, meeting his requests as best he could and, of incalculable importance, granting him the leeway to report directly to the U.S. Fleet's commander in chief, first Kimmel and now, Rochefort hoped, Nimitz.

Not surprisingly, Rochefort took a dim view of the OP-20-G makeover. Unaware of Safford's contradictory memos and perhaps too forgiving of his friend's slack managerial style, Rochefort assumed the worst when he heard of Safford's banishment. He instantly thought that opportunists, in the kind of stealthy maneuvering that was always going on at Main Navy, "had wrested control from Safford."[13] The story of his demise was far more complicated than Rochefort could possibly have known, but there was still some truth to his suspicions.

With Safford now history, Rochefort had to adjust to a new set of Washington superiors: John Redman and Joe Wenger. He knew little about them, what they thought or what they stood for. The notice announcing their appointment provided few clues. It included none of the language from Wenger's 26 January memo calling for centralization of cryptologic activity in Washington. It simply proclaimed a new structure with new people at the top. Nevertheless, Rochefort braced for changes and worried about the possibility of interference with his Hypo operation.

Even with those changes, the comint world remained relatively small. Rochefort no doubt had heard of Wenger. They had both studied cryptanalysis under Safford, though never at the same time. Wenger had served as RI officer in the Asiatic Fleet in the early 1930s, while Rochefort had served in various staff capacities under Admiral Reeves, first with the Battle Force and then the U.S. Fleet. Their paths may have crossed once, but it wasn't a momentous event.

As for John Redman, Rochefort might have asked, and probably did ask, Who the hell is John Redman? At age forty-three, he was first and foremost the boisterous and fun-loving younger brother of the increasingly powerful Joseph Redman, now number two at naval communications but clearly an officer on the rise. At Annapolis (class of 1919), John Redman had played football and lacrosse and been captain of the wrestling team—experience that, one writer suggested, might have given him his instinct to go for the jugular.[14] He demonstrated his competitiveness and wrestling skills at the 1920 Olympics in Antwerp, where he placed fourth in the light heavyweight category.[15]

Like his older brother, John had a long background in naval communications, usually alternating shore duty in Washington with sea duty on board a mixture of battleships, cruisers, and destroyers. In 1935–36, he'd served as communications officer on board the flagship of Admiral Hepburn, commanding destroyers in the U.S. Fleet—the same years Rochefort had served on the staff of Fleet Commander Reeves. Rochefort and Redman had been in the same fleet, but there was never any indication they'd met. They'd had different connections and loyalties; Redman was associated with the Office of Naval Communications, while Rochefort was linked with its archrival Office of Naval Intelligence. The two never stopped squabbling.

At the time of the Pearl Harbor attack, John Redman was holding down a vague staff job at Main Navy in something called the Interdepartmental Communications Liaison Division, in the office of the chief of naval operations. A few weeks later, sometime in January 1942, he was ordered to report as executive officer on board the *Lafayette*, formerly a French luxury liner that had been seized in New York and was being converted into a U.S. troopship.[16] Redman never reported. Instead of going to sea, he received new orders to direct the Navy's top-secret—and rapidly growing—communications intelligence program. Redman now ran OP-20-G.

Years later, Redman admitted he was a curious choice to head a unit previously directed by one of the Navy's cryptologic giants. "I wasn't a cryptanalyst," he said. "I was just a communicator, a ham that kind of grew up with the business."[17]

In fact, Redman had been a communications specialist, concentrating on the nuts and bolts of fleet traffic—working out the intricacies of ship-to-ship and ship-to-shore communication, learning call signs, sorting out frequencies, mastering radio hardware. This was the above-board world of general-services naval communications. Virtually the only link between this domain and the subterranean realm of communications intelligence was the fact that both employed radio equipment.

But Redman had other attributes. First and foremost he was a gifted self-promoter, blending likeability and competitiveness with an aptitude for winning the support of influential officers, not the least of whom was his well-placed older brother. He also had a knack for spotting emerging issues that would take on critical importance in the Navy in future years. One that he'd identified in late 1940 turned out to be particularly serendipitous, at least for his own career: the role of radio deception in naval warfare.

His rapid ascent up the Navy ladder began with a seven-page memorandum submitted to the chief of naval operations, Admiral Stark, on 25 October 1940, more than a year before Pearl Harbor. Titled "The Practice of Deception" and subtitled "Are We Ready?" the memo charged that the Navy was "unprepared in the matter of practicing deception" in wartime. Declaring that "deception is a powerful offensive weapon," Redman called for the creation of an independent section in OPNAV to develop such operations through radio technology. An added advantage of an entity like this, he wrote, was that it would "place us more on alert to practice defense against" radio deception.[18] Circulated for review to the directors of intelligence and communications as well as to the Navy's advisory General Board, the memo touched off an old-fashioned Navy melee.

Some groups were favorable. ONI, for example, liked Redman's idea and endorsed it. But the General Board, consisting of some of the Navy's most senior officers, was unimpressed. Worse, director of naval communications Leigh Noyes blew up and, in due course, answered with a sharp memorandum of his own, this one also to Stark. Taking a somewhat condescending line, Noyes called deception "a minor part" of comint and pointed out that if necessary, his department had five officers and twenty-nine enlisted men trained to practice radio deception against the Japanese. He maintained that the new "independent section" advocated by Redman would duplicate work already being done and, therefore, would be "detrimental to efficiency." He concluded that the "the U.S. Fleet had little to fear from deception at the present time."[19]

Redman didn't let the matter rest. He fired back another memo to Stark, challenging Noyes on each of his objections. He disagreed that deception was a minor part of comint—"no offensive weapon should have a minor role"—and cast doubt on Noyes' view about the fleet having little to fear.[20] Submitted on 1 April 1941, Redman's new memo came to rest somewhere on Stark's desk, and there it remained. Months passed. Redman never heard back from OPNAV.

But Redman wasn't going to let his idea vanish into the Navy's bureaucratic limbo. Sometime in January 1942, one month after Pearl Harbor and shortly after receiving his orders to report to the *Lafayette*, he checked on the status of his proposal. Looking for Stark or someone high up in that office, he encountered Vice Admiral Frederick L. Horne, Stark's principal assistant and soon to become vice chief of naval operations.

As luck would have it, Horne was familiar with Redman's "deception" memo, having read it months earlier as a member of the General Board. Unlike the other members of the group, Horne liked it and now decided to help Redman. The first thing he did was to call Rear Admiral Randall Jacobs, chief of the bureau of personnel, and get Redman's orders to report to the *Lafayette* cancelled. "I want him retained here in Washington," Horne told Jacobs. "I want him to stay here indefinitely."[21]

The second thing Horne did was to keep Redman in communications, albeit in an undefined slot, where he was to concentrate on the deception issue. His transfer to communications coincided with the reorganization proposals then being written by Safford and Wenger at the request of Noyes. Sometime between 23 January and 10 February—the period during which the reorganization memos were flying back and forth—something happened to Noyes' authority. On 12 February his old nemesis, John Redman, the same officer with whom he had clashed over the deception issue, was appointed head of OP-20-G, an increasingly valued domain in Noyes' communications empire. The development was almost certainly engineered by Horne. There was no other way to explain Redman's meteoric rise.

Redman tied his success to the deception memos. "As a result of this business, of writing a paper, I ended up in a subject I wasn't trained in," he said later. Trying to link the various aspects of his career, he added, "Of course, the use of deception and those kinds of things is kindred to intelligence; but not exactly the same line or procedure."[22]

Rear Admiral Noyes could not have been pleased. OP-20-G had been under his jurisdiction for years. And John Redman had openly disagreed with him—indeed, openly challenged him—on the deception issue. He was the last person Noyes would have put in that job. But there was no denying Horne, who had become Redman's protector, in effect his chief sponsor. Redman was on Noyes' staff whether Noyes liked it or not.

Under normal circumstances Redman would have reported to the prickly Noyes, just as Safford did. That would have been awkward now. Fully aware of the tension between the two officers, Horne relieved Redman of that necessity. "Admiral Noyes is pretty bitter at you about the things you've said in this paper," Horne told Redman. He assured the younger officer he would handle things. "Don't worry about your future," Horne said. "I'll write your fitness reports from now on."[23] Horne also ordered Redman to let him know if Noyes gave him any trouble as he carried out his duties at OP-20-G.

Noyes gave him trouble. Settling into his new job, Redman proceeded to turn out directives apparently intended to help the Navy protect itself against the danger of radio deception. Under the Navy chain of command, such directives needed the approval of Noyes before they could be circulated as Navy policy. As Redman explained the situation later, he submitted no fewer than six—all ignored by Noyes. Finally he took his problem to Horne. "I'll take it from here," Redman quoted Horne telling him.

"The next day I heard that the afternoon before, in late afternoon, Admiral Noyes had been detached and gone to the Pacific for duty," Redman said.[24] Whatever the events that had led to Noyes' departure, and whatever Redman's role had been in that change, it is a matter of public record that on 24 February 1942, Noyes was relieved as DNC. The following month he arrived at Pearl Harbor and reported to Nimitz, who ordered him to assume administrative command of Carriers, Pacific Fleet.[25]

Shortly after Noyes' departure his deputy, Joseph Redman, was appointed DNC. Like the others, that change almost certainly was orchestrated by Horne, but with King's approval. With Joseph Redman's younger brother, John, and Joe Wenger now occupying the number one and two positions at OP-20-G, the division's new lineup was in place. The sweeping reorganization of communications that had begun on 23 January with Safford's memo to Noyes was now complete. The changes were ominous for Joe Rochefort.

Rochefort didn't know much about Joseph Redman, but what he did know was troubling. His information came from his top cryptanalyst, Tommy Dyer, who had encountered Redman in the early 1930s when both had served in naval communications, Dyer as head of the old research desk, Redman occupying a higher post up the organizational ladder. Dyer recalled an officer who, like many others in communications, displayed a fashionable disdain for everything connected with the cryptanalytic field.

"Usually when he spoke to me," Dyer remembered, "it was with that sort of sneering smile on his lips that said, 'You poor, ignorant bastard, you think you're doing something useful. You're just wasting your time and the government's money.' When it looked as if the activities of that poor dumb bastard were going to pay off, then he wanted to get in on the gravy train."[26] Rochefort would have no illusions about Joseph Redman.

He and Joe Rochefort almost certainly had never met, but their careers had intersected many years earlier. They had been in proximity once, in 1929, when Rochefort had written to the Navy's high command charging radio officers afloat with laxity in their handling of secret codes. Redman at the time was fleet radio officer on the *Texas*, flagship of the U.S. Fleet's commander in chief, Admiral Wiley. If the memo had been called to Redman's attention, he wouldn't have been amused. But would he have remembered the name Rochefort from an incident thirteen years earlier?

Joseph Redman aside, Rochefort's immediate superiors at OP-20-G, John Redman and Joe Wenger, posed problems of their own. John styled himself as an expert on radio deception as it might be practiced by the Japanese. Given that background, he was in a perfect position to make trouble for Rochefort. Had he instigated the whispering campaign, hinting that Station Hypo might have been suckered by the Japanese at Pearl Harbor? If Redman indeed held such a view, and if Rochefort picked up any sense of that, their relationship would have been poisoned at the outset.

Then there was Wenger, John Redman's principal assistant and the architect of a new plan to tightly centralize the Navy's far-flung comint units around OP-20-G at Main Navy. The Redmans had already embraced the desirability of such a change. OP-20-G and Station Hypo were on a collision course.

। ।■।।

If the Navy suspected Rochefort had been remiss at Pearl Harbor, hoodwinked by Japanese radio deception, it had a perfect forum available to explore the matter. To "ascertain" key facts relating to the Pearl Harbor attack, President Roosevelt a few days after 7 December established the Roberts Commission, chaired by Supreme Court Associate Justice Owen J. Roberts and composed of five high-level admirals and generals.[27] Convened in Honolulu on 18 December, the panel over the next three weeks heard testimony from more than one hundred witnesses, Rochefort among them.

On Saturday 2 January 1942, Rochefort imparted his version of events leading up to the Pearl Harbor strike. In contrast to the grilling of Admiral Kimmel and General Short, who were treated virtually like defendants in a criminal trial, the questioning of Rochefort was tame, albeit relentless. Panelists subjected Rochefort to more than a hundred questions, covering nearly every aspect of the intelligence scene at Pearl Harbor. Like Nimitz, they encountered the quintessential Rochefort, polite but terse, self-protective, given to volunteer as little as possible, at times almost brusque.

Unfamiliar as most panelists were with Station Hypo and its unique mission, they sometimes expressed bafflement as Rochefort, in his laconic, just-the-facts style, walked them through the arcane world of communications intelligence. No, his unit had nothing to do with unearthing spies. That was done by the district offices of Navy intelligence and Army intelligence. No, his unit didn't intercept the Japanese consulate's messages. That was done by the Federal Communications Commission under Army control. Why didn't you do it? It was illegal, sir. But didn't you receive some messages from the consulate? Yes, sir, either Thursday (4 December) or Friday (5 December). Did you decode them? Yes, sir. When? Ten December. Why not earlier? The fellow assigned the task didn't do his job properly. So it went, one bare-bones answer after another.

Rochefort spoke more expansively when the questioning turned to tracking the Imperial Japanese Navy. He felt his unit had done a reasonably good job, good enough to enable him and his analysts to conclude in early November that there was something afoot. He described the buildup of Japanese forces around Palau in the Caroline Islands—all part of an expanding force that was pointed south, toward the resource-rich countries of Southeast Asia. And he described what seemed to be a buildup of Japanese submarine and carrier strength in the Marshall Islands. "We were quite positive the carriers were there. We knew that." He went on to explain that just when he and his analysts were getting somewhere, everything went silent, and around 1 December the carriers vanished. "Never heard another word from them. . . . Battleships likewise."[28] Six days later, the *kido butai* hammered the Pacific Fleet at Pearl Harbor.

What, the panelists wanted to know, could Rochefort tell them about the striking force? How many carriers were involved in the raid? "I estimate three, sir." Only three? "A possible four, but I am inclined to believe three." Wouldn't there have been more? "The others were, I would say, in the immediate area within 500 miles." In reserve? "Perhaps."[29]

Rochefort erred in that estimate. Astonishingly, three weeks after the 7 December attack, he and his Hypo analysts still hadn't grasped the number of carriers. Rather than three or possibly four, no fewer than six carriers had sortied with the *kido butai*. The mistake wasn't entirely Rochefort's. His incorrect estimate was symptomatic of a larger American blind spot about aircraft carriers. American strategists simply couldn't imagine that as many as six might be massed together in a single striking force. In one stroke the Imperial Navy had changed naval warfare, and American thinking hadn't yet caught up with that fact.[30]

Rochefort's testimony exemplified the strengths and weaknesses of America's comint effort as of 2 January 1942. Relying almost entirely on traffic analysis, in a feat of inspired intelligence work, Stations Hypo and Cast had forecast weeks in advance the Imperial Navy's coming offensive in Southeast Asia. If there had been no attack on Pearl Harbor, both stations would have competed for bragging rights. "It was generally agreed," Rochefort testified, "that there was a definite offensive movement. . . . The only error was in direction."[31]

But there was an attack on Pearl Harbor. The analysts of Cast and Hypo were only half right—correct about the offensive in Southeast Asia, but missing the operation in the central Pacific aimed at Hawaii. The lapse reflected the shortcomings of traffic analysis. Unable to read the Japanese navy's main operational code, Rochefort had turned to TA as the only tool available. Traffic analysts worked wonders when conditions were right—when IJN radio operators cooperated by transmitting signals.

But when radio traffic ceased or when Japanese captains changed their fleet configurations without changing their call signs, they were blinded. They started making mistakes, as when they mistakenly placed carriers in the Marshalls that weren't there.

The possibility that Station Hypo might have been duped by the Japanese never came up. No member of the Roberts panel asked him about Japanese deception, nor was he quizzed about it at the Pearl Harbor probes that soon followed—the Hart Inquiry in early 1944, the Army Board hearing in mid-1944, the Navy Court of Inquiry held about the same time, or the Clausen Investigation that commenced on 23 November 1944 and continued for months. It wasn't until the Hewitt Inquiry, launched on 14 May 1945, that Rochefort was expressly queried about Yamamoto's deception program.

Rochefort didn't hold back. "There was perhaps a certain amount of padding or repeating of messages," he testified, "but in our opinion at the time, and our opinion today, of all of the trained [radio intelligence] personnel, there was no attempt on the part of the Japanese to practice radio deception in any of its forms."[32]

Rochefort was wrong.[33] As noted earlier, the Imperial Navy did practice radio deception. Using the target ship *Settsu* and several shore stations, Yamamoto's radiomen maintained a drumbeat of phony signals from the Inland Sea during the crucial weeks when the First Air Fleet was relocating, under radio silence, to Hitokappu Bay in the Kuriles. The bogus signals continued after the fleet departed Hitokappu for Oahu on 25 November (Hawaii time). Such trickery no doubt led Stations Hypo and Cast to make mistakes, as both did on 30 November, when they placed the carrier *Akagi* near Sasebo, in the East

China Sea, when, in fact, she was part of the *kido butai* proceeding toward Hawaii.[34]

But did the Japanese navy's deception effort explain why Pearl Harbor—and Washington—had been caught off guard? In truth, Japan's raid succeeded for many reasons, with deception just one in a matrix of critical factors. To the extent that the U.S. Navy's eavesdroppers were suckered, that failing applied across the board to all its listening posts, Stations Cast and Negat as well as Hypo. They were all listening to the same traffic, and all had approximately the same capabilities to detect trickery. Some cryptologists argued that the issue was overblown. Tommy Dyer, as noted, thought that the Japanese navy's fraudulent traffic may have been wasted effort.[35]

Yet, along with the radio silence scrupulously observed by the *kido butai*, the phony transmissions almost certainly reinforced Rochefort, Layton, and, indeed, all of Navy officialdom in their mistaken conviction that Japan's carriers remained in home waters and would stay there during the early stages of the war about to break out in Southeast Asia. In effect, the entire U.S. Navy, Rochefort along with everybody else, was suckered. Rochefort's insistence that there was no deception probably had more to do with his loyalty to his hardworking crew at Pearl than any professional assessment.

⊪∎⊪

Rochefort finally escaped from the Roberts Commission's proceedings. He was not called on the carpet, then or later, for failing to detect the approaching Japanese striking force—a fact he never hesitated to bring up later on. "Nobody has ever blamed us for lack of effort or failure to come up with the right answer," Rochefort said after the war. "Nobody has ever done this. They were very kind."[36]

Indeed, the Pearl Harbor debacle went unmentioned in his next fitness report. His immediate Pearl Harbor superior, Commandant Bloch, went so far as to advocate his promotion. "Outstanding performance of duties of paramount importance," Bloch said of Rochefort in his remarks covering the December period. "Recommended for immediate promotion to temporary captain."[37] The storm over Pearl Harbor abated, but the Main Navy buzz that associated the surprise attack with radio deception would return.

Unlike Rochefort, Layton, and most others at Pearl, Admiral Kimmel and General Short did not emerge from the Roberts proceedings unscathed. On 23 January, two weeks after departing Hawaii, Chairman Roberts submitted the panel's findings to President Roosevelt. The commission held the two officers "in dereliction of duty" for not conferring with each other "respecting the meaning and intent of the warnings," and for failing to implement "appropriate means of defense required by the imminence of hostilities."[38] Kimmel and Short soon retired, leaving their respective services scorned by much of the public.

Rochefort was now disgusted with the whole business. He believed then, and continued to believe later, that Kimmel and Short were unjustly treated, set up as scapegoats to cover up the even greater sins of omission perpetrated by higher-ups in Washington. Referring to the "so-called Roberts thing" years later, he called it "a travesty of justice."[39]

By 10 January, when the Roberts Commission packed up to leave Hawaii, Rochefort's world was rapidly changing. Along with the civilian relatives of all servicemen posted to Hawaii, Rochefort's family was about to be evacuated. Fay, Janet, and Cora would be gone by the end of January, transported to California, where they would find housing in Pasadena. Rochefort hated to see them go but saw the need for it. (Son John was already living with relatives in the Los Angeles area.) Rochefort gave up his bungalow in Manoa Valley and moved into the bachelors officers' quarters near the basement.

One consolation for Rochefort in the comings and goings at Pearl was that Nimitz decided to retain Eddie Layton as fleet intelligence officer—a decision that would prove momentous in the months ahead. For the moment, all Rochefort knew about that was that Layton's retention gave him a friend at court, with the possibility that he might establish, through Layton, the relatively close working relationship with the U.S. Fleet's new commander in chief that he had enjoyed with Nimitz's predecessor. He would in due course.

The war was heating up. As Yamamoto predicted it would, the Imperial Navy was running wild in the waters of Southeast Asia, vanquishing everything in its path. There were hints that Pacific Fleet task forces might be operating soon. Rochefort's team wanted to be part of that effort. Day after day and sometimes into the night, Dyer, Wright, and Holtwick struggled with JN-25(b). Four weeks after they'd been assigned the code, it still hadn't yielded its secrets.

Some in the basement continued to reel from the events of 7 December. Rochefort wanted to move on. Shortly after the Roberts panelists departed, he got everybody together and said it was time to turn the page on 7 December. Rochefort sounded a new dictum: "Forget Pearl Harbor and get on with the war."[40]

16

Strike Up the Band

The hell with the FBI. Bring those guys in here.
—Joe Rochefort

Getting on with the war turned out to be harder than Rochefort thought. The problem wasn't only that Dyer, Wright, and Holtwick, four weeks into it, were getting nowhere with JN-25(b). It was also Hypo's exploding workload. Rochefort could limp along with his small crew as long as the volume of radio traffic remained trifling. But after 10 December, when Washington ordered Hypo to tackle JN-25(b), that changed. Japanese naval messages encrypted in the intractable code that had been forwarded to OP-20-G now stayed in the basement. Also, as the war intensified the Imperial Navy sent more messages in JN-25(b). Rochefort's traffic analysts and codebreakers grappled with more traffic than they could handle.

Early in January 1942, Rochefort got additional manpower with the arrival of eight Navy Reservists—five ensigns, two lieutenants (jg) and one lieutenant commander—each with some background in cryptanalysis. Of those, Lieutenant Commander Thomas B. Steele, recently the registrar at the University of California, had advanced skills and soon became a mainstay on the cryptanalytic desk.

The new arrivals helped, but they weren't enough. They left unfilled another hole in the Hypo system: men to run the tabulating machines in Holtwick's boiler factory. The work was crucial to the codebreaking process. Men were needed to transfer key elements from an intercept onto IBM punch cards. That work could be grueling. Each intercept might require anywhere from seventy-five to as many as two hundred punch cards, depending on the complexity of the message.[1] If it was about a tanker arriving at a port in the Marshall Islands, every obtainable fact about that ship needed to be recorded: its call sign, port of origin, time of arrival, fleet or task-force connection, communication with other vessels, time in port, time of departure, destination, apparent mission—information gathered from traffic analysis and, when possible, cryptanalysis.

The twenty-plus enlisted men Rochefort had on his staff to perform routine clerical chores couldn't keep up with all the intercepts. With hundreds of IJN messages pouring into the basement each week, thousands of cards needed to be punched every five or six days. Messages piled up unrecorded. This slowed the linguists, who prided themselves on their ability to unravel the code groups and translate them into readable sentences. But they couldn't get very far without printouts from the IBM machines, now serving as Hypo's electronic memory bank, a storehouse of vital ship information that enabled analysts to make crucial connections.

Ironically, in his quest for manpower Rochefort now competed with commanding officers whose personnel needs were very different from his. Rochefort's rivals didn't need exotic specialists. Rather, they wanted all the enlisted men they could get their hands on. Now, so did Rochefort. In this competition he was aided by an unusual resource in the person of Chief Petty Officer Rorie, his right-hand man and the basement's chief fixer and problem solver.[2]

Rorie, in turn, was aided by his own network of chiefs scattered around the base. Some were located at the Pearl Harbor receiving station through which all enlisted men were required to pass upon their arrival from the West Coast. Rochefort already had a deal with the Fourteenth Naval District that Hypo would have the first pick of new sailors, who generally weren't assigned billets until after their arrival at Pearl.[3]

It took Rorie to implement the policy. Whenever a transport was due in, one of his pals at the receiving station alerted him, and Rorie drove over to the station near Pearl's main gate to look over the new crop. Among his esoteric skills was what cryptanalyst Tommy Dyer called an "uncanny knack" to judge which of the newly arrived sailors would be right for Hypo.[4] The basement began to fill up with yeomen.

Then one day Rochefort hit the jackpot. Toward the end of December, Admiral Bloch tipped him off that the *California*'s twenty-member band remained unattached. With their instruments at the bottom of Pearl Harbor, the men weren't doing much of anything, and they might be Rochefort's for the asking. Was he interested? "I'll take them," he told Bloch.[5] He sent Rorie over to the receiving station, where the band had taken up temporary residence. Rorie did what he always did; he lined them up and subjected them to his usual grilling.

"I just walked out there and I said, 'Any of you keep your damn mouth shut?'" Rorie recalled asking the group. "Well, they all held up their hand. I said, 'Any of you want a good job?' They all held up their hand. I said, 'We can get even with the Japs. Maybe we can give you a job that can give some satisfaction, [now] that your instruments have been blown up."[6] The men liked what they heard and wanted the mysterious job Rorie was talking about, whatever it was. They seemed headed for Hypo.[7]

But securing the *California*'s musicians turned out to be trickier than anyone expected. The first difficulty stemmed from the FBI and the Navy security office. They had no trouble with the vast majority of the band's members, but they noticed that some had foreign-sounding names—Garbuschewski, DeStalinska, Palchefsky—that might be heard in some of the European countries the United States was fighting. In a Navy suddenly obsessed with security, several musicians were weeded out and dubbed security risks. Because of their names, they were denied permission to serve in the top-secret world of Rochefort's basement.

One of those names belonged to Seaman Second Class Mike Palchefsky, the young *California* trumpeter who'd been poised to play the "Star Spangled Banner" when the first bomb fell on Ford Island. "About five or six or seven of us had different, you know, names from foreign countries," said Palchefsky, whose father had been born in Poland. "They weren't going to take us."[8]

Rorie had the unpleasant task of explaining this to the *California*'s bandmaster, a hot-tempered musical virtuoso named Lovine B. "Red" Luckenbach, an enlisted man himself. "We'll take these guys but I can't take these [other] guys," Rorie said, singling out several. "The FBI won't allow us to do it." But Luckenbach, suspecting what was coming, had conferred with the musicians and rejected Rorie's offer. "Like hell," he told Rorie. "Either you take them all or you're not going to get any."

Rorie blinked. He seldom got that kind of talk from an enlisted man or anybody else. Holding his own ferocious temper, he said he'd go back and check with his boss, the manpower-hungry Joe Rochefort. Rochefort didn't agonize over the matter. "The hell with the FBI. Bring those guys in here," he ordered Rorie, who went back and told Luckenbach, "OK, the whole band is coming in."[9]

Not long afterward, around the first of the year, the musicians filed into Rochefort's unventilated, smoke-filled basement. Not everybody there was happy to see them. Dyer threw his hands up in despair when he heard that a gaggle of horn players would be invading his domain.[10] Then he calmed down. "When Rochefort came and told me we had just gotten the band, complete with bandmaster, I said, 'I figure we can use the band at labor of some kind, but what are you going to do with the bandmaster?'"[11]

Rochefort assigned the men a lot of work, much of it routine and virtually none requiring the skills of a musician. Many did little more than typing, filing, and other clerical chores. Others performed more demanding tasks. In time they became a vital adjunct to Hypo's codebreaking effort, taking over the job of running the IBM tabulating machines and transferring information from intercepted messages onto punch cards.[12]

Palchefsky, for example, found himself operating one of four keypunch machines in Hypo's cramped, sharply pungent machine room, filled with clattering gadgets that all radiated heat and their own distinct odors. "It wasn't a real pleasant place to work but you could stand it," said Palchefsky, who for months worked a schedule of six hours on, six off. "All I did was just punch," he added. "Sit there and punch for six hours, stop and get a drink of water or something, come back and continue punching."[13]

Unappealing as the environment was, Palfchefsky said he never complained, grateful for being able to contribute to the war effort without the risks that attended other types of duty. "You knew this work had to be done," he said, "so you might as well go along with it, you know, and just do the best job that you could."[14] Even the band's outspoken leader, Red Luckenbach, found a niche in the basement operation, first running one of the tabulating machines and then moving on to more responsible jobs. He ended the war as a commissioned officer.

As the months passed, the musicians won over the codebreakers. Even the initially skeptical Dyer was impressed: "To the best of my knowledge, there wasn't a one of them—some of them were better than others—who didn't turn out to be perfectly satisfactory for our purposes."[15] Rochefort liked them from the start. "They were pretty good, as a matter of fact."[16]

Even after the musicians seemed safely ensconced in the basement, the deal nearly came unglued. No sooner had they started performing their tasks than Rochefort had to fend off the maneuvers of a powerful senior officer who wanted them returned to the Pacific Fleet. This was Captain Russell Train, acting chief of staff to Admiral Nimitz.[17] Train was responding to a request from Vice Admiral Pye. After finishing his stint as acting commander in chief of the Pacific Fleet, Pye was put in command of Task Force 1, comprising the U.S. Fleet's remaining battleships, all now based in San Francisco. He wanted the bandsmen to resume their musical duties, apparently as part of an effort to boost the morale of beleaguered battleship crews. When Bloch turned down his request, Pye's staff went over his head to CINCPAC, claiming the commandant didn't have jurisdiction in the matter.[18] Train sided with Pye.

Seeing that he might lose his precious bandsmen, Rochefort called on Layton for help. "I went to Nimitz," Layton recalled, "and said we wanted the band because they could help Joe with [his work]." Nimitz cited every reason he could think of why Rochefort shouldn't get the band, but Layton persisted. "I said, 'they're not doing a thing. They're not even playing their instruments' . . . [Nimitz] finally agreed."[19] Rochefort got the band for good.

ıı ∎ ıı

Rochefort didn't win every battle. Shortly after the Pearl Harbor attack, he came in second best in a bruising encounter with his own people at the Fourteenth Naval District over competing claims to new facilities in Oahu.[20] The fight swirled around a communications complex that Admiral Bloch had ordered built a year earlier—months before Rochefort took over Hypo—near Wahiawa, a farming community on the plains of central Oahu, surrounded by pineapple fields and Oahu's Koolau Mountain Range in the distance.

As envisioned by Bloch, the move would concentrate all the district's communications personnel at one modernized post, believed to offer advantages over the many radio sites scattered around Oahu. Security would be better, radio reception improved. Scheduled to make the move were all of Rochefort's radio and DF men, the sixty or so from Heeia's Station H and the half-dozen from Lualualei. They would be joined by the many radiomen in general services who were responsible for the Navy's regular radio traffic, in contrast to Rochefort's shadowy crew that functioned in their ill-defined netherworld, not quite legal or illegal.

Under an arrangement Rochefort worked out with Bloch, Hypo's radio intelligence men, because of the highly sensitive work they did, would move into the site's one bomb-proof building. The general services group would also get their own building, but one not bomb-proof. The big move was scheduled for 11 December. Just when Heeia's RI men were getting ready to pack up their gear, the Japanese hit Pearl Harbor, an event that ruptured communications between Pearl Harbor and Heeia, caused intercept operators to go on around-the-clock duty, and pushed back the date radiomen could consider any move.

General services' radiomen were also busy, but not as preoccupied as Rochefort's operators who were trying their best to pick up signals from Nagumo's retreating *kido butai*. Thus the Station H team was in no position to prevent the general services group from arriving at Wahiawa first, on 14 December, and moving into the bomb-proof building intended for radio intelligence. When Rochefort's officer in charge at Heeia, Lieutenant P. P. Leigh, arrived on the scene, it was too late. He confronted a fait accompli, one apparently engineered by the district's communications officer, Commander Roy W. M. Graham.

When Leigh tried to reason with him, Graham shrugged and blandly suggested he put his men in the facility built for general services. Leigh refused. He called the basement, got Dyer first, then Rochefort. Neither could forestall Graham's slick maneuver. Admiral Bloch, Rochefort's longtime champion, provided no help this time. Perhaps because Graham represented a more sizable group, Bloch let his coup stand. Rochefort refused to accept it. He told Leigh to take the Station H team to the site just vacated by general services, a rundown facility located in Wailupe, a small town on the coast some seven miles east of Honolulu.

With his Station H radiomen in tow, Leigh marched the entire caravan the thirty miles from Wahiawa to Wailupe's weathered, beachfront site. Although just abandoned by the general services radiomen, Wailupe's radio equipment remained intact and was still usable for intercept purposes. The move was completed by Christmas Day. Rochefort and his crew decided to make the best of a bad deal. "Intercept conditions," Leigh wrote later, "though far from ideal due to proximity to the highway and the civilian community, were satisfactory, and the location was convenient for delivery to Pearl Harbor," some fifteen miles to the west, still closer than Heeia had been. [21]

Soon wiser heads prevailed. Rochefort and his radio intelligence group reached an armistice with general services. Under terms that were never spelled out, Rochefort's RI men moved back to Wahiawa and occupied building no. 1, the facility originally earmarked for general services. The change made sense.

Just sixteen miles from Pearl Harbor, the new site reduced the distance couriers would have to travel to convey intercepts to Hypo's basement. That was an improvement. The messages still had to be transported by jeep or truck, but the stage was set for major advances.

With Hypo's radiomen now adjusting to their new (non–bomb proof) facilities at Wahiawa, and with the *California*'s bandsmen learning the intricacies of the IBM tabulators and collators in Holtwick's machine room, the hardware side of Rochefort's operation was just about in place. There remained one huge gap. That hole was filled partially in late March 1942, when the Navy installed the first teleprinter line connecting Rochefort's basement with Wahiawa's radiomen.

The line was too slow to convey all the traffic. Jeeps and trucks were still needed to make daily deliveries (usually one in the morning and another in the afternoon), but some intercepts started reaching Rochefort's analysts faster than before, thanks to the teleprinter. Advances in hardware were matched by progress on the analytic side, thanks in part to new linguists and the so-called cryppies brought in to support Rochefort's core team. They meshed well, in time forging a well-drilled operation in which the various players tapped one another's skills and leaned heavily on the IBM machines that were always clacking away in the back room. An unusual merger of man and machine squeezed every available morsel of information from intercepts pouring in.

⑈■⑈

As previously noted, breaking into JN-25(b) didn't come easily. Hypo's effort didn't proceed in a straight line. Rochefort's cryptanalysts made mistakes, went down blind alleys, and ran into roadblocks. Three months would pass before they were able to consistently shred the stubborn defenses of the Imperial Navy's main operational code. But analysts didn't always come up empty. As early as mid-January, they sometimes decrypted a small portion of a particular intercept. The message still had many blanks, and Rochefort and his linguists filled in as many as they could, sometimes just enough to make sense of it. In some instances that was all they needed. Very soon Rochefort and his Hypo team would display their ability to predict at least a few IJN moves—sometimes into places nobody expected.

17

Koryaku Butai

Joe had a capability—the built-in ability "to smell something
fishy," to "suspect something's in the air"—to put a lot of bits
and pieces together to form . . . a picture.

—Edwin T. Layton

Admirals Nimitz and King didn't wait for Rochefort's cryptanalysts to
solve JN-25(b) to push ahead with their own plans to strike back at the
Japanese. As they shaped the broad outlines of a Pacific War strategy in early
January, they would have welcomed any news that might have flowed from
decrypts of Imperial Navy messages, still confounding both Hypo's analysts
in their basement and Cast's in their tunnel on Corregidor. But the admirals
couldn't delay. They wanted the Pacific Fleet to get back into the fight. King
was adamant about the need for action.

Tall and strapping, overbearing in manner and sometimes intimidating,
King lived up to his reputation as an aggressive, hard-boiled leader. Sworn in
on 30 December 1941 as the Navy's commander in chief (now COMINCH),
King wasted no time making his presence felt at Pearl Harbor. His orders were
tough but not unreasonable and, to a large extent, had been anticipated by
Nimitz. He told the Pacific Fleet commander he had two chief tasks: "Hold
the Hawaii-Midway line," and "Keep open the sea route to Australia."[1]

But these were defensive goals, and if there was one thing King didn't like
it was being on the defensive. Despite the Pacific Fleet's reduced capability,
King pressed Nimitz to pursue quickly a bold plan of attack. In a 2 January

The Central Pacific

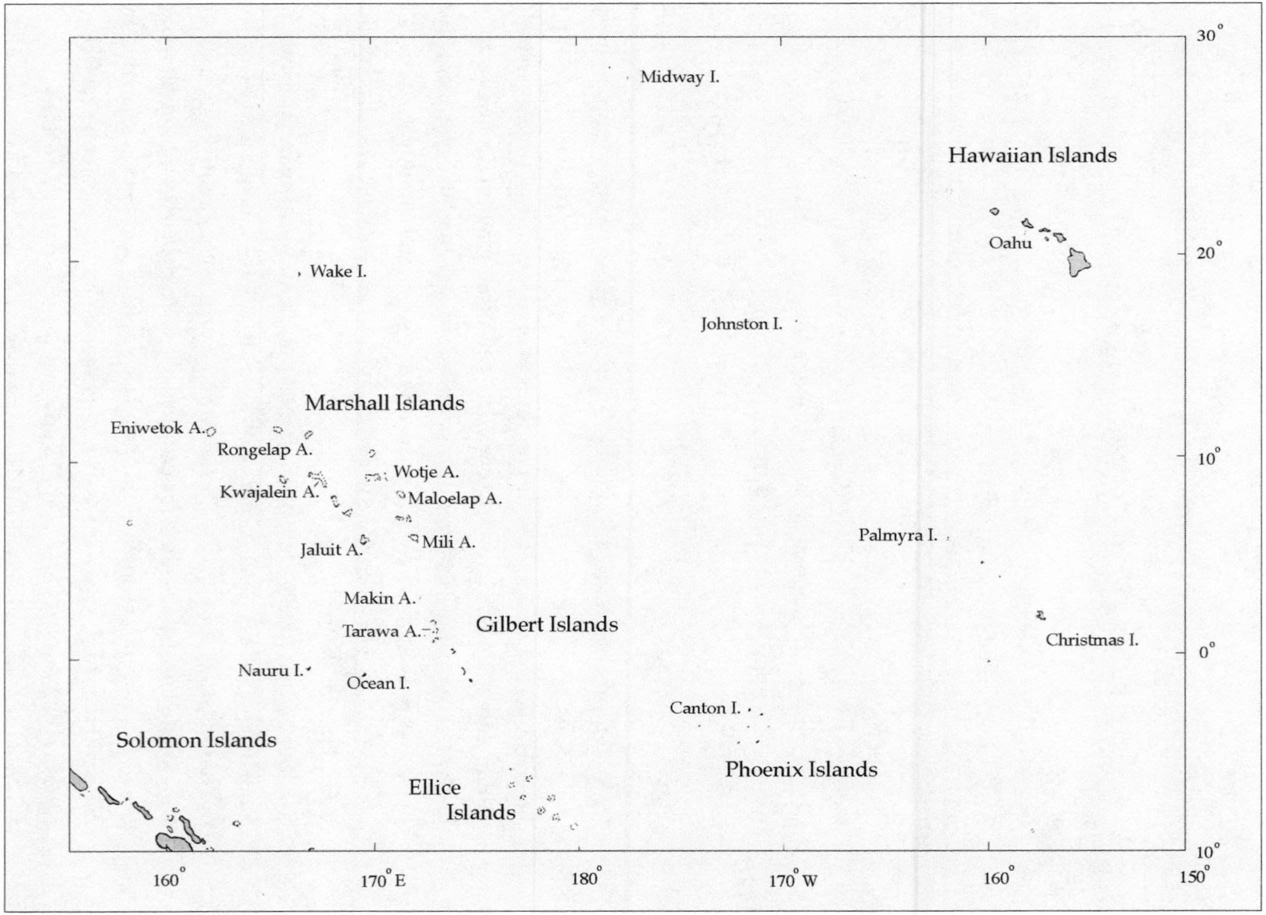

Hawaiian Islands

Oahu

Christmas I.

Palmyra I.

Midway I.

Johnston I.

Canton I.

Phoenix Islands

Wake I.

Marshall Islands

Eniwetok A.
Rongelap A.
Kwajalein A.
Wotje A.
Maloelap A.
Mili A.
Jaluit A.

Makin A.
Tarawa A.
Ocean I.

Gilbert Islands

Nauru I.

Ellice
Islands

Solomon Islands

30°

20°

10°

0°

10°

150°

160°

170° W

180°

170° E

160°

1942 dispatch to Nimitz, King called for an "expedition of raid character against enemy bases" in the Gilbert and Marshall Islands in the central Pacific. As King bluntly put it: the operation should "check increasing enemy threat to Samoa-Fiji area," an action he believed essential to calm Australia's growing fears about Japan and at the same time bolster the U.S. Navy's "general morale."[2]

A few days later, Nimitz's staff presented him with proposals for a series of "hit-and-run" carrier strikes against the Gilbert and Marshall Island chains, to be conducted before the end of the month.[3] Now it was more vital than ever that Nimitz know the disposition and movements of the Imperial Navy, particularly Nagumo's First Air Fleet.

No less than King, Nimitz wanted to strike back at the Japanese. The two admirals had the same goals but, with vastly different personalities, they differed in many respects. In contrast to the touchy and slightly bombastic King, Nimitz was unassuming and quiet, always respectful of the feelings of subordinates. Trim and vigorous at fifty-six, with a fair complexion and very blue eyes that darkened when something bothered him, there was a calmness about him that impressed his fellow admirals.[4] But Nimitz was no shrinking violet. He could be as tough and unyielding as King when he had to be, as Rochefort would soon find out.

From Rochefort's perspective, Nimitz turned out to be a very different leader from Kimmel. Unlike Kimmel, who'd given Rochefort free rein in shaping his fact-gathering agenda, Nimitz wanted specific types of information. Hypo now had to track the "deployment of enemy carriers and carrier strike forces, the disposition and strength of the Fourth Fleet in the Mandates, plus its associated submarine force—the Sixth Fleet," as Layton explained Nimitz's requirements. "Accurate information was needed on the deployment and strength of the Twenty-fourth Air Force, which was scattered through the Marshalls. Nimitz also wanted to be kept informed of the enemy reinforcements that were likely to reach the area by the end of January."[5]

All that was okay with Rochefort, since it accorded with his own concept of Hypo as a forecasting intelligence unit. But Nimitz's stronger demands on Rochefort may not have been an unmixed blessing. Historian Frederick D. Parker suggested that Nimitz's detailed requests had the unintended consequence of twisting Hypo's analysts in knots, causing them to concentrate so intensely on gathering data on Japanese navy capabilities that they missed the big picture: spotting trends that might illuminate Japanese intentions.

"The new approach," Parker wrote, "represented an immense departure from the past and indicated that the symbiotic relationship between Hypo and the CINCPAC intelligence staff had ended."[6] Whatever the reasons, Hypo's estimates during the first two weeks of January would have been a poor guide for action. The unit got a number of things wrong, placing Nagumo's *kido butai* carriers where they were not. The *Akagi* and *Kaga* were not in the Yokosuka-Chichijima area, nor were the *Shokaku* and *Zuikaku* nearing the Philippines, as Hypo calculated. Rochefort did not know that on 8 January four *kido butai* carriers—the *Akagi*, *Kaga*, *Shokaku*, and *Zuikaku* (CarDivs 1 and 5)—weighed anchor in Empire waters and started steaming toward the Imperial Navy base at Truk, a large atoll in the Caroline Islands.[7] A superior anchorage with a lagoon sometimes filled with dozens of ships, Truk was a natural staging area for Japanese operations to the south—toward New Guinea, the Bismarck Archipelago in the Bismarck Sea.

Hypo tried to meet CINCPAC's intelligence needs as Nimitz carried out King's order to strike the Gilbert and Marshall Islands. Commanded by Vice Admiral Halsey on board the carrier *Enterprise*, Task Force 8 departed Pearl Harbor on 11 January, steaming toward American Samoa, some 2,300 miles southwest of Hawaii. Once in that vicinity, Halsey's task force was to link up with Task Force 17, commanded by Rear Admiral Fletcher, approaching from the west on board the carrier *Yorktown*, which had been redeployed from the Atlantic.

Fletcher first had to wind up his mission escorting a convoy—ships carrying a Marine brigade and a detachment of six seaplanes—from the West Coast to Samoa, then join forces with Halsey in the Pacific waters near Samoa. Together the two forces were to proceed north toward the Marshalls and Gilberts. Around 31 January, they were to deliver coordinated blows, Fletcher's against the Gilberts in the south central Pacific, Halsey's against the Marshalls, a little farther north in the central Pacific.

As the operation got under way, there was much Nimitz still didn't know. He had no really good idea where the Imperial Navy carriers were located. Rochefort told him only that they were probably near Empire waters. As noted, neither he nor Rochefort knew that on 8 January, four carriers from Nagumo's First Air Fleet were hundreds of miles away from the Gilberts and Marshalls. Nor did Nimitz have a very good idea what kind of opposition his task forces would face once they neared their target area.

⚫

The Fletcher-Halsey squadrons started moving toward their rendezvous amid indications they might run into trouble earlier than expected. On 11 January, just as Halsey was departing Pearl Harbor, a Japanese submarine surfaced off Tutuila, the largest island in the Samoan chain, and briefly bombarded the U.S. naval station there. The barrage inflicted little damage, but caused Nimitz to worry about what might happen next.[8] A day later, the carrier *Saratoga* was torpedoed southwest of Oahu and severely damaged. Now Nimitz was left with only the small task force built around the carrier *Lexington* to protect the Hawaii-Midway line.

Japanese submarines were far from being CINCPAC's only concern. Hypo's daily summaries also generated unease. On 14 January, Hypo's analysts submitted an alarming new estimate, citing "rather definite clues" that some of Nagumo's carriers might be operating in the central Pacific. If this was correct, it would put Nagumo in the Marshalls—precisely where Halsey and Fletcher were headed.

After reading Hypo's intelligence summary for 14 January, CINCPAC's war plans officer, Soc McMorris, wrote in his daily log, "further information [about the] Marshall Islands indicates larger movements than previously estimated and that CarDiv 5 [the *Zuikaku* and *Shokaku*] are probably with this force."[9] Nimitz might have wondered whether he was sending Fletcher and Halsey into a trap.

Hypo's slips proved temporary. In mid-January, Rochefort's team "reclaimed its role as a valued source of strategic intelligence to new commanders in the Pacific and Washington," as Parker put it.[10] The tone of Hypo's daily summaries changed; they became sharper in their assessments. Between 16 and 19 January, Rochefort and his analysts corrected earlier estimates that had indicated sizable forces might be arrayed against Fletcher and Halsey.

Hypo's changed evaluation stemmed from traffic analysis. Huckins and Williams had spotted a shift in IJN radio traffic away from the Gilbert and Marshall Islands (the Fletcher-Halsey target areas) toward the region around Truk atoll in the Caroline Islands. Rather than concentrating in the Marshalls, as earlier communications had suggested, Japanese naval forces now appeared to be gathering to the southwest, many hundreds of miles away from the Gilberts and Marshalls.[11] Fletcher and Halsey would have clear sailing.

Rochefort's TA team had figured this out on 16 January, when IJN radiomen at Truk called the *Akagi* on a radio circuit. That transmission showed the carrier in the Truk area and presumably its CarDiv 1 partner, *Kaga*, as well. A day later Hypo analysts concluded that the elusive CarDiv 5, *Zuikaku* and *Shokaku*, the same ships placed three days earlier in the Marshalls, had joined CarDiv 1 at Truk, where many Japanese warships were now seen to be massing.[12] For Fletcher and Halsey steaming toward the Marshall and Gilbert Islands, that was a reassuring discovery: they could strike hard without having to worry about nasty surprises.

Hypo's radio intelligence had a flip side. While it was good news for Fletcher and Halsey, the buildup at Truk was still an ominous development.[13] If CarDivs 1 and 5, joined by all those transports and warships, were about to move south, where might they be going? Rochefort had a theory.

So far Hypo's estimates had been based primarily on traffic analysis: inferring ship movements from call signs and changing patterns of radio activity. But Rochefort was aided in this instance by contributions from his cryptanalysts and linguists. They had just decrypted enough of a JN-25(b) message to lay bare some of the code groups hidden in the overall system. Rochefort worked on the translation.

Around 18 January, after confirming his suspicions, Rochefort called Layton. He told the fleet's intel officer that three recent intercepts contained a common code group recovered as *koryaku butai,* a phrase Rochefort and Layton translated initially as "occupation force," then, after thinking about it, "invasion force" or "assault landing force."[14] Whichever term was used, it was clear the Japanese navy was getting ready to mount an invasion. Figuring out where was the next challenge. In each instance the code group had been preceded by another identified as the letter "R," resulting in a fragment that read "R occupation force." "Joe had a hunch that *R* stood for Rabaul, the fine natural harbor at the tip of New Britain," Layton remembered.[15]

Rochefort reasoned that Nagumo's carriers in all likelihood were assembling in Truk for a move against Rabaul, some seven hundred miles to the south.[16] An Australian port on the large island of New Britain in the Bismarck Sea, Rabaul was the gateway to New Guinea. The defense of New Guinea was crucial to Australia's security—a King-Nimitz priority.

Layton agreed with Rochefort that the messages indicated a Japanese plan to drive south and seize New Britain and Rabaul. He dutifully reported all this to Nimitz. Grasping the double-edged nature of the news, Nimitz was of two minds. "He realized that although we had no forces with which to frustrate Japan's occupation of Rabaul, neither would they be able to send strong forces in the Marshalls and Gilberts to oppose our carrier raids," Layton wrote.[17]

Rochefort turned out to be right about R. On 20 January *kido butai* warplanes attacked the Bismarck Archipelago, situated between New Guinea and New Britain. Japanese forces landed on New Britain three days later and occupied Rabaul in short order. The Imperial Navy turned Rabaul into a stronghold from which it landed forces on New Guinea. The moves put the Japanese closer to Port Moresby, the capital and largest city of New Guinea, located on the southwestern coast of that island. The Imperial Navy could seriously threaten Australia if its forces occupied Port Moresby. But there was nothing Nimitz could do about that now.

Rochefort's acumen forecasting the Rabaul attack made an impression on Nimitz. It also exemplified his emerging role as a sort of hybrid intelligence officer, a crypto-linguist who could make sense out of dispatches riddled with holes. Rochefort was coming into his own as a leader and analyst, not by cracking codes but by filling in the blanks of partially decrypted intercepts. Through inspired guesswork he could figure out what the fragments meant and what the Japanese intended. "Joe had a capability—the built-in ability 'to smell something fishy,' to 'suspect something's in the air'—to put a lot of bits and pieces together to form a vague, but definite suggestion of a picture—like the developing picture in a jigsaw puzzle," marveled Layton.[18] In following weeks Rochefort wouldn't always bat a thousand, but in this instance he had given Nimitz a hint of things to come.

❚ ▮ ❚

As Nagumo's warships mopped up Australia's vanquished warriors in New Britain and at Rabaul, Fletcher and Halsey closed in on the Gilbert and Marshall Islands. On 26 January, Hypo noted again the absence of radio traffic from the two island areas, a finding that seemed to confirm its view that IJN defenses in the region were minimal.

Halsey, as he neared the Marshalls, learned to his delight that Task Force 8 had gone undetected by Japanese patrols. His certainty was based on solid evidence. He had on board the *Enterprise* one of Rochefort's linguists, Marine Captain Holcomb. Before leaving Pearl Harbor, Halsey had asked Nimitz for a Japanese-speaking officer to make sense out of pilots' radio chatter. He got Holcomb. On 30 January, Holcomb overheard a pilot from Taroa saying he had reached the end of his patrol sector and was returning to base, having seen "no enemy."[19]

So cheered was Halsey by this news that he asked Holcomb to take down a message and put it in Japanese. "From the American admiral commanding the attack force to the Japanese admiral commanding the Marshall Island defense force," Halsey dictated as Holcomb scribbled away, "thank you very much for your very poor security and your very poor patrolling activities to allow me to make a surprise attack on you."[20] Holcomb put the message on a stencil and ran off some four hundred copies. Early the next morning, on Halsey's order, the leaflets were handed out to pilots with instructions to drop them on the Japanese targets along with their bombs.

With the Imperial Navy occupied in the Bismarcks, the Fletcher-Halsey task forces on 1 February carried out their long-awaited strikes—the first offensive blows delivered against Japan by the Pacific Fleet. Halsey's Task Force 8 attacked Wotje, Kwajalein, and Taroa in the northern Marshalls, sinking three gunboats and a freighter and damaging ten other ships. In exchange Halsey lost five aircraft, and his *Enterprise* flagship sustained light damage from Japanese air attacks, as did the cruiser *Chester*.

Farther south, Fletcher's Task Force 17 hit Jaluit and Mille in the southern Marshalls and Makin in the Gilberts. But his aviators, plagued by bad weather and poor visibility, didn't fare as well as Halsey's. Fletcher lost eight aircraft while bombing Japanese shore installations and damaging several auxiliary vessels.[21]

Both Halsey and Fletcher were pleased with the results, even though they hadn't wiped out everything in their target areas, as Nimitz's war plans officer, Soc McMorris, wanted. The feisty, plainspoken McMorris was disappointed, scoffing that the Japanese would deem the raids of "secondary importance" unless followed up by "further offensive operations," impossible at that moment. A day after the attack he was still vexed, writing in his daily commentary: "No evidence that our action in the Marshalls has had any effect on Japanese plans."[22]

But Yamamoto's chief of staff, Admiral Matome Ugaki, did assign importance to the raids, writing in his diary: "The enemy's attempt was most timely because our operations were focused in the Southwest Pacific and the defensive strength in the Marshalls was thin." He added: "In addition to a fairly big result, they achieved their purpose of diverting our strength. Carriers closed in and heavy cruisers' bombardment was also most daring. It seems we have been somewhat fooled."[23]

But it was primarily Japanese pride that had been hurt. Halsey and Fletcher, in truth, could point to little significant damage inflicted on the Japanese, but they had fulfilled one of King's main purposes: the U.S. Navy was striking back. "The raids provided a tremendous boost to the morale of the Pacific Fleet," Pacific War historian John Lundstrom observed.[24] Task Force 8 returned to Pearl Harbor on 5 February, followed by Task Force 17 the next day.

┃┃■┃┃

If Fletcher and Halsey could take some satisfaction in their daring raid, so too, in his own way, could Rochefort. For the first time in the war, he put on display the potential of radio intelligence to enhance the Pacific Fleet commander's ability to control a combat operation. By bringing to bear critical information about IJN defenses in the Marshalls and Gilberts at just the right time, Hypo strengthened Nimitz's hand, enabling his two task forces to exploit Japanese weaknesses in their target areas.

Another milestone was Hypo's gradually improving ability to make use of codebreaking in its estimates. This new resource emboldened Rochefort to eventually take a step that seemed out of character for this security-conscious officer. He did indeed agonize. When Jasper Holmes, his chief ship plotter and a former submariner, asked Rochefort if he could pass Hypo-generated information about IJN ship movements to the Pacific Fleet's Submarine Force, he at first refused, thinking it risky. If a submarine captain getting tips based on cryptanalysis should fall into IJN hands and be tortured, he might reveal that the U.S. Navy had broken its operational code.[25]

But Rochefort quickly saw that the potential benefits outweighed the risks. He then sanctioned cooperation with the Submarine Force, but instructed Holmes to "sanitize" the material: He could pass on Hypo's findings but he had to conceal their source. Rochefort imposed other strictures. Holmes couldn't take any piece of paper reflecting Japanese ship movements out of the basement. "I used to then copy the latitude and longitude on the palm of my hand," Holmes said, "and go over to SUBPAC [headquarters]. I told them here was the target at such and such a point on such and such a day."[26]

Soon information about routes taken by IJN carriers was circulated to two U.S. submarines, the *Grayling* and *Narwhal*, both patrolling waters off the Carolines. Both subs got off shots but missed. The *Gudgeon,* on patrol near Kwajalein in the Marshalls in late January, fared better, sinking the Japanese sub *I-173.* It was the first major Japanese man-of-war sunk in the war and the first directly traceable to leads supplied by radio intelligence.[27] Although they wouldn't come right away, more successes would follow.

Hypo still had a long way to go before it could read more than shards of JN-25(b). But as Rochefort's mid-January translation of an Imperial Navy code fragment demonstrated, Hypo's cryptanalysts could often break enough of JN-25(b) to indicate the direction of a Japanese offensive. By accurately forecasting the Japanese navy's strike against Rabaul several days in advance, Rochefort provided the Navy's high command a preview of the role Hypo's comint product would play in Nimitz's own offensive actions in the months ahead.

Two months into the war, Rochefort's RI operation was gaining greater visibility at CINCPAC headquarters. But it wasn't only through Hypo's daily summaries or Rochefort's flashes of insight that the unit was making its presence felt. It was also coming to the attention of Pearl's top brass because of another Hypo contribution to the war effort, one about which Rochefort at first had mixed feelings. However, this effort was one initiated by Nimitz himself.

Nimitz was so impressed with what he had heard from Halsey about Captain Holcomb's translating accomplishments on board the *Enterprise* that he wanted to expand that activity. He ordered Rochefort to assign—in effect, to "volunteer"—as many as three linguists and at least nine radio operators for service on board the Pacific Fleet's carrier task forces. The prospect that Hypo would lose to sea duty several of its prized, hard-to-come-by linguists for months at a time created a furor in the basement.

"There was considerable argument about whether these teams were more valuable on board carriers or back at [Hypo] and the intercept station, where they were badly needed," Holmes wrote later.[28] However Rochefort felt about the matter, there was nothing he could do about it. Orders were orders; he looked for suitable "candidates" and found two.

As Tex Biard remembered his recruitment, Rochefort called him and Gil Slonim to his desk on the morning of 14 February. "Looking quite seriously, [he] turned to me and said, 'Tex, you are senior, so you call the toss.'" With that Rochefort took a coin from his pocket. "Heads, commander," Biard said. "All right, Tex, if it comes up heads you will go on *Enterprise* with Admiral Halsey. If it comes up tails, you go on *Yorktown* with Admiral Fletcher."[29] Rochefort tossed the coin; it came up tails, ticketing Biard for the *Yorktown*.

Biard called the coin toss the poorest choice he ever made, the consequence of the stormy relationship he would have later with Fletcher.[30] But he didn't know that on 15 February, when he clambered on board the *Yorktown*. The carrier sortied from Pearl the same day, bound for Japanese-controlled Marcus Island, only to be diverted to the south Pacific where it would soon participate in a strike against Salamaua, New Guinea. Later the *Yorktown* would play a critical role in what became known as the Battle of the Coral Sea, but that was months away. Biard would be at sea 101 days.

Slonim, meantime, was attached to Halsey's staff and departed on board the *Enterprise*, part of a task force that would make strikes against Wake and Marcus Islands in late February and early March.[31] Rochefort tapped one other officer for intelligence duty afloat: Ranson Fullinwider, Lasswell's longtime partner on the linguists' desk. Rochefort put "Fully" on the carrier *Lexington*, which in May joined the *Yorktown* in the Coral Sea.

Why Rochefort singled out Holcomb, Biard, Slonim, and Fullinwider for sea duty and not others was never clear. Of course, he didn't have an infinite number of language officers from whom to choose. He had to pick somebody. But Rochefort could be quirky. He had his moods, his silences, times when he wanted to do nothing but focus on a problem. He had his own way of enforcing the calm he cherished. Officers who liked to visit or talk often were assigned to sea duty, recalled Rear Admiral Showers. "He didn't like anyone around who he considered noisy or disruptive," Showers said.[32]

The four linguists formed the advance guard of what would turn out to be a sizable phalanx of linguists and RI operators serving afloat during the Pacific War. Navy brass regarded them as one of the U.S. Navy's more successful ventures into radio intelligence.[33]

By the end of February 1942, Rochefort's Hypo team functioned as an integral part of the Pacific Fleet both ashore and afloat. Rochefort could take some satisfaction in this. His analysts and radiomen were now making an impact. Along with all other branches of the Navy, they were taking the war to the Japanese. The last thing Rochefort, or for that matter anyone else at Pearl Harbor, expected was that the Japanese would take the war back to Hawaii.

18

Not a Very Glorious Incident

> I just threw up my hands and said it might be a good idea to
> remind everybody concerned that this nation [is] at war.
>
> —Joe Rochefort

Around the middle of February 1942, Rochefort's traffic analysts spotted something unusual in Imperial Navy messages flowing in and out of the Marshalls Islands. They picked up clues indicating that a new operation, decidedly out of the ordinary, was in the works against American positions in the central Pacific.[1] But the data were sketchy: much remained unknown.

For weeks Hypo's analysts struggled to find out more: How big was the attack going to be, and when would it occur? They also weren't sure of the target. Midway Island (1,225 miles northwest of Pearl Harbor), Palmyra Island (994 miles to the southwest), Johnston Island (720 miles southwest), and even Oahu all seemed like possibilities. About the only thing analysts knew definitely was that the operation would involve seaplanes, now arriving at a Japanese base in the relatively nearby Marshalls.

Oddly, Hawaii's defenders had gotten used to the occasional IJN recon plane flying overhead. On 16 December 1941, then on 4 January 1942, and even later, on 19 February, aircraft launched from Japanese submarines had flown over Pearl Harbor, seemingly interested only in monitoring the U.S. Navy's progress repairing damage at the Navy yard.[2] No bombs had fallen.

The relaxed mood didn't last. During the first two days of March Hypo turned up more details, leading Rochefort and his group to surmise that what the Japanese navy had in mind was by no means a routine overflight. To grasp what was going on, Rochefort could now tap his new resource of codebreaking. The growing ability of his two top cryptanalysts, Dyer and Wright, to crack JN-25(b) allowed him to paint a much fuller picture of the impending action.

On 2 March, drawing on a new decrypt, Rochefort forwarded to King and Nimitz an ominous translation of an IJN dispatch: The commander of an air group in the Marshalls had ordered a subordinate to transfer four-engine bombers from one base to another, where the planes were to stay "until a pending offensive operation has been completed."[3] Then Hypo extracted from another intercept two pieces of crucial information: the date of the attack (4 March Hawaii time) and the target.[4] Pearl Harbor would again be hit, in two days. Nimitz wanted to know more, but Hypo didn't have all the answers. Rochefort told Layton that Hypo had solved only the "when and where," but not the "what."[5] The intercepts left unclear the magnitude of the offensive. Rochefort thought for a time that two *kido butai* carriers, the *Zuikaku* and *Shokaku*, might be involved, although it wasn't clear how, since neither flattop was near the central Pacific.

Still, the two carriers were doing a lot of talking. "Both ships in constant and direct radio communication with each other," Rochefort radioed King and Nimitz. "There may be a connection these two ships with operations scheduled commence about 5 March"—which was 4 March in Hawaii. If in the unlikely event those two monster flattops were part of the operation, the strike contemplated by the Japanese would be sizable. But Hypo's traffic analysts placed the carriers in the Yokosuka area, far from Hawaii. Their role remained unclear.

Hypo was on firmer ground identifying Pearl as the target. In his dispatch to King and Nimitz, Rochefort added a morsel of information that nailed down the where. He noted that the Japanese used the Roman letter "K" to designate the mission, calling it Operation K.[6]

Hypo unraveled K through a combination of codebreaking, traffic analysis, and timely sleuthing from Station Cast, whose codebreakers continued to track the Imperial Navy from their beleaguered outpost in Corregidor's tunnels. Working together, Cast and Hypo isolated the two-kana designators for certain regions in the Pacific. They were aided by a message from Japan's Fourth Fleet addressed to AA (believed to be Wake Island) asking for information about the number of ships in harbor at AK.[7]

Hypo's linguists translated a telltale reply from AA: "Aviation facilities repairs completed . . . three battleships present." The message nailed down Cast's suspicions that AA was Wake and AK was Pearl Harbor.[8] That meant there could be little doubt about which Pacific island would soon be hit. Operation K was Operation Pearl Harbor.

Nimitz was convinced and alerted Pacific Fleet forces.[9] But COMINCH wasn't so sure. In a 3 March radiogram to the Fourteenth Naval District, King raised the possibility that the signals picked up from the *Shokaku* and *Zuikaku* might be radio deception, intended to throw the U.S. Navy off the scent from where the real attack would take place. Rather gratuitously, he suggested that "intercepts connected with these movements be most carefully watched and analyzed."[10] The dispatch baffled Rochefort and Layton. "It left us wondering why Washington assumed we were *not* watching and analyzing all pieces of this (and every other) radio intelligence puzzle," Layton wrote later (emphasis in original).[11]

Soon more evidence showed up pointing to a raid against Pearl Harbor. One piece of it was the extraordinary cooperation noted between the Japanese navy's air and submarine forces. Hypo's traffic analysts noticed the commander of the Fourth Fleet's 24th Air Flotilla asking the commander of the Sixth Fleet, the Japanese navy's submarine force, to deploy at least four subs to the operation. Hypo's mid-Pacific direction-finding net located two of the boats east of Midway, near French Frigate Shoals, a large atoll some 560 miles northwest of Pearl.[12]

Rochefort wasn't alone in sounding the alarm. Just as Station Hypo had for several weeks reported indications of an offensive building in the Marshalls, so had Station Cast. Now Cast added one more ingredient to the intelligence picture: a list of coded designators indicating geographic areas that would somehow be involved in Operation K. Translating a badly garbled dispatch from Tokyo, Cast linguists read enough to determine that forces in the "AH, AFH and AF" regions would play a role in the 4 March attack. "Orange operations [may be] scheduled for these areas," Cast radioed COMINCH and CINCPAC, with a copy to Rochefort.[13]

Of course, neither Cast's nor Hypo's analysts knew what islands those letters designated. AH, AFH, and AF could be anywhere. But if AK was Pearl Harbor, as they were sure it was, then the other places must be in the same vicinity—somewhere in the Hawaiian chain. They also knew that DF plots had put Japanese submarines east of Midway and in the area of French Frigate Shoals.

As 4 March approached, Rochefort didn't know what to expect. He had no doubt that Oahu would be bombed, as Steve Horn pointed out in his book *The Second Attack on Pearl Harbor*.[14] But Rochefort was stumped by how the Japanese navy planned to carry out the operation. Giving up on the idea that the *Zuikaku* and *Shokaku* might be involved, he now thought in terms of the enemy's unique *Chitose*-class seaplane carriers, the only such ships in use by any naval power. Rochefort also knew that seaplanes transported by those carriers could carry only a small bomb load, and thus could inflict little damage.

Given the absence of *kido butai* carriers, Rochefort now believed that seaplane carriers offered the best solution to the Imperial Navy's problem: how to transport warplanes from the Marshalls to Hawaii. The idea made sense. Rochefort knew, or at least thought he knew, that the Japanese lacked aircraft capable of reaching Pearl from any of its land bases. But neither Rochefort nor anyone else in the U.S. Navy knew that the enemy had recently developed a long-range flying boat very nearly capable of flying nonstop from the Marshalls to Hawaii and back.[15] If Rochefort had been aware of such an aircraft, he might have paid more attention to recent reports putting submarines in the vicinity of French Frigate Shoals, where a flying boat might refuel for the last leg of a flight to Hawaii.

On 4 March 1942, King signaled a change in his thinking. In a "priority" message radioed to Nimitz, he told CINCPAC that he no longer subscribed to "suggestions"—presumably advanced by OP-20-G—that messages from the *Zuikaku* and *Shokaku* might be radio deception. (As soon became clear, the two carriers were steaming southeast from Japan to chase Admiral Halsey, whose task force had just raided Marcus Island in the northwestern Pacific.)[16]

King also rejected OP-20-G's forecast setting the Japanese navy's raid in the central Pacific around 11–13 March. After receiving the latest reports from Hypo and Cast, King stated his new opinion. "Implications in [the Hypo-Cast estimates] that the attack will occur March 5th either Tokyo or Oahu date have some foundation and cannot be ignored."[17] Through a process of reasoning that mystified people at Pearl, COMINCH now embraced Rochefort's point of view. King wouldn't always be so flexible. But this time, it didn't matter anyway: By the time his new view reached Hawaii, 4 March, it had been overtaken by events.

Shortly after midnight on 4 March 1942, a U.S. Army radar station on the Island of Kauai—occupying the western approach to Hawaii's seven islands—picked up two blips at a true bearing of 290 degrees and a distance of 204 miles. The station reported the sighting to the Oahu air warning system, located at Fort Shafter, where the blips were placed on a large plotting board. Army and Navy liaison officers tracked them as they neared Oahu.[18]

What they were watching were two Kawanashi H8K flying boats ordered aloft by the Imperial Navy to carry out Operation K. Japan's navy chieftains had two goals. They wanted to get more information on activity at Pearl Harbor and, as one IJN officer put it, they wanted "to try anything that would keep the enemy off-balance and worried."[19] To do all this they employed their new flying boat, with its impressive range and performance, later dubbed "Emily" by the U.S. Navy.

The Emily was a huge four-engine seaplane capable of conducting patrols or delivering bombs over very long distances approaching 3,000 miles. The seaplanes caught by Kauai's radar had taken off early on 3 March (Hawaii time) from Wotje in the Marshalls, each carrying four 550-pound bombs. They'd flown nonstop 1,900 miles to French Frigate Shoals, taken on 3,000 gallons of fuel from three tanker submarines waiting for them, then proceeded toward Oahu, some 560 miles away. A fourth submarine part of the operation, I-23, moved closer to the Hawaiian Islands to provide any news about the weather.

Weather had been a big factor in Japanese planning. For weeks the navy had enjoyed access to timely weather reports, provided unintentionally by U.S. naval stations in Hawaii. Japanese codebreakers had solved the U.S. Navy's weather code. But their luck ran out on 1 March, when the Americans changed their code, which required the attacking planes to rely on what reports they might get from I-23.[20] When they didn't hear from their sub, the Japanese pressed ahead anyway. Expecting a full moon over Pearl Harbor, they were optimistic.

Acting on Rochefort's hunch that the raiders might have originated from seaplane carriers, CINCPAC around 1:15 a.m. ordered Patrol Wing 2 to launch five torpedo-laden PBY Catalina patrol bombers to search for the ships. Also, four Army P-40 fighters were scrambled to intercept the fast-closing "bandits."

As the two Emilys, Y-71 and Y-72, neared Oahu, they ran into trouble. First they encountered a tropical rainstorm, then mile after mile of nimbus clouds. Unaware they were being tracked on radar, they proceeded as best they could. As for the U.S. Army and Navy, they knew the planes were up there, but not exactly where. Three Oahu radar stations tracked several bogeys, but some were probably Army pursuit planes sent up to shoot down the intruders. People on the ground were alerted. Air raid sirens sounded in Honolulu; all military bases on Oahu were called to general quarters.

In the meantime, the Japanese flying boats continued to have problems. Coming in at 15,000 feet, the pilots could see little or nothing through the thick cloud cover. Catching what he thought was a glimpse of Ford Island, Y-71's pilot banked and circled over what he calculated to be his intended target: Pearl Harbor's Ten Ten Docks. He released his four bombs at around 2:10 a.m. All seemed to go well. But while making his maneuver, he became separated from Y-72, whose pilot proceeded, only later realizing he had over-shot his target. He turned back and, by dead reckoning, released his bombs. It was 2:30 a.m.[21]

For the Japanese, Operation K ended as farce. Unaware how far he had strayed off course, the pilot of Y-71 had dropped his bombs harmlessly on the slopes of Mount Tantalus behind Honolulu, at least ten miles from Pearl Harbor. Only a few algarroba and monkey pod trees were destroyed. Y-72's pilot wasn't any more successful, splashing his bombs into the sea at the entrance of Pearl Harbor. This raised geysers but caused no damage. Both seaplanes returned safely to the Marshalls, bringing back with them only a photograph and three sketches of Pearl Harbor. Even so, the Japanese navy didn't get through Operation K without casualties. Shortly before the attack the Japanese sub *I-23,* ordered to provide weather reports near Oahu, disap-peared.[22] It was never heard from again.

For the Americans, Operation K ended as an embarrassment. Two Jap-anese floatplanes laden with bombs had flown over Oahu untouched and returned to their bases in the Marshall Islands without sustaining so much as a scratch. Five PBY reconnaissance planes had scoured the area for seaplane carriers that didn't exist. Four Army fighters dispatched to intercept the in-vaders found nothing. True, there were reasons. Lacking radar, little trained in night fighting, the pilots were at a disadvantage. Still, the overall effort seemed lame.

Tommy Dyer and his wife were in bed when Y-71 dropped its bombs on Mount Tantalus, about a mile and a half from their home. Edith nudged her husband, saying she thought the explosion sounded like "the real thing." But Tommy was undisturbed: "Never mind, we'll go on back to sleep."[23]

Rochefort didn't take the matter so calmly. With Japan's surprise attack on Pearl Harbor still burning in his mind, he couldn't understand how two Japanese bombers could fly over Oahu without so much as a shot being fired. He couldn't understand why American forces hadn't acquired enough prowess to fend off an assault that conceivably could have done far more damage. And he was troubled that better use hadn't been made of the intelligence Hypo had supplied CINCPAC and the Fourteenth Naval District. Rochefort was angry.

He got even angrier the next morning when his immediate superior, Commandant Bloch, ordered him to report to his office. Bloch said he hadn't known a thing about the impending attack and wondered why he hadn't been told. He "was quite irritated because these people had appeared and had flown more or less unmolested over the Island of Oahu," Rochefort recalled. "It was actually incredible." Bloch had reason to be concerned. He shared with the Army responsibility for the defense of Pearl Harbor. "I told him that this information had been furnished his office and had similarly been furnished to the commander in chief Pacific somewhat in detail and in sufficient time for them to take any action which they wished to take," Rochefort said. "Apparently they decided to take no action."[24]

Why Bloch's staff hadn't informed him of the fast-developing Operation K was never cleared up. Nor could Rochefort understand the excuses given by the Army and Navy for their tepid effort in the early morning hours of 4 March. He doubted the Navy's explanation that it didn't have planes capable of repelling the attack. And he wondered why the Army couldn't have used better-equipped planes to go after the intruders rather than the more limited single-seat fighters. Of course, Rochefort hadn't gotten everything right either. His preoccupation with Japan's unusual seaplane carriers turned out to be a distraction. His estimate had led the Navy to send five PBYs on a wild goose chase searching for ships nowhere near Hawaiian waters.

But Rochefort believed he and his analysts had done their job well. They had supplied CINCPAC with timely warning about Operation K. He thought it was sufficient to have produced a different and more satisfactory result. But he declared it wasn't his job to follow through on the information passed along to superiors or tell them what to do.

So when 4 March passed without any harm done to Japan's invading floatplanes, Rochefort felt he had no choice but to accept it. "I just threw up my hands and said it might be a good idea to remind everybody concerned that this nation [is] at war," Rochefort recalled. "That's all I could say. I mean I [couldn't] say any more. We can give them the information, but if they don't wish to act on it for some reason or other, this was beyond my control and it was none of my business." But even though Pearl's 4 March performance had not been, as Rochefort put it, "a very glorious incident," the Navy's encounter with the Japanese that night did have a positive side.[25]

It yielded valuable information about IJN operations and code designations for specific Pacific regions. Radio activity between Japanese subs operating in the Midway area and aircraft in the eastern Marshalls enabled Hypo's analysts to establish that Pearl's floatplane attackers had refueled at French Frigate Shoals.[26] Nimitz promptly sent the *Ballard*, a seaplane tender, to patrol the area.

A few anxious days followed. Concern that the Japanese navy might repeat Operation K was supported by radio intelligence, which continued to detect the presence of subs near the Shoals.[27] But Rochefort now saw Japan's focus shifting away from Pearl Harbor. On 6 March he informed King and Nimitz that the flagship of the Japanese submarine fleet was now operating in the Midway–French Frigate Shoals area in close association with Japan's Yokohama air base.[28]

Also, the designator AF now appeared more frequently in the Imperial Navy's radio traffic, clearly indicating a region the Japanese navy intended to visit. On 9 March, Hypo translated a Tokyo message to air group commanders in the mandates providing a two-day forecast of wind force and direction at AF. Rochefort read the message as one more sign of an impending air attack, aimed this time not at Pearl Harbor but at U.S. bases within range of the Marshalls.[29] In Washington, King saw the situation differently.

On 10 March 1942, COMINCH radioed CINCPAC that a renewed bombing attack on Pearl Harbor might be planned. On the same day Rochefort fired off dispatches of his own. First he alerted U.S. naval stations at Palmyra, Johnston, and Midway Islands that they might be bombed, stating: "Possibility exists attack by flying boats tonight or tomorrow night."[30] Then he dispatched a note to King and Nimitz. "AF probably somewhere in this area," he informed his two superiors. He added a kicker: "AF is probably Midway."[31]

Rochefort's hunch turned out to be right. Around mid-morning on 11 March, two blips turned up on Midway's radar. One dropped out of sight, but the other continued to be tracked as it followed a strange, irregular path.

Approaching Midway from an unexpected direction, the blip moved 74 miles away, then headed toward the island. The Emily's pilot didn't know he was being tracked. When he was 45 miles distant, coming in at 10,000 feet, Midway's Marine air command sent up four "Buffalo" fighters to take a look.

The craft they encountered was Emily Y-71, the same flying boat that had bombed Mount Tantalus seven days earlier, this time on a photoreconnaissance mission. No sooner did the pilot spot the fast-approaching fighters than he dived sharply and, looking for an escape route, headed for what clouds he could find. The ungainly, four-engine seaplane couldn't outrun the Buffaloes. All four caught up with the Emily, now forced to employ one of its 7.7-mm machine guns. The Buffaloes zeroed in. "Fighters engaged an enemy plane last seen in vertical turn losing altitude with white smoke pouring from outboard engines," Midway radioed CINCPAC. "Fighter pilot observed object resembling burning plane in water immediately thereafter."[32]

No one knew which fighter scored the fatal hit. All four returned to Midway safely, although one Buffalo pilot, Marine Gunner Robert L. Dickey, the only enlisted pilot in the group, was wounded, his left arm badly shot up. He received the Distinguished Flying Cross and a Purple Heart. Two of the others also received DFCs. The fourth, group leader Captain James L. Neefus, was awarded the Navy Cross.[33]

Commandant Bloch also recommended Rochefort for a medal, in his case a Distinguished Service Medal. He didn't get it. The rejection might have stemmed from a memo from "Pfeiffer" to "Murphy" found in Navy correspondence concerning the award, and unearthed by historian Steve Horn. It read: "These two communications should be handled together. I can't see Rochefort's part on the evidence presented. The actual attack took place just about as far from the time he predicted it was possible to do. Suggest asking Midway whether the message affected their readiness. If the answer is 'Yes'—more power to Rochefort and he should be recognized. [Initialed "P"]."[34]

Pfeiffer turned out to be Marine Lieutenant Colonel Omar T. Pfeiffer with Pacific Fleet staff. Murphy was Captain Vincent R. Murphy, assistant war plans officer under Kimmel and now on Nimitz's planning staff. There had been bad blood between Rochefort and Murphy, who apparently resented Rochefort because he thought Hypo's officer in charge had somehow encroached on his planning function.[35]

Rochefort probably wasn't surprised. He harbored a jaundiced view of many of his superiors and, as has been shown, often let his opinions be known.

And he had experienced setbacks before. Just eighteen months earlier, he had been denied a crucial promotion yet managed to rebound. Furthermore, he knew some Navy officials regarded cryptanalysis as esoteric nonsense, an attitude that caused them to downplay the importance of codebreaking.

Still, Rochefort could not have been happy. He would have had no doubts that his warning to Palmyra, Johnston, and Midway Islands had paid off, even though he hadn't been able to determine in advance which island would be visited. By 10 March, he suspected but hadn't yet confirmed that AF designated Midway, so he warned all three islands. And Y-71's partner, Y-72, did fly over Johnston on a picture-taking assignment. But, lacking fighter aircraft, Johnston wasn't able to interfere, and Y-72 returned safely to Wotje.

Because of Rochefort's timely alert, Midway's fighters were standing by and, in due course, engaged the raider. Yet he didn't get a decoration for his role in the Midway shootdown. It wouldn't be the last time Rochefort would have trouble getting a medal.

While sharing in the delight Marine fliers took in their aerial victory, Rochefort's analysts also derived satisfaction from the encounter. Because of all the IJN radio traffic surrounding the mission, they had been able to confirm the designators for each island or region involved in the operation. In a dispatch to King and Nimitz sent late on 11 March, Rochefort stated: "Recoveries of code place designations as follows X AF is Midway X AH is Hawaiian Islands X AI is Oahu (probable) and AG is Johnston (question)."[36] By 11 March Rochefort was certain that AF was Midway. And both AI and AG were confirmed as Oahu and Johnston.

Rochefort was satisfied with Hypo's work in the Operation K affair. Aside from the warnings that had assisted in the shooting down of an IJN bomber, they had identified Japan's coded designators for certain Pacific islands. Their decoding of Operation K would prove especially significant in just a few short weeks.[37]

For now, fixing AF as Midway seemed to Rochefort a useful, if not especially controversial, piece of information, just another routine morsel secured through the art of radio intelligence. Months would pass before he discovered just how valuable—and, against all common sense, how contentious—this finding was. AF would open a hornet's nest.

19

The Dungeon Comes Alive

[Rochefort] was just fantastic. . . . Always a calm manner, never a harsh word to an inferior and always a little humorous twinkle in his eye.

—John Roenigk

Four months into the war, Rochefort's cryptanalysts were widening the existing cracks in JN-25(b), permitting Hypo to reconstruct ever larger fragments of Imperial Navy messages. Breaches into the system stemmed primarily from the work of Dyer, Wright, Holtwick, and, in his own distinctive way, Rochefort. But they were aided by a steady stream of code recoveries from their beleaguered colleagues on Corregidor, who continued to decrypt intercepts despite almost daily bombardments. They wouldn't be able to do so much longer.

With Manila in Japanese hands and the fall of Corregidor just a matter of time, the Navy early in 1942 started to remove Cast's seventy-four comint personnel from their rock. Seventeen officers and men, including officer-in-charge Lieutenant Fabian, had been evacuated by submarine on 5 February. A second batch of thirty-six followed on 16 March, and the remaining twenty-one escaped on 8 April, just a month before the Philippines fell on 8 May. They left behind smashed top-secret machines and burned codebooks.[1] The unavoidable exodus would temporarily transfer virtually the Navy's entire cryptanalytic burden to Station Hypo.

Washington moved to lighten, or at least share, Hypo's load. Anticipating Cast's imminent departure from Corregidor, the Navy on 18 March ordered OP-20-G's decrypt subsection, OP-20-GY (Negat), to abandon its long-standing research role in which it focused primarily on old Japanese naval traffic, or back traffic as the cryppies called it. Negat was directed to work with Hypo's analysts and the remnants of Cast's people on Corregidor in decrypting current traffic. They would now work on radio traffic in real time.

To bring Negat up to speed, Corregidor forwarded all its code and additive recoveries to Washington via the COPEK channel. So did Hypo. Negat put this material to good use. "As a result of the close collaboration established by radio, [JN-25(b)] fell apart rapidly," said one Navy history written from the perspective of OP-20-GY.[2] But in truth, the code didn't collapse rapidly.

In Hypo's basement and in Cast's tunnel, JN-25(b) had already been unraveling for months, bit by bit. "By January and February we were well into the breaking process," as Rochefort put it. As a result, Hypo could occasionally read some portion of an encrypted dispatch. It had done so in January, as described previously, when Rochefort had alerted Layton to the Imperial Navy's impending occupation of Rabaul; and in early March, when he'd warned CINCPAC about the Japanese navy's second attack on Pearl Harbor. And before March ended, "we were able to glean a considerable amount of information from [IJN] traffic," Rochefort said.[3]

Such progress didn't mean Hypo analysts now read whole messages. Rochefort said he never had that much luck, even once. As of April he and his colleagues could decrypt, translate, and therefore read no more than 10 or 15 percent of a message, a situation that required them to fill in the gaps with sometimes inspired guesswork.[4] They soon were piecing together many more JN-25(b) slivers into partially coherent messages.

But that proved enough to give Nimitz something he didn't have before: a new window into the sometimes surprising movements of the Imperial Navy. Nimitz got an intriguing glimpse into IJN activities right after 10 March, when Task Force 11, commanded by Vice Admiral Wilson Brown Jr. on board the *Lexington*, attacked a Japanese assault force advancing on Lae and Salamaua, two port cities on the northern coast of New Guinea. Of the eighteen ships in the assault force, four were sunk and thirteen damaged, delivering to the Japanese navy its heaviest losses of the war to date.

Some U.S. Navy planners belittled Brown's action as just another pinprick. They would not have done so had they read even small portions of the many urgent messages that now passed between Japanese naval commands. IJN dispatches showed the navy stepping up air and submarine searches and concentrating forces in the approaches to Tokyo Bay. The moves indicated to Rochefort that Japan might be expecting an attack on its home islands.

When he passed on to Layton and Nimitz the news that Yamamoto's sudden interest in defense was "creating more panic than seems reasonable," CINCPAC was delighted. Nimitz relished the idea that the Pacific Fleet's carrier raids were causing havoc in Japanese thinking and causing the navy to deploy its forces against a "nonexistent force."

"A major reason for the success of Nimitz's strategy was this: In just three months we had established a reliable basis for tactical and strategic intelligence to support the Allied war effort in the Pacific," Layton wrote later. "It was our ability to intercept and break significant portions of the enemy's operational traffic that gave us the edge."[5]

Rochefort's ability to deliver such results reflected, in part, sweeping changes taking place in Station Hypo's basement. New cryppies trained by OP-20-G at Main Navy had arrived, bolstering the core cryptanalytic team. New linguists also appeared, and many more would come when the Navy's Japanese Language School, hastily created late in 1941 at the University of Colorado's Boulder campus, started producing graduates. Lasswell wasted no time finding room for the new arrivals at the linguists' table, emptier than usual because of the absence of Slonim, Biard, and Fullinwider, now on seemingly permanent duty with the fleet.

Not all the newcomers were novices. Three additions to Lasswell's team had learned their Japanese in Tokyo. Lieutenants John Roenigk and Arthur Benedict had been pulled out of Japan abruptly in fall 1941.[6] After a brief stint in the Philippines, they'd been assigned to Layton at Pearl. Believing their language skills could be put to better use at Hypo than with the fleet, Layton redeployed them to a grateful Rochefort, always happy to get another linguist.

Easily the most seasoned new arrival was Lieutenant Commander Joe Finnegan, the intense, serious-minded Irishman who'd briefly served in the basement after his battleship, the *Tennessee*, was damaged during the Pearl Harbor attack. Having rejoined the fleet in late December, he was soon reassigned to Hypo, much to his delight and certainly to Rochefort's. Steeped in Japanese and familiar with the elements of cryptology, Finnegan was a perfect fit in the basement.

Another important newcomer was an eager, bright-eyed ensign, Donald "Mac" Showers, fresh out of the Northwestern University Naval Reserve

Midshipman's School at Chicago. His arrival in the basement was a happy accident. Trained briefly in counterintelligence at COM 13 in Seattle, Showers had been shipped to Hawaii after Pearl Harbor with orders to report to the district intelligence office in Honolulu, presumably to work in counterintelligence. The DIO had other ideas.

Asked what experience he had in counterintelligence, Showers said he had none. "Well, you're no good to me. I need people with experience," the DIO's operations officer declared. But, he added, "I'm going to use you. I have a billet out at the navy yard that I've been tasked to fill for a long time, and I've never had anyone I can spare. I'm going to send you out there." If Rochefort minded getting one of DIO's rejects, he never said so. He needed all the bright young men he could get. He turned Showers over to Jasper Holmes, who promptly put the young ensign to work assisting with ship plotting, helping with code group recoveries, and aiding the linguists in their research into code groups. Showers in this way began a thirty-one-year career in naval intelligence that was to peak in 1965 with his promotion to rear admiral. He thereby became the only member of Rochefort's team to achieve flag rank. Showers embraced his new job, which he always regarded as an example of "dumb luck."[7]

Welcome as the newcomers may have been, they created a population explosion. After beginning with 10 officers in June 1941, Rochefort now found himself in charge of nearly 40, an assorted mixture of regular Navy and Reserve officers, cryptanalysts and linguists, lowly ensigns and uppity lieutenant commanders, and all the ranks in between. There were even a couple of Marines, Lasswell (now a major) and Captain Holcomb. On top of that swelling officer corps, the number of enlisted men had jumped from 23 to more than 60, raising total personnel in Rochefort's basement to well over 100.

The basement was bursting at its seams. To relieve the pressure, Rochefort ordered the west wall behind his desk to be knocked out, a move that doubled the size of the basement and opened for use an almost-forgotten staircase in the rear of the big room. It was the same staircase Jasper Holmes had used in August 1941, when he'd merged his ship-plotting activity with Rochefort's cryptanalytic unit. He would skulk in from the rear almost unnoticed. Now a full-fledged member of Rochefort's group, Holmes, along with everybody else, entered from the main staircase.

Officers and enlisted men entering the basement for the first time passed into a world unlike any other they had encountered in the Navy. In place of the antiseptic offices typical of the Navy, they found themselves in a huge, smoke-engulfed room strewn with clutter.

With its informality and atmosphere of seeming equality, the basement fulfilled an enlisted man's dream. "We never had an inspection the entire time I was there," said Ferdinand Johnson, a petty officer third class when assigned to Hypo in the spring of 1942.[8] "There was no uniform. You could wear dungarees down there. And there was none of this 'yes, sir,' 'no, sir' stuff or anything like that." The basement wasn't, in Johnson's words, a "gung ho" kind of place, and that suited Johnson just fine. Officers also liked the casual dress code, routinely wearing khaki shirts and trousers, with or without a necktie.[9] Rochefort, of course, shuffled around the cellar in his customary slippers and smoking jacket, required by the late-night chill that always set in.

The balky air-conditioner didn't trouble only Rochefort. Overactive late at night, it often underperformed during the day, giving the basement a clammy, muggy feel.[10] At times the machine would burst into sudden activity, wreaking havoc in parts of the cellar. "We had about ten thousand cards all stacked up on the tables," Ham Wright recalled. "They all got dry in the air conditioning and they exploded all over the place—static electricity. We had to spend half a day putting those cards back together again."[11]

The basement's relaxed atmosphere masked an underlying tension, generated in part by the extraordinary hours everybody worked. Even before the Battles of the Coral Sea and Midway, still weeks away, no one had been working a normal day since 7 December, as previously detailed. Schedules varied at different stages of the war. Finnegan for a time worked "a type of thirty on and eighteen off" schedule—in effect, every other night. The "normal procedure was to come in about ten o'clock one morning and leave about two o'clock the next afternoon," Finnegan said.[12]

Beginning early in 1942, Rochefort and Dyer alternated twenty-four on, twenty-four off, enabling one or the other always to be present in the basement. "We didn't see too much of each other the first six months of the war," Dyer said. "I would go in in the morning and stay until the next morning. Instead of going home when [Rochefort] showed up, we would overlap for four or five hours. But I had my head buried in what I was doing and he had his buried in what he was doing, and we were at opposite ends of the basement. We'd occasionally see each other, but only occasionally, casually."[13]

Rochefort and Dyer now had different domestic situations. Having arrived in Oahu in 1936, Dyer was considered a permanent island resident and wasn't required to evacuate his wife to the U.S. mainland, as was Rochefort. The Dyers continued to live in Honolulu. Rochefort "may have put in a little more time [in the basement] than I did," Dyer said, "because he did sleep down in the basement occasionally. He had a cot. I didn't."[14]

Junior officers generally put in fewer hours but still worked demanding schedules. A young ensign such as Showers, just arrived from the mainland, worked twelve hours on, twelve off, a schedule he would keep up for seven days, after which time he would get twenty-four hours off. "I usually went down to Waikiki for a day," said Showers.[15]

                        ıı∎ıı

The growing number of officers and men in Rochefort's basement quickened the pace of its underground life. A distinct culture emerged. Seemingly relaxed and casual, the dungeon developed its own class system. Dyer's cryptanalysts occupied the top rung, followed by Lasswell's linguists, Huckins' traffic analysts, and then everybody else—all the newcomers looking for a way to be part of the dungeon's mysterious world.

What unified these disparate groups, what brought them together into a coherent whole was the relentless work ethic: the fact that no one, from the loftiest officer to the lowliest yeoman, worked a normal day. Even those on duty eight hours worked eight on, eight off for long stretches. Others put in twelve-, fifteen-, or twenty-hour days, sometimes longer. A kind of democracy of the weary emerged. The grinding hours turned the basement into something resembling a monastic order.

Strenuous schedules aside, there were few places officers and men could go to unwind other than the beer halls in nearby Pearl City and small towns around Pearl Harbor. A stray ensign might also occasionally find his way to Waikiki. But neither that fabled playground nor the notorious haunts of Honolulu figured much in the life of the basement's denizens. Honolulu was blacked out for nearly all of 1942, making nighttime travel there difficult and dangerous. Rochefort, who managed to make one trip during the ten months following Pearl Harbor, found it "as dark as the inside of a Derby hat."[16]

Further dampening the basement dwellers' social life was the absence of female companionship. Somewhat surprisingly, women were in short supply—a situation running counter to popular stereotypes of island folkways in the 1940s. In his hard-hitting novel dramatizing Army life in pre-war Hawaii, *From Here to Eternity*, James Jones depicted a wide-open Honolulu. And in

War and Remembrance, Herman Wouk's novel of the Pacific War, there were always plenty of nurses and Waves to spice the lives of Navy men stationed at Pearl Harbor and elsewhere in the Pacific.

The reality was different. Bringing curfews and blackouts, the martial law clamped on Hawaii after 7 December 1941 quieted Honolulu's clubs. There were few places soldiers or sailors could go to meet women. Local parents weren't eager to have their daughters date sailors and soldiers, and young Caucasian women from the mainland were scarce.[17] Many had been evacuated after Pearl Harbor. Female nurses, of course, were present in Hawaii, but not Waves. The reason was Nimitz. A gentleman of the old school, "He didn't like women in uniforms, except nurses' uniforms," noted E. B. Potter.[18]

From Potter's account, Nimitz, while heading the Bureau of Navigation in prewar Washington, couldn't get used to women jumping up and snapping to attention when he entered a room. For that reason or some other reason, he saw to it that no Wave or female Marine was assigned to Pearl Harbor, and none would be until he moved his headquarters to Guam late in the war. Waves didn't show up in Hawaii until early in 1945, when Nimitz's deputy at Pearl, Vice Admiral John Towers, welcomed them.[19]

"[The] sad part of it is that Herman Wouk, when he wrote his book on the Pacific, didn't know that," Potter noted. "He had WAVES there from the beginning, but they weren't there."[20] Sad or not, the paucity of women in Hawaii was certainly inconvenient for the officers and men of the basement. Dyer and Holmes could return to their wives at night, since they were permanent residents. But many of the others were bored and lonely. "There was no social life in Hawaii during the war," Lieutenant Roenigk wrote. "We all mostly stayed on the [Makalapa] Hill twenty-four hours a day," he said, referring to the incline behind the Pearl Harbor Navy Yard where officers had quarters. "It was tough even to drive to town."[21]

For relaxation, a favorite pastime for some was visiting ships just back from the war zone, a habit that let them catch up with old friends while getting firsthand accounts of how the war was going. Back on the Hill, Roenigk and his colleague Arthur Benedict, "Benny," pitched horseshoes and played poker and bridge with Red Lasswell. With his legendary cigar always clenched between his teeth, Lasswell relished chess games with Rochefort's cryptanalyic wizard, Ham Wright.

Wright's personal quarters near the submarine base, where CINCPAC was headquartered, served as a kind of ersatz lounge for the basement crew.

Wright himself idled away many hours listening to his opera records, very often with a lot of company. Refugees from the dungeon, sometimes even Nimitz, routinely dropped in to listen to his records and play the slot machine he had on the premises. Wright maintained an "open house for everyone to come in, any time of day, play the slot machine, have a drink and leave a quarter," Roenigk recalled.[22]

If Joe Rochefort engaged in any of the basement's merry-making, no one ever recorded it. He probably didn't. He wasn't one to socialize and, more important, didn't allow himself the time. People heard stories of his bridge-playing prowess, but those tales referred to activities before 7 December. Now Rochefort focused on one thing. He also was mindful of the stomach ailment that had plagued him since 1927. As a result, he drank sparingly. For relaxation he probably did little more than meet his friend Layton occasionally at the officers' club, where Layton quaffed his cherished martinis and Rochefort, if he drank at all, sipped a bourbon and water, his drink of choice.

Inside the basement, Rochefort was all business. He didn't talk a lot, hold meetings, or give speeches. He didn't spend much time walking around to see how people were doing. Rochefort didn't like a lot of fuss. He assumed people knew their jobs and would do them. He let everyone know that he respected them as professionals and would leave them to their tasks, becoming involved only if there was a compelling reason. They didn't need a lot of leadership. "Joe was not a slave driver," said Roenigk, now working with Lasswell and Finnegan at the linguist's desk. "His own example of working around the clock was enough to motivate anyone who associated with him. He seldom left the office, but napped an hour or two on a couch just off the office."[23]

Enlisted men especially warmed to Rochefort's low-key style. "He wasn't a rah-rah person or anything like that," said Petty Officer Third Class Johnson. He liked his boss' hands-off approach.[24] So did Yeoman Third Class Walter Jester, assigned to the basement in early May 1942. "Rochefort set a good tone," he said. "He wasn't a loudmouth. He was very quiet when he spoke to you. And he set an example for the men. He was working more hours than any of us and we were all on about an eighty-four hour week."[25]

Emotionally distant and introverted as he may have been, Rochefort nevertheless remained accessible and fully involved in the life of the basement. Newcomers as well as more seasoned analysts liked being around him. They enjoyed his dry sense of humor, laconic style, and independence of mind. They brought him their questions.

As the weeks passed, Rochefort's stature grew. Not only was he admired for his competence and work ethic, but all in the basement, officers and enlisted men alike, regarded him as a "stand-up" guy, a leader who would back them if they ever got into a scrape. "When some of our enlisted men got into trouble, Rochefort would send Rorie out [to bring them back]," recalled Johnson. "He said those people don't do me any good in the brig."[26]

Jasper Holmes also benefited from Rochefort's quick action. Assigned to plot ship locations, he carried out this task day after day by relying on information received from Hypo's radiomen and his own knowledge of navigation. When one of his plots was challenged by the district's operations officer, a captain noted for his antagonism to Rochefort, Holmes was summoned to that officer's desk, two decks above. He collected his charts and headed for the door.

"I'll answer that call," Rochefort said, relieving Holmes of his charts. Rochefort shed his smoking jacket and slippers, donned his tie and hat, and marched upstairs. "Ten minutes later he returned, barely suppressing a grin," Holmes wrote later. A green watch officer had misinterpreted Holmes' data and, as a result, put a ship where it wasn't. Operations blamed Holmes. Rochefort caught the error (the young officer had failed to distinguish between east and west longitude) and delivered the parties a lecture on elementary geography. "Rochefort was amused, but I was not," Holmes remembered. "I was impressed with his instant assumption of complete responsibility for his organization, and his readiness to stand between one of his junior officers and wrath from without."[27]

⁍▐⁌

Keeping his sometimes rambunctious young officers out of trouble was minor compared with another problem Rochefort faced: bringing them up to speed in the art of intelligence analysis. Many newcomers were strangers to this arcane activity. They might know how to unravel a cryptogram or translate a sentence of Japanese text, but they didn't always know how to interpret ambiguous data from a field report, or how to draw the right conclusions from contradictory material, or how to think skeptically and question everything.

Rochefort brought to the teaching task his own idiosyncratic, sometimes mischievous theory of education, as Roenigk discovered to his embarrassment. "At my first contact with Rochefort he said 'Hi' and went next door and brought out a light chair and told me to sit down. Then he pointed out what was going on in other sections of the cellar and who was in charge, telling me to 'go see what they are doing.'" Then, Roenigk recalled, "he gave me a pack of 'coast watcher' dispatches from Down Under and told me to prepare a summary of Japanese intentions against Lae [New Guinea]. I thought any guess from that 'muck' would be as good as any other."

Four hours later, Rochefort pointed out that each conclusion the lieutenant had reached was wrong and explained why. Roenigk got red in the face, feeling very uncomfortable. Rochefort grinned. "Then," Roenigk said, "he gave his usual giggle, indicating that he was pulling my leg and that there were no real answers to that kind of intelligence guess-work, without a background of 'pattern watching.'" While Roenigk learned about the danger of jumping to harebrained conclusions, he also learned something about Rochefort, who "let me down gently and I developed confidence in him," Roenigk said. "He was just fantastic. I swore by him from those days forward and I could never have let him down. Always a calm manner, never a harsh word to an inferior and always a little humorous twinkle in his eye."[28]

Rochefort's training efforts paid off. Four months into the war, Station Hypo had emerged as the U.S. Navy's center of codebreaking activity. Shortly after receiving thousands of additives from Negat and Cast in late December, "Honolulu swung into full production, recovering over twenty-five thousand text additives in the space of four months," according to a wartime OPNAV history. "By late February both Corregidor and Honolulu could read some traffic." In March, when Station Negat switched to current traffic, the pace of cryptanalytic activity accelerated even more. "[COPEK] dispatches show a flood of information flowing from all three units: additives by the hundreds each day, long lists of code recoveries, and more and more translations of the full text of Japanese messages."[29]

Recovery of code values slowed only slightly when the remnants of Cast were evacuated from Corregidor. Then a reconfigured decrypt network emerged. After a harrowing journey, Cast's officer in charge, Lieutenant Fabian, made his way to Melbourne, Australia, where he put together a new comint troupe. It consisted of Australian cryptanalysts drawn from that country's codebreaking structure and as many of his former Cast colleagues as he could round up.[30] Fabian's outfit was codenamed Belconnen for its associated Australian radio site.[31]

On 20 March 1942, Belconnen began disseminating daily intelligence summaries to Hypo, OP-20-G, and the latest addition to the Navy's Pacific force hierarchy, commander, South Pacific (COMSOPAC), based in Auckland, New Zealand. That post was held first by Vice Admiral Robert L. Ghormley and later Vice Admiral Halsey. Until the last of Corregidor's comint team was removed on 8 April, Cast cryptanalysts could be found at two sites: Melbourne and Corregidor. All the while, British cryptanalysts continued to recover code values from Colombo, Ceylon, to where they withdrew after Singapore's fall on 15 February.[32]

For a time these widely scattered units worked well together. They pooled their knowledge and relied on each other for certain kinds of help. The relatively close cooperation that marked dealings between OP-20-G and Station Hypo didn't last. Some tension started creeping into the Washington–Pearl Harbor relationship in March, when Negat moved to break codes in real time. Yet by early April, the split between the two units was still weeks away. The Navy's jerry-built comint operation continued to function. It would get its first real test soon in the Coral Sea. Rochefort's codebreakers would be right in the middle of it.

20

A Silk Purse Out of a Sow's Ear

In the basement, we lived and breathed and schemed
in the atmosphere of the Coral Sea.
                    —Wilfred J. "Jasper" Holmes

By spring 1942, Rochefort found himself fighting a war on two fronts. Fully engaged in the war against Japan, he now also had to contend with another battle percolating not in the Pacific, but in Washington. This one seemed directed at him, or at least he had a pretty good idea that it was. Rochefort sensed the resumption of the whispering campaign about which Laurance Safford had warned him in January 1942. Some at Main Navy were again hinting that Hypo, and therefore Rochefort, might have been tricked by Japanese radio deception before Pearl Harbor.

The campaign was launched in the form of a secret publication entitled "Black Magic in Communications," written with the signature of Vice Admiral Horne, vice chief of naval operations.[1] But according to Safford, by now long gone as head of OP-20-G, the publication was sponsored and supervised by his successor, Commander John Redman.[2] Circulated in April to many communication officers, undoubtedly including Rochefort, the twenty-eight-page document purported to be a tip sheet alerting them to deception techniques used by the Germans and Japanese.

One portion of the manual was provocatively subtitled, "Did the Japanese Paint Us a Picture?" It didn't try very hard to document that the enemy had used radio deception prior to Pearl Harbor; however, it noted that the

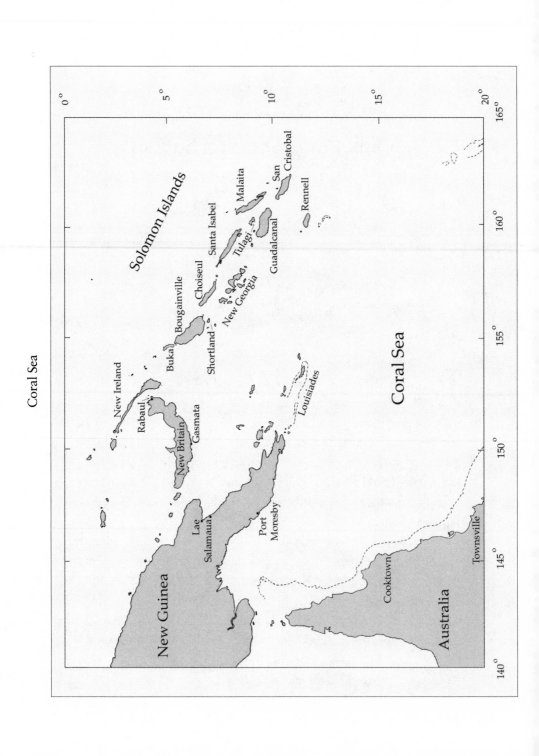

Japanese navy had padded its circuits with dummy messages during 1941, changed communication procedures and call signs, withdrawn its merchant ships from the Atlantic and Pacific, and maintained radio silence. The manual didn't explicitly charge that Hypo had been fooled by the Japanese. It just asked: "Did they paint us a positive 'Radio Picture'?" Then it let the question hang in the air unanswered. The insinuation was clear to all. Oddly, not long after "Black Magic" was published, Safford answered it in a publication of his own, an anonymous essay in which he defended Hypo and sought to debunk the idea that the Japanese had used radio deception. He pointed out that the examples cited by Horne weren't instances of trickery but "positive indications of approaching hostilities," understandable as such to everyone.

Rochefort didn't directly address the "Black Magic" publication, but he did apparently share his views on the matter with his old friend Safford. "Rochefort and the other officers at Pearl Harbor took offense at the contemptible way in which their reputations had been smeared," Safford wrote in 1944.[3]

Whatever his opinion of "Black Magic," Rochefort was too busy in spring 1942 to let it divert him from his central focus. Since 5 February, Japanese warplanes based in Rabaul had been pounding Port Moresby, a key Australian base on the southwestern coast of New Guinea. As noted previously, occupation of Moresby would put IJN fliers within easy striking range of important Australian sites and would move Japan deeper into the southwest Pacific.

In Washington, Admiral King regarded the security of Australia, nearby New Zealand, and all of the southwest Pacific as among his highest priorities.[4] But he didn't worry only about the security of that region. Shortly after the attack on Port Moresby, COMINCH fired off a dispatch to Nimitz that reflected a dizzying range of security concerns. King visualized the possibility of "strong raids against Midway, Oahu, New Hebrides, northeast Australia, possibly the [U.S.] west coast and Canada."[5] To say that King was scattered in his thinking would be an understatement.

Nevertheless, he had just put Nimitz on notice to be vigilant in all directions, including his own backyard. Nimitz shared King's concerns about Oahu. He recognized that the island was far from the "impregnable fortress" it was supposed to be, but he was doing everything he could to strengthen its overall security. He remained steady and calm, alert to the danger but not alarmed. In his unflappability he stood in sharp contrast to the Army's new commander in Hawaii, Lieutenant General Delos Emmons.

If King painted the dangers facing America in the Pacific in the broadest possible strokes, seeing peril in nearly every sector of the Pacific Basin, Emmons focused narrowly. His canvas was Oahu. He seemed agitated, almost rattled, a state of mind he wasted no time in conveying to his superiors in Washington. The "Japanese are opportunists and by their operations have proved they are capable of carefully weighing the war situation [in Hawaii] and making sound plans for the capture of Oahu," Emmons told Washington on 19 February 1942. Emmons worried "they would first seize one or more of the outlying islands of this group as a base for operations against Oahu," then occupy Pearl Harbor.[6]

These concerns weren't altogether outlandish. By the end of March, aside from bombing Pearl Harbor, Japanese forces had occupied British Borneo and all of the Dutch East Indies. Their army was advancing in Burma and was about to complete the conquest of the Philippines. Japanese warplanes continued to strike Moresby, while farther west a large IJN armada was believed to be heading toward the Indian Ocean. The U.S. Navy had no very good idea where the Japanese were going to strike next.

The Navy's comint groups provided little help. As late as 2 April, Rochefort's team confessed bafflement as to the Imperial Navy's next move. "Present location and probable destination of the so-called striking force now in southeast Asia obscure," Hypo's traffic analysts wrote in their daily summary, adding, "There has been no definite association in calls or addressees upon which to predict a move to the Indian Ocean or Australia."[7] Nimitz's new war plans officer, Captain Lynde McCormick, who'd relieved Captain McMorris the previous month, noted the presence of a Japanese submarine squadron in the Sea of Japan and, reading the tea leaves in his own idiosyncratic way, suggested Japan might be getting ready to attack Siberia.[8]

⚫

Three days later Japanese intentions cleared up when Nagumo's *kido butai*— essentially the same striking force that had surprised Pearl Harbor on 7 December—hammered Colombo, Ceylon, in the Bay of Bengal, in the process sinking two British cruisers. On 6 April Japanese naval forces continued their raids on Allied shipping off the east coast of India, leading some of Nimitz's war planners to conclude the Imperial Navy was about to shift its main activities to the Indian Ocean. "Japs are committed to a seaborne offensive in the Bay of Bengal," one planner wrote in Nimitz's Pacific Fleet log, commonly known as the *Greybook*.[9]

While Nagumo's striking force looked for targets in the Indian Ocean, U.S. Navy RI analysts picked up signs pointing in an altogether different direction. The Navy's comint specialists now started to make their presence felt; they estimated that an altogether new Japanese operation was in the works. The first indication of such an offensive showed up on 25 March, when cryptanalysts in Melbourne and at Pearl decrypted a message from the commander of the South Seas Air Force ordering his fighters to assist in "the RZP campaign." No one at Belconnen or Hypo had ever heard of an RZP campaign. Then, on 8 April Rochefort's team decrypted an intercept noting that the *Kaga*, one of Nagumo's six fleet carriers, was scheduled for RZP. In a message to Nimitz, King, and OP-20-G, Rochefort stated: "RZP is Moresby."[10]

To arrive at that conclusion, Rochefort brought to bear all his analytic skills. As was his practice by now, he reached his verdicts by a combination of deduction and guesswork and an uncommon ability to fill in blanks. It was a way of working that amazed Layton. "Very shortly there would arrive by messenger a copy of the decrypt in its actual condition of non-completion, or non-comprehension," Layton said. "It contained many blanks—it would say: 'so-and-so,' blank, blank, blank, and 'so-and-so,' blank. I would call Joe and say, 'Have you got any ideas what these blanks are?' He would say, 'No, we don't know but we're working on them. But I have a hunch that the first blank in there represents'—and he'd use the Japanese word—'and the second blank might be' such-and-such word (in Japanese), etc.—'but I don't *know* this'"[11] (emphasis in original).

Rochefort's intelligence analysis was his outstanding special skill, as detailed previously. He "did not attempt to predict very much, unless he had something in the way of concrete evidence to base the prediction on. It might be fragmentary. But that was his ability—to make a silk purse out of a sow's ear," as Tommy Dyer put it. "The early messages about Coral Sea were perfectly capable of being read in a totally different way than the correct way. Knowledge of the character of the Japanese and this, that and the other, enabled him to get the right meaning."[12]

However Rochefort figured out RZP, his dispatch turned out to be important for two reasons. As Pacific war historian John Lundstrom observed: "The knowledge that the *Kaga* was to sail at the end of April to the New Britain area provided the first concrete indication that the Japanese were planning offensive action in the South Pacific."[13]

Also, Rochefort's RZP pronouncement added a crucial building block to the picture of Japanese intentions now taking shape. For weeks Hypo, Cast, and Belconnen analysts had been painstakingly working out the two- and three-character terms (sometimes known as digraph/trigraph terms) that the Imperial Navy used to designate specific geographic sites. They were aided by Japanese predictability. Weeks earlier, Hypo's analysts had determined that designators beginning with A were U.S. possessions in the central and northern Pacific; on 11 March they'd nailed down AF for Midway, AG for Johnston Island, AH for Oahu, and AK for Pearl Harbor.[14]

Then on 23 March, the remnants of Station Cast on Corregidor, in one of their last reports before their escape on 8 April, enlarged the pool of identified regions in the Pacific when they circulated to OP-20-G and Rochefort a list of digraph/trigraph designators covering more than seventy areas. The Japanese, it turned out, consistently used the letter R in their designations for Australian targets in the Papua/Solomons region. Among others, RR was Rabaul, RXS was Nouméa in the southwest Pacific, RZM was Lae on the northern coast of New Guinea. RZP, however, was listed as unknown.[15]

When Rochefort on 8 April informed Navy brass he believed that RZP was Moresby, pieces of the puzzle started falling into place. A few days earlier, Hypo's traffic analysts had picked up what they called "numerous indications which point to [an] impending offensive from Rabaul." The indications stemmed from radio traffic that showed "movements of air tenders from Truk to Rabaul, and transfer of air strength from the west to Rabaul."[16] The puzzle seemed solved. Rabaul was the home of the Japanese navy's formidable South Seas Fleet, commanded by Vice Admiral Shigeyoshi Inoue. It was also a natural staging area for operations. All that hardware moving into the base suggested preparations for a major campaign somewhere, in all likelihood Port Moresby. Or so Rochefort concluded.

But King, Nimitz, and their top lieutenants lived in a world different from Rochefort's. They didn't doubt the Imperial Navy was gearing up for a major offensive, but they couldn't assume the objective was Moresby just because Rochefort said so. They needed stronger confirmation, but this was not forthcoming. After 8 April, the trigraph RZP dropped out of radio traffic, inviting some Navy planners to consider other possibilities—instead, the Imperial Navy might be contemplating targets in the Solomon, Ellice, and Gilbert Islands, far to the east of Port Moresby.[17]

Layton disagreed. While conceding that such areas might be secondary targets, Layton in mid-April returned the focus to Moresby, telling Nimitz that the "enemy has a campaign in mind . . . probably against Moresby and

Tulagi," referring to an island in the Solomons area near Guadalcanal.[18] In other words, Layton thought in terms of a double target: the Japanese were going to seize both Moresby *and* Tulagi. But Layton was guessing; neither Hypo nor anybody else could substantiate the idea of a double attack.

By mid-April Hypo's codebreakers could fill in only some blanks of the many intercepts arriving on their desks, but it was enough to construct a more detailed picture of the forces assembling at Rabaul. The size of the buildup there amazed them. They knew the fleet carrier *Kaga* was due soon; now they picked up signals alerting them to the arrival of the light carrier *Shoho* (although they misidentified it as the *Ryukaku*), about to depart Yokosuka for Rabaul with aircraft. Still more jarring news followed.

Shortly after "seeing" the *Kaga* and *Shoho* en route to the Rabaul area, Rochefort's analysts spotted what they called an "old-timer" showing up again in traffic: the Japanese navy's powerful CarDiv 5, the huge fleet carriers *Shokaku* and *Zuikaku*, both veterans of the attack on Pearl Harbor and, more recently, the raids on Colombo and other targets in the Indian Ocean.[19] Hypo put CarDiv 5 back in Empire waters near Yokosuka, emitting signals that led Rochefort's traffic analysts to infer it could be headed for Rabaul.

Hypo's inference was a classic example of traffic analysis. Until just recently, the *Shokaku* and *Zuikaku* had been "talking" with Kure and other naval bases on the mainland of Japan. No longer. They were "now talking with Truk or maybe Rabaul," Rochefort explained. "Well, what's the purpose of this? Well, the purpose is that obviously they have some dealings with Truk or Rabaul, and this can only be for future operations and they are moving down to that area or through that area."[20]

But traffic analysis had its limitations, as noted previously. It could suggest possibilities, but it couldn't always confirm them. For now CarDiv 5's destination couldn't be confirmed; it might or might not be steaming toward Rabaul. Rochefort thought the appearance of the *Shokaku* and *Zuikaku* fit a pattern now beginning to emerge: a large, sweeping movement of IJN forces away from the Indian Ocean and the Dutch East Indies toward the Southwest Pacific—toward Rabaul, toward the RZP campaign.

Spurred by Rochefort's estimate and reinforced by similar reports from Belconnen and Negat, Nimitz on 17 April convened his staff to discuss the Imperial Navy's impending offensive. As a working hypothesis, he accepted Rochefort's assumption that CarDiv 5 would join the forces assembling in Truk and Rabaul, almost certainly for a massive thrust southward. "The Japs are expected to use as many as 4 [carriers] with suitable cruiser and destroyer escort and land-based air from [the] Rabaul area," Captain J. M. Steele, a new member of the fleet's war plans staff, wrote in the *Greybook*, adding: "We are planning opposition."[21]

Nimitz dispatched a memo to King. Assuming Moresby was indeed Japan's target, he told COMINCH he expected the Japanese to marshal an armada consisting of at least four fleet carriers in a campaign that would begin around the end of April. He proposed that two carrier task forces be moved into the Coral Sea to block its advance—Task Force 11, commanded by Rear Admiral Aubrey Fitch on board the *Lexington*; and Task Force 17, commanded by Rear Admiral Fletcher on board the *Yorktown*. As the senior of the two, Fletcher would command.[22]

King agreed. He differed with Nimitz only about the timing, asserting that the carriers at Truk "point to Moresby as objective of seaborne and possibly land attack first week of May."[23] The stage was now set for the first major engagement between the naval forces of the United States and Japan. It would take place in the Coral Sea, in waters south of New Guinea, east of Australia. The Imperial Navy seemed to have the advantage. At least that's what Nimitz had every reason to believe. Relying on Rochefort's evaluation, Nimitz thought he was going to be outnumbered four carriers to two. Although he didn't know it at the time and, in truth, wouldn't know it for weeks, the situation wasn't that bad.

Rochefort and his codebreakers had made a mistake, albeit one of omission. They had failed to fully translate—more precisely, to fill in all the blanks—of a crucial dispatch from the Carrier Division 5 to Vice Admiral Inoue, commanding the Fourth Fleet, usually called the South Seas Fleet. The message let Inoue know that CarDiv 5 would *replace* the *Kaga* in the Fourth Fleet's order of battle, not be an addition to it. As a result, Nimitz's ad hoc task forces would face no more than three carriers—two fleet carriers (the *Shokaku* and *Zuikaku*) and one light carrier (the *Shoho*).[24]

Nimitz also didn't know positively that Port Moresby was the Imperial Navy objective. This was just everybody's best guess. Nor did he know whether the Japanese would have a single objective, as most thought, or wage a double offensive, as Layton suspected. He didn't know these things because Hypo's comint analysts, proficient and hard-working as they were, hadn't been able to come up with irrefutable confirmation.

Nimitz's information gaps reflected the state of communications intelligence as of mid-April 1942. Rochefort's radiomen at Wahiawa weren't able to intercept everything. Many messages were missed and, as a result, much critical information didn't reach Nimitz and King. None of that was anybody's fault. Hypo was limited in the volume of signals it could intercept by technology and manpower. Receivers and radiomen to operate them had roughly doubled over the past five months, but Hypo still lacked sufficient men and machines to listen in on every relevant frequency used by the Imperial Navy.

And while Rochefort's cryptanalysts had solved the cipher that protected the JN-25(b) code, his codebreakers still confronted tens of thousands of unidentified code groups. They had a lot of blanks to fill in before they could make a sizable number of messages readable. They could always fall back on traffic analysis, but in the end they still had to do a lot of guesswork.[25]

Given all the uncertainties that surrounded almost every decision he made, it was hardly surprising that Nimitz had mixed feelings about the Navy's intelligence operation at Pearl. "The general condition of our intelligence set up is not the best," reads one entry in Captain Steele's "running estimate," another term for the *Greybook* and a barometer of Nimitz's thinking. "We get *excellent* radio intelligence and communications intelligence, but we are not yet employing all means which can be placed at the disposal of CINCPAC"[26] (emphasis in original).

What Nimitz regarded as the shortcomings of his intelligence system weren't spelled out, but he seemed not to be blaming Rochefort for his problems. His opinion of Rochefort had improved; it could hardly have gotten worse from their initial encounter. Nimitz discerned the potential of communications intelligence to sharpen his thinking. Recognizing the great harm that might result should Hypo's work become known to the enemy, he clamped a tight secrecy lid on that unit's activities, going so far as to keep the very existence of comint from some of his commanders.

CINCPAC's strict rules limited the amount of communicating Rochefort could do. He could not, for example, contact task force commanders directly.[27] That prerogative belonged exclusively to appropriate officers assigned to the Pacific Fleet. Only they could send out messages—cleared by Nimitz or one of his top lieutenants—via the Navy's general fleet radio broadcast, designated "Fox" by naval communicators. As CINCPAC's intelligence officer, Layton could communicate with commanders afloat via Fox, but Rochefort could not.

Still, Rochefort had at his disposal ample means of communication. His main information tool was the daily intelligence summary, a compilation of radio traffic reflecting the highlights of IJN messages intercepted the previous twenty-four hours, delivered each morning to the fleet intelligence officer.

To circulate fast-breaking information, Rochefort could go "on the air"—Hypo lingo for the stream of urgent dispatches the unit radioed OP-20-G throughout the day, always with copies to Nimitz. Rochefort also produced a radio digest summarizing each day's major findings. It was conveyed to the Pacific Fleet almost word for word, but without any hint where the words came from. And, as noted, he constantly chatted with Layton, using their secure phone to alert his friend about unfolding developments, amplify on dispatches already circulated, and share problems.

In turn, Layton put whatever he got from Rochefort to good use. He passed on the most compelling items to Nimitz in the morning, and throughout the day if the news warranted it. Layton also tapped Hypo's reports for the *Fleet Intelligence Bulletin* he produced daily for dispatch to task force commanders. In that way, information generated by Hypo found its way to U.S. forces afloat, albeit in disguised form. Material from Hypo was attributed to anonymous sources to maintain security.

Commanders were never the wiser, although some had their suspicions. Whatever they knew officially, many continued to hold a dim view of code-breaking and cryptanalysis without realizing the extent to which they relied on it. Rochefort didn't complain. Security-minded himself, he supported Nimitz's strictures. "I would give [the information] to Layton," Rochefort explained. "Or rather Layton would receive it, and Layton would act on it, but Layton never, as far as I know, ever mentioned our organization."[28] Rochefort heartily approved.

He had his own information network. It included COPEK, the Navy's secret cryptochannel that linked Hypo, Belconnen (formerly Cast), and Negat for the exchange of technical comint data. He was kept abreast of what was going on at CINCPAC headquarters and elsewhere by Layton, Commandant David W. Bagley (who had just relieved Admiral Bloch), and all manner of dispatches from Washington. But Rochefort wasn't always kept in the loop, as his subordinate officers discovered to their dismay on the evening of 17 April.

॥■॥

Rochefort returned to the basement that night after a conference at CINC-PAC headquarters. He brought with him the startling news that planes from

Halsey's Task Force 16—consisting of the *Enterprise* and a carrier new to the Pacific, the *Hornet*—would bomb Tokyo the night of 18 April (Honolulu time). In the past Hypo had been alerted to carrier raids, if for no other reason so that Wahiawa's radiomen could pick up reports of the weather at the target. Not this time.

This time King and Nimitz felt justified in deciding to keep a closely guarded secret. This operation was the now-legendary raid in which Lieutenant Colonel James H. Doolittle led sixteen B-25 bombers over targets at Tokyo, Nagoya, Yokohama, Yokosuka, Kobe, and Osaka. They didn't want anything to go wrong with the Japanese navy lurking nearby. That thinking didn't mollify Hypo's chief traffic analyst, Thomas Huckins. He was irked that he hadn't gotten more time.

Huckins had good reason to be upset. In charge of direction finding and interception of Japanese messages, he was responsible for staffing the radio hardware at Wahiawa. But he operated on a shoestring, rotating limited personnel around the clock as best he could. With proper notice he could have juggled schedules and doubled the watch the night of 18 April. Because of the short notice, he realized he wouldn't be able to bring together enough kana operators to cover more than a few Japanese naval radio circuits. That was unfortunate for many reasons, one in particular.

With limited intercept capability, Hypo would be unable to exploit the large volume of Japanese naval traffic that inevitably would follow the raid. That meant Hypo would be constrained in the amount of useful radio intelligence it could pass on through CINCPAC to the *Enterprise*, where one of Rochefort's linguists, Lieutenant Slonim, served as Halsey's resident language officer. Charged with tracking IJN ship movements, Slonim would have welcomed reports from his friends in the Hypo basement. He didn't get any that night.

During the evening of 18 April, many hours passed before radiomen generated a sizable number of intercepts for Hypo's analysts to work on, and by then it was too late to help Slonim. Happily, he didn't need the help, because Halsey got away untouched.[29]

The extra effort expended by Wahiawa's intercept operators didn't go to waste. The IJN transmissions pulled out of the air on the night of 18 April may not have figured in Halsey's escape, but they did provide CINCPAC with crucial information. They confirmed Rochefort's earlier suspicion that Nagumo's *kido butai* had departed the Indian Ocean and returned to Empire waters. In fact, it arrived back just in time to join the search for Halsey. Intercepts also showed the Japanese mighty Second Fleet, as well as portions of Vice Admiral Inoue's Fourth Fleet, now patrolling the north Pacific in an attempt to head off Halsey. They hunted for days.[30]

Back at Pearl Harbor, Rochefort's analysts drew what they thought was an obvious conclusion. Inoue's forces couldn't patrol the north Pacific and also gear up at Rabaul for a campaign in the southwest Pacific. The Moresby campaign would be delayed.[31] But the pause turned out to be short-lived. Radio traffic showed the Imperial Navy quickly resuming preparations for the RZP campaign.[32] Rochefort on 21 April got the confirmation he had been waiting for about the *Shokaku* and *Zuikaku*.

That's when Wahiawa's radiomen intercepted a message to CarDiv 5. Rochefort's analysts usually struggled to read more than 10 to 15 percent of any particular message. They decrypted enough of this one to learn that CarDiv 5 had been detached from the *kido butai* and ordered to proceed to Truk for duty with the Fourth Fleet, under Admiral Inoue.[33]

Hypo's discovery was offset by a lapse. On 22 April Rochefort's analysts correctly saw "evidence of a powerful concentration" of forces in the Truk-Rabaul area, an aggregation that included CarDiv 5, CruDiv 5, and the light carrier *Shoho*. So far, so good. But Hypo's analysts repeated an earlier error when they again incorrectly included the *Kaga* and the carrier *Kasuga Maru* in the Fourth Fleet.[34] If confirmed, that would give Inoue five carriers to Fletcher's two.

The widening carrier gap between the two opposing forces caught the attention of analysts in the basement. Rochefort was troubled by it, as was just about everybody else privy to what was going on. They saw taking shape an unfair fight between two hugely uneven combatants. Jasper Holmes thought Rochefort should do something to improve Fletcher's odds. He proposed that his boss go over to CINCPAC headquarters and suggest to Nimitz that Halsey, now returning to Pearl from the Tokyo raid with the carriers *Enterprise* and *Hornet*, take a cutoff, bypass Pearl, and make a high-speed run for the Coral Sea. "[Rochefort] shrugged off my impertinent suggestion with a typically cynical remark," Holmes recalled. "I had a lot to learn as an intelligence officer."

Rochefort explained the difficulties that would frustrate such a detour—the complications of logistics, shortage of tankers, and hazards of running short of fuel. Successful action required many elements other than intelligence, he lectured. "Like most naval and military intelligence officers," Holmes wrote later, Rochefort "subscribed to the principle that intelligence organizations should gather, collate, and disseminate information and not attempt to make operational decisions."[35]

Whether Rochefort was correct about this previously discussed mandate would remain part of a larger debate that continued for decades. The feasibility of Holmes' plan wasn't tested. Rochefort did nothing with it. He was vindicated in this instance not because he had the superior argument, but by the drift of events. It turned out that Inoue did not have five carriers in the South Seas force; he had only three. But neither Rochefort nor Nimitz knew that as of 22 April.

Flawed as it may have been, Hypo's intelligence provided the basis for Nimitz's 22 April "estimate of the situation," an appraisal circulated via Fox to Fletcher, now taking Task Force 17 to the Coral Sea; and to Fitch, commanding Task Force 11, also en route to the Coral Sea, where the two squadrons were to rendezvous on 30 April. Nimitz remained guarded in his outlook, portraying Port Moresby as Japan's "probable objective" and adding his lingering uncertainties: "Will [the offensive] be only for Moresby, or Moresby and the Solomons?" Or, he wondered, would it include New Caledonia and the Fijis as well?[36]

⊪■⊪

If Pearl needed any more evidence confirming the magnitude of the Japanese effort, they got it on 24 April when one of Rochefort's newest codebreakers, Japanese linguist Joe Finnegan, discovered a reference to a new organization, the "MO covering force."[37] Unraveling a dispatch from Vice Admiral Inoue to his invasion force, Finnegan found that Inoue had assigned a sequence of special call signs and designators for the approaching Coral Sea campaign. It listed no fewer than seven separate forces: MO fleet, MO occupation force (listed twice), MO attack force, RZP occupation force, RXB occupation force, RY occupation force.

RZP was back, making its first appearance in radio traffic since 8 April. That was helpful. It seemed to bring with it a whiff of clarity, strengthening Hypo's long-standing view that RZP was Moresby. RXB wasn't a problem. This was Tulagi, a small island in the Solomons off the northern coast of Guadalcanal.[38] Layton and Nimitz had speculated earlier that the Japanese might have two targets. So they did. They would try to occupy both Moresby and Tulagi. RY was a puzzle. It was conjectured to be in the Gilberts; it turned out to be two small volcanic islands adjacent to U.S. supply lines to Australia, Ocean and Nauru, west of the Gilberts.

The big question concerned MO. What did it designate? No one had ever heard of it. Intelligence officers were mystified. Why did MO, whatever it was, merit no fewer than four occupation forces? Was this another term for Port Moresby? If so, what was RZP? Or did MO designate an altogether different target? The surfacing of MO ignited a new debate. The Imperial Navy's over-all strategy was by no means considered certain. Writing in CINCPAC's war plans diary, Captain Steele commented that "some indications appear which might mean that naval activity will be resumed in the Indian theatre"—a curious suggestion given that Nagumo's striking force had just returned to Empire waters.[39] An entry in the CINCPAC *Greybook* reported indications the Japanese "may be changing the direction of their effort to the east now instead of south from Rabaul. This may only be wishful thinking."[40] Indeed it was. The Fourth Fleet was going south, but where?

To settle the MO matter, Rochefort turned the investigation of this two-kana diagraph over to his two top linguists, Lasswell and Finnegan. Proficient in Japanese and adept at codebreaking, with some skill at cryptanalysis, they should have been an ideal team. In practice, it was fortunate they got along so well, given their differences in personality and problem-solving styles. They were a study in opposites.

Methodical, painstaking, relentlessly logical, Lasswell approached code-breaking like a chess player maneuvering to outwit an opponent on some imaginary game board. "His desk was usually clear of everything but his current puzzle," remembered Jasper Holmes. Finnegan, in contrast, was more the free spirit: highly intuitive, given to sudden insights and wild guesses. He "barricaded himself behind a desk with two flanking tables," Holmes recalled, "all piled high with IBM printouts, newspapers, messages, crumpled cigarette packs, coffee cups, apple cores, and sundry material, through which he searched intently, usually with success, for some stray bit of corroboratory evidence he remembered having seen days or weeks before."

Rochefort got the best out of both of them. "A Finnegan hunch checked out by Lasswell's siege tactics made a firm foundation on which to build," Holmes observed.[41] That turned out to be the case with MO. Finnegan insisted it was Port Moresby. The two-kana digraph showed up in messages with places named Deboyne and Misima, small islands in the Louisiade Archi-pelago, a string of ten volcanic islands off the eastern tip of New Guinea, jutting into the Coral Sea. The islands would make ideal bases from which Japanese seaplanes could search for U.S. task forces. The Louisiades could be traversed via the Jomard Passage, an opening through which IJN warships and transports could slip around New Guinea's tail and make their run north toward Port Moresby. MO had to be Moresby.

But Rochefort was skeptical, or at least pretended to be. He often played the role of the doubter to force his analysts to do more digging and support their contentions. "When Lasswell backed up Finnegan, Rochefort was convinced," Holmes said.[42] So was CINCPAC.

On 29 April, five days after the MO digraph first appeared in traffic, all doubts vanished. Rochefort's analysts decrypted and translated Operation Order No. 1, in which Yamamoto communicated to Inoue, CarDiv 5, CruDiv 5, and his Eleventh Air Force to state the mission: "The objective of the MO will be first, to restrict the enemy fleet's movements and will be accomplished by means of attacks on outlying units and various areas along the north coast of Australia. The Imperial Navy will operate to its utmost until this is accomplished."

Rochefort commented: "The sense of the above message is that CinC Combined Fleet is exhorting the Task Force on the eve of starting operations, to do its utmost."[43] The message also established that RZP and MO both stood for Moresby; RZP was Moresby's geographic designator, MO the codename for the Moresby mission.

From Operation Order No. 1 and related messages that followed in quick succession, Rochefort's analysts pieced together the Fourth Fleet's order of battle, the disposition of its forces and objectives. What emerged from these and other decrypts was a picture of three invasion convoys assembled at Truk and Rabaul, all under Vice Admiral Inoue, getting ready to move, some of them already steaming from Truk toward Rabaul and points farther south.

The largest convoy was destined for Port Moresby, the campaign's ultimate objective. The MO invasion force, covered by the light carrier *Shoho* and her escorts, would steam southward down the eastern coast of New Guinea; capture the islands of Deboyne, Samarai, and other islands in the Louisiades, at the easternmost tip of New Guinea; then enter the Coral Sea, en route to Moresby.

As the MO force steamed toward the Coral Sea, a second invasion force would sail eastward and, on X minus 7 Day (3 May), seize Tulagi (RXB) in the Solomons, desired by the Japanese for its excellent harbor. Once that island was occupied, part of the Tulagi convoy would rejoin the MO invasion force near New Guinea. Meantime, other elements of the Tulagi force would steam east from the Solomons into the south central Pacific, where it would capture Ocean and Nauru (RY).

Providing extra security for each attacking force would be a striking force consisting of CarDiv 5 (the *Zuikaku* and *Shokaku*), two heavy cruisers, and six destroyers. If all proceeded the way Hypo expected, the force would enter the Coral Sea from the northwest, escorting the invasion transports, all the while watching for the approach of any Allied naval forces in the area. Operating in tandem, the three forces—invasion, occupation, and striking—would slip around New Guinea's eastern tip and steam north toward Moresby.

Rochefort and his Hypo analysts didn't get everything right. As already noted, they put more carriers in Inoue's Fourth Fleet armada than he possessed. A more serious error was Hypo's failure to note that the *Zuikaku* and *Shokaku* would *not* advance with the invasion force from the northwest, but separately from the northeast, from Fletcher's right flank. Fletcher would find out that for himself in a few days.

Lapses aside, Hypo now provided CINCPAC and COMINCH with a steady stream of estimates pinpointing the direction and timing of Fourth Fleet ship movements. On 27 April 1942, Hypo reported that the Japanese appeared ready to change their codes and ship call signs—moves that usually preceded a major attack. The Japanese did change their call lists but, astonishingly, they retained their old JN-25(b) code for another month, a fatal mistake that enabled U.S. Navy codebreakers to continue reading major portions of IJN traffic in real time.

As ships' comings and goings betrayed Fourth Fleet schedules, Rochefort went on the air, passing on new developments to King and Nimitz. On 30 April he alerted King, Nimitz, and Belconnen to "'RZP' Occupation Force Operation Order #1," which reported that two IJN troop transports would "depart Rabaul Xray minus seven day, and rendezvous off Deboyne Islands with the Saipan Base Force scheduled to arrive Deboyne Xray minus 5 day."[44]

From this intercept, the departure of the transports from Rabaul was fixed at 3 May, the rendezvous of the transports with the Saipan force—the light carrier *Shoho* and her escorts—at 5 May, and the invasion of Port Moresby at X day, or 10 May. The force that earlier had invaded Tulagi would then move against Nauru and Ocean Islands and, if all went the way the Japanese planned, seize both on 15 May.

Arrayed against the IJN armada were Task Forces 17 and 11, assembled around the *Yorktown* and *Lexington* respectively, and a third task force of Australian and U.S. cruisers under British Rear Admiral John Crace. Rear Admiral Fletcher on the *Yorktown* was both the Task Force 17 commander and overall tactical commander for all three task forces. Under the plan, Fletcher and TF 17 would rendezvous with Rear Admiral Fitch's TF 11 near Caledonia on 30 April, then proceed northwest to intercept CarDiv 5 and the Moresby invasion force.

ıı ◼ ıı

"In the basement the chart desk was strewn with charts of New Britain, New Guinea, and the Solomon Islands. The air was thick with conversations about . . . the Moresby Occupation Force, and Rabaul," Holmes wrote later. "We lived and breathed and schemed in the atmosphere of the Coral Sea." Up above, in the ground-level world where most Navy people did their work, no one talked about the Coral Sea. "Everyone was concerned with his own special problem, and no one outside the basement seemed aware of the gathering tornado."[45] They would hear of it soon.

21

King Comes Calling

We were a little surprised that [King] would ask us
what our views were. I personally felt that he was not
even aware of our existence.

—Joe Rochefort

For Rochefort, as for Nimitz, the fast-approaching Battle of the Coral Sea was an all-consuming reality. Their preoccupation, shared by all at Pearl Harbor who were privy to that event, was hardly surprising. The clash would be the first major encounter between the two combatants since 7 December. After months of sparring in hit-and-run raids, frontline forces of each navy would now meet head-on. The outcome wouldn't decide the war, but it seemed likely to have far-reaching implications: if the Imperial Navy prevailed it would strengthen Japan in the southwest Pacific and, probably, doom the Fijis, Samoa, New Hebrides, and New Caledonia. It would imperil Australia.

Five thousands miles away at Main Navy, Admiral King saw the world in different terms. COMINCH didn't doubt the importance of the looming battle, which he deemed crucial for Allied security in the south Pacific. But for King the engagement was just one of many treacherous issues bearing down on him. Aside from the action in the Coral Sea, he had to focus every day on the harrowing struggle in the Atlantic to stymie German U-boats—now destroying millions of tons of crucial U.S. war goods bound for Great Britain and the Soviet Union—and a host of other issues connected with the war against Germany.

Sitting as a member of the Joint Chiefs of Staff, King joined Army Chief of Staff George Marshall and Army Air Forces Commander Henry H. "Hap" Arnold in shaping U.S. military and naval policy against the Axis powers: Germany, Japan, and Italy. Like Marshall and Arnold, King subscribed to FDR's overarching "Atlantic first" goal. Known as Plan Dog, named for paragraph D of a plan advanced in 1940 by former CNO Stark, the policy envisaged a defensive posture in the Pacific while the United States and Britain aimed first at defeating Germany and Italy.[1]

By May King had relieved Stark, now transferred to London to command U.S. Naval Forces, Europe. Stark relinquished his OPNAV post in March 1942, believing the war effort would run more smoothly with the hard-driving King wearing both the COMINCH and OPNAV hats. Always his own man, fiercely independent in his thinking, King nevertheless continued to endorse the objectives of Plan Dog, albeit grudgingly at times.[2]

But King did not neglect the Pacific. He looked for opportunities to shift resources there. He imposed conflicting priorities on Nimitz, urging him to be more aggressive against the Japanese while also warning him not to put the Navy's precious carriers at risk. King's contradictions had many sources. While agreeing that Germany should be tackled first, King also thought it would be mistake to let the Japanese consolidate their holdings. He wanted to keep them off balance and lay the groundwork for stronger action later.[3] Many on the West Coast, concerned about the Imperial Navy, wanted a bigger war against Japan.[4]

Especially strong pressure came from the ambassadors of Australia and New Zealand, both of whom feared invasion. Their concerns were reasonable, considering that their armed forces were engaged elsewhere in the British Empire and that England could provide no aid after the fall of Singapore. Inevitably the two countries looked to the U.S. Navy for protection—in particular, they looked to Admiral King. Now King had to be a politician as well as a naval strategist. He sympathized with their plight, agreeing that both countries were vital to America's strategic position in the Pacific. He promised he would keep a carrier or two in the south Pacific. He practically guaranteed their security. Subjected to pressure from disparate sources and many different sectors of opinion, "King was in an absolutely awful position," naval historian Robert W. Love Jr. said in a telephone interview. Besides everything else King had to contend with, "[FDR trouble-shooter] Harry Hopkins keeps beating on him about those North Sea Russian convoys."[5]

Given the difficulties facing him, it was hardly surprising King would want the latest intelligence on future Japanese moves. What *was* surprising was that he didn't make that desire known to Nimitz, with whom he met in San Francisco on 25–27 April, the first of many conferences they would hold during the war. Of course, King may have thought he already knew what the Japanese planned to do next: move in force into the southwestern Pacific and, after occupying Moresby, attack Samoa, the Fijis, and New Caledonia—steps that both he and Nimitz viewed as "part of an attempt to conquer all Australia," as CINCPAC's *Greybook* noted on 23 April.[6]

Beacuse of Japan's strategic situation, both Navy leaders figured the Imperial Navy would concentrate primarily on building up its position in the southwestern Pacific, at least for now. To counter anticipated moves in this region, King approved Nimitz's proposal that the bulk of the U.S. Navy's offensive power be shifted to the Coral Sea area—the waters around Samoa, the Fijis, and New Caledonia.[7]

There was only one problem with such a deployment: It would require that many of the Pacific Fleet's most potent warships, especially its carriers, be positioned some three thousand miles from Hawaii, a shift that would leave the crucial Hawaii-Midway line only thinly protected. King and Nimitz nevertheless decided to proceed with that risky course. One reason was that, as of 27 April, none of the Navy's three main intelligence centers—Hypo, Belconnen, and Negat—had detected any new or unexpectedly strong interest by the Imperial Navy in U.S. possessions in the central or northern Pacific.

But were they correct? Was that evaluation of Japan's naval priorities well grounded? Always a bit wary, Nimitz never took anything for granted. Nor did King. King had been worried about the relatively exposed positions of Midway and Hawaii since early in the year—concerns he'd never hesitated to pass on to Nimitz. Yet, during their San Francisco meeting, King made no effort to obtain additional intelligence from Nimitz.

For that information King turned to Rochefort, officer in charge of the Navy's reclusive codebreaking unit at Pearl Harbor, Station Hypo. By so doing, King touched off another of what would be many controversies to swirl around Joe Rochefort. Did King violate his own chain of command and go straight to Hypo, in the process bypassing Nimitz? Or did he just use a more roundabout channel to reach Hypo, thereby giving Rochefort the impression, albeit a false one, that he was being contacted directly?

Rochefort entertained no doubts that he had heard directly from King. Shortly after the Imperial Navy pulled out of the Indian Ocean, "I received, as I recall, a message from COMINCH asking for Station Hypo's estimate of further Japanese or future Japanese intentions," Rochefort said. Nimitz's name appeared in the message heading, but only as an addressee for an "information copy." Rochefort and his Hypo colleagues thought the request unusual, but they were pleased. "We were a little surprised that [King] would ask us what our views were," Rochefort said. "I personally felt that he was not even aware of our existence."[8]

Some questioned whether Rochefort had received such a message, at least directly from King. One doubter was Fleet Intelligence Officer Layton. Although one of Rochefort's closest friends, he was protective of Nimitz's prerogatives, as well as his own. And he knew how the chain of command worked. In giving orders or making requests, admirals at King's level would deal directly only with other admirals. "The message *did not*, in my opinion, originate in Admiral King's office," Layton later told naval historian John Lundstrom (emphasis in original). "King would have addressed Nimitz."[9]

Layton suggested another pathway by which the message could have reached Rochefort and still seemed to have come from King. Two months earlier, King had assumed duties as chief of naval operations, meaning he commanded not only the fleet but also the Navy's Washington departments, one of which was OP-20-G, the entity that, among other things, directed Station Hypo. A message from OPNAV might have been from King or, just as plausibly, from OP-20-G or some other OPNAV department. "Personally, I am inclined to think that this was a request from OP-20-G," Layton said, "'representing' CNO, for such an appraisal, to be used in planning future intercept facilities and personnel requirements."[10]

Layton's viewpoint gained support from naval historian Love, a longtime expert on King. "For King not to go through Nimitz would have been almost unthinkable," Love said. "It not only would have been improper, but Nimitz would have gone through the ceiling if King had communicated directly with Rochefort."[11]

That wasn't how Rochefort remembered it. He believed King actually troubled to contact Hypo directly. Writers who met Rochefort after the war favored his viewpoint. They found the former intelligence officer an enthralling storyteller, even a bit exotic, but still a rock-solid, just-the-facts sort of fellow who wouldn't make things up.[12] In shaping their narratives of the Pacific War they accepted the Rochefort version, as did Walter Lord, author of the 1967 best-selling account of the Battle of Midway, *Incredible Victory*.

"One day toward the middle of April a totally unexpected message arrived from Washington," Lord wrote. "It was, in fact, the first and only communication Rochefort ever received directly from Admiral Ernest J. King, Commander in Chief of the U.S. Fleet. COMINCH wanted Rochefort to give, based on the current flow of intercepts, his long-range estimate of Japanese naval intentions."[13]

No such message ever turned up in any of the Washington–Pearl Harbor message files preserved after the war. (But thousands of memoranda and pieces of correspondence deemed routine were destroyed in the months following the war.) Origins of the message aside, Lord did get one thing wrong in his account: The message delivered to Rochefort did not arrive in mid-April; It was handed to Hypo's leader on 30 April, just days before the Battle of the Coral Sea.

ıı■ıı

Washington's fabled message couldn't have arrived at a busier time for Hypo's analysts. Six days earlier, on 24 April, they had unearthed from the flurry of intercepts conveyed from Wahiawa reference to a new organization, the "MO covering force." It had taken Finnegan and Lasswell a few days to establish that MO and RZP, in their different ways, represented Port Moresby. Then, on 29 April, Rochefort's analysts had decrypted the Japanese navy's Operation Order No. 1, confirming MO as Moresby. From that the Hypo team had been able to piece together the Fourth Fleet's order of battle for the impending Coral Sea engagement. Now, on 30 April, Rochefort and his crew were handed the King request.

Immersed as he was tracking the movements of the Fourth Fleet, now sailing toward the southeastern end of New Guinea, Rochefort dropped everything to prepare a response for King. Giving the request his highest priority, he assigned six of his top analysts to ponder Washington's query.[14] Eight hours later the team (himself plus Dyer, Wright, Lasswell, Finnegan, Huckins, and Holtwick) finished what they called "Hypo's Evaluation of the Picture in the Pacific." A lengthy, four-part message, it was dated 30 April, and on 1 May was transmitted via COM 14's radio connection to OPNAV at Main Navy, with copies to Belconnen and Nimitz.[15]

The fact that the message was addressed to OPNAV, not COMINCH, didn't go unnoticed in later years; it bolstered the Layton-Love view that the information request had originated from a unit in the Office of Naval Operations, maybe OP-20-G, not King himself. Whoever set in motion the request, Rochefort was pleased with Hypo's reply. "This was the combined opinion of possibly six of us, of which I was responsible," Rochefort said. "I had the responsibility for this."[16]

Neither King nor Nimitz was startled by Hypo's first point: "Major fleet operations in Indian Ocean are completed for present," the message stated. Rochefort had reached that conclusion two weeks earlier and circulated the finding to CINCPAC and OP-20-G. Even though the finding contradicted British fears of continued Japanese attacks in the Indian Ocean, no one at Main Navy or CINCPAC disagreed.[17]

King and Nimitz were more surprised—perhaps even jolted—by Hypo's second conclusion. The Japanese weren't going to invade Australia: "No indications of any large scale operations from Java, Bali or Timor to the south," said Hypo, noting the sites from which such an attack would begin.[18] This finding did not mean that Japan no longer sought to cut off Australia from U.S. supply lines. Japan's drive into the southwest Pacific would still pose a threat to Australia and America's strategic position in the Pacific.

Hypo's third major point restated what U.S. Navy war planners already knew: Japan's powerful Fourth Fleet, beefed up with one carrier division, a light carrier, two cruiser divisions, plus numerous destroyers and transports, was on the move. It was heading toward southeast New Guinea and the Louisiade Archipelago, en route to Port Moresby, all part of an operation code-named MO. Just to make sure no one doubted the target, a matter of dispute just a few weeks earlier, Rochefort repeated it: "Suggest Moresby for MO."

The fourth point captured the attention of both admirals. Rochefort stated that large portions of the Imperial Navy, just back from the Indian Ocean, were gathering in home waters—"now available for offensive or defensive tasks." He cited BatDivs 1 and 2 (which included the massive battleships *Yamato* and *Musashi*); CruDivs 4 and 6; two fleet carriers, *Soryu* and *Kaga*, ready to sortie; and other carriers in home yards, but "on a 2 or 3-day sailing orders basis."[19] Where might these warships go? From their anchorages, they could move south—or east.

Until Rochefort's 1 May evaluation, Navy strategists probably would have answered "south." They would have figured the forces assembling in Japan's home waters were poised to strike south toward the Solomons and the Coral Sea islands of Samoa, the Fijis, New Caledonia, and New Hebrides, in support of the Fourth Fleet's MO operation to isolate Australia. Rochefort didn't contradict this thesis, but he did call attention to the "great interest shown by Tokyo" in other regions: Canton Island in the south-central Pacific, the Baker-Howland Islands just to the north, and Palmyra Island, a mere 990 miles southwest of Pearl Harbor. Rochefort guessed those IJN activities were intended to support the MO campaign, but he did note other possibilities.

Looking beyond the southwest Pacific, he pointed out Japan's stepped-up radio surveillance of "Hawaiian areas" and Alaska's Aleutian Islands. He noted that earlier in the year, Hypo had reported signs in Tokyo's radio traffic suggesting the Aleutians might be a candidate for Japanese operations, and now those signs were showing up again. Therefore, after the MO campaign, "second choice for operations of available forces is raid on the Aleutians," Rochefort wrote. "This considered unlikely at this time but certainly probable at a later date."[20]

In later years Rochefort claimed that Hypo's evaluation unveiled "an operation different and distinct from the operation planned off New Guinea"— and was, therefore, "generally the first information we had on Midway."[21] In truth, Rochefort's estimate didn't go that far. He didn't mention Midway or, for that matter, the central Pacific as such. But his evaluation was still far-sighted. It captured the Imperial Navy as it started to tilt away from the southwest Pacific and toward east and central Pacific waters.

Rochefort's picture added a jarring element of uncertainty to Navy thinking. With the Imperial Navy assembling in home waters, positioned to move in any one of several directions, it would be harder to assume that future Japanese naval activity would be confined to the New Guinea–Coral Sea area. It would therefore be more difficult to justify concentrating U.S. forces in the south Pacific at the expense of the Hawaii-Midway line, as King and Nimitz had considered.

What King and Nimitz thought of "Hypo's evaluation" doesn't show up in naval records. Rochefort never knew. As Lord said, Rochefort never again heard from King. The only comments he received came from CINCPAC headquarters. "I did get a negative response from one or two members of Admiral Nimitz's staff," Rochefort said. "[They] considered that making such an estimate was their responsibility and not mine." Unable to resist a dash of his trademark sarcasm, Rochefort said the criticism came from "several members—oh, let's say the least competent members" of the CINCPAC team, people "who were not exactly appreciative of, they said, me taking over their functions, which was true."[22]

Who were these critics? Rochefort named two: Nimitz's chief planning officer, Commander Vincent R. Murphy, and a war plans officer, Captain Steele, who, Rochefort said, "reprimanded" him for "usurping" his job.[23]

What, then, is the verdict of history? Did Rochefort really hear directly from Admiral King, or did he just imagine that he did? There can be no conclusive answer, but it's hard to believe Nimitz's staff would have been so upset with Rochefort if King had gone through regular channels and this had been a normal communication.

⸭

Unhappy as some CINCPAC staffers were with Rochefort, the gist of Hypo's evaluation found its way into the fleet's *Greybook*. "The preliminaries of the Japanese offensive in the Southwest Pacific are underway," the diary stated. "While there is no good information as to moves in the Central and Northern Pacific at this time," the diarist added, "all positions as far east as Pearl Harbor and Dutch Harbor may possibly be recipients of a raid."[24]

Did Nimitz read the evaluation? No doubt, but he may have been too busy with his next project to have done so immediately. On 1 May, the same day the memorandum was circulated, Nimitz flew the 1,200 miles out to the lonely Midway Atoll for a personal inspection of its defenses. He spent all of 2 May checking the fortifications of the atoll's two islets, Eastern and Sand. He visited gun pits, hangars, underground command posts. He questioned officers and Marine defenders. He liked what he saw, and promised them all the supplies and reinforcements they would need to defend the place.[25]

Guarding against the possibility of an attack by large flying boats or some other kind of air raid, "Nimitz's inspection of Midway had nothing to do with any hint of a future Midway assault," Layton wrote later.[26] In this assertion Layton was on firm ground. As of 1 May, neither Hypo nor Belconnen nor Negat possessed any intelligence indicating a land invasion of Midway.

The Midway visit was King's idea. Nimitz made the trip "after King expressed concern about this island," the *Greybook* noted on 2 May.[27] King's concern, shared by Nimitz, had to do with their anxiety about shifting so much of the Pacific Fleet to the southwest Pacific. "As far as King was concerned, Midway had to be made as secure as possible if the Pacific Fleet was to be committed to the south," observed naval historian H. P. Willmott.[28]

As things turned out, events did more to decide the disposition of the Pacific Fleet than the planning done by King and Nimitz or the possibilities raised by

Rochefort's 1 May evaluation. Nimitz returned to Pearl Harbor on 3 May, the same day the Fourth Fleet's striking force seized Tulagi in the Solomons and one day before Fletcher's *Yorktown* planes pounded the invading forces at that island. Japan's Fourth Fleet commander, Admiral Inoue, then knew a U.S. carrier task force was in the area. It was just a matter of days before Inoue's and Fletcher's squadrons would meet in an all-out clash.

Back at Pearl, Nimitz could see that Hypo was tracking the Fourth Fleet's every move. But what neither he nor Rochefort grasped was that some of the estimates by his analysts were problematic, based often on partially decrypted messages that left out crucial information. That was nobody's fault. Hypo's codebreakers still had recovered only a relatively small percentage of JN-25-(b)'s fifty thousand code groups. They believed partially decrypted messages were better than none at all and had grown accustomed to making educated guesses. "You'd have to guess the gaps," Rochefort told Walter Lord.[29] But this could be risky, and some of the decrypts circulated to CINCPAC had the potential to mislead Fletcher. Three may have done so.

Between 3 and 5 May (local time), Fletcher received two dispatches from CINCPAC that led him to misconstrue, at least for a time, the movements and combat mission of the *Zuikaku* and *Shokaku*. One message told Fletcher, incorrectly, that Japanese carrier-based planes would soon raid land targets in northern Australia and some south Pacific islands to pin down Allied naval forces. A second dispatch told him, also incorrectly, that CarDiv 5 was moving to a point southeast of Port Moresby in order to strike Moresby by air on 7 or 8 May, two to three days before the projected invasion.[30]

But, as cryptanalysts determined later, Yamamoto had actually ordered the *Zuikaku* and *Shokaku* to search for U.S. carriers that might be in or near the Coral Sea. The misinformation radioed Fletcher stemmed from a flawed reading of Yamamoto's original message, which, Hypo admitted in its decrypt, was "difficult to read due to lack of code groups."[31] Hypo had filled in some blanks erroneously and, in doing so, inadvertently told Fletcher IJN planes would be hitting land targets when in fact they were looking for him.

A third dispatch might also have led Fletcher astray. After attacking Tulagi on 4 May, he took the *Yorktown* south into the Coral Sea to rendezvous with Fitch's *Lexington* and ponder his next move. Fletcher now received information from CINCPAC based on another Hypo decrypt, this one indicating that if the Japanese found the U.S. task force, CarDiv 5 would link up with the invasion force in the Solomons, then proceed southward, presumably toward Jomard Passage through the Louisiades Archipelago.

The order seemed to make sense; Fletcher believed he had been spotted. Such a move would enable the *Zuikaku* and *Shokaku* to join the invasion convoy and escort it as it moved through the Louisiades at the tip of New Guinea, then north toward Moresby. CarDiv 5 would then be well-positioned to strike Moresby as previously ordered. Convinced the convoy and its carrier escort were approaching the Louisiades from the north, Fletcher turned his task force north-northwest toward the archipelago to intercept them. Steaming toward New Guinea's eastern tip early on 6 May, he thought CarDiv 5 was in Bougainville waters, far out of range of his planes. What Fletcher didn't know, nor did Rochefort nor Nimitz, was that the order Hypo had decrypted putting the carriers near Bougainville applied to an altogether different Fourth Fleet element, the MO main force, not the MO striking force with its two carriers. Nor did they know that CarDiv 5 was approaching not from the northwest, but from due north on Fletcher's right flank. Around noon on 6 May, CarDiv 5 was three hundred miles away and closing.

Fletcher got lucky. As 6 May wore on, the MO striking force ran into troubles of its own, stemming from a mixture of poor intelligence, weak reconnaissance, and terrible weather. By six o'clock that evening, the Japanese carriers had moved to within ninety miles of Fletcher's task forces, but neither side knew it.[32] The two forces wouldn't begin searching for each other in earnest until early the next morning, 7 May, when they first engaged. Swayed by imprecise intelligence and blinded by the fog of war, both sides continued to make mistakes.

Striking force planes from the *Shokaku* and *Zuikaku* made the first one. Flying to an area where they thought they would find one or more American carriers, they discovered only the U.S. fleet oiler *Neosho* and escort destroyer *Sims*, parked in a remote spot where Fletcher thought they would be safe. CarDiv 5's pilots had been misinformed. Now they erred again, this time misidentifying the *Neosho* as a carrier. They hit the ill-starred vessels, sinking the *Sims* and turning the *Neosho* into a floating shell. The Japanese fliers departed, thinking they had smashed a major portion of the U.S. task force.

Fletcher also slipped up. Scanning the area north of the Louisiades, where he expected to find the striking force carriers, Fletcher's search planes did indeed spot enemy ships. Told the previous day that the *Zuikaku* and *Shokaku* were north of him, Fletcher assumed his planes had spotted the two fleet carriers—he proceeded to fling his *Lexington* and *Yorktown* planes against the ships.[33] They turned out to be only transports, escorted by the light carrier

Shoho. Fletcher's fliers hammered the *Shoho*, making it the first Japanese carrier sunk by U.S. aircraft. That was fine, but the striking force was still on the loose.

It wasn't until the following day, 8 May, that the main elements of each opposing force located each other and launched all-out strikes. The two sides were about evenly matched: 121 Japanese planes against 122 American. Both sides handed out heavy blows, CarDiv 5 sinking the *Lexington* and impairing the *Yorktown*, the U.S. task force badly damaging the *Shokoku* and severely depleting the *Zuikaku*'s aircraft strength. The encounter forced Inoue to withdraw his armada from the Coral Sea. Was the fight really over? No one was sure, but it certainly was suspended.

The Battle of the Coral Sea marked a major milestone in the Pacific War. It would be the first naval action in which the opposing ships never sighted one another. It was arguably a tactical success for Inoue, in that his forces destroyed one U.S. fleet carrier while losing only a light carrier. But it ended up a strategic failure for the Japanese because they were thwarted in their drive to secure Port Moresby, one of their key objectives in the war.

II▮II

For the first time since Pearl Harbor, a Japanese advance had been turned back, a feat that changed the tone of the Pacific War in one stroke. Nimitz was satisfied with the outcome and, for the most part, so was King, although he wondered whether Fletcher had been sufficiently aggressive. Nimitz harbored no such doubts and sought Fletcher's promotion to vice admiral, eventually approved by King.[34] Nimitz also was pleased with Rochefort and the role played by radio intelligence in the Coral Sea.

He had good reason. Rochefort and his analysts, joined by their colleagues at Belconnen, early on had pinpointed Port Moresby as the primary objective of the RZP operation. In their daily reports to CINCPAC and OP-20-G, they had shown the ceaseless buildup of aircraft and carrier strength of the Fourth Fleet at Truk and Rabaul. In early May they'd established a reasonably accurate timetable for Fourth Fleet movements through the Solomons, around the tip of New Guinea into the Coral Sea, and the projected conquest of Moresby.

Besides their tracking of Inoue's South Seas force, Rochefort and his team had also provided the Navy's high command with a broad picture of the Imperial Navy. They'd shown its shift back to home waters and its positioning for action in any one of several directions. They had noted its renewed interest in the Aleutians in the northern Pacific and the islands east of the Solomons, including Palmyra and Hawaii.

But the Coral Sea engagement also exposed some of the shortcomings of radio intelligence. At critical moments during the days leading up to the battle, Hypo had based some estimates on partially solved messages, estimates about the enemy's likely moves that could have confused Fletcher. As naval historian Lundstrom described the pros and cons of comint, "radio intelligence proved immensely useful in strategic matters, [but] in the fast-moving, tactical situations in which Task Force 17 found itself, much of it turned out to be incomplete or incorrect or very misleading." Even if Nimitz had been aware of such findings, he probably would have still recognized Hypo's larger contribution, also spelled out by Lundstrom: "Radio intelligence was responsible for the American carriers being in the Coral Sea in the first place, and this provided Nimitz with a tremendous strategic advantage in knowing in a general way his opponent's future moves."[35]

Whatever doubts Nimitz may have retained about Rochefort since their unfortunate first encounter, they were erased by the Battle of the Coral Sea. Comint had proved itself. So had Rochefort and his team of cryptanalysts, traffic analysts, linguists, and other "crazy" people, as their boss called them. Rochefort and his crew now enjoyed unprecedented credibility, at least as far as CINCPAC was concerned. "By this time Nimitz had come to recognize the value and effectiveness of the Intelligence furnished him," Layton told Lundstrom. "He had become Intelligence conscious and accepted the analysis of intelligence as forming a recognizable picture, and was (perhaps subconsciously) placing more faith in it than he had before."[36]

Rochefort would put Nimitz's faith in intelligence to the test in the weeks ahead. It would be strained at times. He would have to draw heavily on the trust he had earned during the preceding months. But Nimitz recognized that Rochefort now saw something new: a buildup of forces larger than anything seen before. He didn't know what it was, but he knew his battered fleet wouldn't get much rest after the Coral Sea. Nor would Rochefort's basement team.

22

Something Is Brewing

The Striking Force to commence operations 21 May . . .
objective or mission not indicated.
　　　　　　　　—Edwin T. Layton, 12 May 1942

Even before U.S. and Japanese carrier forces collided in the Coral Sea,
Rochefort at Pearl Harbor and Rudy Fabian in Melbourne caught hints
of another Imperial Navy offensive in the works. As early as 27 April the
commander of the Japanese navy's powerful Second Fleet, Admiral Nobutake
Kondo, radioed Tokyo for navigational information, requesting charts of the
area 50–61 degrees north, 140–165 degrees west.[1] "All that was necessary
was to glance at an atlas," naval historian Stephan Howarth observed. "The
section requested covered the Gulf of Alaska, part of the Alaskan coast, and
the eastern Aleutians."[2]

On the same day Melbourne picked up Kondo's request, Rochefort's unit
published an IJN message concerning the number of American planes in AOE
and KCN—identified by Hypo as IJN geographic designators for Dutch Harbor and Kodiak respectively.[3] Layton's assistant, Lieutenant Robert Hudson,
inferred what seemed obvious: Japan was actively considering an operation
against the Aleutians. "The date is purely conjecture," he said, "but a guess
would put it during the last part of May."[4]

More perplexing messages followed. On 2 May Station Negat decrypted
and translated a message from Admiral Kondo's chief of staff, Kazutaka Shiraishi, to the Japanese navy's 5th Naval Base at Saipan concerning plans to

assemble something called "the 'A' force and the Striking Force" at Truk for two weeks after 20 June.[5] The message confused U.S. Navy planners. It led some to think that the Japanese navy's new offensive would be launched *after* 20 June instead of before.

There were other puzzles. Why was Shiraishi talking to Saipan, a major Fourth Fleet base in the Marianas? Was the Second Fleet going south? What was the A Force? Had the Japanese created a second striking force to complement Nagumo's *kido butai*? Why the rendezvous at Truk, a huge IJN naval base in the Carolines? The most troubling question was how the Second Fleet would occupy itself before reaching Truk on 20 June.

On 4 May Rochefort's linguists translated another troubling message, this one a partially decrypted "priority" dispatch from the battleship *Kirishima* to Yamamoto, commanding the Combined Fleet. "This ship will be undergoing repairs during the time of the said campaign," the message stated. Noting the work would be completed around 21 May, the message concluded: "Will be unable to accompany you in the campaign."[6]

From this dispatch it appeared that whatever campaign loomed ahead, it would materialize around 21 May. But what campaign was it? Rochefort and his Hypo colleagues had no idea. Always guarded in his estimates, Rochefort radioed the translation to Washington, then sent it over to Nimitz with the following comment: "No substantiation of [the ship's projected schedule] nor any indication of nature of so-called campaign or operations."[7]

Rochefort may have hesitated to speculate, but Layton offered a couple of ideas. They were recorded in his "scorecard," as he and Nimitz referred to Layton's "enemy's file," which he produced daily.[8] Layton conjectured that the buildup of Japanese naval strength in home waters "may be preparatory to another raid in force on Oahu," as well as some kind of an offensive in the Aleutians, possibly around 15 May.[9]

Layton's guesswork about Oahu gained credence on 6 May, when Hypo's analysts decrypted another curious message. This dispatch originated from the Japanese navy's Fourth Air Attack Force, based at Kwajalein in the northern Marshalls, and was directed to Japan's large naval base at Yokosuka. Fourth Air asked to be supplied—before 17 May—ten crystals for frequencies 4990 and 8990 kilocycles for use in aircraft in something called the "number 2" or "second King campaign."[10] The target was Affirm King, or AK.

Rochefort had no trouble figuring this one out. Already legendary in the basement for his phenomenal memory, he recalled some recent history and fired off a priority dispatch to Negat, Belconnen, and CINCPAC, this one hand-delivered to Nimitz via Layton. Rochefort noted that the Fourth Air Group message carried the same addressees as a similar dispatch that had preceded the 4 March flying-boat attack on Oahu. He also noted that Affirm King, or AK, was the Japanese navy's geographic designator for Pearl Harbor, identified during the 4 March attack.[11]

Other aspects of the mystery now resolved themselves. The frequencies cited in the Japanese message were used for communication between submarines and aircraft. Those plus the "King campaign" led Rochefort and colleagues to reach a conclusion that seemed unavoidable: Pearl was going to get hit again, this time in a coordinated air-submarine attack around 17 May.

No one, either at CINCPAC headquarters or at Main Navy contested Rochefort's estimate. King, Nimitz, and their staffs were busy, preoccupied with the Battle of the Coral Sea, which was now entering its critical phase. But those analysts who looked at Rochefort's evidence found it solid. After receiving Hypo's translation, the Office of Naval Intelligence worked it into the summary of radio intelligence it prepared daily for Admiral King. "Although by no means definite, it is believed possible that after 17 May a new attempt will be made to carry out long range raids on the Hawaiian islands," ONI's Marine analyst Lieutenant Colonel R. A. Boone ventured.[12]

Once the furious clash in the Coral Sea had ended, Nimitz turned his attention to Hypo's latest information and found it credible. "It is indicated that the Japs will try a seaplane bombing raid on Oahu between May 15 and 20," stated the *Greybook*.[13] COMINCH, for his part, continued to worry primarily about the south Pacific. But he recognized, as did CINCPAC, that Hawaii was not well defended. Neither admiral was surprised that the Japanese navy might attempt another strike at Pearl. Rochefort's second-attack theory was now widely accepted. Very soon he would run into heavy weather with some of his estimates, but not yet.

On 7 May (local time), Nimitz and his staff rejoiced at the outcome of the desperate air battle that had just been waged in the Coral Sea, ending with the Fourth Fleet now retiring rapidly to the north. "This was a red letter day for our forces operating in the Coral Sea area," intoned CINCPAC's diarist. The news wasn't all good. As noted, the *Lexington* had been sunk and the *Yorktown* banged up by a 500-pound bomb. Unclear about the extent of the damage and believing any carrier less than 100 percent effective operated at a grave disadvantage, Nimitz ordered Fletcher to retire from the area.[14]

Unavoidable as it was, the *Yorktown*'s departure did have one unfortunate consequence: It wouldn't be available to defend the Australian-controlled
islands of Ocean and Nauru. Layton feared both would be occupied soon,
certainly by the middle of May.[15] While the islands weren't of great strategic
importance, they could serve as staging areas for attacks on the Fijis and
Samoa to the south, islands figured to be high on the Japanese list for occupation. As much as the United States and Australia would have liked to prevent
their loss, there seemed little the Navy could do.

With the Moresby campaign apparently postponed and Nauru and Ocean
Islands as good as gone, the Navy's high command wondered what the Japanese navy would do next. Driving U.S. concerns were those heavy naval units
assembling in Japan's home waters, cited by Rochefort in his 1 May memo,
"Hypo's Evaluation of the Picture in the Pacific." At least four battleships
from Battleship Divisions 1 and 2 could be ready to sail within two days,
three at most. So could the carriers *Kaga*, *Soryu*, and *Akagi*, scheduled to
be available after 15 May. An unknown number of destroyers and cruisers
were also in home waters. Together they constituted the mightiest elements of
Yamamoto's fleet, all set for an operation to be launched on or about 21 May.
"Nothing is known of the nature of this operation, but the forces mentioned
are available in Japanese waters," ONI's Boone cautioned on 10 May.[16] Where
was that force going?

No one at Main Navy or Pearl Harbor knew. Navy brass certainly agreed
that the Aleutians were in IJN sights, either for a sizable raid or possibly occupation. But if for occupation, how extensive would it be? The far western tip?
The islands of Kiska and Attu? Or, unlikely as it seemed, all the way down to
Unalaska and Dutch Harbor? Such a development couldn't be ruled out, but
the Aleutians, remote, cold, rainy, and fogged in much of the year, seemed an
improbable target for all that naval fire power.

A likelier action in King's view was a renewed Imperial Navy push down
to the south Pacific islands of New Caledonia, Efate, the Fijis, and Samoa,
possibly coordinated with an IJN offensive against northeast Australia. Nor
did he think the Japanese would give up going after Port Moresby. King
placed great weight on the Second Fleet's plan to assemble an A force and a
striking force at Truk around 20 June, after which he believed the Japanese
navy would move south.

Nimitz, too, worried about the south Pacific, and he had no doubts that
the Japanese would try again to take Port Moresby. But now, thanks to Hypo's

decrypts, he focused more on signs the Imperial Navy was gearing up for some kind of offensive against Pearl Harbor, possibly Hawaii itself. Nimitz wasn't alone in these concerns. Even King thought the Japanese had something in mind with regard to Hawaii. But what?

Questions abounded. Was the impending Operation K just about Oahu? Or did it involve the entire Hawaiian chain including Midway? What kind of operation was it going to be? Another pinprick? A repeat of the 4 March flying-boat raid? Or did the Japanese navy contemplate something more ambitious? Was Operation K linked to the Aleutian offensive, or were they separate operations, each likely to be carried out independently?

Nimitz suspected the Japanese contemplated more than the jab delivered on 4 March. After all, Layton had already warned of "another raid in force on Oahu," and now Rochefort had provided intelligence about a second Operation K. A few on Oahu feared something far worse—an IJN attempt to invade and occupy Hawaii. The concern wasn't frivolous. U.S. war planners had long assumed that Yamamoto wouldn't rest until his forces had stormed the Hawaiian Islands.

ı∎ı

For insight into these and other questions, Nimitz turned to Rochefort and his codebreakers. They didn't have the answers, but Rochefort had a strategy for getting them. More precisely, he had an operating methodology that was distinctly his own and not necessarily appreciated by his OP-20-G superiors. Early in the year Rochefort's Washington bosses, DNC Joseph Redman and OP-20-G chief John Redman, parceled out the workload to be handled by the Navy's three comint branches: Negat at Main Navy, Hypo at Pearl Harbor, and the Belconnen group at Melbourne.

Under the division of labor ordered by Washington, each unit was responsible for intercepting Japanese radio traffic in a particular sector of the Pacific, called a block. The boundaries were vague (none showed up in Navy literature). Presumably Rochefort would have been directed to concentrate Hypo's collection efforts on the nearby Marshall Islands, the south-central Pacific, and almost certainly some portion of Japan's home waters. The rest of the Pacific— the block comprising the northwest area (including the Mariana Islands), Southeast Asia, and, again, Japan's home waters—would be the domain of Negat and Belconnen.

Rochefort didn't pay any attention to the blocks handed down from Washington. He didn't ignore the Marshalls or south-central Pacific, but he didn't limit Hypo's work to the boundaries assigned. He thought it was more important to cover particular Imperial Navy fleets, not geographic sectors. He ordered his radiomen and analysts to track Kondo's Second Fleet and Nagumo's First Air Fleet as best they could, a focus traceable at least in part to Nimitz himself. "Nimitz said the information we really wanted was, what was the First Air Fleet going to do?" Layton remembered. "Why didn't Rochefort concentrate on all messages to and from the First Air Fleet?" Rochefort did just that.

Predictably, OP-20-G protested Rochefort's freewheeling approach. "He waited a couple of days, let them cool down but kept breaking messages out of his area," Layton said. "Then he told them what he was doing and why, 'Just following orders from the Pacific Fleet Commander.' Of course, that made them mad."[17]

Another factor that might have colored Washington's thinking was that Rochefort's show of independence coincided with circulation of the Horne–John Redman "Black Magic" publication. Did OP-20-G believe that Rochefort was again letting the Japanese "paint us a picture" of what was going on in the Pacific? There would be no way to know, but the question raised by Horne and Redman continued to hang in the air. However OP-20-G viewed Rochefort, Hypo's broader net didn't immediately produce results. Rochefort and his analysts couldn't irrefutably establish Yamamoto's intentions. But Hypo did observe and mark down for all to see the extreme lengths to which the Japanese were going to disguise whatever action they were planning.

Unable to spot radio deception before Pearl Harbor, Hypo's analysts now identified the various techniques IJN radiomen were using to throw eavesdroppers off the scent. They noted that shore stations originated dispatches of major fleet commanders, while many of those commanders generated traffic in the name of other commanders. And vessels that clearly were not flagships acted as flagships in their radio traffic.[18] The tricks obscured some ship movements, but they also alerted Hypo's team.

Wherever the Japanese were going, speed was of the essence. Drawing on one of Hypo's translations, ONI told King that the Japanese navy had arranged for the fueling at sea of two large cruiser divisions and a destroyer squadron—an action that clearly indicated a long-distance operation of some kind. ONI analyst Lieutenant Ethelburt Watts added: "Every indication points to the urgency with which ships now in home yards are having their overhauls completed or even curtailed."[19]

Another thing bothered Rochefort and, for that matter, just about everybody at CINCPAC headquarters. Where was Admiral Kondo's mighty Second
Fleet? Rochefort's concern, shared by his superiors in operations, wasn't idle
curiosity. Created in 1903 as a mobile force of cruisers and destroyers to
pursue the Imperial Russian Navy's cruiser squadron, the Second Fleet had
evolved into the strongest surface force in Yamamoto's Combined Fleet. It was
essential that Nimitz know the whereabouts and, if possible, the intentions of
Admiral Kondo at all times.

But the Second Fleet hadn't emitted a sound for days, suggesting that Kondo's ships were observing strict radio silence, never a good sign. Indications
that the fleet might have moved north into the Sea of Japan suggested to some
that it might have returned to home waters. Were they right? Uncertain about
what Kondo and Yamamoto were up to, Rochefort's sleuths proceeded like
sleepwalkers trying to make their way through a trackless labyrinth, bumping
into walls and doorjambs before making their way through an opening.

Hypo finally scored a breakthrough on 8 May. Rochefort's top traffic
analysts, Huckins and Williams, correctly associated Nagumo's First Air Fleet
with key elements of the Second Fleet, most notably the fast battleships *Hiei*
and *Kongo* and the cruisers *Tone* and *Chikuma*, still in Empire waters.[20] The
analysts called attention to what they believed was the reappearance of Nagumo's old striking force—the same *kido butai* that had slammed Pearl Harbor,
now consisting of four carriers (the *Akagi*, *Kaga*, *Soryu*, and *Hiryu*), two battleships, two cruisers, destroyers, and other warships. A merging of Kondo's
Second Fleet with Nagumo's *kido butai* would put under one umbrella the
most formidable naval force the Imperial Japanese Navy had yet assembled.
Rochefort brought this new information together and told his superiors at
Pearl and Main Navy what he thought: "Something is brewing."[21]

Confirmation of a new *kido butai* arrived the next day, when Hypo intercepted and translated "Striking Force Operation Order No. 6." This dispatch
to the "Commander Destroyer Striking Force" ordered destroyer screens for
many of the carriers and capital ships in the striking force, with instructions
to the *Akagi* to depart Yokosuka on 15 May, rendezvous in home waters with
unidentified ships on 18 May, and proceed to Sasebo, from where the entire
striking force would depart on 21 May. Rochefort sent the translation to King
and Nimitz, adding: "Destination of the above force is unknown."[22]

But Rochefort had a good idea where it was *not* heading: south toward the Coral Sea and the islands of the south Pacific. In his 8 May dispatch to King and Nimitz regarding the First Air Fleet's new striking force, Rochefort noted: "While the center of activity is the Coral Sea, signs of renewed activity in other areas were seen." Hypo noted little radio traffic or ship activity that concerned the south Pacific. Rochefort wrote: "Efforts to locate any additional fleet units en route to reinforce the Jap fleet in (the Coral Sea) have failed to disclose any major units headed that way."[23]

The southern route seemed like a dead end. But as of 9 May, neither Rochefort nor Layton nor anyone else in intelligence could say definitely where the Imperial Navy was heading. Rochefort and Layton did think they knew some things. There was that mystery raid on Oahu, now getting closer, possibly fewer than ten days away. And there was that strange thrust toward the Aleutians, now pegged for late May. But neither locale seemed to be the full answer. For that, Rochefort would keep watching the movements of the Second Fleet and the First Air Fleet.

All the while intercepts poured in suggesting the magnitude of the operation that clearly was on the way. Through the fog generated by deception and radio silence, Hypo translated a "partially readable" message from Tokyo alluding to a unit called "the Yokosuka landing force," which, Rochefort told CINCPAC and Main Navy, "will carry out some kind of training" at Guam.[24] A landing force implied occupation. With Port Moresby now out of the question, the landing contemplated by the Japanese navy would take place somewhere else.

U.S. Navy planners gained an important clue on 11 May, when Belconnen translated Admiral Kondo's "2nd Fleet Operations Order No. 22." Addressing all elements of his fleet, including a newly formed "2nd Fleet No. 1 Occupation Force," Kondo showed an unexpected interest in the Mariana Islands. "This force will proceed direct to the Saipan-Guam area and wait for the forthcoming campaign," he ordered.[25] There was Saipan again. Why would Kondo send his occupation force to Saipan?

To OP-20-G, Saipan seemed a likely site for drills that might precede King's predicted IJN thrust into the south Pacific. Rochefort disagreed. "Suggest possibility," he told CINCPAC and COMINCH, that forces convening at Saipan could be components of an "actual campaign or operation with two CarDivs and two BatDivs still not mentioned," an operation that, in his view, was getting ready to move, but not south.[26] He based his estimate on Hypo's traffic analysis showing that almost every destroyer command in Yamamoto's Combined Fleet had been assigned to the mid-Pacific region.[27]

Still, how Saipan fit into Yamamoto's plans remained unclear. The second-largest of the Marianas, a chain of volcanic islands in the northwest Pacific, Saipan housed a sizable IJN base, but it seemed an unlikely starting point for operations in the Hawaiian or Aleutian areas. Rochefort's radiomen did their best to monitor transmissions to and from Kondo's Second Fleet and Nagumo's famed *kido butai*. The two fleets seemed to hold the key to what was going to happen. But as of 12 May Saipan continued to puzzle, as did the main target of the Japanese navy's impending campaign. Layton on 12 May commented in his daily scorecard: "The Striking Force to commence operations 21 May . . . objective or mission not indicated."[28]

꜄ ꜄ ■ ꜄ ꜄

As the Imperial Navy assembled its far-flung forces, creating new striking and occupation forces, assigning new anchorages, switching around its ships like pieces on a giant oceanic chessboard, Japanese naval communications exploded. At first the increase seemed a blessing, as it gave analysts more traffic with which to work. But then the volume got ridiculous.

During the first two weeks of May 1942, the Japanese generated many more messages than the Navy's listening posts could possibly snare. Wahiawa's fifty or so radiomen were overwhelmed. They hauled in as many transmissions as their limited manpower and receivers would permit, then transmitted or trucked the collection down to Pearl, confronting Rochefort's cryptanalysts with huge bundles of raw intercepts.

Station Hypo now received somewhere between 500 and 1,000 intercepts per day, a sizable number but far fewer than the Japanese transmitted.[29] According to an estimate by CINCPAC staff, Hypo's intercept men copied no more than 60 percent of all "possible messages," while the unit's Pearl Harbor analysts decoded just 40 percent of "messages copied."[30] Put another way, Hypo was translating or partially translating only about a quarter of all IJN messages then being transmitted. That may not have seemed like much, but under the circumstances it represented an astonishing feat. It proved to be enough.

As more and more intercepts poured into Hypo, the character of the basement changed once again. From a monastery the place turned into a pressure cooker. Rochefort set the tone. During the run-up to the Coral Sea engagement he had begun working twenty- and twenty-two-hour days, taking time off only to sleep an hour or two in a small room in a corner of the basement where he had a cot. "I would personally translate about one hundred and forty messages a day," Rochefort said. "You can't do this in eight hours."

Rochefort's core group—Dyer, Wright, Holtwick, Lasswell, Finnegan, Huckins, and Williams—worked similar hours, settling into a routine they would observe through May and into June. "Normal would be possibly twenty hours a day," Rochefort said. "In the days immediately preceding, say, Coral and Midway, it would be unusual to have these people put in less than twenty hours a day."[31]

Gradually life in the basement took on a surreal quality. The only reality was the basement itself, the world of codebreaking. The outside world, the war itself, receded. "By and large, I would say, throughout the war, what I knew about U.S. operations was what I read in the *Honolulu Advertiser*," Dyer said. The problem was time. "There are only twenty-four hours in a day. . . . Trying to do a job [for which] thirty-two hours a day would not have been enough, you don't have time to waste on unessential things."

Dyer later found his own way to retain a sense of identity with combat forces: He kept on his desk a lacquered abacus, called a *soroban*, liberated from a previously occupied Japanese island. "Sometimes we would get something to remind us of operations," Dyer said. "Somebody in our outfit landing out there was thoughtful enough to bring it to me." It was a perfect gift for a math wizard breaking the Japanese code.[32]

Staying awake was almost as much of a problem as solving JN-25(b). Rochefort recalled people using amphetamines. "Dyer had buckets full of pills sitting on his desk, and every so often he would just grab a couple and put them in his mouth."[33] That was one of Rochefort's few statements that elicited a strong rebuttal.

"That is pure unadulterated fiction," Dyer said later. "I had nothing on my desk for the benefit of anybody else, or even myself. I did not supply anyone else with them." But Dyer did take pills prescribed to alleviate a case of inflammatory colitis, a condition he said was brought on by the frustration of sitting long hours at a desk struggling with an intractable code. For this problem, Dyer took both uppers and downers. "I couldn't keep awake sitting at my desk," he recalled. "I complained about that, so [my doctor] gave me some Benzedrine sulfate. I would take that in the morning and Phenobarbital at night. They worked pretty well."[34]

II ■ II

Outside the basement, at CINCPAC headquarters and Main Navy in Washington, Nimitz and King were increasingly uneasy about what they were hearing. The seemingly contradictory reports about the timing of the various offensives—17 May or later for an attack on Oahu, and 20 June or later for a still-unidentified operation—unsettled both admirals. They weren't precisely in conflict, but they weren't in agreement, either. They drew different conclusions from the comint crossing their desks.

Those dissimilarities surfaced around the middle of May. Originally the more aggressive of the two, King now became more cautious. Clearly a lot was on his mind. Worried about the south Pacific, as always, and upset by the loss of the *Lexington*, King on 12 May told Nimitz he considered it "inadvisable" for Halsey's Task Force 16, centered around the carriers *Enterprise* and *Hornet*, to operate "in forward areas beyond own shore-based air cover and within range of enemy shore-based air," until "necessity requires" such operations.[35]

Believing the next enemy move would be against the "inadequately defended" islands of the south Pacific, King advanced an unusual idea. To preserve U.S. carriers during attacks on the islands, he proposed that Nimitz "operate one or more carrier groups from shore" and reinforce those bases with land-based bombers flown in from Hawaii and Australia.[36]

By the time King's proposal arrived at CINCPAC headquarters, Nimitz's appraisal of the danger in the Pacific had changed.[37] Nimitz had come to believe that the main threat posed by the Imperial Japanese Navy was close to home rather than in the south Pacific. Having taken note of Hypo's finding that the Japanese planned a "second King campaign" against Pearl Harbor, he doubted it would be a glancing blow like the 4 March attack. Nimitz took stock of Hypo's 8 May finding that the First Air Fleet, in close association with the Second Fleet, had formed a new striking force, a sizable armada that could move by the end of May 1942.

Taking into account all the warning signs, Nimitz thought he understood where the new *kido butai* was headed. The 12 May *Greybook* recorded his evolving viewpoint about what the Japanese navy was going to do: "Commence an operation May 21 with a force of about 3 BB, 2–4 CV, and usual light forces. The objective may be Oahu."[38]

Given his drastically different reading of the situation in the Pacific, there was no way Nimitz could comply with King's proposal. Replying late on 13

May, Nimitz diplomatically presented King his own estimate of the peril arising in the Pacific. He told King the Imperial Navy probably would delay any further action against Port Moresby until it had built up more strength at Rabaul.

He stated, as everybody did, that the Japanese navy would soon occupy Ocean and Nauru Islands and, possibly, keep moving eastward—a course that would take it toward Howland and Baker Islands in the central Pacific. Nimitz figured it was likely the enemy would continue on its eastward path and "attack Oahu in the near future with long range sea planes." The type of fuel being loaded on board Japanese tankers led Nimitz to conjecture that the large striking force now assembling in Japan's home waters was preparing for an "attack on [a] populous area—probably Oahu, possibly the West Coast."[39]

Why Nimitz mentioned the West Coast can't be explained, unless it was to jolt King's attention away from the south Pacific. Nimitz pledged to do all he could to make Oahu impregnable. He tactfully set proposals before King that were aimed at securing the Hawaiian chain.

Before King could respond, he and Nimitz were faced with a startling IJN dispatch, decrypted and translated by Station Negat on 13 May. It seemed to clarify what the Imperial Navy was up to in the Hawaiian and Aleutian Islands. The originator of the message (not identified in the heading) asked to be resupplied with charts covering the following geographic areas: Niihau to Oahu, Oahu to Hawaii, Hawaii, Pearl Harbor, Oahu, Seward Anchorage and Wells Bay, and the Western Hawaii Group.[40]

If there was a trace of good news in the decrypt, it was the absence of any interest in the West Coast; Nimitz and King could relax about that threat. But the heavy focus on the Hawaiian chain and the Aleutians caused the always surprising King to revise his earlier opinion, if only briefly. Fearing that an attack on the Hawaiian chain might come sooner than anyone expected, COMINCH ordered Nimitz to declare a state of "Fleet Opposed Invasion"— a condition of heightened alert in which warships and shore facilities would be at maximum readiness.

Nimitz fretted more about the massive offensive he saw building in Empire waters than the quick, flying-boat raid that King seemed to have in mind. But he knew such a raid was possible, maybe within a few days. To prevent IJN flying boats from refueling again at French Frigate Shoals, Nimitz ordered the waters around the Shoals mined and directed patrol boats to remain in their vicinity. He implemented the King directive for the Hawaiian and Aleutian Islands, including Midway.

The moves by King and Nimitz showed the two admirals improvising and adjusting as nimbly as they could to changing conditions as their assessment of the situation evolved. They would change their minds again in just a few days.

23

Five Days in May

I've got something so hot here it's burning the top of my desk.

—Joe Rochefort

Everything changed on 13 May. The day marked a turning point in the long-simmering debate over where the next Imperial Navy blow would fall. Before that day a fair case could have been made for any number of sites in the Pacific area, but after 13 May, reasonable grounds for doubting the main Japanese objective vanished.

On that day Hypo analysts decrypted, and Rochefort translated and interpreted, an Imperial Navy message pointing emphatically in one direction. The intercept left room for the Aleutians and Pearl Harbor only as secondary targets. It would take a while for this news to sink in; not all would accept it. Some would harbor doubts for weeks, but for those who examined Hypo's latest decrypt, there was now powerful evidence that the Japanese intended to invade two small islands 1,200 miles northwest of Pearl Harbor: the Midway Atoll.

The critical player in this discovery was an ordinary Japanese supply ship called the *Goshu Maru*. Since the outbreak of the war, she had plied the waters from Nagoya and Yokosuka on the Japanese mainland to Empire bases at Rabaul, Wake, and the Marshall Islands, ferrying fighter aircraft, aircraft engines, and spare parts. Early on Wednesday 13 May, while anchored at Wotje Atoll in the eastern Marshalls, the *Goshu Maru* received an important transmission from the commander of the Japanese navy's Fourth Air Attack

Squadron, based in the Marshalls. Wahiawa's radiomen intercepted the message and speeded it to Station Hypo, where it was decrypted and translated that afternoon by Rochefort and his analysts. The message told the *maru* to advance to Imieji, a small IJN base near Jaluit, "load air base equipment and munitions of the Imieji (sea plane unit) and proceed to Saipan."

Once there, the message made clear, the ship was to join the assembling occupation force—the by-now familiar term *koryaku butai*. It was then to "load its base equipment and ground crews and advance to Affirm Fox ground crews. Parts and munitions will be loaded on the *Goshu Maru* . . . Everything in the way of base equipment and military supplies which will be needed in the K campaign will be included."[1]

Two elements in the message jumped out at Rochefort: Affirm Fox, or AF, clearly a geographic designator, and the K campaign. How long it took Rochefort to connect AF with Midway is impossible to know. It might have been a few minutes, maybe longer. After all, AF hadn't made a significant appearance in radio traffic since 9 March, shortly after the Japanese seaplane attack on Pearl Harbor. Hypo's linguists at that time linked AF with Midway, an identification confirmed by Station Cast on 23 March.

AF almost certainly existed somewhere in the basement's files, but those tended to be scattered. Each Hypo team, and often each analyst, kept separate files. Some analysts were tidy, such as Red Lasswell who maintained meticulous records. Others were less structured, and Rochefort fell easily into the latter category. His desk was surrounded by piles of paper through which he rummaged when he wanted something. Rochefort wasn't better organized "because I could remember," he said later. "I could remember back maybe three or four months. This fellow sends a message to some other command. He sends this. So we dig back in here to produce this from the stack of junk [around my desk]. In other words, everything was in my head."[2]

Hypo officers who worked with Rochefort attested to his remarkable memory. "He had a photographic mind and never, to my knowledge, forgot a single detail," marveled Lt. John Roenigk.[3] However he made the AF connection with Midway, through memory or finding the list of geographic designators on his desk, Rochefort was satisfied. He had no doubts that AF stood for Midway. Nor did any other analyst in the basement. They were all just as convinced as Rochefort, especially linguist Joe Finnegan, who remembered working on the AF translation back in March when the linkage with Midway had first been made.[4]

From a few translated lines within an IJN message sent to one of their obscure *marus*, Rochefort and his Hypo colleagues identified the Imperial Navy's impending target. And they tied the K campaign to the Japanese forces now concentrating at Saipan.

Rochefort didn't circulate that news instantly. There was always a lag of several hours between the arrival of an intercept by either teleprinter or jeep, its decryption and translation, and its release to the Navy's high command in Washington and at Pearl Harbor. Still, while the AF message was in raw form, intelligible but not fully translated and not ready for release, Rochefort knew he had something of the greatest importance. He knew what to do with it.

He called Layton on their secure phone, realizing that Nimitz might require additional explanation. "I've got something so hot here it's burning the top of my desk." When Layton asked what it was, Rochefort told him what he had. "You'll have to come over and see it. It's not cut and dried, but it's hot! The man with the blue eyes will want to know your opinion of it."[5]

After meeting with Rochefort and conferring with the Hypo analysts who had worked on the decrypt, Layton agreed his friend did indeed have something hot. He returned to CINCPAC headquarters to look for Nimitz. "I wanted Admiral Nimitz to see these pieces first hand and urged him to do so," Layton said.[6]

What Layton told Nimitz about Rochefort's find wasn't clear. Layton knew Navy brass tended to brush off estimates derived from cryptanalysis because they believed them to be exaggerated. To compensate for this tendency and make sure that Hypo's calculations got the attention they deserved, sometimes he inflated Rochefort's numbers. The practice infuriated Rochefort. "Layton used to upgrade [the estimates]," Rochefort said. "If I said four carriers Layton would make it six."[7]

Whatever Layton said to Nimitz didn't get the desired response. The admiral was interested but, as luck would have it, tied up. He said he couldn't spare the time.[8] But he did agree to send over to the basement his new war plans officer, Captain McCormick, a seasoned Navy officer who had served on battleships and commanded destroyers and submarines. McCormick would give Rochefort's material the hard-headed review Nimitz needed. He arranged to drop by the next morning, 14 May.

In the meantime, Rochefort and his linguists put the finishing touches on the *Goshu Maru* message. They completed the translation, double-checked the code groups, and filled in all the blanks as best they could. Rochefort had the message hand-delivered to CINCPAC headquarters in the early evening of 13 May. He then radioed it to OPNAV and COMINCH and copied Belconnen via COPEK. And he attached to the decrypt some comments of his own: "While there are some 'blanks' in above believe gist of message is as given. No explanation as to why tender loads at Imieji. Goes to Saipan then returns to Midway except that she will join Task Force at Saipan, proceeding direct to destination from there. Note mention of K Campaign as connected with AF movement."[9] The message arrived at Main Navy early Thursday 14 May, available for Rochefort's Washington superiors to include as part of their morning reading.

Back at Pearl Harbor, McCormick showed up in the basement early Thursday, accompanied by Layton. Rochefort couldn't have asked for a better reviewer. Square-jawed and quiet-spoken, McCormick was old-line Navy, reserved in manner, radiating authority. He looked every inch the admiral he would soon become. But he combined his regal bearing with a sense of ease. McCormick's fellow officers liked and respected him. A subordinate remembered him as "a delightful, smart, clean-cut gentleman."[10] Even the hard-to-impress Rochefort thought well of him, stating later that he "thoroughly respected his ability."[11] What McCormick thought would count with Nimitz.

Rochefort was ready for the two officers. He presented his exhibits on sheets of plywood laid over sawhorses in the middle of the basement, near the desks of Lieutenant Holmes and Ensign Showers. He "didn't have enough tables or desks on which to lay out his 'exhibits'—many pieces of paper, here and there, but all inter-related," Layton said later. Rochefort started out by giving McCormick a tutorial on traffic analysis, explaining how radio intelligence had captured the Imperial Navy changing its command structure and fleet arrangements to accommodate a massive invasion of Midway. He showed the captain intercepts gathered during recent days—fragments of code and partial decrypts that fleshed out the picture he was painting. "We went over the papers, one by one," Layton said. "We went through the whole compilation of traffic analysis, how each command, or unit, became associated with others and then continued in association with still others, where there had been no association before; how these new associations continued to be together, how there had been general association between commanders, but now all the ships of a division [were] brought into common association."

"It's like Virginia Reel or a square dance," Layton mused. "Those concerned 'become associated' and thereafter follow an intricate pattern in relation, one to the other; they would nearly always 'do-se-do' back with their partners, or with another 'set.'"[12]

Then Rochefort got to the meat of the matter. Making use of the *Goshu Maru* intercept, he called McCormick's attention to the words *koryaku butai*—a phrase he and his fellow linguists had translated as "occupation force" or "invasion force" just before the Japanese navy had occupied Rabaul on 23 January. He noted that the same phrase had also appeared in Japanese transmissions just prior to the Japanese invasion of the New Guinea ports of Lae and Salamaua on 5–8 March.[13]

Rochefort walked McCormick through the *Goshu Maru*'s projected route—first stopping at Imieji, bringing on board air base equipment and munitions; proceeding to Saipan, loading supplies needed for the K campaign; joining the *koryaku butai* and advancing to AF. How did Rochefort know AF was Midway? "It was only logic," Rochefort said later. "There was no brainstorm involved in this thing at all. . . . The Japanese developed a simple little code referring to cities, counties, states, countries and areas by two or three Roman letters." He added: "Very quickly it became apparent that these [letters], in the Pacific at least, where the letter A appeared, were invariably American." He noted that the Japanese had reported on 7 December that they had attacked a place called AH. "Now obviously this has to be either the island of Oahu or some part of the island."[14]

Still more evidence linking A to American sites piled up. During the early months of 1942, Hypo had confirmed more than fifty such sites to its own satisfaction: AA as Wake, AD as Samoa, AO as the Aleutians, AOB as Kiska, AOE as Dutch Harbor, AH as Hawaii, AK as Pearl Harbor, to name just a few.[15] There was also a very strong suspicion that AFH was French Frigate Shoals, the large atoll 560 miles northwest of Pearl Harbor that the Japanese had used to refuel seaplanes en route to their 4 March Pearl Harbor attack. "It naturally follows that A followed by another letter was somewhere in this area," Rochefort said.

IJN transmissions following the 4 March raid proved to be the clincher for AF as Midway. "The Japanese in their orders to the planes made mention of the fact that the Americans maintained a rather extensive air search from AF," Rochefort said. "So AF then had to have some airfield on it or seaplane bases and the only thing we had was, of course, Midway."[16]

But if the case for AF was closed, as Rochefort believed it to be, much else about the Imperial Navy's fast-developing offensive remained unknown, including the two next most important facts about the operation: the date and time. Hypo did not know the routes various attacking forces would take in approaching Midway. Nor did Rochefort and his analysts have, at least at this stage, an order of battle—a definitive lineup of the IJN forces that would be arrayed for the engagement.

Right now, Rochefort could say only a few things with certainty: the Japanese navy's mighty Second Fleet was assembling an invasion force at Saipan; in conjunction with that force, at least four *kido butai* carriers—the *Akagi*, *Kaga*, *Hiryu*, and *Soryu*—were to rendezvous soon in Japan's Inland Sea, then head toward an unknown destination after 21 May. The operation wouldn't be a little stab like the 4 March attack, Rochefort said. If carriers were involved, "this would signify an air attack," he said. "Now, if in the same outfit you find a movement of ships carrying personnel and transports, then this would give you reason to think about possibly an occupation."[17] That's what all signs indicated, Rochefort said. Hypo's intercepts showed the Imperial Navy organizing a massive amphibious operation intended to culminate in the occupation of Midway.

McCormick was impressed. "He asked questions, went through our files and remained in the basement the better part of the day," recalled Ensign Showers, whose desk was near Rochefort's sawhorses. "He seemed thoroughly interested in what we had."[18]

McCormick returned to CINCPAC headquarters convinced that Rochefort was correct about AF. He conferred with Nimitz, presented Rochefort's findings, and, in due course, told CINCPAC that "seeing the raw material at first hand had reinforced his own conviction of an impending invasion of Midway."[19] Coming from a seasoned officer like McCormick, this view carried weight. CINCPAC harbored a doubt or two, but he agreed that the case for Midway was strong. On 14 May 1942, Nimitz became a convert to Hypo's Midway analysis.

⁞⁞■⁞⁞

Even before embracing the Midway theory, Nimitz had been in a bind. His boss, Admiral King, wasn't blind to the dangers facing Hawaii, but he saw things differently. On 12 May King told the Joint Chiefs in Washington that the Japanese could strike anywhere along the Alaska-Hawaii-Australia line by 1 June.[20] He even ordered Nimitz to declare a state of emergency, fearing the Japanese navy planned another flying-boat raid on Pearl Harbor. But King still believed that the enemy's overarching goal at this stage remained the isolation, if not the conquest of Australia, to be accomplished in piecemeal steps—occupying Port Moresby first, then driving farther south to seize key south Pacific islands, all part of a master plan to erase Australia as an Allied base.

To protect Australia, King on 27 April instructed Nimitz to keep at least two carriers on permanent patrol in the south Pacific, where the *Hornet* and *Enterprise* (Halsey's Task Force 16) now cruised. That order troubled Nimitz, but he carried it out. Nimitz was even more disturbed by King's 12 May dispatch directing him to keep Halsey on a short leash. King didn't want Halsey to operate in forward areas beyond shore-based air cover. And he wanted Nimitz to transfer some support personnel and relief pilots to air bases in the south Pacific.

King's instructions ran against Nimitz's grain. The last thing he wanted was to get tied down to a static defense in the south Pacific.[21] He wanted more, not fewer carriers on patrol in Hawaiian waters. CINCPAC wanted Halsey's carriers operating in the central Pacific.

The problem for Nimitz was how to bring that about without nettling his mercurial boss. He needed to say something to King and did so on Wednesday 13 May, the same day he told Layton he couldn't see Rochefort and one day *before* he would hear back from McCormick on his visit with Rochefort. With King's latest messages in hand, Nimitz drafted a response.[22]

Walking a kind of tightrope, he tried to deflect COMINCH away from the strictures he had put on Halsey's movements. He cited the looming Imperial Navy threat to the central Pacific, requesting that King reconsider his 27 April order that two carriers remain stationed in the south Pacific. He asked that King "give consideration to moving Halsey to the Central Pacific."[23]

What Nimitz proposed was nothing less than a fundamental rethinking of COMINCH's whole Pacific strategy. He told the U.S. Fleet's commander in chief where he thought the Japanese were going to strike—either Oahu or the West Coast—and put forward what he thought were realistic measures to counter the enemy's projected moves. CINCPAC radioed his message to COMINCH late in the day on Wednesday 13 May. He did so around the time Rochefort transmitted his fully decrypted AF message to Washington, about which Nimitz had not yet been briefed. In this instance, Rochefort circulated the translation to Washington when it was ready for release, without waiting for Nimitz. This might have seemed strange, since Rochefort usually reported important news to Nimitz first. But Rochefort no doubt reasoned that he had already alerted Layton. Given the urgency of that decrypt, in all likelihood Rochefort figured he'd better get it to Washington fast. It was to OP-20-G, after all, to which he was ultimately accountable.[24]

Both the Nimitz and Rochefort transmissions would be decoded in Washington and available for reading first thing Thursday morning, 14 May, but Nimitz's would have priority. It went directly to COMINCH. Hypo's AF message, once processed by the OP-20-G watch officer, would proceed through the hierarchy, stopping off at OP-20-G's lead officers, moving on to ONI, and making it finally to King, who in fact read as many Hypo translations as he could. COMINCH would have a lot to think about on Thursday.

In his message to Washington, CINCPAC told COMINCH quite a lot about what he *did* and *did not* want to do. But Nimitz didn't tell King everything he wanted to do and in fact had already done. On the evening of 13 May (14 May in the New Hebrides) Nimitz passed on to Halsey COMINCH's advice from a day earlier that Task Force 16 not advance into forward areas beyond U.S. shore-based air cover. That message was routine. He was keeping Halsey informed of King's wishes. What Nimitz did next wasn't routine.

First he indicated to Halsey that the fifty-plus Wildcats he had on his two carriers would provide a better defense for Task Force 16 than land-based air cover. Then, in an unusual display of independence, Nimitz followed up this communication with an "eyes only" message for Halsey.[25] Unlike nearly all CINCPAC messages, COMINCH was not an addressee. "Nimitz directed Halsey to be seen [by the Japanese the next day] and reported," Layton told historian John Lundstrom years later.[26] He told Halsey to take Task Force 16 the next day toward Ocean and Nauru Islands, a route that would require him to pass within 500 miles of Tulagi, from where Halsey and Nimitz knew IJN flying boats scanned as far out as 700 miles. After being spotted, Halsey was to withdraw quickly to the south to avoid any further contact with IJN forces.

Nimitz was taking a calculated risk. He strongly believed that once the Japanese discovered Task Force 16—a sizable armada consisting of two carriers and their supporting vessels—they would pull back their weaker Ocean-Nauru invasion force, now unsupported by carriers, since the *Shokaku* and *Zuikaku* had retired to the north. Nimitz gambled that the retreat of the Ocean-Nauru force would clear the way for Halsey to return his carriers to Pearl.[27]

Halsey went along with Nimitz's directive. Exercising the discretion Nimitz requested, he never logged CINCPAC's message (it's unlikely King ever learned of it). Irked by King's cautionary advice of 12 May, the aggressive Halsey was only too happy to be released from what he regarded as a straitjacket. Late on 14 May (local time) he set course to the northwest on a heading that put him on a direct line toward the center of the Japanese navy's Tulagi search zone.[28]

II ■ II

Early on Thursday 14 May, watch officers at Main Navy started reading newly arrived traffic from the Navy's distant listening posts. One item was Rochefort's AF message. Reaction to it was slow in coming from OP-20-G (primarily John Redman and Joe Wenger), naval communications (Joseph Redman), and war plans (Rear Admiral Richmond Kelly Turner). But the Office of Naval Intelligence, in its summary of IJN movements prepared each day for COMINCH, weighed in with a review that clearly reflected a reading of Rochefort's AF dispatch.

"Evidence of a forthcoming coordinated air and submarine attack on the Hawaiian Islands continues to mount," ONI analyst Boone reported. "Although uncertain at present there are indications that an actual landing may be attempted on Midway or possibly Johnston Island. Every effort is being made to determine more exactly the reliability of this report and which of the two locations is correct." ONI labored under the misapprehension that AF might be Johnston Island, a small atoll 720 miles southwest of Pearl Harbor where the U.S. Navy maintained an airfield. It seemed an unlikely target for the Imperial Navy. But the Japanese were aware of Johnston Island and, accordingly, had given it the geographic designation AG, identified as such by both Hypo and Cast back in March. Cast at that time had circulated the information to Washington, but ONI, for whatever reason, had failed to make a note of it. Even though Johnston Island got equal billing with Midway, ONI's 14 May summary represented progress. It was the first time Midway had shown up in any of that office's daily summaries as a possible IJN objective. Midway at least was now on ONI's radar.[29]

Others had trouble seeing AF as Midway. Among them, strangely, were the analysts at Belconnen in Melbourne. Just two months earlier, with many of the same officers as it had now, Cast's Corregidor team had joined Hypo in identifying AF as Midway and had circulated that news to Washington.[30] Now, after the move from the Philippines to Australia, the unit's analysts displayed some slippage in institutional memory. After decrypting the same

Goshu Maru message Hypo had picked up on 13 May, Belconnen's analysts thought AF might be Jaluit Island in the Marshalls or Wake.[31]

Rochefort's view that AF represented Midway fared better on his home turf. CINCPAC's intelligence staff, headed by Layton, agreed that Midway was targeted for invasion and occupation. Even Captain Steele, McCormick's war plans assistant whose ideas sometimes drew scoffs from his intel counterparts, concurred: "An attack on Midway seems indicated."[32]

The sudden emergence of Midway as an Imperial Navy objective was reflected in Layton's daily scorecard of "enemy activities": On 14 May Midway moved up closer to the top of his list of looming IJN threats. He cited the *Goshu Maru* picking up supplies needed for the still-pending K campaign and "advancing to Midway (AF) via Saipan." Layton described the operation as a "large-scale assault and raid by [a carrier] group to remove our advanced [submarine] base." He noted "vague indications Aleutian area may be included in campaign."[33]

Far-sighted as Layton may have seemed, there was an unresolved quandary at the center of his estimate. He figured the Midway operation to be part of the Japanese navy's Second K Campaign—the mystery attack on Pearl Harbor that Hypo had forecast on 6 May. Unclear in Layton's outlook was which of the two attacks—the thrust against Oahu or the invasion of Midway—was to constitute the main IJN blow. Was Midway going to be the tail of a major offensive against Oahu? Or was Oahu going to be the tail of a massive campaign against Midway?

Layton had it both ways. In his 14 May scorecard he summarized the battle taking shape as "a campaign designed to take Midway and Dutch Harbor, followed by an assault on Oahu," the latter of which would also include carriers.[34] Layton's ambivalence would continue. He remained undecided whether the main target was Oahu or Midway.[35] So did other people. The specter of a major assault on Oahu coinciding with an invasion of Midway—or whatever target was represented by AF—would confound U.S. Navy planners at both Pearl Harbor and Main Navy. Nimitz sorted it all out eventually. So did King, but not before he took a few detours.

Admiral King got around to answering Nimitz's message two days later, Friday 15 May. By that time King knew the Japanese had spotted Halsey the day before, about 500 miles southeast of Tulagi.[36] King wasn't happy about the sighting and so informed Nimitz. But that wasn't the main thing he had on his mind.

King had given himself twenty-four hours to digest the two Pearl Harbor dispatches received on 14 May. One, of course, was CINCPAC's pre–*Goshu Maru* dispatch citing Oahu and possibly the U.S. West Coast as Japanese focal points for attack. The other was Rochefort's report on the *Goshu Maru.* COMINCH didn't directly question AF as Midway. He did, however, advance an altogether different scenario of likely Imperial Navy activity, one that downplayed the importance of both Midway and the central Pacific as major IJN targets. COMINCH remained preoccupied with the south Pacific.

He cited other decrypts that he believed created "the presumption of offensive starting from Truk 15–20 June and lasting more than one month." He visualized an attacking force consisting of four battleships, five to seven carriers, six cruisers, and numerous destroyers, all moving south: "It seems probable that not only Moresby but also either Northeast Australia or New Caledonia and Fiji may be objectives." Yes, King conceded, Midway would be part of the campaign, but a modest part. He figured the Imperial Navy had provided for "an expeditionary force for capture of Midway," a force that would probably leave Saipan around 24 May and include one carrier division, consisting of the light carriers *Ryujo* and *Hosho.* But Midway wouldn't be the main show. "This [move] may be for eliminating Midway as sub refueling base and also to divert our forces away from SoPac" (the south Pacific). "Alaska is associated but not clear to what extent."[37]

King did, however, make one concession to Nimitz's point of view: He temporarily lifted the requirement he had imposed on 27 April that Nimitz keep two carriers on permanent patrol in the south Pacific. Nimitz now had some leeway with Task Force 16.

But differences remained. What CINCPAC viewed as the centerpiece of Japan's major offensive, an attack in the central Pacific, COMINCH saw as a mere diversion. While Nimitz gathered his staff on the evening of Friday 15 May to prepare a reply, he was interrupted by Layton, this time the bearer of good news. Layton handed Nimitz a Japanese communication picked up by Hypo reporting that the enemy had postponed indefinitely the Ocean-Nauru occupation.[38] Nimitz promptly used his new authority to redeploy Halsey's task force. He fired off an instruction to Halsey (with King included as an addressee), "desire you proceed to Hawaii area."[39]

Later Friday, Nimitz radioed Washington. It was his first full-length report to King since he had heard from McCormick regarding Rochefort and Midway. CINCPAC now presented COMINCH a sharply revised estimate of

IJN intentions. "Present indications that there may well be three separate and possibly simultaneous enemy offensives," Nimitz started out.[40]

He projected first an attack against the Aleutians, probably Dutch Harbor, involving cruisers and carriers. Second, he thought, along with everyone else, the Imperial Navy would again move against Port Moresby, but only with the modest forces already in the area. Third, contrary to King's estimate, Nimitz predicted a move "against Midway-Oahu line probably involving initially a major landing attack against Midway for which it is believed the enemy's main striking force will be employed." It was this third offensive, Nimitz told King, that led him to order Halsey's quick return to Hawaii. He also crowed a little, telling King that in all likelihood it was the sighting of Halsey's task force nearing Nauru and Ocean that had led the Japanese navy to call off the invasion of the two islands.[41]

By Saturday 16 May, Nimitz's thinking had crystallized into a Midway first, Oahu second scenario. But he did leave the door open just a crack for possible error. "Unless the enemy is using radio deception on a grand scale, we have a fairly good idea of his intentions," Nimitz told his staff that day. "It seems quite possible that Orange will attack Midway and raid Oahu the first part of June."[42] He was close to figuring out what the Japanese had in mind.

Late Saturday afternoon, having still not heard back from COMINCH, Nimitz dispatched to King yet another message, this one possibly intended to reduce some of the tension that seemed to be building up between Pearl Harbor and Washington. "Considerable difference in estimates based probably on the same data," Nimitz pointed out. He cited as one example the differing conclusions the two headquarters had drawn from the alleged buildup at Truk. Tactfully as he could, he suggested that King's intelligence analysts reassess their data. "Latest information here does not confirm future enemy concentration at Truk," Nimitz wrote. Then he sounded a conciliatory note: "Will watch situation closely," he said, "and return Halsey to southwest if imminent concentration that direction is indicated."[43]

Rochefort and Layton were impressed by the confidence Nimitz had placed in their estimates. "We were aware that by challenging King and his intelligence staff head on, Nimitz had put himself out on a limb—and we were clinging onto it behind him," Layton wrote later.[44]

Rochefort gave Nimitz even more credit. "The best thing—possibly the best thing that happened to the Navy during the war—was Nimitz's acceptance of Station Hypo's estimate of what the Japanese were going to do," Rochefort said. "He acted on this, for which I am forever grateful, somewhat respectfully grateful, to Admiral Nimitz."[45]

॥ ▪ ॥

On Sunday evening, 17 May, at Pearl Harbor, CINCPAC received an "urgent and confidential" cable in the Navy's most secret flag officer's code.[46] Happily for everyone concerned as well as the war effort itself, King had not lost his capacity to astonish. He did something close to an about-face, accepting in large measure Nimitz's strategic evaluation. He attributed any misunderstanding between the two admirals to the possibility that Pearl Harbor had received decryption intelligence first.[47] King wrote: "I have somewhat revised my estimate and now generally agree with you except I believe enemy attempt to capture Midway and Unalaska will occur about May 30th . . . or shortly thereafter, while enemy South Pacific campaign will be started middle or latter part of June and will be strong attempt to capture Moresby plus Northeast Australia or New Caledonia and Fijis."[48]

King had come around to the point that Rochefort had been trying to make all along in separate dispatches to Washington, but, from all indications, that had been rejected by King's staff. Rochefort's point had been that whatever the purpose of the future buildup scheduled for Truk, it was to *follow* the earlier occupation of Midway and flying-boat attack on Oahu.[49]

King was now comfortable with the Rochefort-Nimitz perspective. Aside from a detail or two, his thinking now closely paralleled Nimitz's: "Estimate that Midway attack may possibly be preceded by shipborne air raid on Oahu and that enemy intention includes effort to trap and destroy a substantial portion of the Pacific Fleet." Rather than just two light carriers, COMINCH now saw the Imperial Navy bringing to bear against Midway four fleet carriers and possibly a fifth, the *Zuikaku*, along with four fast battleships, other warships, and a landing force. To blunt the IJN force, King recommended that Nimitz "make strong concentration Hawaiian area [and] employ strong attrition tactics and not repeat not allow our forces to accept such decisive action as would be likely to incur heavy losses in our carriers and cruisers."[50]

Nimitz had in mind something a little more aggressive but, that being said, the two admirals were now on the same page. Nimitz had a green light to take whatever action he deemed appropriate. Any lingering doubts anyone might have had about King's commitment to CINCPAC's Midway scenario were dispelled a day later, Monday 18 May, when COMINCH heard concerns lodged by the British government about the removal of Task Force 16 from the south Pacific.

King quickly sent instructions to the Navy's special representative in London, ex-Chief of Naval Operations Harold Stark: "Request you say to First Sea Lord in person that indicated imminence of enemy attacks on Midway and Alaska perhaps Hawaii has required withdrawal of carrier-cruiser groups from South Pacific."[51] He suggested the British shift a carrier from their eastern fleet to the south Pacific—a step he likely doubted the British would take.

U.S. Navy officials now appeared unified in recognizing the threat they faced in the central Pacific and what to do about it. But as Rochefort suspected and as he would soon experience firsthand, the Americans at Main Navy weren't quite as united as they seemed.

24

Rochefort's War

We were quite impatient at Station Hypo that people
could not agree with our reasoning.

—Joe Rochefort

Rochefort and Layton were pleasantly surprised by King's 17 May about-
face on Midway. They knew him to be stubborn, strong-willed, and
preoccupied with the southwest Pacific. They didn't think he would instantly
embrace their point of view. But they suspected other factors might have
stiffened his resistance to Pearl's intelligence. The two longtime friends and
allies figured that COMINCH had been ill-served by what they regarded as a
pandering, poorly trained, and even self-aggrandizing OP-20-G staff.

Layton conjectured later that King's turnabout had followed a stormy
encounter between COMINCH and OP-20-G's director. "Evidently Jack Redman had been hauled over the coals and made to eat his previous predictions,"
Layton wrote. "It must have been an uncomfortable twenty-four hours spent
reviewing and revising intelligence estimates. King did not appreciate being
anyone's fall guy, but now he had admitted that Hypo had been right and his
staff wrong."[1]

Whether King had in fact dressed down Redman in a heated confrontation was never verified. No Navy record supports Layton's contention. Even
though King was a perfectionist and a tough taskmaster with little patience
for half-hearted performance, he also was a man of many contradictions who
at times backed people he liked even when they were wrong. Redman may or

may not have been taken to task. Whatever King did or did not say to Redman, the OP-20-G leader showed no signs of having been chastened.

The stage had been set for trouble early in the year when naval communications had eased Rochefort's friend Laurance Safford out of his job as head of OP-20-G. "As long as Safford was in Washington, I just about knew what to expect from him, and he knew what he could expect from me," Rochefort said later. "It worked out very nicely on a personal basis. It was only when other people became involved in it as part of the expansion that we began to have trouble."[2]

Early in the year, naval communications and Hypo started squabbling over a variety of issues.[3] Tension between the two offices heightened in March 1942, when OP-20-G announced that it would join Hypo and Cast working on current Japanese radio traffic to break JN-25(b). OP-20-G then tried to exert greater control over the entire decrypt operation. "Washington wanted to take complete charge and tell us what to do in detail," Ham Wright said. "Well, we'd have no part of that. Not any of us, Rochefort or me or any of us. We had the [job], we knew what we were doing, and we were quite happy with it."[4]

Rochefort probably aggravated the situation in April with a move of his own. He had the Fourteenth Naval District's new commandant, Rear Admiral Bagley, send a message to COMINCH suggesting that Hypo be granted primary responsibility for current IJN radio traffic.[5] Such an arrangement would have relegated Negat to a backseat. The proposal was resented by Redman's team. As Layton observed, the episode added fuel to a rivalry that was slowly developing between OP-20-G and Hypo over which unit best evaluated intelligence.[6]

And, of course, OP-20-G was annoyed when Rochefort declined to restrict Hypo's intercept activity to the sectors assigned by Washington. As described earlier, Rochefort went ahead with his own plan to monitor particular IJN fleets, not naval activity in pre-assigned blocks.[7]

Then on 14 May, Redman and his OP-20-G analysts found themselves reading Rochefort's *Goshu Maru* dispatch indicating an Imperial Navy plan to invade and occupy a placed called AF, defined by Rochefort as Midway. They doubted the finding and conveyed their skepticism to King, who, after several days of indecision, came down on the side of Hypo on 17 May, as noted.

King's message to Nimitz should have settled the matter, but didn't. Even though COMINCH was now convinced that AF was Midway and would very soon be assaulted by all the sea and air forces the Japanese navy could muster, he hadn't yet persuaded everyone at OP-20-G, naval communications, or war plans, entities that quarreled as bitterly among themselves as they did with Hypo. Even after King had made clear his accord with Nimitz, the bickering between John Redman's analysts and Rochefort's continued.

Rochefort could have chosen to ignore the protests he received almost daily from OP-20-G that his AF estimate was faulty. He must have been baffled, having seemingly won the argument. But Rochefort couldn't take that approach. He probably recognized what one historian called "the highly fluid views of Admiral King" and assumed Hypo would have to continue to work to keep in place its estimate that AF was Midway.[8] He figured the game could still be lost.

          II ■ II

And, as noted earlier, Melbourne also doubted Hypo's conclusions about AF. This must have astonished Rochefort. Except for an occasional difference of opinion during the weeks preceding Pearl Harbor, Hypo and its sister decrypt unit, first at Corregidor and now at Melbourne, usually saw things the same way. Rochefort probably found Belconnen's position unfathomable.

As recently as 23 March, Cast had circulated to OPNAV a finding that confirmed Hypo's 11 March estimate that AF represented Midway. But on Wednesday 13 May, the same day Rochefort rediscovered AF thanks to the *Goshu Maru* intercept, Belconnen decrypted the same message and speculated that AF might be Jaluit or Wake. A day later, on 14 May, the unit's officer in charge, Lieutenant Fabian, joined Rochefort and Hypo's analysts in recognizing that the Second Fleet was working with Carrier Divisions 1 and 2 (the First Air Fleet). But they drew different conclusions. "This may be another striking and occupation force but *no* definite hint has been given as to where it will operate" (emphasis in original), Fabian told Washington.[9]

Fabian didn't see Midway in Imperial Navy sights. In fact, he advanced a scenario that soon became the template for much thinking at Main Navy: "Suggest that the first striking force is to operate offensively against the Aleutians and that the second may attempt another attack on Hawaii or attack with intent to occupy other islands in the Southern Pacific in order to cut Allied supply lines," wrote Fabian. Apparently he had concluded there were two equal striking forces, one headed for the Aleutians, the other toward either Hawaii or the south Pacific.

As the days passed, Belconnen intercepted still more messages indicating that an occupation force would soon descend on a place called AF, but each time in his daily report Fabian put Midway in parentheses with a question mark. It wouldn't be until 21 May (Hawaii time), under an extraordinary circumstance, that Fabian would finally confirm AF as Midway.[10] But that was several days away.

In Washington, ONI proved more flexible. On 14 May, Rochefort's *Goshu Maru* decrypt was interpreted to mean that AF could be either Midway or Johnston Island. But on 17 May, ONI analysts changed their story. In their daily summary of Japanese radio activities, prepared for King, they saw Japan's naval forces concentrating in the Saipan-Guam area "for an attack on the Hawaiian Islands, including the seizure of Midway."[11] Midway was now in ONI's picture.

But not in OP-20-G's. The problem wasn't that John Redman and his colleagues were unaware of the supposed link between AF and Midway. They knew of nearly all the Japanese designators for Pacific area sites that had been worked out by Hypo and Belconnen. But OP-20-G analysts often questioned the rationale used by Hypo and Belconnen in determining the designator of a particular place. Earlier John Redman, along with one of his assistants, Commander C. H. Murphy, had simply rejected the Hypo/Belconnen identifications for Bougainville and other sites in the Solomons, as well as several in the Aleutians.[12]

Given OP-20-G's demonstrated weakness for hair-splitting and exaggerated pedantry, it was hardly surprising that Redman and Murphy should question AF as Midway. Redman had doubted the AF identification as early as 18 April, three weeks after receiving that finding from Station Cast. In the margin of a memo from Murphy citing it, Redman had scrawled a note that AF was a communication zone designator, not an area designator.[13] Five days later, in a memorandum to Murphy, Redman restated his view that AF referred to communication zones, "the designators for which may not indicate the same areas as the corresponding geographical area designators."[14]

Rochefort knew he had a battle on his hands shortly after dispatching his *Goshu Maru* decrypt to Washington on 13 May. How long it took Redman and his intelligence people to express their doubts isn't known, but sometime between 14 May and 17 May Rochefort started to hear from the OP-20-G group. The first thing he heard was that AF was a communication zone, not an area designator.

Of course, Rochefort didn't accept that verdict. "He didn't suffer fools lightly," Layton observed of his friend years later.[15] Rochefort tried to walk

OP-20-G through Hypo's thinking. "AF has to be in the Pacific," Rochefort explained. "AF has to be under American control. It was a place which was in close proximity to the place that the Japanese used as a refueling [site] for their attack" in March 1942, referring to French Frigate Shoals (AFH).

OP-20-G wouldn't budge. "We were quite impatient at Station Hypo that people could not agree with our reasoning," Rochefort said after the war, "because they had the same information we had, and they should have without any particular stress on their brain, have come up with the same answers."[16]

Very soon the discussion between OP-20-G and Hypo assumed a darker tone. "They didn't trust our additives and would not use them," Ham Wright said. During the preceding months, Hypo, Cast/Belconnen, and Negat had routinely exchanged additives as they worked them out, circulating them via COPEK channel. The practice enabled the three stations to build up large inventories of additives, without which the underlying code groups could never have been exposed. But now Negat rejected those circulated by Hypo. "It was a mess," Wright said. "We'd fight with OP-20-G all the time; we couldn't get together." The bad feeling soon found expression in the junk sentences, or "padding" that each unit's radiomen inserted before and after actual messages as a security measure, to confuse potential eavesdroppers. "We were getting these nasty remarks," Wright said. "The guys would say these Hawaiian additives were no good." He added, "It got to be more than a game."[17]

It turned out to be far more than a game. From rejecting Hypo's additives it was an easy step to rejecting the conclusions Hypo reached with those additives, one being Hypo's identification of AF as Midway. "Washington did not buy [the] Midway attack at all," Tommy Dyer later said. "They very stubbornly insisted there's nothing to Midway."[18]

He and other Hypo analysts were perplexed by Washington's rigidity. Like OP-20-G, Hypo had developed categories for the reliability of their estimates, conjectures, and guesses about the meaning of messages and message fragments. An "A" message was considered positive, the finding having been determined by more than one source and having turned up in radio traffic numerous times, removing any possibility of doubt. "B" was considered all but certain, established by analysis, but with a wrong identification not impossible; "C" was probable; "D" was possible and likely.[19] A fifth category, "WAG," was also used occasionally: "wild-assed guess."[20]

As far as Hypo's analysts were concerned, AF fell into the A category. It had been identified as Midway by Hypo and, despite their current skepticism, by Belconnen personnel at Cast on 11 and 23 March. AF had turned up more than once in radio traffic over several months in connection with other A designations that were indisputably American possessions in the central Pacific, primarily the Hawaiian chain. "From various things that occurred, there was little doubt in the minds of people at [Hypo] that AF was Midway," Dyer said.[21]

But if Hypo's analysts were stumped by OP-20-G's reasoning, they were not altogether surprised. The two units had been sparring for months. Part of the problem had to do with personalities. Laurance Safford, OP-20-G's ousted director, had been one of the Navy's pioneers in cryptanalysis. John Redman, however, wasn't a trained cryptanalyst and appeared to owe his job to his brother's influence.

Rochefort had little respect for him, referring to him constantly as "little r" Redman. "He was something less than capable or competent," Rochefort said, responding to what he believed, rightly or wrongly, to have been a power grab by OP-20-G. "We were having trouble with them," he said, "because they were attempting to exercise control over us by what I termed bullying tactics or brow-beating tactics, something to bring us in line."[22] Rochefort refused to give in on AF.

As was his habit, he didn't try to disguise his low opinion of his Washington counterparts. After a particularly acerbic exchange, Rochefort would call Layton on their secure phone to fill him in on the points covered. "Joe would say, 'Listen to what these clowns are saying now,'" Layton recalled.[23] "Clowns" became one of Rochefort's favorite terms for the people at OP-20-G.

⊓⊔■⊓⊔

In the days immediately following Rochefort's *Goshu Maru* dispatch, the AF area designator turned up in more intercepts, bolstering Hypo's theory about an attack on Midway. A 16 May intercept would be one of the milestone messages decrypted during the weeks leading up to the Battle of Midway. Of incalculable importance, it indicated the position from which the Japanese planes would be launched for their attack. The *kido butai*'s Nagumo was highly specific about what he intended to do in this request to the 6th Communication Unit: "As we plan to make attacks [roughly] from a northwesterly direction from N-2 days until N-day, request you furnish us with weather reports 3 hours prior to the time of take off on said day. Also, would like to be informed of enemy activity or anything else which might be of importance.

. . . On the day of the attack we will endeavor to . . . at a point 50 miles NW of AF and move pilots off as quickly as possible."[24]

Not all blanks were filled in, but they didn't have to be. An intelligence officer didn't have to be a genius to figure out that Nagumo planned to move to a point within fifty miles of Midway, from where the *kido butai*'s planes would pound the target for two days before the occupation force attempted its landing. The scenario fit Midway perfectly because almost any striking force would approach from the northwest.

Rochefort might have thought the case for Midway was sealed when radiomen intercepted a dispatch from an unidentified originator to the Second and Fourth Fleets and the Eleventh Air Fleet. Translated on 19 May, the message reported that fleet elements concerned with the occupation of a previously unheard-of place called Mike Item, or MI, would hold an operation conference on 26 May, then depart for rendezvous points on 27 May.[25] It was the first time MI had turned up in traffic, a wrinkle that left some analysts wondering if it designated yet another region.

Rochefort's codebreakers didn't think so. The two-kana diagraph was so close to the MO the Japanese navy had used in connection with the Port Moresby campaign that analysts had no trouble figuring it out. Just as MO had served as the codename for the Japanese mission to occupy a place designated RZP (Moresby), MI was the codename for the operation to invade AF (Midway). The Imperial Japanese Navy removed any doubt about the matter a few days later with a dispatch explicitly linking MI with AF.[26] And yet the debate continued.

Six days after Rochefort circulated his *Goshu Maru* dispatch linking AF with Midway, skeptics remained. They were by no means confined to high-echelon posts in naval communications or OP-20-G. They also turned up in unlikely places, as Hypo linguist Red Lasswell discovered to his dismay during 16–20 May.

By mid-May, more than a thousand daily intercepts streamed into Hypo. But during the night of 19–20 May the basement was swamped by an unusually large volume of traffic, including at least fifty intercepts identifiable as high-priority dispatches. The bulk of those showed up during Lasswell's watch, making him the appropriate analyst to tackle the crucial transmissions. He threw himself into the task. So much material was contained in the messages that the impression emerged that Lasswell had stumbled onto Yamamoto's order of battle for the entire Midway campaign—a possibility that proved controversial, even hotly debatable (it will be discussed in detail in the next chapter).

Lasswell's colleagues recalled him working on that particular batch for several days.[27] But he processed a few quickly enough to know what he had. One concerned the location of certain destroyer squadrons to be employed in the AF campaign, translated by Lasswell as Midway.[28] After Rochefort had reviewed his translation and it circulated to Washington, Lasswell ran into trouble. "I was sure of myself," he said. "The element of doubt was thrown into it by the Washington office; [they] thought I was wrong."[29]

The doubter with whom Lasswell clashed was not one of John Redman's cryptanalysts, but a fellow language officer. The antagonist was Commander Redfield "Rosey" Mason, head of OP-20-GZ, the Japanese language unit of OP-20-G and sister unit of OP-20-GY (Negat), specializing in cryptanalysis. Mason had impeccable credentials. A Naval Academy graduate, he had completed mandatory sea-duty tours, then gone to Japan in 1930 to learn Japanese, arriving one year after Rochefort and Layton. Mason was part of the Navy's small clan of linguist-codebreakers in which everybody knew everybody.

He'd served in Manila during 1940–41 as fleet intel officer for Admiral Hart, commander of the Asiatic Fleet. When the Japanese had invaded the Philippines in the waning days of 1941 and early 1942, Mason had joined evacuees from Station Cast in their escape to Melbourne, Australia, where he'd helped set up Belconnen.[30] After Rudy Fabian showed up to lead Belconnen, Mason returned to Washington, where ONI detailed him to OP-20-GZ.

Now Mason served as OP-20-G's chief Japanese linguist. A balding, cherubic-faced man given to flashes of brilliance and outbursts of profanity, he wasn't an easy man to work for.[31] His driving personality intimidated aides, some of whom found him scary, others inspirational. "A highly competitive individual, Mason wanted his unit in Washington, not its rivals at Pearl Harbor and Melbourne, to decode and translate that vital message," one historian observed.[32]

Now Lasswell, no shrinking violet himself, ran into the Mason buzzsaw. A few hours after Lasswell had circulated his AF finding, "Rosey Mason, my counterpart at 'Negat' came on the circuit and agreed with my translation, but thought the target might be elsewhere in the Pacific," Lasswell told Navy historian Roger Pineau.[33] Mason rejected the whole idea that AF might be Midway. Whether he was taking his cues from his nominal boss, John

Redman, or (more likely, given his fierce independence) acting on his own instincts, Mason remained adamant.

So did Lasswell. Over the next several days the two officers argued back and forth via COPEK. "I stuck by my guns," Lasswell said. "I saw no reason to change [my mind]."[34] His tussle with Mason became something of a cause célèbre inside the basement. Just about everybody working the cryptanalytic and codebreaking desks was aware of it and groaned, worried Hypo's case for AF might lose steam at Main Navy. "Rosey Mason was the guy in Washington who wouldn't buy AF for Midway," Ham Wright said. "A very nice guy, an able linguist, but he wouldn't buy it."[35]

Although no one at Main Navy seemed to notice, there was a muddle at the heart of OP-20-G's thinking with regard to Midway. Its various players, from the cryptanalysts in OP-20-GY to the linguists in OP-20-GZ, concurred on one big thing: AF wasn't Midway. They could agree on what AF did *not* stand for, but they couldn't come together on what it *did* represent. They were all over the lot in their estimates.

Around 13 May, the same day Rochefort circulated to Main Navy his *Goshu Maru* dispatch linking AF with Midway, King got an estimate from OP-20-G pointing in a different direction. "Although the available information is vague," John Redman told COMINCH, "it would appear that the 2nd K campaign will be on a considerably larger scale than the first one and may involve a large scale attack starting from the Mandates (as far west as the Marianas) with the CinC 2nd Fleet in direct charge."[36] He saw Hawaii as the Imperial Japanese Navy's principal target.

Redman was right about one thing: The commander in chief of Japan's Second Fleet, Admiral Kondo, was in direct charge of the Imperial Navy's new occupation force now assembling at Saipan. But when the time came, that force would steam toward Midway, not Hawaii.

Ironically, the contents of Rochefort's 6 May decrypt disclosing a Second K Operation had morphed into the centerpiece of the impending Japanese offensive, at least in the minds of some at Main Navy. The view wasn't completely unreasonable. Nimitz too had worried that the coming attack might fix primarily on Hawaii, a view he'd abandoned only after hearing McCormick's report on his meeting with Rochefort.

OP-20-G didn't give up its ideas about Hawaii being main target of the coming campaign, but its analysts raised other possibilities.[37] John Redman's team fashioned two scenarios. One of his section leaders, Lieutenant (jg) J. S.

Lehman, theorized that the K Campaign would involve an attack on Oahu, with Japan's submarines acting as lookouts. After that those subs would "move on eastward"—toward the eastern Aleutians, Alaska, and the West Coast—"to be used as advance lookouts for the 'AF' Campaign. They should be one week to 10 days apart."[38]

In other words, ten days after Oahu was hit, some other target in the areas listed would be bombarded by Admiral Kondo's Second Fleet, which included an occupation force. Was the U.S. West Coast going to be occupied?

Another possibility was envisioned by a second OP-20-G section leader, Lieutenant P. L. Joachim. In a rare reference to Midway, he visualized the Japanese navy's Fourth Air Attack Force, based in the Marshalls, striking Midway as part of the Second K Campaign, but not as the main thrust of the offensive. Joachim had another region in mind. Alluding to recent traffic involving destroyers, he conjectured: "Here is more than a hint that Samoa is to be an objective in the not too distant future, by at least a portion of the forces now concentrating at Saipan."[39] Joachim had the Second Fleet going to Samoa.

Another dissenter was Rear Admiral Turner, director of the War Plans Division, known around Main Navy as "Terrible Turner" because of his hot temper and combative style. "Lean and quick-acting and over six feet tall, he cut an imposing figure, with lantern jaw and beetling black brows that gave him a Mephistophelean aspect," said Layton, who later in the war would feud with Turner and nearly come to blows with him. "Turner was intimidating both in appearance and personality."[40]

Selected for the War Plans post by former CNO Stark early in 1941, Turner quickly proved himself a brilliant thinker and planner, writing the first draft of the Navy's Rainbow 5 war plan that envisaged the United States, in any conflict that might arise, joining with Great Britain to defeat Germany and Italy first. But Turner didn't confine himself to planning. Incorrigibly restless, he also fancied himself an intelligence specialist and expert on Japan.

There were difficulties with that. Turner's background in intelligence was limited, and the basis for his claim to expertise on matters Japanese was flimsy. His declared prowess in this area, from the testimony of his fellow officers, proceeded from his duty as commanding officer of the heavy cruiser *Astoria* when that ship had returned the ashes of the deceased Japanese ambassador to Japan in April 1939. "As a result of the approximately ten days he had spent in Japan on the mission, Turner felt he knew a great deal about the Japanese," wrote one naval officer.[41]

Turner parlayed his ten-day encounter with the Japanese into a power position. He wrangled with various directors of naval intelligence, insisting the authority to evaluate intelligence should rest with War Planning, not ONI. He brought matters to a head in August 1941, when he inserted in ONI's *Intelligence Digest* an article predicting a Japanese attack on, of all places, Siberia—an article that had not been cleared by ONI's Far Eastern desk. When Commander McCollum protested, Turner asked CNO Stark to turn the evaluating function over to War Plans. Stark did.

Now, in the second half of May 1942, Turner was at it again. This time he was challenging not just Hypo but also OP-20-G and naval communications. Turner had been at loggerheads with the two Redman brothers since early March, when DNC Joseph Redman and OP-20-G chief John Redman had created a new entity, OP-20-GI (combat intelligence), to produce current intel reports based on input from Hypo, Belconnen, and Negat. Turner regarded this new intelligence product as a rival to the evaluations put out by War Plans. He didn't like GI's work, and didn't hold back saying so. Soon the analysts in War Plans and GI were bickering in much the same way Hypo and OP-20-G did.

Oddly, the squabbling tended to be over relatively minor issues, such as details about IJN logistics and battle preparations rather than objectives. Even more oddly, both War Plans and OP-20-G appeared unaware of the decisions and words exchanged between CINCPAC and COMINCH, particularly during the critical 8–23 May period.

Around 20 May, Turner and John Redman clashed openly in a face-to-face confrontation that very shortly would reverberate in Rochefort's basement. Turner told Redman bluntly that he was dissatisfied with the intelligence emanating from Hypo and Belconnen as well as from Negat. He said he was particularly unhappy with the failure of all three units to make a distinction between the impending AF and K campaigns, which, he insisted, were unrelated.

Turner's assertion contradicted Rochefort's 13 May report concerning the *Goshu Maru*'s planned track from Saipan to AF (Midway), carrying equipment that included "military supplies which will be needed in the K campaign." The decrypt had made the connection between AF and K an article of faith at Hypo. Pacific Fleet intelligence had accepted the link, as did ONI at Main Navy.

Now Turner tried to undo it. In an extraordinary directive reflecting his boundless self-confidence, he ordered that his view be accepted by all, unless unequivocally refuted by fresh evidence. Turner ordered the officer in charge of OP-20-G's Combat Intelligence Section (GI), Lieutenant Commander Gordon W. Daisley, to circulate a memo to OP-20-G's Washington and field units. "Admiral Turner says that we have been erroneously associating the AF Campaign with the 2nd K Campaign," wrote Daisley. "In his opinion, these will be independent operations, the AF Campaign involving a relatively heavy striking force, while the 2nd K Campaign will use subs and aircraft."[42]

Daisley's subordinates didn't like being told what to think. Lieutenant Joachim, an OP-20-GI section chief, reported that Turner's views were "not entirely" shared by his analysts.[43] What Rochefort thought of Turner's directive hasn't survived, but it can be imagined. In truth, it didn't matter. Soon the Turner thesis would be rendered null and void, turned into a historical curiosity. But for now, Turner still held sway at Main Navy, at least in certain quarters. What, then, did he think the Imperial Japanese Navy was going to do? Where was it going to strike? What was AF?

Drawing on internal correspondence between OP-20-G and War Plans, historian Frederick D. Parker proposed that it was actually Turner who shaped, and may have originated, King's 15 May dispatch to Nimitz depicting the assault on Midway as a diversion from the Japanese navy's main attack. From all indications, Turner believed that attack would not be against Midway, but would be aimed at northeast Australia, New Caledonia, and the Fijis, scheduled to start between 15 and 20 June.[44]

ıı▆ıı

Midway doubters stiffened their resistance. Rochefort picked up ominous murmurs from Washington. The whispering campaign about which Safford had warned him after Pearl Harbor resumed. Now he heard new rumbles, which he traced to the people at OP-20-G, that he was leading the Pacific Fleet into a trap at Midway.[45]

Even his friend Layton, reflecting the concerns of Admiral Nimitz, now wanted stronger confirmation. Nimitz had, of course, received the same alarms being directed at Rochefort. Some high-ranking Army and Navy officers insisted that all the indications pointing toward Midway were part of an elaborate Japanese hoax to disguise a massive offensive against Hawaii or even the West Coast.[46] No evidence ever surfaced putting Admiral King in this camp; in fact, as recently as 17 May King had told Nimitz he now accepted his view on Midway. Still, Nimitz might have wondered. King could be changeable.

Levelheaded, shrewd at assessing people and at calculating risk, Nimitz wasn't one to panic. He still believed the Japanese were preparing a powerful thrust at Midway, but he also knew he was staking the Pacific Fleet—nearly his entire command—on radio intelligence, on information provided by Joe Rochefort. Now that information was coming under withering fire. On 18 May, he imparted his unease to Layton. "[Nimitz] said that, as commander in chief, he could not be satisfied with Rochefort's or my 'guess' as to where [AF] was," Layton said later. "That I was to tell Rochefort that he was to do anything he could within his power to try to solve this problem and to pin down the fact that AF was or was not Midway. I told Joe this and we had a long talk."[47]

Early Tuesday morning, 19 May, Rochefort convened a small group of Hypo's analysts around Jasper Holmes' desk in the basement. He stated the problem and what needed to be done. "We've got to prove to the world that AF is Midway," Rochefort told them. Did anyone have any ideas? Holmes did, and Rochefort liked it. "Very good, Jasper. Very good," he said.[48] Holmes' idea would require Nimitz's approval. Rochefort reached for his secure phone to Layton.

25

Affirm Fox Is Confirmed Here

When in doubt, you compel the enemy himself to produce
the conclusive evidence you seek.

—Ronald Lewin[1]

Rochefort on 20 May found himself having to calm down a furious
Tommy Dyer. Dyer had just decoded a troubling Imperial Navy message from its base on Wake Island to Tokyo. Dated that day, the transmission passed on news taken from a U.S. Navy dispatch—radioed in plain language—intercepted by the Japanese. It revealed what appeared to be an emergency at AF: a mishap at the island's water-distillation system had left it critically short of freshwater. AF was reported as asking Pearl for water—quickly.

What upset Dyer wasn't the contents of the U.S. Navy message from AF (Midway) to AK (Pearl Harbor), but the fact that it was transmitted by radio unencrypted, a violation of all that was sacred in wartime communication. "Those stupid bastards on Midway," Dyer fumed. "What do they mean by sending out a message like this in plain language?"[2] He didn't know that the naval air station on Midway had done just what Pearl Harbor had told it to: send Pearl a message in plain language reporting this exact problem. The message had been a ruse, cooked up by several Hypo analysts who'd convened around Jasper Holmes' desk early Tuesday morning, 19 May.

No one in the group had been to Midway. But Holmes noted that as an engineer on the faculty of the University of Hawaii before the war, he had participated in an investigation of the effect of using coral and saltwater in mixing concrete for construction on Midway. "I was familiar with some of Midway's problems," Holmes wrote later. "I suggested to Rochefort that fresh-water supply was a constant problem at Midway, and a breakdown of its new fresh-water distilling plant would be a serious matter." Joe Finnegan remarked that if the Japanese learned that Midway was short of freshwater, the Wake radio unit would report that information to Tokyo immediately. "That's all right, Joe," Rochefort said, obviously pleased.[3] He also commended Holmes for his useful idea.[4]

Rochefort called Layton on their secure phone. Layton liked what he heard and consulted Nimitz, who quickly approved what Rochefort had in mind. Rochefort then talked the matter over with Commandant Bagley.[5] Together they framed a message for the Navy's commander on Midway, Captain Cyril T. Simard, conveyed by an undersea cable that connected the two sites, permitting communication between Midway and Oahu without use of the airwaves.

The dispatch ordered Simard to radio COM 14 the emergency message in plain language. Simard did so. Bagley then replied, also in a plain-language radio message, that a water barge was on the way. Rochefort told no one about the gambit, not Belconnen, nor OP-20-G, nor, for that matter, his friend Dyer.

Wake picked up this traffic and did just what Finnegan thought it would. The first sign that the Japanese had taken the bait was Wake's 20 May message that landed on Dyer's desk. He reported his "find" to Rochefort along with his exasperation. Rochefort explained.

Given Hypo's strained relations with OP-20-G, Rochefort didn't immediately pass on to Washington the news that AF's identity had been verified. He apparently thought it would appear self-serving for Hypo to be the bearer of this information, since OP-20-G had been disputing Rochefort's AF claim for six nerve-wracking days. He decided to wait and see if anyone else picked up the same transmission. Belconnen picked it up.

A day later, on 21 May, Belconnen passed on to OP-20-G a translation of the Japanese dispatch from Wake to Tokyo: "The 'AF' air unit sent the following radio message to commandant 14th District 'AK' on 20th. . . . At present time we have only enough water for 2 weeks. Please supply us immediately." Belconnen's Rudy Fabian found the message curious, and he let Washington know he would check the report with the Fourteenth Naval District. "If authentic it will confirm identity 'AF' as Midway," Fabian wrote.[6] Rochefort waited until later on 21 May before sending his own dispatch to OP-20-G:

"Connection Melb units despatch regarding water situation at Affirm Fox x Plain language was sent by Midway to 14 on subject of feed situation there for animals x As stated previously Affirm Fox is confirmed here as Midway."[7] The nonsense about a feed situation for animals was probably Rochefort's satiric way of saying the whole thing had been a setup, a hoax to trick the Japanese into disclosing their target. Nor could Rochefort resist a little dig in closing, with "as stated previously." The Redmans surely got the point.

 ı ı ■ ı ı

The ruse had worked. Nimitz relaxed. He ordered the Midway air station to begin reconnaissance flights on 24 May covering an area seven hundred miles northwest of the island. "The enemy is indicated leaving Saipan on the 26th for Midway," CINCPAC's *Greybook* reported on 23 May.[8]

In Washington, ONI informed King that AF had been corroborated as the designator for Midway.[9] Yet, bewilderingly, the AF debate still didn't go away. While the skeptics at Main Navy had been silenced, doubts persisted among the Army's leadership and even in the Roosevelt administration.

Secretary of War Henry L. Stimson questioned the Midway scenario. Rather than mount an invasion against that small central Pacific atoll, he feared the Japanese were gearing up for something more ambitious—"a revenge attack upon us for the bombing of Tokyo," he wrote in his diary on 21 May. Stimson conjectured that the Imperial Navy might be planning to strike Alaska, Panama, or, as many others before him had also believed, the U.S. West Coast.[10]

Army Chief of Staff George Marshall shared Stimson's doubts. Indeed, he suspected that Nimitz and his intelligence team might be falling for an ingenious Japanese trick. The last straw for Marshall was a 20 May decrypt in which the Japanese navy's Fourteenth Air Corps, based near Imieji in the Marshall Islands, requested the Yokosuka Personnel Bureau to forward all its mail to AF.[11] Rather than reflecting Japanese complacency, Marshall thought the message might be part of an IJN stratagem to deliberately call attention to Midway and thereby draw U.S. naval forces away from the real target. "We were very much disturbed because one Japanese unit gave Midway as its post office, and that seemed a little bit too thick," Marshall told Congress later."[12]

Looking for a Doolittle-type raid, Stimson and Marshall on 21 May met with Army Air Forces and G-2 (Intelligence) officials about the possibility that Japanese raiders might strike U.S. plants in San Diego, then escape to Mexico, much in the way Doolittle's planes had flown to China after their stunning attack on the Japanese homeland in April. At Stimson's request the State Department alerted its representatives in Mexico to the danger. The following afternoon Marshall flew to the West Coast to survey the region's defenses, "because we think there is a very real danger of a Japanese raid very soon on some part of the coast and very likely in the southern part," Stimson noted in his diary.[13]

Back at Pearl Harbor, Nimitz heard an echo of the Army's thinking through General Emmons, commander of the Army's Hawaiian Department. Emmons advanced a line of thinking of his own. His concerns resulted in part from Nimitz's use of CINCPAC's emergency powers to place all forces in the Hawaiian area, except Army ground forces, under Navy control.[14]

The emergency condition had been ordered by King in response to a 13 May decrypt in which a Japanese naval unit asked for navigation charts covering the Hawaiian Islands and portions of the Aleutians. Although the Army remained responsible for the defense of Hawaii, an Army-Navy agreement authorized Nimitz to assume control of the Army's Seventh Air Force bombers if conditions warranted such a move.[15] The chart intercept—pointing toward an attack on Hawaii and possibly the Aleutians—seemed to justify Nimitz's action. But when Nimitz started moving the bombers to Midway, Emmons balked.

Around 16–17 May, Emmons sent Nimitz an Army intelligence critique that reflected his own view that the Navy was carrying too far its belief that the Japanese navy now contemplated the conquest of Midway. Worried that the Navy was putting all its eggs in one basket, Emmons pointed out that Nimitz's planning was based upon estimated enemy intentions rather than capabilities—which, Emmons warned, included another attack on Oahu. Emmons visualized a repeat of the 7 December attack.

Nimitz promptly summoned Layton. When he passed the general's memo on to his intelligence officer for comment, Nimitz watched in amusement as Layton exploded, as he'd thought Layton would. Nimitz had received Emmons' concerns good-naturedly, recognizing that he had a point. The memory of 7 December remained fresh at Pearl Harbor as a reminder of what could happen if the Americans dwelled too much on what the Japanese might do rather than on what they could do.[16]

Nimitz also appreciated that Emmons didn't have all the intelligence available to CINCPAC. Just as Kimmel had declined to fully apprise General Short of the radio intelligence supplied by Hypo before the 7 December attack, Nimitz continued to regard Rochefort's decrypts as an exclusive Navy preserve. He believed he couldn't tell Emmons everything he knew.[17] But he did feel he should address at least some of the Army's concerns. He devised a plan he hoped would pacify Emmons. It involved Layton, albeit not in a way Layton welcomed.

Nimitz's solution, conveyed to Layton around the time of the AF water message, was to assign Captain Steele of his war plans staff to reassess the findings of Pacific Fleet intelligence. When Nimitz told his thin-skinned intelligence officer what he planned to do, Layton cringed. Since 13 April Steele had been carrying out a task originally handled by Captain McCormick: offering war plans' analysis of Hypo's daily intelligence. Layton was familiar with Steele's cryptic, sometimes erratic comments and was unimpressed. He regarded Steele as a "boob"—a perplexing officer who tended to be stubborn and obtuse.

Steele's mission was to serve, in effect, as a devil's advocate. His job, quite simply, was to challenge every estimate circulated by Layton and Rochefort. Layton was unenthusiastic about Steele's task, but there was nothing he could do about it. Orders were orders. He grudgingly accepted Steele's larger role in Pacific Fleet intel.[18] The lingering question was whether the Steele appointment would satisfy Emmons. Nimitz and Layton would have to wait and see.

ıı▪ıı

While Layton coped with Steele's greater presence in his daily routine, Rochefort grappled with problems of his own. To the question whether the water message convinced all the unbelievers, Rochefort supplied a blunt answer: "It didn't."[19] The problem bedeviling Rochefort wasn't only the whispering about how he and his Hypo colleagues had been suckered before by Japanese radio deception and now were being duped again. Equally disturbing was an OP-20-G grievance that had been building for some time: Hypo was exceeding its authority in the way it conducted business. The breaking point for OP-20-G was Rochefort's water message. Even though the message elicited new information, John Redman and his entourage didn't like the fact that Rochefort had carried out the ploy—ironically, an example of radio deception *against* the Japanese—without consulting his Washington superiors. They viewed the move as a high-handed act verging on insubordination.

Redman and Wenger regarded Rochefort's stewardship of Hypo dimly, believing it was undermining their effort to centralize Navy intelligence in Washington. They had a point. Under Wenger's reorganization plan instituted in February, OP-20-G was supposed to acquire "central coordinating authority for all communication intelligence activities," as Wenger's memo put it.[20] In theory, that meant OP-20-G's far-flung units were to be less autonomous and more technical in their mission. They would supply Washington the raw material and leave the thinking to OP-20-G. But when Redman looked at what was happening at Pearl Harbor, that was not what he saw. He noticed that Hypo was doing the thinking. This distressed him, and he imparted the message to Rochefort through the usual channels.

Rochefort didn't like what he heard. "We had this ridiculous situation where some people were fully informed," as Rochefort told it later, "but they had no knowledge whatever of the Japanese mentality or of the language or anything else, and yet they were making the decisions based on their own hunches or whatever it might have been." From his point of view, the difficulty resulted in part from Washington's failure to understand the people they were dealing with at Pearl Harbor. They weren't number crunchers or narrow specialists who didn't see the big picture. "The estimates that came from Station Hypo were not the estimates of technical people such as cryptanalysts or translators or communications intelligence people," Rochefort tried to explain. "They were the considered opinions of people who had these capabilities as well as the experience of having served in the operations of the various staffs of the fleet."[21]

Of course, Rochefort was talking primarily about himself. Other officers at Hypo did have experience in various aspects of communications intelligence, from translating Japanese to codebreaking to cryptanalysis, but no one brought to the comint task all those facets the way Rochefort did. With his background in all phases of intelligence, he didn't like being lectured by people he regarded as inferiors, to say the least. Nor did he enjoy being treated like a mere functionary who was supposed to simply pass on data to OP-20-G.

"I felt that I had the knowledge and experience of being able to estimate and form a judgment on what the traffic actually meant," Rochefort said.[22] For whatever reasons, Washington didn't accept Rochefort's definition of his proper role, and the bickering continued. The two sides moved toward the inevitable showdown. But first there was work to be done.

❚❚■❚❚

Nimitz didn't wait for Rochefort's water-shortage ploy to devise a plan of action of his own. Even before the 13 May *Goshu Maru* message revealed Midway to be the Imperial Navy's primary objective, Nimitz had started taking steps to retrieve his Pacific Fleet carriers. As noted, King on 15 May approved Nimitz's request that Halsey's carriers be brought back to Hawaii, with the proviso that they be returned to the south Pacific if new intelligence should warrant such a move. Three days later, on 18 May, Nimitz radioed Halsey: "Expedite return to Hawaii area."[23]

The same day CINCPAC addressed a similar dispatch to Fletcher on board the badly damaged *Yorktown*, now being refueled at Tongatapu Island, near the Fijis. Ten days earlier the carrier had been limping eastward toward the Bremerton Navy Yard. Then, on 9 May, CINCPAC ordered Fletcher to proceed to Tongatapu and await further orders.

But COMINCH had his own plan for the *Yorktown*, which he wanted sent to the shipyard at Puget Sound. Nimitz had no intention of giving up the flattop, but fetching it back to Pearl Harbor required all of his diplomatic acumen. He assured King, "If [repair] not feasible [at Pearl] contemplate sending to Puget."[24] King went along with that. Nimitz promptly summoned Fletcher.

CINCPAC's carriers were coming home. The *Hornet* and *Enterprise* were expected 26 May, the *Yorktown* was due back 27 May. Nimitz's plan was unfolding just about the way he had hoped. From radio intelligence provided by Hypo, he knew the Japanese believed that the *Lexington* had been sunk in the Coral Sea, and that the *Yorktown*, if not sunk, had at least been severely damaged. He also knew from Rochefort that the Japanese thought Halsey's task force was heading toward the area around New Hebrides, some three thousand miles from Pearl.

Nimitz wanted the Japanese to keep believing all of it. On 21 May he told Fletcher and Halsey to observe "strict radio silence" during their return to Pearl. Task force planes flying ahead to Oahu also were told to refrain from any transmissions "when coming in to land." CINCPAC's order resulted from a Hypo discovery that Japanese radio intelligence had been learning of U.S. carrier movements in and out of Pearl by monitoring air-ground radio chatter.

While the operating forces would find Nimitz's radio silence order hard to obey over the next few months, it did reflect the "undiluted confidence" he now placed in Layton and Rochefort as well as the entire intel team at Pearl. Nimitz also employed some radio deception of his own. He arranged for the seaplane tender *Tangier*, on station in the Coral Sea, to start transmitting the radio calls typical of a carrier task force operating in the south Pacific. On 28 May PBYs assigned to the *Tangier* bombed Tulagi, surprising the Japanese and giving them the impression they were being attacked by carrier planes.[25] They took the bait again. After reporting both Halsey's carrier force south of the Solomons and the raid on Tulagi, Japanese radio intelligence provided Yamamoto with some good news: it appeared unlikely the U.S. Navy would have any carrier strength available to throw against the Midway invasion.[26]

For all their differences over Japanese intentions and how best to employ the Pacific Fleet's carriers, King and Nimitz by 25 May pretty much agreed on what they were up against in the central Pacific. The turning point in their deliberations had come on 17 May, when King had told Nimitz he accepted CINCPAC's view that Japan planned to capture Midway and bomb Unalaska. They disagreed only on the time, King pegging the campaign for 30 May while Nimitz thought it would happen later, sometime during the first week of June.

COMINCH and CINCPAC both got some things wrong. Like Nimitz, King looked ahead quite mistakenly to a "shipborne air raid on Oahu" that would precede the Midway attack. But King correctly grasped that Japan's intent was to destroy the Pacific Fleet. The fact that he and Nimitz could agree on so many major principles at this stage of the campaign reflected the profound change that had taken place in top brass thinking toward communications intelligence. Maligned for years as crackpots or worse, cryptanalysts and RI people had become the "go to" professionals who from now on would leave their imprint on practically every action taken by the Navy's high command.[27]

Strides made in communications intelligence had been jaw-dropping. As early as April, improvements in direction finding and other aspects of radio intelligence had enabled Rochefort and his Hypo analysts to know the location of most Japanese ships within a range of three hundred to four hundred miles. Gains registered in cryptanalysis and codebreaking permitted Rochefort to practically look over Yamamoto's shoulder as he moved his forces around the Pacific. Comint's fortunes had stemmed largely from the explosion of IJN radio transmissions, the sine qua non for results in codebreaking. Codebreakers not only now processed more intercepts, they also extracted more meaning from them. Rochefort recalled that by late May, analysts were recovering at least a third of the code groups encountered, compared with roughly one-fifth in April. "Thus by May 25 we had a clear picture of what the Japanese were up to," Rochefort said.[28]

        ıı∎ıı

From the later testimony of many, Rochefort's clear picture owed much to the large batch of high-priority messages that poured into the basement around 19–20 May. As seen in the previous chapter, Hypo linguist Red Lasswell happened to be on duty the evening they showed up. Like all members of Rochefort's core team of analysts, Lasswell had been putting in absurdly long hours, rarely taking time off. "Just prior to the Battle of Midway," as he told the story, "we were working around the clock and [I] still didn't have enough time to process everything that came over my desk."

But suddenly Lasswell got even busier. "While scanning the day's traffic [I] detected what I thought was an important message," Lasswell said. "It was directed to just about every important naval command. I spent all night identifying the unknown code groups and by eight o'clock the next morning," had solved enough of the intercept to circulate it to Washington.[29]

Whether he decoded and translated the entire transmission in one night or processed pieces of it over several days remained unclear. Ensign Showers carried away a vivid memory of Lasswell working on this major intercept over three days.[30] However long it took, there was no question the dispatch or dispatches that engaged Lasswell contained valuable information. Lasswell certainly thought so. "The message was a copy of the Japanese Navy's operations order for the attack on Midway," he said.[31]

With that assertion, Lasswell embroiled himself in one of the great mysteries of World War II Navy cryptology. This riddle was unrelated to the AF controversy, a debate now shelved at Main Navy. The new puzzle involved an altogether different issue: Had Lasswell decrypted and translated on 20 May and the days thereafter part or all of Yamamoto's operations order for the Battle of Midway? Or had he rendered readable just another important transmission, but not the famed operations order? Lasswell wasn't the only one who thought he had translated the order. "On 20 May Yamamoto issued an operation order detailing the complete Japanese order of battle for the assault on AF and the Aleutians," Jasper Holmes wrote later.[32] Ham Wright believed the same. "The message that led to the battle of Midway was a single message," he recalled. "It was a single operations order. It told who was to do what and what ships were to go where. It was a very long message."[33]

By 25 May, Rochefort recalled, Hypo's analysts had completed "the final translation of the Japanese operation order of the 20th," the approximate date Lasswell remembered tackling the "important message" he'd detected that night. From Rochefort's account, this lengthy intercept yielded its secrets sparingly, only in chunks and segments, revealing initially "the strength of the attack force and [its] composition," but holding back critical pieces of the puzzle such as the date and time of the attack.[34]

Authoritative as Rochefort's story seemed to be, it wasn't accepted by all. Even some at Pearl Harbor found holes in it. One, oddly, was Rochefort's best friend, Eddie Layton. Like Rochefort, he was in an excellent position to know what happened. Layton was emphatic in his later view, asserting in 1970 that all previous conclusions about the alleged operation order had been "absolutely, unqualifiedly false." If such an order had been decrypted, "I'd have known about it," Layton insisted.[35] He declared that he'd never heard of it.

According to Layton, Rochefort's claim that Hypo had intercepted such an order was weakened by a fatal flaw. It failed to cite a key component that necessarily would have had to appear in any battle plan: Yamamoto's Main Body—a formidable armada consisting of thirty-four ships, including Battleship Divisions 1 and 2, with Yamamoto personally on board the monster battleship *Yamato*. That was no small omission. Under Yamamoto's battle plan, the Main Body would trail six hundred miles behind Nagumo's *kido butai* descending on Midway. Once that force had smashed the island's defenses and presumably lured Nimitz's carriers from Pearl, Yamamoto would close in from behind to support Nagumo. If all went according to plan, Main Body battleships would arrive in time to annihilate the U.S. carrier threat in the Pacific—Yamamoto's rationale for the Midway operation.

As it turned out, Nimitz ordered the Pacific Fleet to Midway unaware that the Main Body lurked in the background. Rochefort would state otherwise in later years, telling one interviewer he had informed Nimitz of the Main Body.[36] But that force didn't turn up in any Hypo estimate and would remain unknown to its analysts until *after* the Battle of Midway. In Layton's view, this information gap proved Hypo didn't have the full operation order. "Had we been able to read the entire battle order, as has been written, we would have [known about] the battleships."[37]

The discrepant accounts may have a simple explanation. Yamamoto and Japanese naval headquarters circulated a variety of operations orders in the days before 20 May. Headquarters outlined the general shape of the approaching battle in Navy Order No. 18, circulated to all operational commands on 5 May. As IJN ships moved toward their assembly points, Yamamoto on 12 May issued initial operations orders, followed up on 20 May with final operation orders for low-level commands.[38] Could these low-level orders have been the orders Lasswell and others tackled on 20 May thinking they were Yamamoto's main operations orders?

The mystery of Yamamoto's missing operation order would never be solved. Pacific War historian John Lundstrom noted that no single order for the battle ever turned up in Hypo's or CINCPAC's files after the war. Nor, he added, did such a document show up in the files of either Belconnen or OP-20-G. He doubted it existed—a view hotly contested by many.[39]

The debate over that elusive order raised questions about the state of Rochefort's knowledge during the weeks leading to the Battle of Midway. How detailed was his intelligence of Yamamoto's approaching force? Did Hypo analysts have at their disposal Yamamoto's prized order of battle? Or did they make do with less? Did they come to grasp Yamamoto's plan by stitching together telltale fragments and other bits and pieces of data that streamed into the basement?

Whatever the answers to those questions, no one ever disputed that around 20 May an unusual intercept or set of intercepts occupied Lasswell and his colleagues. Even if not the fugitive battle order, the messages contained information that amounted to the same thing. When combined with what Rochefort called all the fragments painstakingly collected over the weeks—"incomplete information and hints, little changes of plan, changes of location"—Hypo and Belconnen were able to piece together a remarkably accurate picture of Yamamoto's plan.[40]

By 24 May Hypo, Belconnen, and Negat agreed that Saipan had been designated as the assembly point for the occupation force ordered to descend on Midway. They saw the transports at Saipan getting ready to move, along with Kondo's invasion force and Nagumo's First Air Fleet preparing for action in Japan's Inland Sea. They expected those forces to converge and depart for Midway (Operation MI) in close coordination with a second operation they figured would begin at almost the same time. That was the so-called Northern Force (Operation AL), believed headed for the Aleutians.

Still, major questions remained. What day would the Japanese strike Midway? When the Aleutians? What was Operation K?

‖ ∎ ‖

Fully briefed on what he was up against, Nimitz on 26 May issued an "Estimate of the Situation, Attack on Hawaiian and Alaskan Bases." The document brought together everything CINCPAC had learned from Hypo, Belconnen, and Negat about the emerging threat facing the U.S. Navy.

Citing his assets, Nimitz included a statement that must have resonated with Rochefort at Hypo, Fabian at Belconnen, and their counterparts at Negat: "Our sole source of information . . . is RI and CI [comint]." Then Nimitz added a kicker that probably jolted Rochefort: "The enemy may be deceiving us."[41] The sentence acknowledged the uncertainty that persisted among the Navy's high command—and would continue to do so for a week. Comint was now on the spot. So was Rochefort. Later on 26 May Nimitz notified Rochefort he wanted to see him the next morning in his office at CINCPAC headquarters. Nimitz wanted him to brief CINCPAC staff and a representative from the Army on everything he knew about the coming battle. Rochefort said he would be there.

But first Rochefort had work to do. Hypo knew just about everything about what the Japanese were going to do except when they were going to do it. So far Rochefort and his analysts had been able to do little more than make rough estimates. By calculating roughly the speed at which the ships might advance to the Aleutians and Midway from their bases at Ominato, Saipan, and the Inland Sea, they had come up with "attack dates" ranging from 1 to 10 June. Rochefort knew Nimitz needed better information than that. He also knew any hope of finding it lay buried somewhere in the long stream of intercepts that had flooded the basement on 19–20 May.

By 26 May most of that material had already been decoded and translated. Roughly 10 to 15 percent had resisted decryption. In that unprocessed portion lay hidden a virtually unsolvable time-date cipher—a sort of superenciphered code within a code. The cipher was tough because it had only turned up three times in all the thousands of intercepts Hypo had worked on since the start of the war, leaving Rochefort's experts with far too few samples to analyze.[42] Cryptanalysts at Belconnen were also struggling with this perplexing code. On 25 May one of Melbourne's analysts began work on an IJN message he pulled at random from a box of garbled traffic. After recovering a code group for "Midway" and one for "attack," he ran into trouble. Finding the message too badly garbled to permit progress, he notified Hypo and Negat. Negat promptly tackled the code; Rochefort's group was already working on it.[43]

Somehow the task of solving this daunting cipher fell into the lap of Lasswell's Japanese-language partner, Joe Finnegan. After making some progress he also found himself stumped. Finnegan was trying to solve a system that employed three katakana code groups incorporated within the original Japanese text prior to its encryption in the JN-25(b) code. "I solved the meanings of the first two *Kana* as the first representing a month and the second the day of the month," Finnegan explained later. "I was puzzled by the use of the third *Kana*."[44]

As night approached, Finnegan took his problem to Rochefort. Ham Wright was standing near Rochefort's desk, having already worked twelve hours and about to head for home before returning for another long spell. But he recognized what was at stake and changed his mind. Wright and Finnegan went over to an empty desk and settled in for the night. The two officers—Finnegan the translator-turned-codebreaker, Wright the quintessential cryptanalyst—started work on the problem, oblivious to the passing hours. Finnegan informed Wright of the three previous uses of the cipher, one of which, it turned out, had been in a message pinpointing the date for the Battle of the Coral Sea. Another was rendered nearly useless by garbled text. Wright assigned four yeomen to search for other instances of the cipher.

He and Finnegan were stymied for hours.[45] But as the night wore on, they worked it out. "By 5:30 a.m. I got it solved," Wright told David Kahn. Much to the annoyance of Finnegan later on, Kahn, in his monumental work *The Codebreakers*, gave most of the credit to Wright.[46] Whoever deserved most of the praise, the fact remained that by early Wednesday morning, 27 May, Finnegan and Wright had solved the astonishingly complex cipher. They accomplished this by improvising a rectangular garble table that revealed the dates they wanted. The table was constructed like a checkerboard, with a box for each date included in the message. When lined up this way, analysts could distinguish the garbled, or incorrect, dates from the real ones.

Even though their solution had a few rough edges, Wright regarded it close enough to show Rochefort. He believed they had delivered dates for the coming attacks. As Wright reported it, those dates were 4 June for Midway and 3 June for the air strike on Dutch Harbor in the Aleutians.

Rochefort didn't immediately cheer. He had noticed weak spots in their work and promptly challenged Wright. "I can't send this out," he said.[47] But Rochefort "was a great kidder," Wright said. "He would question us to make sure that we were certain of our work; he did not question us because he was uncertain of us. He had great faith in his men. I told him, 'If you don't send it out, I will.'" Rochefort laughed and said, "go ahead."[48]

Hypo's solution was circulated to Belconnen and Negat via the COPEK channel.

॥■॥

The time for Rochefort's early morning meeting at CINCPAC headquarters had come and gone. He had decided not to leave the basement until the time-date cipher had been worked out. Now satisfied with Wright's solution, he shed his old red smoking jacket and carpet slippers and changed into a fresh khaki uniform. Rochefort hustled up the basement's steps out into the admin building's parking lot. He was running late.

26

Nimitz Comes Around

I would look over and I would see four stars. And I would answer this question to the very best of my ability.

—Joe Rochefort

Admiral Nimitz didn't have to check his watch. He knew from the fidgeting of his distinguished guests, among whom were two generals, two rear admirals, and a bunch of captains, that something was amiss. His star attraction, a commander not well known to all in the room, was overdue.

Time mattered on Wednesday morning, 27 May 1942. The generals were on a tight schedule, as was Nimitz. He was expected soon at the *Enterprise*, which had steamed into Pearl on the 26th. He was supposed to hand out decorations.[1] Then he planned to welcome home the battle-scarred *Yorktown*, due early that afternoon after one hundred days at sea. Nimitz wanted to look at the vessel and, of course, meet with a bone-weary Frank Jack Fletcher, commander of Task Force 17.

At last, half an hour late, Rochefort showed up. Rumpled and unshaven, bleary-eyed from lack of sleep, he made his way into CINCPAC's modest quarters on the second deck of the old submarine building, now packed with stony-faced officers. Nimitz shot him an icy glance, a look Rochefort later remembered as "coldly impersonal." The chill he felt didn't come only from Nimitz. Everyone seemed grim. "The atmosphere was very impersonal," Rochefort said.[2]

348

For his part, he wasn't all that happy to be there either. "I would have much preferred to have been back at our place working on other things," Rochefort said later. His ambivalence didn't stem from shyness or any reluctance to consort with high-ranking officers. "I had been around," he said. "Fortunately, I had served under half a dozen or eight or nine extremely capable naval officers. And they didn't frighten me."

What gnawed at Rochefort was that he had always tried to keep his distance from the world of operations. Since taking over as Hypo's officer in charge a year earlier, he had scrupulously observed his own code. Now he was in CINCPAC's quarters on the eve of one of the most critical battles in U.S. Navy history. He was trapped. Nimitz had called him in. Rochefort was in a room full of operations people, and he would have to give advice whether he wanted to or not. As the meeting got under way he apologized, explaining that he and his analysts had been up all night trying to work out the timing of the Japanese navy's impending attack. Nimitz relaxed a little.

"Very fortunately, Admiral Nimitz being the type of man he was, accepted this," Rochefort said. He then handed Nimitz a copy of the dispatch Hypo had just rushed to COMINCH in Washington. "This will explain everything," he said. "This is the operation order under which the Japanese are going to operate."[3]

Whether the material Rochefort handed Nimitz was indeed Yamamoto's prized order of battle or simply the summary of some very good decrypts would never be cleared up, as previously detailed. The officers didn't immediately respond. Many didn't know what to make of Rochefort. They didn't know him well, but some with whom he was acquainted remained skeptical of the Midway scenario. One was General Emmons.

Nimitz had been trying to resolve the general's doubts for days. In an effort to turn around his thinking, a week earlier he had assigned Captain Steele of his war plans staff to reexamine the Rochefort-Layton file on Midway and, presumably, brief Emmons. In so doing Nimitz had divulged to Emmons at least some of the Navy's cherished intelligence from Hypo.[4] But the effort didn't produce the result Nimitz had hoped for. Emmons remained unconvinced that AF was Midway.

Two days earlier, on 25 May, the general had jarred Nimitz with another challenging memo. "Though I do not have full details of enemy info, believe there is some danger drawing definite conclusions that major Japanese effort in Hawaiian area will be directed against Midway," Emmons warned. "Japs may be practicing deception with radio orders intercepted by U.S."[5] Emmons would doubt that Midway was Japan's principal target right up until the battle, now just days away. So would the other general present, Major General Robert C. Richardson, General Marshall's personal representative. Richardson was on assignment from Marshall to conduct a personal reconnaissance of the whole Pacific theater to assess strengths and weaknesses of the Allied situation. As Marshall's close associate, he shared that general's misgivings about Midway.[6]

Predictably, the Navy officers present saw things differently, but not all were privy to everything Nimitz knew, and not all were as convinced about Midway as was Nimitz. Included in the Navy group was a newcomer to CINCPAC's inner circle, Rear Admiral Raymond A. Spruance, pinch-hitting for Vice Admiral Halsey. Halsey had arrived the day before on board the *Enterprise*, commanding Task Force 16. Nimitz had taken one look at him and sent him to the base hospital. Not only was Halsey utterly exhausted after six months of intense, uninterrupted service on the *Enterprise*, he was also seriously ill. He had contracted dermatitis, a painful skin disease that had worsened over the weeks, undoubtedly the result of nervous strain.

Realizing he was in no shape to hold down a command in the fast-approaching Midway battle, Halsey recommended that Spruance, his cruiser commander, be given temporary command of TF 16. Nimitz, who had already gained enormous respect for the soft-spoken Spruance, agreed.[7] What Spruance knew or didn't know about IJN plans for Midway remained unclear. Away from Pearl Harbor for as long as Halsey, he would not have been acquainted with daily developments having to do with Midway. Nor would he have been on Nimitz's short list of officers granted some access to intelligence from Hypo's decrypts. So he would have been hearing many details of the coming battle for the first time.

Rounding out the Navy contingent were Captain McCormick, head of CINCPAC's war plans staff and a strong advocate of Nimitz's Midway plan; his assistant Captain Steele; Captain DeLany, fleet operations officer; and finally Nimitz's chief of staff, Rear Admiral Milo F. Draemel. Of all those present, few were more familiar with Rochefort's work than Draemel, having acquired familiarity with cryptology while commanding the Code and Signal Section from 1918 to 1921. Spruance would relieve him in late June.

Missing from this conference was Fleet Intelligence Officer Layton, who would have strongly supported Rochefort's Midway story if called upon. But as a mere lieutenant commander, he probably didn't have sufficient rank to warrant an invitation. Layton didn't find out about the session until the next day, when he brought Nimitz the news that Hypo had broken the time-date cipher for the Midway attack—only to discover that Rochefort had already done so.[8]

Layton was understandably disappointed, even a little hurt, by his exclusion from the meeting. He had always taken great pride in his role as Rochefort's intermediary with CINCPAC. He later blamed Commandant Bagley for "hastening over with Rochefort to give Nimitz the report that they had solved the date" for the Midway bombardment, thereby scooping Layton.[9] Bagley had not, however, pulled a fast one on Layton. Nimitz simply wanted to see Rochefort and called him in.

।।▆।।

Rochefort had no illusions about the purpose of the meeting or his own role there. The staff conference hadn't been called to settle anything. "It was obvious when Nimitz sent for me that he had already decided his course of action," Rochefort said. "He had already made up his own operation orders by this time and the matter was closed."[10]

Why, then, had Nimitz bothered to summon Rochefort? He had a pretty good idea what he was *not* there to do. Rochefort was not there to discuss Station Hypo's mission or reveal its success in breaking the Imperial Navy's operational code. "Up to that period of time [Nimitz] had never divulged the source of his information to anyone," Rochefort said. Even some officers at this meeting would have had only a vague notion of what Rochefort did. A few may even have assumed, as did other officers at Pearl, that CINCPAC's tips came from clandestine sources in Tokyo. "The admiral would never disabuse anybody of that idea," Rochefort said. "He would merely say that information had reached him which, in his opinion, was sufficient to act upon."

All of which put Rochefort in a tight spot. "Nimitz didn't go into any discussion of my activities," he said. Rather than a codebreaker, Rochefort had probably been presented as an intelligence officer familiar with Japanese messages who had pieced together what the enemy was up to. He was there to answer questions and, by so doing, add weight to CINCPAC's plan of action. Rochefort was there to tell some of the things he knew, but not how he knew them.

"What do you think the Japanese are going to do?" was the first question that popped up.[11] Given the limits of codebreaking, Rochefort couldn't know everything the Japanese planned, and he didn't. Yet by 27 May, he had learned a great deal. Assuming he proceeded in his usual logical way, he would have put first things first: IJN warships were on the move. They had weighed anchor the previous day. He knew this because Yamamoto's carriers had not emitted a radio signal in three days. "Lack of carrier traffic usually means they are at sea," Rochefort had informed Nimitz the day before.[12] In other words, the Japanese navy's two distinct striking and invasion forces were now steaming toward their respective targets, Midway and the Aleutians.

Drawing on Hypo's recent decrypts, Rochefort presented the following scenario: Within days the *kido butai*, composed of four carriers (the *Kaga*, *Akagi*, *Soryu*, and *Hiryu*) and possibly a fifth, the *Zuikaku*, supported by three battleships, four to five cruisers, and a destroyer squadron, would approach Midway from the northwest at a bearing of 315 degrees, close to within fifty miles and, beginning at around 7:00 a.m., launch their planes against Midway's ground and air defenses.[13]

Both Ham Wright and Rochefort later said that the date Hypo's officer in charge gave at this meeting was 4 June. But were they remembering accurately? As will be seen, they may have been off by a day. Yamamoto originally ordered Nagumo to strike Midway on 3 June, and that is the date that would have appeared in his time-date cipher. This was also the date arrived at by Nimitz and King for Nagumo to begin his air attack.

Did Rochefort and Wright later misremember and, albeit inadvertently, push back the date they "recollected" to fit that of the actual attack: 4 June? The question proved impossible to answer.[14]

The attack-date issue aside, Rochefort's scenario in most respects matched the events about to unfold. With CINCPAC's guests listening intently, he continued his briefing: Nagumo's initial assault would be followed two days later by the arrival of an occupation force, sailing in due west from Saipan, to begin landings on Midway's two islands, Eastern and Sand.[15]

Rochefort's guess was that the Northern Force, consisting of at least one fleet carrier, one light carrier, two cruisers, three destroyer divisions, a submarine squadron, and a host of support ships, had already departed Ominato.[16] He figured one element was en route to Kiska and Attu in the western Aleutians for occupation, while the other was heading toward Dutch Harbor to bombard that place and keep U.S. forces away from the invasion site.

Astonishingly prescient as Rochefort and his analysts may have been, they did err in some aspects of the coming campaign. Rochefort described the Imperial Navy drive into the Aleutians as a ploy to divert the Pacific Fleet away from Midway—a notion accepted by writers for decades until challenged in 2005 by historians Jon Parshall and Anthony Tully.[17]

That miscue would have no bearing on the Midway campaign. Nagumo's *kido butai* and Kondo's invasion force had just departed Japan's Inland Sea. Both moved in concert with a third force, the occupation transports now exiting Saipan. In all, Rochefort believed, the forces converging on Midway and the Aleutians consisted of more than one hundred warships, transports, tankers, and submarines—a major portion of the Japanese Imperial Navy.[18]

He was besieged with questions. Nimitz jumped in first. Rochefort could be impatient with officers, even superiors, who failed to follow his reasoning. Not this time. "I would look over and I would see four stars," he later explained. "And I would answer this question to the very best of my ability"—and do so, he added, "without being impertinent or nervous or anything of this nature." Nimitz accepted Rochefort's overall scenario, but not everyone was so agreeable.

Some of the queries now directed at Rochefort were prickly. What makes you think there are going to be four carriers? Why not six? Why are you so sure the attack will be June 4th? Why not June 6th? Why not have the major attack against Alaska?[19] They also wondered why the Japanese navy would mobilize so huge a force to invade two tiny islands in the central Pacific. Or, for that matter, why should they bother with two remote islands in the Aleutians at all? Might not these messages be fakes transmitted to deceive the U.S. Navy? Would the Japanese be so naive as to put their most treasured secrets on the air where they could be picked up?[20]

Nimitz came to Rochefort's rescue, pointing out that the enemy could be operating in strength to overcome any American opposition that might arise. Japan's "main objective might even be to draw out the inferior U.S. Pacific Fleet so that it could be destroyed," Nimitz explained. "The transmission of plans by radio could mean that Yamamoto was operating on so tight a schedule that he could get them distributed in time by no other means."[21]

But Nimitz couldn't help Rochefort with another question that came up: What did the Japanese have in mind for Oahu? Even those who had never heard of Operation K feared that it would be high on the list of prospective Imperial Navy targets. Emmons, for example, thought Oahu was in for something far worse than a mere raid. As noted, for weeks he had preached that the Japanese would, at a minimum, mount an attack in force on Hawaii. Even Admiral King worried that Oahu might be hit hard, either just before or just after the assault on Midway. Nimitz, too, looked for some kind of assault, possibly an expanded version of the flying-boat attack back in March. Layton subscribed to that view.[22]

Rochefort could only say that he had no fresh information on the mysterious K Campaign, although he probably didn't use that term (Operation K was a phrase peculiar to Hypo's comint culture). That answer probably didn't satisfy anyone. What he didn't know, and therefore couldn't report, was that Operation K, whatever it was, would be conducted in just two days. There was another hole in Rochefort's presentation. Neither he nor any other intelligence officer knew about Yamamoto's Main Body. That potent force wasn't part of the discussion.

⸎

Despite the misgivings of some members of CINCPAC's staff, Nimitz had already decided to base his plans on the assumption that Hypo's estimates were essentially correct.[23] Rochefort's briefing concluded, Nimitz proceeded to lay out his plan of action for foiling the Imperial Navy at Midway. The scheme he devised, released later in the day as Operation Plan No. 29-42, was based heavily on Hypo's decrypts of IJN messages during the past ten days.[24]

Nor had Nimitz waited for this 27 May staff conference to put his plan into action. He already had ordered Midway's PBYs to scout daily as far out as 700 miles along an arc stretching from southwest of Midway to due north. He'd directed thirteen fleet submarines to patrol along a similar arc as far out as 200 miles from Midway. He also had ordered a destroyer to patrol French Frigate Shoals to guard against any repetition of the 4 March flying-boat attack.

By comparison with Yamamoto's multi-pronged operation, Nimitz's plan was relatively simple. Under Plan 29-42, Spruance would depart Pearl the next day on board the *Enterprise*, commanding Task Force 16, consisting of two carriers (the *Hornet* and *Enterprise*) supported by five cruisers, one light cruiser, and twelve destroyers, and proceed to an area labeled "Point Luck" (latitude 32 degrees north, longitude 173 degrees west), a spot 350 miles northeast of Midway. Assuming the *Yorktown* could be repaired in time, Spruance would be joined on 2 June by Task Force 17, commanded by Fletcher on board the *Yorktown*, supported by two cruisers and six destroyers.[25] As the senior officer, Fletcher would be in operational command of both task forces.

After linking up at Point Luck, the two task forces would await Nagumo's armada, believed to be steaming toward Midway from the northwest. Nimitz's next step involved careful timing. Once the *kido butai*'s approach and location had been confirmed, Fletcher was to promptly move his two task forces south and west, until they reached a point from where they could deliver a surprise blow against Nagumo.

The operation would be tricky. Fletcher would have to move his task forces close enough to the Japanese ships so that he could bring back his pilots (fuel was always a worry), but not spend so much time as to risk discovery by Nagumo's scouts. What Nimitz, Fletcher, and Spruance hoped to do was surprise the *kido butai* before the planes it had launched against Midway had returned—a time of maximum vulnerability for Nagumo's carriers, because they would be preoccupied with recovering their aircraft.

CINCPAC didn't ignore the Imperial Navy's threat to the Aleutians, but there wasn't much he could do about it. He had no carriers to spare, and he had already decided against employing the fleet's slow-moving battleships in either the Midway or Aleutian campaigns. They remained based in southern California under Vice Admiral Pye, having returned to battleship duty.

To engage the Northern Force advancing on the Aleutians, Nimitz on 22 May formed Task Force 8, a modest force of five cruisers, fourteen destroyers, and six submarines under the command of Rear Admiral Robert A. Theobald. Nimitz provided Theobald a survey of the Northern Force order of battle and a preliminary timetable, information assembled by Hypo. He told him on 28 May that the Imperial Japanese Navy planned to "seize and secure" U.S. naval bases at Kiska and Attu.[26]

But Nimitz didn't tell Theobald everything. As was his practice by now, he didn't divulge to commanders afloat the fact that his information was derived from Hypo's success in breaking the Japanese navy's operational code. It probably wouldn't have made any difference if he had; Theobald no doubt guessed the source was radio intelligence. He dismissed it, figuring the Japanese were using radio traffic to mislead the U.S. Navy. Also, Theobald refused to believe the enemy would go after what he regarded as two useless hunks of land in the remote northern Pacific. He thought that CINCPAC had been taken in by a hoax, devised by the Japanese navy to lure Theobald to the western Aleutians so they could maneuver behind him for a landing at Dutch

Harbor or even the Alaskan mainland.[27] Nicknamed Fuzzy years earlier at the Naval Academy, Theobald now earned that moniker again. Ignoring Nimitz's suggested defense of Kiska and Attu, he kept his task force well to the east, closer to Alaska and the West Coast.

As noted, other Pacific Fleet task force commanders also worried more about Alaska and America's coastal region than Midway. On 28 May, the same day Nimitz tried to alert Theobald to the danger in the Aleutians, CINCPAC received an unsettling dispatch from Vice Admiral Pye. Pye told Nimitz he had put his battleship force on alert status and ordered all antiaircraft batteries fully manned. "Intelligence indicates probability of Japanese air raid on Alaska or San Francisco–Los Angeles area during coming week," Pye wrote.[28]

This notion had probably come from the Army. It had only been one week since General Marshall had flown to California to assess that region's defenses. Now, with the Midway engagement fast approaching, General Hap Arnold, commanding general, U.S. Army Air Forces, was on the West Coast conducting another inspection. The Army still considered that area as a possibility for AF.[29]

For this Rochefort blamed Admiral King. Whenever Rochefort and his Hypo colleagues heard that some misguided officer was anxious about the western United States, they tended to reprove COMINCH. Now, once again, Rochefort was hearing about an invasion threat to that coastal region and thought of King. "I never have been able to understand why COMINCH gave any more than a couple of thoughts to the idea that this operation was to be directed against the mainland of the United States," Rochefort said later, "because it was simply beyond the capability of the Japanese." By the time of Midway, Rochefort said, Hypo had pretty much figured out what the Japanese could and couldn't do. The idea of an attack on the western United States was "sort of ridiculous," he said, "because they didn't have any ships. We could tell with a reasonable degree of accuracy what they had available and where these things were."

Put simply, Rochefort said, the Japanese navy "didn't have the tankers, they didn't have the transports, they didn't have the refrigeration ships, they didn't have the supply line. This was why they couldn't go to San Francisco." Not only would logistical problems have ruled out such an attack but, he added, so would military common sense: The Japanese would not have put their fleet between Pearl Harbor, with its carriers, and the West Coast, where "they'd be subject to our shore-based planes off San Francisco. . . . Obviously, this was stupid."[30]

Rochefort was right about the impossibility of a Japanese advance on America's coastal states, but he was wrong about Admiral King. From all indications, King doubted Midway for only three days—14 May through 16 May—a period during which he received Rochefort's *Goshu Maru* dispatch and Nimitz's pronouncement on Midway. During that time COMINCH worried primarily about Port Moresby, New Caledonia, the Fijis, and other islands guarding the approach to Australia, as well as northeast Australia itself.

But, as discussed previously, on 17 May King radioed Nimitz that he had revised his estimate and now believed that Midway, along with some islands in the Aleutians, would be IJN targets for occupation around 30 May. He still held that view, except for the date, which he now put at 3 June. Although King may have been as troubled as Nimitz by the Army's doubts and those of some on his staff, he showed no signs of wavering. If he did have such concerns, he appeared not to have expressed them officially. Though the two admirals had differences, they were primarily in terms of emphasis: King thought the Japanese navy might come at Oahu with more force than did Nimitz, who now thought the attack on Oahu would be no more than another raid similar to the one on 4 March.

Pearl Harbor's impression that King viewed the U.S. mainland as a Japanese objective stemmed almost entirely from Hypo's bare-knuckle encounters with OP-20-G, which *did* postulate some type of IJN action against the American coast. It was natural for Rochefort and his analysts to suspect this thinking came from COMINCH. But as historian Frederick Parker has pointed out, OP-20-G wasn't always in sync with King and, at times, seemed oddly unaware of the exchanges between King and Nimitz.[31]

Also, King didn't rely exclusively on OP-20-G for his information about Imperial Navy moves. While he did read decrypts of IJN traffic produced by Negat, Hypo, and Belconnen, King also received daily intelligence memoranda from ONI, some written by the independent-minded Arthur McCollum. And he had his own personal intelligence team, headed by an extremely capable captain, George Dyer, who later in the war would rise to flag rank. King was by no means hostage to OP-20-G for his intelligence about the Japanese. Nevertheless, Rochefort and his analysts sometimes thought King was behind all their troubles with OP-20-G, which, after all, operated under King's organizational umbrella.

Vagaries of OP-20-G aside, Rochefort and his colleagues received in late May what they probably regarded as welcome news: One of their Washington tormentors, Richmond Kelly Turner, had been dismissed as chief of War Plans. He was removed at the insistence of General Marshall, said historian Eric Larrabee, because during his tenure on the joint planning staff, the Army found him hard to get along with. Turner landed on his feet. He was given command of amphibious forces in the Pacific, and he later commanded the successful invasions of Guadalcanal, New Georgia, Tarawa, Eniwetok, the Marianas, Iwo Jima, and Okinawa. King later teased Turner by addressing him as "the Army's single greatest contribution to the war in the Pacific."[32]

ıı▩ıı

Twenty-seven May found Nimitz and Rochefort first pleased, then sobered, by the news coming in. The good news related to the *Yorktown*, which arrived at Pearl early in the afternoon trailing an oil slick ten miles long. Greeted with sirens and steam whistles, the carrier maneuvered through Pearl's narrow entrance straight into Dry Dock No. 1, where Nimitz and his party waited nearby. Nimitz pulled on boots and led an inspection of the carrier's hull.

From the assessment of his engineers, he concluded the ship could be patched up quickly, not in the ninety days estimated earlier by some Navy officers. Speaking to the work crews that gathered around, Nimitz pulled no punches: "We must have this ship back in three days."[33]

As the first batch of some 1,400 workers swarmed over the carrier, Nimitz met with Frank Jack Fletcher, thoroughly exhausted after his ordeal in the Coral Sea. If Fletcher thought he was due some respite, he was quickly disabused of that notion. Nimitz delivered two pieces of solemn news: King had doubts about some of his decisions made in the Coral Sea (eventually resolved in Fletcher's favor, with Nimitz's help), and the Japanese were expected to invade Midway in about a week. Nimitz told Fletcher he would have to lead Task Force 17 on board the *Yorktown* to Point Luck, join forces with Spruance, and thwart the enemy.

If everything was going CINCPAC's way with the *Yorktown*, things were not going so well for Rochefort in Hypo's basement. The day before, on 26 May, Hypo had decrypted a message from Japan's publication office to all units throughout the Empire indicating a "forthcoming distribution."[34] Analysts for weeks had dreaded just such a development. Radio traffic on 27 May confirmed their worst suspicions when the Imperial Navy announced that effective midnight, it would introduce a new general-purpose code system. The change would render unreadable the IJN's main operational code after the 27th.[35]

The switch meant the end of JN-25(b), unveiled on 1 December 1940. Realizing the dangers of leaving a single code system in place too long, the Japanese had planned to replace JN-25(b) much earlier, first on 1 April, then, when that didn't work out, 1 May. They'd delayed the changeover each time because of the difficulties they faced circulating the new code to an ever-increasing number of units scattered around an expanding horizon of Japanese bases. Now that they had finally made the change, it was too late. U.S. code-breakers at Negat, Belconnen, and Hypo had already gleaned from JN-25(b) what they needed to know about IJN plans for Midway. The Japanese had paid a price for their growing empire.

With the demise of JN-25(b) came the arrival of JN-25(c). Happily, the new code didn't represent an altogether new cryptanalytic system. Like the original JN-25(a), it remained a five-digit code with some 50,000 code groups. Dyer and Wright would have to find new pathways through an altogether revised cipher employed to protect the codebook. Lasswell, Finnegan, and their fellow codebreakers would have to start all over again building up a new codebook, matching thousands of five-digit numbers with all the possible meanings. That would take time. "You might say the curtain went down and we weren't reading anything in JN-25 for a period of possibly a month or so," Rochefort said.[36]

In the meantime, all was not lost. Wahiawa continued to intercept IJN transmissions and convey them to Hypo. As he had in the months before JN-25(b) was shelved, Rochefort fell back on his traffic analysts, still led by Huckins and Williams, to track the Imperial Navy. Through direction finding and analysis of message headings, they did remarkably well keeping Roche-fort, and thereby CINCPAC, abreast of IJN activities.

Unable to read current traffic, Rochefort's cryppies started reevaluating old JN-25(b) messages for valuable information that might have been over-looked. They hit paydirt on 31 May. An IJN dispatch noted that fighter pilots from the carrier *Zuikaku* had been transferred to a Northern Force unit that departed Ominato 26 May. The discovery ruled out any possibility that the *Zuikaku*—now with few planes and no fliers—would see action in the Mid-way campaign.[37]

··■··

The CINCPAC operation plan that Nimitz unveiled on 27 May started to unfold on 28 May. That morning Task Force 16, with Rear Admiral Spruance on board the *Enterprise* and in command, steamed out of Pearl Harbor, took on planes, and headed northwest. Two days later, electricians and mechanics, after working around the clock for three days, put the finishing touches on the *Yorktown*. Task Force 17, with Rear Admiral Fletcher in command, filed out of the harbor, formed up, and headed toward its rendezvous with Task Force 16 at Point Luck. Before the *Yorktown* sortied, Nimitz stopped by to wish the crew "good luck and good hunting."[38]

The crews of Task Forces 16 and 17 had already been the beneficiaries of one extraordinary piece of good luck. Yamamoto's original plan had ordered that a line of thirteen submarines be established southeast and east of Midway, where they could intercept any U.S. Navy ships coming to Midway's rescue from Pearl Harbor. Stretching hundreds of miles athwart the expected sea routes, the subs were supposed to be in place on 30 May, the same day Fletcher exited Pearl. But they were a day late. Both American task forces were well on their way to Point Luck by the time they arrived on station.

That favorable development could have been nullified if it hadn't been for another instance of good fortune. Without realizing it, the U.S. Navy had prevailed in a contest it hadn't known was under way: the much-dreaded Operation K. Since Rochefort on 6 May had translated a decrypt referring to such an operation, Nimitz and his lieutenants had braced for a repeat of the 4 March flying-boat raid on Pearl Harbor, if not an onslaught far more serious.

Operation K turned out to be something quite different. Rather than an invasion, it was only a reconnaissance mission in support of the Midway offensive, not an attack on Oahu. Under the IJN plan, two Kawanishi flying boats were to land at French Frigate Shoals late in May (just as they had in March), refuel from tanker submarines, and proceed to Pearl Harbor not to bomb, but to observe—to make sure that America's carriers were in port, safely out of the way.

But when the Japanese sub *I-123* reached French Frigate Shoals on 29 May, it found three U.S. Navy warships—the seaplane tenders *Thornton* and *Ballard* and the destroyer *Clark*—on patrol, posted there earlier by Nimitz as a preventive measure without any precise knowledge of what the Japanese had in mind. When the Japanese received the *I-123*'s findings, they rescheduled the operation for 31 May. But they canceled the operation altogether after finding the three ships still in the area, perhaps denying themselves information that could have alerted them to the danger they faced. So ended Operation K.[39]

Back at Pearl Harbor, Nimitz, Rochefort, and their assistants had no idea of the mini-adventure that had just played out below the surface. Like many others at Pearl, they wondered if the long-awaited Operation K attack would materialize. They also wondered about 3 and 4 June, and what would happen on those dates.

27

Our Man in Tokyo

This officer deserves a major share of the credit
for the victory at Midway.
—Chester W. Nimitz

Rochefort wasn't on board the *Enterprise* as it steamed out of Pearl Harbor on the morning of 28 May, but the work he and his Hypo analysts had done tracking the Japanese forces approaching Midway was reflected in the paperwork that Admiral Spruance now circulated.

The document was CINCPAC Operation Plan No. 29-42, prepared by Admiral Nimitz and distributed the day before to commanders ashore and afloat who would have to fight the battle, including Admirals Fletcher and Spruance. In preparing that order Nimitz and his staff drew heavily on the decrypts, translations, and estimates churned out by Rochefort and his staff.

As Task Force 16 speeded northward, Spruance made Nimitz's operations plan (op-plan) available to the officers who needed to know its contents.[1] Without revealing the source of its information, the order laid out in matter-of-fact detail what the Imperial Navy had in mind for Midway ("a full-scale attack for its capture"), how it expected to begin that operation ("high speed approach by carriers"), the direction from which those carriers would arrive ("a northwesterly bearing will be favored"), and when the Japanese would show up (around 3 June). First revealed by Nimitz at his 27 May staff conference, the op-plan told Spruance's officers what U.S. forces would be up against in about five days: 4 to 5 carriers (the *Zuikaku* remained on the list as a possibility), 2 to 4 fast battleships, 8 to 9 cruisers, 16 to 24 destroyers, 8 to 12 submarines, and a landing force with seaplane tenders.[2]

Astonished by the inside knowledge disclosed in the order, officers wondered where all that information came from. Inevitably, rumors circulated that the Navy had broken the Japanese code.[3] Some officers fostered the notion that Nimitz had a direct pipeline to Tokyo. Not many believed that but a few played along. After reading the op-plan, Commander Richard Ruble, navigator of the *Enterprise*, remarked wryly: "That man of ours in Tokyo is worth every cent we pay him."[4]

In preparing the plan, Nimitz honored King's admonition that his forces exercise caution.[5] CINCPAC directed his task force commanders to "be governed by the principle of calculated risk," meaning they were to do everything they could to "inflict maximum damage on the enemy" while avoiding action that could result in heavy loses to carriers and cruisers.[6] That was the Navy's way of saying its pilots were to surprise enemy ships, stop them, destroy them if possible, and do so without taking unnecessary risks.

On 2 June 1942, Task Forces 16 and 17 arrived within visual signaling distance at Point Luck, some 350 miles northeast of Midway. They established contact—and waited. They waited for the Japanese to arrive at their predicted location, if not someplace else, as some skeptics feared. A few admirals and generals still worried about the West Coast. There were other uncertainties.

If there was a difference between Nimitz's and Rochefort's views of what would happen at Midway, it had to do with dates, as previously noted. Rochefort might have thought he had settled the matter on 27 May when he'd presented Hypo's painstakingly deciphered timeline at Nimitz's staff conference. The Imperial Navy's Northern Force would strike first in the Aleutians on 3 June, preceding by one day Nagumo's massive air strike against Midway on 4 June (N-2). That bombardment, intended to take out Midway's defenses, would be followed two days later by attempted landings on Eastern Island, Saturday 6 June (N-day). Nimitz didn't accept all of Rochefort's proposed dates. He didn't think the Japanese would begin the operations by assaulting their two targets on different days. Nor did he think the only possibility was an early morning attack; he cautioned that a night attack couldn't be ruled out.

On 31 May, as they proceeded toward Point Luck, Fletcher and Spruance received Nimitz's projected sequence of events. Nimitz told his two task force commanders that he expected Nagumo's *kido butai* to deal its first blows against Midway on the night of 2 June or the morning of 3 June.[7] As did

Midway Campaign

Map labels: TG-11.1, Hawaiian Islands, Oahu, TF-17, TF-16, joined, Midway, Dutch Harbor, Aleutian Occupation Forces, 2nd Carrier Force, 1st Carrier Force (Nagumo), Main Force, Second Fleet, Midway Occupation Forces, Saipan

King, Nimitz figured N-day would be 5, not 6 June as predicted by Rochefort. But in his 31 May dispatch, Nimitz did draw on Rochefort's latest information to update the composition of Yamamoto's assorted fleets advancing on Midway.[8]

The revised picture differed only slightly from that provided by Rochefort four days earlier. It retained the four carriers that all comint units now agreed constituted the heart of the *kido butai*, but it omitted the *Zuikaku*, considered a possibility on 27 May but not after 31 May, when Hypo found that the carrier's crew had been redeployed to other commands. Task force commanders wouldn't have to worry about a fifth flattop.

ıı ■ ıı

Back at Pearl Harbor, Rochefort and his analysts also waited. With IJN forces observing strict radio silence, Hypo found the pickings slim, leaving codebreakers little to do but work on back traffic and continue efforts to break into JN-25(c), a task that would stymie them for weeks. Day after day Rochefort's radiomen strained to hear something. "Carriers quiet and unheard," Huckins and Williams wrote in their 28 May intelligence summary.[9]

Spotty direction finding led to a serious mistake on 29 May, when traffic analysts picked up a transmission from the Fourth Air Attack Force to Yamamoto. Hypo's TA team assumed the dispatch reached the Combined Fleet's commander in chief at his headquarters in the Inland Sea. "It appears that CinC Combined is busy 'coaching from the sidelines' and is not identified with any particular task force," they stated.[10] They were wrong. Yamamoto was on board the battleship *Yamato*, flagship of his Main Body force, trailing six hundred miles behind Nagumo's First Air Fleet.

Tension mounted inside the basement as Rochefort's eavesdroppers failed to get a line on Yamamoto's various fleets. But if Yamamoto and his commanders used their radios sparingly, the same couldn't be said for some of their U.S. Navy counterparts. While the Fletcher-Spruance task forces remained silent, some Navy units and their superiors at Pearl weren't so restrained. They were doing a lot of "talking." Rochefort's analysts reported on 1 June that the Imperial Japanese Navy's RI crews were having "a field day" with U.S. naval communications, collecting large quantities of U.S. naval traffic and distributing their findings to commanders afloat.[11]

Rochefort's radiomen were listening to Yamamoto's radiomen listening to Pacific Fleet activity, and they didn't like what they heard. The Japanese could draw inferences from radio traffic just as easily as could Hypo's analysts. They didn't have to break the U.S. Navy's operational codes (they never did). They just had to be able to make informed guesses about U.S. operations based on patterns of radio traffic.

Even after Rochefort sounded the alarm, nothing changed.[12] Yamamoto's eavesdroppers noticed a sharp intensification of communications traffic out of Hawaii. Out of 180 U.S. naval messages intercepted in early June, 72 were labeled "urgent," indicating that heavy-duty American operations almost certainly were under way.[13] Hypo's analysts worried the Japanese might put two and two together, grasp what was going on, and spring a trap of their own.

Incredibly, the intel suggesting greater U.S. naval activity was not passed on to Nagumo's striking force.[14] Yamamoto declined to transmit those reports because he didn't want to break radio silence and he figured Nagumo had already copied them from the Japanese navy's fleet broadcast. Also, Yamamoto's staff officers dismissed the danger on grounds that drawing out the U.S. Fleet was, after all, the purpose of their campaign.[15] As it turned out, Nagumo had picked up some but not all of those clues.

In the basement and elsewhere at Pearl Harbor, long hours of waiting for the action to begin, coupled with fears that the Navy's ambush of Nagumo had been compromised, led to a bad case of the jitters. No one was immune. When officers didn't get news from or about Midway, they worried about the possibility of an attack on Oahu. They remained concerned about Operation K.

During the latter part of May, even though Admiral King had begun to doubt whether Operation K would materialize, that view wasn't shared at Pearl. "A seaplane raid on Oahu is still to be expected," Captain Steele stated on 31 May in his daily war plans comments.[16]

3 June: Noon to Midnight (Hawaii)

No bombs fell on Oahu, but they did fall elsewhere early in the morning of Wednesday 3 June. Just as Rochefort had predicted, planes from the carriers *Ryujo* and *Junyo*, constituting Japan's Second Carrier striking force, bombed Dutch Harbor on Unalaska Island shortly after 8:07 (local time), inflicting considerable damage and killing about twenty-five soldiers and sailors. This action was followed by an attack on nearby Makushin Bay.[17] The Battle of the Aleutian Islands had begun.

It took a while for the news to reach Nimitz and Rochefort at Pearl Harbor. The first reports went no further than Admiral Theobald, commanding Task Force 8, which was far from any possible contact with the enemy. Doubting the reliability of Nimitz's intelligence, Theobald had stationed his small flotilla farther to the east, some 400 miles south of Kodiak, where, as E. B. Potter mused, "it proved about as useful as if it had been in the South Atlantic."[18] Operating under strict radio silence, Theobald had no way of passing his information on to Pearl Harbor.

Nimitz and Rochefort knew something was happening, they just didn't know what. Even if Nimitz could have been sure about the Aleutians, he still lacked proof that Nagumo's striking force was bearing down on Midway. Then he got the proof he wanted. Just after 1:30 p.m. at Pearl (11 a.m. Midway time), Midway's naval air station relayed to CINCPAC headquarters a bulletin from a PBY patrolling 700 miles southwest of Midway: "Main Body . . . bearing 262, distance 700 . . . eleven ships, course 090, speed 19." The message noted that Midway's commanding officer, Captain Simard, had dispatched nine B-17s to bomb the oncoming enemy force.[19] The Battle of Midway had begun.

What Simard's B-17s had set out to bomb was the vanguard of three different IJN fleets now converging on Midway from the west. Two of the fleets, a transport group made up of 28 troopships and a close support force comprising 15 destroyers and cruisers, had sortied from Saipan. The third, and deadliest, was Admiral Kondo's invasion force. Consisting of 21 warships and a mix of battleships, cruisers, destroyers, and the carrier *Zuiho*, the invasion force had departed from the Inland Sea on 25 May. It had just rendezvoused with the transport and support forces as the two groups neared Midway. Rochefort's traffic analysts would discover in the days ahead that the transports included 2 freshwater tankers sent along to supply an island rendered desperate for water following a mishap the Japanese believed had ruined its distillation plant on 20 May.[20]

The news that Yamamoto's lead forces had appeared approximately where and when Hypo had predicted evoked an almost audible sigh of relief in the basement. The dungeon's no-nonsense culture ruled out displays of riotous emotion. Rather than applause or wild cheering, there was just a feeling of profound satisfaction. "We were all on tenterhooks until word had been received that contact had been made," Tommy Dyer said.[21]

Rochefort, too, felt relieved. His spirits had lifted earlier when the signals coming out of the Aleutians were indisputably linked with the bombardment of Dutch Harbor: The Japanese navy's Fifth Fleet was on schedule. "I must admit that I felt much better when the contact reports from the Aleutians came in on time," Rochefort said.[22] He'd felt even better after learning of the PBY sighting west of Midway. For weeks the meaning of AF had been contested; it would not be again.

At CINCPAC headquarters, Nimitz smiled what Layton called "that brilliant white smile." If Nimitz had been unduly concerned, he had disguised it. But he made no attempt to conceal his relief as he showed Layton the dispatch just received from Midway. "This ought to make your heart warm," Nimitz said. "This will clear up all the doubters now. They just have to see this to know that what I told them is correct." The first thing he did after that was radio his task force commanders at Point Luck a correction, in case they had picked up the PBY's "Main Body" sighting. Nimitz knew from Rochefort's 27 May briefing that Nagumo's striking force would arrive from the northwest, not the southwest. So what the PBY had spotted wasn't Nagumo. "That is not, repeat not, the enemy striking force," he told Fletcher and Spruance. It was the invasion force, the lead elements of Admiral Kondo's Second Fleet escorting the occupation transports.[23]

There remained a nagging question. Nimitz and King both expected Nagumo's four carriers to begin their bombardment of Midway no later than Wednesday morning 3 June. It was now Wednesday afternoon, and there was no sign of Nagumo's carriers. So where was the *kido butai*? Was it possible that Rochefort had been correct once again? Were Nagumo's carrier planes going to strike early Thursday morning 4 June, just as Ham Wright and Joe Finnegan had predicted on the morning of 27 May?

Rochefort and his analysts were ultimately proven correct, but their accuracy might have been the result of a fluke. What no one in the U.S. Navy could have known, as noted, was that Nagumo's *kido butai* was behind schedule, running a day late. Much to Yamamoto's unhappiness, Nagumo's carriers couldn't depart the Inland Sea on 26 May (25 May in Hawaii) as originally scheduled, a date that would have put his carriers in a position to strike Midway on 3 June. When Nagumo reported that the First Air Fleet needed more time for provisioning, Yamamoto had no choice but to accept that. But he told Nagumo the other units in his vast armada would sail on time, meaning they would be one day ahead of the *kido butai*. The *kido butai* would have one less day to knock out Midway.[24]

Of course, all Nimitz knew was that Nagumo's carriers hadn't arrived when expected. True, the invasion force had been spotted, so from all indi-

CINCPAC link: In 1942 Rochefort's best friend at Pearl, Lt. Cdr. Edwin T. Layton (shown here as a rear admiral), served as Station Hypo's liaison with commander in chief, U.S. Pacific Fleet, first Adm. Husband E. Kimmel, then Adm. Chester W. Nimitz. The Rochefort-Layton connection proved vital in the weeks leading up to the Battle of Midway. *NARAII*

The band played on: One member of USS *California*'s band died when the battleship was torpedoed and bombed during the Japanese attack on Pearl Harbor on 7 December 1941. With their instruments lost, the remaining bandsmen were unemployed. Rochefort got them released to Station Hypo, where they did everything from typing and filing to punching intercepted messages onto punch cards. Even the *California*'s bandmaster, Lovine B. "Red" Luckenbach (left), got a job—running an IBM tabulating machine. *Courtesy Mike Palchefsky*

Rear Adm. Leigh H. Noyes, director of naval communications and a longstanding Rochefort antagonist, was reassigned to the Pacific in 1942 and given command of Task Force 18. On board his flag ship, the carrier *Wasp*, Noyes (left) confers with Capt. Forrest Sherman during the 7 August 1942 assault on the Eastern Solomons. After the *Wasp* was torpedoed on 14 September 1942 he never received another sea command. *NARAII*

"Fusser": Living up to his Naval Academy nickname, Rear Adm. Russell Willson wrote a memo in 1942 to Adm. Ernest J. King, commander in chief, U.S. Navy, recommending against a Distinguished Service Medal for Rochefort. One of his reasons: Rochefort hadn't served in combat. *Naval Security Group*

"Terrible Turner": Rear Adm. Richmond Kelly Turner, head of War Plans, lived up to his nickname in May 1942 when he rejected key aspects of Rochefort's estimate that AF represented Midway. Adm. Ernest J. King, commander in chief, U.S. Navy, reassigned him to the Pacific in June 1942, where he distinguished himself as head of amphibious operations. *NARAII*

Midway skeptic: in charge of OP-20-G's Japanese-language section in May 1942, Lt. Cdr. Redfield "Rosey" Mason (shown here as a rear admiral) refused to believe Station Hypo's estimate that AF designated Midway. *Naval Security Group*

Mentor: a long-time Rochefort crony, the Office of Naval Intelligence's Capt. Arthur H. McCollum warned his blunt-spoken friend against speaking insultingly to superior officers he didn't respect. "Rochefort stepped on toes of a lot of people who later got to be pretty important guys," McCollum recalled. *U.S. Naval Institute Photo Archive*

Rochefort confidant: nicknamed Socrates for his "well ordered brain," Capt. C. H. "Soc" McMorris (left), CINCPAC's war plans officer, was dubbed by Rochefort "the ugliest man alive"—but he was "smart as hell and could curse with anyone." McMorris shared Rochefort's view that Pearl Harbor was an unlikely target for Japanese aggression. *NARAII*

Capt. John Redman pictured here having just received a Legion of Merit medal. Running the Navy's cryptographic unit in 1942 (OP-20-G), Redman encountered a skeptical Rochefort, who scoffed that Redman had no background in cryptanalysis and owed his position to his powerful brother, Rear Adm. Joseph Redman, director of naval communications. John later helped engineer Rochefort's ouster from Station Hypo. *Naval Security Group*

Shortly after the Battle of Midway, Rear Adm. Joseph Redman masterminded the plot to expel Rochefort from Station Hypo. Redman later changed his view of this officer. In a strange twist of fate, in 1944 he asked his onetime adversary to head the planning team set up to determine Japan's future naval capabilities. *Naval Security Group*

The deputy: as John Redman's assistant at OP-20-G, Lt. Cdr. Joseph Wenger (shown here as a rear admiral) worked to centralize the Navy's communications intelligence (comint) activity in Washington, a move that strained relations with Station Hypo analysts at Pearl. Wenger joined forces with the Redman brothers in the plan to evict Rochefort. *Naval Security Group*

Nemesis: as Vice Chief of Naval Operations, Vice Adm. Frederick J. Horne (shown here as an admiral) championed the careers of the Redman brothers, sponsoring Capt. John Redman as head of OP-20-G and Rear Adm. Joseph Redman as director of naval communications. This led him to support the Redmans when they moved to oust Rochefort as officer in charge of Station Hypo. *NARAII*

Rochefort's relief: Here with his wife earlier in his career (as a commander), Capt. William B. Goggins took charge of Hypo in October 1942, following Rochefort's departure. Goggins had no experience in cryptanalysis but was considered by Adm. Ernest J. King to be a good administrator. *NARAII*

Famed as the founder of the Seabees, Rear Adm. Ben Moreell, chief of the Bureau of Yards and Docks, wanted Rochefort to supervise the building of a floating drydock, advanced base sectional dock (ABSD-2), in June 1943. Rochefort seized the opportunity. *NARAII*

Floating drydock: relieved as Station Hypo's boss, in 1943 Rochefort was ordered to supervise the building of the Navy's second floating drydock, known as an advanced base sectional dock, or ABSD-2. Built in ten sections and later towed to an assembly site in the South Pacific, the vessel was one of seven such drydocks constructed during World War II. *U.S. Naval Institute Photo Archive*

Rochefort in charge: After returning to Washington in 1944, Rochefort headed a new Pacific Strategic Intelligence Section (OP-20-G50), centered in the Communications Annex on Nebraska Avenue in northwest Washington. Rochefort's team did long-range studies on Japan's future naval capabilities. *Courtesy Ferdinand Johnson*

Winding down: Eighteen months after returning to the Navy Department in spring 1944, most of them spent running the 300-member Pacific Strategic Intelligence Section, Rochefort was tiring of the Washington scene. Shortly after Japan surrendered on August 15, 1945, he applied for sea duty, a request that was first granted, then rescinded. *Credit: Naval History & Heritage Command*

Joe (left) with Joe Jr. in Army uniform and Fay, circa 1945–46. Young Joe graduated from West Point in 1945, while Joe Sr. retired from the Navy effective 1 January 1947. *Courtesy Janet Rochefort Elerding*

Captain Joe Rochefort finally received the Distinguished Service Medal denied him in 1942 when President Reagan awarded it to him posthumously at a White House ceremony May 30, 1986. Above, Reagan awards duplicates of the medal to Rochefort's son, Colonel Joseph J. Rochefort Jr., left, and his daughter, Mrs. Janet Rochefort Elerding. *Official White House Photo by Pete Souza; courtesy Ronald Reagan Library*

During the ceremony honoring Rochefort, President Reagan greeted two Station Hypo survivors, Capt. Gilven Slonim, USN (Ret.), facing the camera, and Rear Adm. Donald "Mac" Showers, shaking hands with Reagan. In the middle is Showers' wife, Billie. *Official White House Photo by Pete Souza; courtesy Ronald Reagan Library*

Rochefort and his wife, Elma Fay, inside their ranch-style home in Palos Verdes, a section of Redondo Beach, CA, circa 1967. Fay predeceased Joe, dying in 1969 of congestive heart failure. Joe was shattered by her death, which rendered him lethargic for months. He lived seven more years, until 1976. *Courtesy Janet Rochefort Elerding*

cations Yamamoto's attack plan was unfolding pretty much the way he and Rochefort had contemplated. But CINCPAC still had questions. Since the *kido butai* was now anticipated 4 June rather than 3 June, Nimitz wanted to know if anything else had changed. Was Nagumo still going to show up from the northwest bearing 315 degrees, as Rochefort had estimated on 27 May?

Nimitz now did what he usually did when he was puzzled: he summoned his fleet intelligence officer. Even though Layton had already subscribed to Rochefort's 4 June attack date, Nimitz now asked him for a fresh estimate, a specific date and time for Nagumo's attack. Layton restated his belief that the *kido butai* would arrive the next day, 4 June. Then, in a projection that differed slightly from Rochefort's, he told Nimitz: "They'll come in on northwest or bearing 325 degrees and they will be sighted at about 175 miles from Midway and the time will be about 0600 Midway time." Nimitz seemed satisfied.[25] Four June was at hand. Few people at Pearl doubted what the morning would bring.

⸎

Rochefort didn't wait for Nagumo's carriers to show up to organize the basement into a state of high readiness. He had already doubled all watches at Wahiawa under what Hypo called Condition 1.[26] He politely informed his underground staff, officers and enlisted alike, that they would have to remain at their stations well beyond their normal duty hours. They would be needed in what Rochefort grasped would be an emergency situation that could last days.

Rochefort's job now differed somewhat from his usual mission of tracking the Imperial Navy. He and his team still had to do that; indeed, they had to do it with even greater precision and speed than before. But they also had to do something different: stay on top of fast-breaking combat developments at Midway and speed the flow of news to CINCPAC.

Rochefort faced obstacles doing that. Station Hypo had been set up to function as a communications intelligence unit, not a communications center. There was a world of difference between the two. He could receive intercepts of IJN messages only if they were picked up by Wahiawa's radiomen and conveyed to Pearl by teleprinter or jeep; he couldn't receive radio traffic from U.S. Navy forces afloat. There were no radio receivers inside the basement. At most he could hope that his Japanese language officers assigned temporarily to Wahiawa might hear something interesting over the air and pass it on to the basement via teleprinter.

Aside from what Wahiawa could tell him, Rochefort had three ways to keep abreast of events at Midway. He could get news informally from Layton via their secure phone line, or he could get fleet operational messages relayed to the COM 14 admin building from the communications station at Wahiawa. The undersea cable from Midway direct to the admin building at Pearl was another resource. Copies of messages received from Midway at COM 14 could be delivered to the basement via a pneumatic message tube.

Rochefort now created a new job for Ensign Showers, who for months had been assisting Jasper Holmes with ship plotting. Now Rochefort had Showers' desk moved from Holmes' area to the support pillar behind his own desk. Attached to that pillar was the pneumatic message tube terminal. The cylinders would plop down on Showers' desk. Beginning early on 3 June, Showers would remain at his desk for what turned out to be seventy-two un-interrupted hours, catching the cylinders when they came down the tube. His routine was to check the messages inside the tube to see if they merited passing on. If so, he walked them over to Holmes, who either used them to plot ship movements on a giant map spread across a table near his desk or, if they were important enough, take them to Rochefort.

"I didn't budge from that spot for three days," Showers said. He survived on snacks brought in from outside and occasional catnaps. For the most part he stayed awake, refraining from taking the stimulant pills favored by some, energized by the tension in the room and the adrenaline that seemed to be surging in all. Twenty-two years old, still unfamiliar with many aspects of the Hypo operation, Showers didn't always know everything that was go-ing on. But he was left with one overwhelming impression: "It was damned exciting."[27]

4 June: 8:30 a.m. to Noon (Hawaii)

Early Thursday 4 June, Rochefort learned what Nimitz had found out around 8:30 a.m.: At 8:00 a.m. (5:30 on Midway), a PBY pilot, Lieutenant (jg) How-ard P. Ady, had flashed to Midway the following message: "Enemy carriers." He'd amplified the dispatch a few minutes later with a bulletin placing those carriers bearing 320 degrees and 180 miles from Midway.[28]

At CINCPAC headquarters, Nimitz compared the *kido butai*'s location just reported from Midway with Layton's estimate from the day before. He was impressed. "Well, you were off only five minutes, five degrees and five miles out,"[29] Nimitz told him. Rochefort received his copy of Ady's message moments later. What Rochefort thought or said when he read it was never recorded. He probably wasn't thinking about his prophecy or Layton's. If he was, he knew that he too had been off only five degrees, having estimated 315 degrees.[30]

Ady's startling report had been followed by another gripping message at 8:22 a.m. (5:52 Midway time) from a second PBY pilot, Lieutenant (jg) William E. Chase, flying in the sector immediately south of Ady. Chase proclaimed in plain language: "Many planes heading Midway, bearing 310 distance 150."[31] Rochefort got the news shortly after Nimitz did.

Both Rochefort and Nimitz knew that Ady and Chase had caught only a glimpse of Nagumo's *kido butai*. Rather than the two carriers Ady soon reported seeing, they knew there were four, in company with at least two battleships, a handful of cruisers, and many destroyers. Nagumo's twenty warships would be pitted against Fletcher's twenty-six—four carriers against Fletcher's three. Midway, jammed with more than eighty B-17s, light bombers, dive bombers, and assorted fighters served as an unsinkable fourth. There was local equality, possibly even an advantage for the Americans if they could retain the element of surprise.

Hypo's men at Wahiawa now strained to pick up whatever sounds they could from the waters around Midway. They didn't hear much. With combat operations finally under way, information suddenly got scarce. Both U.S. task forces remained on radio silence; they received radio traffic but didn't send any. Rapidly closing on Midway, the *kido butai* remained silent, as did the Main Body trailing some six hundred miles behind Nagumo.

At Midway communications halted abruptly. Once bombs started dropping—the first smashed into Eastern Island around 6:30 a.m. (9:00 at Pearl)—radio operators ducked for cover. Few cylinders plopped down on Showers' desk. Then news began to trickle in, some of it relayed to Rochefort by the U.S. Fleet's communications center, some picked out of the air at Wahiawa and relayed to Pearl. Rochefort called Layton whenever an interesting morsel showed up. Layton did the same for Rochefort. They talked on their direct line more than forty times on 4 June.[32]

From Midway's naval air station, its radiomen back in business around 9:30 (Hawaii time), Hypo and CINCPAC got their first sense of the events unfolding at Midway. "Only 3 undamaged fighting planes remain," Midway cabled. "No contact our dive bombers." A follow-up cable noted that things could have been worse: The island's two power stations had been destroyed, along with two clusters of fuel tanks, a hangar, and a mess hall, but some assets survived. Midway's runways were only slightly damaged and, amazingly, its main supply of aviation gasoline remained intact. Midway also reported shooting down eight Japanese planes.[33]

Less heartening was the news that flowed in from Midway's pilots attempting to strike the *kido butai*. They were having a hard time getting close, as was painfully clear from the brief reports Midway cabled Pearl just before 10:00 a.m. (Hawaii time). Six of the island's recently arrived Avenger (TBF) torpedo planes ran into heavy fighter opposition. So did four B-26 bombers and sixteen SBDs. Few seemed to have gotten near the enemy to inflict any damage, although one SBD pilot did report hitting a "carrier either in the center or forward" part of the ship.[34]

Another glimmer of good news came in from the Army's sixteen B-17s taking part in the attack. They dropped their bombs from 20,000 feet and headed for home, reporting one carrier smoldering.[35] Told that at least one and possibly two *kido butai* carriers had sustained hits, Nimitz by 10:30 a.m. (Hawaii time) had reason to be guardedly optimistic. He had no way of knowing that Midway's valiant fliers, through no fault of their own, overwhelmed by the *kido butai*'s brutally efficient combat air patrol, had scored no hits and, in the fog of combat, had failed to distinguish between genuine strikes and the geysers created by near misses.

All the while the *kido butai* remained silent. It emitted no detectable signal during the entire early morning onslaught, lasting from approximately 6:30 to nearly 9:00 a.m. (Midway time), during which Midway hurled fifty-three planes at the IJN carriers (some thirty fighters remained behind on combat air patrol).

One burst of Japanese radio activity early 4 June was ominous. At 7:40 a.m. Midway time, 10:10 at Pearl, Hypo's language officers at Wahiawa heard the pilot on scout plane Tone 4, launched earlier that morning from the cruiser *Tone*, blurt out a voice message to the *kido butai* in plain language: "Te-te-te" three times, meaning *teki*, the Japanese word for enemy.[36] The excited message was followed by an encrypted dispatch in Japanese Morse. Neither Rochefort nor his analysts could read the encrypted message, but they had no doubts that the Japanese scout had spotted the Fletcher-Spruance task forces.[37]

The same pilot that Wahiawa heard at 7:40 radioed another encrypted message around 8:20 a.m. Midway time (10:45 in Hawaii), now reporting in code that the ships he had seen earlier were "accompanied by what appears to be a carrier bringing up the rear."[38] The message couldn't be read. But any doubt about what it meant was cleared up by the voice message from Seso (the call sign of the sending party) to Tone 4: "Inform us of position of enemy carrier."[39] The Americans now knew the Japanese had discovered their carriers, or at least one of them.

Shortly before noon at Pearl, the teleprinter linking the basement with Wahiawa crackled to life again. Rochefort's radiomen had intercepted a signal from the *Akagi*. They had no doubt that it was the *Akagi* because they recognized the touch on the key as that of the heavy-fisted operator recognizable on that carrier on 7 December.[40] Having repulsed or evaded everything that Midway had been able to throw at his striking force, Nagumo had concluded it was time to talk to Yamamoto, still trailing six hundred miles behind. He broke radio silence at 8:55 a.m. Midway time (11:25 at Pearl), informing the Combined Fleet's supreme commander of Tone 4's sighting. Nagumo told Yamamoto: "At 0800 Enemy 1 CV, 5 CA, 5 DD were 10 degrees 240 miles from Midway. Heading for them."[41]

Nagumo's message was one of eighty-seven encrypted transmissions collected by Wahiawa over three days, twenty-six of them on 4 June.[42] Ordinarily the 8:55 a.m. dispatch and others that flowed in throughout that day would have been an information windfall, but that wasn't the case this time because of the change to JN-25(c) on 27 May.

The IJN dispatches beginning to arrive from Wahiawa weren't wasted, however. Dyer and Wright couldn't make sense out of them, but Huckins and Williams could. As Nagumo and his commanders broke radio silence later in the day, Hypo's traffic analysts could determine the *kido butai*'s various frequencies and use them to calculate the bearings and call signs of some Japanese ships, a few in desperate trouble.[43]

One piece of news Rochefort and Nimitz did get Thursday morning was baffling. Shortly before noon Hawaii time, they learned from a Midway cable that eleven SBD dive bombers from the *Hornet* (VB-8) had landed at Eastern Island to refuel. The planes had been in the air for hours searching vainly for Nagumo's carriers. Unable to find any trace of the *kido butai* and low on gas, the planes landed at Midway. They were refueled and sent on their way with orders to resume their search for Nagumo's carriers, then look for the *Hornet*.[44]

The roaming dive bombers turned out to be part of a larger story. None of the *Hornet*'s thirty-five SBDs and ten F4F fighters located the *kido butai* that morning, an exercise in futility subjected to careful scrutiny by historians in later years. In what writers called "the flight to nowhere," researchers found that the commander of the *Hornet* air group, Commander Stanhope Ring, incomprehensibly led his planes on a wild goose chase far to the north of the *kido butai*'s actual position. Ring never satisfactorily explained the course he flew that morning or why he flew it.[45]

None of this was known to Nimitz, Rochefort, or anyone else at Pearl on 4 June. Nor did they know that one *Hornet* squadron—the fifteen Devastator torpedo planes (VT-8) led by Lieutenant Commander John Waldron—did perform gallantly that morning, as did the fourteen Devastators from the *Enterprise* (VT-6), led by Lieutenant Commander Eugene E. Lindsey; and the twelve from the *Yorktown* (VT-3), led by Lieutenant Commander Lance E. Massey. Days would pass before Fletcher, Spruance, and Nimitz learned the fate of their three torpedo squadrons. They had no way of knowing that between 9:18 and 10:20 a.m. at Midway, the torpedo planes of Task Forces 16 and 17 had set the stage for the most decisive naval engagement of the Pacific War. News about the Devastators would be slow in coming.

If there was a silver lining to Midway's report about the *Hornet*'s lost dive bombers, it was the confirmation they provided that Fletcher and Spruance had indeed launched their aircraft against Nagumo's carriers early Thursday. How those planes were faring was anybody's guess. "So little came over the radio that Fletcher and Spruance had no idea whether their attacks were successful," observed Pacific war historian John Lundstrom.[46]

4 June: Noon to 6:00 p.m. (Hawaii)

By early afternoon Rochefort and Nimitz had only the dimmest idea of what was going on at Midway. But very soon the Wahiawa-Pearl teleprinter and Showers' cylinders started bringing news. It turned out to be mixed. Bulletins indicating success one moment alternated with reports portending disaster the next. The clashing reports put Rochefort, Nimitz, and their aides on an emotional rollercoaster ride that wouldn't let up until well into the next day.

One sobering development concerned the *Yorktown*. At 12:15 p.m. (2:45 at Pearl), Rear Admiral Fletcher broke radio silence to tell Nimitz that the carrier had been attacked by Japanese fighters 150 miles north of Midway.[47] With the carrier's stability uncertain, Fletcher moved quickly to transfer his flag to the cruiser *Astoria*, a development that probably led Rochefort to turn his thoughts to Hypo's translator on board the *Yorktown*, the seemingly snakebit Ranson Fullinwider, who had lived through the destruction of the *Lexington* four weeks earlier.[48]

Rochefort needn't have worried. Fully joined Fletcher at 12:38 (Midway time) as the admiral and his staff made a cautious descent to the boat sent over to fetch them. Already having survived the sinking of the *Lexington*, the apparently indestructible Fullinwider showed everybody how to do it. He remarked that he was getting to be an old hand at this.[49]

On board the *Astoria*, Fletcher turned tactical leadership of the two task forces over to Spruance. Then, shortly after 4:30 p.m. at Pearl, Nimitz received a more welcome report when Spruance radioed his first dispatch of the day. He informed CINCPAC that between 9:00 and 10:30 a.m. Midway time (11:30 to 1:00 at Pearl) air groups from Task Forces 16 and 17 had attacked Nagumo's *kido butai*, leaving "all four carriers badly damaged."[50]

Nimitz was saddened to learn about heavy plane losses, but he could hardly have asked for better news. All four *kido butai* carriers appeared to have been put out of action. There was more good news. The *Yorktown*'s blazes had been stanched, and the ship was moving ahead on her own steam.

Then, an hour after getting Spruance's upbeat report, Nimitz got a rude jolt. At 2:44 p.m. Midway time (5:15 at Pearl) the *Yorktown* was bombed a second time, sustaining two torpedo hits and listing badly, apparently sinking. Her captain, Elliott Buckmaster, soon ordered the ship abandoned. Fletcher told Nimitz: "Have no idea location carriers attacking Task Force 17."[51] Obviously, Spruance's earlier report of an obliterated *kido butai* had been premature. All four of Nagumo's carriers had not been eliminated.

Now Task Forces 16 and 17 stopped talking, as planes from the Navy's two surviving carriers and Midway searched for the *Yorktown*'s assailant. Nagumo's ships, meanwhile, had been transmitting confusing signals. Radiomen picked up traffic from a carrier—later determined to be the *Hiryu*—after her planes had smashed the *Yorktown*. Oddly, the *Hiryu* didn't address Nagumo on board his flagship, the *Akagi*, but instead sent her messages to the light cruiser *Nagara*.[52]

As the day wore on, Rochefort's traffic analysts noticed something else unusual: an absence of plain language air-to-ground chatter from Japanese pilots.[53] "We came to believe they were unable to communicate," Layton said. "You can learn by not hearing anything. To be sure I would talk to Rochefort and say, 'Don't we hear anything on this?' He says, 'Not a thing.' And I said, 'Have we tried the other frequencies?' He says, 'We've tried every frequency that we know they've got.'" Rochefort and Layton reached the same conclusion: "The only reason they weren't talking was because they weren't able to do anything," as Layton put it.[54] The two intelligence officers didn't conclude from this that all the *kido butai* carriers had been destroyed, just that they had been incapacitated. But they didn't know for sure.

4 June: 6:00 p.m. to Midnight (Hawaii)

For hours no illuminating reports came in from either Midway or Wahiawa, let alone the task forces. "There were long stretches where we didn't get any news from the outside," Showers recalled.[55] Finally around 8:15 p.m. Hawaii time, Pearl got some news. A PBY pilot flying out of Midway, Ensign Ted Thueson, reported that the three burning ships he had spotted two hours earlier had indeed been Japanese carriers—the first confirmation obtained by any U.S. scout plane that Nagumo's force had sustained severe damage.[56] Then Thueson's PBY was jumped by a Zero. He got away, but the incident left no doubts that an IJN carrier remained "on the loose."[57]

As time passed without word one way or the other about that loose carrier, Nimitz grew agitated, coming very close to losing his fabled cool. He carped at the paucity of information. "There wasn't a report, there wasn't anything and Admiral Nimitz was frantic," Layton said later. "I mean, as frantic as I've ever seen him because he wasn't getting any reports."[58] As midnight approached, Nimitz finally got the news he had been waiting for. Spruance radioed him that Task Force 16 had attacked the remaining Japanese carrier, which, he declared, was "last seen burning fiercely."[59] From all the evidence, an overriding fact emerged: Nagumo's carrier threat had ceased to exist in the waters around Midway.

CINCPAC now radioed a message of his own, this one addressed to all task force commanders, with copies to Admiral King and General Emmons: "You who participated in the battle of Midway today have written a glorious page in our history x I am proud to be associated with you."[60]

5 June: Midnight to 6:00 a.m. (Hawaii)

Even with all four *kido butai* carriers smashed, Nimitz didn't assume the Battle of Midway had been won, or was over. Early in the morning of 5 June, CINCPAC radioed his commanders and cabled Midway and COMINCH that the Japanese "will attempt assault and occupation Midway regardless past losses."

He told his forces that "another day of all out effort" would be required to "complete the defeat of the enemy."[61]

Nimitz was right to be cautious. Admiral Yamamoto, whose Main Body for a time had closed on Spruance from the northwest, now briefly considered a night action. That concern, coupled with the possibility of a morning invasion, put Rochefort, Nimitz, and everybody else at Pearl Harbor on edge. They didn't feel reassured when in the hours just after midnight, Midway reported that a Japanese submarine had shattered the night's calm by hurling at the atoll several rounds of shell fire.[62]

Navy brass might have rested more easily had Rochefort's codebreakers been able to read a detailed, four-part dispatch that Nagumo sent to Yamamoto toward morning, entitled "Striking Force Battle Report." Nagumo said all his carriers had been either sunk or damaged beyond repair.[63] That message wasn't decrypted for weeks, nor was the follow-up dispatch from Kondo's Second Fleet to the occupation force: "Cancel Midway Operation."[64]

Yamamoto had quit, and Hypo couldn't read his message calling off the fight. "The night after the battle, I came across a message in a tactical code that I was then working on," Dyer remembered. "It said, 'Line fleet operation order number so-and-so, the Midway operation is . . .' And then—blank. I worked for hours trying to fill in the blank, without success."[65]

5 June: 6:00 a.m. to 6:00 p.m. (Hawaii)

As Rochefort's team early Friday morning braced for another day, the mood in the basement was somber. Even though Yamamoto's invasion forces showed signs of withdrawing, as usual in the basement, there was no exhilaration. After nearly three days of ceaseless activity, much of it fruitless struggle with a code they hadn't been able to break, Hypo's analysts were too numb to feel much of anything. Talk of victory seemed rash in the early morning hours of 5 June.

Yet, as the analysts went about their work, more evidence surfaced indicating that events had gone America's way. Hypo found on Friday 5 June that the previous morning, Nagumo had transferred his flag from the *Akagi* to the *Nagara*. "[Message] heading definitely states [Nagumo's] Chief of Staff is aboard the *Nagara* and in view of this fact coupled with collateral information it is fairly well indicated the *Akagi* has probably been abandoned, possibly sunk," Rochefort's traffic analysts wrote in their summary for 6 June, covering traffic that was intercepted 5 June.[66]

The TAs also brought forth a revelation: Admiral Yamamoto himself had been present in the north Pacific during the Battle of Midway, in company with two battleship divisions (with Yamamoto on board the *Yamato*), a cruiser division, a destroyer division, and two light carriers. That finding represented Hypo's first discovery of Yamamoto's Main Body, a formidable force of thirty-four warships intended to deliver a knockout blow to the U.S forces that Yamamoto assumed would rush to the aid of Midway.[67]

Even with the *Akagi* a goner, Nagumo on board the *Nagara*, and PBYs reporting burning *kido butai* carriers, Rochefort and his analysts remained unsure about what had happened at Midway. Ensign Showers didn't feel certain about the outcome until late in the afternoon of Friday 5 June. That's when a Midway PBY fished out of the water Ensign George Gay Jr., the lone pilot to survive Lieutenant Commander Waldron's doomed Devastator attack on the *kido butai* early on 4 June. Shot down just after making a torpedo run at a carrier, Gay had avoided being seen by the Japanese by taking cover under a floating seat cushion. Barely keeping his head above water, he'd caught glimpses of SBDs bearing down on Nagumo's carriers.[68]

In an action that was unplanned and uncoordinated, the dive bombers of the *Enterprise* and *Yorktown* appeared over Nagumo's carriers at about the same time. The two groups had taken different paths to wind up in the same place. The *Enterprise*'s thirty-two planes, led by Lieutenant Commander C. Wade McClusky, took a more circuitous route, first finding nothing, then, by sheer luck spotting the IJN destroyer *Arashi* returning to the *kido butai* after a fruitless pursuit of a U.S. submarine. McClusky maneuvered his group in the same direction the *Arashi* was taking.

The *Yorktown*'s seventeen SBDs, led by Lieutenant Commander Maxwell F. Leslie, proceeded on a more direct path straight to Nagumo's flattops.[69] The two squadrons showed up over the *kido butai* around 10:15 a.m. local time, just as Nagumo's Zeros were preoccupied with the *Yorktown*'s Devastators, too busy to notice the threat from the high-altitude dive bombers. Even though only nine of forty-seven torpedo squadron pilots and six of their planes survived on 4 June, historians would credit them for pulling Nagumo's fighters out of position and making possible the successful unexpected attack on the carriers.[70]

Ensign Gay, struggling to stay afloat, claimed to have watched the whole spectacle. He said he inflated his life raft after dark, then climbed in, and saw three IJN carriers—later thought to be the *Akagi*, *Kaga*, and *Soryu*—blaze into the night and then sink.[71] The *Hiryu* escaped long enough to launch two waves of dive bombers and torpedo planes against the *Yorktown* early in the afternoon. The *Hiryu* was found by planes from the *Enterprise* around 5:00 p.m. Midway time (7:30 at Pearl) and smashed by four direct hits. She was scuttled the next day.

Thirty hours later, Gay was picked up by a Navy PBY and rushed back to Midway, where he reported what he had seen. "Many of us weren't sure what had happened on Thursday at Midway until we heard Gay's story," Showers said. "When he said he saw three carriers burning, that's when we first realized we had actually won the battle."[72]

But what kind of victory was it? There remained doubts about how complete the triumph had been. "There was a feeling of general satisfaction in the cryptanalytic unit when the first contacts with the Jap fleet at Midway were made [on 3 June] where and when we said they would be," Dyer commented later. "But there was never a moment when we were aware that Midway had been a completely successful operation. Only later did we recognize that the battle was won, but by then the moment of jubilation had passed."[73]

Rochefort remained his laconic self. Whatever was going through his mind at that time, he kept his thoughts to himself. He had never been a cheerleader or, for that matter, particularly effusive. Yet Rochefort must have been pleased with how everything had turned out during Hypo's three-day ordeal, both for himself and his crew, a group he always referred to as "the best communications intelligence organization that this world has ever seen."[74]

Aftermath: Midway and Hawaii

Spruance pursued the retreating Japanese for a couple of days. His thoroughly exhausted SBD pilots managed to sink the cruiser *Mikuma* and severely damage her sister ship the *Mogami*, which had to struggle to make Wake. Spruance decided not to push ahead any farther. Recognizing his force had done as much as he could reasonably expect, he called off the chase on 7 June.

The Japanese had little to show for their massive effort. Their main trophies were two small islands on the far western tip of the Aleutians Islands. With Admiral Theobald's Task Force 8 hundreds of miles out of position, IJN transports on 7 June faced virtually no opposition when they landed troops on Attu and Kiska. Although occupation of the islands made no sense without Midway in Japanese hands as well, the navy decided to keep both, "partly as a block to invasion, partly for nuisance and morale value," historian Samuel Eliot Morison observed.[75]

The only other prize the Imperial Navy could claim was the *Yorktown*. Crippled by the *Hiryu*'s two attacks on 4 June, the carrier and her escort destroyer, the *Hammann*, were torpedoed by the Japanese sub *I-168* on 6 June. The *Hammann* sank immediately; the *Yorktown* went down the next day, marking the end of the Battle of Midway.

For Rochefort and his analysts 4 June had been frustrating. After weeks of being at the epicenter of the Midway debate, they suddenly found themselves on the sidelines. They had followed the engagement as best they could. Rochefort's radiomen and linguists at Wahiawa, and his traffic analysts and linguists at Pearl, had done their best to "read" Midway's message traffic.

But the dispatches copied by his radio operators couldn't be decrypted by his cryptanalysts. In the chaotic, fast-breaking situation, traffic analysts could make only limited sense of signals exploding out of the Midway area. When Nimitz fully grasped the magnitude of his fleet's victory over the Japanese, that knowledge came not from the communication intelligence produced by Rochefort's team, but from fliers and commanders at sea.[76]

None of that mattered. Against resistance from their superiors in Washington, Rochefort and his analysts had provided Nimitz with information that enabled him to put his carriers where they needed to be on Thursday 4 June. By the time combat operations began that morning precisely where and when Rochefort and his team had predicted, Hypo's job was done.

Even with that stunning forecast, American success on 4 June had by no means been inevitable. "The closest squeak and the greatest victory [in the Pacific] was at Midway," General Marshall said later. As factors in that victory he cited the "magnificent and self-sacrificing" performance of the Navy.[77] There could be no question that the bravery of individual pilots, the wise tactical moves of Spruance and Fletcher, and the bold strategy of Nimitz all were crucial to the outcome.

One other group proved indispensable to America's success at Midway: the U.S. Navy's comint specialists, Rochefort's team in particular. Without the smarts and unshakable resolve of Rochefort and his codebreakers, Nimitz's carriers might well have been 3,500 miles away, somewhere in the southwest Pacific during Yamamoto's extravagant campaign to seize Midway and key islands in the Aleutians. "Midway would be one of those cases when intelligence strikes like lightning," military historian John Ferris said in an interview. "Intelligence was so fundamental to the event, that the battle could not have happened without intelligence"—in particular, without that produced by Rochefort and the U.S. Navy's entire comint community.[78]

Eventually the Battle of Midway would be compared with Trafalgar, Jutland, and other major campaigns at sea that turned the tide of history. The battle transformed the conflict between the United States and Japan. Many agonizing years of combat loomed ahead, but after Midway the United States would remain on the offensive. "Midway was the crucial battle of the Pacific War, the engagement that made everything else possible," Nimitz said after the war.[79]

Back at Pearl, Nimitz wasted no time giving credit where he thought it was due. His chance came on 6 June, shortly after King had sent him a radio message of congratulations for the effort expended by all branches of the military—Navy, Marines, Coast Guard, Army—at Midway. It was broadcast in plain English so it could be read by all, including the Army.

When General Emmons read King's message, he decided to concede he had been wrong about Midway. He promptly showed up at CINCPAC headquarters bearing a jeroboam of cold champagne decorated with Navy blue and gold ribbons. Emmons gave a speech of congratulations, after which Nimitz ordered the bottle opened and the champagne served.

When Layton suggested that Rochefort be invited to the party, Nimitz agreed. A staff officer phoned him, requested his presence, and sent over a staff car to the basement to fetch him. Rochefort was late as usual. Nimitz's call caught him busy at his desk, unshaven, rumpled, wearing his trademark smoking jacket and carpet slippers. By the time he'd cleaned himself up and made his way over to the party, it had been replaced by a staff conference at which Nimitz was presiding. Nimitz welcomed him, introduced him to those present, and said: "This officer deserves a major share of the credit for the victory at Midway."[80]

Caught off guard by Nimitz's praise, "I muttered something to the effect that I was merely doing what I was being paid to do," Rochefort recalled. He went on to say that any praise to be handed out should go to all at Station Hypo, not just one person. "Oh, naturally, I was pleased," Rochefort said later. "We felt that we had earned our pay." He added, "I do think in all honesty we did probably an outstanding job insofar as the Battle of Midway is concerned.

This didn't detract at all from the fact that we failed at Pearl Harbor."[81] Rochefort would remain haunted by Pearl Harbor the rest of his life.

॥ ▆ ॥

Three days later in the basement, when it was clear Yamamoto was taking his numerous forces back to Empire waters, Rochefort gave his team a respite from the crushing hours they had been working. "I ordered all these people home and told them I didn't want to see them for three or four days," Rochefort said later. "Their answer to this was to set up a party."

One of the analysts had a house on Diamond Head, to where some thirty of the basement's denizens now repaired. "They got me up to this thing and this thing was a great big drunken brawl," Rochefort said. "It was in a house—it wasn't a hotel—we had enough sense to stay away from a hotel," where Hypo's finest might have encountered the shore patrol.

Did Rochefort join the revelry? He wasn't a teetotaler. Given the occasion, he might well have sipped a bourbon and water. Because of the ulcers he traced back to his days on the research desk, he probably kept his drinking within bounds, out of deference to his health if for no other reason. The partying eventually ended. "We gradually drifted back and started off again," Rochefort said. His analysts didn't resume the killer schedules they had followed for weeks, but they still had hard work to do. They had to break JN-25-(c). They were getting heat from Washington. "We had to start reading [the code] as of yesterday," Rochefort said.[82]

28

By Any and All Means

Under Com 14 direct control of the Radio Intelligence Unit
has been, by virtue of seniority, in the hands of an ex–Japanese
language student (a Commander).

—Joseph R. Redman

Shortly after the Midway campaign Rochefort learned that his immediate
superior, Rear Admiral Bagley, wanted to recommend him for a Distinguished Service Medal, then the Navy's second-highest decoration after the
Medal of Honor. The paperwork had been completed, Admiral Nimitz had
endorsed it, and all that remained to be done was for Bagley to send the proposal to Washington. Rochefort voiced reservations.

The proposal hadn't come out of the blue. Two days after the battle,
King's staff asked Bagley to recommend awards for those in radio intelligence
deserving recognition for their role in that battle. Bagley kicked the request
over to Rochefort, who handed it off to Jasper Holmes with the advice that
he form a committee. Holmes then met with cryptanalysts Holtwick and
Steele, who decided that medals should go to Hypo's "old-timers," as they
called the veterans, with a DSM to Rochefort. They took their list to Bagley,
who consulted Nimitz.[1] Now, with Bagley about to follow through, "I advised
against it," Rochefort explained later. "I advised against doing anything like
this, because it's going to make trouble."[2]

His hesitation wasn't surprising. Ordinarily Rochefort opposed medals
for codebreakers during wartime, fearing that such public recognition after

a highly publicized military success would tip off the enemy that his codes had been broken.[3] Security would be jeopardized. But something more was behind Rochefort's attitude than his well-known concern about security. "If COMINCH approves [the medal], he is admitting that the intelligence work at Midway was done by Station Hypo and *not* by Washington," Rochefort said (emphasis in original). "If you admit this, then you admit that the statements that have been made the past three or four months by Washington—Station Negat—were incorrect."[4]

Quite apart from the security issue, Rochefort also had mixed feelings about decorations in general. Since taking over as Hypo's officer in charge, he had tried to foster a culture of group-mindedness and disinterest in personal recognition. The sign on his desk—"We can accomplish *anything* . . . provided . . . no one cares who gets the credit"—helped everyone maintain that value.[5]

But when it came to the Battle of Midway, Rochefort did care who got the credit. And he believed he knew who deserved it in this instance: his Hypo crew, the people he called "the best damn" intelligence team in the world. Rochefort wasn't blind to the merits of others; he recognized the huge contributions made by Lieutenant Fabian's team at Belconnen. But he drew the line at Station Negat. Coral Sea and Midway were Rochefort's benchmarks of worthiness. "We backed up and helped Belconnen on the Coral Sea job," he commented years later. "Belconnen backed us up, perhaps to a lesser extent due to lack of talent, and helped us on the Midway job, while Negat kibitzed and complained on both jobs."[6]

Now medals were being weighed for all those who, deservedly or not, had helped bring about the stunning victory at Midway. The whole business made Rochefort uneasy, but none of his concerns made any impression on Admiral Bagley, who ignored them. On 8 June 1942 he submitted the following one-paragraph proposal to Admiral King: "It is recommended that Commander Joseph J. Rochefort, U.S. Navy, be awarded, at a suitable future time to be determined by the Navy Department, the Distinguished Service Medal for especially meritorious conduct in the performance of secret duties, the nature of which is well known to the Commander-in-Chief, U.S. Pacific Fleet."[7] Bagley proposed somewhat lesser awards for several of Hypo's old-timers. Everybody sat back and waited.

Rochefort's plainly wasn't at his best in the days right after Midway. The grinding weeks before the battle, along with the bad air conditioner, had taken their toll. He had a persistent bronchial cough and had lost 15 pounds, dropping from his usual 175 down to around 160.[8] The wear and tear were beginning to show. "I was exhausted," he said.[9]

Yet new challenges kept arising, some of which would bear directly on his future at Pearl. One onslaught stemmed not from his old adversaries at OP-20-G but, ironically, from his friends at ONI. This move had its origins in March, when the commandant of the Marine Corps, Lieutenant General Thomas Holcomb (the uncle of Hypo's Bankson Holcomb), recommended to Admiral King that the Navy create advanced intelligence centers at five sites around the Pacific.[10]

Proposed for Dutch Harbor, Pago Pago, Auckland, Brisbane, and Pearl Harbor, the centers would be unlike anything that currently existed. They would provide crucial intelligence to Army, Navy, and Marine commands in the Pacific. The plan looked ahead to the day when combined U.S. Navy, Marine, and Army forces would go over to the offensive and need new kinds of intelligence to support amphibious operations against Japanese forces entrenched in their island fortresses in the central and western Pacific.

As envisioned by Holcomb, the centers would be supervised by CINC-PAC. But Nimitz let it be known that he didn't want the centers under his direct authority. He proposed they be managed by naval intelligence. That was fine with ONI, which had ideas of its own about the centers. As sculpted by ONI, the centers would produce information about enemy forces and installations from "all sources"—a term that covered not only the likes of mapping, aerial reconnaissance, photo interpretation, and geographic research, but also comint, which then belonged to naval communications. ONI put a joker in the deck.

"By designating the centers as all source," observed historian Fred Parker, "the Holcomb proposal . . . threatened the DNC with losing control to ONI of communications intelligence."[11] Whether he intended it or not, Holcomb had just given ONI a weapon in its long-standing effort to gain control of the Navy's comint program. Previous attempts had always failed. But with the emergence of the Holcomb plan, a new opportunity presented itself. Convinced such centers would soon be needed, King in April approved a variant of the Holcomb proposal. He so informed Nimitz. But he also gave Nimitz a voice in shaping the organization of the centers. He ordered ONI's Arthur

McCollum to Pearl in early April to meet with Nimitz and work out details for what Holcomb referred to as an Advanced Joint Intelligence Center.[12]

ONI's chieftains didn't think Nimitz would be a pushover. They knew his preference for a small, streamlined staff, and what they had in mind was anything but small or streamlined. They envisioned about 120 specialists of one kind or another for the Hawaii center. McCollum's task was to "sell" Nimitz on the ONI version of the concept. He expected to find Nimitz skeptical.[13] McCollum remained at Pearl several weeks, talking first with Nimitz's staff before making his big pitch to Nimitz. Chief of staff Draemel, war plans chief McCormick, and operations chief DeLany were amenable, as was the new COM 14, Rear Admiral Bagley. McCollum also approached his old friend Rochefort, whose viewpoint would be critical because under the ONI plan, the Hypo unit would be integrated into the center. Rochefort could be back with ONI.

Rochefort was in an awkward spot. As officer in charge of the Hypo radio intelligence unit, he served multiple bosses. Administratively he was accountable to Bagley, operationally he reported to CINCPAC. But Hypo was a field office of naval communications and took direction on policy issues from OP-20-G. Rochefort may have preferred to serve under the ONI banner, but the last thing he wanted was to get caught up in a power struggle between ONI and ONC. Yet, presented with the idea of an advanced intelligence center at Pearl, "Joe Rochefort welcomed it," McCollum said. "He said it was just exactly what we needed. There was no ill-feeling, nothing but the greatest of cooperation on Rochefort's part." Whether McCollum accurately gauged Rochefort's opinion can be questioned.

But if Rochefort did indeed welcome the center in May, it was an attitude that wouldn't last. Before many weeks passed, he would see the center in a different light. In the early days of May, however, no strong voice was raised in opposition to an advanced intelligence center at Pearl. Nimitz finally accepted the overall concept, telling McCollum he would "give it a whirl," and agreed to designate one of his officers as the temporary chief of the center until a specially trained ONI officer could be named to replace him. But he approved the plan with caveats, itemized in a 28 May memo to King.[14] A major stipulation concerned Joe Rochefort. Nimitz had come to value the timely intelligence supplied by Hypo. In fact, he had just approved Rochefort's request that overall staffing at Hypo be increased from 170 intercept operators, cryptanalysts, linguists, yeomen, and clerks to more than 400. Now Nimitz worried that the manpower required by the new centers might drain away people needed for Hypo. Thus, in his letter to King Nimitz asked that the manpower for Rochefort's unit be brought to Pearl immediately and be drawn from the Washington force, that is to say, from OP-20-G.

CINCPAC wanted the intelligence center's personnel to be assigned to the Fourteenth Naval District, as were the officers and men of Hypo. Nimitz also sought to the keep the center small. Aside from Hypo, which he put in a class by itself, he figured that no more than eight or nine officers and men would be required to man the center, at least for now. Nimitz didn't think the Hawaii center should be called an Advanced Joint Intelligence Center.[15] He proposed Intelligence Center, Pacific Ocean Areas—thus was born ICPOA, a unit that shortly would evolve into one of the Navy's most ambitious intelligence enterprises.

As agreed upon by Nimitz, ICPOA would be a shore-based establishment under the umbrella of COM 14, organized primarily to serve the fleet. It would be a Navy operation, with liaison to the Army and Marine Corps. Nimitz would retain operational control; he would appoint a temporary chief until ONI named a permanent director. Manpower would be supplied by ONI, with Hypo dependent as always on OP-20-G for staff, but now shifting into a gray area.

Reaction in Washington to Nimitz's changes was mixed. ONI was delighted to have CINCPAC on board; with Nimitz's essential approval in hand they could go ahead and do pretty much what they wanted. Naval communications was another matter. DNC Joseph Redman had played no role in the original formulation of the advanced centers. Nor had his brother John, still running OP-20-G. The concept confronted them with the likelihood that they would lose their grip on Hypo.

From the Redmans' point of view, integrating Hypo with the ONI-managed intelligence center was bad enough. But now Nimitz had made things worse. Not only did CINCPAC want the center to operate under the aegis of the Fourteenth Naval District, he proposed that Hypo's immediate staffing needs be met by shifting people to Pearl Harbor from OP-20-G—a request the Redmans had no intention of granting.

"Any attempt to transfer activities now being carried out in Washington in support of the Pacific Centers at this time would interfere seriously with operations and result in a decided loss in general efficiency," stated Joe Wenger, John Redman's deputy, in a memo to Vice CNO F. J. Horne, with a copy to DNC Joseph Redman.[16] Joseph Redman agreed with Wenger.

But the Redman brothers and their associates had to be careful. They couldn't be seen in any way objecting to a concept that had the full support of Admiral King. Even their patron at court, Vice Admiral Horne, championed the centers. If both King and Horne wanted them, the Redmans had to want them also. They did better than that. Not only did the Redmans support the centers, they presented themselves to King and Horne as guardians of the concept.

There was only the problem that if the new centers materialized as proposed, Hypo could end up an arm of naval intelligence, as previously noted. The Redmans suspected Rochefort might have played a role in the Nimitz plan. Without any evidence, they blamed Rochefort for Nimitz's amendments. "Reactions to the Nimitz comments on the Holcomb/ONI plan from within the communications directorate were decidedly hostile and directed personally against Rochefort and, to a lesser extent, against Layton," wrote historian Parker.[17]

Layton was getting it from both ends—communications and intelligence. During his weeks at Pearl, McCollum got the impression that he opposed the ONI proposal. In truth, Layton's only "fault" in the affair was that he defended Nimitz's view that staffing for the center should be kept limited.[18] Nevertheless, word spread around Main Navy that Nimitz's intelligence officer was working against ICPOA. The Redmans exploited the rumor, depicting Layton as a malcontent. They also looked for a way to picture Rochefort in an unflattering light.

Now Rochefort himself did something that aided their effort. It coincided with a development that seemed favorable. On 15 June 1942, Nimitz's assistant chief of staff handed Rochefort an order to report to the Pacific Fleet.[19] The order appointed Rochefort CINCPAC's temporary chief of ICPOA, a job that would be in addition to his current duties as officer in charge of Hypo. Rochefort didn't altogether welcome his new assignment. He thought his workload was heavy enough. But the order was vague, the center was weeks away from reality, and Rochefort saw advantages in attachment, if only briefly, to CINCPAC's staff. He thought it provided an extra layer of protection against his adversaries in Washington. What he did next can only be attributed to overconfidence or extreme fatigue.

Responding to an unexpected message from John Redman in which he actually asked Rochefort what Washington could do to aid Station Hypo, Rochefort answered heedlessly. He used the message as an opportunity to try to separate himself from John Redman and OP-20-G. But he did so in a way that had the opposite effect from what he intended—it boomeranged. "I eventually prepared a dispatch which said in effect that what is history is history," Rochefort said later. "What happened in Midway, happened in Midway, I'm not at all interested in anything like that now. We've got other problems such as future operations in the Pacific . . . and therefore I'm not going to discuss any longer with Washington or anybody else matters which I consider as not important." He told his OP-20-G masters that beginning immediately, "I'm operating under the instructions of Admiral Nimitz [and Admiral King]."[20]

"And I showed this to Layton," Rochefort recalled. "Layton said the admiral has seen this and he agrees with it, and he said send it. Which I did send." Through this dispatch, Rochefort believed he had made his break irreversible. "I am working for COMINCH and CINCPAC," he informed them, "and I'm not working any longer for you clowns back in Washington."[21]

What the Redmans thought of Rochefort's message wasn't recorded. But they must have felt they had had just about enough of this officer. First they had Nimitz's request to supply Hypo with extra staff. Then they had to review Bagley's recommendation—endorsed by Nimitz—for a Distinguished Service Medal for Rochefort. Now they had on their desks Rochefort's own declaration of independence from OP-20-G. Many of their long-standing complaints against Rochefort bubbled to the surface. "These people in Washington were somewhat jealous of Rochefort's position out there," said Arthur McCollum, who was at Main Navy at the time. "Rochefort [sending] stuff directly to Nimitz without their knowledge" was a particular sore point. "Their nose was a little bit out of joint. They wanted very much to get into the driver's seat so that nobody got any information except with their okay. That was a difficult thing."[22]

The Redman brothers and their associates now started playing a high-stakes game of their own. Their objective was to defend the new Hawaii intelligence center while at the same time doing everything they could to keep Hypo part of ONC's domain. Their means of achieving that goal was to use their influence at Main Navy to arrange for an officer loyal to naval communications to relieve Rochefort as officer in charge of that unit.

On 20 June, less than three weeks after the Battle of Midway, Joseph Redman took his first concrete action to bring about the downfall of Joe Rochefort. Ostensibly responding to Nimitz's 28 May memo to COMINCH, Redman prepared a memorandum to Vice Admiral Horne, who supervised communications as part of King's leadership team. Entitled "Radio Intelligence Organization," the memo purported to be an even-handed review of ONI's bid to extend its sovereignty over radio intelligence. Redman began generously, observing, "Intelligence as such properly belongs under the jurisdiction of ONI." Then he proceeded to tick off all the reasons why, in this instance, intelligence wouldn't be an appropriate home for the personnel and equipment of communications. People in ONI "just don't speak our language," he lamented. He noted that all the hardware used in RI belonged to naval communications. And he pointed out that traffic analysis and direction finding, for example, involved personnel who were, in their training and thinking, creatures of communications. "Thus," he asserted, "my conclusion is that Radio Intelligence cannot thrive and function efficiently except under direct control of Naval Communications."[23]

To illustrate the incompatibility of intelligence with the rigorous world of communications, Redman directed Horne's attention to Pearl Harbor, where, he stated, the Navy's RI operation was faltering under the weak leadership of two ONI-oriented officers, one shore-based, the other fleet-based, both allegedly ill-equipped by training and temperament to perform the hard technical work required by communications. Redman wrote: "Under Com 14 direct control of the Radio Intelligence Unit has been, by virtue of seniority, in the hands of an ex–Japanese language student (a Commander). On CinCpac's staff the intelligence received from the Com 14 Radio Intelligence Unit is handled by an ex–Japanese language student (a Lt. Cmdr.). They are not technically trained in Naval Communications, and my feeling is that Radio Traffic Analysis, Deception, and Tracking, etc. . . . are suffering because the importance and possibilities of the phases of Radio Intelligence are not fully realized."

Whether Redman believed any of this can be doubted. While there's no record of his ever having met Rochefort, their career paths had intersected at various points. They had both served in naval communications in the 1920s, Rochefort in Washington and on board the destroyer *Macdonough*, Redman as communications officer on board the Pacific Fleet's flagship, *Texas*. (Rochefort's 1929 memo to the U.S. Fleet Commander criticizing communications officers afloat for sloppy handling of classified material might or might not have been seen by Redman.)

Also, Joseph Redman served in naval communications with officers familiar with Rochefort. If naval history ever came up in conversation, Redman would have learned that Rochefort had been a pioneer in shaping the Navy's codebreaking program, which had operated from the beginning under the banner of naval communications. Yet Redman's description of Rochefort as an ex–language student would have conjured in the mind's eye the image of someone fresh out of graduate school. Layton, too, was far more than an ex–Japanese language student, having by this time acquired a wide-ranging background in every aspect of naval intelligence and fleet operations.

Redman carried on: "Strong people should be in strong places, and I do not believe the Pacific organization is strong because the administration is weak in so far as Radio Intelligence is concerned. I believe that a senior officer trained in Radio Intelligence should head up these units rather than one whose background is Japanese language. They should confine their activities to Intelligence as such, i.e., the product of Radio Intelligence."

He wrapped up the memo by forwarding to Horne background material prepared by John Redman, or OP-20-G as his older brother called him. Finally, "in the interest of immediately improving this situation," he suggested that OP-20-G "make a quick trip to Honolulu to get first-hand information on which to base recommendations for remedial action."

OP-20-G's accompanying memorandum, entitled "Establishment of advanced intelligence centers," was written by Joe Wenger and signed by John Redman.[24] This one argued for a strong Washington office where the real brain work of OP-20-G could be done. In making his case, the memo's author betrayed a surprisingly uninformed view of how OP-20-G's field offices actually worked. "Experience has indicated that units in combat areas cannot be relied upon to accomplish more than the business of merely reading enemy messages and performing routine work necessary to keep abreast of minor changes in the cryptographic systems employed." This opinion, coming three weeks after Midway, would have startled Nimitz and elicited a fiery oath from Rochefort.

∎

On 22 June, two days after the Redman brothers submitted their highly charged memoranda to Vice Admiral Horne, Rochefort figured in still another memo, this one to COMINCH from Rear Admiral Russell Willson, King's chief of staff. Willson and Rochefort had a history.

Their mutual enmity went back at least to 1936, when both had served on board the *Pennsylvania*, Willson as captain and Rochefort as a member of Admiral Reeves' staff. Rochefort later came to believe it was this rear admiral who had defeated his initial bid for promotion to commander in 1940. Now, once again, Willson was in a position to influence Rochefort's career. His memo to King was in response to the Nimitz-Bagley proposal that Rochefort be awarded a DSM. Willson weighed in before the Navy's recently created board of awards could consider the recommendation, and didn't pull any punches: "I do not concur in the recommendation that Commander Rochefort be awarded a Distinguished Service Medal."[25]

Rochefort didn't deserve the award, Willson wrote. Although performing his duties in a highly successful manner, "he has merely efficiently used the tools previously prepared for his use," Willson contended. Nor would it be appropriate, he continued, "to award a medal only to the officer who happened to be in a position to reap the benefits, at a particular time, unless in actual combat with the enemy." Cast, Belconnen, and Negat, he averred, had done work of as high an order as Hypo's. "However, these Officers in Charge performed a more or less mechanical, technical job in utilizing a tool already forged to their use," Willson wrote, dismissing the entire cryptanalytic enterprise as little more than a clerical function. Rather than award medals to such officers, he proposed that King send a "well done" to the Navy's three main decrypt units.

Willson's view jibed with King's hard-boiled attitude toward awards and decorations. Even in the early months of the war, King had griped that too many people were getting medals. He generally believed that officers shouldn't get recognition for doing jobs they had been trained to do.[26] He didn't always follow his own policy in practice, but he did take Willson's advice now.

In a cover letter to Secretary of the Navy Frank Knox, he adopted Willson's language in explaining why he didn't concur with Nimitz's recommendation that Rochefort get a DSM. High on the list of factors: while Rochefort's performance of duty was of a high order, the results he obtained stemmed from "the thought and work of a large number of officers." Also, his "performance of duty was not in combat operations with the enemy."[27]

⁌⁍

Back in the Hypo basement, Rochefort's officers and men received on 23 June a message from Admiral King bestowing on them a well done in connection with the Midway campaign.[28] They didn't know that it had been prompted by Russell Willson's memo recommending against a DSM for Rochefort. Nimitz and Bagley got King's reply on Rochefort's medal at about the same time RI personnel got their well done. Bagley passed that word on to Rochefort, who was not surprised. He probably confided the development only to Holmes and a few others; most officers at Hypo wouldn't learn of COMINCH's action until years later. Like their colleagues everywhere, the Hypo people had a healthy interest in medals. They were good for an officer's career and they boosted morale. The men in the basement knew that an awards board was in place to consider proposed decorations for men involved in RI work, including their boss.

Rochefort may have lost his DSM, but he was still in the running for some kind of medal, along with many of his top officers. Their names were before the board of awards, consisting of top brass pulled from different sectors of Main Navy. The board's activities percolated all summer. King's staff and the leadership at naval communications agonized over what type of awards should be meted out to deserving individuals in the Navy's RI network.

Finally, early in September 1942 King's chief intelligence officer, Captain Dyer, and Captain Carl Holden, pinch-hitting for Joseph Redman who was away, agreed on a plan that was accepted by the board, headed by Admiral Thomas C. Hart (just back in Washington after commanding the now-defunct Asiatic Fleet). The plan called for King to send a letter of commendation to each individual on two different lists prepared by Vice Admiral Horne; consideration for medals would be deferred until the end of the war.[29] Twenty-four officers and men were on an A list, another forty-one on a B list. Topping the A list were three commanders: John Redman and Joe Wenger from OP-20-G, and Joe Rochefort from Hypo. For now, officers and men in radio intelligence would get letters of commendation but no medals.

When Hypo's officers and men learned decorations would not be forthcoming soon, they shrugged. They understood the need for secrecy. Most took the news philosophically, some satirically. One was the basement's jokester, Jack Holtwick, noted for his pranks. Sometimes showing up at parties with a monocle in one eye, he had a way of flipping it so it always ended up in his shirt pocket. When Holtwick heard the news, he rigged up a mock ribbon for himself. It had a veil over it indicating the decoration was for secret intelligence work that couldn't be revealed. "Everybody got the point," remembered Admiral Showers. "This eased the tension."[30]

Rochefort knew on 23 June he had been denied a DSM, but he didn't know why or how that decision had been made. Nor did he have any way of knowing about the memoranda that Joseph and John Redman had submitted three days earlier to Vice Admiral Horne. He didn't know that John was coming to Hawaii to look things over and, possibly, propose "remedial action."

But early in July, Rochefort and Layton did get the feeling they were being "investigated," as Layton put it. They weren't altogether surprised. Rochefort got a hint from someone in Washington that an enlisted man attached to the OPNAV staff at Main Navy—an individual known to Rochefort as Chief Yeoman Richman—was en route to Pearl Harbor to question Rochefort and Layton about their working relationship.[31] Apparently Rochefort had at least one ally at Main Navy (possibly McCollum or Safford) who tipped him off. "Rochefort told me," Layton said, "that he had 'private information from a friend in Washington that a special agent from a certain naval officer on Admiral King's staff was coming out to investigate you and me.'" Still fatigued from the Midway ordeal, Rochefort now made another mistake. Assuming Washington didn't like the very close way he and Layton worked together, he framed a strategy intended to give the opposite impression. Under the plan, the two intelligence officers agreed to say, if asked, that they got "along officially" but, each would make clear, "we're not real personal friends," Layton remembered.

Sure enough, Chief Yeoman Richman showed up. He stopped by Layton's office, ostensibly to ask about equipment needed for the intelligence center about to be set up. Then he changed the subject. "After some talk he asked me about my relations with Rochefort and I gave the 'agreed reply,'" Layton said later. "He merely grunted and said that Rochefort had said the same thing concerning me." The Rochefort plan backfired. "[Richman] went back and reported—I've been told—that Joe and I were not friendly, that we didn't get along well," Layton said.[32] The idea that the two were at loggerheads would take root in Washington and, incredibly, be used against Hypo's officer in charge.

⸻ ■ ⸻

Besieged as he already was by problems and pressures, Rochefort now found himself shouldering a new responsibility. On 25 June he received orders from the COM 14 chief of staff that confirmed his "temporary additional duty as Officer in Charge" of ICPOA.[33] ICPOA opened for business officially on 14 July, with a very unhappy Rochefort running the center from his basement desk. He didn't like the job.

Now the long months of tension inside the basement seemed to catch up with Rochefort. He succumbed to something resembling paranoia. Although he knew perfectly well that the idea for ICPOA had originated with ONI and that Nimitz wanted him to help get it started, he saw his new job as a Washington trick to "get me away from communications intelligence," as he put it later. As a result, "I refused to accept that," Rochefort said. "I just flatly refused to have any part of it."[34]

But he did take part in it. Whether he liked it or not, ICPOA was a reality, a shore-based establishment created to serve the Pacific Fleet. Rochefort delegated at least some of the work. "One morning, late in July, Rochefort dropped a mass of papers on my desk and told me to find some space to put the new organization," Holmes wrote. He was relieved to find that only 46 of the more than 200 officers and men ultimately approved for ICPOA were expected soon. But by basement standards that was a lot of people, enough to worry Hypo's cryptanalysts, always concerned that newcomers in the basement could jeopardize security. Holmes solved the problem. He integrated the new people into his own unit, then moved his entire operation, with its many charts and files, to the far end of the basement. The newcomers "filled urgent needs" and stayed out of the way, Holmes said.[35]

If Rochefort had come to see ICPOA very nearly in conspiratorial terms, so had the Redman brothers. They saw it as a power grab by ONI. They now thought it was more important than ever to put a communicator in charge of Hypo, slated to play a key role in ICPOA. On 18 July, four days after ICPOA opened for business, Joseph Redman approached the Bureau of Personnel (BUPERS). He requested orders for Commander William B. Goggins as "officer in charge of the Radio Intelligence section of the Fleet Intelligence Center at Pearl Harbor."

BUPERS ignored what must have seemed an odd request, unaccompanied as it was by no similar call for action from the Fourteenth Naval District or CINCPAC. It could have appeared to BUPERS, as Parker has pointed out, that the DNC was seeking "to replace a highly qualified analyst of Japanese communications in the communications directorate with a person who had no experience whatsoever in this highly specialized field."[36] With his background in the nuts and bolts of regular communications, Goggins was available. He had been severely wounded in March while serving as executive officer of the cruiser *Marblehead* in the Java Sea. Eventually he was recalled to Washington, and, while awaiting orders, assigned to the radio division of the Bureau of Ships, then transferred to OP-20-G to familiarize himself with the world of codebreaking.

Weeks passed and everybody waited. The Redman brothers waited for BUPERS to act. So did Goggins, who thought he was going to Hawaii. BUPERS didn't act. Seeing no strong rationale behind the DNC's request, BUPERS let the matter rest. Joseph Redman's request gathered dust. More time passed.

If Rochefort had any inkling of what was going on in Washington, he gave no indication of it. He had other things on his mind. Like most people in the Navy, he did have a war to fight. Rochefort returned to tracking the Imperial Navy, which had gotten harder since 27 May when the navy had changed its operational code. But during the afternoon of 5 July, Rochefort's team scored a major success against JN-25(c).

It broke a radio dispatch disclosing that a Japanese naval party had landed on Guadalcanal. Of special interest was the fact that the party included an engineering unit, a clear indication that the Japanese navy was about to build an airfield on that island. The news was transmitted to Nimitz and King, meeting in San Francisco to discuss the Navy's forthcoming drive into the Solomon Islands. They had just mapped out plans to recapture Tulagi and seize Santa Cruz Island on 1 August.

The possibility of an IJN airfield on Guadalcanal caused King and Nimitz to rethink their priorities. An airfield there would put Port Moresby within easy striking distance and give the Japanese a forward base close to U.S. supply lines to Australia. Time now became a factor. The United States couldn't let the airfield be finished. So while Tulagi remained a target, the plan to occupy Santa Cruz was dropped in favor of Guadalcanal.[37]

To thwart the Japanese buildup, the U.S. 1st Marine Division landed on Guadalcanal and Tulagi on 7 August 1942. Thus began the battle for the Solomon Islands. Nimitz looked to Hypo for help. Having made some dents in the Imperial Navy's new code system, Rochefort's analysts seemed poised to play a critical role. Then, on 14 August, ten weeks after introducing JN-25(c), the Japanese navy again changed its main code. With lighting speed, JN-25(d) was ushered in. Hypo would have to start all over, from scratch.

Why had the Japanese jettisoned JN-25(c) so quickly? Yamamoto's cryptographers may have been attempting to get back to their original schedule. But some officers advanced another theory. One was Laurance Safford, still bitter after losing out in OP-20-G's reorganization. In a bizarre memorandum, unsigned and undated, Safford traced the 14 August code change to events he said had begun with an article on the front page of the *Chicago Tribune* for Sunday 7 June.

Under a headline screaming the U.S. Navy at Midway "Had Word of the Jap Plan to Strike at Sea," the article itemized the order of battle for Nagumo's forces. It attributed the information to "reliable sources" in the Navy, but any moderately informed reader would have inferred the U.S. Navy had broken the Japanese code. The story had created a furor at Main Navy. King had been enraged, as had been Nimitz and just about all high-echelon officers.[38]

King wanted to hush up the story. But according to Safford's highly charged tale, the Redmans wanted to pursue the matter and somehow tie the unauthorized story to Rochefort. "The Redmans were out for blood," Safford wrote in his anonymous essay, and hinted it was Rochefort's blood.[39] Layton shared Safford's view of what the Redmans were up to: "[They] may well have concluded that Rochefort or I must have been involved in the leak."[40]

An internal Navy investigation turned up that the *Chicago Tribune* story was based on information taken from the summary of Yamamoto's order of battle transmitted by CINCPAC to Fletcher and Spruance on 31 May. The cipher system used was common to that of Admiral Fitch, late of the *Lexington*, now on board the transport *Barnett*, carrying survivors of that destroyed carrier. Nimitz's message reached the *Barnett*, where it was passed to the former executive officer of the *Lex*, Commander Morton T. Seligman. Seligman carelessly let the message fall into the hands of the *Tribune*'s reporter, Stanley Johnston, who happened to be on board the *Barnett*.[41]

Even though it was now clear that the leak had not originated in Pearl Harbor, the Redmans still pushed the Navy Department to continue the case. So did many others. As a result, on 7 August 1942 Attorney General Francis Biddle ordered the *Tribune* to be investigated by a federal grand jury for disclosing secret intelligence operations, prohibited by the Espionage Act.[42] When Biddle's order was announced on 8 August, it triggered headlines across the country. "Barrages of publicity surrounded the case," Layton and his coauthors wrote in *And I Was There*. "They could not possibly have escaped the watchful eyes and ears of Tokyo."[43]

Six days later, on 14 August, the Imperial Japanese Navy substituted JN-25(d) for JN-25(c). Layton laid the blame for the change at the feet of the Redman brothers, as did Laurance Safford, who maintained that Rochefort joined him in condemning the Redman brothers. But did he? Rochefort faulted the Redmans for many things, but probably not this. If he had an opinion, and he almost certainly did, it probably was similar to Tommy Dyer's.

"I am relatively convinced that the change in code and cipher that took place shortly after Midway had nothing to do with the leak," Dyer said. "To distribute the new material and place it in effect requires a little bit more time. . . . In other words, the changes followed too closely upon the *Tribune* story to be occasioned by it."[44]

No evidence surfaced to support Safford's hint and Layton's charge that the Redmans pursued the *Tribune* case in order to smear Rochefort. That deed, along with the Redmans' alleged culpability for the Japanese navy's 14 August code change, must stand as pure conjecture. Whatever the motives of the brothers in pursuing the *Tribune* leak, the issue quickly vanished. The Navy Department later in August withdrew its support for the investigation; the government dropped the case. The Navy correctly worried that the additional publicity sure to surround any continuing probe would imperil security. Reason prevailed.

Safford's portrait of the Redmans madly pulling strings to somehow ensnare Rochefort in the *Tribune* case reflected that officer's bias. This does not mean the brothers weren't doing a certain amount of plotting. Months earlier, they had hatched a conspiracy to dislodge Joe Rochefort from Pearl Harbor by any and all means available to them. Just how far they would go to get rid of Rochefort would soon be clear.

29

Remedial Action

He appears to have been the main obstacle
to full coordination.

—Ernest J. King

Ten weeks had passed more or less quietly since Rochefort had, at least
in his own mind, severed ties with OP-20-G. The only annoyance from
Washington had been the Navy's on-again, off-again, pursuit of the *Chicago
Tribune* case, thankfully dropped late in August. Rochefort didn't think he
had heard the last of the Redman brothers, but the last thing he expected was
that one of them would invade his Pearl Harbor sanctuary.

That's what happened on 10 September 1942, when a newly promoted
Captain John R. Redman showed up at Pearl to take the job of communications officer for the Pacific Fleet.[1] Redman's arrival was part of an elaborate
game of musical chairs intended to meet, at least ostensibly, the changing duty
requirements of five officers. In assuming his new post, Redman relieved Captain Maurice "Germany" Curts, who in turn succeeded Captain Holden, who
had served as deputy to DNC Joseph Redman. Holden took the place of his
former boss, who had gone to sea upon being promoted to rear admiral. (He
would return as DNC in six months.) As for John Redman, by relinquishing
his post at OP-20-G, he created an opening for Captain Goggins who, despite
his inexperience in radio intelligence, was appointed officer in charge of the
Navy's comint agency.[2]

If the rotations accomplished nothing else, they advanced the plan concocted by the Redman brothers to eject Joe Rochefort from Station Hypo. John Redman now occupied a position where he could, as his brother had suggested to Vice Admiral Horne on 20 June, "get first-hand information on which to base recommendations for remedial action."[3]

Redman showed up just as Rochefort was beginning to relax. His mood had improved earlier in September, when Captain Roscoe H. Hillenkoetter had reported to COM 14 for duty as officer in charge of ICPOA. Rochefort now had one less thing to worry about: ONI had kept its word that his ICPOA duty would be brief. And Hillenkoetter turned out to be a blessing in more ways than one. Not only did he relieve Rochefort of an unwanted task, but he soon moved ICPOA's forty-six officers and men out of Hypo's crowded basement into Pearl's new supply building.[4] Rochefort could get back to business.

But now Rochefort had a new concern. John Redman's appearance heightened his sense that he was being targeted, and his intuition was correct.[5] Redman came equipped with a memorandum from Joe Wenger entitled "Matters for discussion with Hypo."[6] This was intended in part to clear up what Wenger called "legitimate complaints" from Hypo's analysts, presumed in advance to be unhappy with OP-20-G. "They will undoubtedly have many other items which bother them and on which we could probably take action to improve matters," Wenger wrote.

To pacify Hypo's headstrong group, Wenger advised Redman to explain the reasons for "our taking over current Orange work in Washington," undoubtedly a reference to OP-20-G's decision in March to work on the latest IJN traffic along with Hypo and Belconnen. That decision, as noted, caused bad feeling in the basement when OP-20-G, as Ham Wright put it, tried "to take complete charge and tell us what to do in detail."[7] Rochefort then proposed to King that Hypo, not OP-20-G, be assigned the "task of reading all of today's traffic today."[8]

Redman's task, as Wenger conceived it, was to explain that OP-20-G didn't intend "to supplant the work of Hypo," but to supplement it. The plan, Wenger advised Redman to say, had paid off at Midway. "[We] believe that [OP-20-G's] contributions [to the Battle of Midway], in a large measure, made it possible to obtain much of the information which was gathered before that action," Wenger continued.[9]

What Rochefort and the officers and men of Station Hypo thought of this version of events isn't known, nor can it be established how Redman presented this message or with whom he met. It is not certain that he engaged Rochefort, whose name didn't appear in the memo. Wenger simply proposed that Redman discuss matters "with the proper people at Hypo." That may or may not have included Rochefort, now well on his way to becoming a nonperson, at least as far as Redman and Wenger were concerned.

Desirable as mending relations with Station Hypo might have been, achieving that wasn't Redman's primary goal. It was secondary to an altogether different objective, in the interest of which Redman now put into action a plan he and Wenger had devised shortly before he'd left Washington. A few days after settling in at Pearl, Redman started communicating with Wenger at Main Navy through a secret code known only to the two of them. They used the Pacific Fleet's radio system, appropriating Nimitz's personal radio call sign to authorize the dispatches. The use of such a code, not to mention the theft of Nimitz's call sign to facilitate the exchange, violated Navy regulations and was done without CINCPAC's knowledge.[10] That didn't slow down John Redman.

Wasting no time to make his move, Redman's dispatches to Wenger characterized Rochefort as uncooperative and unacceptable as officer in charge of Hypo.[11] On 20 September he sent the following message to Wenger (now Goggins' deputy): "OIC of the Radio Intelligence Section, Navy Department: Conditions such [that] even more important than we thought [that] Goggins come out. DF management deplorable. Studying against obstacles and trying to obtain reversal of Hypo's position [regarding] RFP personnel. Suggest you send anyway [to] establish equipment."[12]

RFP referred to radio finger printing, a new process of identifying enemy ship radio transmitters by the characteristics of the emission from the particular transmitter. A process involving oscilloscopes, high-speed photographic equipment, and other new technology, RFP was in its infancy at that stage of the war. Rochefort evidently didn't want to divert his limited resources to the activity.[13] As for the DF operation, Rochefort had inherited a flawed system a year earlier, and over the months had frequently pleaded with Washington for better equipment.

Redman's 20 September message stirred action in Washington. BUPERS, no doubt under heavy pressure from naval communications, finally responded to Joseph Redman's 18 July request proposing Goggins as relief for Rochefort. The bureau consented to that change on 5 October 1942, when it detached Captain Goggins from OP-20-G and published orders for him to report to COM 14 as officer in charge of Hypo.

On 7 October Redman sent another secret message to Wenger: "Be certain Goggins orders read Officer in Charge." Goggins arrived at Pearl on 14 October apparently unaware of the hornet's nest into which he was stepping. Also, his new job wasn't as certain as he thought. Redman still had more work to do to displace Rochefort. On 18 October he fired off another secret message to Wenger: "Suggest Rochefort be ordered immediately to Department for visit by air [with] a weeks delay via coast. This will give him much needed physical rest and be beneficial otherwise. Hillenkoetter and Goggins both concur." That was followed sixteen hours later by yet another Redman-to-Wenger dispatch: "Delay action regard Rochefort pending further word."[14]

Redman had good reason to think twice at this stage. Through his own channels he'd learned that Rochefort was taking defensive measures. Rochefort had gone to Rear Admiral Spruance, Nimitz's new chief of staff, to find out where he stood and request a transfer if his work had not been satisfactory.[15] Such an action might have seemed rash, but it was consistent with Rochefort's character to bring issues to a head and put his career on the line.

Commandant Bagley had also jumped into the fray. No pushover, he had strong ideas about who should be Hypo's officer in charge, a position under his administrative jurisdiction. He wanted to keep Rochefort, as did Nimitz, and they'd both said so. Shortly after getting BUPERS orders regarding Goggins, Bagley had dispatched a message to the bureau, written in the usual radio jargon, describing a change he wanted in Goggins' orders. It was received in Washington on 19 October: "190050 BUPERS orders October Third to Captain William Baker Goggins being modified to report for Executive Officer Intelligence Center Pacific Ocean Areas. CINCPAC concurs. Request confirmation."[16]

In other words, rather than see Goggins replace Rochefort, Bagley and Nimitz wanted him to be appointed the deputy to ICPOA's new director, Captain Hillenkoetter. Realizing Bagley's message would trouble Wenger, Redman secretly advised his OP-20-G collaborator on 20 October: "See COM 14 response to BUPERS 190050. Suggest you wait my private letter to Admiral Horne mailed [via airmail] today." In this letter, Redman restated his brother's 20 June memo to that admiral, as well as the messages he had dispatched to

Wenger during the past four weeks. He reminded Horne that Joseph Redman's memo had been "prompted by certain difficulties which had been experienced in coordinating the work of the Washington and Pearl Harbor radio intelligence units." And he noted that at the time, "it was decided to order an experienced communication officer to the 14th Naval District to assume duties as administrative head of the radio intelligence unit located there."[17]

In effect, Redman was asking Horne to stand against Nimitz. He did not inform Horne that he had conveyed his messages to Wenger surreptitiously, using Nimitz's call sign without his knowledge. Whether it would have made any difference to Horne if he had been fully aware of Redman's machinations can be doubted. When Redman's activities finally were divulged to Horne in late October, he didn't flinch, having found Redman's arguments persuasive.

Rochefort didn't believe the orders he received on 22 October 1942. Signed by Commandant Bagley, the orders were stamped "temporary additional duty." He was to proceed by the earliest plane available to Los Angeles then go on to Washington, where he was to report to Vice Admiral Horne. Upon completion of this temporary duty, Bagley's order stated, he was to proceed to San Francisco and report to the Commandant of the Twelfth Naval District "for the first available government or commercial air transportation as he may assign to Pearl Harbor, T.H. [Territory of Hawaii], and upon arrival resume your present duties."[18]

This all sounded fine in theory, but Rochefort didn't believe it. Even with support from Nimitz and Bagley, he suspected that his tenure at Pearl was ending. One reason, as noted, was his immediate suspicions about the presence of John Redman, who seemed to be taking greater interest in the activities of Station Hypo than was appropriate for the CINCPAC communications officer. Rochefort thought that at the very least, Redman intended to diminish the independence Hypo had carved out from Washington.[19]

Another factor in Rochefort's thinking was the 14 October arrival of Captain Goggins. A certain amount of mystery surrounded Goggins, who clearly was in a state of limbo. He might have gone out to Hawaii with the intent of assuming duties as officer in charge of Hypo, but no sooner did he meet his new boss, Commandant Bagley, than he learned that an effort was under way to change his orders to executive officer for Hillenkoetter. Goggins would have passed that information on to a disconcerted John Redman.

Goggins probably remained unclear about his future until at least 22 October, when Rochefort received his orders. But even that development, assuming Goggins knew of it, would not have dispelled all the confusion. After all, Rochefort's order expressly directed him, upon the completion of his temporary duty, to return to Pearl Harbor and resume his present job.

So why was Goggins in Hawaii? He might have wondered. He might also have wondered what, if anything, he should say to Joe Rochefort. How the two got along during their brief overlap at Pearl isn't known. The vignettes provided by Layton and Safford strain credulity. Safford depicted Goggins as an almost comical character who was denied admission to the basement until he established his identity and the purpose of his business.[20] That was probably a tall tale. Goggins would have been accompanied by a high-ranking officer, just as Bloch had escorted Kimmel and Nimitz. Goggins wouldn't have just wandered into the basement.

Layton improved on Safford's story, picking it up and embroidering it. He showed a more pushy Goggins, first, getting stopped by armed guards as he tried to enter the basement, then, once in the basement, giving Rochefort direction on how to run Hypo and ICPOA. "Rochefort, naturally, resented Goggins's intrusion," Layton wrote.[21] Layton's story would not have convinced many who had been on the scene. First, there were no armed guards near the heavy door that led to the basement.[22] Second, those who came to know Goggins found him modest, reserved, and a sensible administrator, a gentleman bearing no resemblance to the caricatures conjured by Safford and Layton.

What Rochefort thought of Goggins never surfaced. Jasper Holmes and Tommy Dyer couldn't recall him ever appearing in the basement while Rochefort served there as officer in charge.[23] Uncertain how the struggle over his role would be resolved, Goggins kept his distance. He wanted to wait until the coast was clear, and, as October drew to a close, the coast remained decidedly unclear.

⁙

John Redman's luck ran out in late October. As Dyer remembered the story, Layton, whose office was near CINCPAC's nerve center, learned that Redman was misusing the fleet's communications system and passed this information on to Nimitz.[24] Nimitz, furious, ordered Redman to cease this activity.[25] Calling Redman's actions "intolerable," Nimitz, from all accounts, refused to speak to his new communications officer for two weeks.[26]

"In looking into the Radio Intelligence set-up," Nimitz told Horne months later, "I discovered that the Communications Officer on my staff had possession of a code, known only to himself, which he used to communicate either with the Director of Naval Communications or the Director of the Communication Intelligence Organization." The outraged Nimitz continued: "It came as quite a shock to me to find that one of my staff, using my call letter, could communicate with other individuals in the Navy in a code which I did not possess. This appeared to me to be an intolerable situation, and I have directed Redman not to make use of this code without showing me the dispatches. The dispatches already sent in this code are not available to me as they have been destroyed."[27]

But Horne was unconcerned. By the time he received Nimitz's letter, he was familiar with nearly every aspect of Redman's stealthy communication arrangement with Wenger. His source, from one account, was Joseph Redman's successor as DNC, a very upset Captain Holden, who in late October learned about the Redman-Wenger messages.

Just as Redman's dispatches vexed Nimitz at Pearl, they troubled some at OP-20-G. One was the unit's new officer in charge, Captain Earl E. Stone, who had relieved Goggins. According to Safford, Stone was not a party to the Redman-Wenger arrangement. Safford believed that Stone learned of it when Wenger received an enciphered message from Redman and didn't know what to do with it. The message read: "Get rid of Rochefort at all costs."

Refusing to have anything to do with this dispatch, Stone ordered Wenger to report the matter to Holden, who "took immediate action," Safford wrote. "First he ordered Wenger to destroy his copy of the private cipher, thus putting a stop to further messages. Then he reported the matter to the Vice Chief of Naval Operations [Horne]." Holden gave Horne the Redman messages that had come in and left the responsibility with him.[28] Rochefort's fate was now in Horne's hands.

Horne, of course, was primed for such a development. He was aware of and had come to share the Redmans' opinion of Joe Rochefort. As already noted, Horne by this time had received John Redman's private letter from Pearl Harbor recounting the history of the brothers' aim to take "remedial action" at Pearl. The same letter disclosed some of the dispatches that had passed between Redman and Wenger.[29] Horne agreed that Rochefort had to go and so informed BUPERS. Goggins was in. Horne briefed King, who agreed and immediately started work on a letter to Nimitz. Dated 28 October, the letter went out by airmail.

Back at Pearl Harbor, Rochefort made arrangements to take the first available plane to the U.S. mainland, as mandated in his 22 October orders. Quite apart from the lingering drama over his future at Pearl, he had every reason to want to travel at least as far east as California. Ten days earlier, on 16 October, he received a telegram from Fay letting him know that his father, Frank J. Rochefort, had died in Los Angeles at age 90. He was to be buried 19 October. With so much uncertainty at Pearl, there was no way Rochefort could get there. He hadn't seen his father in years, nor, for that matter, any family members living in California. Family issues were no doubt on his mind.

As far as his job was concerned, Rochefort had few doubts that his duty at Pearl Harbor had come to an abrupt halt. He packed and started saying his goodbyes, letting his closest friends and colleagues know he probably wouldn't be back. Nobody believed him. "I told everybody, 'When I leave Pearl, I'm not coming back,'" Rochefort said later. "I knew this. 'I know I'm not coming back.'

"'Oh, yes you are, too,'" Commandant Bagley shot back, "'Don't forget, now, you come back. I was just talking to Admiral Nimitz and he wants you back here.'

"I said, 'Well, I'll tell you one thing. I'll bet I'm not coming back.' He said, 'Well, you've got to come back, because Admiral Nimitz says so.' I said, 'Well, then Admiral Nimitz had better straighten this out with Admiral King. But I'm predicting right now that I won't be back.'"[30]

Another doubter was Tommy Dyer. Like just about everybody else in the basement, Dyer had no idea of the clandestine effort under way to ease Rochefort out of his job. "He never talked to me beforehand about any difficulties," Dyer said later. "All of a sudden out of a clear sky, as far as I was concerned, they sent orders for Rochefort to come to Washington for temporary duty and conferences. At first I took it for a routine sort of thing, but before he left, he said, 'I'll never be back.' And he wasn't."[31]

Jasper Holmes also was caught by surprise. In fact, when Rochefort received his temporary orders, Holmes cheered. "It would be an opportunity for him to gather up some of the loose ends of our relations with OP-20-G," Holmes recalled thinking. "We needed more trained cryptographers, more translators, more *kana* radio operators, more communication and radio direction-finding equipment, and Washington was our only source of supply."

Holmes figured the trip would be a welcome respite for Rochefort. Then he got a sense his friend saw it differently. "Before he left, Rochefort turned over to me a package of personal papers and the keys to his desk," Holmes wrote. "I somehow got the feeling that he anticipated being away longer than we expected, but I did not even suspect that I would not see him again until long after the war was over."[32]

Rochefort departed Hawaii on 25 October 1942.[33]

He didn't proceed immediately to Washington. After all, he had fifteen days' leave. The first thing he did was reunite with Fay, Janet, and Cora, all living in an apartment in Pasadena. Then he reconnected with his brothers, finding to his relief that Harold, who had become disabled and resided with their now-deceased father, had been relocated to a new home, thanks to the intervention of his sister, Margaret. Sister Mary Francis now held the office of treasurer with the Sisters of St. Joseph of Carondelet, a distinguished Catholic order in Los Angeles. Rochefort visited his father's gravestone, and after a few days he and Fay boarded a train for Washington, leaving eleven-year-old Janet in Pasadena with her grandmother.

Things didn't go Rochefort's way at Main Navy. The news he had been dreading was provided by his old friend and mentor, Captain Zacharias, now assistant director of ONI. "Upon my arrival in Washington I was informed by Zacharias that he had just been informed that orders had been issued for my transfer to Op Nav," Rochefort wrote Holmes on 16 November 1942, a few days after his arrival. "ONI had not been consulted prior to the orders having been issued."[34] Nor had CINCPAC, nor COM 14. The waiting was over. Rochefort was hardly surprised, having braced for just such a development weeks ago. However, he was surprised by what he learned next.

Through the new DNC, Captain Holden, he found out about the back-channel communication arrangement that had linked Redman at Pearl Harbor with Wenger and perhaps other officers at OP-20-G. "Carl Holden, the D.N.C., said that several msg's had been received from CincPac (Redman), urging that COM 14's orders to Goggins as exec. NOT be confirmed, and that I be transferred at once," wrote Rochefort, expressing himself in his usual shorthand fashion to Holmes. "Holden ordered those msg's be burned and issued orders that no more be sent. He disclaimed all knowledge of the whole deal and seemed disinclined to become involved in it."[35]

Rochefort was incensed. He "determined to run the story down," as he put it. He proceeded to confront Captain Stone, OP-20-G's new director, and Joe Wenger, Stone's deputy. Rochefort didn't know either officer. He had met Wenger only once, fleetingly, when Wenger had passed through Honolulu in summer 1941. He had never met Stone. The two officers "professed ignorance of the whole thing," Rochefort wrote. "They were both satisfied with Combat Intell at Pearl and did not desire any changes."[36]

Given his short history at OP-20-G, Stone's denial seemed plausible. He clearly was baffled by the whole situation. "I never quite understood the personal animosity that existed between some of the people on duty in Washington and those in Hawaii," Stone said later. As for Rochefort, he liked and respected him ("He was one of the most able people that we had"), and thus found himself puzzled by the sentiment against him.

Was there an OP-20-G conspiracy against Rochefort? "Well, I knew there was an argument going on and I must say I didn't realize that it was [as] serious as it proved to be when Rochefort was summarily relieved, which was an awful mistake," Stone said. "But I must say I had no part in that. That sort of thing I let Joe Wenger handle completely."[37]

Whatever it was that Stone let him handle, Wenger protested his innocence. Recalling Rochefort's visit to Washington, Wenger years later characterized himself as little more than a bystander in the affair. "What precipitated this visit, I'm not sure, but I believe it came about as the result of a recommendation by Commander [sic] Redman, who was then at Pearl Harbor on Admiral Nimitz's staff," Wenger wrote. "Exactly what took place between Redman and Rochefort I do not know. Rochefort, in fact, refused to discuss it with me when he arrived in Washington but was obviously disturbed about something."[38]

Wenger's portrayal of himself as a mere witness would have amused Rochefort. In fact, Wenger was in deep. He had, after all, drafted John Redman's 20 June memo to Vice Admiral Horne that helped cut the ground out from under Rochefort and, to a lesser extent, Layton. The memo signed by Redman was originated by "GA," the organizational symbol for Wenger.[39] Also, Wenger had prepared the 3 September memo for Redman entitled "Matters for discussion with Hypo," intended to help reconcile Hypo to OP-20-G's leadership.

And when Redman in September had started sending secret dispatches from CINCPAC headquarters to OP-20-G, those had to go to someone. If they didn't go to Wenger, already established as a close collaborator with Redman, then to whom? Even without knowing all there was to know, Rochefort put Wenger in the enemy camp.

Rochefort wasn't through yet. In addition to his testy run-ins with Holden, Stone, and Wenger, he also waylaid Captain George Dyer, King's personal intelligence officer. In fact, their encounter probably emerged as the premier event among Rochefort's various engagements at Main Navy. Dyer was primed and ready for the meeting. He wasted no time laying out the bill of particulars against Rochefort, beginning with Chief Yeoman Richman's spurious finding that Rochefort had been squabbling with Layton.

"I asked Dyer if he was taking the word of an enlisted man regarding the state of affairs at Pearl, particularly when referring to officers," Rochefort stated. "He made no reply." Dyer then charged that the newly created ICPOA was being actively and passively opposed by unknown parties. "I was suspected of this," Rochefort noted. "I was blamed for not keeping Cominch informed of Intell matters. Also, I had forgotten that I was an 'op nav' man and should have worked for them instead of Com 14 and the Fleet, presumably."

Rochefort fired back. Indeed, he indulged himself in an old-fashioned tirade. "By this time I was in good form and told Dyer what I thought of the whole setup, that he and Opnav and Cominch had apparently not realized that CincPac was in command in the Pacific and I took orders from Com 14 and CincPac," Rochefort declared. He also pointed out that COM 14 and CINCPAC staff were "quite capable" of taking corrective action if he was seen in any way to be remiss in his duties, as suggested by Dyer and, apparently, some at OP-20-G.

"In short the story was too flimsy to even merit discussion and boiled down to either Holden and Dyer being stupid which they are not or else being a party to a deal of putting their friends in charge of [radio intelligence] organizations regardless of experience and ability," Rochefort fumed. "All the above I communicated to all concerned in words of one syllable."[40]

How Dyer responded to Rochefort's counterattack wasn't recorded. No log of the meeting from Dyer's end ever turned up. The only glimpse of the encounter was provided by Wenger, once again the all-seeing witness. "Shortly after [Rochefort's] arrival, a conference took place between him and one or more persons on COMINCH's staff," Wenger noted. "What occurred at this meeting was never disclosed to me but obviously some heat was generated, as Rochefort was visibly angry when he returned to OP-20-G. He left soon thereafter without commenting any further on the matter to me."[41]

ıı▪ıı

By the time Rochefort and his Main Navy superiors got around to discussing his next duty, his situation had deteriorated beyond repair. With the atmosphere thoroughly poisoned, amicable conversation became impossible. Rochefort never said with whom he met during this second phase of his Washington appearance, but it was probably the same people with whom he had clashed earlier: Holden, Stone, Wenger, and possibly Dyer, who might have been present to keep King and Horne informed of developments. Certainly not Horne, the master operator who usually let his vassals handle messes of this type.

Rochefort was the first to admit that the fault was not all the Navy's. Once it had been established he wasn't going back to Pearl, "I made several mistakes in a great big hurry," Rochefort said later.[42] Obstinate, emphatic, and angry, he put on display a range of attitudes and opinions that clearly hurt his chances to snatch from his worsening situation some kind of opportunity that fit his abilities. "I was just not well," Rochefort said, describing himself as "overtired" and "exhausted" at the time. "I think that was the problem. I was just not well and I was not thinking well."

That being said, "I still was well enough to have kept the job in Pearl," Rochefort insisted. But when he found out what Main Navy had in mind for him, that it was some kind of "special work" in Washington vaguely related to the activities of OP-20-G, he exploded. "I flatly refused," he said. He wasn't going to work for OP-20-G. "Unless I go back [to Pearl] as the officer in charge, then I'm not going to perform the duty in Washington," Rochefort told his superiors. "I'm not going to work for you guys. I'll tell you that right now."

"Oh, yes, you are, too," he was told. "Well, I've got news for you," Rochefort replied. "No, Sir." During a lull in his meetings, which stretched over several days, Rochefort discussed the problem with some of his old friends, including retired Admiral Reeves, commander of the U.S. Fleet in the mid-1930s and Rochefort's longtime mentor. "They volunteered to assist me," Rochefort said. "I told them I didn't need any assistance."

Finally Rochefort's Main Navy bosses agreed to consider some kind of sea duty for him. "Well, what do you want?" Rochefort was asked. "I want to go to sea, preferably in a combatant ship. That's what I've been trained to do, and that is what I want to do. I do not want any shore job." Rochefort's superiors would have to think that over. Admiral King had a policy that naval personnel involved in communication intelligence couldn't serve in war zones. Should such an individual be captured and tortured, he might compromise one of America's most cherished secrets—the fact that the U.S. Navy had broken the Imperial Navy's main operational code. Rochefort regarded the policy as "sound," but he still pressed for duty in a combatant ship.

Amazingly enough, King consented. "I got that clearance by calling everyone I could think of, and in order to get rid of me they said, 'Okay, we've turned you loose.'" The offer he got from BUPERS was desirable: command of an ammunition ship scheduled to sail the next day from San Francisco. But the job had to be filled right away; he would have to leave Washington at once. Rochefort turned it down.

Days earlier he had promised Fay they would visit Joe Junior at West Point, where their son was a student. They were to make the trip in a couple of days, spend a day or two in the West Point area, then return. "I told them I couldn't leave Washington until after that," he said. When Rochefort returned to Main Navy, he found that the time for discussion had passed. There would be no more haggling over what duty he might or might not find acceptable. The Navy had made up his mind for him. Rochefort was handed a new set of orders.

He thought the situation he was in "could have been avoided actually by Admiral Nimitz . . . expressing himself forcefully to Admiral King," Rochefort later opined. "But again, this is Admiral Nimitz."

⁙

In Rochefort's view, Nimitz hadn't done enough to protect him. But there was much Rochefort didn't know. He didn't know, for example, that Nimitz hadn't learned of his permanent reassignment until around 3 or 4 November, after his departure from Pearl. At that point the situation was irretrievable. That was also when Nimitz had received King's 28 October letter spelling out what COMINCH regarded as just grounds for Rochefort's removal.

King began condescendingly, telling Nimitz that "you may not be fully apprised of the radio intelligence situation" at Pearl Harbor. Then he explained Rochefort's transfer by relying on rumor and gossip: "Much of the information that has come to my attention is unofficial—through personal messages and letters exchanged between the personnel at Honolulu and in Washington," King wrote. "In addition, there have been comments made by officers who have returned from the Pacific. This information, though unofficial, definitely indicates that Commander Rochefort has been actively opposing the successful functioning of the intelligence center as set up by the Vice OPNAV," meaning Vice Admiral Horne. Contending that "petty jealousy and bickering" had weakened coordination between the Washington and Honolulu RI units, King stated that Horne had ordered Goggins to Pearl as officer in charge of Hypo as a "corrective measure."

"Although Commander Rochefort apparently has contributed a great deal to the results obtained by radio intelligence unit at Honolulu," King continued, "he appears to have been the main obstacle to full coordination." King did more than slam the door shut on Rochefort; he also invited Nimitz to take action against Layton. "The attitude of Commander Layton also seems not to have been very helpful," King told Nimitz. "I suggest you consider what should be done in the case of [Lieutenant] Commander Layton in view of his reported resistance to most effective coordination."[43]

Nimitz called in Layton and let him know that he had an enemy somewhere in Washington. Layton was dumbfounded, but Nimitz seemed unruffled. "Go back to your office and don't think any more about it," Nimitz told him with a reassuring chuckle.[44] He could shield Layton but not Rochefort. Though assigned to CINCPAC for temporary duty, Rochefort still belonged to COM 14 and thus was beyond Nimitz's span of control.

Although faced with a fait accompli with regard to Rochefort, Nimitz didn't let the matter rest. In his response to King's letter, and in separate messages to Rear Admiral Harold Train (now director of ONI) and Vice Admiral Horne, Nimitz let Washington brass know that he didn't like the way Rochefort's removal had been handled, or the fact that he, Nimitz, hadn't been consulted. And he reminded King that he had recommended Rochefort for a DSM.

"I have no information other than what you have furnished, of bickerings and jealousy between the Washington and Pearl Harbor RI units," Nimitz wrote King, "but I observed enough out here to know that Rochefort's sin was probably one of doing too much rather than too little,—a hard thing for which to condemn a man." He told Train, now spearheading the growth of ICPOA from Washington, that Goggins had shown up at Pearl without any advance word to CINCPAC, and that Rochefort had been detached just as abruptly. He invited Train to pass his complaint on to Horne, who had made the final decision on Rochefort.[45]

Answering, Horne reminded Nimitz gently but firmly that operation of the radio intelligence organization was the responsibility of the vice chief of naval operations. "The Main Unit at Washington," Horne said, "exercises control as necessary over the RI units at Pearl Harbor and Melbourne in order to coordinate all efforts for the maximum efficiency of the entire organization." Goggins had been selected to relieve Rochefort because he was believed to be a better administrator. That was that.[46]

Nimitz knew how the Navy worked. He knew what Horne's job was. But he remained dissatisfied with what he heard from Washington. He dispatched another letter to Main Navy, this one to Horne, repeating his earlier concern. "While I did not consider Rochefort as a member of my staff, I was so dependent on the work of his organization, that I was unpleasantly surprised to find that he had been replaced without one word to me." Nimitz added, "There was never, to my knowledge, the slightest bit of friction between Rochefort and my Intelligence Officer."[47]

Nimitz pushed his campaign to vindicate Rochefort about as far as the Navy and the always irascible King would permit, as Layton was bluntly reminded one day. When he asked Nimitz whether he planned any additional effort with regard to Rochefort's DSM, Nimitz blew up. "Layton, I've got enough to do to fight this war. I've got other things, bigger issues. When the time comes, I hope to take those up. But right now, I can't be bothered with it."[48] And he didn't bother with it the rest of the war. The Rochefort case was closed.

⚬ ▪ ⚬

The basement crew didn't learn Rochefort wasn't coming back until about two weeks after his departure, when Captain Hillenkoetter came down the staircase with Captain Goggins in tow. When Hillenkoetter introduced him to Holmes as "your new boss," Holmes thought he was kidding. He thought Hillenkoetter might be referring to his own expected relief as officer in charge of ICPOA, a job Hillenkoetter had never wanted and would in due time relinquish.[49] It wasn't until he handed Holmes written orders from the Office of Naval Operations that Holmes realized Goggins had actually shown up to relieve Rochefort as officer in charge of Station Hypo.

He immediately took Goggins over to the cryptanalyst's area to meet Dyer, in charge of the basement during Rochefort's absence. Dyer was equally astonished and didn't know quite what to make of Goggins. He and other basement dwellers continued to view Goggins warily for a week or two, until around the time Holmes received Rochefort's 16 November letter explaining what had happened to him at Main Navy.

Passed around and discussed for days, Rochefort's letter produced two very different results in the life of the basement. The first and immediate consequence was to embitter many of Rochefort's closest friends and colleagues in the big room who had come to respect the acumen and quirky humanity of their boss. They couldn't fathom the charges leveled against him—that he had "squabbled" with Layton and CINCPAC staff. Or, equally ridiculous, that he had opposed the creation of ICPOA and failed to keep COMINCH informed on intelligence matters.

"The only probable explanation of what happened to Rochefort," Holmes concluded, drawing on his friend's 16 November letter, was "that he became the victim of a Navy Department internal coup." If so, it was one with far-reaching implications. And "it was," said Holmes, "another blow to our morale."[50]

Rochefort's summary relief did more than demoralize. At least for a while, his absence also weakened the Hypo operation. The unit's effectiveness was impaired not so much because analysts missed his leadership, said Dyer, although some officers would have disagreed. Hypo "wasn't the kind of an organization where leadership played a very large part," Dyer maintained. "In my own bailiwick, I had people in key positions and I gave them their head." Where Rochefort was missed, Dyer thought, was precisely in the area where Joseph Redman deemed him lacking: his all-around prowess in every aspect of communications intelligence, from cryptanalysis and communications to translating and analysis. And, of course, Rochefort could use his memory, intuition, and knowledge of Japanese to flesh out partially decrypted message fragments. "We were missing out on his expertise in analyzing and supporting the intelligence," Dyer said. "We were bound to suffer to some extent. No one could step into his shoes."[51]

Goggins certainly could not. He had no background in cryptanalysis and didn't know Japanese, but he did have a solid background in communications. And, as Vice Admiral Horne told Nimitz, he was known to be "a good executive type officer" who, it was hoped, would "attempt to eliminate an apparent lack of coordination between the Honolulu unit and other units of the organization."[52] He had one other attribute: He was OP-20-G's man at

Pearl Harbor, the personal choice of Joseph and John Redman. "Difficulties over cooperation led the DNC, Captain Redman, to take the position that no officer would be assigned as head of any comint activity who was not under his full and direct control," Joe Wenger commented later. "It was under these circumstances, as I remember, that Goggins came into the picture."[53]

Goggins may or may not have been a proxy for Joseph Redman, but he managed to gain the confidence of Hypo's officers and men. Ironically, he was aided by Rochefort. This was the second major consequence of his 16 November letter to Holmes. Rochefort asked his former colleagues to give their new OIC the benefit of the doubt. Speaking to the group as a whole, Rochefort said: "I hope you will be as loyal to Goggins as you have been to me."[54]

And they were. "The last paragraph of Rochefort's letter facilitated Goggins's smooth take-over of an organization that had been badly shaken," Holmes wrote later. "Fortunately, Goggins was an able administrator and an expert in naval communications. He and I became close and enduring friends."[55]

Even the skeptical Dyer came around. "Initially I concluded that [Goggins] was in on the plot, if there was one," Dyer said. "I think I treated him with the minimum politeness that a commander should show a captain. But I soon had to reform that opinion. I was forced to the conclusion that he was an innocent bystander who sort of got caught in a little jam."[56]

Pleasantly surprised as many of the basement dwellers turned out to be, life in what many still called the dungeon nevertheless changed markedly. Goggins brought an altogether different style to his job as officer in charge. Gone was the old atmosphere of casual informality. Goggins was a strict, by-the-book officer who wanted things done the old Navy way, as one yeoman found to his unhappiness shortly after Goggins' arrival.

Petty Officer Third Class Ferdinand Johnson occupied a desk near that of the unfortunate yeoman. As Johnson recalled the incident, the young man had been put in charge of the basement's coffee pot. One day the yeoman asked the new officer in charge, "Would you like a cup of coffee?" Goggins instantly and sternly corrected him. "Would you like a cup of coffee, Captain?" as Johnson remembered the scene. Officers would now be addressed by their titles. "That was the basic difference between Goggins and Rochefort," Johnson recalled. "Goggins was Navy-conscious. Not Rochefort. There was none of this rank business with Rochefort."[57]

II■II

As for Joe Rochefort, now at age forty-two, his career was about to take another unexpected turn. He got his new orders shortly after his return to Main Navy from West Point. He was to proceed to San Francisco and report no later than 28 November 1942 to the commander, Western Sea Frontier, for duty. The duty wasn't specified.[58]

30

Drydocked

This was very interesting duty.
—Joe Rochefort

Rochefort accepted his fate calmly. The assignment handed him wasn't one he would have picked had he been given a choice. Indeed, it was the type of activity he thought he had left behind in Hawaii. But there was no getting away from what he was expected to do now: set up an advanced intelligence center on the West Coast.

His new boss was adamant about that. Shortly after showing up on 28 November 1942 at the Federal Building in San Francisco, where the Western Sea Frontier was headquartered, Rochefort got his new orders. They were delivered by Rear Admiral John W. Greenslade, an imposing officer who doubled as commander of the Western Sea Frontier and commandant of the Twelfth Naval District.[1]

What Greenslade wanted Rochefort to do was organize an intelligence center similar to ICPOA but that served the Western Sea Frontier, a sprawling entity comprising three naval districts (the Eleventh, Twelfth, and Thirteenth), responsible for the sea defense of all U.S. Pacific coastal areas stretching from southern California to northern Alaska.

Rochefort was now well versed in intelligence centers. Contrary to George Dyer's charge that he had opposed ICPOA, he strongly favored the Pearl Harbor center and said so (Arthur McCollum could attest to that). His only objection to the intelligence center was his belief—a foolishly incorrect notion reflecting his fatigue at the time—that it was being used as a wedge to pry him away from communications intelligence.

That misconception aside, Rochefort had doubts about what Greenslade had in mind. With the Japanese shifting to defense and combat operations headed away from the U.S. mainland, he questioned the need for an intelligence center on the West Coast. But Greenslade wanted it, and Rochefort didn't argue. Although his heart wasn't quite in it, he followed orders. Settling into a routine, Rochefort spent a lot of time on the road, meeting with high-echelon officers of all three districts in his territory. Over the next few months, he would grow to like his new job. It offered amenities he treasured: He was his own man; no one interfered with his work; he didn't get any carping from Washington. "It was a lot of fun," Rochefort said later.[2]

Other jobs opened up, but Rochefort wasn't interested. Late in May 1943 he received what might be called a feeler from his old friend Jasper Holmes back at Pearl. Holmes now wore two hats. He still headed the Combat Intelligence Unit, responsible for plotting Japanese ships. But the unit had been integrated into ICPOA, separating him physically for part of each day from the Hypo group. His second hat was to serve as a link, or liaison, between ICPOA and Hypo, now an arm of ICPOA but operating more or less as a separate entity. ICPOA's Hillenkoetter needed Holmes to tie the two groups together.[3]

In this enlarged role, Holmes was charged with developing additional intelligence capabilities. One new activity contemplated was an intel site in the south Pacific headquarters of Admiral Halsey (who had relieved Vice Admiral Robert L. Ghormley in October 1942), based in Nouméa, New Caledonia. ICPOA was thinking of sending an analyst there to evaluate raw intelligence originating in that region for the benefit of Pearl and, of course, Washington.

Holmes thought of his old boss. "I personally think that you would be the man for the job," Holmes wrote Rochefort. "I know that a good man in that job would be in a good position to help win the war and I think you would be the best man for the job." But before taking the matter to Admiral Nimitz, Holmes wanted to know if Rochefort was interested. "It would do a lot of harm to lay a lot of groundwork and then find that it is contrary with your wishes," Holmes stated. If he did indeed want the job, Holmes assured Rochefort there would be "powerful backing" for his appointment.[4] Would Rochefort give the green light?

He wasn't even tempted. Rochefort gave his friend several reasons for begging off. Fed up with the Navy's intelligence bureaucracy, he told Holmes he had "no desire for a second installment" in an organization in which, he implied, he had lost trust. He had another, even more compelling reason to spurn what he called Holmes' "very kind" offer: his new job was beginning to look intriguing. "I have received orders and leave today to a command at sea," Rochefort wrote Holmes on 2 June 1943. "I have always wanted it and am delighted at the opportunity."[5] He exaggerated slightly; he hadn't received an order to a command at sea. But there still was some truth to his story.

⁞⁞■⁞⁞

Shortly before receiving Holmes' letter, Rochefort was given reason to believe there might be a ship in his future. It wouldn't be the cruiser he had always wanted, but the concept presented to him piqued his imagination: the prospect of commanding a new type of vessel slotted for the dangerous waters of the south Pacific. There was only one catch. The ship would first have to be built and a crew specially trained. The good news was that if he signed on, he would manage both tasks. Rochefort signed on.

This would be no ordinary ship. It didn't have a ship's proper name, and it never would be given one. It would always be known by the category of seagoing vessels into which it fell: advance base sectional dock two or, as it was usually called, ABSD-2. It was to be a floating drydock. Aside from the fact that this vessel would have to be towed (it lacked any means of propulsion), it would resemble other ships in that it was designed to operate on water. If all went well, Joe Rochefort would be its captain.

Rochefort had known for weeks about the ABSD-2 possibility. On 18 May, he was detached from the Western Sea Frontier and ordered to Washington on 7 June to meet yet another new boss, Rear Admiral Ben Moreell, chief of the Bureau of Yards and Docks.[6] Beefy, square-jawed, plainspoken, Moreell was well on his way to becoming a Navy legend by the time Rochefort met him. In March 1943 the Navy had granted his request to recruit men in the building trades for assignment to three naval construction battalions (CBs, the personnel in which would become known as Seabees). Adopting the motto provided by Moreell, "We Build. We Fight," the Seabees built advanced bases under perilous combat conditions in hundreds of locales in all theaters of the war.[7]

Now Moreell was pioneering another form of advanced base: the floating drydock. The concept wasn't new. The U.S. Navy had first ventured into such activity in 1851, when it ordered a wooden one built for the Portsmouth Navy Yard. A second one, five hundred feet long, was built of steel after the Spanish American War for use in the Philippines.[8] For many years the Navy did little more than study the concept. Then in 1937, with Moreell running the Bureau of Yards and Docks, the Navy put renewed emphasis on floating drydocks. The service recognized that U.S. warships crippled in remote areas could be lost for months unless repaired quickly. As one officer put it, "The fleet needed drydocks close to where the action was."[9]

Moreell and his engineers helped to develop a wholly new version of the floating drydock: one consisting of sections, each of which could be towed to an assembly area near a war zone. This would be the advance based sectional dock, and this was what Moreell wanted to discuss with Rochefort. Only one had been built so far, ABSD-1, commissioned at Everett, Washington, on 10 May 1943. Moreell wanted Rochefort to oversee the building of ABSD-2.

Rochefort liked the idea. He was directed to report again to Admiral Greenslade "for duty in connection with the fitting out of the U.S.S. ABSD No. 2 and for duty as commanding officer of that vessel when placed in commission."[10]

Much in Rochefort's life now changed. First he was assigned to carry out his work in a new locale—a place called Paradise Cove, a bucolic haven on the Tiburon Peninsula jutting into San Francisco Bay, near the small town of Tiburon and a short boat ride from San Francisco. The Navy used this site to build the Floating Drydock Training Center, where Rochefort would supervise the training of personnel to operate ABSD-2.[11]

Also, he resumed his family life. With his new duty looking reasonably permanent, he relocated Fay, daughter Janet, and mother-in-law Cora from Pasadena to Navy housing near Paradise Cove. They moved in like every Navy family, not sure what the future might bring, but pleased to enjoy a reprieve from the usual vicissitudes of Navy life. Tiburon didn't hold much appeal, noisy as it was with taverns and sailors on liberty. But the peninsula itself, with its rustic hideaways and proximity to the bay, was a place where a man could relax.

Rochefort didn't do much relaxing. As always when he got immersed in something, he threw himself into his work. He now divided his time among Tiburon and three building sites—at Stockton and Eureka in California, and

Everett on Puget Sound—where tests were being run on components of the ten sections that would make up ABSD-2.

Then, on 14 August he was ordered to Eureka for the commissioning of the fifth section of the floating drydock (Section Easy), now christened and commissioned the USS *ABSD-2*. Upon accepting the vessel he was detached from COM 12 and ordered to assume duty as the ship's first CO.[12] That change pleased Rochefort. Not only did he now command a Navy vessel but he could remain in Tiburon, where he was needed to train personnel and fit out the *ABSD-2*.[13]

Aside from her predecessor the *ABSD-1*, Rochefort's craft would be like no other that existed in the U.S. or any other navy. Equipped with cranes and other lifting equipment, each of the ten sections making up *ABSD-2* would be shaped like a small ship, with a length of 256 feet and a width of 80 feet. On each side would rise walls, called wingwalls, 56 feet high, 20 feet wide, and 80 feet long.[14]

When welded together, the ten sections would form a deck 827 feet long (927 when allowing for outriggers added to each end) and 256 feet wide, with 140 feet between the wingwalls. The space between the wingwalls would be occupied by ships needing repair. A damaged ship would float into the dock while her lower deck was submerged. The water would be pumped out after closing the dock's entryway, leaving the ship ready for work.[15] Once in service, the *ABSD-2* would be able to lift 90,000 tons, more than enough to accommodate any battleship, cruiser, or aircraft carrier in the U.S. Navy. Had she survived Midway, the carrier *Yorktown*, displacing 36,800 tons with a length of 872 feet, would have been a perfect fit.[16]

From August 1943 into the early months of 1944, Rochefort supervised trials of the ten sections. He arranged for them to be moved to Hunter's Point, near San Francisco, from where they were to be towed to a war-zone assembly point and made ready for operation. For Rochefort it was an amazing ten months. With no background in this type of work, he managed a building process that prepared the *ABSD-2* for deployment. Admiral Moreell praised his efforts. "This officer has taken on an unusual assignment with commendable enthusiasm and the indications from what he has accomplished to date are that he will complete the difficult task assigned him in a very workmanlike and satisfactory manner," Moreell wrote.[17]

"Under [Rochefort's] capable guidance the basis for the successful assembly and operation of the dock was laid," said an official Navy history of the drydock written in 1945.[18] The only question was whether Rochefort would command the *ABSD-2* once she departed for her distant assembly point. There was no question he liked this strange craft. He would not have agreed with his old friend, Eddie Layton, and others who bemoaned his fate, declaring that he had been consigned to a Navy backwater. If Tiburon was a backwater, it was one he respected. "This was very interesting duty," Rochefort said.[19] But he doubted the Navy would let him near a war zone. He believed his Main Navy superiors wanted him to supervise the construction of the *ABSD-2*, but not take the ship to sea.

His prediction would never be tested. Before the big drydock could leave Hunter's Point, Admiral Hart, recently commander of the Asiatic Fleet, appeared in San Francisco. Now stationed in Washington, Hart was in town on Navy business, conducting yet another inquiry into the Pearl Harbor disaster. He needed Rochefort to be a witness.[20]

Rochefort and Hart were already acquainted. "[He] asked me what my duties were, and I told him," Rochefort remembered. Hart apparently thought, as did many others, that Rochefort's talents were being wasted. "He made no comment when I urgently requested that he not interfere but just leave me where I was performing duties on the West Coast not involving intelligence."[21]

Whatever Hart did or did not say back in Washington, the *ABSD-2* sailed on 2 May 1944 without Rochefort, each of her sections pulled by a separate tug. Moving at a speed slower than six knots, the convoy arrived in Manus, Admiralty Islands, on 22 June and was assembled and made ready for operations by 13 September. The *ABSD-2* turned out to be one of 7 section-type drydocks constructed during World War II. She was one of 147 floating drydocks of all types put into service during the war.[22]

ıı▮ıı

With fresh orders in hand sending him to Washington, Rochefort headed east. He suspected Hart had ignored his plea that he be permitted to remain on the West Coast.[23] Nine days after testifying before Hart's panel on 28 March 1944, he received orders to report to Admiral King at Main Navy.[24] He did so on 19 April and was promptly directed to his new billet: the Far Eastern Section of the Office of Naval Intelligence, still located in the seventh wing.

Rochefort didn't want to be in Washington but soon reconciled himself to his new situation. He found a modest apartment in southeast Washington, barely adequate for himself plus Fay, Janet, and Cora. Janet enrolled in a nearby public school, and Joe commuted to Main Navy. But the ONI job didn't last. Rochefort never said what his ONI assignment had been, but from his letters it was clear he felt underutilized.[25] After a few weeks he was reassigned to, of all places, naval communications, now based on a thirty-three-acre site in northwest Washington in buildings that had formerly housed the Mount Vernon Seminary, a girls' school.[26] The transfer doubled his commute, but Rochefort nevertheless welcomed the change of scene.

He had been extricated from the stifling confines of Main Navy by an unlikely savior: Rear Admiral Joseph Redman, the same who two years earlier had slandered him in a memo to Vice Admiral Horne as "an ex–Japanese language student" unfit to run a vital communications intelligence unit. Rochefort had no way of knowing about that memo.[27] If he had, he might have been less inclined to engage Redman in conversation, or to offer what he thought was a pretty good idea.

One day Rochefort suggested, almost casually, that unused comint material available in the back files of OP-20-G might be profitably incorporated into the long-range planning for the naval war against Japan.[28] "It was a perfectly innocuous remark on my part," Rochefort said later. "I merely pointed out that it would be helpful to these planners if they had some indication or some estimate based on fact or logic regarding Japanese capabilities," especially at a time when the United States was beginning to plan the initial invasion of the Japanese home islands.

"It was my opinion," Rochefort said, "that a unit, a rather small unit, if it was competent and had the required materials, such as captured documents and all the [comint] messages going back to, say, 1941 or 1942, could have been of some value to the planners at the Joint Chiefs of Staff level."[29]

Redman liked what Rochefort had to say and promptly had him detached from ONI to develop the concept. Somebody might have wondered why Redman had suddenly warmed to Rochefort. Had he reconsidered the merits of his 20 June 1942 memo to Horne in which he'd disparaged Hypo's officer in charge? Had he reassessed Hypo's role in Midway's intelligence, now giving Pearl—and therefore Rochefort—greater credit?

Probably not, although his thinking might have been jolted a few months earlier, in October 1943, when Hypo cryptanalyst Jack Holtwick passed through Washington. Holtwick called on Redman. During their chat Redman remarked that Station Hypo had "missed the boat" on Midway, requiring

Station Negat to jump in and save the day. The comment took Holtwick's breath away, but he managed to say that Admiral Nimitz thought the reverse was true. When Redman stated that Nimitz must have been misinformed, Holtwick replied: "Admiral Nimitz read the official dispatches and drew his own conclusions. Also, he has just given me a letter of commendation for my part in the work."[30]

Redman might have pondered what Holtwick had to say, or he might have ignored the officer's remarks. Perhaps he brought Rochefort on board for an altogether different reason: Rochefort no longer posed a threat to OP-20-G's control of Station Hypo. He had been relieved of that duty and could now be viewed as an asset. His obvious talents could be exploited.

If Redman was the latest in a long line of flag rank officers to push Rochefort forward, he also would be the last and the oddest. Aggressive, manipulative, a master practitioner of Navy politics who seemed always to get his way, Redman also indulged in eccentricities that turned him into a source of amusement at the communications annex, as the complex was called. "We learned that he kept a doghouse in his outer office," reported a Wave, a young woman who worked near Redman's office. "It was a real doghouse and inside usually stood a toy Scotty dog. If someone on Redman's staff blundered, the person's name was inscribed on a plaque and that plaque was hung on the front of the doghouse. Although unorthodox, his method of discipline was most effective."[31]

Redman's doghouse held no terrors for Rochefort. By this time he would have figured Redman had done just about all the damage to his career that could possibly be done. He probably felt that because of some curious quirk of fate, the officer who had once schemed against him now found him useful. Despite feeling estranged from the Navy's career system, due in part to burning too many bridges, Rochefort remained the consummate professional and still wanted to be of use. He would work for Redman, albeit with his eyes wide open.

Even though he couldn't know the full extent of Redman's role in the plot to oust him from Hypo, Rochefort still had good reasons to distrust his new boss. He would, of course, have remembered how OP-20-G and the DNC had rejected Hypo's finding that AF represented Midway. Without knowing all the details, Rochefort would have associated Joseph Redman with his brother John's campaign to eject him as officer in charge of Pearl's decrypt unit. As a result, in later years he always included both brothers on his list of those he regarded as "opportunists"—people who he thought were motivated primarily by a drive for "personal glory" and "promotion and pay."[32]

Redman would not have cared the slightest about any of Rochefort's reservations, even if he had suspected them. No one knew what he thought. There was never the slightest hint that the two ever discussed Midway or the circumstances that had led to Rochefort's departure from Pearl. That was ancient history. Rochefort wasn't a whiner. Redman was in charge and knew what he wanted done. He ordered Rochefort to head a new arm of OP-20-G, this one called OP-20-G50.

Rochefort was back where he'd started, working under the umbrella of OP-20-G, a unit headed by an individual about whom he had doubts, Commander Joe Wenger, who had relieved Captain Stone. Still, he felt at home. Joseph Redman granted him considerable independence, and he started building a staff. He relished working on a concept that he not only liked but had helped originate.

❚❚❚❚❚

Rochefort's career now took a more promising turn. On 23 September 1944, five months after rejoining OP-20-G, Rochefort received a terse, three-word message from Redman: "Delivered with congratulations." Redman's note announced that James Forrestal, the new secretary of the navy, had approved Rochefort's promotion to captain.[33] Now a four-striper, Rochefort had reached an exalted pinnacle: one step below flag rank.

The promotion had required Redman's recommendation, and by now he was pleased with Rochefort's effort at OP-20-G50. Rochefort had worked all summer and into the fall putting together a team equipped to do long-range studies on Japan's future naval capabilities. On 14 November 1944, Rochefort's work at OP-20-G50 was transformed into hard Navy reality: Admiral King formally announced the establishment of the section that had preoccupied Rochefort for months. It now had a name: the Pacific Strategic Intelligence Section (PSIS). King stated that its mission "shall be the study, compilation, and dissemination of Pacific strategic intelligence, based upon Japanese communications intelligence and such collateral information as may be available or necessary to accomplish its mission."[34]

King's statement meant that Rochefort's new unit was open for business. Drawing on existing staff already assigned to the communications annex, Rochefort had put together an organization of some three hundred officers and enlisted personnel. PSIS included cryptanalysts, linguists, and a mix of both regular and reserve officers and sailors, including Waves. Many were young people on their first major assignment.

Rochefort's PSIS work differed sharply from what his task had been at Hypo. Rather than tell the commander in chief today what the enemy would do tomorrow, he now concerned himself "solely with the long range view."[35] So once the Navy's three decrypt units—Hypo, Negat, and Belconnen—had provided their operational intelligence, the work of the PSIS would begin. Rochefort described it as "what might be called the clean-up group." PSIS would not break Japanese codes in real time. Instead, "we reconstructed all the Japanese codes which we didn't have time to do previously. We reconstructed all of these, we developed a whole complete communications file, so we were prepared to state," for example, "where all Japanese submarines were at all times during the war."[36]

With unusual expertise at his command, Rochefort was now besieged with requests for insight into important but hitherto neglected aspects of the Pacific War. One of his most demanding customers was Commander W. J. Sebald, representing COMINCH. First he wanted "a study on the Japanese viewpoint concerning the current situation in Germany." He followed up that request a day later with another asking for "a study showing what success the Japanese have had in sweeping acoustic mines." Then he wanted "a study on the present oil situation in Japan."[37]

Rochefort and his analysts turned up information that shed new light on what the Imperial Japanese Navy was doing to survive. Late in March 1945, Rochefort told Sebald that the Japanese had produced a new oil tanker that could be converted easily to a dry cargo ship. "A possible explanation for the development of this type of tanker," Rochefort wrote, "can be found in Japan's frenzied efforts to throw everything into the transportation of oil as long as the oil producing areas were in Japanese hands and the sea lanes were open."[38]

Not all PSIS reports gained favor. Reviewing a study on the willingness of Japanese diplomats to make concessions to Russia in order to maintain the Japanese-Soviet Neutrality Pact, Sebald scolded the team for naïveté about power relations inside Japan's leadership. "This study is hardly a complete index of the best thought of the Japanese High Command," Sebald wrote Rochefort.[39]

Rochefort probably didn't let Sebald's criticism pass unchallenged. Historian Roger Pineau, then a PSIS staffer, said he had a strong "readiness to stand up for his subordinates when he believed them to be in the right." Whatever Rochefort said or didn't say in this brush with authority (he outranked Sebald but Sebald represented King), he won the loyalty of his people, most of whom found him "an inspiring leader and morale-builder," Pineau said. Like his crew at Hypo, Rochefort's PSIS team appreciated his casual management style. "I recall him not being one for spit and polish," Pineau wrote later, "and there was no academic haughtiness in his attitude toward juniors." Moreover, "When he commented on our work—good or bad—it was directed to the point, but with an avuncular air, usually a friendly hand on our shoulder if he stopped by our desk. Corrections were usually made with a tolerant smile."[40]

Pineau and Rochefort remained close friends after the war. Pineau went on to a distinguished career as a naval historian, collaborating with other writers on books about the Pacific War. He ultimately joined forces with John Costello to coauthor Edwin Layton's *And I Was There*, a detailed account of comint during the war from Layton's perspective as CINCPAC's intel officer. As noted earlier, after Layton's untimely death Pineau and Costello finished the book, which was the first to detail at length Rochefort's achievements at Hypo.

What struck Pineau about his two years at the communications annex was how little he or anyone else learned about Rochefort or his prior experience. Rochefort never talked about his naval history, nor did he in any way indicate a controversial past. "He got along amicably with officers of his rank," Pineau said. "To us reservists all senior officers seemed to be academy graduates, and it never occurred to me at the time even to wonder about his professional credentials. One thing was certain, however: he knew the Japanese language and people, and knew them very well."[41]

⸱⸱■⸱⸱

Despite his reputation as a dissident, Rochefort didn't usually appear that way in Washington. Month after month he managed to avoid conflict with superiors he had once tangled with. But the old undercurrents were still there. Every so often he experienced something that resembled the Midway-era power plays he associated with OP-20-G. When he did, such as the time some senior officers tried to tell him to whom he should and *should not* send his PSIS studies, the old Rochefort reappeared.

"I made a report dealing with Japanese submarine activities at the beginning of 1941 and extending on up to 1944," Rochefort recalled, "and I wished to send a copy of this to CINCPOA's [commander in chief, Pacific Ocean Areas, a secondary title for Nimitz] headquarters to the Fleet intelligence officer and was directed by COMINCH's representatives not to send such a report to CINCPOA."[42] In other words, Rochefort wasn't to send material to his old friend, Nimitz's intel officer, Edwin Layton, whom King two years earlier had wanted CINCPAC to expel. Rochefort never said who applied the pressure, but the two likeliest candidates were his immediate superior, Joseph Redman, and Redman's immediate superior, Vice Admiral Horne, still King's deputy.

Rochefort regarded the "blacklist" as an encroachment on his prerogatives as the director of PSIS. "I sent the report to CINCPOA," he said later. "I don't know what the reason for [the blackout] was, and I was not particularly interested, as a matter of fact, in the reason." Whatever King's objections, "I saw that [Layton] got a copy of it."[43] Rochefort's new duty brought him back into contact with his old friends at Pearl Harbor. When Nimitz and his staff transferred CINCPAC to Guam early in 1945, Layton kept Rochefort informed of developments and gossip concerning the admiral and his entourage. Still smarting from their run-ins with top Navy officials during the Midway period, Rochefort and Layton fashioned their own code words to represent the Navy chieftains they encountered.

Rochefort told Layton about the stirrings of "the phantom," a moniker known only to Layton but in all likelihood Rochefort's term for Joseph Redman. And when Rochefort ran into heavy weather sending out PSIS' submarine study to Layton, he alerted his friend in Guam that there remained anti-Layton sentiment in Washington: "the ghost [is] rising again," was Rochefort's way of expressing it. Layton thanked Rochefort for the tipoff and, in turn, let him know that "lower case r"—their term of disrespect for John Redman—would soon leave his post as the Pacific Fleet's communications officer.[44] Redman was succeeded in March 1945 by Earl Stone, who been relieved as director of OP-20-G by Joe Wenger in March 1944, and had then gone on to command the battleship *Wisconsin*. Now it was Redman's turn to command a battleship; he was given the *Massachusetts*—the type of combatant ship, incidentally, that Rochefort was told he couldn't have because he knew too much.

Absorbing as all the gossip tended to be, there remained a war to fight. Assignments coming Rochefort's way became more challenging. With the

United States closing in on Japan in mid-1945, and with the likelihood of an invasion of Japan itself appearing greater every day, U.S. war planners now wanted detailed information about Japanese capabilities regarding "personnel and materiel at any given point in the future," as Rochefort put it.[45] Deadlines got tighter.

On 6 May 1945 Rochefort heard again from Sebald, who asked for information on the current situation in Japan with regard to food, fuel oil, gasoline, steel, aluminum, coal, and other critical materials. He also wanted information on Japanese shipping: present tonnage available, and tonnage required per year to transport all necessities to Japan. "It is requested that answers be short and specific and be in my hands by Wednesday, 9 May," Sebald directed.

Three days later Rochefort fired back a crisp, three-page memo providing specific answers to each of Sebald's questions. The picture of Japan that emerged from Rochefort's memo was that of a country on the verge of ruin. Present stocks of salt and coal were depleted, while current stocks of aluminum and steel were "critically short." Stocks of fuel and diesel oil were little more than half of Japan's military and civilian requirements. If there was a bright spot for Japan, it was in the area of aviation gasoline: its backlog at least approximated the 5 to 5.5 million barrels required by the military. "[The] figures do represent the Japanese economic position with a reasonable degree of accuracy," Rochefort wrote.[46]

⁙

How useful PSIS' findings would have been to U.S. armed forces had they landed on Kyushu on 1 November 1945, as called for under Operation Olympic, would never be known. On 6 August, as U.S. ground forces were being redeployed from Europe to the Pacific, the first atomic bomb fell on Hiroshima. Three days later, as the Soviet Union entered the war, the second bomb struck Nagasaki. Together the two bombs killed between 100,000 to 200,000 Japanese. On 14 August 1945, Japan surrendered. The war was over.

Rochefort and his PSIS analysts now had nothing to do. Like just about every other Navy activity, Rochefort's work had been premised on the near-certainty of a long air and ground war in Japan.[47] With no studies to be done, a pall fell over Rochefort's sector of the communications annex. He now idled his time away. A Wave who wandered by his office noticed him engrossed in a puzzle. "He had lost interest and spent most of his time doing double acrostics" (similar to but more complicated than crossword puzzles).[48]

What consideration Rochefort now gave to his Navy career remained a mystery. He never said. He probably could have found a slot at OP-20-G or remained in communications under Redman if he'd wanted. He had made a strong impression on his onetime archenemy. In one of the supreme ironies of Rochefort's career, his former nemesis now praised him. "Capt. Rochefort is in charge of a section which compiles intelligence of a strategic nature in the Pacific, such information being supplied to Cominch and Cincpac," Redman wrote on 29 November 1945. "He has performed this duty in an outstanding manner. His skill and long experience in his specialty coupled with his executive ability have contributed materially to the prosecution of the war. He is recommended for promotion."[49]

Whether Redman noticed the variance between his current appraisal of Rochefort and the hatchet job he'd done on him three years earlier in his memo to Horne would never be known. Rochefort didn't see the positive fitness report until many months later. By the time Redman wrote it, Rochefort was long gone from Washington. Redman never succeeded in winning over Rochefort.

During the weeks following Japan's surrender, Rochefort made a fateful decision of his own. He'd never wanted to be in Washington, and now he did something about it. On 15 September 1945, he submitted a memo to the Navy's chief of personnel. "Subject: Sea Duty, Request for. It is requested that I be assigned to sea duty," Rochefort wrote. "My preferences for duty are: First, Heavy Cruiser; Second, Light Cruiser; Third, Any other cruising vessel."[50]

Ten days later, his wish appeared to have been granted. The orders Rochefort received typified the sort of runaround he'd experienced during much of his career. First he was detached from the Office of Naval Operations, effective 1 October. Then he was to proceed to San Diego for a week of indoctrination in the shipboard combat information center system. That was to be followed by a week of damage control training in San Francisco.[51]

Finally he was to get a ship of his own. At the end of those weeks of instruction and indoctrination, Rochefort was to report for duty as commanding officer of the *Stokes*, a cargo ship designed to carry military cargo and landing craft. The *Stokes* may not have been a heavy cruiser or even a light one, but at least it met Rochefort's third preference. It was a "cruising vessel." He looked forward to the *Stokes*.

But before he could report to the ship, Rochefort's orders were changed.[52] He was told to command a different vessel, the *Telfair*, an attack transport now in the far Pacific but expected to reach San Francisco on 25 November, at which time Rochefort was ordered to assume command. He was amenable; Rochefort would still have his own ship.

The *Telfair* didn't work out either. Rochefort's orders were canceled on 11 November 1945, before the *Telfair* got anywhere near San Francisco. He was ordered back to Washington, where he didn't want to be, this time to stand by and wait to be called as a witness before the Joint Committee on the Investigation of the Pearl Harbor attack, the seventh probe into that disaster.[53]

If there was a silver lining to his situation, it was that he was home for the holidays. Except for Joe Junior, now in the Army, the family was intact. Fay, Janet and Cora had stayed behind at the apartment in Washington to wait for Janet's school year to end and Joe to light somewhere.

Marking time in the early months of 1946, Rochefort wasn't always in the best of moods. Always strict where Janet's studies were concerned, he now became even more severe. When she had trouble grasping certain concepts in mathematics, Rochefort taped them on the wall and then, when he came home from work, he drilled Janet. "If I still got them wrong, he'd get mad as hell," Janet recalled. "He'd say, 'you're not using your head.'" Her father could be tough. "It was his way or nothing."[54]

Rochefort was not having his way early in 1946. He remained in Washington for months. After testifying before Congress in January, he returned to Main Navy, the old Navy building on Constitution Avenue.[55] There he was assigned to OP 23, a department of OPNAV responsible for coordinating construction, repair, and disposal of Navy vessels.[56] Important during the war, the office was a backwater now. Rochefort was in a dead end job, and he knew it.

Among the many things Rochefort never talked about was when the idea of retirement took hold. He had considered the notion once before, late in 1940, when his bid for promotion to commander had been rejected. He'd been saved then by Vice Admiral Brown, who'd seen to it that he was reexamined and, in due course, upgraded. Now he considered retirement again.

Whether Rochefort would have stayed in the Navy if he'd received command of a ship would never be known. No powerful admiral came this time to his aid. Rochefort probably didn't care. He wanted out of the Navy and requested retirement on 24 June 1946.[57] The request was granted on 9 July,

and he was put on the retirement list effective 1 January 1947.[58] Joe Rochefort's twenty-eight-year Navy career came to an end when he was forty-six
years old.

II ■ II

Some people who retire after many years in one job suddenly find themselves
lost or rudderless. Not Rochefort. He didn't mope around or wonder what
to do; he had something in mind. Rochefort wanted to enroll in a university,
take advanced courses, and complete a bachelor's degree. But first he had to
obtain a high school diploma.

Rochefort could keep a secret. The number of people in his circle who
knew that the onetime head of the Navy's decrypt unit at Pearl Harbor didn't
have a high school diploma could probably have been counted on the fingers
of one hand. They may not even have extended beyond Fay. Even his best
friends thought he had been to college, either the Stevens Institute or, as Layton and Pineau thought, the University of California.[59] He had taken a Navy
training course at Stevens, but hadn't been registered there as a student. Nor
had he been to Cal.

The fact that Rochefort was a high school dropout had never been an
issue in the Navy. No one knew. But it did become a problem in 1948, after
he had relocated his family back to California, this time to Manhattan Beach,
a burgeoning town south of Los Angeles on the Pacific Coast. Early that year,
when trying to enter the University of Southern California, Rochefort found
he wouldn't be admitted without a high school diploma.

He wrote a letter. On 25 June 1948, he wrote to the principal of Polytechnic High School, J. G. Goodsell, asking that his Navy training in engineering,
cryptanalysis, and the Japanese language be accepted as credit toward his
diploma. Striking a personal note, he added: "As I have indicated, a boy of
18 is not gifted with the foresight of an adult, and after I joined the Navy, I
did not foresee the necessity of acquiring my diploma. It was my firm understanding in 1918 that those of us who left school to enter the service would
be given our diploma by mail, provided, of course, that our records were
satisfactory."[60]

Goodsell accepted Rochefort's story. "We are granting you a high school
diploma and we are marking your record as having graduated," Goodsell
wrote Rochefort on June 28.[61] Still young at forty-eight and with his entrance
to USC now assured, Rochefort surveyed a postwar future that seemed filled

with possibilities. Using the G.I. Bill, he enrolled at USC in the fall of 1948, majoring in international relations but taking special courses in Russian and higher mathematics. No one except possibly Fay knew exactly what he had in mind with those courses but, as he told Goodsell, he was guided in his choices by "the general world situation," which made him "most anxious to start my studies right away."[62]

Rochefort's college career didn't last; he cut it short after two years. Nothing was ever simple with Rochefort. Did he find college life not to his liking? Did he have a hard time listening to lectures on world politics from professors who knew less than he did? He may have. If so, that wasn't why he left USC. His reason for not pressing on can be summed up in four words: the United States Navy. The Navy wanted him back. The duty sounded appealing.

ıı ■ ıı

The Navy's renewed interest in Rochefort stemmed from the Korean War, ignited on 25 June 1950 when North Korea's army crossed the border and swept down South Korea all but unopposed, stopping only when it hit the southern tip of the peninsula. U.S. armed forces later regained the initiative and in due course pushed back the North Koreans. But the first phase of the war was a debacle for the United States, catching its military off guard and unprepared.

To find out "how we could have been so surprised," as Rochefort put it, the Navy created the Fleet Evaluation Group, a small party of officers experienced in key Navy activities: gunnery, operations, logistics, and, of course, intelligence. A big stipulation for membership in this select clan was that the officer not be in a responsible position—not, in other words, have a vested interest in the outcome of the study. ONI's chief, Rear Admiral Felix Johnson, proposed Rochefort for the intelligence section. "There's this fellow Rochefort still kicking around," as Rochefort explained his selection, "and he still has some knowledge of fleet activities despite four years had gone by and he is still familiar with the general layout and the general personalities involved, and he has no axe to grind." Rochefort said he would be "delighted [to] perform this service."[63]

Rochefort returned to active duty on 16 October 1950.[64] Three months later, on 4 January 1951, he received his orders from Admiral Arthur W. Radford, now commander in chief, Pacific Fleet.[65] After a brief stint in Washington with OPNAV, Rochefort proceeded to Hawaii, met Radford, then joined the rest of his group for the first phase of a "flying inquiry" that took him and fellow investigators to key Navy installations throughout the Far East. Rochefort returned to Japan for the first time in twenty years.

Naturally, he didn't hold back stating his views. "The level of intelligence—at least as it was practiced in the Pacific—was even more unacceptable than it [was] in 1941," Rochefort said. "In other words, nothing had been accomplished. The three services were using different grid systems for reporting. It was a very unfortunate system of command relationships." After making some recommendations to Admiral Radford, he was ordered to report to the director of ONI in Washington. Rochefort did so, then found himself ordered back to Japan for a second look to see if any of his proposals had been implemented. Some had been; still, "I could see no real improvement in the overall situation."[66] Rochefort returned to Washington and asked to be put on the retired list again. He almost was, but this time a Navy commodore intervened.

Upon being detached from the Evaluation Group on 31 May 1951, Rochefort was ordered to the Naval War College at Newport, Rhode Island.[67] He wasn't going as an officer to take courses as preparation for higher rank down the road. Rochefort was back in business as a translator.

Early in the year, he'd received a note from Commodore Richard W. Bates, head of the Special Projects Section at the Naval War College. For years Bates' section, composed of two captains and two commanders with various specialties, had been producing critical analyses of major naval battles of World War II. They had already completed studies of the battles of the Coral Sea, Midway, and Savo Island. Two slots opened up just as Bates directed his team to work on the Battle of Leyte Gulf—the 24–25 October 1944 naval action in which Japanese forces had attempted to destroy U.S. landings on the Japanese-occupied Philippine island of Leyte. "I am particularly anxious to obtain your services to assist me in working up the ORANGE side for the battle," Bates wrote Rochefort.[68]

Beginning 1 July 1951, Rochefort, along with his fellow analysts, spent the next twenty-one months doing little else but studying the Battle of Leyte Gulf. "This is all we were engaged in," Rochefort said. His primary task was to translate Japanese documents and use them to understand why the admiral commanding the striking force, Vice Admiral Takeo Kurita, had failed to press his advantage when he appeared able to demolish the undersized U.S. naval force guarding the Leyte beachhead, choosing instead to disengage.[69]

Rochefort didn't have a chance to complete his role in the study. He had joined Bates' staff with assurances from the Navy Department that he could remain on active duty at least two years, longer if his work required it. Even though that was the case, late in 1952 Bates heard from BUPERS that budgetary constraints demanded Rochefort's duty be cut short after just twenty-one months. Bates tried to keep him, but the effort failed.[70]

Rochefort's active duty ended on 2 March 1953. He and Fay, who had joined him in Newport, returned to Manhattan Beach. He had no hard feelings about the way his duty had ended. He always said his months in Newport were among the most pleasant of his naval career. Everything considered, "it was most enjoyable duty," Rochefort said. "Most enjoyable."[71]

Rochefort's life now took on the shape of that of a comfortably situated retiree with time on his hands. Only fifty-three, he got involved in a lot of things. Besides studying Russian and taking more courses at USC, he started a career in real estate and, from all indications, acquitted himself respectably. He also plunged into a major volunteer project, starting work on a civil defense plan for Manhattan Beach and surrounding cities. The work evolved into a paid job as coordinator for civil defense for fifteen area cities.[72]

Rochefort was now through with the Navy. He tried to put World War II behind him and pursue his new interests. But the Navy, or at least those remnants of the old service that remembered him, wasn't yet through with him. One group in particular sought out Rochefort. It included former Navy people now involved in a dubious project: They aimed to prove that the Roosevelt administration in late 1941, to trick the United States into war, had ignored warnings that Japan intended to strike Pearl Harbor. They thought Rochefort might be a kindred spirit because of his own bumpy history with some of the Navy's leadership.

The group's nominal leader was Laurance Safford. One of Rochefort's oldest friends, he had introduced Rochefort to cryptanalysis in the 1920s and backed him for the Hypo slot in 1941. Safford may have thought that Rochefort could now help him in return. He had retired from the Navy a captain in 1953. His career had veered off course late in the war, when he'd told Congress and other panels investigating the Pearl Harbor debacle about an alleged conspiracy—the Navy destroying papers that, if preserved, would have shown that Washington knew three days before Pearl Harbor that Japan would strike. The attack was allegedly revealed by a Tokyo message that Rochefort's linguists at Heeia and Navy radiomen elsewhere were listening for early in December—the "east wind rain" message.

Safford maintained that the Navy's listening post at Cheltenham, Maryland, had extracted from a Japanese weather report this phrase, the so-called execute message intended by Tokyo to alert its posts around the world that Japan would soon be at war with the United States. Safford claimed the Navy got that message on 4 December.[73] But his testimony failed to hold up before Congressional scrutiny. The report issued by the Joint Congressional Committee in 1946 concluded: "No genuine message . . . was received in the War or Navy Department prior to December 7, 1941." Safford, the JCC said, was "honestly mistaken."[74]

Safford didn't let the matter rest. Unyielding in his conviction, during his retirement he orchestrated a massive research effort to prove he had been correct all along. Not only did he hope to show that the government had lied, but also that its alleged destruction of records had been part of a larger plan to black out information from reaching Kimmel and Short that could have alerted them to the coming attack. To assist him in his endeavors, Safford joined forces with a like-minded Navy officer and two controversial historians whose views paralleled his own. Together they intended to write a revisionist history that would challenge the official story line: Pearl Harbor was hit without warning in a surprise attack that forced the United States into a war it didn't want.

Safford wanted Rochefort to join the team.[75] His timing was good. For years Rochefort had been brooding about Pearl Harbor. He had always accepted part of the blame, believing he had failed in his primary task to give his commander timely warning about what the enemy would do. But he didn't think the fault was only his or, for that matter, all Kimmel's or Short's. He thought both had gotten a raw deal from the Roberts panel and, more broadly, from their superiors in Washington.

Quite simply, Pearl's commanders "were not given 'sufficient warning' nor were they kept advised as to developments," Rochefort told the author A. A. Hoehling in 1963. "If one is inclined to be charitable, one could say that Washington was guilty of a serious error in judgment." He added: "But if they withheld information from the military commands in the Pacific, and I believe they did, they must accept responsibility for what later occurred."

Rochefort believed responsibility for the attack "must be placed on the war-time Commander in Chief"—President Roosevelt and his chief aides, General Marshall and Admiral Stark.[76]

Rochefort granted members of Safford's group several interviews over the next two years. The first showed promise, at least from the point of view of the interviewer, revisionist historian Harry Elmer Barnes. "He is a genial man with a fine sardonic sense of humor," Barnes wrote a colleague. "He is decidedly on our side and eager to help us." Barnes felt that Rochefort shared their conspiratorial view of Washington's actions. "He fully agrees that there was deliberate blackout at Washington, and for the purpose of assuring war and attack."[77]

Without a transcript of Rochefort's words, it is impossible to know exactly what Rochefort said. He may have shared Barnes' deepest suspicions about FDR. Or he may have told Barnes what he told Hoehling: If FDR and his aides withheld information, and he believed they did, they must accept responsibility. Rochefort was unclear whether he thought FDR and his team deliberately withheld information to set up Pearl for attack, or whether they held it back for some other reason.

Safford's team was encouraged by what Rochefort had to say, but it wouldn't be for long. Soon it ran into a major stumbling block: east wind rain. The allegation that Japan had transmitted that phrase on 4 December 1941 and that the U.S. government had destroyed the message, then covered up having received it, was crucial to Safford's case.

Rochefort proved unmovable. In truth, Rochefort told Barnes, his team at Heeia never heard any such message. Moreover, he added for good measure, he doubted it was ever sent. Barnes was discouraged. "It is quite obvious," Barnes wrote a colleague, "that it is not going to be easy to debrainwash him about the Winds execute message."[78]

It turned out to be impossible. Nobody ever made Rochefort subscribe to a view he didn't believe. He couldn't be brainwashed or debrainwashed. Safford's interviewers gave up on Rochefort. "He is a slick duck," one member of Safford's team wrote in 1965. "I've been reviewing some of the material I have on Rochefort and I am satisfied that that gentleman is and has been, all along, holding out on us."[79] In time Safford's group broke up. Their revisionist history was never published. Rochefort went his own way.

From his encounter with the Safford group and, indeed, from his entire naval career, Rochefort emerged as the consummate loner, very nearly the "lone wolf" that one member of Safford's team made him out to be.[80] For Safford and for others who tried to understand him, Rochefort's persona was enigmatic; no one ever quite knew where he stood. He could believe the worst about Roosevelt (and he did) but still refrain from joining a crusade intended to expose FDR's alleged crimes. He would walk away if he thought the campaign got the details wrong, as he did in this case. Rochefort's integrity was wrapped up in those details.

Something else might have given him pause. Unlike Safford, who appeared angry at the entire Navy, Rochefort's beef wasn't with the service, but directed at officers he regarded as "glory seekers." His postwar musings belied the image of Rochefort as some sort of maverick. Even though he nursed his grudges and could flirt with revisionist theories of the Pearl Harbor attack, in the end Rochefort contained the fires that raged within. His daughter never detected any bitterness in him. "My father never talked about it," Janet said, referring to the post-Midway events of 1942. She said her mother was "far more bitter about the deal he got from the Navy than Joe was."[81]

As mentioned earlier, Rochefort was later asked why he hadn't written a book about Midway and his battles with OP-20-G. "If I were to be frank," he said, "then I would have to be extremely critical of some people by name." Who might they be? "[People] such as Masons, such as Redmans, such as Wengers, and other individuals. . . . If I thought it were to the advantage of the Navy to prepare some sort of factual account, then I would be the first to do it. But you'd have to convince me that this was in the best interest of the Navy."[82]

⁣⁣⁣I I ■ I I

No longer pestered by Safford's chroniclers, after 1965 Joe and Fay Rochefort found themselves beset by other irritants. A big problem was health. Joe continued to be plagued by the recurrence of old ills: stomach trouble and a bad back that in early 1941 had landed him in Pearl's base hospital for three weeks. Fay's health was particularly precarious. She continued to suffer from aftereffects of the rheumatic fever she had battled as a child. The household was held together by Fay's mother, the indomitable Cora, now nearing ninety, who still did a lot of the cooking and household managing. The family lived comfortably, having moved years earlier from their residence in Manhattan Beach to a more spacious ranch-style home in Palos Verdes, an affluent section of Redondo Beach.

With both Joe and Fay ailing, the Rochefort home was no longer the high-spirited place it had been in the 1930s, when, Janet recalled, her mother "used to give fantastic parties."[83] Visitors to Rochefort homes in the 1950s and early 1960s found them more sedate, almost forbidding at times. "My grandfather was not a warm or welcoming person," said Karen Rochefort Ballew, Joe Junior's daughter. At age eight or nine, she was an occasional guest. "He was stern. He sat is his chair, he read a lot. The expectation at their house was that if you were a child, you were quiet. You spoke only when spoken to."[84] Rochefort still ran a quiet operation.

Despite their health issues, the Rocheforts were able to enjoy the accomplishments of their children. Joe Junior graduated from West Point and served in Korea and Vietnam in the Army Corps of Engineers. He married a young woman with the Red Cross whom he met while on duty in Austria, raised two daughters, and settled in the San Diego area. He retired a full colonel in 1973 (he died in San Diego on 8 December 1994). Janet in 1951 married a promising medical student, Charles Elerding, who launched a successful practice in dermatology. They raised three sons and settled first in Santa Ana, California; later in Newport Beach.

Fay's health declined slowly but steadily in the late 1960s. She died 12 July 1969 of congestive heart failure. Joe was shattered. The Rocheforts had been a devoted couple, always supporting each other. He had considered taking Fay to Washington, D.C., to visit Joe Junior, now stationed near the nation's capital and living there with his family. But her death rendered Rochefort lethargic, virtually numb for months, as he indicated in his October 1969 letter to his Hypo linguist friend Joe Finnegan, also living in Washington: "Fay, my wife, passed away very suddenly in July, and I have had problems in getting back to battery; hence don't feel like going back east at this time."[85]

Blunt-spoken as always, Rochefort in his letter to Finnegan exhibited his lingering bitterness, not toward the Navy but toward some of his old antagonists. He worked in a little dig aimed at a few. Closing his letter, Rochefort suggested to his former colleague, who had medical woes of his own: "In the meantime say hello to my friends (if any are left), ignore the Redmans, Wengers, et al., and most important take care of yourself."[86]

॥ ▪ ॥

By 1976 Rochefort was beginning to experience some of the spinoffs of being a burgeoning celebrity: he was in demand. His recognition had been a longtime coming. The first time Rochefort's name reached a broader audience had probably been in 1949, when the *Saturday Evening Post* carried an article entitled "Never a Battle Like Midway." One of the first detailed accounts of that naval engagement, it called attention to the cryptanalytic prowess of "a smart young officer, Cdr. Joseph J. Rochefort," who confirmed for Nimitz that Yamamoto's target was indeed Midway.[87]

Eighteen years later, in 1967, three historians dug deeper into the role Navy codebreakers had played in the Pacific War, in the process shedding new light on the activities of Joe Rochefort. In his suspense-filled account *The Broken Seal*, Ladislas Farago focused in part on Rochefort's pre–Pearl Harbor effort to solve one Imperial Navy code. Rochefort was depicted as the dean of U.S. Navy cryptanalysts.[88] His activities before and after Pearl Harbor, including his key role in the Battle of Midway, were captured in David Kahn's monumental history of cryptanalysis, *The Codebreakers*. Kahn accurately described Rochefort as the only man in the Navy with expertise in three critical fields: cryptanalysis, radio, and the Japanese language.[89] And he came vividly to life in Walter Lord's compelling account of the Midway campaign, *Incredible Victory*. Lord portrayed Station Hypo as a shambles of a place, littered with paper and stacks of folders piled on desks. Presiding over it all was the humorously caustic Rochefort, wearing his legendary red smoking jacket and carpet slippers.[90]

Hollywood discovered Rochefort in 1970. He served as a consultant for the Twentieth Century Fox blockbuster *Tora! Tora! Tora!* the American-Japanese film dramatizing the attack on Pearl Harbor. Six years later he again served as a consultant for a war film, this one the Mirisch Corporation's *Midway*, another giant production. The movie was shot in part at the Terminal Island Naval Base in San Pedro's harbor, near the site where Rochefort had enlisted in the Naval Reserve fifty-eight years earlier. He had come full circle.

There was a complication. By 1976 Rochefort's health had declined. Besides ulcers, he now also suffered from low blood pressure and heart disease. When his health permitted, he lived at his home in Redondo Beach, still managed by the ageless Cora.[91] But increasingly he had to stay at the Earlwood Nursing Home in nearby Torrance. Each morning during the shooting of *Midway*, a studio limousine picked him up at Earlwood and took him to the set, where he coached actor Hal Holbrook, playing Hollywood's version of Joe Rochefort. He seemed not to mind Holbrook's tangy characterization.

The movie added another element to the Rochefort story. On 12 May, Rochefort's birthday, Holbrook and civic leaders from Torrance and Redondo Beach held a luncheon in his honor. Afterward, Rochefort told a reporter he was living comfortably in a retirement motel, "though I hate like hell to think that's how I'll spend the rest of my life."[92]

But that was where he spent most of his remaining months. Rochefort died of a heart attack on 20 July 1976 at age seventy-six, in the Little Company of Mary Hospital in Torrance. He had decided not to be buried in the Calvary Cemetery, the Los Angeles Catholic cemetery where both his parents had been laid to rest. He elected to be buried next to Elma Fay in Los Angeles' Inglewood Park Cemetery. Near a monument carrying the single name Aery (Fay's surname) are markers for the two Rocheforts. Joe now came clean on his year of birth:

Joseph John Rochefort
Capt, US Navy
World War I & II Korea
1900–1976

Epilogue

The Medal

This is a promise fulfilled.

—Wilfred J. "Jasper" Holmes

Early Friday morning, 30 May 1986, a bright spring day in the nation's capital, nine high officials of the Reagan administration and various other dignitaries filed into the Roosevelt Room in the West Wing of the White House. Among those making their way into the stately meeting room were Vice President George H. W. Bush, Secretary of Defense Caspar W. Weinberger, Chairman of the Joint Chiefs of Staff Admiral William J. Crowe, Chief of Naval Operations Admiral James D. Watkins, and Deputy Director of Central Intelligence Robert M. Gates.[1]

The highest-ranking official was the last to arrive: President Ronald Reagan. He walked over to the belt-high lectern, gave his customary nod to all present, and got quickly to business. "It is especially fitting to honor this man so close to Memorial Day," Reagan started out. "Joseph J. Rochefort's contribution to our nation's defense was for many years cloaked in secrecy."[2]

Going straight to the material that had been cloaked, Reagan narrated Rochefort's role in the Battle of Midway, a story known to his friends but not the general public: Rochefort laboring in his basement with a few handpicked experts, breaking the enemy's secret code, tracking Japan's powerful fleet and fixing its target, rejecting rival scenarios focusing on Alaska and the Panama Canal, pinpointing the date, time, and launch point of the carrier attack—

442

discoveries that enabled U.S. forces to sink four carriers and win a victory that would make Midway the crucial naval battle of World War II in the Pacific.

With that background now on the record, Reagan proceeded to the heart of the matter: presenting the Distinguished Service Medal posthumously to Captain Joseph J. Rochefort, United States Navy, Retired, in recognition of his "exceptionally meritorious service" from March through June 1942.

At long last, Rochefort had his DSM.[3] Reagan's ceremony ended a quest that had begun on 8 June 1942, when Rear Admiral David Bagley, commandant of the Fourteenth Naval District, had dispatched to Admiral King a proposal endorsed by Admiral Nimitz, recommending Rochefort for a Distinguished Service Medal. That proposal was rejected by King on the advice of his chief of staff, Rear Admiral Russell Willson.

King clearly was persuaded by Willson's opinion that no one individual should be singled out for excellence in the intelligence arena. That argument was obviously flawed, for if carried out to its logical extreme, no one would ever receive an award for anything, because, as one historian pointed out, "human achievement is largely a cooperative matter."[4]

Many different factors worked against cryptanalysts in the awarding of medals during World War II. Some officers serving on award boards were unfamiliar with the concept of communications intelligence and tended to be skeptical of claims advanced on behalf of codebreakers. There also was the security factor. Awards for comint people had to be downplayed so as not to alert the enemy that his codes had been broken.

Rochefort, of course, had problems quite apart from his work in cryptology. His feisty personal style surely didn't aid his cause. One other factor worked worked against him, as detailed in this book: he was a mustang who'd been commissioned in the regular Navy without attending the Academy. That deprived him of the coterie of friends and the professional network that inevitably follow four years at Annapolis, resulting in a bias that followed him throughout his career.

Asked years later whether his mustang status had impeded his career, Rochefort treated the question lightly, musing only that an Academy education might have equipped him with better manners. "If I had gone to the Naval Academy, I would have been well-trained in things that you just don't do—that you don't get away with," he answered. "For example, you don't fight City Hall. I would have had that brainwashed into me a long time ago. I didn't have that, so I would be more inclined to speak up when I should have kept my mouth shut."[5]

Fighting City Hall was Rochefort's trademark. So when Admiral Bagley's memo proposing a DSM for him showed up at Main Navy on 8 June, it generated consternation. King's 22 June 1942 decision to deny Rochefort the medal didn't settle the matter. The issue came to life again when the Navy's board of awards began considering medals for all deserving officers in the Navy's three comint units: Hypo, Belconnen, and Negat. That put the Bagley-Nimitz proposal for Rochefort back on the table.

The question of how to recognize people in communications intelligence, Rochefort among them, tied Main Navy in knots. But the Rochefort part of the puzzle bothered them the most. Memoranda with the same subject sailed around Main Navy for months: "Recommendation for Medal Award for Commander Joseph J. Rochefort, U.S. Navy." The problem moved toward a solution on 4 September 1942, when Vice Admiral Frederick J. Horne proposed that officers and men on what he called an A list—composed of Rochefort, John Redman, Joe Wenger, and twenty-one others—be granted recognition for meritorious service. He proposed lesser awards for forty-one others.

The awards board, headed by Rear Admiral Thomas C. Hart, accepted Horne's suggestion, stipulating the recognition should be in the form of the Legion of Merit, to be awarded when "circumstances permit," presumably after the war. There was no talk of a Distinguished Service Medal for anybody, certainly not for Rochefort. When Layton, back at Pearl, prodded Nimitz on the DSM for Rochefort, the Pacific Fleet commander exploded, reminding Layton that he had a war to fight. The time never came, not even at the war's end. Either Nimitz was too busy with other pursuits or he simply forgot about it. Rochefort seemed to have slipped through the cracks, at least as far as that medal was concerned. Other comint people fared better. By fall 1945 a new awards board was in place. It made some use of the work done by Admiral Hart's 1942 board but didn't feel bound by its preferences.

Soon the new board submitted to Admiral King a modified list of candidates for recognition. After doing his own appraisal, King in October 1945 proposed to Secretary of the Navy James Forrestal the names of officers and men from the world of radio intelligence whom he thought should get medals.[6] Among seventy-nine ultimately awarded, six were Distinguished Service Medals. Ranked in order of merit, as determined by King, the recipients were Captain Joseph Wenger (OP-20-G), occupying the number one spot, followed by Captain Redfield "Rosey" Mason (OP-20-GZ), Captain Howard T. Engstrom (OP-20-G), Captain Wilfred J. "Jasper" Holmes (recognized for his work at ICPOA), Commander Jefferson R. Dennis (OP-20-G), and Captain Thomas H. Dyer (of Hypo).[7]

Rochefort's name was not on that list, but it did appear among the names of twenty-seven officers King recommended for a lesser medal, the Legion of Merit, a substantial award but one occupying a niche one level below the DSM in prestige. Again ranked in order of merit, as determined by King, Rochefort ranked fifth.[8] Shrugging off his own place in King's universe of merit, Rochefort was pleased by a number of things. He was delighted that the DSM honor was going to his good friend Holmes and his gifted colleague Dyer. And he was glad that five other members of his core team had been selected for the Legion of Merit: Hypo's ace translators, Captain Joseph Finnegan and Colonel Alva "Red" Lasswell; the unit's premier traffic analyst, Captain John Williams; and two of Dyer's comrades on the cryptanalyst's desk, Captain Wesley "Ham" Wright and Captain Jack Holtwick Jr.[9] In reviewing the medal winners, one thing would have jumped out at Rochefort. He would have noted that Admiral King, in approving six comint officers for the Distinguished Service Medal, ignored the criteria he had used in 1942 to rule him out for a DSM: no one person who had served in comint should be singled out for a medal. Also, none had done their work in combat operations. Nor were any solitary performers, officers who did their work by themselves without drawing on the help of others. Like Rochefort, they were team leaders, members of a community that shared resources and benefitted from the contributions of all. But some team leaders had been more effective than others. Rochefort's champions believed that on this score, Hypo's officer in charge was shortchanged by the Navy's award boards and, ultimately, by King.

Rochefort was contradictory when it came to medals, yet he cared about the DSM and resented King for killing his. Twenty-five years after King and Willson torpedoed that medal, Rochefort remembered just about every detail of the episode. He recalled Nimitz and Bagley recommending him for the DSM and what happened to their proposal in Washington (copies of their memoranda turned up in his personal papers). As for the Legion of Merit, Rochefort remembered that Nimitz and Bagley considered it should be granted "to some juniors, but as officer in charge I should be given the Distinguished Service Medal." He added, "That was overruled in COMINCH's headquarters."[10]

As a result, rather than being included in the outstanding comint officers receiving the DSM, he ended up grouped with twenty-seven very capable officers awarded the Legion of Merit. That wouldn't have bothered Rochefort except for one thing: One of the recipients of that medal was a naval officer he held in particularly low regard, his bitter adversary John Redman, recognized for his work as head of OP-20-G during a period in which he not only resisted AF as Midway but maneuvered Rochefort's exit from Hypo.

Rochefort retained a damning view of those running OP-20-G, as shown throughout his story. "One of these people," he asserted, "would be a chap named Jack Redman who saw a chance here to do what Rudyard Kipling used to say—the promotion and pay."[11] Whether John Redman was the opportunistic conniver Rochefort made him out to be would be for others to judge. Rochefort never changed his mind about Redman and others in Washington he didn't like. He thought their subsequent careers showed them to be the "glory seekers" he always claimed they were.

John Redman did indeed go on to have a solid, some might even say distinguished, career in the Navy. Unlike Rochefort, he got command of a combatant ship, the battleship *Massachusetts*, which made its presence felt in the Kyushu area in the final months of the war. Redman later served as deputy commander of the Western Sea Frontier, director of the Office of Naval Communications (the post held earlier by his brother) and Communications-Electronics director for the Joint Chiefs of Staff. Along the way he gained a slew of medals. He never earned the Distinguished Service Medal, but he did receive the Legion of Merit three times, the third time getting a Combat "V" enhancement. He retired a vice admiral in 1957.

Joseph Redman received a Distinguished Service Medal for his work as DNC from 3 April 1943 to 31 August 1945. During this time he emerged as the Navy's dominant voice in communications policy, serving on many boards and representing the United States at international communications conferences. Upon retiring from the Navy in 1946 he was named a vice president of Western Union, a position he held for twenty years.

Joining the Redmans atop Rochefort's list of glory seekers was Joe Wenger, easily the most consequential of the three. After heading OP-20-G during the final year of the war, he worked later to ensure the continuity of the Navy's cryptologic efforts. In 1949 he became deputy director for communications intelligence for the Armed Forces Security Agency, the forerunner of the

National Security Agency. When the NSA was established in 1952, he became its vice director. Wenger retired in 1958 a rear admiral.

He had been the brains of OP-20-G during the war. His memo calling for greater centralization within the comint establishment served as the basis for the reorganization of OP-20-G implemented in February 1942. The revamping that followed led soon to the ouster of Laurance Safford as director of OP-20-G and the rise of John Redman as his replacement and Joe Wenger as Redman's deputy. Far-sighted as he was about the potential of radio intelligence, Wenger had his blind spots. He emphasized traffic analysis over cryptanalysis, telling Tommy Dyer in the early 1930s that codebreaking would yield little information of value in any future war.[12]

Nor was he above the bureaucratic infighting and petty politics that marked Navy life. Because of his belief in centralization, Wenger joined forces with John Redman in his machinations to expel Rochefort from Pearl Harbor. He was on the receiving end of Redman's surreptitious dispatches from Pearl in October 1942 aimed at undermining Rochefort. With considerable justification, Rochefort viewed Wenger as one of the OP-20-G plotters who helped derail his career in comint.

But if Rochefort thought ill of Wenger, there was every reason to believe the feeling was mutual. Although he never discussed Rochefort, there is evidence that Wenger regarded him as something of a menace, a blatant threat to the efficient workings of the Navy's comint organization. Two years after retiring in 1958, Wenger put on paper the closest thing that ever surfaced as a rationale for OP-20-G's bare-knuckle campaign against Rochefort. Without mentioning him by name but leaving no doubt about to whom he referred, Wenger provided his own version of the lead-up to the Battle of Midway:

> The Hawaiian unit had by then recovered from the shock of the Pearl Harbor attack and established itself as the principal supplier of vital intelligence to the Commander in Chief, Pacific. In these circumstances the initial efforts by OP-20-G to establish control met with strong opposition at Pearl Harbor. The attitude there was "give us what we need and let us alone; CINCPAC is running the war. You are too far away to control." In Washington, however, a much broader view was fortunately taken. Not only was it possible there to comprehend more clearly the global nature of the conflict but to see, in the German problem, the inevitable increase in complexity and sophistication that would have to be dealt with.

Thus began a struggle to impose the authority of OP-20-G. This eventually reached the point where Admiral King had to step in personally to settle the matter. His intervention resulted in the basic organizational charter which welded together the various comint activities, and established OP-20-G in a position of unassailable operational and technical control which transcended the authority of all Naval Commanders. It may be said parenthetically that although this action completely violated the traditional concepts of command and was at first bitterly opposed, it was not only finally accepted completely, but at the end of the war was generally acknowledged to be one of the most important contributions to the Navy's success.[13]

Missing from Wenger's view of OP-20-G's superior global perspective was any mention of the Battle of Midway, which stood then as a rebuke to the notion of centralized comint far from the battle zone. Wenger gave no hint that he had even briefly considered the possibility that Station Hypo, obstreperous and unruly as it may have seemed, had gotten Midway right, while OP-20-G, with its estimates of Yamamoto's target ranging all the way from Samoa to the U.S. West Coast, had not.

Wenger's picture of an out-of-control Hypo directed by a recalcitrant, narrowly focused officer did not go unchallenged. It was contested by the people who had been on the scene and knew from firsthand experience the critical events of May and June 1942. The thesis they advanced wasn't only Hypo's primacy in pinpointing Midway, but Rochefort's decisive role in shaping that evaluation.

Tommy Dyer's testimony is a case in point. Longtime colleague though he was, Dyer was no shill for Rochefort. He wasn't blind to his friend's peccadilloes and shortcomings. He knew that Rochefort had a tendency to shoot himself in the foot, as he did shortly after Midway when he told Washington, as Dyer put it, "to send us more men and leave us alone." Rochefort "was very undiplomatic—and that was one thing they literally resented," Dyer recalled.[14]

Dyer didn't buy into the Rochefort mythology that took root after the war. He debunked the widely accepted notion that his former boss was the Navy's top cryptanalyst. "Anyone who really knows about it, knows that he wasn't the world's greatest cryptanalyst, as he's been painted," Dyer stated. "Even in the Japanese field he did not do any real original cryptanalysis." Nevertheless,

"In the total combination, in the value to the war effort and the country, I unhesitatingly step aside for Rochefort," Dyer said.[15]

Where Rochefort shined, Dyer maintained, was in intelligence analysis: seeing the big picture, making connections, filling in the blanks, using his language skills and knowledge of the Japanese to foresee Imperial Navy moves, understanding the enemy. He might have added bringing those facets together to grasp the flow of events and, when challenged, displaying the character and leadership skills needed to make his estimates stand up.

"There is no confusion in my mind," Dyer said in 1982. "Rochefort was almost solely responsible for producing the intelligence, which resulted in the Battle of Midway." Dyer recalled vividly OP-20-G insisting "until the last minute" that Alaska was the objective and that anything in the direction of Midway was a feint. "I can swear on a stack of Bibles that Negat initially said Alaska was the target."[16]

Against enormous pressure from Washington, Rochefort did not budge. "Something I've never forgiven and I don't know who to hate for it, but Rochefort was right," Dyer said on another occasion. "We won the Battle of Midway primarily on his guts and then Nimitz recommended him for a DSM and that made Washington see redder than ever so they eventually eased him out towards the end of '42."[17] A year before his death, Dyer summed up his thinking on the issue. "I have given a great deal of thought to the Rochefort affair," Dyer wrote in 1984, "and I have been unwillingly forced to the conclusion that Rochefort committed the one unforgivable sin. To certain individuals of small mind and overweening ambition, there's no greater insult than to be proved wrong."[18]

ıı▪ıı

Jasper Holmes didn't let the DSM matter rest. He stayed on the case, even after retiring from the Navy as a captain in 1946. Holmes returned to the University of Hawaii faculty, from where Admiral Bloch had recruited him for Fourteenth Naval District intelligence work in June 1941. He proceeded to hold a number of posts, including dean of engineering. He never forgot his promise to himself to pursue Rochefort's DSM.

He resumed the crusade in November 1957, when he visited Admiral Nimitz at his home in Berkeley, California. Nimitz had just given up his position as a regent of the University of California and now had some free time. He revisited the Rochefort matter at Holmes' request. Holmes said he thought

Hypo's onetime officer in charge had never been adequately recognized, following up with a letter to Nimitz laying out the case for a DSM for Rochefort. He took note of Admiral King's grounds for disapproving the original recommendation—that many individuals, distributed broadly in time and geography, had contributed to the successful intelligence at Midway.

"Without detracting in the least from the value of what was done in other units," Holmes wrote, "I believe the major share of the Midway intelligence was developed in the Hawaii unit." Holmes attributed this unit's success to Rochefort's "qualities of leadership"—specifically the example he set of unremitting effort, which kept the unit at a high pitch for long hours, working to the point of utter and absolute exhaustion. "During this period in which I was able to observe him, I am convinced that no one made as great a contribution as Rochefort did," Holmes wrote. "It is my opinion, that for his work in Communication Intelligence between the attack on Pearl Harbor and the Battle of Midway, Commander Rochefort thoroughly earned and deserved and should be awarded the Distinguished Service Medal."[19]

This time Nimitz acted. A month after getting Holmes' letter, on 2 January 1958 Nimitz wrote a letter of his own, a two-page handwritten note to Secretary of the Navy Charles Thomas. He urged that his letter and Holmes' be referred to the Navy's board of awards for a reconsideration of Rochefort's earlier award, which, he added, "I think should have been a Distinguished Service Medal rather than a Legion of Merit."[20]

The Navy didn't waste much time saying no. In a two-page letter dated 1 March 1958, Assistant Secretary of the Navy Richard Jackson walked Nimitz through the history of award board actions with regard to Rochefort's medal, noting the board's 17 September 1942 decision to award him a Legion of Merit and its 14 February 1946 action reaffirming the earlier verdict. On both occasions, board members had "the benefit of advice from Captain Rochefort's contemporaries and superiors," Jackson told Nimitz. "It is my belief," Jackson stated, "that those who considered the award before were in a much better position to evaluate correctly and equitably the achievements of Captain Rochefort than are the members of the present Navy Department Board of Decorations and Medals at this date after so many years."

To reverse a decision after this much time, Jackson continued, the case should be so clear cut "that no doubt would be left in my mind that a great injustice would otherwise be done." He concluded: "Such does not appear to me to apply to the case of Captain Rochefort." Just so there wouldn't be any doubts in Nimitz's mind that the case was closed, Jackson noted that statutory limits for awarding the DSM had run out.[21]

Jasper Holmes had played his last card. There the matter rested, apparently one of those lost causes that constantly dot the history of war. Not this time. Twenty-three years later the case came unexpectedly to life again.

In 1981, a new player appeared on the scene: retired Rear Admiral Donald "Mac" Showers, the former ensign who'd arrived in Rochefort's basement in February 1942, now a special assistant to the director of Central Intelligence, William Casey. The whole trajectory of Showers' Navy and post-Navy career had led him to a place where he'd always wanted to be: a spot where he could do something for Joe Rochefort.

Showers brought new savvy to the Rochefort crusade, combining as he did Navy accomplishment with know-how in the ways of Washington. Top brass knew him. After World War II he had risen quickly up the ladder, serving in a succession of important posts: assistant intelligence officer to the commander, U.S. Naval Forces in the Eastern Atlantic and Mediterranean; fleet intelligence officer for the First Fleet, based at Pearl Harbor (Layton's old job); and, after ascending to rear admiral, assistant chief of staff, Plans and Programs; followed by chief of staff, Defense Intelligence Agency, Washington, to name just a few.

Three days after retiring from the Navy on 31 December 1971, Showers joined the Central Intelligence Agency, where he served in a range of analytic and administrative capacities. By 1981, as a special assistant to Casey, he managed a little-known counterintelligence program, an activity that required liaison with National Security Council staffers based in the White House and the nearby old Executive Office Building.

One day at that building, he met with an NSC staffer and friend, Gus Weiss, who knew of Showers' interest in Rochefort. Because of recent posthumous medals awarded by President Reagan, Weiss suggested now might be a good time to resume the Rochefort campaign, possibly for a National Defense Medal. Showers ran the notion by his boss, William Casey. Casey liked the idea but told him the honor should be a Navy medal, not a civilian one. "We concluded the Distinguished Service Medal would be the appropriate honor," Showers said.[22]

He picked up where his onetime mentor, Jasper Holmes, had left off. Holmes, now aging and frail, still retained the hope that Rochefort might one day receive greater recognition for his exploits at Station Hypo. Toward that end, in 1979 he'd published *Double-Edged Secrets: U.S. Naval Intelligence Operations in the Pacific During World War II*, recently republished by the Naval Institute Press. The book highlighted Rochefort's achievements and pointed out the power plays mounted against him after Midway, but the slim volume did not reach a wide national audience.

Showers spent the next three years working on the project, first as a side-line, then, after retiring from the CIA in 1982, as close to a full-time effort. He began work on a justification for the medal to be submitted to the secretary of the navy. And he joined forces with two historians, John Costello and Captain Roger Pineau, U.S. Naval Reserve (Retired), who were working with Edwin T. Layton on his World II memoirs. The three researchers were helped in their effort by the declassification of more than 300,000 decoded Japanese military and diplomatic documents. The records detailed the U.S. Navy's secret radio surveillance of the Imperial Navy's wartime communications. The documents were invaluable to the researchers, who were working in tandem with Layton, since one of his own goals was also to highlight Rochefort's deeds at Pearl Harbor.

In summer 1983, Showers submitted to the Navy Department his dossier recommending a DSM for Rochefort. The outlook seemed good. Both the Naval Security Group Command, the successor organization to OP-20-G, and the Navy's Board of Awards and Decorations approved the medal. Then Showers' package went to Secretary of the Navy John F. Lehman for final approval. Nothing happened. Months passed; two years went by. Showers heard nothing.

Concerned his effort on behalf of Rochefort "had come to naught," as he put it, on 26 September 1985 Showers appeared before a standing-room-only audience at a naval history symposium in Annapolis. Its subject was "Naval Intelligence at Midway," based on Layton's soon-to-be published book *And I Was There*, completed by Costello and Pineau after Layton's death. Joining Showers at the symposium was Pineau, who reported on Rochefort's performance at Midway as documented in the Layton book.

Then it was Showers' turn to speak. He told the audience that, sadly, his effort appeared to have failed. He feared that Navy Secretary Lehman might have rejected the proposal. With the impetus of the Pineau and Showers presentations, a number of scholars and high-ranking officers in the audience rose to speak, arguing that the Rochefort issue should not be allowed to rest. Their pleas made a strong impression on a representative from Lehman's staff who happened to be present.[23]

That official, Arthur Davidson Baker III, said that none of the facts voiced by Pineau or Showers had been known to the secretary. He pledged to go back to Lehman's office and look into the matter. Two weeks later Baker called Showers with two pieces of news. First, his dossier in behalf of Rochefort had been found; Lehman had never seen it. It had gotten sidetracked as it traveled from office to office for review, and had never made its way to Lehman. Second, Lehman had just signed the authorization awarding Rochefort the Distinguished Service Medal. Showers' efforts had borne fruit.

The first thing he did was call his old friend and former boss Jasper Holmes, who by now was critically ill and living a nursing home in Honolulu. It took a while for Holmes to grasp what Showers was trying to tell him. Then he got it. He said, "This is a promise fulfilled."[24] Holmes died two months later, on 1 January 1986.

It didn't take long for the news to get out. On its front page for 17 November 1985, the *New York Times* reported that the Navy had reversed itself after forty-four years and now planned to award a posthumous Distinguished Service Medal to Joseph Rochefort. A Navy Department spokesman said the decision was based "solely on the merits of the case."[25] But Rochefort admirers attributed the turnaround to new details revealed in the Layton book and, of course, Showers' dossier.

What Rochefort's antagonists—primarily Joseph Redman, John Redman, and Joe Wenger—thought of his restoration would never be known. The three had passed away well before the Navy Department did its about-face. Joseph Redman had died in 1968 after choking on food during a banquet in Arlington, Virginia.[26] John Redman had died of natural causes two years later, in 1970, the same year Wenger died.

⚊⚊

Spearheading the effort that produced a Distinguished Service Medal for Rochefort was one thing. Getting that medal into the hands of the right people in the right way was a different problem. Showers found himself engaged in that matter as well. The Navy Department wanted to just mail it to Rochefort's son and daughter, both living in California, and let it go at that. Taking a different tack, Showers wrote to Vice President Bush suggesting that he present it to the families himself. Bush declined, citing scheduling problems.

The matter remained unresolved. Then one day Showers got a call from Kenneth de Graffenried, a staffer with the National Security Council. He was calling on orders from a Showers friend, National Security Adviser John Poindexter, who had acted at the behest of President Reagan. The president was concerned about the morale of the intelligence community. It had gotten a black eye recently in the press, the result in part of news that the NSC had approved an arms deal with Iran in return for the release of hostages. Reagan thought the NSC was getting a "bad rep." Wasn't there any good news? Couldn't something upbeat be said about the intelligence community? Did Showers have any ideas?

"Yeah, I have an idea," Showers told de Graffenried, who seemed amenable. Showers called his friend Poindexter. "That's perfect," Poindexter told Showers. So it was decided. The White House scheduled a ceremony for 30 May 1986, at which Reagan would present the Distinguished Service Medal to members of Rochefort's family, surrounded by top-ranking members of his administration and the military. (It turned out that Bush's schedule would permit.)

Showers organized the event, aided by the White House staff. They arranged for Rochefort's son, Colonel Joseph Rochefort Jr., U.S. Army (Retired); his wife, Elinore Mae; Rochefort's daughter, Janet Rochefort Elerding; and her three sons (her husband, Charles, couldn't be present) to be brought to Washington to attend the ceremony as Reagan's guests. Rochefort family members, along with more than twenty dignitaries and their spouses, filed into the Roosevelt Room to hear the president's words.

In paying homage to Rochefort, Reagan said, "we also celebrate the achievements of thousands of other men and women of our nation's intelligence community who anonymously serve our country without any expectation of recognition or reward." Reagan had made good his pledge to honor the intelligence community. After his talk on behalf of Rochefort, he greeted each member of the family, presented daughter and son twin versions of their father's DSM, chatted briefly with dignitaries, and was gone. The ceremony lasted about ten minutes.

If there was a downside to the occasion, it was that so few of Rochefort's onetime colleagues were able to be present. Other than Showers, those who attended were retired captains Gilven Slonim and Willis Thomas, the latter having served in Hypo's basement in 1942; plus Pineau, who had served on Rochefort's PSIS staff. A large number of his associates and friends from Station Hypo had passed from the scene. Tommy Dyer had died in January 1985 at Silver Spring, Maryland. His partner on the cryppie desk, Ham Wright, also having moved to Silver Spring, died there on 1 January 1986, the same day Jasper Holmes passed away in Honolulu. Other members of Rochefort's core team had died or soon would.

More honors awaited Joe Rochefort. Later in 1986 he received the Presidential Medal of Freedom for his contribution to the Battle of Midway. In 2000 he was awarded what many among his various teams might have regarded as the ultimate prize: He was inducted into the National Security Agency's Hall of Honor, created in 1999 to pay special tribute to the pioneers in the military and civilian realms who had invented and shaped American cryptology.

In receiving this honor, Rochefort joined such luminaries as William F. Friedman, Frank B. Rowlett, Abraham Sinkov, and Solomon Kullback, cryptanalysts who, as part of the Army's Signal Intelligence team, broke Japan's main diplomatic code in 1940; Herbert O. Yardley, who in the 1920s was chief of the first U.S. peacetime cryptanalytic organization; Captain Laurance F. Safford, considered "the father of U.S. Navy cryptology"; and Agnes Meyer Driscoll, one of the originals who, as a civilian Navy cryptanalyst, broke a multitude of Japanese systems.[27]

Some still questioned whether Rochefort actually deserved to be included in such august company. They wondered whether the belated recognition had gone too far and blurred into a form of overcompensation for a past wrong. The case for Rochefort to be included among the "giants" of U.S. cryptology was weak, contended Robert Hanyok, former senior historian at the National Security Agency.

"Rochefort was a very talented intelligence analyst," Hanyok said. "But if you look for long-term impact, meaning cryptanalytic techniques, a philosophy of analysis, organization left behind, there are no traces." He contrasted Rochefort with people like Safford who, for all his troubles, helped set up the original OP-20-G organization, and even Joe Wenger. "For all Wenger's Byzantine practices, he turned out to be very important because he helped set up post-war cryptological organizations." In Hanyok's view, Rochefort belonged in the category of people who perform well, do wonderful things, but leave nothing behind but anecdotes about their ability to do those things. There was, of course, Midway. "He really shines only during that one period," Hanyok conceded. "But the rest of the time, there's nothing left behind. You don't see his imprint on post-war or even wartime organization."[28]

Not so, countered Admiral Showers. Rochefort's influence on the evolution of U.S. intelligence went beyond the Battle of Midway. In Showers' opinion, Rochefort helped change intelligence as it was practiced in 1941–42. He did so by carving out greater autonomy for the Pearl Harbor decrypt unit. In a move sanctioned by his old friend OP-20-G head Safford, Rochefort reduced the layers of bureaucracy separating Hypo's radio intelligence from the people who needed it most—U.S. fleet commanders on the scene.

Like his predecessors at Hypo, Rochefort took overall direction from Safford and OP-20-G. But unlike the previous regime, he reported Hypo's RI findings directly to the U.S. Fleet's commander in chief, first Kimmel, then Nimitz, a relationship facilitated by his friend Fleet Intelligence Officer Layton, his unwavering link with the fleet's commanders. As a result, Showers contended, Rochefort took a giant step toward shaping a concept later called actionable intelligence—intelligence developed at the local level, in this case a shore-based unit called Station Hypo, aimed at informing the commander in chief today what the enemy is going to do tomorrow. That, of course, was Rochefort's mantra, constantly repeated during the sixteen months he led Hypo.

As for a modest legacy, Showers rejected Hanyok's view. He pointed out that Rochefort's intelligence career was essentially over when he was pulled out of Pearl Harbor in 1942. Because of the circumstances surrounding his expulsion and his clashes with various high-echelon officers, he didn't get the opportunity to ascend higher up the Navy ladder or play a major role in its future intelligence system, said Showers.[29]

Decades after he was eased out of Pearl Harbor and denied the medal Admiral Nimitz wanted him to have, Joe Rochefort remains controversial. His significance in the history of Navy intelligence will no doubt be debated for many years to come. Whatever the outcome of that argument, it's probably safe to say his reputation will hinge largely on his contributions during the critical days leading up to the Battle of Midway.

Given the crucial importance of Midway in U.S. naval history, it's fitting to give President Reagan the last word on Rochefort. "If ever there was a battle involving tens of thousands of men in which victory was attributable to one man," Reagan said in his Roosevelt Room remarks, "this one was attributable to Joseph J. Rochefort."

Appendix 1

Rochefort's DSM Citation

THE SECRETARY OF THE NAVY

WASHINGTON

The President of the United States takes pride in presenting the DISTINGUISHED SERVICE MEDAL posthumously to

CAPTAIN JOSEPH J. ROCHEFORT
UNITED STATES NAVY

for service as set forth in the following

CITATION:

For exceptionally meritorious service to the Government of the United States in a duty of great responsibility while serving the Commander-in-Chief of the Pacific Fleet as Officer in Charge of the Combat Intelligence Unit (Station HYPO) from March 1942 through June 1942.

By virtue of his superb professional knowledge, astute guidance, and personal dedication, Captain (then Commander) Rochefort provided technical expertise and inspiring leadership to discover, analyze, and provide to the Fleet Commander-in-Chief astoundingly timely and accurate intelligence on Japanese naval plans and intentions leading to the Battle of Midway in June 1942. The information provided by Captain Rochefort's Radio Intelligence Unit served as the singular basis for the Fleet Commander-in-Chief to plan his defenses, deploy his limited forces, and devise strategy to ensure U.S. Navy success in engaging the Japanese forces at Midway. His unrelenting efforts in this endeavor and the intelligence information he developed resulted in a Naval engagement with the Japanese fleet that is acknowledged as the turning point of the Pacific War.

Captain Rochefort's distinctive accomplishments, tenacious commitment to excellence, and steadfast devotion to duty reflected great credit upon himself and were in keeping with the highest traditions of the United States Naval Service.

For the President,

Secretary of the Navy

Appendix 2

Breaking JN-25(b)

Just how difficult JN-25(b) was to solve can be appreciated by following the steps taken by the Japanese code clerk sending a message.

Handed a dispatch by a superior officer, the clerk began by breaking the message in two. He encoded the second half first—a trick intended to avoid the weakness inherent in stereotyped beginnings ("the honorable so and so"). He then placed at a predetermined spot in the dispatch a special indicator, or key, meaning "begin reading here"—a crucial instruction that would tell the code clerk at the receiving end of the transmission where to begin the decryption process.[1]

After that was done, the clerk began encoding the message. He turned first to his codebook and looked up the five-digit number representing each plain text value in the dispatch. As noted in this book, this could represent a word, phrase, syllable, numeral, ship name, place name, area designator, or something else. With that task completed, the clerk proceeded to the next step: enciphering the message. He turned to his book of additives, with 100 groups of random five-digit numbers on each page (adding up to more than 50,000 groups). The additives were intended to disguise each code group, digit by digit.[2]

The disguise was accomplished by adding a five-digit additive to each five-digit code group, which was done through "false" arithmetic—that is, by failing to carry over as one does in true addition. Thus, if the total exceeded ten, the amount would not carry over to the next number. To avoid using the same additive twice, the clerk was instructed to begin using additives on a page and a line assigned only to him, usually somewhere in the middle of the book. When all additives had been used, he was permitted to start over again.[3]

The five-digit groups resulting from that false addition were then transmitted. At the receiving station, another code clerk—equipped with an identical cipher book—reversed the process to decipher the message, subtracting the additives from the fake code groups, revealing the true code groups hidden underneath. Then he looked up the resulting sums in an exact copy of the JN-25(b) codebook to find the Japanese words, phrases, or numbers represented by the code groups.[4]

The following example illustrates the process.[5]

Plain text:	from	*Kaga*	estimated time	of		arrival	19th	2130
Code text:	21936	48222	01905	38832	87039	64527	11520	99708
	From	next	*Kaga*	stop	ETA	19th	2130	stop
		group						
		upper						
		case						
Additive key:	02923	41338	00989	15861	28959	90024	23693	18229
Code plus additive:	23859	89550	01884	43693	05988	54541	34113	07927

There was another wrinkle. Besides the additive group, yet another five-digit code group was inserted at a known point in the message to tell the clerk on the receiving end which pages in the additive book the random numbers were taken from. That was called the indicator, or key. The indicator told the receiving clerk two things: where the message began, and where to look for the additives that needed to be subtracted from the numbers on the page to reveal the actual code.

For Tommy Dyer or Ham Wright sitting at the cryptanalysts' desks in the basement, the first challenge was clear: find the indicator group, or key, that would tell them where the message began and where the additives were. Finding the key wasn't easy. The Japanese put in place yet another hurdle to confound people like Dyer and Wright—a separate list of random numbers to disguise the indicator group. Just as JN-25(b) included a separate book of more than 50,000 additives to disguise the five-digit code groups, it also came with 999 key additives—that is, false five-digit groups used to disguise the indicator group. Code clerks chose key additives for the indicator group by the date of the message. The indicator code group might change weekly or even daily.[6]

Obviously, Hypo's cryptanalysts had their hands full. Their job was less to decode intercepts landing on their desks than to get *inside* the JN-25(b) system—a process that, if successful, would lead them to the actual code groups hidden underneath the five-digit numbers they saw on the page. As Hypo's Tommy Dyer liked to put it, "You don't break messages; you break systems."[7] Dyer and Wright weren't so much codebreakers as system breakers.

Daunting as breaking into JN-25(b) might have seemed, Rochefort's cryptanalysts gained aid from an unexpected source: the Japanese themselves. Japanese mistakes encrypting messages gave the Americans a toehold into the code they would not otherwise have had. A critical error committed by code clerks was to ignore orders to select their first additive numbers in the middle of the book and work through to the end, and only then turn to the front for additional additives. That way the whole book would have been used.[8]

But clerks got complacent. Figuring that JN-25(b) was unbreakable anyway, clerks sometimes relaxed their vigilance and took the easy path; they started at the beginning of the additive book and did not move very deeply into it. As a result, they often used the same additives over and over, yielding patterns that cryptanalysts, with the help of Hypo's IBM machines, could discern and exploit. It turned out that 10,000 additives were enough to read 60 percent of those messages decrypted, even when the additive book had 50,000 entries.[9]

Another Japanese lapse was their fondness for stereotyped openings to their messages (discernible even when buried in the messages). Repeated again and again, the terms gave cryptanalysts cribs, or clues, into code-group meanings. An equally helpful weakness was the fact that all code groups in JN-25(b) were divisible by three. This aspect of the code was supposed to help message recipients protect against garbles in the transmitted code and thereby prove the validity of a group. But the practice served the same function for U.S. codebreakers; it enabled them to confirm that they had arrived at the correct numeric values of a code group.[10]

Appendix 3

The Meaning of Midway

Historians likened America's victory at Midway to great naval battles in the past that turned the tide of history. To some the outcome at Midway ranked with Salamis, the fifth-century-B.C. naval battle in which vessels of the Greek city-states repelled warships of the mighty Persian Empire. Midway reminded others of Trafalgar, scene of the most decisive British sea victory of the Napoleanic Wars; or Jutland, the major World War I sea battle after which the German navy never again challenged the British navy.

The Battle of Midway was as decisive in its own way as were the battles of Salamis, Trafalgar, and Jutland. Indeed, the battle had ripple effects that extended well beyond the central Pacific and, as will be seen, affected the conduct of World War II in virtually every theater where Allied forces confronted the Axis powers.

Japan's failure at Midway diminished that country's importance to its Axis partners. "After Midway, Japanese priorities in the Pacific Ocean and strategic necessity drastically curtailed any appreciable military cooperation with the European Axis powers," wrote military historian Carl Boyd. Much to Germany's disappointment, it all but eliminated the already slim possibility of a Japanese attack on the Soviet Union.[1]

In the Pacific, Midway changed the nature of the war between the United States and Japan. For six months the Japanese Imperial Navy had "run wild," as Yamamoto had predicted. He had hoped to continue that run—advance into new sectors of the Pacific. He had visualized Midway as a jumping-off point to areas south and east, e.g., Hawaii, as well as a vital element in a defensive

461

shield that would stretch from the Aleutians in the north through the Marshall and Caroline Islands to the Marianas in the west.

But the destruction of the *kido butai* at Midway shattered Yamamoto's grand design. Not only did the U.S. victory end Japan's unchallenged domination of the western Pacific, it halted the Imperial Navy's forward movement. Japan remained a formidable adversary nevertheless. Frantic, desperate battles loomed ahead everywhere from Guadalcanal to Iwo Jima to Okinawa, but in each of those fights it was America that would be on the offensive, not Japan. The era of Japanese expansion was over.[2]

Because of Midway, many battles that otherwise would have had to be fought didn't occur. If by some twist of fate the *kido butai* had prevailed at Midway, that outcome would have left the Imperial Navy with its carrier fleet intact, and America with just the *Saratoga* (recently repaired, approaching from the West Coast) and the *Wasp* (a carrier soon to arrive from the Atlantic). Such an event would have left Nagumo holding the initiative in the Pacific.

With Midway in Japanese hands, Nagumo sometime between 16 and 20 June would have taken his carriers to Truk to prepare for the next phase of conquest in Yamamoto's master plan.[3] From that island fortress, the *kido butai* would have moved into the southwest Pacific, first to complete unfinished business at Port Moresby, then to subdue New Caledonia, Fiji and Samoa—all slated for occupation in July.[4]

With Australia isolated, the *kido butai* would have turned eastward and almost certainly seized Johnston Island in August.[5] That occupation would have put Pearl Harbor within easy striking distance of Japan's long-range Kawanishi flying boats. Meantime, the Imperial Japanese Navy's Fifth Fleet would have moved eastward up the Aleutians toward Dutch Harbor. Hawaii would have been caught in a vice between two forces: the Fifth Fleet to the north and the *kido butai* to the west and southwest.

Given the complicated logistics that would have been involved, Hawaii might have been beyond the Imperial Navy's reach. Yamamoto didn't think so. "Such an operation was not only contemplated but was in the advanced planning stage as the Midway operation was launched," military historian Theodore F. Cook Jr. observed. "To Yamamoto, at least, the 'Eastern Operation' was the logical follow-up to his Aleutians and Midway strikes, hitting at the most significant real estate in the Pacific Ocean."[6]

Even if Hawaii had eluded Yamamoto's grasp, Alaskans and residents of the states of Washington, Oregon, and California would have been anxious, to say the least. The panic that briefly swept portions of the West Coast after Pearl Harbor would have returned with greater force, causing lawmakers in Washington to rethink priorities about how the Axis powers should be defeated. In all likelihood, "Roosevelt could not have persevered with a Europe-first policy," former U.S. defense secretary James Schlesinger declared at a 2003 Midway Night dinner. "Public opinion would not have allowed it."[7]

If Schlesinger's judgment is correct, the result would have been a massive and potentially catastrophic shift in policy and planning. Resources intended for the fight against Germany and Italy would have been diverted to the Pacific theater. Britain may not have received the Sherman tanks that enabled it to win its milestone victory at El Alamein. Allied landings in North Africa—the operation that eventually led to the destruction of Rommel's Afrika Korps—could not have happened in the fall as scheduled. The whole Allied timetable for the war would have been pushed back: the invasions of Sicily and Italy and, eventually, the D-day landings in Normandy. Germany would have had more time to beef up its defenses and dig in on the western front.

Another ripple effect would have involved the Soviet Union. With the Imperial Navy now controlling the Pacific, with American resources targeted elsewhere, the Soviet Union would have been harder to supply. Under Schlesinger's grim scenario, the Soviet Union may not have survived. Or if it had, somehow prevailing with less help from the West, it would have proceeded farther west, in all likelihood occupying the whole of Germany. Postwar Europe would have been a different place.

All that was avoided by the U.S. victory at Midway. "It was far more than the turning of the tide in the Pacific War," Schlesinger contended. "In a strategic sense, Midway represents one of the turning points of world history." Schlesinger's argument—what can only be called a worst-case scenario—may overstate the consequences of an American defeat at Midway. It is hard to imagine that war leaders as determined and fiercely realistic as FDR, Marshall, and King would have let the Allied war effort drift away from what they believed to be the paramount threat facing the United States: a robust and undefeated German military machine.

Even so, an American setback at Midway certainly would have weakened the overall U.S. war effort. Hawaii would have come under tremendous pressure. America's Pacific policy would have been aimed almost exclusively at the recapture of Midway. That development probably would have had to await the arrival of the newly minted *Essex*-class carriers in 1943. Other U.S war aims in the Pacific would have been deferred.

Deprived of its three main fleet carriers, the United States would not have invaded Guadalcanal in August 1942, a change that would have given the Japanese more time to increase their possessions in the southwest Pacific and strengthen their grip on those islands. The island-hopping that Nimitz commenced late in 1943—a strategy that took U.S. Navy, Marine, and Army forces from the Gilbert and Marshall Islands through the Carolines and Marianas to the doorstep of Japan—would have been pushed back many months. So would have been the advance of General MacArthur up through New Guinea and into the Philippines.

With its enormous industrial capacity, America would have prevailed in its war against Japan, but it would have taken longer. The Pacific War would have been prolonged many months, possibly as long as a year, at the cost of many thousands of additional lives.

The calamity of a longer war was averted by America's smashing victory at Midway. Because of that milestone event, America could keep its main war policies on track. As Admiral Nimitz put it, Midway was the crucial battle of the Pacific War that made everything possible.[8]

Appendix 4

The Kido Butai *and Radio Silence*

Around 10:30 in the morning of 25 November 1941 (Hawaii time), the thirty-three ships of the First Air Fleet, under the command of Vice Admiral Chuichi Nagumo, slipped out of Hitokappu Bay and steamed into the icy waters of the north Pacific.

The striking force proceeded under absolute radio silence, as ordered by Admiral Isoroku Yamamoto in Combined Fleet Secret Operation Order Number One. Precautionary measures were put in place to ensure that silence was maintained. At a conference on board Nagumo's flagship the *Akagi* on 23 November, Lieutenant Commander Kenjiro Ono spelled out the rules ships were to observe: radio transmission keys must be sealed and fuses removed. Ships could receive messages but send none. Communications would be by flags in the daytime and narrow-beamed blinkers at night.[1]

Yamamoto's rules permitted one narrow exception: Nagumo could radio Tokyo in case of an *extreme* emergency. But the situation would have to be grave, one involving an accident that might jeopardize the *kido butai*'s mission and require its return. Even in that circumstance, the message would have to be disguised as emanating from a merchant vessel. No other exceptions were permitted. Even if the receipt of a message from headquarters was uncertain, vessels in the *kido butai* were prohibited from transmitting acknowledgments.[2]

The remainder of Yamamoto's warships, such as those organized in the southern expeditionary force moving into the South China Sea, also observed radio silence, but they operated under a somewhat more lenient order. Southern force vessels could use their radios only in case of an emergency, but, unlike the strictures imposed on the *kido butai*, it didn't have to be an *extreme* emergency.[3]

In Tokyo, the Naval General Staff employed extraordinary means to ensure that messages radioed to the *kido butai* would not go astray. All communications were given a special number. Particular messages were broadcast repeatedly to make sure the flagship *Akagi* picked them up, thereby making it unnecessary for the *Akagi* to reply, said Lieutenant Commander Susumi Ishiguro, communications officer on board the *Soryu*.[4]

Every odd-numbered hour, day and night, messages were conveyed to the striking force. Message Number Thirteen, for example, was sent at 9:00 a.m., 1 December 1941. According to Ishiguro, it was sent again on every odd hour for a day, unless newer information made it unnecessary. Another means the General Staff used to pass on information to the *kido butai* was through regular broadcasts on Radio Tokyo. At the end of certain broadcasts intended for Japanese nationals living abroad, there would sometimes be an extra statement, albeit well disguised, directed at the striking force.[5]

Some Tokyo messages were especially important. No sooner did the force exit the Kuriles than it received an alert that it might encounter two Russian supply ships, the *Uzbekistan* and *Azerbaidzhan*, westbound from San Francisco. But no radio signal was sent by either ship, fueling conspiracy theories that the Soviets knew of Japanese plans in advance and might even have tipped off President Roosevelt. A recent study of the sea routes traversed by the two Soviet ships has found that neither was ever within visual range of Nagumo's task force, obviating the need for any signaling.[6]

During the *kido butai*'s twelve-day journey to Hawaiian waters, Tokyo radioed daily reports about the weather it would face as it moved eastward. Forecasts were invariably peculiar to conditions in the northern Pacific and would have been identifiable as such if the messages could have been read. But all were encrypted in the unreadable JN-25(b), buried in transmissions disseminated to Japanese ships across the Pacific, none seen as directed expressly to the northern Pacific.[7]

On 2 December (Hawaii time), Yamamoto radioed Nagumo the most iconic message of the *kido butai*'s passage. "This is Top Secret. . . . Climb Niitaka 1208, repeat 1208." Decrypted and translated in 1945, the message was understood by OP-20-G to be: "Attack on 8 December" (Tokyo time).[8] Referring to a mountain in Formosa, the highest in the Japanese Empire, the message would have been meaningless to U.S. Navy codebreakers even if they had been able to read it in 1941, which they were not.

As the *kido butai* moved across the northern Pacific, the Imperial Navy employed various tricks to conceal the whereabouts of the striking force. In one attempt at deception, it assigned to a warship moving toward the Philippines a radio operator with approximately the same fist (touch) as the radioman regularly assigned to the *Akagi*.[9]

Presumably U.S. Navy eavesdroppers, when picking up traffic sent by this operator, would assume the *Akagi* was moving south, not east toward Hawaii. Meantime, the carrier's regular radioman couldn't have used the *Akagi*'s radio if he had wanted to, because the transmitter room was kept locked during the entire cruise to Hawaii.[10]

All the while, the five sending stations already established on Kyushu to simulate radio traffic between carriers, planes, and other ships continued their drumbeat of bogus messages, thereby creating the impression, or so the Japanese hoped, that IJN carriers were still holding drills in the Inland Sea. By late November, land-based stations at Yokosuka and Sasebo had joined Kyushu's in the phony traffic effort.

Were traffic analysts at Hypo, Station H, and Cast taken in by these spurious communications? The question can't be answered with certainty. What is clear is that U.S. Navy radiomen recorded nothing unusual in the traffic collected on 25 November 1941, the day the striking force departed Hitokappu Bay. Traffic volume was reported normal. Station H at Heeia did make one mistake that day, reporting: "The *Kirishima* is believed to be at Yokosuka."[11] In fact, that battleship was hundreds of miles to the north that morning, having just left Hitokappu Bay on her way to Hawaii.

Rochefort's traffic analysts made a mistake of their own two days later in Hypo's daily intelligence summary covering IJN radio traffic for 27 November (Hawaii time). They stated flatly: "Carriers are still located in home waters."[12] Kimmel initialed the summary on the morning of 28 November. The striking force had exited the Kuriles three days earlier.

Notes

INTRODUCTION: THE RIDDLE OF JOE ROCHEFORT

1. Interview with Joe Rochefort, conducted by Walter Lord, 14 April 1966, Lord Papers, Operational Archives, Navy History and Heritage Command (NHHC), Washington Navy Yard. The author is indebted to Rear Adm. Paul Tobin, USN (Ret.), director of the Naval Historical Center in 2005, and Kathleen M. Lloyd, head, Operational Archive Branch, for retrieving the Rochefort interview from the Lord Papers, now in storage at NHHC.

2. Walter Lord, *Incredible Victory* (Harper and Row, 1967), p. 17. Lord erred in tagging the "junior" on to Rochefort's name.

3. Rear Adm. Edwin T. Layton, USN (Ret.), John Costello, and Capt. Roger Pineau, USNR (Ret.), *And I Was There* (William Morrow, 1985), pp. 367–69, 449–56.

4. Ronald Lewin, *The American Magic* (Penguin Books, 1983), p. 138. Wilfred J. Holmes, *Double-Edged Secrets* (Naval Institute Press, 1979), p. 167. Ladislas Farago, *The Broken Seal* (Arthur Barker, 1967), p. 164. John Costello, *The Pacific War* (Rawson, Wade, 1981), p. 247. Alan Schom, *The Eagle and the Rising Sun* (W. W. Norton, 2004), p. 122.

5. Lewin, *The American Magic*, p. 138. Clay Blair Jr., *Silent Victory* (J. B. Lippincott, 1975), vol. 1, p. 237. Holmes, *Double-Edged Secrets*, p. 3. Steve Horn, *The Second Attack on Pearl Harbor* (Naval Institute Press, 2005), p. 121.

6. Report on the Fitness of Officers, for Joseph John Rochefort, 31 March 1929, signed by Lt. Cdr. O. L. Downes, Commanding, USS *Macdonough*, Rochefort service record, Military Personnel Records (MPR), St. Louis, MO. Hereafter Fitness Report.

7. Capt. Joseph J. Rochefort, USN (Ret.), oral history conducted by Cdr. Etta-Belle Kitchen, USN (Ret.), 14 August 1969, U.S. Naval Institute, pp. 294–95. Rochefort's oral history was declassified by the National Security Agency (hereafter NSA) and released to the U.S. Naval Institute (hereafter USNI) in 1982.

8. Rear Adm. Donald M. "Mac" Showers, USN (Ret.), quoted in Ronald W. Russell, *No Right to Win* (iUniverse, 2006), p. 38. Russell is moderator of the Internet-based Battle of Midway Roundtable, where Showers' quote originally appeared.
9. David Kennedy, "Victory at Sea," *Atlantic Monthly*, March 1999, quoted in Hervie Haufler, *Codebreakers' Victory* (New American Library, 2003), p. 152.
10. Lewin, *The American Magic*.
11. Harry Elmer Barnes letter to Percy Greaves, 11 May 1962, Redondo Beach, CA, Hiles Papers, Accession 1448, Box 29, American Heritage Center, University of Wyoming (hereafter Barnes-Rochefort interview).
12. The author is indebted to Rochefort's daughter, Janet Rochefort Elerding of Newport Beach, CA, for making available her father's papers (hereafter Rochefort Papers).

CHAPTER 1: TROLLEY TO SAN PEDRO

1. Church records in London, Ontario, establish the names of Francis Rochefort's parents as Patrick Rochford [*sic*] and Elizabeth Kavangh of Dublin, Ireland. The occupation of Rochefort's father as a pawnbroker was confirmed by John McDermot of McDermot Research, Dublin.
2. The date of Frank Rochefort's departure from Ireland is recorded in his U.S. naturalization papers filed with the probate court, State of Ohio, 4 November 1892. A copy of Rochefort's papers was provided by the Ohio Historical Society.
3. The author is indebted to Dan Brock, a London, Ontario, historian for the work he did to document the history of Frank Rochefort and Ellen Spearman in London.
4. The residences and work history of the Rochefort family in Dayton are established by city directories going back to 1891 and continuing through 1912, sections of which were provided by the Ohio Historical Society.
5. No birth certificate for Joe Rochefort shows up in the Montgomery County, OH, probate court birth record index. This indicates that he was born at home, according to Bill Markley of the Research Services Department, Ohio Historical Society. Confirmation that he was born in the year 1900 was provided by St. Joseph Catholic Church in Dayton, where Joseph John Rochefort was baptized on 27 May 1900. His State of California death certificate gives his birth date as 12 May 1900.
6. Interview with Janet Rochefort Elerding, Newport Beach, CA (author's files); hereafter Elerding interviews.
7. For this characterization of Los Angeles and the neighborhood into which the Rocheforts moved, the author is indebted to LA historian Mark Wanamaker (telephone interview, author's files).
8. The Los Angeles residences and work history of the Rochefort family were documented through city directories available at the Los Angeles public Library.

9. Rochefort oral history, USNI, p. 1.

10. Elerding interviews; Records Division, Los Angeles Unified School District.

11. Polytechnic School Student Yearbook, 1917, p. 92 (high school now located in Sun Valley).

12. *The Poly Optimist*, Polytechnic High School newspaper, 19 March 1918; 25 September 1917; 23 October 1917; 26 March 1918.

13. Rochefort oral history, USNI, p. 2.

14. James Hornfischer, *Ship of Ghosts* (Bantam Books, 2006), p. 22.

15. Joe's deed is confirmed by two sets of Rochefort service records, one part of the Rochefort Papers, the other included in the National Personnel Records Center, Military Personnel Records, St. Louis, Missouri. On the U.S. Naval Reserve Force enrollment form signed by Rochefort on 20 April 1918, he reported his birth date as 12 May 1899.

16. Rochefort oral history, USNI, p. 3.

17. John Lukacs, *Democracy and Populism* (Yale University Press, 2005), p. 81.

18. Polytechnic School Student Yearbook, 1919.

19. Second endorsement, 29 August 1918, Cdr. Guy Whitelock, Commanding Officer, San Pedro Naval Reserve Training Camp, to Bureau of Navigation, Navy Department, Washington, D.C., National Personnel Records Center, MPR.

20. Letter, 16 September 1918, Twelfth Naval District, San Francisco, to Joseph J. Rochefort, E. 3/c (Gen) USNRF, citing Bureau of Navigation letter of 11 September 1918 disapproving Rochefort request for flight training, MPR.

21. Rochefort service record, Rochefort Papers.

22. Rochefort probably thought he was in fact a high school graduate. He said after the war he expected the school to extend diplomas to students who had dropped out to join the military. In this he was mistaken; he received no diploma.

23. In paperwork filled out 17 March 1919 for the Naval Auxiliary Reserve in New York, Rochefort reported his date of birth as 12 May 1898. Rochefort service records, MPR.

24. Information Bulletin, U.S. Navy Steam Engineering School, archives, Stevens Institute of Technology, Hoboken, NJ.

25. Ship's log, USS *Koningin der Nederlanden*, April 1919, RG 24, vol. 187, National Archives and Records Administration, Washington, D.C. (NARAI).

26. Fitness Report, 5 May 1919, signed by Capt. W. P. Cronan, Commanding, USS *Koningin der Nederlanden*.

27. Rochefort service record, MPR.

28. Rochefort oral history, USNI, p. 3.

29. See John R. Schindler in "Joseph J. Rochefort Dedication," anthologized in *Leadership Embodied* (Naval Institute Press, 2005); Norman Polmar and Thomas B. Allen, *Spy Book: The Encyclopedia of Espionage* (Random House, 1998); and Layton et al., *And I Was There*.

30. Email to author, 28 June 2006, from Doris A. Oliver, assistant curator, Stevens Institute of Technology: "Unfortunately there is no listing in our records of Joseph J. Rochefort, from 1917–1922."

31. Letter, 25 June 1919, Acting Commandant, Third Naval District, to Ensign Joseph J. Rochefort, USNRF-3, Rochefort Papers.
32. Rochefort travel expenses, 16 August 1919, signed by Lt. (jg) Charles Butz, USNRF, U.S. Submarine Base, San Pedro, CA, certifying Rochefort traveled 3,111 miles at a cost to the government of eight cents per mile, or $248.88. Rochefort Papers.
33. Los Angeles City Directory, 1920, Los Angeles Public Library.
34. *The Tidings*, Los Angeles, 2 April 1971 (newsletter of St. Joseph of Carondelet).
35. Elerding interviews.
36. Letter, 19 September 1919, Navy Department, Bureau of Navigation, Washington, D.C., to Ensign Joseph J. Rochefort; first endorsement, USS *Cuyama*, San Diego, CA, 7 October 1919, signed by his CO, Cdr. Isaac Smith, Rochefort Papers.

CHAPTER 2: MUSTANG

1. Rochefort oral history, USNI, p. 3.
2. Stephen Puleo, *Due to Enemy Action* (Lyons Press, 2005), pp. 6, 64.
3. Elerding interviews.
4. Fitness Report, 1 February 1921 to 16 May 1921, signed by Isaac B. Smith, Commander, USNRF-3, commanding USS *Cuyama*.
5. Memo, 14 November 1921, from Bureau of Navigation, to Commanding Officer, USS *Cardinal*, MPR.
6. Ronald H. Spector, *At War at Sea: Sailors and Naval Combat in the Twentieth Century* (Viking, 2001), p. 137.
7. Ronald Spector interview with the author, 14 June 2005, George Washington University, Washington, D.C.
8. Spector, *At War at Sea*, p. 262.
9. As noted, *Cuyama* captain Cdr. Isaac Smith described Rochefort as qualified for a commission in the Regular Navy. Rochefort's next CO, Lt. Harold G. Billings, commanding officer of the *Cardinal*, described the young officer as "calm, forceful, active," with "above average" professional ability.
10. Spector, *At War at Sea*, p. 136.
11. Rochefort oral history, USNI, pp. 53–54. See also Peter Karsten, *The Naval Aristocracy* (Free Press, 1972), pp. 12–16.
12. Rochefort, ibid.
13. Memo, second endorsement, 16 November 1921, from Capt. H. O. Stickney, *Connecticut*, flagship, U.S. Pacific Fleet, to Chief of the Bureau of Navigation, Washington, D.C., File 45287; third endorsement, 18 November 1921, Capt. W. H. Standley, *New Mexico*, U.S. Pacific Fleet, to Chief of the Bureau of Navigation, File 21–4-Ro, MPR.
14. Rochefort service record, Rochefort Papers.
15. Fitness Report, 14 August 1922, signed by Cdr. John H. Blackburn, commanding officer, USS *Cuyama*.

16. Fitness Report, 22 April 1924, signed by Cdr. C. C. Moses, commanding officer, USS *Cuyama*.
17. Letter, 25 June 1948, Capt. Joseph J. Rochefort, USN (Ret.), to J. G. Goodsell, principal, Polytechnic High School, Los Angeles, CA; letter provided author 6 December 2006, by Phil Lopez, supervisor for student records, Los Angeles Unified School District.
18. Memo, 6 October 1923, Rear Adm. A. T. Long, Bureau of Navigation, to Lt. (jg) Joseph J. Rochefort, USS *Cuyama*, Rochefort Papers.
19. Ibid., 8 December 1923.
20. Memo, 23 June 1924, Lt.(jg) J. J. Rochefort, USS *Cuyama*, to Bureau of Navigation, Rochefort Papers.
21. Record of proceedings of a court of inquiry convened on board the USS *California*, by order of Commander in Chief, Battle Fleet, to inquire into the dragging of the USS *Cuyama*, 27 September 1924. Received by the Navy Department 30 October 1924, File Number 26835–2672. RG 80, Box 1922, NARAI.
22. Ibid. This section also draws on ship's log USS *Cuyama*, 27 September 1924, RG 24, vol. 8, NARAI.
23. Record of proceedings; ship's log, USS *Cuyama*, 27 September 1924.
24. Confidential memo, 12 November 1924, Rear Adm. George R. Marvell, Commander, Fleet Base Force, USS *Procyon*, to Lt. (jg) J. J. Rochefort, USS *Cuyama*, attached to Fitness Report, 12 January 1925.
25. Fitness Report, 17 November 1924, signed by Cdr. C. C. Moses, commanding officer, USS *Cuyama*.
26. Rochefort oral history, USNI, p. 5.
27. Rochefort service record, Rochefort Papers.
28. Fitness Report, 14 December 1925, covering quarter 28 June 1925–22 September 1925, signed by Capt. H. P. Perrill, commanding officer, USS *Arizona*.
29. Rochefort service record, Rochefort Papers.
30. Rochefort oral history, USNI, p. 7.
31. Rochefort service record, Rochefort Papers.

CHAPTER 3: ODYSSEY OF A CODEBREAKER

1. *On the Treadmill to Pearl Harbor: The Memoirs of Admiral J. O. Richardson*, as told to Vice Adm. George C. Dyer, USN (Ret.), Naval History Division, 1973, p. 66.
2. Navy personnel dropped sharply from its peak of 501,425 in 1918 to 114,708 in 1925. Source: *A Statistical Abstract Supplement, Historical Studies of the United States from Colonial Times to 1957* (U.S. Department of Commerce).
3. Known in 1925 as the Communication Office, the entity by 1930 had evolved into the Communication Division; later it was referred to as the Office of Naval Communications (ONC). To maintain consistency, the latter title is used throughout this volume.
4. See Layton et al., *And I Was There*. When Willson, as captain of the *Pennsyl-*

vania, learned that one of his subordinates, Lt. Wesley "Ham" Wright, was engrossed in codebreaking, he gave him hell for "fooling around with that stuff."

5. Rochefort oral history, USNI, pp. 13, 32.

6. Vice Adm. George C. Dyer, USN (Ret.), oral history conducted by John T. Mason Jr., 13 November 1969, USNI, pp. 232–33.

7. David Brinkley, *Washington Goes to War* (Knopf, 1988), pp. 53–54, 61, 74; Ernest J. King and Walter Muir Whitehill, *Fleet Admiral King: A Naval Record* (W. W. Norton, 1952), p. 647.

8. Navy Department, Directory of Bureaus, Boards, and Offices, August 1925, on file at Navy Department Library, NHHC.

9. L. S. Howeth, *History of Communications-Electronics in the United States Navy* (Bureau of Ships and Office of Navy History, 1963), pp. 261–63.

10. See Capt. Laurance Safford, USN, "A Brief History of Communications Intelligence in the United States," SRH-149, pp. 3–5, NHHC.

11. For accounts of Herbert O. Yardley's controversial career, see David Kahn, *The Reader of Gentlemen's Mail* (Yale University Press, 2004), pp. 21, 27, 28–49; David Kahn, *Codebreakers* (Scribner, 1967), pp. 324, 352–55; Steve Budiansky, *Battle of Wits* (Free Press, 2000), pp. 25–27; Safford, "Brief History of Communications Intelligence," p. 3.

12. Kahn, *Reader of Gentlemen's Mail*, pp. 72–80.

13. Safford, "Brief History of Communications Intelligence," p. 5.

14. Layton et al., *And I Was There*, pp. 31–36.

15. Interview with Capt. L. F. Safford, undated, conducted by Raymond Schmidt, p. 4, Naval Cryptologic Veterans Association (NCVA), Corry Station Library, Pensacola, FL (hereafter Safford-Schmidt interview).

16. John Prados, *Combined Fleet Decoded* (Random House, 1995), p. 77.

17. Safford-Schmidt interview.

18. Letter, 23 June 1985, Mrs. Eunice Willson Rice to Roger Pineau, quoted in Layton et al., *And I Was There*, pp. 32–33.

19. Rochefort oral history, USNI, pp. 10–11.

20. See Robert Hanyok, "Still Desperately Seeking 'Miss Agnes,'" *NCVA Cryptolog*, fall 1997, p. 3.

21. Safford, "Brief History of Communications Intelligence." See also NCVA, *A History of Communications Intelligence in the United States with Emphasis on the United States Navy* (Special Publication, fall 2003), pp. xi–xix.

22. For the definitive history of U.S. Navy war planning against the Japanese, see Edward S. Miller, *War Plan Orange* (Naval Institute Press, 1991). For the status of Navy war planning during the early and mid-1920s, see pp. 122–31.

23. Memorandum from Chief of Naval Operations to Chief of Bureau of Navigation, 24 February 1932, subject: "Developing a reserve of expert cryptanalysts," signed W. R. Sexton, Acting, A-6–3(1)/P11–1, RG 38, Box 104, CNSG Library, National Archives and Records Administration, College Park, MD (hereafter NARAII).

24. Layton et al., *And I Was There*, pp. 33–34.
25. Rochefort oral history, USNI, p. 12.
26. Ibid., p. 7.
27. See Ronald Clark, *The Man Who Broke Purple* (Little, Brown, 1977), pp. 23–27. See also Kahn, *Reader of Gentlemen's Mail*, pp. 22–27; and Kahn, *Codebreakers*, pp. 371–86.
28. Rochefort oral history, USNI, p. 8.
29. William F. Friedman, *Elements of Cryptanalysis* (Aegean Park Press, 1976), pp. 1–37.
30. Rochefort oral history, USNI, p. 16.
31. Rochefort recognized that mainstream Navy officers often viewed cryptanalysts as "odd characters," a description he thought had some validity (Rochefort oral history, USNI, p. 13).
32. Fitness Report, 17 February 1926, signed by Ridley McLean.
33. David Alvarez, *Secret Messages* (University of Kansas Press, 2000), p. 23.
34. Budiansky, *Battle of Wits*, p. 4.
35. Rochefort oral history, USNI, p. 6.
36. Ibid., p. 14.
37. Edwin T. Layton tape, p. 80, Pineau Papers, Box 10, folder 17, archives, University of Colorado at Boulder Libraries. See also Layton et al., *And I Was There*, p. 58.
38. Layton tape.
39. Rochefort oral history, USNI, pp. 29–30.
40. Ellis Zacharias, *Secret Missions* (G. P. Putnam, 1946), p. 83.
41. Laurance Safford to C. C. Hiles, 22 August 1964, Safford Collection, Box 2, Accession 1357, American Heritage Center, University of Wyoming.
42. Layton et al., *And I Was There*, p. 31.
43. The story of ONI's secret fund is told by Laurance Safford in "The Undeclared War," in *History of Radio Intelligence*, 15 November 1943, SRH-305, Navy Department Library, NHHC. Also anthologized in NCVA, *History of Communications Intelligence*, pp. 202–21.
44. Layton et al., *And I Was There*, p. 31.
45. Safford, "Undeclared War"; see also Layton et al., *And I Was There*, p. 33.
46. The numeral 20 in OP-20-G appears to have been arbitrary. A history of the Navy Department shows no more than sixteen divisions in the Office of Naval Operations. War Plans was OP-12, Intelligence (ONI) was OP-16 and Ship Movements was OP-38. See Rear Adm. Julius Augustus Furer, USN (Ret.), *Administration of the Navy Department in World War II* (Department of the Navy, 1959), pp. 115–17. For background on OP-20-G's reorganization, see Capt. Jack S. Holtwick Jr., USN (Ret.), "Organizational Development of the Naval Security Group," RG 38, Box 83, Folder 5400/13, CNSG Library, NARAII. See also Rear Adm. Joe Wenger, USN (Ret.), "The Evolution of the Navy's Cryptologic Organization," SRMN-084, RG 457, NARAII.
47. Rochefort oral history, USNI, pp. 58–59.

48. Rochefort interview with Percy Greaves, 7 January 1964, Civil Defense Office, Redondo Beach, CA, Hiles Collection, Accession 1448, Box 29, American Heritage Center, University of Wyoming (hereafter Greaves-Rochefort interview).
49. Jeffrey W. Dorwart, *Conflict of Duty* (Naval Institute Press, 1983), p. 31.
50. Zacharias, *Secret Missions*, pp. 84–90.
51. A useful description of this code can be found in Budiansky, *Battle of Wits*, p. 5.
52. Rochefort oral history, USNI, p. 17.
53. Zacharias, *Secret Missions*, pp. 84–90.
54. This portrait of Rochefort's health is drawn from his medical records (medical history, data for annual consultation, 10 January 1927, MPR; medical history, COMSERVPAC Headquarters Dispensary, 29 January 1951), MPR.
55. Rochefort oral history, USNI, pp. 46–47.
56. Report of annual physical examination, Naval Dispensary, Washington, D.C., 14 January 1926; medical history, case data for health records, 1926, MPR.
57. Rochefort oral history, USNI, pp. 30–31. In his "Undeclared War" Safford agreed with this assessment, noting that "Mrs. Driscoll was responsible for the initial solution."
58. Safford, "Undeclared War."
59. Rochefort oral history, USNI, pp. 37–40.
60. Safford, "Undeclared War"; see also Layton et al., *And I Was There*, pp. 35–36.
61. Rochefort, "Memorandum for Captain Ogan," 21 December 1932, Rochefort Papers.
62. Safford-Schmidt interview.
63. Rochefort oral history, USNI, p. 299.
64. Fitness Report, 13 October 1926, signed by Capt. Ridley McLean.
65. Rochefort oral history, USNI, pp. 45–49.
66. Medical History, COMSERVPAC Headquarters Dispensary, 29 January 1951, MPR.
67. Rochefort oral history, USNI, pp. 32, 45–49.

CHAPTER 4: FLEET GADFLY, TOKYO WHIZ
1. Rochefort oral history, USNI, p. 56.
2. Rochefort oral history, USNI, p. 49.
3. Fitness Report, 17 April 1928, signed by Cdr. Arthur S. Carpender.
4. Memorandum to Lt. Meyers, 25 November 1927. Rochefort misspelled the name. He undoubtedly submitted his memo to Lt. Ralph O. Myers, radio officer on board the *Litchfield,* the destroyer squadron's flagship. No reply from Myers showed up in Rochefort's papers (Rochefort Papers).
5. Rochefort's service record, Rochefort Papers.
6. Capt. Thomas H. Dyer, USN (Ret.), oral history conducted by Paul Stillwell, 15 August 1983, at Dyer's home in Sykesville, MD, USNI, pp. 86–88.
7. Admiral Wiley was succeeded later in 1929 by Admiral Pratt, who in 1930 was appointed CNO, a post he held until April 1933. Admiral Stark served as CNO from 1 August 1939 to 26 March 1942. Admiral Kimmel served as

commander in chief of the Pacific Fleet from 1 February 1941 until 17 December 1941. Lieutenant Commander Downes commanded the *Macdonough* from April 1928 until January 1930.

8. Rochefort memorandum, 23 February 1929, "Suggestions for Improvement: Naval Communications," Rochefort Papers.

9. Ibid.

10. Fitness Report, 31 March 1929, signed by Lt. Cdr. O. L. Downes, Rochefort service record.

11. Ibid., 8 October 1928.

12. Bureau of Navigation memo, 18 May 1927, signed by BuNAV chief Rear Adm. R. H. Leigh, to Lt. Joseph J. Rochefort, Rochefort Papers.

13. Change of duty order, Bureau of Navigation, 3 August 1929, signed by BuNAV chief Rear Adm. R. H. Leigh, to Lt. Joseph J. Rochefort, Rochefort Papers.

14. Bureau of Navigation memo, 8 August 1929, signed by BuNAV chief Rear Adm. R. H. Leigh, to Lt. Joseph J. Rochefort, Rochefort Papers.

15. Rochefort oral history, USNI, pp. 57–60.

16. Fitness Report, 12 April 1928, signed by Cdr. A. S. Carpender.

17. Rochefort oral history, USNI, p. 60.

18. Kahn, *Reader of Gentlemen's Mail*, pp. 97–103.

19. Ibid.

20. Memorandum from Lt. Cdr. Walter McClaran to Director of Naval Communications S. C. Hooper, 3 November 1930, Naval Security Group History to World War II, part 1, compiled by Capt. J. S. Holtwick Jr., SRH-355, p. 70, Navy Department Library, NHHC. SRH-355 is also available from NCVA.

21. Layton et al., *And I Was There*, p. 39. Layton wrote that the meeting took place in August, but he is wrong about the date. Rochefort's orders clearly specified a 6 September boarding date and the dates obviously had to be the same for both men.

22. Rear Adm. Edwin T. Layton, USN (Ret.), oral history conducted by Cdr. Etta-Belle Kitchen, USN (Ret.), 30 May 1970, USNI, pp. 7–10.

23. *Lucky Bag*, Naval Academy yearbook, 1924.

24. For this portrait of Layton on Guam the author is indebted to Rear Adm. Donald "Mac" Showers, USN (Ret.), hereafter Showers interviews (author's files).

25. Capt. Thomas H. Dyer, USN (Ret.), oral history conducted by R. D. Farley and H. P. Schorreck, 29 January 1982, NSA, NSA-OH-01–82, Sykesville, MD.

26. Layton et al., *And I Was There*, pp. 39–40.

27. See Rochefort oral history, USNI, p. 61; and Layton et al., *And I Was There*, p. 39.

28. Rear Adm. Arthur H. McCollum, USN (Ret.), oral history, 8 December 1970, USNI, pp. 1, 38–40.

29. Testimony of Capt. Arthur H. McCollum, Hearings before the Joint Congressional Committee Investigating the Pearl Harbor Attack, February 1946, Part 8, p. 3404 (hereafter PHH).

30. Rear Adm. Edwin T. Layton, USN (Ret.), oral history conducted by Robert D. Farley, Carmel, CA, 7–8 February 1983, NSA, pp. 10–12.

31. Interview with Rear Adm. Edwin T. Layton, conducted by John Costello and Roger Pineau, 11 May 1983, Edwin T. Layton Papers, Box 30, Folder 1, Naval War College, Newport, RI (hereafter Layton-Costello interview, NWC).

32. Rochefort oral history, USNI, pp. 62–63.

33. Layton et al., *And I Was There*, p. 40.

34. Rochefort oral history, USNI, pp. 64–65.

35. Besides Rochefort and Layton, the group present in 1929 included five Navy officers: Edward S. Pearce, Thomas B. Birtley, Kenneth D. Ringle, Louis D. Liebnow, and Ethelbert Watts. The Marines included F. P. Pyzick and J. F. Burke.

36. Layton et al., *And I Was There*, p. 41. See also Kahn, *Reader of Gentlemen's Mail*, pp. 130–36. "The book ignited a firestorm in Japan," Kahn writes. "Book sales skyrocketed. On a per capita basis, the Japanese total of 33,119 copies in the first year was almost four times better than in the United States."

37. Rochefort oral history, USNI, p. 36.

38. Kahn, *Reader of Gentlemen's Mail*, p. 131.

39. See Layton et al., *And I Was There*, pp. 41–42.

40. Rochefort oral history, USNI, p. 66.

41. Memorandum, "Examination in the progress of the Japanese language of Lieutenant J. J. Rochefort, U.S. Navy: final examination," from Capt. I. C. Johnson, 11 October 1932 (American Embassy, Naval Attache's Office, Tokyo, Japan), Rochefort service records, MPR.

42. Rochefort oral history, USNI, p. 80.

43. Ibid., pp. 78–79.

44. Dorwart, *Conflict of Duty*, p. 55.

45. Safford, "Undeclared War," pp. 205–7.

46. Ibid., pp. 203–9.

47. Pratt's "blackout" order wasn't revoked until a new CNO, Adm. William H. Standley, was named in mid-1933, long after Rochefort had returned to sea.

48. Rochefort, "Memorandum for Captain Ogan," 21 December 1932, Rochefort Papers.

49. Rochefort oral history, USNI, p. 81.

CHAPTER 5: THE ADMIRAL'S CONFIDANT

1. Rochefort oral history, USNI, pp. 81–86.

2. Fitness Report, 11 July 1933, signed by Adm. William H. Standley.

3. Reeves' Naval Academy classmates dubbed him "Bull" to describe his vigorous, risk-taking style of playing football. See Thomas Wildenberg, *All the Factors of Victory* (Brassey's, 2003), p. 23.

4. See Wildenberg's *All the Factors of Victory* for origins of Billy-Goat (p. 104);

see oral history of Rear Adm. Arthur H. McCollum, USN (Ret.), for origins of "the old man with the beard" (p. 191).

5. Wildenberg, *All the Factors of Victory*, pp. 120–24, 226, 248.
6. Fitness Report, 24 October 1933, signed by Adm. J. M. Reeves.
7. "Notes on Combat Intelligence, Fleet Problem, 7–10 July," memorandum to Battle Force Commander Reeves, 12 July 1933, signed by Cdr. O. L. Wolford, Rochefort Papers.
8. Ibid.
9. Wildenberg, *All the Factors of Victory*, pp. 235–36. *Time* magazine, 4 June 1934, p. 14; *Pittsburgh Press*, 16 June 1934, p. 2.
10. Wildenberg, *All the Factors of Victory*, pp. 244–45.
11. Layton et al., *And I Was There*, p. 49.
12. *Lucky Bag*, 1906 Naval Academy Yearbook, Navy Department Library, NHHC.
13. Bernard Godwin, *Journal-Sentinel*, Winston-Salem, NC, 13 February 1944.
14. McCollum oral history, USNI, p. 486.
15. Wildenberg, *All the Factors of Victory*, pp. 238–39; Rochefort oral history, USNI, p. 86.
16. Rochefort oral history, USNI, pp. 83–86.
17. McCollum oral history, USNI, pp. 191–93.
18. See Paolo E. Coletta, ed., *United States Navy and Marine Corps Bases: Domestic* (Greenwood Press, 1985), p. 602.
19. Layton et al., *And I Was There*, p. 49.
20. Wildenberg, *All the Factors of Victory*, p. 240.
21. Rochefort, "Memorandum for Admiral: courses of action open to Orange," 17 August 1934; Rochefort Papers.
22. Ibid.
23. Fitness Report, 18 October 1934, signed by Adm. J. M. Reeves, MPR.
24. Wildenberg, *All the Factors of Victory*, p. 231.
25. Greaves-Rochefort interview.
26. McCollum oral history, USNI, pp. 166–77.
27. Ibid.
28. Dorwart, *Conflict of Duty*, p. 66; see also Zacharias, *Secret Missions*, pp. 166–69.
29. Rochefort letter to H. F. Kingman at Office of Navy Communication, 24 January 1935, RG 38, Box 94, CNSG Library, NARAII.
30. H. F. Kingman letter to Rochefort, 20 March 1935, RG 38, Box 94, CNSG Library, NARAII.
31. Layton et al., *And I Was There*, p 49.
32. McCollum oral history, USNI, p. 486.
33. Ibid.
34. Layton et al., *And I Was There*, p. 49.

35. McClaran letter to Rochefort, 16 October 1935, RG 38, Box 94, CNSG Library, NARAII.
36. Rochefort letter to McClaran, 19 November 1935, RG 38, Box 94, CNSG Library, NARAII.
37. Fitness Report, 1 April 1936.
38. Rochefort oral history, USNI, p. 84.
39. Ibid.
40. Ibid., pp. 54–55.
41. Ibid.

CHAPTER 6: ASSIGNMENT PEARL HARBOR

1. Orders from commanding officer to Lt. Cdr. Joseph J. Rochefort, U.S. Navy, 29 September 1939, Ref.: BuNAV dispatch 6425–1245 of 26 September 1939, Rochefort Papers.
2. David Reynolds, *From Munich to Pearl Harbor* (Ivan R. Dee, 2001), p. 60.
3. *On the Treadmill to Pearl Harbor: The Memoirs of Admiral J.O. Richardson*, p. 162.
4. Fitness Report, 24 April 1940, signed by Vice Adm. Adolphus Andrews.
5. Greaves-Rochefort interview.
6. Rochefort oral history, USNI, p. 96.
7. *On the Treadmill to Pearl Harbor: The Memoirs of Admiral J. O. Richardson*, pp. 327–29.
8. Ibid. According to U.S. Fleet Commander J. O. Richardson, the reenlistment rate in the Navy fell from 80.81 percent in fiscal 1939 to 75.45 percent in fiscal 1940.
9. Rochefort oral history, USNI, p. 94.
10. Gordon Prange, with Donald M. Goldstein and Katherine V. Dillon, *At Dawn We Slept* (Penguin Books, 1982), p. 621.
11. Eric Larrabee, *Commander in Chief* (Harper and Row, 1987), p. 177.
12. Miller, *War Plan Orange*, pp. 227–29.
13. Ibid.
14. Greaves-Rochefort interview.
15. Elerding interviews.
16. Ibid.
17. Memo from BuNAV Chief Chester Nimitz to Judge Advocate General, 14 November 1939, ordering selection board to convene 6 December 1939, board consisting of the following rear admirals: R. Sexton (president); Clark Woodward, Wilson Brown, Herbert Leary, Russell Willson, John Wainwright, Andrew Pickens, Wilhelm Friedal, and Leigh Noyes. RG 24, see Boxes 105, 969, NARAI.
18. Nimitz memo to JAG, 25 November 1939, RG 24, Boxes 105, 969, NARAI.
19. "Report on the Operation of the Officer Promotion System in Effect in the

U.S. Navy and of the System of Graduate Education or Training of the Officer Personnel of the U.S. Navy," 8 July 1939; RG 24, see Boxes 105, 969, NARAI.

20. Ibid., p. 19.
21. Nimitz letter to Senator James J. Davis, 1 August 1939, RG 24, Boxes 105, 969, NARAI.
22. Ibid. See also "Report on the Operation of the Promotion System," pp. 18–21.
23. Nimitz letter to Senator James J. Davis, 1 August 1939; "Report on the Operation of the Promotion System," p. 22.
24. Fitness Report, 6 June 1938 (Gannon); 28 December 1938 (Beauregard); and 30 October 1940 (Andrews).
25. McCollum oral history, USNI, p. 486.
26. Showers interviews (author's files).
27. Fitness Report, 13 February 1941, signed by Vice Adm. Adolphus Andrews.
28. Greaves-Rochefort interview.
29. Ibid.
30. Fitness Report, 23 April 1941, signed by Vice Adm. Wilson Brown.
31. McCollum oral history, USNI, p. 486.
32. Layton et al., *And I Was There*, p. 49.
33. Fitness Report, 23 April 1941 and 22 May 1941.
34. Layton, et al., *And I Was There*, p. 54.
35. As commander in chief, U.S. Fleet (CinCUS), Bloch through Navy custom held the temporary grade of full admiral. After his reassignment he reverted to his permanent grade, rear admiral.
36. Capt. Thomas H. Dyer oral history, USNI, pp. 188–99.
37. The Rochefort-Safford correspondence from this period hasn't survived; no trace of it can be found in either Rochefort's papers or the Safford Collection at the University of Wyoming. All that's known about the correspondence is from Rochefort's oral history.
38. Fitness Reports, 1933 through 23 April 1941.
39. Rochefort oral history, USNI, pp. 98–103.
40. Email from Fred Parker to author, 2 June 2010, author's files.
41. Layton et al., *And I Was There*, pp. 92–95.
42. Ibid.
43. Showers interviews (author's files).
44. Undated comments, Laurance Safford to C. C. Hiles, Safford Collection, Accession No. 1357, Box 2, American Heritage Center, University of Wyoming.
45. When Admiral Bloch learned in mid-1938 that Rochefort was about to be rotated back to sea, he wrote a glowing appraisal to the district commandant, stating, among other things, that Rochefort had performed his liaison tasks "in a uniformly excellent manner." See memo to Rear Adm. Sinclair Gannon, 15 May 1938, signed by Adm. Claude Bloch, Rochefort Fitness Reports.
46. Prange et al., *At Dawn We Slept*, p. 93.
47. Congress of the United States, *Report of the Joint Committee on the Investiga-*

tion of the Pearl Harbor Attack (Government Printing Office, 1946), pp. 83–84 (Aegean Park Press, 1994).

48. Ibid.

49. Layton et al., *And I Was There*, p. 91.

50. Ibid.

51. Ibid., pp. 112–14.

52. Naval Security Group History to World War II, prepared and compiled by Capt. J. S. Holtwick Jr., USN (Ret.), pp. 427–28; SRH-355, Part 1, Navy Department Library, NHHC (hereafter Holtwick, SRH-355).

53. Personal and confidential letter, Bloch to Stark, 2 June 1941, Bloch Papers, Container No. 3, Stark Folder, Library of Congress.

CHAPTER 7: A MOST UNUSUAL PLACE

1. Disagreement has persisted over when Rochefort moved his group into the basement. Dyer thought it was in September; others believed it was later. On 18 August 1941, Rochefort radioed the following one-sentence dispatch to OP-20-G in Washington: "We are now doing business in the new office— plenty of room and very nice" (Holtwick, SRH-355, p. 431).

2. Capt. Wesley A. "Ham" Wright, USN (Ret.), oral history, 24 May 1982, NSA, NSA-OH-82, p. 67.

3. The basement has given rise to many exaggerated depictions. One historian stated: "To see anyone in [the basement], it was necessary first to buzz a locked door at the top of the cellar" (Lord, *Incredible Victory*, p. 27). Another declared: "Vault-like doors protected [the basement's] secrets; steel-barred gates at the top and bottom of the stairs kept out visitors; guards stood a round-the-clock watch" (Kahn, *Codebreakers*, p. 562). In truth, the metal door separating the staircase from the basement measured five and one-half inches thick—barely qualifying as vault type. Forrest Biard, who reported to the basement on 30 September 1941, activated no buzzer, encountered no steel-barred gates, and spotted no guards in front of the basement entrance (see Capt. Forrest R. "Tex" Biard, USN [Ret.], oral histories conducted by Etta-Belle Kitchen, 15 and 21 August 1984, USNI). Mac Showers, who reported in February 1942 and remained on duty through March 1943, said he never saw a guard near the basement entrance, nor did he ever find the entrance locked, as maintained by some writers.

4. Biard oral history, USNI, p. 520.

5. Letter from Capt. John Roenigk, USN (Ret.), to Capt. Roger Pineau USNR (Ret.), 21 February 1987, Pineau Collection, Box 24, Folder 1, Archives, University of Colorado at Boulder Libraries.

6. Holmes, *Doubled-Edged Secrets*, p. 56.

7. Speech given by Capt. Forrest R. Tex Biard, USN (Ret.), to National Cryptologic Museum Foundation, 14 June 2002, reprinted in *Cryptologia* 30, no. 2 (April 2006): pp. 151–58.

8. Holmes, *Double-Edged Secrets*, pp. 16–17, 56.
9. Rochefort oral history, USNI, p. 126.
10. Ibid., pp. 154–55.
11. Capt. Thomas H. Dyer oral history, USNI, p. 199.
12. Rochefort oral history, USNI, pp. 12–13.
13. Holmes, *Double-Edged Secrets*, p. 22.
14. Rochefort oral history, USNI.
15. Capt. Thomas H. Dyer oral history, USNI, p. 324.
16. Ibid., pp. 197–99.
17. Holmes, *Double-Edged Secrets*, p. 54.
18. Showers interviews (author's files). Serving under Holmes, Showers was stationed in the basement from February 1942 to March 1943, when the Hypo crew was moved to Makalapa Heights at Pearl Harbor.
19. Rochefort oral history, USNI, p. 103.
20. See Kahn, *Codebreakers*, p. 20; and Prados, *Combined Fleet Decoded*, p. 163.
21. Holmes, *Double-Edged Secrets*, p. 18.
22. Rochefort oral history, USNI, p. 104.
23. Methods of Procedure, RG 38, Box 83, Folder 5400/13, CNSG Library, NARAII.
24. Ibid. In addition to ships' call signs and their relationships, traffic analysts also established frequencies employed, traffic routing methods, secret calls and address systems, station and message serial numbers, zone time, volume of traffic, station activity, signal strength, distinctive characteristics of transmitters and operators, methods in relaying, and priority of indications.
25. Rochefort oral history, USNI, p. 104.
26. Holmes, *Double-Edged Secrets*, pp. 15–16.
27. Capt. Thomas H. Dyer oral history, USNI, p. 201.
28. Showers interviews (author's files).
29. Holmes, *Double-Edged Secrets*, pp. 36–37.
30. Ibid.
31. Col. Alva B. "Red" Lasswell, USMC (Ret.), oral history, 1 April 1968, Historical Division, Headquarters, U.S. Marine Corps.
32. Brig. Gen. Bankson Holcomb, USMC (Ret.), oral history, 8 May 1983, Naval Security Group, Naval Cryptologic Museum Library, Pensacola, FL.
33. Biard speech, 14 June 2002, Naval Cryptologic Foundation Museum. Biard repeated this story in a telephone interview with the author on 29 March 2005.
34. Biard speech, 14 June 2002.
35. Rochefort oral history, USNI, p. 13.
36. Holtwick, SRH-355, p. 427.
37. Capt. Wesley A. Wright, USN (Ret.), 24 May 1984, interview with John Costello and Roger Pineau, p. 4, Papers of Edwin T. Layton, Box 46, Folder 8, NWC.
38. Rochefort Papers. Layton et al., *And I Was There*, p. 453.
39. Rochefort oral history, USNI, p. 102.

40. Ibid.
41. Capt. Thomas H. Dyer oral history, USNI, p. 126.
42. Frederick D. Parker, *Pearl Harbor Revisited: United States Communications Intelligence 1924–1941* (Center for Cryptologic History, NSA, 1994), pp. 18–19.
43. Pacific War historian Robert Hanyok points out that the Navy's numbering of its codes was arbitrary. For example, he notes, JN-39 appeared a few years before JN-25 and was exploited earlier. JN-21, on the other hand, appeared after JN-25.
44. Parker, *Pearl Harbor Revisited*, pp. 18–19.
45. Rochefort's cryptanalytic team was well aware of the hole in his experience. See Capt. Thomas H. Dyer oral history, USNI, p. 87.
46. Rochefort oral history, USNI, pp. 90–91.
47. Ibid., pp. 12, 105.
48. Roenigk letter to Pineau, 22 April 1989.
49. Holmes, *Double-Edged Secrets*, pp. 21–22; see also Capt. Thomas H. Dyer oral history, USNI, p. 208.
50. Roenigk to Pineau, undated 1983 letter, Box 23, Folder 4, Archives, University of Colorado at Boulder Libraries.
51. Interview with Joe Rochefort conducted by Gordon Prange, 26 August 1964, Redondo Beach, CA, Papers of Gordon W. Prange, Accession 2002–78, Boxes 20, 21, Manuscript Division, University of Maryland Library, College Park, MD (hereafter Rochefort-Prange interview).
52. As of 26 June 1941, the unit's three key sections included the following personnel: linguists Capt. Lasswell, Lt. Fullinwider, with Lt. Cdr. Rochefort head of the section; cryptanalysts Lt. Cdr. Dyer, Lt. Cdr. Holtwick, Lt. Cdr. Wright, Ens. Werner, and four comint-trained enlisted men completing the section (CY Conant, CY Rorie, CY Johnson, and CRM Woodward); traffic analysts Lt. Cdr. Huckins, Lt. Cdr. Williams, Lt. Cdr. Moore, and two enlisted traffic analysts (CRM Hopkins and CRM Willis). See Holtwick, SRH-355, pp. 427–28.
53. Lt. Cdr. Durwood G. Rorie, USN (Ret.), oral history, 5 October 1984, NSA, NSA OH-27–84, p. 23.
54. Rorie oral history, NSA, pp. 17–18.
55. Holmes, *Double-Edged Secrets*, pp. 14, 21–22.
56. Rorie oral history, NSA, p. 18.
57. Holmes, *Double-Edged Secrets*, p. 14.
58. Ibid.; and author's interview with Pacific war historian Ron Russell.
59. Showers interviews (author's files).
60. Fred B. Wrixon, *Codes, Ciphers, Secrets and Cryptic Communication* (Black Dog and Leventhal, 1998), pp. 256–58; see also "History of Invention and Development of the Mark II ECM (Electric Cipher Machine)," SRH-360, Navy Department Library, NHHC.
61. Rochefort oral history, USNI, pp. 148–49.
62. Ibid., p. 141.

CHAPTER 8: ROCHEFORT'S WORLD

1. Edward S. Miller, *Bankrupting the Enemy* (Naval Institute Press, 2007), pp. 191–205.

2. Jonathan Utley, *Going to War with Japan, 1937–1941*, quoted in Miller, *Bankrupting the Enemy*, p. 203.

3. Miller, *Bankrupting the Enemy*, p. 192.

4. Layton et al., *And I Was There*, pp. 127–28.

5. Combat Intelligence Summaries (hereafter CIS), 16 July–31 December 1941, SRMN-012, pp. 19–26, Navy Department Library, NHHC.

6. Layton et al., *And I Was There*, pp. 127–28.

7. CIS, 16 July–31 December 1941, SRMN-012, pp. 19–26, NHHC.

8. Ibid. See also Layton et al., *And I Was There*, pp. 126–27.

9. Rochefort oral history, USNI, pp. 136, 180.

10. Showers interviews (author's files).

11. Kimmel's initials appeared on all Hypo's daily summaries from 16 July 1941 through 6 December 1941; see RG 80, Box 41, NARAII. See Layton's testimony before the Joint Congressional Committee in 1946, PHH, Part 10, p. 4831.

12. Rochefort oral history, USNI, pp. 146–48.

13. Ibid.

14. Memorandum, Chief of Naval Operations to the Fourteenth Naval District, 21 August 1937, "History of the Pearl Harbor Unit," Navy Department, RG 38, Box 84, NARAII.

15. Rochefort letter to Harry Elmer Barnes, 8 June 1962, Safford Papers, Accession No. 1357, Box 1, American Heritage Center, University of Wyoming.

16. Howeth, *History of Communicatons-Electronics*, pp. 261–65. During the European War, the Navy manipulated copper-wrapped poles to monitor German U-boats along the Atlantic coast.

17. Rochefort memorandum, "High Frequency Direction Finding in the Pacific Ocean Prior to December 7, 1941," OP-20-G/nmcg, 9 August 1944, Rochefort Papers.

18. Holtwick, SRH-355, p. 374.

19. Rochefort memorandum, "High Frequency Direction Finding," Rochefort Papers.

20. Parker, *Pearl Harbor Revisited*, p. 39. The twenty-one radio receivers at Heeia consisted of one low-frequency XRI type, one low-frequency RAA type, thirteen high-frequency RAO-RAS types, one ultra-high-frequency (30–300 mcs) type, and one Diversity RAE-RAO type. See memorandum from Commandant, Fourteenth Naval District, to Chief of the Bureau of Ships, via Chief of Naval Operations, subject: "Communication Intelligence Stations, Fourteenth Naval District, Material Requirements for, January 17, 1941," RG 38, Box 84, Inactive Stations, NARAII.

21. George P. McGinnis, ed., *U.S. Naval Cryptologic Veterans Association History Book* (Turner, 1996), pp. 62–63.

22. CWO James B. Capron Jr., USN (Ret.), oral history, 3 October 1984, NSA, p. 29. A member of the On-the-Roof Gang (OTRG) class of 1940, Capron served as an RMC 2d Class at Heeia from 1940 to 1941.

23. Between 1928 and 1941, 176 Navy and Marine Corps radiomen (150 sailors and 26 Marines) reported for special training in copying Japanese radio messages. For a history of the OTRG, see Elliott Okins, *To Spy or Not to Spy* (Pateo, 1985), pp. 39–42; see also History of the Naval Cryptologic Veterans Association, www.usncva.org/history.shtml.

24. There are actually two sets of kana. Each set contains forty-eight letters. One set is called *hiragana* and the other is called katakana. Generally the former are used to form grammatical endings, while the katakana are used to write in Japanese foreign words that the Japanese have borrowed. Thus the focus here is on katakana. See Len Walsh, *Read Japanese Today* (Charles E. Tuttle, 1969), p. 155. For the Navy's description of katakana, see CNSG History of OP-20-GI-P, RG 38, Box 116, Folder 5750/200, CNSG Library, NARAII.

25. For a description of katakana and the RIP-5 typewriter, see Holtwick, SRH-355, pp. 40–41; Layton et al., *And I Was There*, p. 56; *RIP-5: The Underwood Code Machine* (NCVA Special Publication, 2006), pp. 19–24; Kahn, *Codebreakers*, p. 356; and Budiansky, *Battle of Wits*, pp. 36–37.

26. Holtwick, , SRH-355; Layton et al., *And I Was There*; Budiansky, *Battle of Wits*.

27. Author's interview with Harold Joslin, 5 December 2007. A member of the OTRG class of 1940, Joslin during 1940–41 served as a radioman second class in Guam.

28. Parker, *Pearl Harbor Revisited*, p. 34.

29. American cryptographers read the first complete Japanese diplomatic message conveyed via the Purple machine on 25 September 1940, the work primarily of the Army's Signal Intelligence Service (SIS), directed by civilian cryptanalyst William Friedman. Army-Navy engineers built eight replicas of the machine between that date and the end of 1941. Four were retained in Washington, two by the SIS and two by the Navy's Communications Intelligence Service. Three others were shipped to London, and in April 1941 the eighth to the Philippines. It was installed in the tunnels of Corregidor Island, where Station Cast was based. (The Navy moved Cast's codebreakers from the Cavite Navy Yard, near Manila, to Corregidor in fall 1940 for security purposes.) See Dundas P. Tucker, "Rhapsody in Purple: A New History of Pearl Harbor, Part I," *Cryptologia*, July 1982, p. 198; Ronald Clark, *The Man Who Broke Purple* (Little, Brown, 1977), p. 157; I. C. B. Dear and M. R. D. Foot, eds., *The Oxford Companion to World War II* (Oxford University Press, 1995), pp. 707–8; and Parker, *Pearl Harbor Revisited*, pp. 45–46.

30. Lt. Cdr. Elliott E. Okins, USN (Ret.), *A Personal Account of Comint*, p. 2, RG 38, Box 10, NARAII.

31. Okins, *To Spy or Not to Spy*, p. 95.

32. Parker, *Pearl Harbor Revisited*, p. 35.
33. Capt. Homer L. Kisner, USN (Ret.), oral history, 23 September 1983, p. 20, NCVA. Kisner was also an OTRG graduate.
34. Rochefort oral history, USNI, p. 112.
35. Layton et al., *And I Was There*, pp. 92–93.
36. Memorandum from Rear Adm. R. E. Ingersoll, Acting, Chief of Naval Operations, to Commander in Chief, U.S. Fleet; Commander in Chief, Asiatic Fleet; Commandant, Fourteenth Naval District; Commandant, Sixteenth Naval District, subject: "Cryptanalytical Activities, Status of: 4 October 1940," RG 38, Box 104, NARAII.
37. Parker, *Pearl Harbor Revisited*, pp. 20–21.
38. Untitled memorandum, summary of a five-page memorandum prepared 15 August 1944 by OP-20-G/nmcg tracing history of the Hypo unit based on information collected by Joe Rochefort. The original memo does not show up, but the summary appears in the Rochefort file at the NCVA Library, Pensacola, FL.
39. Comments of Tommy Dyer, quoted in National Security Group History, SRH-355, p. 398.
40. Wright oral history, NSA.
41. Untitled memorandum, summary of a five-page memorandum prepared 15 August 1944 by OP-20-G/nmcg, pp. 3–4, Rochefort file, NCVA Library.
42. Memorandum for Lt. Cdr. John F. Sonnett, USNR, 17 May 1945, from Capt. L. F. Safford, USN, Exhibit No. 151, PHH, Part 18, pp. 3335–38.
43. Capt. Thomas H. Dyer oral history, USNI, pp. 196–97.
44. Wright oral history, NSA, p. 30.
45. Alva B. Red Lasswell to Capt. Roger Pineau, USNR (Ret.), undated letter, William F. Hudson Papers, Box 12, Folder 2, Archives, University of Colorado at Boulder Libraries.
46. Holmes, *Double-Edged Secrets*, p. 20.
47. OP-20-GY monthly report, stamped 1 October 1941, included in "History of OP-20-GYP," RG 38, CNSG Library, Box 115, Folder 5750/198, NARAII.
48. CIS, 16 July–31 December 1941, SRMN-012, pp. 78–83, NHHC.
49. Ibid., p. 116.
50. Ibid., p. 124.

CHAPTER 9: SHADOWING YAMAMOTO

1. Zacharias, *Secret Missions*, pp. 92–97.
2. Layton et al., *And I Was There*, pp. 58–59.
3. Rochefort testimony, PHH, Part 26, p. 217.
4. Ibid.; Rochefort oral history, USNI, p. 169.
5. Stephan Howarth, "Admiral of the Fleet," in *Men of War*, Stephan Howarth, ed. (St. Martin's Press, 1992), pp. 108–28. David C. Evans and Mark R. Peattie, *Kaigun* (Naval Institute Press, 1997), pp. 308–9.
6. Howarth, "Admiral of the Fleet."

7. Biard oral history, USNI, p. 30.

8. Evans and Peattie, *Kaigun*, p. 360.

9. PHH, Part 36, Exhibit 3, pp. 467–69.

10. Ibid. See also Mark Stille and Tony Bryan, *Imperial Japanese Navy Aircraft Carriers* (Osprey, 2005).

11. Telephone interview with Pacific War historian John Lundstrom.

12. CIS, 22 October 1941, PHH, Part 36, pp. 747–48. See also Parker, *Pearl Harbor Revisited*, Appendix C, p. 73.

13. CIS, 1 November 1941, RG 80, Box 41, NARAII.

14. Author's interview with Harold Joslin.

15. CIS, 3 November 1941, RG 80, Box 41, NARAII.

16. Ibid.

17. Evans and Peattie, *Kaigun*, p. 349; see also *The Campaigns of the Pacific*, U.S. Strategic Bombing Survey (Naval Analysis Division, 1946), p. 21.

18. Layton et al., *And I Was There*, p. 174.

19. PHH, Part 36, pp. 467–69.

20. Edwin T. Layton testimony, PHH, Part 10 (Joint Congressional Committee), p. 4834.

21. Joseph J. Rochefort testimony, PHH, Part 23, p. 679.

22. Holmes, *Double-Edged Secrets*, p. 18.

23. CIS, 3 November 1941.

24. Ibid.

25. OPNAV radiogram to CINCPAC, CINCAF, and the commanders of naval districts 11, 12, 13, 14, 15, and 16, 5 November 1941, RG 80, Box 41, NARAII.

26. Greaves-Rochefort interview.

27. For Zacharias' warning about the withdrawal of Japanese merchant ships, see Capt. Ellis M. Zacharias testimony, PHH, Part 7, p. 3245. Precisely what Captain Zacharias said to Admiral Kimmel in their March 1941 conversation has been in dispute since Zacharias' 1946 congressional testimony. He told lawmakers he also warned Kimmel that, if Japan decided to go to war with the United States, "it would begin with an air attack on our fleet on a weekend and probably a Sunday morning . . ." (Zacharias testimony, PHH, Part 7, pp. 3237–44). Kimmel said he remembered the Zacharias conversation, but stated emphatically he received no such warning from Zacharias. Kimmel's version was supported by his chief of staff, Capt. W. W. "Poco" Smith. The Kimmel-Zacharias differences are recounted in Smith's PHH testimony, Part 7, pp. 3256–59.

28. Rochefort oral history, USNI, p. 213.

29. CIS, daily summaries, 3, 6, and 7 November 1941.

30. Rochefort oral history, USNI, pp. 166–67.

31. Yamamoto issued a series of orders on days following the 1 November order. Translations vary, but it's clear X-day was to be the attack on Pearl Harbor and Y-day, X-day minus 16, when ships would depart the Kuriles for Pearl

Harbor. Y-day turned out to be 25 November (Hawaii time). For an interpretation of Y-day see Prados, *Combined Fleet Decoded*, p. 159. For a copy of the 5 November order see PHH, Part 13, pp. 713–17. Copy of the 1 November order is from the Papers of Philip H. Jacobsen, author's files.

32. Interview with Susumi Ishiguro, conducted by Gordon W. Prange, 6 April 1948, Papers of Gordon W. Prange, Accession 2002–78, Box 19, Manuscript Collection, University of Maryland Library, College Park. The author is indebted to Pacific War historian J. Michael Wenger for transcripts of the Ishiguro-Prange interview.

33. For an authoritative study of Yamamoto's radio silence policy, see Philip H. Jacobsen, "Radio Silence and Radio Deception: Secrecy Insurance for the Pearl Harbor Strike Force," in *Intelligence and National Security*, winter 2004, pp. 695–718.

34. Ishiguro-Prange interview; see also Jacobsen, "Radio Silence and Radio Deception."

35. CIS, 9 and 10 November 1941; see also Prange et al., *At Dawn We Slept*, p. 338.

36. Ishiguro-Prange interview; Jacobsen, "Radio Silence and Radio Deception," pp. 695–718.

37. Letter to author from Japanese navy Capt. Noritaka Kitazawa (Ret.), researcher at the National Institute for Defense Studies in Tokyo. The author is grateful to Captain Kitazawa for his considerable assistance, which included Special Duty War Fleet Act Chart Part 2, charting the movements of the *Settsu* from 1 May 1941 through 23 December 1941 (author's files). The author is also indebted to Rika Seya of George Washington University for her translation of this material, and to American historian Jon Parshall for putting him in touch with Captain Kitazawa.

38. Ishiguro-Prange interview; Jacobsen, "Radio Silence and Radio Deception," pp. 695–718.

39. Donald M. Goldstein and Katherine V. Dillon, eds., *Fading Victory: The Diary of Matome Ugaki, 1941–1945*, Masataka Chihaya, trans. (University of Pittsburgh Press, 1991), p. 29.

40. From undated notes of 1963 David Kahn interview with Capt. Thomas Dyer, Dyer Papers, courtesy of Ann L. Dyer (daughter of Thomas Dyer).

41. Jacobsen, "Radio Silence and Radio Deception," pp. 695–718.

42. CIS, daily summaries, 12, 14, 17, 18, 24 November 1941.

43. Ibid., 20–21 November 1941; 23 November 1941.

44. Ibid., 23 November 1941.

45. Ibid., 25 November 1941.

46. Ibid., 19 November 1941.

47. Station Hypo communication intelligence summary and chronology of OPNAV dispatches to CINCAF, CINCPAC, naval district commandants, RG 80, Box 41, NARAII.

48. Layton testimony, PHH, Part 26, p. 230.

49. COM 14, 260110, November 1941, to OPNAV, Info: CINCPAC, CINCAF, COM 16, No. 197, Communications Intelligence Reports, Japanese Navy: Organization of Fleets, "The 'Magic' Background of Pearl Harbor," vol. 4, Appendix, p. A-106, Navy Department Library, NHHC. Copy of original in Rochefort Papers, author's files.

50. Holmes, *Double-Edged Secrets*, p. 26.

51. COM 16, 261331, 27 November 1941, to CINCPAC, COM 14, OPNAV, CINCAF, No. 198, Japanese Navy: Organization of Fleets, "The 'Magic' Background of Pearl Harbor," vol. 4, Appendix, p. A-107.

CHAPTER 10: ENCOUNTER WITH KIMMEL

1. PHH, Part 6, pp. 2814–15.

2. Memorandum from Capt. Laurance Safford to Admiral Stark, cited in Safford memo to John F. Sonnett, counsel to Hewitt Inquiry, 17 May 1945, PHH, Part 18, Exhibit No. 151, pp. 3335–36.

3. Ibid.

4. Layton oral history, NSA, p. 90.

5. CIS, COM 14, RG 80, Box 41, NARAII. Gordon Prange identified Turner as the author of the war-warning dispatch. See Prange et al., *At Dawn We Slept*, p. 406.

6. *Oxford Companion to World War II*, p. 928.

7. Gordon W. Prange, with Donald M. Goldstein and Katherine V. Dillon, *Pearl Harbor: The Verdict of History* (McGraw-Hill, 1986), pp. 291, 428–29.

8. *Lucky Bag*, 1912 Naval Academy yearbook, p. 168, Navy Department Library, NHHC.

9. Rochefort-Prange interview.

10. Rochefort oral history, USNI, p. 210.

11. Prange et al., *Pearl Harbor: The Verdict*, p. 651; see also Layton's testimony describing Kimmel's 27 November staff meeting, PHH, Part 10, pp. 4862–63.

12. Testimony of Vice Adm. William Ward Smith, PHH, Part 7, p. 3361.

13. Testimony of Capt. Charles Horatio McMorris, PHH, Part 22, pp. 526–27.

14. Layton et al., *And I Was There*, p. 169.

15. Prange et al., *At Dawn We Slept*, p. 406; see also PHH, Part 7, pp. 3026–27.

16. Holmes, *Double-Edged Secrets*, p. 25.

17. Greaves-Rochefort interview.

18. Gordon W. Prange, "A Portrait of Admiral Kimmel and His Staff on Oahu in 1941," Prange Papers, Box 33, University of Maryland, Manuscript Division. This essay, based on Prange's interviews with Kimmel and his closest advisers, provides the foundation for Prange's description of Kimmel that appears in *At Dawn We Slept* and *Pearl Harbor: The Verdict of History*.

19. Prange, "A Portrait." See also Vice Adm. George C. Dyer oral history, USNI, pp. 215–16. Dyer's comment: "His wife's absence provided Admiral Kimmel with an excuse, in my opinion, for not doing his job properly . . . It was a fun-

damental error. He should have brought his wife out there and put her to work on other wives. Having her back in the states was just no good at all."

20. Layton oral history, USNI, p. 68.
21. Alan Schom states in *The Eagle and the Rising Sun*: "Kimmel, along with Claude Bloch, disappeared behind the door of Commander Rochefort's office" (p. 123). However, Rochefort had no private office.
22. Rochefort testified before the Hewitt Inquiry that his meeting with Kimmel followed the admiral's receipt of the war warning message from Washington. He said he had learned of the message by the time of the meeting. See PHH, Part 36, p. 34.
23. Rochefort, testimony, PHH, Part 26, p. 216.
24. Prange interview with Vice Adm. William W. Poco Smith, USN (Ret.), November 14, 1962, Prange Papers, Box 23.
25. Rochefort oral history, USNI, p. 148.
26. Rochefort-Prange interview.
27. Rochefort testimony, PHH, Part 10, p. 4694.
28. CIS, 27 November 1941, RG 80, Box 41, NARAII.
29. Rochefort testimony, PHH, Part 28, p. 870.
30. Ibid., Part 10 , p. 4702.
31. Ibid., Part 36 , p. 33.
32. Layton testimony, PHH, Part 10, p. 4836.
33. Rochefort testimony, PHH, Part 26, p. 217.
34. Rochefort-Prange interview. Asked by interrogators at the Army Pearl Harbor Board whether he regarded the Japanese force gathering in the Marshalls as a threat to Hawaii, Rochefort answered, "Personally, no sir." See PHH, Part 28, p. 871.
35. Rochefort testimony, PHH, Part 28, p. 871.
36. CIS, 27 November 1941.
37. Ibid.
38. Rochefort-Prange interview.
39. Layton testimony, PHH, Part 26, p. 237.
40. Rochefort oral history, USNI, p. 115.
41. Ambassador Kurusu arrived in Washington from Tokyo on 15 November 1941 to assist Nomura in his negotiations with Secretary of State Hull. See "The 'Magic' Background of Pearl Harbor: From Tokyo to Washington," vol. 4, item 61, p. 47.
42. Prange et al., *At Dawn We Slept*, p. 82.
43. "The 'Magic' Background of Pearl Harbor," Message No. 812, 22 November 1941, vol. 4, Appendix, p. A-89.
44. Kahn, *Codebreakers*, pp. 11–12.
45. Holmes, *Double-Edged Secrets*, p. 49.
46. Rochefort-Prange interview.
47. Rochefort testimony, PHH, Part 10 , pp. 4697–98.

48. Rochefort oral history, USNI, p. 159.
49. The 24 September 1941 Bomb Plot message from Teijiro Toyoda to Nagao Kita read as follows (from PHH, Part 12, p. 261):

> Strictly secret. Henceforth, we would like to have you make reports concerning vessels along the following insofar as possible:
> 1. The waters (of Pearl Harbor) are to be divided roughly into five sub-areas. (We have no objections to your abbreviating as much as you like.)
>   Area A. Waters between Ford Island and the Arsenal.
>   Area B. Waters adjacent to the Island south and west of Ford Island.
>   (This area is on the opposite side of the Island from Area A.)
>   Area C. East Loch.
>   Area D. Middle Loch.
>   Area E. West Loch and the communicating water routes.
> 2. With regard to warships and aircraft carriers, we would like to have you report on those at anchor (these are not so important), tied up at wharves, buoys, and in docks. (Designate types of and classes briefly. If possible we would like to have you make mention of the fact when there are two or more vessels along side the same wharf.)

50. Pacific war historian Robert Hanyok informed the author that no grids resembling that called for by the Bomb Plot message turned up in the cockpits of any of the downed Japanese planes on 7 December, suggesting that material was not intended for use by *kido butai* pilots.
51. Rochefort testimony, PHH, Part 10, p. 4674.
52. Layton et al., *And I Was There*, pp. 163–65.
53. Prange et al., *At Dawn We Slept*, pp. 249–55.
54. Ibid.
55. Barnes-Rochefort interview.
56. Ibid. Rochefort softened his view of Purple's importance in 1969 when he said only that if Pearl had possessed such a machine, "I am sure that at least Layton and myself could have made a better evaluation of the significance of that traffic than the people in Washington apparently made" (Rochefort oral history, USNI, p. 160).
57. Stephan Budiansky, "Too Late for Pearl Harbor," U.S. Naval Institute *Proceedings*, December 1999, pp. 47–51.
58. From September 1945 to May 1946, the Navy Department decrypted 26,581 Imperial Navy dispatches encrypted in JN-25(b), that had been intercepted at Hypo, Cast, Negat, and Guam between September 1941 and 4 December 1941. Of those, 2,413 were considered by the Office of the Chief of Naval Operations to be of sufficient interest for translation; 188 are reprinted in "Pre-Pearl Harbor Japanese Naval Despatches," Appendix 1, prepared by the CNO, SRH-406, Navy Department Library, NHHC. See also Parker's *Pearl*

Harbor Revisited, pp. 43–49. No evidence emerged that any of the JN-25(b) intercepts had been decrypted prior to the Pearl Harbor attack.

59. "Pre-Pearl Harbor Japanese Naval Despatches," SRH-406, p. 11.

60. Ibid., p. 63.

61. "A minimum depth of 75 feet may be assumed necessary to successfully drop torpedoes from planes," 15 February 1941 letter from CNO Adm. Harold Stark to Adm. Husband Kimmel, cited by Kimmel in Proceedings of the Joint Committee, PHH, Part 6, p. 2508.

62. "Pre–Pearl Harbor Japanese Naval Despatches," SRH-406, p. 16.

CHAPTER 11: ILL WIND

1. Memorandum from Tokyo to Washington, No. 148, 19 November 1941, circular 2353, trans. 28 November 1941, "The 'Magic' Background of Pearl Harbor," vol. 5, Part D: Special Studies, p. 51. See also vol. 4, Appendix, p. A-81, Navy Department Library, NHHC.

2. Memorandum from Tokyo to Washington, No. 162, 22 November 1941, 812, trans. 22 November 1941, "The 'Magic' Background of Pearl Harbor," vol. 4, Appendix, p. A-89.

3. Layton, et al., *And I Was There*, p. 219.

4. Biard oral history, USNI, p. 524.

5. Ibid., pp. 537–38.

6. Rochefort testimony, PHH, Part 10, p. 4700.

7. Ibid., Part 26, p. 216.

8. Layton testimony, PHH, Part 26, p. 234.

9. CIS, 30 November 1941.

10. Ibid.

11. Jacobsen, "Radio Silence and Radio Deception," pp. 700–701. Jacobsen noted that Station Cast also reported hearing a call sign purporting to represent the *Akagi* on 4 December, nine days after striking force call signs were changed. Use of the old call sign "was positively due to continued radio deception activity from Kure," Jacobsen wrote.

12. Rochefort testimony, PHH, Part 10, p. 4680.

13. CIS, 2 December 1941.

14. Combat Intelligence Unit message file, originator OPNAV 290110, priority message to CINCPAC, RG 80, Box 41, NARAII.

15. Layton oral history, USNI, pp. 87–89; Layton et al., *And I Was There*, p. 237–44.

16. CIS, 1 December 1941.

17. Memorandum from Fleet Intelligence Officer to Admiral, 1 December 1941, subject: "Orange Fleet: Location of." This memo by Layton was attached to his Memorandum to the Commission, submitted by Layton to the Roberts Commission on 5 January 1942 (RG 80, Box 41, NARAII).

18. Layton testimony, PHH, Part 36, pp. 127–28.
19. Kimmel testified before the Joint Congressional Committee: "The failure to identify Japanese carrier traffic, on and after December 1st when the call signs were changed, was not an unusual condition . . . As to the carriers, during the six months preceding Pearl Harbor, there existed a total of 134 days—in twelve separate periods—each ranging from nine to 22 days, when the location of the Japanese carriers from radio traffic analysis was uncertain" (Joint Committee, Part 6, p. 2523).
20. Rochefort testimony, PHH, Part 26, p. 216.
21. Memorandum for the Roberts Commission, prepared by Lt. Cdr. Edwin Layton, submitted 5 January 1942, RG 80, Box 41, NARAII.
22. CIS, 1 and 2 December 1941, RG 80, Box 41, NARAII.
23. CIS, 2 December 1941; see also Layton et al., *And I Was There*, pp. 229–30.
24. Layton et al., *And I Was There*, pp. 229–30; see also Prados, *Combined Fleet Decoded*, p. 177.
25. Holcomb oral history, NSG.
26. Combat Intelligence Unit message file, OPNAV to COM 16, CINCPAC, COM 14, CINCAF, message 031850, 3 December 1941, RG 80, Box 41, NARAII.
27. Testimony of Adm. Richmond Kelly Turner, *Report of the Joint Committee on the Investigation of the Pearl Harbor Attack*, p. 206.
28. Rochefort testimony, PHH, Part 10, p. 4784.
29. Layton et al., *And I Was There*, p. 250.
30. Kimmel testimony, PHH, Part 6, p. 2764.
31. Henry C. Clausen and Bruce Lee, *Pearl Harbor: Final Judgment* (Da Capo Press, 1992), pp. 303–5.
32. Layton et al., *And I Was There*. Layton died early in the writing of his memoir. Most of the book was written by his coauthors, historian John Costello and Capt. Roger Pineau, USNR (Ret.), using extensive notes from Layton's files.
33. Kimmel told Congress in 1946 he dismissed the radiogram because of the way it was worded. If "the Navy Department had considered [this news] of such vital importance as they now say they do, they should have taken the precaution to tell me to give this message to General Short" (Part 6, p. 2764). Four years earlier at the Roberts panel, Kimmel admitted his mistake with regard to the code burning: The "codes burned from time to time, and in a time of tension like this we receive a great many scary reports . . . I didn't draw the proper answer, I admit that. I admit that I was wrong" (PHH, Part 22, p. 379).
34. Layton testimony, PHH, Part 36, p. 137.
35. Affidavit of Robert L. Shivers, signed 16 March 1945, Clausen Investigation, PHH, Part 35, pp. 43–44; see also Part 9, pp. 4360–61.
36. Layton testimony, Part 36, p. 137; see also affidavit of Capt. Edwin T. Layton, PHH, Part 9, pp. 4370–71.

37. Clausen Investigation, PHH.

38. Layton testimony, Part 36, p. 137, PHH. See also Layton et al., *And I Was There*, p. 250.

39. Affidavit of Brig. Gen. Kendall J. Fielder, signed 11 May 1945, Clausen Investigation, PHH, Part 9, p. 4355–56; see also Part 39, pp. 274–75.

40. Affidavit of Col. George Bicknell, signed 25 February 1945, Clausen Investigation, PHH, Part 35, pp. 30–31; see also Part 9, p. 4346.

41. Affidavit of Capt. Joseph Rochefort, signed 20 February 1945, Clausen Investigation, PHH, Part 35, p. 26–27.

42. Clausen and Lee, *Pearl Harbor*, pp. 301–3.

43. Rochefort testimony, PHH, Part 10, pp. 4675–98.

44. Ibid.

45. Affidavit of Brig. Gen. Kendall J. Fielder, signed 11 May 1945, Clausen Investigation, PHH, Part 9, p. 4355–56.

46. Ibid.

47. In *The Ultra-Magic Deals* (Airlife, England, 1993), World War II historian Bradley F. Smith points out: "It was not until 1 February 1942, seven weeks after the Japanese attack, that the American army command in Hawaii finally established a liaison arrangement with its naval counterpart regarding cryptanalytic information matters" (p. 85).

48. PHH, Part 3, p. 1445.

49. Bratton testimony, PHH, Part 9, p. 4596.

50. Rochefort was not ONI's man in Hawaii. As officer in charge of Station Hypo, he was responsible, administratively, to Fourteenth Naval District Commandant Bloch, and in Washington to OP-20-G's Safford, who reported to the director of naval communications, Rear Adm. Leigh Noyes. ONI supplied linguists to one subsection of OP-20-G: OP-20-GZ. The arrangement gave ONI some voice in OP-20-G activity, but OP-20-G was primarily the responsibility of naval communications.

51. Proceedings of the Clarke Investigation, PHH, Part 34, p. 126.

52. Clausen and Lee, *Pearl Harbor*, p. 95.

53. Affidavit of Col. George Bicknell, signed 25 February 1945, Clausen Investigation, PHH, Part 35, pp. 30–31.

54. Despite claims by OP-20-G's Laurance Safford during and after the war, no "winds" execute message was broadcast before 7 December 1941, according to NSA historians Robert Hanyok and David P. Mowry. Their study of Japanese radio traffic did show that one execute message was sent, but on 7 December, six to seven hours after the attack on Pearl Harbor. The dispatch included the phrase "west wind clear," indicating war against Great Britain. For what is probably the definitive account of Safford's strange crusade, and for details surrounding the Navy's quest for the winds message, see Hanyok and Mowry's monograph *West Wind Clear: Cryptology and the Winds Mes-*

sage Controversy: A Documentary History (Center for Cryptologic History, NSA 2008), p. 88.

55. Rochefort testimony, PHH, Part 10, p. 4702.

CHAPTER 12: COMEDY OF ERRORS

1. Note from Lt. (jg) Yale Maxon, Fourteenth Naval District Intelligence Office, to Lt. Cdr. (sic) Rochefort, District Communications Office, 2 December 1941, Dyer Papers.

2. Rochefort testimony, PHH, Part 10, p. 4701.

3. "If we could have solved the Flag Officers System, Admiral Kimmel would probably have known of the Japanese plans and the Pacific Fleet would not have been surprised on December 7, 1941": Capt. Laurance Safford to Hewitt counsel, Lt. Cdr. John F. Sonnett, USNR, Exhibit No. 151, PHH, Part 18, p. 3335.

4. Rochefort testimony, PHH, Part 10, p. 4696. See also Layton et al., *And I Was There*, p. 245.

5. Hanyok and Mowry, *West Wind Clear*, p. 24; see also Kahn, *Codebreakers*, pp. 15–18.

6. For the Washington perspective of the U.S. Army's G-2 and U.S. Navy's intelligence analysts with regard to Hawaii's consular traffic, see Prange et al., *At Dawn We Slept*, pp. 248–51.

7. PHH, Part 12, Exhibits of the Joint Committee, pp. 260–71.

8. Holmes, *Double-Edged Secrets*, p. 38. Captain Mayfield's assistant, Lt. Donald Woodrum, supported Holmes' impression that it was Bloch who intervened with Sarnoff to produce the cables from the Japanese consulate: "It is my understanding that Admiral Bloch requested David Sarnoff, who was visiting in the islands at the time, to make available to the naval service copies of messages handled by RCA Radio. Sarnoff agreed and ordered the local office to do this." See PHH, Part 36, p. 224.

9. Pearl Harbor investigators Henry Clausen and Bruce Lee faulted Rochefort for failing to realize the significance of the fact that the Japanese consulate could communicate with Tokyo only via two low-level codes (PA-K2 and LA). There is some merit to that criticism, but none in their judgment that if Rochefort had cracked that traffic it would have unambiguously revealed Pearl Harbor as a target. Leaving aside the cable traffic from Saturday 6 December that Rochefort didn't get, there was no mention of Pearl Harbor as a target in the cable traffic he did receive from Captain Mayfield on Thursday or Friday. See Clausen and Lee, *Pearl Harbor*, pp. 306–7.

10. Rochefort testimony, Part 10, p. 4708; Part 23, p. 686.

11. Ibid., Part 23, p. 673. See also Rochefort's testimony before the Army Pearl Harbor Board, in which he restated his belief that obtaining the consulate's cables from RCA was against the law (Part 28, p. 865).

12. Rochefort on 16 February 1946 told the Joint Congressional Committee that he received Mayfield's batch of Japanese consulate cables "on the night of the 3rd or the morning of the 4th" (Part 10, pp. 4677, 4708). He told the Roberts Commission, meeting in January 1942, that the material was forwarded "either Thursday night, the 4th of December, or Friday, the 5th of December. I believe it was during the night, sir" (Part 23, p. 673).

13. In a memorandum to the Roberts Commission dated 2 January 1942, Captain Mayfield stated that messages were received from the communication company and delivered via messenger to Rochefort's office on either 4 or 5 December 1941. See Proceedings of the Roberts Commission, Part 23, p. 692. In testimony before the Hewitt Inquiry on 4 July 1945, Mayfield stated: "I called personally at the office of RCA at the beginning of the forenoon, late forenoon, and received from the manager a blank envelope containing copies of these messages. To the best of my recollection my first visit was about the 3rd of December. The envelope I received contained plain sheets of paper with the messages written thereon. I immediately forwarded these messages by officer messenger to Commander Rochefort. As I did not keep a written record of receipt and delivery of these messages, I am unable to give exact dates of receipts and deliveries to Commander Rochefort" (Part 36, p. 331).

14. Lieutenant Woodrum testified before the Hewitt Inquiry: "On the morning of 5 December the District Intelligence Office received the first copies of these [consulate] cables, and it is my understanding that these were immediately sent to Commander Rochefort's unit" (Part 36, p. 224).

15. Testimony of Lieutenant Farnsley Woodward, PHH, Part 36, p. 320.

16. Cable from Tokyo (Togo) to Honolulu, 2 December 1941, J-19, No. 123, Army 27065, JD 8007 (Japanese). See Exhibits of the Joint Committee, Part 12, p. 266. This message was also collected by the Army's MS-5 intercept unit at Fort Shafter and flown to the U.S. mainland by Pan Am Clipper. It arrived in Washington on 23 December and was translated by the Army on 30 December.

17. Woodward's signature can be seen affixed to the following LA-encrypted cables: items 154, 155, 156, Exhibit 56, PHH, Part 38.

18. Woodward testimony, PHH, Part 36, pp. 350–51.

19. Reports and conclusions, PHH, Part 39, p. 453.

20. Rochefort testimony, Part 10, p. 4677.

21. Kahn, *Codebreakers*, p. 48.

22. Among these were items 247 and 248, Exhibit 56, Part 12, pp. 268–69. The first was a 3 December message reporting a U.S. military transport sailing out of Pearl Harbor toward the U.S. mainland; the second was a 3 December message noting that a battleship (misidentified as the USS *Wyoming*) and two seaplane tenders had departed Pearl Harbor. Both messages were among several translated on 10 December by Hypo linguist Alva Red Lasswell.

23. Capt. Thomas H. Dyer oral history, USNI, p. 204. Dyer's impression that Woodward received no substantive help from any other codebreaker was supported by the recollection of Hypo cryptanalyst Wesley Ham Wright, who testified: "Woodward, I believe, did all the decryption with some clerical assistance" (PHH, Part 36, p. 263).

24. Woodward testimony, PHH, Part 36, p. 320.

25. Rochefort testimony, PHH, Part 26, p. 214.

26. Ibid., Part 23, p. 674.

27. Memorandum from Honolulu (Kita) to Tokyo, 3 December 1941, PA-K2, No. 245, Trans. 11 December 1941. Exhibits of the Joint Committee, Part 12, pp. 267–68. This message was also picked up by the Army at its Fort Hunt, Virginia, intercept site and turned over to OP-20-GZ for translation. The dispatch was partially translated on Saturday 6 December 1941 by a newly hired linguist, Mrs. Dorothy Edgers, who thought it important enough to bring to the attention of her supervisor, Lt. Cdr. Alwin D. Kramer. He thought it was not of "sufficient importance" to require her continued effort on Saturday; he suggested she finish the translation on Monday. "The lights message did not get the attention it warranted from Kramer because it was in a low-grade PA-K2 consular cipher," wrote Layton in Layton et al., *And I Was There* (pp. 281–83).

28. Layton et al., *And I Was There*, p. 245.

29. Joseph C. Harsch, "A War Correspondent's Odyssey," in *Air Raid: Pearl Harbor!* Paul Stillwell, ed. (Naval Institute Press, 1981), p. 264.

30. CIS, 5 December 1941, RG 80, Box 41, NARAII.

31. Ibid.

32. Layton oral history, USNI, pp. 74–75.

33. Layton et al., *And I Was There*, pp. 274–75.

34. Author's telephone phone interview with John Lundstrom.

35. Rochefort testimony, Part 23, p. 679; Part 10, p. 4689.

36. Secret naval message, COM 14 to OPNAV, 6 December 1941, Rochefort Papers.

37. Layton et al., *And I Was There*, pp. 274–75.

38. I am indebted for this information about the role of officers in determining the priority status of messages to CTRCM Chief John A. Gustafson, USN (Ret.), now membership secretary with the Naval Cryptologic Veterans Association. Author's interview, Pensacola, FL.

39. Layton et al., *And I Was There*, pp. 274–75.

40. Rochefort testimony, Part 23, p. 686.

41. Rochefort-Prange interview.

42. Rochefort testimony, PHH, Part 28, p. 867.

43. Rochefort-Prange interview.

44. Robert B. Stinnett, *Day of Deceit* (Free Press, 2000), pp. 214–16.

45. Station H Chronology, 6 December 1941, RG 38, Box 10, NARAII.

46. Exhibits of the Joint Committee, PHH, Part 12, p. 261.
47. *The Honolulu Advertiser*, 6 December 1941.
48. Rochefort testimony, Part 10, p. 4709.
49. Associated Press article, the *Honolulu Star-Bulletin*, 27 November 1941.
50. "[How] could the Japanese have done [all] this and still remain the great power? There was no way for them to go" (Rochefort oral history, USNI, pp. 68–69).
51. Rochefort testimony, Part 23, p. 687.

CHAPTER 13: AIR RAID PEARL HARBOR!

1. On duty elsewhere were the Pacific Fleet carriers *Lexington, Enterprise,* and *Saratoga.* After seeing the first Japanese bomb fall on Ford Island, Lt. Cdr. Logan Ramsey ordered the radioman at the Ford Island Command Center to send out the following message: "Air raid, Pearl Harbor. This is *no* drill." The clock read 7:58 a.m.
2. Prange et al., *At Dawn We Slept,* pp. 490, 501–2.
3. Tommy Dyer letter to Robert Stinnett, 7 October 1983, Dyer Papers.
4. "War Diary of Fourteenth Naval District for Period 7 December to 1 January," Hewitt Inquiry, Part 37, pp. 1266–76. See also Gordon W. Prange, with Donald M. Goldstein and Katherine V. Dillon, *December 7, 1941: The Day the Japanese Attacked Pearl Harbor* (McGraw Hill, 1988), pp. 92–93, 100–114.
5. Prange et al., *At Dawn We Slept,* pp. 499–501.
6. Rochefort-Prange interview. See also Prange et al., *December 7, 1941,* p. 107.
7. The whereabouts of these officers on Sunday 7 December 1941 are documented by their oral histories. See Capt. Thomas H. Dyer oral history, USNI, pp. 217–19; Wright oral history, NSA, pp. 18–19; and Lasswell oral history, USMC.
8. Author's interview with Michael Palchefsky, Laurel, MD.
9. Ibid.
10. Wright oral history, NSA.
11. Capt. Thomas H. Dyer oral history, USNI, p. 219.
12. Forrest Tex Biard letter to John Roenigk, 8 February 1981, Pineau Collection, Box 7, Folder 29, Archives, University of Colorado at Boulder Libraries.
13. Holmes, *Double-Edged Secrets,* pp. 1–3.
14. Layton oral history, USNI, pp. 91–95.
15. Rochefort testimony, PHH, Part 10, p. 4688.
16. Holmes, *Double-Edged Secrets.*
17. Rochefort-Prange interview.
18. Holmes, *Double-Edged Secrets.*
19. Rochefort oral history, USNI, pp. 112–13.
20. Author's interview with Andy Cooper, 16 September 2004, NCVA reunion, Charleston, SC. Cooper died 3 December 2007. See "The Journey of Andy Cooper 1918–2007," by his wife, Nancy Cooper, *NCVA Cryptolog,* summer

2008. She wrote: "On the morning of 7 December 1941, Andy was on duty at the CXK. Was he able to detect enemy messages? No! Why? Because someone had ordered all power to this equipment to be shut off. Unable to carry out his duties, Andy passed the time on that watch by writing Christmas cards. Many a time in later years, he commented on the mysterious turn of events, but never heard or read an explanation."

21. Rochefort oral history, USNI, pp. 112–13.

22. Layton et al., *And I Was There*, p. 317.

23. After action memo, "Air Raid Attack by Japanese, Report on," from District Communication Officer to Commandant, Fourteenth Naval District, 18 December 1941, RG 181, Box 2, Accession 68, NARA, Pacific Region, San Bruno, CA.

24. Rochefort testimony, Roberts Commission, Part 23, pp. 682–83; see also COM 14 radio log for 7 December 1941, titled "Radio Bearings Received from Fourteenth Naval District," Pearl Harbor Liaison Office, RG 80, Box 41, NARAII.

25. Rochefort testimony, Roberts Commission, pp. 682–83; COM 14 radio log for 7 December 1941, RG 80, Box 41, NARAII. Rochefort told the Roberts Panel: "About 10:30 Sunday morning we received one bearing from our radio station at Heeia . . . We couldn't reach [Lualualei] through any communication, so we had to use the station at Heeia, which is a radio direction finder that can give only a reciprocal" (PHH, Part 23, p. 683). The COM 14 operator's log supports Rochefort's testimony with this entry for 7 December: "1040 LCT YUNE 8 bearing (bilateral) 357 degrees or 178 degrees T from Heeia. YUNE 8 is COMCARDIVS (AKAGI)."

26. Asked years later whether he had gotten any useful intelligence from his DF net, Rochefort answered dismissively, "I didn't get anything from Dutch Harbor and Samoa." Rochefort testimony, PHH, Part 28, p. 868.

27. Interview with Rear Adm. Edwin T. Layton by John Costello and Roger Pineau, 11 May 1983, Edwin T. Layton Papers, Box 30, Folder 1, NWC.

28. Skipper Steely, "Attacking Pearl Harbor: Time and Again Mock Exercises Were Successful," *flightjournal.com*, December 2008, pp. 81–82.

29. Kimmel testimony, PHH, Part 6, pp. 2601–3.

30. Testimony of Vice Adm. William Ward Smith, PHH, Part 7, pp. 3357–58.

31. Ibid.

32. Layton told Congress in 1946: "This plane-guard destroyer division, it later turned out, had been detached from the carriers and had gone to Mandates to reinforce the Mandate Fleet. The deduction was right at the time but incorrect in fact." Layton testimony, Part 10, p. 4836.

33. Smith testimony, PHH, Part 7, pp. 3357–58.

34. Hewitt Inquiry Exhibit No. 71, U.S. Naval Communication Service, CINCPAC and CINCPOA, from CINCPAC to Minneapolis, info to COMTASKFORCE 8, Msg. 072230, Part 37, pp. 1208–9.

35. William F. Halsey and J. Bryan III, *Admiral Halsey's Story* (Zenger, 1947), pp. 77–81.
36. Hewitt Inquiry Exhibit No. 71, U.S. Naval Communication Service.
37. Hewitt Inquiry Exhibit No. 67, U.S. Pacific Fleet Radio Unit, "Record Telephone Communications In and Out," 7 December 1941, Part 37, p. 1145.
38. Author's interview with Janet Rochefort Elerding.
39. Tommy Dyer said his wife didn't find out until the late 1960s that her husband was a cryptanalyst. "She knew I had something to do with communications and that's about all. Maybe I was operating a key and sending Morse." Capt. Thomas H. Dyer oral history, USNI, pp. 207–8.
40. Elerding interview.
41. Capt. Gilven M. Slonim, USN (Ret.), "Have We Learned the Lesson of Pearl Harbor?" *Navy Magazine*, December 1966, pp. 12–15.
42. Layton et al., *And I Was There*, p. 317.
43. Lasswell oral history, USMC, pp. 30–38.
44. Testimony of Rear Adm. Arthur C. Davis, Assistant Chief of Staff for Operations to the Commander in Chief, U.S. Fleet, served as Fleet Aviation Officer on the staff of Fleet Commander Husband Kimmel in December 1941, PHH, Part 26, p. 110.
45. Layton oral history, USNI, p. 93.
46. Smith testimony, PHH, Part 36, p. 564.
47. Rochefort testimony, PHH, Part 23, p. 683.
48. Wright interview with Costello and Pineau, NWC.
49. Testimony of Col. George W. Bicknell, PHH, Part 22, p. 192.
50. Hewitt Inquiry, Kita messages, PHH, Part 37, p. 999.
51. Holmes, *Double-Edged Secrets*, p. 37.
52. Capt. Joseph Finnegan, USN (Ret.), oral history, 20 July–11 October 1969, obtained from NSA through the Freedom of Information Act. Transcript, session No. 6. Comprising eleven volumes of taped interviews and written manuscripts, Finnegan's history was prepared during his tour of duty with the Navy History Division between 20 July and 22 November 1969. The volumes are now under the jurisdiction of the NSA.
53. PHH, Exhibits of the Joint Committee, Part 12, p. 269.
54. Finnegan oral history, NSA.

CHAPTER 14: THE LONG WAIT FOR JN-25(b)
1. "The History of GYP-1," RG 38, CNSG Library, Box 116, 5750/202, p. 28, NARAII.
2. Rochefort oral history, USNI, p. 117.
3. Tucker, "Rhapsody in Purple," *Cryptologia*, pp. 220–27.
4. Layton et al., *And I Was There*, p. 231.
5. Parker, *Pearl Harbor Revisited*, pp. 42–45.
6. Layton et al., *And I Was There*, p. 231.

7. Ibid., p. 95.

8. Writer Robert B. Stinnett asserted that Rochefort's testimony that Station Hypo was assigned to work on the Flag Officers' Code rather than JN-25 "appears to be a cover story," presumably to obscure Hypo's alleged success against JN-25(b); see Stinnett's *Day of Deceit*, pp. 81–82, 347. The author believes Stinnett's contention to be groundless. Testifying under oath on 16 February 1946, Rochefort told Congress: "We were specifically told to keep away or not to exploit the so-called five-number system, which was a naval system [renamed during the war JN-25]. That was being done elsewhere" (Part 10, PHH, p. 4697).

9. OP-20-GY monthly reports for October, November, December, stamped 1 January 1942, included in "History of OP-20-GYP," RG 38, CNSG Library, Box 115, 5750/198. For an excellent summary of the Navy's limited success against JN-25(b), see Budiansky, "Too Late for Pearl Harbor," *Proceedings*, pp. 47–51.

10. Letter from Capt. Laurance F. Safford, USN (Ret.), to Percy Greaves Jr., 10 April 1963, Laurance Frye Safford Collection, Accession No. 1357, Box 1, Greaves Folder, American Heritage Center, University of Wyoming.

11. "The Activities and Accomplishments of GY-I During 1941, 1942, 1943," in "History of OP-20-GY," RG 38, CNSG Library, Box 115, 5750/197, pp. 7–8.

12. "The Baker Ciphers before Pearl Harbor," chap. 2 of "The History of GYP-1," RG 38, CNSG Library, Box 116, 5750/202, pp. 25–26. Pacific War historian Robert Hanyok informed the author that the Japanese used a separate system to encode ship movements, not JN-25(b), a point that further weakens the case that messages encrypted in JN-25(b) were being routinely read.

13. Testimony of Lt. Cdr. Rudolph J. Fabian, 17 May 1945, PHH, Part 36, p. 48. Fabian was a lieutenant in 1942 and 1943, the time period covered by this volume.

14. Rochefort's testimony that the Navy could handle only about 10 percent of intercepted traffic (Part 10, PHH, p. 4674, 4678).

15. Budiansky, "Too Late for Pearl Harbor," *Proceedings*.

16. Layton et al., *And I Was There*, pp. 339–40.

17. "The Baker Ciphers," chap. 2 of "The History of GYP-1," RG 38, CNSG Library, Box 116, 5750/202, p. 52.

18. Rochefort oral history, USNI, p. 119.

19. Ibid., p. 144.

20. For helpful descriptions of the JN-25(b) code, see Fred B. Wrixon, *Codes, Ciphers, Secrets and Cryptic Communication* (Black Dog and Levanthal, 1998), pp. 370–71. See also Geoffrey Sinclair, *JN-25, Operational Code of the Imperial Japanese Navy* (2004), a useful monograph based on four Navy histories from RG 38: 5750/197 (Box 115); 5750/198 (Box 115); 5750/199 (2 of 3, Box 116); 5750/202 (Box 116). For other descriptions of this code,

see Kahn, *Codebreakers*, pp. 7, 10, 564, 565, 567; and Budiansky, *Battle of Wits*, pp. 3, 6–9, 12, 216–18.

21. Tommy Dyer letter to David Kahn, 27 December 1963, Dyer Papers.

22. They were also called "book builders." See Michael Lowe, "Japanese naval codes," included in F. H. Hinsley and Alan Stripp, eds., *Codebreakers: The Inside Story of Bletchley Park* (Oxford University Press, 1993), pp. 257–63. See also Hugh Denham, "Japanese naval codes and ciphers," Hinsley and Stripp, eds., *Codebreakers*, pp. 276–79.

23. Layton et al., *And I Was There*, p. 340.

24. Navy history from RG 38, 5750/198, p. 15.

25. Holmes, *Doubled-Edged Secrets*, p. 40.

26. Costello, *The Pacific War*, p. 162.

27. Edwin P. Hoyt, *How They Won the War in the Pacific: Nimitz and His Admirals* (Lyons Press, 2000), pp. 14–24.

28. Tucker, "Rhapsody in Purple," *Cryptologia*, p. 233.

29. CIS, 20–23 December, 1941, SRMN-012, pp. 253–76, Navy Department Library, NHHC. See also Rochefort's testimony, PHH, Part 23, pp. 680–83.

30. Rochefort-Prange interview.

31. Rochefort oral history, USNI, pp. 317–19.

32. Hoyt, *How They Won the War in the Pacific*, p. 23.

33. Hoyt in *How They Won the War in the Pacific* captures the disarray in the weeks immediately following the Japanese attack. See his chap. 1 "Confusion," pp. 1–25.

34. Rochefort oral history, USNI, pp. 122–23.

35. Wright oral history, NSA, p. 33.

36. E. B. Potter, *Nimitz* (Naval Institute Press, 1976), pp. 16–19.

37. Thomas B. Buell, *Master of Sea Power* (Naval Institute Press, 1980), p. 153.

CHAPTER 15: PEARL HARBOR AFTERMATH

1. Rochefort oral history, USNI, pp. 110–11.

2. Ibid., pp. 186–87.

3. Ibid., pp. 235, 186–87.

4. Potter, *Nimitz*, p. 64.

5. Confidential letter from Laurance Safford to Joe Rochefort, 21 January 1942, Serial 03320, RG 38, CNSG, Inactive Stations, Box 83, NARAII. I am indebted to the late Phil Jacobsen for calling my attention to this letter, from the Jacobsen Papers, in author's files.

6. Rochefort is quoted in "The Inside Story of the Battle of Midway and the Ousting of Commander Rochefort," an undated and unsigned memorandum. For years this twenty-one-page memo circulated among members of the naval intelligence community as a mystery document, its authorship disputed and authenticity questioned. From internal evidence inside the memo itself, the

author has established it as having been written sometime in 1944 by Laurance Safford. Copies of Safford's "Inside Story" memo can be found in the Rochefort Papers owned by his daughter, Janet Elerding; Edwin T. Layton, NWC; Donald Mac Showers, Arlington, VA; and Roger Pineau, Archives, University of Colorado at Boulder Libraries. This mystery memo has now been published by the U.S. Naval Cryptologic Veterans Association in *Echoes of Our Past*, with its authorship attributed to Safford, pp. 25–32.

7. Memorandum for Admiral Noyes, 23 January 1942, from Capt. L. F. Safford, U.S. Navy, reprinted in Holtwick, SRH-355, pp. 450-64.

8. Holtwick, SRH-355, commentary, p. 450.

9. After graduating from the Naval Academy in 1923, Wenger in 1929 took instruction in cryptanalysis in the Office of Naval Communications.

10. Wenger said in 1970 that he prepared his recommendations at the request of Joseph Redman before he ever saw the Safford reorganization plan. See Holtwick, SRH-355, pp. 460–63.

11. Memorandum for Rear Admiral Noyes, 10 February 1942, subject: "Reorganization of Communications Division," from Capt. L. F. Safford, OP-20-G, RG 38, CNSG Libraries, Inactive Stations, Box 83, NARAII.

12. Office of Naval Communications, memorandum for all section heads, 12 February 1942, subject: "Reorganization of Sections 20-G and 20-K," from Joseph Redman, RG 38, CNSG, Inactive Stations, Box 83, NARAII. A third spinoff from OP-20-G was OP-20-K, turned over to Lt. Cdr. Densford, now responsible for analyzing and authenticating the Navy's own radio traffic.

13. Rochefort oral history, USNI, p. 256.

14. Prados, *Combined Fleet Decoded*, p. 300. See also Potter, *Nimitz*, p. 177.

15. Vice Adm. John R. Redman, USN (Ret.), oral history conducted by John T. Mason Jr., San Francisco, CA, 6 June 1969, interview no. 2, USNI, p. 8.

16. The French-built *Normandie* was seized from Vichy France in 1941 and renamed the *Lafayette* for the Marquis de Lafayette. Partially destroyed by fire early in 1942 during her conversion to a troopship in New York, she was later sold for scrap.

17. John Redman oral history, USNI, p. 51.

18. "Memorandum for the Chief of Naval Operations," 25 October 1940, via Director, Radio Liaison Division, subject: "The Practice of Deception," from John R. Redman, Commander, U.S. Navy, Secret, Serial 0814, RG 38, Box 94, NARAII.

19. "Fourth Memorandum Endorsement," from Director of Naval Communications to Chief of Naval Operations, subject: "The Practice of Deception," undated, Secret, Serial 040220, RG 38, Box 94, NARAII.

20. "Memorandum for the Chief of Naval Operations," 1 April 1941, subject: "The Practice of Deception," from John R. Redman, Commander, U.S. Navy, RG 38, Box 94, NARAII.

21. John Redman oral history, USNI, pp. 43–49.

22. Ibid.

23. Ibid.

24. Ibid.

25. In June 1942 Noyes took command of Task Force 18, with the carrier *Wasp* his flagship. On 15 September, while the Task Force was supporting reinforcements at Guadalcanal in the Solomon Islands, the *Wasp* was torpedoed and sunk. After the loss of the *Wasp*, Noyes served with Commander Air Force, Pacific Fleet. In December 1942 he reported as senior member of the Pacific Coast Section, Board of Inspection and Survey, headquartered in San Francisco. He held this position for the remainder of the war. See Navy biography file, Navy Department Library, NHHC.

26. Capt. Thomas H. Dyer oral history, USNI, pp. 268–69.

27. In addition to Justice Owen J. Roberts, serving as chairman, members of the commission were Adm. William H. Standley, USN (Ret.); Rear Adm. Joseph M. Reeves, USN (Ret.); Major Gen. Frank R. McCoy, USA (Ret.); and Brig. Gen. Joseph T. McNarney, USA.

28. Rochefort testimony, Part 23, pp. 673–83.

29. Ibid.

30. See comments of John Lundstsrom, Chapter 12.

31. Rochefort testimony, Part 36, p. 37.

32. Ibid. Inexplicably, Kimmel's fleet intelligence officer, Edwin T. Layton, gave two contradictory accounts regarding Japanese radio deception, telling the Army Board in 1944 that "the Japanese practiced deception," then, in his 1985 book *And I Was There*, stating: "Contrary to popular myth and the assumption of many historians, there was no sustained deception plan put into operation by Japan" (pp. 228–29).

33. For a critique of Rochefort's views on the radio deception issue, see Robert J. Hanyok, "Catching the Fox Unaware," *Naval War College Review*, autumn 2008; and Hanyok, "How the Japanese Did It," *Naval History*, December 2009.

34. Jacobsen, "Radio Silence and Radio Deception," p. 701.

35. Capt. Thomas Dyer interview with Kahn, Dyer Papers.

36. Rochefort oral history, USNI, pp. 110–11.

37. Fitness Report, 1 October 1941–31 March 1942, signed by C. C. Bloch, stamped 20 April 1942. Bloch also gave Rochefort a 4.0 grade for this period, the highest possible grade.

38. Prange et al., *At Dawn We Slept*, pp. 600–603.

39. Rochefort oral history, USNI, p. 269.

40. Holmes, *Double-Edged Secrets*, p. 53.

CHAPTER 16: STRIKE UP THE BAND

1. Rochefort oral history, USNI, pp. 128–30; see also Layton et al., *And I Was There*, p. 358.

2. Rochefort said of Rorie: "[Details] I left to the chief yeoman that we had. [He] was quite capable of getting the things we wanted, and I never inquired where he got them or anything else. He produced these things from somewhere, being a good chief petty officer." See Rochefort oral history, USNI, p. 154.

3. Prados, *Combined Fleet Decoded*, p. 405.

4. Capt. Thomas H. Dyer oral history, USNI, p. 273.

5. Rochefort oral history, USNI, p. 120.

6. Rorie oral history, NSA.

7. The recollections of Tommy Dyer support Rorie's story: "Getting people, we broke all the rules and so forth. A draft would come in from the Coast on a transport. We'd send Tex Rorie over and they would be lined up and he'd go down and say 'I'll take you and you and you.' They all looked after a trip . . . rather unkempt and unprepossessing." Interview with Capt. Thomas H. Dyer, USN (Ret.), conducted by Griff Chiles, 26 August 1976, NCVA, folder 16.

8. Author's interview with Michael Palchefsky.

9. Ibid.

10. Dyer letter to David Kahn, 27 December 1963, Dyer Papers.

11. Capt. Thomas H. Dyer oral history, USNI, pp. 234–35, 273.

12. Layton et al., *And I Was There*, p. 358.

13. Author's interview with Michael Palchefsky.

14. Ibid.

15. Capt. Thomas H. Dyer oral history, USNI. Neither Dyer nor Rochefort supported Jasper Holmes' extravagant appraisal of the bandsmen: "Many of these musicians turned out to be such competent cryptanalysts after a short period of instruction that a theory was advanced that there must be a psychological connection between music and cryptanalysis." See Holmes, *Double-Edged Secrets*, pp. 37–38. Some bandsmen may have helped the linguists identify code groups, but none did cryptanalysis, the highly technical effort that is entailed in deciphering an encrypted message. Dyer commented: "There seems to be an affinity between musical ability and cryptanalytic ability. If there is, I'm the great exception that proves the rule" (oral history, USNI, p. 235).

16. Rochefort oral history, USNI, p. 120.

17. Rochefort letter to Roger Pineau, 8 June 1971, Pineau Papers, Box 22, Folder 20, University of Colorado Archives at Boulder.

18. Holmes, *Double-Edged Secrets*, p. 62. "We had to carry the case to Admiral Nimitz to save our ex-bandsmen cryptanalysts from becoming bandsmen again, making music to improve the morale of the Market Street Commandos."

19. Layton oral history, NSA.

20. Holtwick, SRH-355, pp. 441–42.

21. Ibid.

CHAPTER 17: *KORYAKU BUTAI*

1. Layton et al., *And I Was There*, pp. 355–59; King and Whitehill, *Fleet Admiral King*, p. 364; see also "King's Strategy for the Pacific War," 5 March 1942, "Memorandum to the President," from E. J. King, reprinted in Buell, *Master of Sea Power*, Appendix 5, pp. 531–33; and Potter, *Nimitz*, pp. 32–36.

2. CINCPAC message file, COMINCH to CINCPAC, 1/1/42, message no. 021718, RG 38, NHC-70, NND 907044, RG 313, Box 1, Microfilm Roll 1, NARAII.

3. Layton et al., *And I Was There*, pp. 355–59; Potter, Potter, *Nimitz*, pp. 32–36; Frederick D. Parker, *A Priceless Advantage: U.S. Navy Communications Intelligence and the Battles of Coral Sea, Midway, and the Aleutians* (Center for Cryptologic History, National Security Agency, CH-E32-93-01, 1993), p. 5.

4. Larrabee, *Commander in Chief*, p. 355.

5. Layton et al., *And I Was There*; Parker, *A Priceless Advantage*, pp. 15–17.

6. Parker, *A Priceless Advantage*, pp. 15–17.

7. John B. Lundstrom, *Black Shoe Carrier Admiral* (Naval Institute Press, 2006), p. 57.

8. Ibid.

9. SRMN-012, Combat Intelligence Unit, 14th Naval District, Traffic Intelligence Summaries with comments by CINCPAC War Plans Section, 15 January 1942, part 2, Navy Department Library, NHHC.

10. Parker, *A Priceless Advantage*, p. 5.

11. Layton et al., *And I Was There*, pp. 355–59.

12. SRMN-012, Hypo's CIS, 16–17 January 1942.

13. Ibid., 18 January 1942.

14. Edwin T. Layton letter to John Lundstrom, 10 January 1974, Edwin T. Layton Papers, Box 48, Folder 1, NWC.

15. Layton et al., *And I Was There*, p. 359.

16. Ibid., pp. 355–59.

17. Ibid., p. 359

18. Layton letter to Rear Adm. Donald Mac Showers, 5 November 1982, Showers Papers (in his personal possession).

19. Holcomb oral history, NSG.

20. Ibid.

21. John B. Lundstrom, *The First South Pacific Campaign* (Naval Institute Press, 1976), pp. 30–31.

22. Comments by War Plans Section, 1–2 February 1942, Intelligence Comments and Summaries, Part 3, SRMN-012, RG 457, NARAII.

23. Goldstein and Dillon, eds., *Fading Victory: The Diary of Matome Ugaki*, pp. 81–83.

24. Lundstrom, *First South Pacific Campaign*, pp. 30–31.

25. Holmes, *Double-Edged Secrets*, pp. 63–64.

26. Interview with Capt. Wilfred J. Jasper Holmes, conducted by NSA historian Henry Schorreck and Naval Security Group historian Raymond Schmidt, 13 September 1977, NCVA.

27. Blair, *Silent Victory*, pp. 95–96.

28. Holmes, *Double-Edged Secrets* p. 58.

29. Forrest R. Tex Biard, "The Pacific War," *Cryptolog*, NCVA, winter 1989, p. 4.

30. Biard's side of the story can be found in his 1989 *Cryptolog* report "The Pacific War." Fletcher's version is reported in Lundstrom's *Black Shoe Carrier Admiral*, see especially pp. 93–94, 122–23, 167–71, 201–2.

31. Ernest Beath, "Pacific Direct Support Units," *U.S. Naval Crypotologic Veterans Association* (Turner, 1996), pp. 50–54.

32. Showers interviews (author's files). In an interview with the author on 11 October 2005 in Dallas, TX, Biard disputed Showers' statement, maintaining that Rochefort respected his work and in 1944 offered him a job. "I [had] tremendous admiration for the man because he made fantastic contributions to our country and to our success," Biard said in his 1984 USNI oral history.

33. For background on the mobile radio intelligence units, see Ernest Beath, "Pacific Direct Support Units," *NCVA*, 1996.

CHAPTER 18: NOT A VERY GLORIOUS INCIDENT

1. COMINCH to CINCPAC, 4 March 1942, Message No. 042227, RG 313, microfilm copies of dispatches, CINCPAC message file, RG 313, Box 1, Roll 5, NARAII.

2. Capt. Edwin T. Layton, USN, "Rendezvous in Reverse," U.S. Naval Institute *Proceedings*, May 1953, p. 480.

3. COM 14 to all Task Force Commanders, COMINCH, CINCPAC, 2 March 1942, 020715, CINCPAC message file, RG 313, Box 1, Roll 5, NARAII.

4. COM 14 to CINCPAC, COMINCH, COM 16, 2 March 1942, 021120.

5. Layton et al., *And I Was There*, pp. 372–77.

6. COM 14 to CINCPAC, COMINCH, COM 16, 2 March 1942, 021120.

7. Layton et al., *And I Was There*, pp. 372–77.

8. COM 14 to CINCPAC, COMINCH, COM 16, et al., 2 March 1942, 021113.

9. Admiral Nimitz's command file "Running Estimate of the Situation," 3 March 1942, *Greybook*, book 1, p. 261, Operational Archives, NHHC.

10. COMINCH to COM 14, 3 March 1942, 032230.

11. Layton et al., *And I Was There*, pp. 372–77.

12. Prados, *Combined Fleet Decoded*, pp. 282–84.

13. COM 16 to COMINCH, CINCPAC, COM 14, et al., 4 March 1942, 040630.

14. Horn, *The Second Attack*, pp. 117–23.

15. Ibid.

16. Layton et al., *And I Was There*, pp. 372–77.

17. COMINCH, Message No. 042227, RG 313, microfilm copies of dispatches, CINCPAC message file, RG 313, Box 1, Roll 5, NARAII.

18. Layton, "Rendezvous in Reverse," U.S. Naval Institute *Proceedings*, May 1953, p. 484.
19. Prados, *Combined Fleet Decoded*, pp. 282–84.
20. David D. Lowman, "Rendezvous in Reverse II," U.S. Naval Institute *Proceedings*, December 1983, pp. 132–33.
21. Horn, *The Second Attack*, pp. 90–94.
22. Prados, *Combined Fleet Decoded*, pp. 282–84.
23. Capt. Thomas H. Dyer oral history, USNI, p. 239.
24. Rochefort oral history, USNI, pp. 204–8.
25. Ibid.
26. CINCPAC to COMINCH, 5 March 1942, 050325.
27. COM 14 to CINCPAC, COMINCH, COM 16, et al., 5 March 1942, 052231.
28. COM 14 to COMINCH, CINCPAC, COM 16, et al., 6 March 1942, 062203.
29. Layton et al., *And I Was There*, pp. 372–77.
30. COM 14 to NAS Palmyra, Johnston, Midway, 10 March 1942, confidential, 100315.
31. COM 14 to CINCPAC, COMINCH, COM 16, et al., 10 March 1942, 100834.
32. NAS Midway to COM 14, CINCPAC, 11 March 1942, 110535.
33. Horn, *The Second Attack*, pp. 141–42. Awarded DFCs were Lieutenants Charles W. Somers and Francis P. McCarthy.
34. Ibid.
35. Rochefort oral history, USNI, p. 176.
36. COM 14 to CINCPAC, COMINCH, COM 16, et al., 11 March 1942, 112132.
37. Operation K would have yet another sequel, played out after the war between Eddie Layton and Jasper Holmes. Layton suggested that an article Holmes wrote in 1940 for the *Saturday Evening Post* under the pseudonym Alec Hudson gave the Japanese the idea for refueling their seaplanes from submarines at French Frigate Shoals. See Layton et al.'s *And I Was There,* p. 374; and Layton, "Rendezvous in Reverse," *Proceedings*, May 1953, pp. 478–85. Holmes rejected Layton's thesis. See his reply in *Proceedings*, August 1953, pp. 897–99, and his book *Double-Edged Secrets*, p. 83.

CHAPTER 19: THE DUNGEON COMES ALIVE

1. See *Intercept Station "C,"* 2nd ed., NCVA, fall 2003.
2. "The History of GYP-1," RG 38, Box 116, CNSG, 5750/202, p. 29–30, NARAII.
3. Rochefort oral history, USNI, p. 143. For a chronology of initial translations of JN-25(b), see RG 38, CNSG Library, Box 22, Folder 3222/82; first translation is dated 8 January 1942.
4. Rochefort interview with Lord, NHHC.
5. Layton et al., *And I Was There*, pp. 374–76.
6. They were preceded in the basement by four other evacuees from America's language program in Japan: Lts. (jg) Forrest Biard, Gilven Slonim, and John

Bromley; and Marine Capt. Bankson Holcomb Jr., all of whom arrived in September 1941.

7. Showers interviews (author's files). See also interview with Rear Adm. Donald M. Mac Showers, USN (Ret.), conducted by Bill Alexander, 13 March 1998, Fredericksburg, TX, Admiral Nimitz Museum and University of North Texas Oral History Collection, No. 1257.

8. Like Showers, PO3/c Johnson reported originally to the district intelligence office, Fourteenth Naval District, in Honolulu, then, after a few days, was "loaned" to the Combat Intelligence Unit at Pearl Harbor.

9. Finnegan oral history, NSA.

10. Author's interview with Lt. Cdr. Ferdinand Johnson, USNR (Ret.).

11. Wright interview with Costello and Pineau, NWC.

12. Finnegan oral history, NSA.

13. Capt. Thomas H. Dyer oral history, USNI, pp. 233–34.

14. Ibid.

15. Showers interviews (author's files).

16. Rochefort oral history, USNI, p. 225.

17. Roger Dingman, *Deciphering the Rising Sun* (Naval Institute Press, 2009), pp. 111–12.

18. Ronald Marcello interview with E. B. Potter, 8 October 1994, Kerrville, TX, University of North Texas Oral History Collection, p. 26. Legislation creating the Waves—standing Women Accepted for Volunteer Emergency Service—was signed by President Roosevelt on 30 July 1942. Within a year more than 27,000 women served as Waves, but not in Honolulu, where they weren't permitted until 1945.

19. Potter, *Nimitz*, p. 287.

20. Marcello interview with Potter, University of North Texas.

21. Roenigk letter to Pineau, 3 May 1985; and 22 April 1989.

22. Roenigk letter to Arthur Benedict, 9 March 1985.

23. Roenigk letter to Pineau, 22 April 1989, Pineau Papers.

24. Author's interview with Ferdinand Johnson.

25. Author's interview with Walter Jester. Jester was called to active duty in March 1942 as a Y3/c and, like Showers and Johnson, ordered to report to the district intelligence office in Honolulu, then assigned to Rochefort's basement.

26. Author's interview with Ferdinand Johnson.

27. Holmes, *Doubled-Edged Secrets*, p. 33.

28. Roenigk to Pineau, 23 August 1981, 22 April 1989, 21 February 1987, Pineau Collection, Box 24, Folder 1, Archives, University of Colorado at Boulder Libraries.

29. "General History of OP-20-3-GYP," p. 23, 5750/199, CNSG, RG 38, Box 116, NARAII.

30. Kahn, *Codebreakers*, pp. 564–65.

31. For the origins of the name Belconnen for the Melbourne site, see Russell, *No Right to Win*, p. 260.
32. See *Intercept Station "C,"* 2nd ed., NCVA, fall 2003.

CHAPTER 20: A SILK PURSE OUT OF A SOW'S EAR

1. "Black Magic in Communications," CSP 1494(A), 15 April 1942, signed by Vice Adm. F. J. Horne, Vice Chief of Naval Operations, RG 38, Crane Library, Box 66, NARAII. The author is indebted to Pacific War historian Robert Hanyok for directing him to this document.
2. Safford, "The Inside Story of the Battle of Midway and the Ousting of Commander Rochefort," unsigned (1944), NCVA.
3. Ibid.
4. Buell, *Master of Sea Power*, pp. 173, 532.
5. COMINCH to CINCPAC, 6 February 1942, 061513, Admiral Nimitz's command file, books 1 and 8, Operational Archives, NHHC (hereafter *Greybook*).
6. General Emmons to Adjutant General, Washington, 19 February 1942, *Greybook*, p. 249.
7. CIS, Combat Intelligence Unit, 2 April 1942, RG 38, Box 3, CNSG, Inactive Stations, NARAII.
8. Comments by War Plans Section, 2 April 1942, Intelligence Comments and Summaries, Part 3, 1 April–30 June 1942, SRMN-012, RG 457, NARAII.
9. *Greybook*, p. 33.
10. Summaries of radio intelligence, Japanese Naval Communications, SRNM 0381, RG 457, Box 1, Entry 9016, NARAII.
11. Layton oral history, USNI, pp. 119–20.
12. Capt. Thomas H. Dyer oral history, USNI, p. 247.
13. Lundstrom, *The First South Pacific Campaign*, p. 77.
14. COM 14 to CINCPAC, COMINCH, COM 16, et al., CINCPAC message file, 11 March 1942, 112132, RG 313, Box 1, NARAII.
15. Summaries of radio intelligence, Japanese Naval Communications, SRNM 0123, RG 457, Box 1, NARAII.
16. *The Battle of the Coral Sea*, SRH-012, Appendix 2, Part 1, p. 213, Navy Department Library, NHHC.
17. Fleet Intelligence Summary, 11 April 1942, Intelligence Comments and Summaries, Part 3, 1 April–30 June 1942, SRMN-012, RG 457, NARAII.
18. Fleet Intelligence Summary, 15 April 1942.
19. CIS, 17 April 1942.
20. Rochefort oral history, USNI, p. 189.
21. *Greybook*, 16 April 1942, p. 352.
22. CINCPAC to COMINCH, 17 April 1942, 172035, *Greybook*, pp. 500–501.
23. COMINCH to CINCPAC, 18 April 1942, 182032, *Greybook*, p. 501.
24. H. P Willmott, *The Barrier and the Javelin* (Naval Institute Press, 1983), p. 179; see also Lundstrom, *The First South Pacific Campaign*, p. 79.

25. Lundstrom, *The First South Pacific Campaign*, p. 76.
26. *Greybook*, 30 April 1942, p. 422.
27. Parker, *A Priceless Advantage*, p. 19.
28. Rochefort oral history, USNI, p. 182.
29. Holmes, *Doubled-Edged Secrets*, pp. 68–69.
30. Ibid.
31. CIS, 19 April 1942.
32. Ibid., 20 April 1942.
33. *The Battle of the Coral Sea*, SRH-012, Appendix 2, Part 1, p. 219, Navy Department Library, NHHC.
34. CIS, 22 April 1942.
35. Holmes, *Double-Edged Secrets*, pp. 72–73.
36. Admiral Nimitz's "Estimate of the Situation," 22 April 1942, *Greybook*, p. 385.
37. Holmes, *Double-Edged Secrets*, p. 70.
38. *The Battle of the Coral Sea*, SRH-012, Appendix 2, Part 1, p. 221, Navy Department Library, NHHC.
39. Comments by War Plans Section, 26 April 1942, Intelligence Comments and Summaries, Part 3, SRMN-012, RG 457, NARAII.
40. *Greybook*, 28 April 1942, p. 416.
41. Holmes, *Double-Edged Secrets*, p. 64–65.
42. Ibid.
43. *The Battle of the Coral Sea*, SRH-012, Appendix 2, Part 1, p. 225, Navy Department Library, NHHC.
44. SRNM No. 0687, COM 14 to OPNAV, COMINCH, CINCPAC, Belconnen, COM 16, 300316, April 1942, summaries of radio intelligence, RG 457, Box 1, Entry 9016, NARAII.
45. Holmes, *Double-Edged Secrets*, pp. 72–73.

CHAPTER 21: KING COMES CALLING
1. Larrabee, *Commander in Chief*, p. 48.
2. Buell, *Master of Sea Power*, pp. 205–10.
3. "King's Strategy for the Pacific War," 5 March 1942, reprinted in Buell, *Master of Sea Power*, pp. 531–33.
4. Author's telephone interview with Robert W. Love Jr.
5. Ibid.
6. *Greybook*, 23 April 1942, p. 386, Operational Archives, NHHC.
7. Willmott, *The Barrier and the Javelin*, p. 184.
8. Rochefort oral history, USNI, pp. 174–78.
9. Layton letter to John Lundstrom, 14 October 1973, Edwin T. Layton Papers, Box 48, Folder 1, Naval Historical Collection, NWC.
10. Layton's oral history, USNI, p. 136.
11. Author's telephone interview with Robert W. Love Jr.

12. Another historian who accepted Rochefort version was *Nimitz* author E. B. Potter, who wrote that King "took the unprecedented step of communicating directly with Commander Rochefort at Station Hypo" (p. 66).
13. Lord, *Incredible Victory*, pp. 18–19.
14. Rochefort oral history, USNI, pp. 174–78.
15. CINCPAC message file, microfilm copies of dispatches, message no. 011108, Roll 10, RG 313, Box 1, NARAII.
16. Rochefort oral history, USNI, pp. 174–78.
17. Lundstrom, *The First South Pacific Campaign,* pp. 90–91.
18. CINCPAC message file, no. 011108, Roll 10, RG 313, Box 1, NARAII.
19. Ibid.
20. Ibid.
21. Rochefort oral history, USNI, pp. 174–78.
22. Ibid.
23. Rochefort letter to Jasper Holmes, 29 September 1959, Showers Papers.
24. *Greybook*, 1 May 1942, p. 432.
25. Potter, *Nimitz*, p. 78.
26. Layton letter to John Lundstrom, 12 June 1974, NWC.
27. *Greybook*, 2 May 1942, p. 433.
28. Willmott, *The Barrier and the Javelin*, p. 184.
29. Rochefort interview with Lord, NHHC.
30. This section is based on COM 14 messages in the CINCPAC message file at NARAII. In drawing conclusions the author has relied heavily on the excellent analysis of John B. Lundstrom, "A Failure of Radio Intelligence," *Cryptologia*, April 1983, more recently summarized in Lundstrom's book *Black Shoe Carrier Admiral*, pp. 152–58.
31. CINCPAC message file, COM 14 to COPEK addressees, message no. 020344 series, Roll 10, RG 313, Box 1, NARAII; see also Lundstrom, *Black Shoe Carrier Admiral*, pp. 106–16.
32. Lundstrom, *Black Shoe Carrier Admiral*, pp. 106–16.
33. Ibid.
34. Potter, *Nimitz*, p. 77.
35. Lundstrom, "A Failure of Radio Intelligence," *Cryptologia*, April 1983.
36. Layton to Lundstrom, 7 April 1975, NWC.

CHAPTER 22: SOMETHING IS BREWING

1. Fleet Radio Unit Melbourne, digest for 27 April 1942, SRNS-1517 (Part 1), p. 78, NARAII.
2. Stephan Howarth, *Morning Glory: A History of the Imperial Japanese Navy* (Hamish Hamilton, London, 1983), p. 296.
3. Parker, *A Priceless Advantage*, p. 43.
4. Fleet Intelligence Summary, 27 April 1942, Intelligence Comments and Summaries, Part 3, 1 April–30 June 1942, p. 190, SRMN-012, RG 457, NARAII.

5. *The Battle of the Coral Sea*, SRH-012, Appendix 2, Part 1, pp. 262–63, Navy Department Library, NHHC; see also Parker, *A Priceless Advantage*, p. 45; Prados, *Combined Fleet Decoded*, p. 316.

6. COM 14 to COMB, message no. 040816, 4 May 1942, microfilm copies of dispatches, CINCPAC message file, RG 313, Box 1, Roll 10, NARAII.

7. Ibid.

8. The author is indebted to John Lundstrom for the information that Layton's daily "enemy activities file" was known at CINCPAC headquarters as the "score card." See Lundstrom, *Black Shoe Carrier Admiral*, p. 124.

9. CINCPAC Enemy Activities File, 4 May 1942, SRH-272, NHHC.

10. COM 14 to COMB, message no. 061848, 6 May 1942, CINCPAC message file, NARAII.

11. Ibid.

12. CNO summaries of radio intelligence, Japanese Naval Activities, 6 May 1942, SRNS-0001–0352, RG 457, NARAII.

13. *Greybook*, 9 May 1942, p. 474.

14. Ibid., pp. 443, 473.

15. Fleet Intelligence Summary, 9 May 1942, Intelligence Comments and Summaries, Part 3, 1 April–30 June 1942, p. 190, SRMN-012, RG 457, NARAII.

16. CNO summaries of radio intelligence, Japanese Naval Activities, 10 May 1942, RG 457, SRNS 0027, NARAII.

17. Layton-Costello-Pineau interview.

18. COM 14 communication summaries, 5 May 1942, RG 38, Box 3, CNSG, Inactive Stations, NARAII.

19. CNO summaries of radio intelligence, Japanese Naval Activities, 5 May 1942, SRNS-0022, RG 457, NARAII.

20. Parker, *A Priceless Advantage*, pp. 44–46.

21. COM 14 to COMB, 090054, 9 May 1942, CINCPAC message file, Layton Notebook, Layton Papers, Box 27, Folder 4, Naval Historical Collection, NWC.

22. Ibid.

23. Ibid.

24. COM 14 to COMB, 052202, 5 May 1942, CINCPAC message file, NARAII.

25. Fleet Radio Unit Melbourne, digest for 14 May 1942, SRNS-1517, p. 146, Navy Department Library, NHHC.

26. COM 14 to COM, 140945, 141222, 141022, CINCPAC message file, Layton Notebook, Layton Papers, NWC.

27. Layton et al., *And I Was There*, p. 411.

28. CINCPAC Enemy Activities File, 13 May 1942, pp. 051–054, SRH-272, NHHC.

29. Rochefort oral history, USNI, pp. 128–33.

30. *Greybook*, 26 May 1942, p. 543.

31. Rochefort oral history, USNI, pp. 128–33, 152.

32. Capt. Thomas H. Dyer oral history, USNI, pp. 236–37.
33. Rochefort oral history, USNI, pp. 124–25.
34. Capt. Thomas H. Dyer oral history, USNI, pp. 206–7.
35. Lundstrom, *Black Shoe Carrier Admiral*, p. 209. COMINCH to CINCPAC, 121945, 121950, CINCPAC message file, Operational Archives, NHHC.
36. COMINCH to CINCPAC, 121945, 121950.
37. See Lundstrom, *Black Shoe Carrier Admiral*, pp. 208–11.
38. *Greybook*, 12 May 1942, p. 479.
39. CINCPAC to COMINCH, 140639, CINCPAC message file, Operational Archives, NHHC.
40. Parker, *A Priceless Advantage*, p. 46–47; *The Battle of the Coral Sea*, SRH-012, Appendix 2, Part 1, p. 272, Navy Department Library, NHHC.

CHAPTER 23: FIVE DAYS IN MAY
1. COM 14 to OPNAV, COMINCH, CINPAC, message no. 140700–140706, Japanese Naval Communications, SRNM 0698–1292, RG 457, Box 2, NARAII.
2. Rochefort oral history, USNI, p. 131.
3. Roenigk letter to Pineau, 22 April 1989.
4. Finnegan oral history, NSA.
5. Layton et al., *And I Was There*, p. 411.
6. Layton oral history, USNI, p. 123.
7. Rochefort-Prange interview.
8. Layton oral history, NSA, p. 143.
9. COM 14, 140700–140706.
10. Michael Isenberg, *Shield of the Republic: The United States Navy in an Era of Cold War and Violent Peace* (St. Martin's Press, 1993), p. 331.
11. Rochefort oral history, USNI, p. 209.
12. Layton oral history, USNI, pp. 123–24.
13. See Layton's two oral histories: USNI, pp. 123–24; NSA, p. 143.
14. Rochefort oral history, USNI, pp. 196–203.
15. For geographic designators confirmed by Stations Hypo and Cast, see COM 16 to OPNAV, 230939, March; COM 14 to OPNAV, 030244 May; Belconnen to OPNAV, 060710, May; and Layton Notebook, Layton Papers, NWC.
16. Rochefort oral history, USNI, pp. 196–203.
17. Ibid.
18. Showers interviews.
19. Layton oral history, USNI, pp. 124–25.
20. Layton et al., *And I Was There*, p. 414; see also Lundstrom, *The First South Pacific Campaign*, pp. 152–53.
21. Lundstrom, *The First South Pacific Campaign*, pp. 152–53.
22. CINCPAC to COMINCH, 140639, 140741, 140829, 140853, Nimitz Papers, Operational Archives, NHHC. See also Lundstrom, *The First South Pacific Campaign*, pp. 152–53.

23. CINCPAC to COMINCH, 140639, 140741, 140829, 140853, Nimitz Papers, Operational Archives, NHHC.

24. Administratively Rochefort was subordinate to the commandant of the Fourteenth Naval District at Pearl Harbor (Rear Adm. David Bagley); operationally he was responsible to OP-20-G (directed by Cdr. John Redman). But as a practical matter, Rochefort deemed it his mission to serve primarily the commander in chief, U.S. Pacific Fleet (Admiral Nimitz).

25. Lundstrom, *Black Shoe Carrier Admiral*, pp. 210–12; Lundstrom, *The First South Pacific Campaign*, pp. 154–57.

26. Layton letter to John Lundstrom, 12 June 1974, Correspondence, Box 48, Folder 1, Papers of Edwin T. Layton, NWC. Layton-Costello-Pineau interview, NWC. Everything known about Nimitz's "eyes only" message to Halsey derives from this 1974 letter to Lundstrom and the 1983 interviews with Costello and Pineau. Nimitz's secret dispatch does not appear in any of the extant hard-copy CINCPAC message files, the absence of which was pointed out to Layton. His explanation to Costello and Pineau was that Nimitz asked him to keep the message in his own files and therefore was given the file copy by the fleet's communications watch officer. See also Lundstrom, *The First South Pacific Campaign*, p. 155.

27. Lundstrom, *Black Shoe Carrier Admiral*, pp. 210–12.

28. Lundstrom, *The First South Pacific Campaign*, pp. 154–57.

29. CNO summaries of radio intelligence, Japanese Naval Activities, 14 May 1942, RG 457, SRNS 0031, NARAII.

30. COM 16 to OPNAV, COM 14, CINCAF, 230939, 230938, 23 March 1942, Japanese Naval Communications, RG 457, SRNM-0123, Box 1, NARAII.

31. Fleet Radio Unit Melbourne, daily digest for 14 May 1942, p. 146, SRNS-1517, Navy Department Library, NHHC.

32. Fleet Intelligence Comments and Commentaries, May 14, 1942, SRMN-012, pp. 317–18, Navy Department Library, NHHC.

33. CINCPAC Enemy Activities File, 14 May 1942, SRH-272, NHHC.

34. Ibid.

35. Fleet Intelligence Comments and Commentaries, 14 May 1942, SRMN-012, pp. 317–18, Navy Department Library, NHHC.

36. *Greybook*, 14 May 1942, p. 480.

37. COMINCH to CINCPAC, message 152130–152136, *Greybook*.

38. Layton et al., *And I Was There*, pp. 415–17.

39. CINCPAC to CTF 16, info COMINCH, 160307, *Greybook*.

40. CINCPAC to COMINCH, 160325, *Greybook*.

41. Ibid.

42. *Greybook*, 16 May 1942, p. 482.

43. CINCPAC to COMINCH, 170407, *Greybook*. See also Buell, *Master of Sea Power*, p. 201.

44. Layton et al., *And I Was There*, pp. 415–17.

45. Rochefort oral history, USNI, p. 301.
46. Layton et al., *And I Was There*, pp. 415–17.
47. COMINCH to CINCPAC, 172220, *Greybook*.
48. Ibid.
49. Lundstrom, *Black Shoe Carrier Admiral*, p. 216.
50. COMINCH to CINCPAC, 172220, *Greybook*.
51. COMINCH to SPENAVO, London, 181255, *Greybook*, p. 492.

CHAPTER 24: ROCHEFORT'S WAR

1. Layton et al., *And I Was There*, pp. 367–68; 408–10, 417.
2. Rochefort oral history, USNI, p. 99.
3. Layton et al., *And I Was There*, p. 358.
4. Wright interview with Costello and Pineau, NWC.
5. COM 14 to OPNAV, COMINCH, 291010, 29 April 1942, CINCPAC microfilm message file, RG 313, Box 1, Roll 10, NARAII.
6. Layton et al., *And I Was There*, p. 394.
7. Costello-Pineau Layton interview.
8. Parker, *A Priceless Advantage*, p. 46.
9. Fleet Radio Unit Melbourne, radio log, digest for 15 May 1942, SRNS-1517, Navy Department Library, NHHC.
10. Ibid., 22 May 1942.
11. CNO summaries of radio intelligence, Japanese Naval Activities, 17 May 1942, RG 457, SRNS-0034, NARAII.
12. Memorandum for Cdr. Murphy, OP-20-G/JAC, 18 May 1942, 5750/171, CNSG, File 287, History of OP-20-GI, RG 38, Box 112, NARAII.
13. Memo for Cdr. Redman, F-111, 18 April 1942, 5750/177, CNSG, History of OP-20-GI, RG 38, Box 112, NARAII.
14. Memorandum for Cdr. Murphy, OP-20-G, 23 April 1942, 5750/177, CNSG, History of OP-20-GI, RG 38, Box 112, NARAII.
15. Layton oral history, NSA, p. 9.
16. Rochefort oral history, USNI, pp. 202–3.
17. Wright interview with Costello and Pineau, NWC.
18. Capt. Thomas H. Dyer interview, NCVA.
19. 5750/188, CNSG, History of OP-20-GI-P, RG 38, Box 114, NARAII. This description of Hypo's rating system also accords with the memory of Rear Adm. Donald Mac Showers, then an ensign in Rochefort's basement.
20. Dingman, *Deciphering the Rising Sun*, pp. 103–4.
21. Capt. Thomas H. Dyer oral history, USNI, pp. 241–43.
22. Rochefort oral history, USNI, pp. 166, 252.
23. Layton-Costello-Pineau interview.
24. COM 14 to COMB, CINCPAC message file, 189000, message received 16 May, translated 18 May; see also *The Battle of the Coral Sea*, SRH-012, Appendix 2, Part 1, p. 277, Navy Department Library, NHHC.

25. *The Battle of the Coral Sea*, SRH-012, Appendix 2, Part 1, p. 271, Navy Department Library, NHHC.
26. COM 14 to COMB, 222100, CINCPAC microfilm messages file, Roll 12.
27. Mac Showers recalls Lasswell working on this message or messages several days after 20 May. Showers interview (author's files).
28. *The Battle of the Coral Sea*, SRH-012, Appendix 2, Part 1, pp. 284–85, Navy Department Library, NHHC.
29. Lasswell oral history, USMC.
30. Dingman, *Deciphering the Rising Sun*, pp. 100–101.
31. Edward Van der Rhoer, *Deadly Magic* (Charles Scribner's Sons, 1978), p. 49.
32. Dingman, *Deciphering the Rising Sun*, pp. 100–101.
33. Col. Alva B. Lasswell, USMC (Ret.), to Capt. Roger Pineau, 31 December 1985, Pineau Papers, Box 17, Folder 6, Archives, University of Colorado at Boulder Libraries.
34. Lasswell oral history, USMC.
35. Wright interview with Costello and Pineau, NWC.
36. Memorandum from John Redman, undated, History of OP-20-GI, File 287, 5750/177, RG 38, Box 112, NARAII. See also Budiansky's *Battle of Wits*, p. 15.
37. Lord, *Incredible Victory*, p. 21; Samuel Eliot Morison, *Coral Sea, Midway and Submarine Actions*, *Coral Sea, Midway and Submarine Actions: May 1942–August 1942* (Castle Books, 1949), vol. 4, pp. 167–68.
38. Memorandum for Lt. Cdr. Gordon Daisley, 22 May 1942, SRMN-008, p. 007, NHHC.
39. Ibid., 23 May 1942, SRMN-008, p. 008, NHHC.
40. Layton et al., *And I Was There*, pp. 19–21, 96–98. See also Layton-Costello-Pineau interview.
41. Capt. Wyman H. Packard, *A Century of U.S. Naval Intelligence* (Office of Naval Intelligence and Naval Historical Center, 1996), p. 22. The information in this section on Turner relies largely on this work. See especially pp. 49–51.
42. Memorandum for OP-20-GI Watch, 20 May 1942, SRMN-008, NHHC.
43. Memorandum for Lt. Cdr. Daisley, 21 May 1942, SRMN-008, p. 007, NHHC.
44. Parker, *A Priceless Advantage*, p. 47.
45. Rochefort letter to Edwin T. Layton, 20 March 1974, Pineau Papers, Box 16, Folders 21–23, Archives, University of Colorado at Boulder Libraries.
46. Morison, *Coral Sea, Midway and Submarine Actions*, p. 80.
47. Layton-Costello-Pineau interview.
48. Showers interviews (author's files); see also Holmes, *Double-Edged Secrets*, p. 90.

CHAPTER 25: AFFIRM FOX IS CONFIRMED HERE
1. Lewin, *The American Magic*, p. 105.

2. Layton et al., *And I Was There*, pp. 421–22, based on a 27 June 1984 interview with Dyer conducted by John Costello and Roger Pineau. See also Dyer's USNI oral history, pp. 241–43.

3. Holmes, *Double-Edged Secrets*, pp. 90–91. Holmes wrote that that was the last he heard of the matter until he read an article by J. Bryan in the March 1949 *Saturday Evening Post*, "Never a Battle Like Midway," disclosing the AF water episode.

4. Showers interviews (author's files). Rochefort after the war couldn't remember whose idea it was to send the water message to Midway. "Somebody—possibly Layton, possibly somebody in my office, possibly me," came up with the idea. See Rochefort's oral history, USNI, p. 211.

5. Holmes in his book stated that Rochefort discussed the matter with Commandant Bloch. That is incorrect. Rear Adm. Bagley relieved Bloch on 2 April, and it would have been Bagley, not Bloch, with whom Rochefort conferred on 19 May.

6. Fleet Radio Unit Melbourne, Daily Digests for 21 May 1942, p. 176, SRNS 1517, Navy Department Library, NHHC.

7. COM 14 to COMB, Secret COPEK, 220732, CINCPAC message file on Midway, Naval Cryptologic Museum Library, Fort Meade, MD. Pioneer historians of Midway stumbled when it came to correctly dating Rochefort's famous water-shortage order. Lord in *Incredible Victory* put it at "around May 10," as did Prange in *Miracle at Midway*, Lundstrom in *The First South Pacific Campaign*, and Willmott in *The Barrier and the Javelin*. The water incident was correctly placed between 19 and 21 May by Layton in *And I Was There*, Prados in *Combined Fleet Decoded*, Budiansky in *Battle of Wits*, and Jonathan Parshall and Anthony Tully in *Shattered Sword* (Potomac Books, 2005).

8. Command summary, CINCPAC files, Book 1, Box 9, 23 May 1942, p. 540, *Greybook*.

9. CNO summaries of radio intelligence, Japanese Naval Activities, 22 May 1942, prepared by Arthur McCollum, SRNS-0040, RG 457, NARAII.

10. Gordon W. Prange, with Donald M. Goldstein and Katherine V. Dillon, *Miracle at Midway* (McGraw-Hill, 1982), p. 66.

11. "The Role of Radio Intelligence in the American-Japanese Naval War," vol. 1, *The Battle of the Coral Sea*, SRH-012, Navy Department Library, NHHC.

12. Pearl Harbor Hearings, Part 3, p. 1158.

13. Prange et al., *Miracle at Midway*, p. 66.

14. Ibid., pp. 46–47; E. B. Potter, *Nimitz*, pp. 79–80.

15. COMINCH to CINCPAC, 141527, CINCPAC messages, Midway File, Naval Cryptologic Museum Library, Fort Meade, MD.

16. Prange et al., *Miracle at Midway*, pp. 38–39; Lord, *Incredible Victory*, pp. 24–25; Potter, *Nimitz*, pp. 79–80.

17. Parker, *A Priceless Advantage*, p. 47.

18. Lundstrom, *Black Shoe Carrier Admiral*, pp. 124–25; Lord, *Incredible Victory*, pp. 24–25.
19. Rochefort oral history, USNI, p. 212.
20. "Naval Security Group History to 1971," Holtwick SRH-355, pp. 460–63.
21. Rochefort oral history, USNI, pp. 212, 144–45.
22. Ibid., pp. 144–45.
23. CINCPAC to CTF 16, 180403, CINCPAC microfilm message files, RG 313, Roll 12, NARAII.
24. Lundstrom, *Black Shoe Carrier Admiral*, pp. 208, 216–17.
25. Ibid.; Parker, *A Priceless Advantage*, p. 52.
26. Mitsuo Fuchida and Masatake Okuyama, *Midway, the Battle That Doomed Japan: The Japanese Navy's Story* (Naval Institute Press, 1955), pp. 138–39.
27. Capt. Thomas H. Dyer oral history, USNI, p. 125.
28. Rochefort-Prange interview.
29. Memoirs of Col. Alva Bryan Lasswell, USMC (Ret.), undated, Lasswell Family Papers, provided through courtesy of the Lasswell family.
30. Showers interviews (author's files). As this book went to press, Showers, now at age ninety-two, continued to believe that Lasswell decoded Yamamoto's operation order.
31. Lasswell memoirs, Lasswell Family Papers.
32. Holmes, *Double-Edged Secrets*, p. 89. Holmes didn't explicitly single out Lasswell as the codebreaker working on this order, but the date given by Holmes for the receipt of this lengthy intercept dovetailed with Lasswell's timeline.
33. Interview with Capt. Wesley A. Wright, USN (Ret.), conducted by David Kahn, 12 December 1963, Silver Spring, MD, Kahn Papers, Naval Cryptologic Museum, Fort Meade, MD.
34. Rochefort oral history, USNI, pp. 215–17.
35. Layton oral history, USNI, p. 125.
36. With regard to Yamamoto's Main Body, Rochefort told Etta-Belle Kitchen in his 1969 oral history that "we knew this"—a contention contradicted by the RI summaries provided CINCPAC at that time.
37. Layton oral history, USNI, pp. 215–17.
38. Parshall and Tully, *Shattered Sword*, p. 67.
39. "So far as I can tell, based upon a great deal of research in original documents, no detailed schedule for the Japanese carrier attack on Midway was ever recovered prior to the battle," Lundstrom told the author. Lundstrom email to Bill Price, Showers, and author on 7 June 2008. Historians supporting the Hypo story of a 20 May operation order include Lord, *Incredible Victory*; Prange, *Miracle at Midway*; Kahn, *Codebreakers*; Prados, *Combined Fleet Decoded*; and Costello, *The Pacific War*.
40. Rochefort oral history, USNI, p. 190.

41. "Estimate of the Situation, Attack on Hawaiian and Alaskan Bases," 26 May 1942, *Greybook*, pp. 506–20.

42. Holmes, *Double-Edged Secrets*, pp. 94–95; see also Kahn, *Codebreakers*, pp. 568–70.

43. Henry F. Schorreck, "The Role of COMINT in the Battle of Midway," June 1972, SRH-230, Navy Department Library, NHHC.

44. Finnegan oral history, NSA.

45. This account of Finnegan's work with Ham Wright during 26–27 May is taken from Kahn's *Codebreakers*, p. 570; Kahn's interview with Wright, cited above; Holmes' *Double-Edged Secrets*; and Finnegan's oral history, NSA.

46. Kahn explained that Wright "discovered that the date-and-time cipher comprised a polyalphabetic with independent mixed-cipher alphabets and with the exterior plain and key alphabets in two different systems of Japanese syllabic writing—one the older, formal *Katakana*, the other the cursive *Hiragana*."

47. Wright-Kahn interview.

48. Ibid. Regarding who deserves credit, Wright was generous, telling John Costello and Roger Pineau: "Finnegan worked that out," but didn't elucidate his own role. See Wright interview with Costello and Pineau, Layton Papers, NWC. Finnegan in his oral history leaves no doubt where credit should go: "I solved it and it was of the greatest importance because it provided the actual date of the Midway attack and the dates for the noon positions of the Occupation Force."

CHAPTER 26: NIMITZ COMES AROUND

1. Potter, *Nimitz,* pp. 82–85.

2. Rochefort oral history, USNI, pp. 218–33.

3. Ibid.

4. Parker, *A Priceless Advantage*, p. 47.

5. COMGENHAW DEPT. to CINCPAC, 251930, CINCPAC message file, Layton's Notebook, Layton Papers, Box 29, Folder 4, NWC; hereafter message 251930.

6. Richardson in little more than a year would relieve Emmons from his post in Hawaii.

7. Potter, *Nimitz,* pp. 82–85.

8. Layton oral history, USNI, pp. 108–9.

9. Layton in his oral history singled out former District Commandant Claude Bloch as the culprit in this episode. But by the time of this staff conference, Bloch had been relieved by Rear Adm. David Bagley, so it was clearly Bagley whom Layton had in mind as the officer allegedly responsible for taking Rochefort over to see Nimitz. See Layton's oral history, USNI, pp. 108–9.

10. Rochefort in his oral history gave 25 May as the date he was invited to brief Nimitz and his staff. But this date is incorrect. Rochefort stated that among

participants was U.S. Army Maj. Gen. Robert C. Richardson. But CINPAC's *Greybook*, the daily log of the fleet staff, reported Richardson's presence at a staff conference on 27 May. Different writers gave different dates for this meeting. Nimitz's biographer E. B. Potter used Rochefort's date. Layton in *And I Was There* gave the date as 26 May. Kahn in *Codebreakers* got the date right: 27 May.

11. Rochefort oral history, USNI, pp. 218–33.
12. COM 14 to COMB, 262226, CINCPAC microfilm file, in and outgoing messages, January–August 1942, RG 313, Box 1, Roll 12, NARAII.
13. Rochefort oral history, USNI, pp. 218–33. See also "Commander Rochefort's Estimate," RG 38, Box 88, Inactive Station, NARAII.
14. No copy of the date-time cipher dispatch prepared by Ham Wright during the morning of 27 May and circulated to Washington ever turned up in Navy files or in CINCPAC's microfilm file. The absence of this document has made it impossible to verify the date he and Joe Finnegan calculated as the date for the *kido butai*'s initial attack on Midway.
15. "Commander Rochefort's Estimate," RG 38, Box 88, Inactive Stations, NARAII.
16. CINCPAC to COMINCH, 260345, CINCPAC file.
17. Parshall and Tully argue persuasively that the Aleutians Operation was not a feint designed to lure the American fleet out of Pearl Harbor. "The simultaneous launch of operations in the Aleutians was designed to capitalize on the Americans being busy elsewhere, so that objectives in the Aleutians could be seized without hindrance. Operation AL was an invasion in its own right, strategically timed, and not merely a diversion," the authors write in *The Shattered Sword*, p. 431.
18. The number of IJN vessels in the Midway and Aleutians operations added up to 186.
19. Rochefort oral history, USNI, pp. 218–33.
20. Potter, *Nimitz*, pp. 82–85.
21. Ibid.
22. "Enemy Activities," 24 May 1942, prepared by E. T. Layton, CINCPAC Enemy Activities File, April–May 1942, SRH-272, NHHC.
23. Potter, *Nimitz*, pp. 82–85.
24. Operation Plan No. 29–42, 27 May 1942, RG 38, Box 21, NARAII.
25. Ibid.
26. CINCPAC to CTF8, 282153, CINCPAC microfilm message file, Layton Notebook, Layton Papers, NWC; see also Parker, *A Priceless Advantage*, pp. 51–52; Potter, *Nimitz*, p. 88.
27. Potter, *Nimitz*, p. 88.
28. CTF 1 to TF 1, Information CINCPAC, 282150, CINCPAC microfilm file, RG 313, Roll 13, NARAII.

29. Holmes, *Double-Edged Secrets*, p. 91.
30. Rochefort oral history, USNI, pp. 192–95.
31. Parker, *A Priceless Advantage*, p. 49.
32. Larrabee, *Commander in Chief*, p. 201.
33. Potter, *Nimitz*, p. 85.
34. COM 14 to COMB 262244, CINCPAC microfilm file, NARAII.
35. Parker, *A Priceless Advantage*, p. 54.
36. Rochefort oral history, USNI, p. 242.
37. COM 14 to COMB, 310545, CINCPAC microfilm file, NARAII.
38. CINCPAC to COMTASKFSOR 17, 292049, CINCPAC microfilm file, NARAII.
39. Hugh Bicheno, *Midway* (Cassell, 2001), p. 82; Robert J. Cressman, Steve Ewing, Barrett Tillman, Mark Horan, Clark Reynolds, and Stan Cohen, *"A Glorious Page in Our History": The Battle of Midway, 4–6 June 1942* (Pictorial Histories, 1990), pp. 34, 40.

CHAPTER 27: OUR MAN IN TOKYO

1. Potter, *Nimitz*, p. 87.
2. Operation Plan No. 29-42, 27 May 1942, Commander in Chief, U.S. Pacific Fleet, RG 38, Box 21, NARAII. Nimitz's Op Plan originally projected the Japanese to arrive "as soon as thirty May," but by the time Fletcher and Spruance sailed he had moved the attack date back to 3 June.
3. Many Midway veterans remember hearing rumors before the Battle of Midway that the U.S. Navy had broken the Imperial Navy's operational code. Their stories have been recorded on the Battle of Midway Roundtable, an electronic forum consisting of about 400 Midway veterans, historians, and interested parties (www.midway42.org). See pp. 39–44 in Russell, *No Right to Win*.
4. Potter, *Nimitz*, p. 87.
5. COMINCH to CINCPAC, 172220, CINCPAC message file, command summary, *Greybook*, p. 489, Operational Archives, NHHC.
6. Operation Plan No. 29–42, 27 May 1942, RG 38, Box 21, NARAII.
7. CINCPAC to TF 16, TF 17, COMINCH, 310357, CINCPAC microfilm message file, Roll 13, NARAII.
8. CINCPAC to all TF Commanders PACFLT, 311221, CINCPAC message file, *Greybook*.
9. CIS, 28 May 1942, Combat Intelligence, Fourteenth Naval District, RG 38, Box 3, CNSG, Inactive Stations, NARAII.
10. CIS, 29 May 1942.
11. Ibid., 1 June 1942.
12. Ibid.
13. Fuchida and Okumiya, *Midway, the Battle That Doomed Japan*, pp. 150–53.
14. Parker, *A Priceless Advantage*, p. 56.

15. Fuchida and Okumiya, *Midway, the Battle That Doomed Japan*.

16. COMINCH to CINCPAC 300050, Fleet Intelligence Comments and Summaries, 31 May 1942, SRMN-012, p. 460, NHHC.

17. Morison, *Coral Sea, Midway and Submarine Actions*, p. 176; Parker, *A Priceless Advantage*, p. 59.

18. Potter, *Nimitz*, p. 88.

19. Ibid., pp. 91–95.

20. Showers interviews (author's files).

21. Capt. Thomas H. Dyer oral history, USNI, p. 245.

22. Rochefort letter to Roger Pineau, 8 January 1968, Showers Papers.

23. Potter, *Nimitz*, p. 88.

24. Parshall and Tully, *Shattered Sword*, p. 69; see also Lundstrom, *Black Shoe Carrier Admiral*, pp. 220–21.

25. Interview with Rear Adm. Edwin T. Layton, USN (Ret.), conducted by E. B. Potter, 19 March 1970, Carmel, CA, p. 30, Layton Papers, Box 30, Folder 5, NWC. Historians disagree on when the Nimitz-Layton exchange occurred. Potter in *Nimitz* and Prange in *Miracle at Midway* place the famed meeting around the time of Nimitz's 27 May staff conference. Lundstrom, in his 2006 biography of Frank Jack Fletcher, *Black Shoe Carrier Admiral*, claimed it took place on the morning of 4 June, at 7:30 a.m. Pearl local time. Lundstrom cited as a source Layton's 22 July 1964 interview with Prange. Unfortunately, what Layton told Prange cannot be authenticated because the Layton interview is missing from Prange's papers at the University of Maryland. Prange and Potter thought 27 May the more logical time for the Layton-Nimitz conversation, but that date cannot be confirmed either. The author believes the meeting took place on 3 June because that date fits the context of Layton's 19 March 1970 interview with Potter. In that interview Layton noted his prophecy during a discussion of Midway's 3 June discovery of the invasion force approaching from the west.

26. Parker, *A Priceless Advantage*, pp. 60–63.

27. Showers interviews (author's files).

28. Lundstrom, *Black Shoe Carrier Admiral*, pp. 239–42.

29. Layton interview with Potter, p. 20, Layton Papers, NWC. See also Lundstrom, *Black Shoe Carrier Admiral*, pp. 239–42; and Layton et al., *And I Was There*, p. 438.

30. Rochefort oral history, USNI, p. 219. Why the *kido butai* launched its planes at 170 to 180 miles from Midway rather than the 50 miles specified in Hypo's famous 18 May decrypt was never explained, but one historian suggested Hypo's translation of the 18 May message may have been flawed. See Parker, *A Priceless Advantage*, pp. 60–63.

31. Lundstrom, *Black Shoe Carrier Admiral*, pp. 239–42.

32. Layton interview with Potter, p. 42, Layton Papers, NWC.

33. Midway to CINCPAC, 042020, 4 June; CINCPAC to all commanders, 042007; Midway to CINCPAC, 041927, CINCPAC message file, RG 313, Box 1, Roll 14 NARAII.

34. Midway to CINCPAC, 042158; CINCPAC to COMINCH, all commanders, 042301.

35. Midway to CINCPAC, 042105; Midway to CINCPAC, 042325.

36. Potter, *Nimitz*, p. 88.

37. Lundstrom, *Black Shoe Carrier Admiral*, pp. 252–53.

38. Potter, *Nimitz*, p. 88.

39. Running Log of Midway Operations, Fleet Intelligence Comments and Commentaries, 4 June, SRMN-012, pp. 499–524, NHHC.

40. Potter, *Nimitz*, p. 88.

41. Parshall and Tully, *Shattered Sword*, p. 198; see also Enemy Dispatches, Battle of Midway, Striking Force to Combined Fleet, 0600, 5 June, SRMN-005, p. 96, NHHC.

42. Memorandum for Fleet Intelligence Officer, regarding Enemy Dispatches, Battle of Midway, from J. J. Rochefort, 15 October 1942, SRMN-005, p. 95, NHHC.

43. Parker, *A Priceless Advantage*, p. 63

44. Midway to CINCPAC, 042325, cable.

45. Evidence gathered by Maryland attorney Bowen Weisheit, a fraternity brother of one of the doomed *Hornet* pilots, indicated that the *Hornet*'s captain, Rear Adm. Marc Mitscher, for reasons never acknowledged let alone understood, directed Ring to follow a heading that took him north of the *kido butai*'s actual position on 4 June; then, after the battle, submitted a map as part of his after action report irreconcilable with the course the air group actually followed that morning. A detailed account of his investigation can be found in his 1996 self-published book, *The Last Flight: C. Markland Kelly, Junior, USNR*. Such authors as John Lundstrom, Robert Cressman, Mark Horan, Alvin Kernan, Jon Parshall, Anthony Tully, James Sawruk, and Robert Mrazek have endorsed his findings.

46. Lundstrom, *Black Shoe Carrier Admiral*, p. 257.

47. CINCPAC to COMINCH, 050131; CTF 17 to CINCPAC, 050035; Midway to CINCPAC, 0430/15.

48. Biard and Fletcher feuded when Fletcher asked the Hypo linguist to brief his staff on the details of his work in radio intelligence. Realizing the officers weren't cleared for comint, Biard refused. They wrangled again during the critical days of the Battle of the Coral Sea when Biard felt Fletcher ignored his warnings, based on Japanese fleet radio traffic, that IJN forces were closer to Fletcher than he wanted to believe. See Layton et al., *And I Was There*, pp. 395, 398–401.

49. Lundstrom, *Black Shoe Carrier Admiral*, pp. 267–68.

50. CTF 16 to CINCPAC, 050204; CTF 17 to CINCPAC, 050035.

51. CTF 17 to CINCPAC, 050315; CTF to CINCPAC, 050415; CINCPAC to Midway, 050052; also see Lundstrom, *Black Shoe Carrier Admiral*, p. 270; Cressman et al., *"A Glorious Page In Our History,"* p. 170.

52. Enemy Dispatches, Battle of Midway, SRMN-005, p. 100, NHHC.

53. Parker, *A Priceless Advantge*, p. 63.

54. Layton interview with Potter, pp. 42–43, Layton Papers, NWC.

55. Showers interviews (author's files).

56. Cressman et al., *"A Glorious Page In Our History,"* pp. 136–39.

57. CINCPAC to commanders, 050647.

58. Layton interview with Potter, p. 34, Layton Papers, NWC.

59. CINCPAC to all commanders, COMINCH, 050915.

60. CINCPAC to all commanders, 050915.

61. Parker, *A Priceless Advantage*, p. 63.

62. Lundstrom, *Black Shoe Carrier Admiral*, p. 279.

63. Enemy Dispatches, Battle of Midway, SRMN-005, p. 121, NHHC.

64. Ibid., p. 127.

65. Capt. Thomas H. Dyer oral history, USNI, p. 245.

66. CIS, 6 June 1942.

67. Parker, *A Priceless Advantage*, p. 63.

68. George Gay, *Sole Survivor* (Midway, 1979), pp. 125–27.

69. Paul S. Dull, *A Battle History of the Imperial Japanese Navy* (Naval Institute Press, 1978), pp. 156–59.

70. Of the forty-one TBD Devastators that attacked the *kido butai* from the carriers *Hornet*, *Enterprise*, and *Yorktown*, six survived. Of six TBF Avenger torpedo planes from Midway, three returned to the island.

71. Historians over the years have questioned whether Gay really saw all he claimed to have seen. One school of thought holds that the *kido butai* had moved far to the north of where he ditched, making it difficult if not impossible for him to have witnessed certain events on 4 June. Experts particularly questioned his claim that he watched three carriers blaze into the night, then sink, unlikely since two of them sank just after sundown. Gay's defenders retorted that critics exaggerated the extent to which the *kido butai* moved away from the pilot's position in the water. All sides of the debate have expressed their views on the electronic forum Battle of Midway Roundtable (BOMRT). See Russell, *No Right to Win,* pp. 198–204.

72. Showers interviews (author's files).

73. Letter from Thomas Dyer to David Kahn, 27 December 1963, Dyer Papers. The Dyer-Kahn correspondence also can be found in the Kahn Papers, National Cryptologic Museum, Fort Meade, MD.

74. Rochefort oral history, USNI, p. 105.

75. Morison, *Coral Sea, Midway and Submarine Actions*, p. 181.

76. Parker, *A Priceless Advantage*, p. 63.
77. Forrest C. Pogue, *George C. Marshall, Ordeal and Hope* (Viking Press, 1965), p. 325.
78. Author's interview with John Robert Ferris, author of *Intelligence and Strategy: Selected Essays* (Routledge, Taylor and Francis, 2005). Ferris is a professor of history at the University of Calgary.
79. Theodore F. Cook Jr., "Our Midway Disaster," published in *What If?* (Berkley Books, 1999), pp. 329–30.
80. Potter, *Nimitz*, p. 101.
81. Rochefort oral history, USNI, pp. 234–35, pp. 238–39.
82. Ibid., pp. 265–66.

CHAPTER 28: BY ANY AND ALL MEANS

1. Holmes, *Double-Edged Secrets*, pp. 108–9. The Distinguished Service Medal was the Navy's second highest decoration after the Medal of Honor at the time Rear Admiral Bagley recommended it for Rochefort (see *Bluejackets' Manual*, 1944, 12th ed., p. 9); Congress in August 1942 displaced it as the Navy's number two medal by the Navy Cross.
2. Rochefort oral history, USNI, pp. 251–52.
3. Holmes, *Double-Edged Secrets*, pp. 108–9.
4. Rochefort oral history, USNI, pp. 251–52.
5. Rochefort Papers.
6. Rochefort letters to Jasper Holmes, 16 November 1942, 29 September 1959, Showers Papers.
7. Confidential memorandum, Serial 01655, 8 June 1942, From Commandant, Fourteenth Naval District to Commander in Chief, U.S. Pacific Fleet, subject: "Recommendation for Medal Award for Commander Joseph J. Rochefort, U.S. Navy, Rochefort Papers."
8. Holmes, *Double-Edged Secrets*, p. 115.
9. Rochefort oral history, USNI, p. 259.
10. Holcomb memorandum from Commandant, U.S. Marine Corps, to Commander in Chief, U.S. Fleet, subject: "Establishment of Advanced Joint Intelligence Centers," 24 March 1942, RG 38, Box 137, Folder 5750/301, CNSG-OP-202, NARAII.
11. Frederick D. Parker, "How OP-20-G Got Rid of Joe Rochefort," *Cryptologia*, July 2000, pp. 212–16.
12. Willson memorandum, from Commander in Chief, U.S. Fleet, to Commander in Chief, U.S. Pacific Fleet, subject: "Establishment of Advanced Joint Intelligence Centers," 13 April 1942, signed by Russell Willson, Chief of Staff, RG 38, Box 137, Folder 5750/301, CNSG-OP-202, NARAII.
13. Parker, "How OP-20-G Got Rid of Joe Rochefort," *Cryptologia*; Dingman, *Deciphering the Rising Sun*, pp. 105–8; Holmes, *Double-Edged Secrets*, pp.

111–17; Layton et al., *And I Was There*, pp. 465; McCollum oral history, USNI, pp. 358–72.

14. McCollum oral history, USNI, pp. 358–72. Parker, "How OP-20-G Got Rid of Joe Rochefort," *Cryptologia*, pp. 219–21; Nimitz memorandum, from Commander in Chief, U.S. Pacific Fleet, to Commander in Chief, U.S. Fleet, 28 May 1942, Serial 0116 W, RG 38, Boxes 88 and 118, Inactive Stations.

15. Parker, "How OP-20-G Got Rid of Joe Rochefort," *Cryptologia*. McCollum in his oral history gave a different interpretation of the ONI and Nimitz visions of ICPOA. McCollum maintained it was ONI, not Nimitz, that originally proposed that the ICPOA staff should be attached to the Fourteenth Naval District. See his oral history, p. 362.

16. Memorandum for Vice Adm. F. J. Horne, 20 June 1942, from John Redman, prepared by Joe Wenger, SRH-268, Navy Department Library, NHHC.

17. Parker, "How OP-20-G Got Rid of Joe Rochefort," *Cryptologia*. See also SRMN 015, "FRUPAC History," RG 38, CNSG library, Box 88, 5400/13, NARAII.

18. Parker, "How OP-20-G Got Rid of Joe Rochefort," *Cryptologia*.

19. Memo from Commander in Chief, U.S. Pacific Fleet, to Commander Joseph J. Rochefort, U.S. Navy, subject: "Orders: temporary additional duty," 15 June 1942, signed by L. J. Wiltse, Assistant Chief of Staff, Rochefort Papers.

20. Rochefort oral history, USNI, pp. 253–54.

21. Ibid. Rochefort's actual dispatch hasn't survived. We have only his description of it in his oral history. Whether he used the word "clowns" in his dispatch can be doubted, but his Washington superiors probably got the point.

22. McCollum oral history, USNI, pp. 461–62.

23. All quotes from this document are from the memorandum for Vice Adm. F. J. Horne, 20 June 1942, "Radio Intelligence Organization," from Joseph R. Redman, SRH-268, Navy Department Library, NHHC.

24. Memorandum for Vice Adm. F. J. Horne, 20 June 1942, "Establishment of advanced intelligence centers," from John R. Redman, SRH-268, Navy Department Library, NHHC.

25. All quotes from this document are from the memorandum for the admiral, 22 June 1942, "Commander Rochefort Recommendation for Medal Award," from Russell Willson, chief of staff, Rochefort Papers.

26. Buell, *Master of Sea Power*, pp. 380–83.

27. Memorandum from Commander in Chief, United States Fleet and Chief of Naval Operations, to Secretary of the Navy, via Chief of the Bureau of Naval Personnel, subject: "Recommendation for Medal Award for Commander Joseph J. Rochefort, U.S. Navy," 23 June 1942, Rochefort Papers.

28. OP-20-GY War Diary, 10 December 1941–30 July 1942, RG 38, Box 111, CNSG, 5750/168, NARAII.

29. Memorandum Seventh Endorsement, 4 September 1942, from Vice Chief of Naval Operations, to Commander in Chief, U.S. Fleet, subject: "Recommen-

dation for Medal Award for Commander Joseph J. Rochefort, U.S. Navy," Rochefort File, NCVA Library.

30. Showers interviews (author's files).

31. Rochefort letter to Jasper Holmes, 16 November 1942, Pineau Papers, Box 13, Folder 27, Archives University of Colorado at Boulder Libraries. Richman appeared only as "Chief Yeoman Richman" in the Rochefort-Holmes correspondence. Layton in his USNI oral history confirmed the existence of such an individual, but didn't name him.

32. Layton oral history, USNI, pp. 141–43.

33. Memorandum from the Commandant, Fourteenth Naval District, to Commander Joseph J. Rochefort, 25 June 1942, Rochefort Papers.

34. Rochefort oral history, USNI, p. 256.

35. Holmes, *Double-Edged Secrets*, pp. 111–14.

36. Parker, "How OP-20-G Got Rid of Joe Rochefort," *Cryptologia*, pp. 226–33.

37. Potter, *Nimitz*, pp. 114–15.

38. Layton et al., *And I Was There*, pp. 453–55. The article also appeared in the *Washington Times-Herald* and *New York Daily News*.

39. Safford, "The Inside Story of the Battle of Midway and the Ousting of Commander Rochefort," unsigned (1944), NCVA.

40. Layton et al., *And I Was There*. Layton and coauthors accepted "The Inside Story" at face value, at times quoting from it word for word, without reservations.

41. For an excellent account of the *Chicago Tribune* affair see Prados, *Combined Fleet Decoded*, pp. 342–46.

42. *"The United States Navy v. the* Chicago Tribune," by Larry J. Frank, printed in *The Historian*, February 1980, pp. 284–303.

43. Layton et al., *And I Was There*, pp. 456–55.

44. Capt. Thomas H. Dyer oral history, USNI, p. 270.

CHAPTER 29: REMEDIAL ACTION

1. Parker, "How OP-20-G Got Rid of Joe Rochefort," *Cryptologia*, p. 226.

2. Safford, "The Inside Story of the Battle of Midway and the Ousting of Commander Rochefort," unsigned (1944), NCVA, p. 19. Layton et al., *And I Was There*, pp. 366–67.

3. Joe Redman to Vice Adm. F. J. Horne, 20 June 1942, SRH-268, Navy Department Library, NHHC.

4. Holmes, *Double-Edged Secrets*, pp. 112–15.

5. Layton et al., *And I Was There*, pp. 366–67.

6. Memorandum for Commander John R. Redman, from Joe Wenger, 3 September 1942, subject: "Matters for discussion with Hypo," RG 38, CNSG Library, File 5750/301, Box 137, NARAII.

7. Wright interview with Costello and Pineau, NWC.

8. COM 14 to OPNAV/COMINCH, 291010, April, CINCPAC message file, RG 313, NARAII.

9. Wenger memo to Redman, 3 September 1942, RG 38, CNSG Library, File 5750/301, Box 137, NARAII.

10. If reports of this covert communication arrangement within the Navy's own system had appeared only in Layton et al., *And I Was There* (pp. 466–67); and Safford, "The Inside Story of the Battle of Midway and the Ousting of Commander Rochefort" (p. 20), a reader might reasonably have asked for more confirmation. Additional proof turned up. NSA historian Frederick Parker established independently the existence of the Redman-Wenger private cipher system; see his "How OP-20-G Got Rid of Joe Rochefort," *Cryptologia*, p. 227. Final corroboration of workings of the Redman-Wenger cipher system can be found in Admiral Nimitz's 8 December 1942 letter to Vice Adm. Horne; see RG 38, Box 94, CNSG Library, NARAII.

11. Parker, "How OP-20-G Got Rid of Joe Rochefort," *Cryptologia*.

12. Memorandum for Vice Adm. Horne, from John Redman, subject: "Officer in Charge, Radio Intelligence Unit, Pearl Harbor," 21 October 1942, RG 38, Box 137, CNSG Library, Folder 5750/301, NARAII. Redman itemized his messages to Wenger, beginning with the 20 September one.

13. Parker, "How OP-20-G Got Rid of Joe Rochefort," *Cryptologia*.

14. Memorandum for Vice Adm. Horne from John Redman, subject: "Officer in Charge, Radio Intelligence Unit, Pearl Harbor," 21 October 1942, RG 38, Box 137, CNSG Library, Folder 5750/301, NARAII.

15. Layton et al., *And I Was There*; Safford, "The Inside Story of the Battle of Midway and the Ousting of Commander Rochefort," unsigned (1944), NCVA, p. 20.

16. Memorandum for Vice Adm. Horne, from John Redman, subject: "Officer in Charge, Radio Intelligence Unit, Pearl Harbor," 21 October 1942, RG 38, Box 137, CNSG Library, Folder 5750/301, NARAII; see also Parker, "How OP-20-G Got Rid of Joe Rochefort," *Cryptologia*.

17. Memorandum for Vice Adm. Horne, from John Redman, subject: "Officer in Charge, Radio Intelligence Unit, Pearl Harbor," 21 October 1942, RG 38, Box 137, CNSG Library, Folder 5750/301, NARAII.

18. Memorandum from Commandant, 14th Naval District, to Commander Joseph J. Rochefort, subject: "Orders: temporary additional duty," 22 October 1942, Rochefort Papers.

19. Layton et al., *And I Was There*, pp. 366–67.

20. Safford, "The Inside Story of the Battle of Midway and the Ousting of Commander Rochefort," unsigned (1944), NCVA, p. 19.

21. Layton et al., *And I Was There*, pp. 366–67.

22. Lt. (jg) Forrest Biard and his fellow linguists, arriving at Station Hypo in September 1941, found no guards protecting the door to the basement.

23. Holmes, *Doubled-Edged Secrets*, p. 115.

24. Capt. Thomas H. Dyer oral history, NSA, p. 56.
25. Nimitz letter to Horne, secret and personal, 8 December 1942, RG 38, Box 94, CNSG Library, NARAII.
26. Layton et al., *And I Was There*, pp. 366–67.
27. Nimitz letter to Horne, secret and personal, 8 December 1942, RG 38, Box 94, CNSG Library, NARAII.
28. Safford, "The Inside Story of the Battle of Midway and the Ousting of Commander Rochefort," unsigned (1944), NCVA, pp. 20–21. Safford's account must be regarded as plausible in this instance because he was physically on the scene, able to serve as an eyewitness.
29. Memorandum for Vice Adm. Horne, from John Redman, subject: "Officer in Charge, Radio Intelligence Unit, Pearl Harbor," 21 October 1942, RG 38, Box 137, CNSG Library, Folder 5750/301, NARAII.
30. Rochefort oral history, USNI, pp. 257–58.
31. Dyer, USNI OH, p. 264.
32. Holmes, *Double-Edged Secrets*, pp. 115–16.
33. Memorandum, 15 November 1942, from Commandant, Fourteenth Naval District, to Vice Chief of Naval Operations, subject: "Commander Joseph J. Rochefort, USN: Orders to duty in Office Chief of Naval Operations, forwarding of. 1. Commander Rocherfort departed this area October 25, 1942, under temporary duty orders to the Vice Chief of Naval Operations," Rochefort Papers.
34. Rochefort letter to Jasper Holmes, 16 November 1942. This letter can be found in both the papers of Admiral Showers and the Rochefort file, Pineau Papers, Box 22, Folder 20, Archives, University of Colorado at Boulder Libraries, hereafter Rochefort letter to Jasper Holmes.
35. Rochefort letter to Jasper Holmes.
36. Ibid.
37. Rear Adm. Earl E. Stone, USN (Ret.), oral history, conducted by R. D. Farley, 9 February 1983, Carmel, CA, NSA, pp. 11–12, National Cryptologic Museum, Fort Meade, MD.
38. Undated Wenger memo, signed J. N. W., Safford Papers, from the collection of Robert R. Frey, National Cryptologic Museum Foundation, Fort Meade, MD.
39. Parker, "How OP-20-G Got Rid of Joe Rochefort," *Cryptologia*, p. 222.
40. Rochefort letter to Jasper Holmes.
41. Undated Wenger memo, Robert R. Frey collection, National Cryptologic Museum Foundation.
42. All quotes in this following section are from Rochefort oral history, USNI, pp. 258–62.
43. King letter to Nimitz, 28 October 1942, RG 38, Box 94, CNSG Library, NARAII.
44. Layton et al., *And I Was There*, pp. 468–69; see also Layton's oral history, USNI, p. 141.

45. Nimitz to Train, 5 November 1942, RG 38, Box 94, CNSG Library, NARAII.
46. Horne to Nimitz, 1 December 1942, RG 38, Box 94, CNSG Library, NARAII.
47. Nimitz to Horne, 8 December 1942, RG 38, Box 94, CNSG Library, NARAII.
48. Layton oral history, USNI, p. 141.
49. Hillenkoetter was relieved as officer in charge of ICPOA on 7 September 1943, in a reorganization in which ICPOA was superseded by the Joint Intelligence Center, Pacific Ocean Area, with Army Col. Joseph J. Twitty named officer in charge of what became a substantially enlarged intelligence organization.
50. Holmes, *Double-Edged Secrets*, pp. 115–16.
51. Capt. Thomas H. Dyer oral history, USNI, pp. 265–66.
52. Horne to Nimitz, 1 December 1942, RG 38, Box 94, CNSG Library, NARAII.
53. Undated notes by Joe Wenger, in Safford Papers, National Cryptologic Museum.
54. Rochefort letter to Jasper Holmes, 16 November 1942.
55. Holmes, *Double-Edged Secrets*, pp. 115–16.
56. Capt. Thomas H. Dyer oral history, USNI, pp. 265–66.
57. Author's interview with Ferdinand Johnson.
58. Orders from Chief of Naval Personnel, Rear Adm. Randall Jacobs, to Commander Joseph J. Rochefort, 5 November 1942, Rochefort Papers. Jacobs' letter indicates that Rochefort's orders to San Francisco were cut before he even arrived in Washington and, presumably, were held back pending the outcome of his meetings with his Navy Department superiors.

CHAPTER 30: DRYDOCKED

1. Orders from Commander, Western Sea Frontier, to Commander Joseph J. Rochefort, subject: "Temporary Additional Duty," 9 December 1942, Rochefort Papers.
2. Rochefort oral history, USNI, pp. 267, 263.
3. Holmes, *Double-Edged Secrets*, pp. 130–31. Later in 1943 ICPOA and Hypo would be reorganized again, with ICPOA evolving into the Joint Intelligence Center, Pacific Ocean Area, and the Hypo unit renamed the Fleet Radio Unit, Pacific Ocean Area. Belconnen was renamed Fleet Radio Unit Melbourne. Both ICPOA and Hypo moved out of the navy yard into a two-story wooden structure built for them on the rim of Makalapa Crater, near the Pacific Fleet's new headquarters, with ICPOA occupying part of one floor, Hypo the rest of the building.
4. Holmes letter to Rochefort, 28 May 1943, Rochefort Papers.
5. Rochefort letter to Jasper Holmes, 2 June 1943, Costello Papers, National Museum of the Pacific War, Fredericksburg, TX.
6. Change of Duty, from Chief of Naval Personnel, to Joseph J. Rochefort, 18 May 1943, Pers-3154-MMG, MPR.
7. Obituary of Adm. Ben Moreell, *Washington Post*, 1 August 1978.
8. A. H. Beggs, "Big Brothers to the Fleet," *Buships Journal*, April 1953; R. G.

Skerrett, "They Also Served," *Compressed Air Magazine*, December 1945. See also *Building the Navy's Bases in World War II*, vol. 1, pp. 209–26 (Government Printing Office, Washington, 1947).

9. Capt. Richard D. Hepburn, USN (Ret.), *History of American Naval Dry Docks* (Noesis, 2003), pp. 133–41.

10. Change of Duty, from Chief of Naval Personnel, to Joseph J. Rochefort, 18 May 1943, Pers-3154-MMG, MPR.

11. *Building the Navy's Bases in World War II.*

12. Change of Duty, from Chief of Naval Personnel, to Joseph J. Rochefort, 14 August 1943, MPR.

13. *History of USS ABSD-2*, 1945, Navy Department, NHHC, Archives Branch, Unnamed Ships Collection, Box 1, Folder "ABSD-2." The author is indebted to NHHC's Daniel O. Jones for locating this folder. There remained much to be done. Using living space inside the water-tight hulls of each section, skeleton crews of 35–65 officers and men stayed on board to familiarize themselves with the deck sections and make them ready for sea.

14. *History of USS ABSD-2.*

15. Ibid.

16. *Ship's Data U.S. Naval Vessels*, vol. 3, Auxiliary, District Craft and Unclassified Vessels, Bureau of Ships, Navy Department, 15 April 1945, U.S. Government Printing Office, Navy Department Library, NHHC.

17. Fitness Report, 20 October 1943.

18. *History of USS ABSD-2.*

19. Rochefort oral history, USNI, p. 268.

20. Rochefort testified before the Hart Inquiry on 28 March 1944.

21. Rochefort oral history, USNI, p. 268.

22. Hepburn, *History of American Naval Dry Docks*, pp. 133–41.

23. Rochefort oral history, USNI, p. 268.

24. Change of Orders, from Commanding Officer, to Commander Joseph J. Rochefort, 7 April 1944, Pl-4/00, MPR.

25. Memorandum for Cdr. W. J. Holmes, from Cdr. J. J. Rochefort, 29 May 1944, RG 38, Box 88, Inactive Stations, NARAII.

26. "Mt. Vernon Seminary Taken Over by Navy for Training School," *Washington Post*, 25 November 1942.

27. The two memos written by Joseph and John Redman to Vice Adm. F. J. Horne on 17 June 1942 were not declassified until 6 January 1984, eight years after Rochefort's death.

28. Rochefort memo to Holmes, 29 May 1944, RG 38, Box 88, Inactive Stations, NARAII; see also Capt. Roger Pineau, USNR, "Captain Joseph John Rochefort," in *Men of War*, Stephan Howarth, ed. (St. Martin's Press, 1992), p. 548.

29. Rochefort oral history, USNI, pp. 268–74.

30. Holtwick's remarks are quoted in Laurance Safford's monograph "The Battle of Midway and the Plot to Oust Joe Rochefort." Safford wrote that Holtwick

told him the story after his meeting with Redman; since Holtwick is known to have read the monograph and never denied the quote attributed to him, the story has credibility.

31. J. Frances Wyckoff, "A Wave in OP-20-GZ during World War II," *NCVA Cryptolog*, fall 2006. The author is indebted to John Gustafson of the NCVA for providing this article.

32. Rochefort oral history, USNI, pp. 100, 166, 253, 294.

33. Memorandum for Joe Rochefort, from Joseph R. Redman, Director of Naval Communications, Serial 364520, 23 September 1944, Rochefort Papers.

34. Draft memorandum, from Commander in Chief, U.S. Fleet and Chief of Naval Operations, to Vice Chief of Naval Operations, subject: "Pacific Strategic Intelligence Section, Establishment of," 14 November 1944, SRMN-039, pp. 28–29, Navy Department Library, NHHC (hereafter PSIS, SRMN-039).

35. Rochefort memo to Holmes, 29 May 1944, RG 38, Box 88, Inactive Stations, NARAII.

36. Rochefort oral history, USNI, pp. 270–78.

37. PSIS, SRMN-039, pp. 45–47.

38. Memorandum to F22: "New Tanker Type Produced by Japan," from Capt. J. J. Rochefort, 19 March 1945. Draft memo, Commander in Chief, U.S. Fleet and CNO, to Vice CNO, "Pacific Strategic Intelligence Section," 14 November 1944, SRMN-039, p. 62, Navy Department Library, NHHC.

39. PSIS, SRMN-039, p.54.

40. Pineau, "Captain Joseph John Rochefort," in *Men of War*, Howarth, ed.

41. Ibid.

42. Rochefort oral history, USNI, pp. 278–79.

43. Ibid.

44. Rochefort letter to Edwin T. Layton, 23 February 1945, quoted in Layton's 2 March 1945 letter to Rochefort; and Layton letter to Rochefort, RG 38, Box 94, Folder 5750/38, CNSG Library, NARAII.

45. Rochefort oral history, USNI, pp. 272–73.

46. PSIS, SRMN-039, pp. 80–84.

47. Richard B. Frank, "Ending the Pacific War," in *The Pacific War*, Daniel Marston, ed. (Osprey, 2005), pp. 240–45, 231.

48. Lucie Anne Porterfield, oral history note in *The Interpreter* (15 September 2005), a newsletter of the U.S. Navy Japanese/Oriental Language School Archival Project, University of Colorado Libraries. The author is indebted to David M. Hays of the Boulder Archives for providing this issue.

49. Fitness Report, 29 November 1945, signed by Joseph R. Redman.

50. Memo from Capt. Joseph J. Rochefort, to Chief of Naval Personnel, via Chief of Naval Operations, subject: "Sea Duty, Request, for," 15 September 1945, MPR.

51. Memo from Chief of Naval Personnel, to Capt. Joseph J. Rochefort, via CNO, subject: "Change of Duty," 25 September 1945, MPR.

52. Modification of Orders, from Chief of Naval Personnel, to Capt. Joseph J. Rochefort, Pers-3115-BJS-6C, 28 September 1945, MPR.

53. Cancellation of Orders, from Commandant, Twelfth Naval District, to Capt. Joseph J. Rochefort, ND12–60t-ld, 11 November 1945, MPR.

54. Elerding interviews.

55. Besides the Communications Annex, some offices of the Navy Department had moved into the new Pentagon Building in Arlington, VA. Other offices remained at Main Navy.

56. Change of Duty, from Chief of Naval Personnel, to Capt. Joseph J. Rochefort, Pers-31533-BB-6B, 19 December 1945, MPR.

57. Memorandum to Pers 31528, Pers-325-fac/CWM, subject: "Capt. Joseph J. Rochefort, Ref: Subj officer's request dated 24 June 1946," 27 June 1946, MPR.

58. Memorandum from Chief of Naval Operations, to Capt. Joseph J. Rochefort, subject: "Orders relieving you of all active duty, Op-211E," 9 July 1946, MPR.

59. Layton et al., *And I Was There*, p. 34.

60. Letter, Joseph John Rochefort to J. G. Goodsell, principal, Polytechnic High School, Los Angeles, 25 June 1948, provided the author 12 December 2006, courtesy supervisor Los Angeles Unified School District.

61. Letter, J. G. Goodsell, principal, to Joseph Rochefort, 28 June 1948.

62. Rochefort to Goodsell.

63. Rochefort oral history, USNI, pp. 282–85.

64. Memorandum from Director of Naval Intelligence, to Chief of Naval Operations, subject: "Rochefort, Joseph J., Captain, USN (Ret.), Request for return to active duty," 13 October 1950, Op-323Pl. "It is requested that subject officer be returned to active duty, for the remaining period of fiscal 1951, for assignment on staff of CINCPAC as member of the Evaluation Group," signed by Rear Adm. Carl F. Espe, Assistant Director of Naval Intelligence.

65. Temporary Additional Duty, from Commander in Chief, U.S. Pacific Fleet, to Capt. Joseph J. Rochefort, P16–4/00 Ser P-21, 4 January 1951, MPR.

66. Rochefort oral history, USNI, pp. 282–85.

67. Orders from Chief of Naval Personnel, to Capt. Joseph J. Rochefort, Pers-B1115d-dda-2, 11 April 1951, MPR.

68. Letter from Commodore R. W. Bates, USN, to Capt. Joseph J. Rochefort, 12 February 1951, Bates Papers, Box 4, Folder 3, NWC online services.

69. Rochefort oral history, USNI, pp. 285–90.

70. Letter from R. W. Bates to Rear Adm. C. L. "Casey" Green, Acting Chief of Naval Operations (personnel), Pentagon Building, 21 October 1952, Bates Papers, Box 4, Folder 9, NWC online service.

71. Rochefort oral history, USNI, pp. 285–90.

72. Ibid., pp. 289–90.

73. The Joint Congressional Committee took testimony from Safford for almost three days on this one issue. The JCC interviewed another two dozen witnesses about various aspects of the winds message. The Clarke Investigation

and the Hewitt Inquiry also heard Safford's testimony that General Marshall had ordered the destruction of papers related to the winds message—a contention strongly denied by Marshall.

74. *Report of the Joint Committee on the Investigation of the Pearl Harbor Attack* (Government Printing Office, 1946), p. 486.

75. Safford's group included Cdr. Charles C. Hiles, USN (Ret.); revisionist historian Harry Elmer Barnes; and Percy L. Greaves, a free-market economist, historian and, for a time, financial editor for *United States News*, precursor of the *U.S. News and World Report*. Greaves was the principal writer of the winter 1983–84 special issue of the Institute for Historical Review, "Pearl Harbor: Revisionism Renewed."

76. A. A. Hoehling, *The Week Before Pearl Harbor* (W. W. Norton, 1963), pp. 210–12.

77. Harry Elmer Barnes letter to Percy Greaves, 14 May 1962, Redondo Beach, CA, Hiles Papers, Accession 1448, Box 29, American Heritage Center, University of Wyoming.

78. Ibid.

79. C. C. Hiles letter to Laurance Safford, 11 January 1965, Laurance Frye Safford Collection, Accession 1357, Box 2, American Heritage Center, University of Wyoming.

80. Hiles letter to Greaves, 19 July 1962, Laurance Frye Safford Collection, Accession 1357, Box 2, Hiles Folder, American Heritage Center, University of Wyoming.

81. Elerding interviews.

82. Rochefort oral history, USNI, pp. 294–95.

83. Elerding interviews.

84. Author's interview with Rochefort's granddaughter Karen Rochefort Ballew, 30 July 2006, at Ballew's residence, San Diego, CA (author's files).

85. Rochefort letter to Joe Finnegan, 14 October 1969, Finnegan Papers, courtesy of Joe Finnegan's son, Gregory Finnegan.

86. Ibid.

87. Bryan, "Never a Battle Like Midway," *Saturday Evening Post*, 26 March 1949.

88. Farago, *The Broken Seal*, p. 164.

89. Kahn, *Codebreakers*, p. 7.

90. Lord, *Incredible Victory*, p. 17.

91. Cora Aery would outlive Joe Rochefort by four years; she died at age 100 on 8 January 1980.

92. Torrance *Daily Breeze*, 13 May 1976.

EPILOGUE: THE MEDAL

1. Other high officials present were Director of Naval Intelligence Rear Adm. William O. Studeman, Commander of the Naval Security Command Rear Adm. Don H. McDowell, Presidential Chief of Staff Donald T. Regan, and Presi-

dential Adviser for National Security Affairs Vice Adm. John M. Poindexter (source: Periscope, Association of Former Intelligence Officers, summer 1986).

2. Remarks transcribed from Rochefort family videotape of the White House ceremony, courtesy of Karen Rochefort Ballew, San Diego, CA.

3. Congress in August 1942 placed the Navy Cross just beneath of the Medal of Honor, displacing the Distinguished Service Medal as second in the order of precedence of Navy medals. See Service Medals and Campaign Credits of the U.S. Navy, www.history.navy.mil/medals/navcross.htm. Also available via NHHC website.

4. Prange et al., *Miracle at Midway*, p. 384.

5. Rochefort oral history, USNI, p. 53.

6. Memorandum from Chief of Naval Operations, to Secretary of the Navy, subject: "Awards of Meritorious Service in the case of certain Communications Intelligence Personnel, Recommendations for," 23 October 1945, Serial 0016620, Showers and Costello Papers.

7. Ibid.

8. The Legion of Merit was originally ranked directly below the Distinguished Service Medal in the Navy's pyramid of honor. This was changed by Navy Directive 49 of 28 January 1946, which placed this medal immediately below the Silver Star, thereby making it the Navy's fifth ranking decoration.

9. CNO memo to SECNAV "Awards of Meritorious Service in the case of certain Communications Intelligence Personnel," 23 October 1945, Serial 0016620, Showers and Costello Papers. In addition to the thirty-three officers awarded either a DSM or a Legion of Merit, forty-six officers were awarded the Bronze Star, including Hypo traffic analyst Capt. Thomas Huckins.

10. Rochefort oral history, USNI, pp. 280–81.

11. Ibid., oral history, USNI, pp. 99–100.

12. Capt. Thomas H. Dyer oral history, NSA, p. 96.

13. Rear Adm. Joseph N. Wenger, USN, "The Evolution of the Navy's Cryptologic Organization," pp. 18–19, 1960, SRMN-084, Navy Department Library, NHHC.

14. Capt. Thomas H. Dyer oral history, NSA, p. 70.

15. Capt. Thomas H. Dyer oral history, USNI, pp. 86–87, 251. In Dyer's opinion, "purely as a cryptanalyst or code breaker, I think I was unquestionably his superior. The only person I know of that came close to me was Wright"—a judgment that most cryptologic authorities today accept.

16. Capt. Thomas H. Dyer oral history, NSA, pp. 57–58, 68.

17. Interview with Capt. Thomas H. Dyer, conducted by Griff Criles, 26 August 1976, University Park, MD, NCVA.

18. *Cryptolog*, summer 1984.

19. Holmes letter to Adm. Nimitz, 6 December 1957, Showers Papers.

20. Nimitz letter to Navy Secretary Charles Thomas, 2 January 1958, Showers Papers.

21. Letter from Assistant Navy Secretary Richard Jackson to Nimitz, 1 March 1958, Showers Papers.
22. Showers interviews (author's files).
23. Publisher's note, Layton et al., *And I Was There*, Morrow paperback edition, 1986.
24. Showers interviews (author's files).
25. *New York Times*, 17 November 1985.
26. *Washington Post*, 9 September 1968.
27. Hypo cryptanalyst Tommy Dyer was inducted into NSA's hall of honor in 2002, Rear Adm. Joseph N. Wenger in 2005.
28. Hanyok interview (author's files).
29. Showers interviews.

APPENDIX 2: BREAKING JN-25(b)

1. "The Baker Ciphers," chap. 2 of "The History of GYP-1," RG 38, CNSG Library, Box 116, 5750/202, pp. 1–16.
2. Ibid.
3. Ibid.
4. Ibid.
5. Hugh Denham, "Japanese Naval Codes and Ciphers," in Hinsley and Stripp, *Codebreakers*, pp. 276–79.
6. "The Baker Ciphers," chap. 2 of "The History of GYP-1," RG 38, CNSG Library, Box 116, 5750/202.
7. Capt. Thomas H. Dyer oral history, USNI, p. 256.
8. "The Baker Ciphers," chap. 2 of "The History of GYP-1," RG 38, CNSG Library, Box 116, 5750/202.
9. Geoffrey Sinclair, *JN-25, Operational Code of the Imperial Japanese Navy*, 2004 monograph based on four Navy histories from RG 38: 5750/197 (Box 115); 5750/198 (115); 5750/199 (2 of 3, Box 116); 5750/202 (Box 116), NARAII.
10. "The Baker Ciphers," chap. 2 of "The History of GYP-1," RG 38, CNSG Library, Box 116, 5750/202.

APPENDIX 3: THE MEANING OF MIDWAY

1. Carl Boyd, *Hitler's Japanese Confidant* (University Press of Kansas, 1993), pp. 55–58.
2. Craig L. Symonds, *Decision At Sea* (Oxford University Press, 2005), p. 260.
3. Parshall and Tully, *Shattered Sword*, pp. 51–52; see also Lundstrom, *The First South Pacific Campaign*, pp. 124–25; Willmott, *The Barrier and the Javelin*, p. 82.
4. Parshall and Tully, *Shattered Sword*, pp. 51–52.
5. Ibid.

6. Theodore F. Cook Jr., "Our Midway Disaster," in *What If?* (Berkley Books, 1999), pp. 329–30. See also John J. Stephan, *Hawaii Under the Rising Sun* (University of Hawaii Press, 1984).

7. James R. Schlesinger, "Midway in Retrospect: The Still Under-Appreciated Victory," archived at the Naval Historical and Heritage Center, accessed at http://www.history.navy.mil/faqs/faq81-12.htm.

8. Cook, "Our Midway Disaster," p. 318.

APPENDIX 4: THE *KIDO BUTAI* AND RADIO SILENCE

1. Pearl Harbor Hearings, Appendix to the Combined Fleet Secret Order Number One, Combined Fleet Commander in Chief Isoroku Yamamoto, 1 November 1941, parag. 4. Joint Congressional Hearings, Part 13, Source Document 16, Exhibits of the Committee, p. 713.

2. Prange et al., *At Dawn We Slept*, pp. 373–77.

3. Jacobsen, "Radio Silence and Radio Deception," pp. 695–718. Jacobsen pointed out that revisionists who contend the *kido butai* broke radio silence on its journey to Pearl Harbor err by citing the lesser order that applied to the Combined Fleet as a whole.

4. Ishiguro-Prange interview.

5. Ibid.

6. For documentation of the sea routes taken by the *Uzbekistan* and *Azerbaidzhan* and a dissection of various conspiracy theories, see Marty Bollinger, "Did a Soviet Merchant Ship Encounter the Pearl Harbor Strike Force?" *Naval War College Review*, autumn 2007, pp. 93–110.

7. Parker, *Pearl Harbor Revisited*, Appendix A, pp. 63–65.

8. Ibid.

9. For this information the author is indebted to Ken Kotani, a research fellow in Military Affairs at the National Institute for Defense Studies in Tokyo. In a 4 November 2007 email to the author, Kotani wrote that he relied on the memoir of Motonao Samejima, chief of signal section of the Imperial Japanese Navy in 1941. In his memoir, Samejima described the radio deception used as follows: "The same type of *Akagi*'s radio sender was installed in [a] certain ship, which was ordered to head to the South [the Philippines]."

10. Ibid.

11. Station H daily chronology, RG 38, Box 10, NARAII.

12. Communication Intelligence Summary, 27 November 1941, RG 80, Box 41, NARAII.

Glossary

additives	numbers added to a code group during encipherment, to conceal its identity
Belconnen	cover name for U.S. radio intelligence unit in Melbourne, Australia
Blue Code	Japanese naval code in use from 1931 to 1938
book breaking	recovering the meaning of code groups, sometimes called book building
Cast	(also Station Cast) cover name for U.S. radio intelligence unit on Corregidor, the Philippines (Sixteenth Naval District)
cipher	a system of cryptography in which each letter or number of the original plaintext is interchanged for another letter or number according to a key
code	messages produced by the use of a code book consisting of code groups
code group	a group of letters or numbers designating a letter or number, a phrase, a whole sentence or a complete thought
COM (n)	Commandant, (n)th Naval District, i.e., COM 14 (or any unit of the Fourteenth Naval District)
Combined Fleet	Commanded by Admiral Isoroku Yamamoto from 1939 through 18 April 1943, the Combined Fleet was the main oceangoing component of the Imperial Japanese Navy
comint	communications intelligence; intelligence produced by the study of foreign communications, including the breaking, reading, and evaluating of enciphered communications
COPEK	communications channel used by U.S. Navy intelligence organizations to exchange encrypted technical information
crib	a section of plain text assumed to be in an enciphered or coded message and is used to decode or decipher it

cryptanalyis	the science of compromising the enemy's codes and ciphers
cryptography	the application of methods of concealment to make codes secure
DNC	director, Naval Communications, Washington, D.C.
DNI	director, Naval Intelligence, Washington, D.C.
DSM	Distinguished Service Medal
ECM	electric cipher machine
FECB	Far East Combined Bureau (British unit)
FRUMEL	Fleet Radio Unit Melbourne (1943–45 name for decrypt unit in Australia)
FRUPAC	Fleet Radio Unit Pacific (1943–45 name for decrypt unit in Hawaii)
GY	element of OP-20-G charged with decryption and cryptanalysis
GZ	element of OP-20-G charged with translation and code recovery
Hypo	(also Station Hypo), cover name for U.S. Navy decrypt unit in Hawaii, a.k.a. Combat Intelligence Unit (CIU) and FRUPAC
ICPOA	Intelligence Center Pacific Ocean Area
J-series	designator for Japanese diplomatic cryptographic systems; for example, J-19
JN-	prefix designator for Japanese naval code and cipher systems, e.g., JN-25, the Allied designation for the Imperial Japanese Navy's main operational code
key	a set of instructions, usually a set of letters or numbers, which controls the sequence of encryption or decryption of text
kido butai	Japanese carrier task force (a.k.a. First Air Fleet and Striking Force)
Magic	American code word for intelligence derived from high-level Japanese diplomatic ciphers
Negat	cover name for OP-20-G, radio intelligence unit, Office of the Chief of Naval Operations, Washington, D.C.
ONC	Office of Naval Communications, Washington, D.C.
ONI	Office of Naval Intelligence, Washington, D.C.
OP-20-G	division of Naval Communications charged with naval cryptanalysis and naval cryptography, Washington, D.C.
Purple	American code word for the high-level Japanese diplomatic cipher machine in use after 1940
Red Code	Japanese naval code in use during the 1920s and early 1930s
Red Machine	cover name for the Japanese diplomatic cipher machine in use from 1936 to 1940
RI	radio intelligence, a term referring to direction finding and traffic analysis, often interchangeable with communications intelligence

SIS	Signal Intelligence Service, the name of the Army's code-breaking bureau in the 1930s and early 1940s
stripping	the process of identifying and subtracting the additive sequence used to encipher a message in an enciphered code, thereby laying bare the basic code groups
traffic analysis	the science of obtaining information from an encrypted message by studying its so-called externals, e.g., its header or preamble
Ultra	Allied codename for intelligence derived from high-level Axis communications

Bibliography

National Archives and Records Administration (NARA)
NARAI (DOWNTOWN WASHINGTON) CONTAINS U.S. NAVAL RECORDS
PRIOR TO WORLD WAR II
  Record Group (RG) 24: U.S. Navy ship deck logs; naval records from the Office
    of the Judge Advocate General
  RG 80: Records of U.S. Navy courts of inquiry

NARAII (COLLEGE PARK, MD) CONTAINS U.S. NAVAL RECORDS
COVERING WORLD WAR II
  RG 38, including documents from the Crane Naval Security Group Library
    (CNSG): U.S. naval records from the Office of the Chief of Naval Opera-
    tions; Office of Naval Intelligence (OP-16); Office of Naval Communica-
    tions (OP-20-G)
  RG 80: Department of the Navy records; Pearl Harbor Liaison Office Series
  RG 313: Microfilm file of secret radio messages to and from Commander in
    Chief, U.S. Pacific Fleet (CINCPAC) and Commander in Chief, U.S. Fleet
    (COMINCH), and subsidiary command systems throughout World War
    II, referred to as the CINCPAC message file
  RG 457: Radio intelligence files released by the National Security Agency.
    SRH: Special Research Histories; SRMN: Discrete U.S. Navy records of
    historic cryptologic importance; SRN: Japanese navy message translations;
    SRNM: miscellaneous records; SRNS: Japanese naval radio intelligence
    summaries; SRMD: Discrete joint service records of historic cryptologic
    importance

PACIFIC REGION (SAN BRUNO, CA)
  RG 181: Radio intelligence materials and records of the Commandant, Four-
    teenth Naval District (Honolulu, Territory of Hawaii)

Collections in Associations, Libraries, Museums, Universities

LIBRARY OF CONGRESS (WASHINGTON, D.C.)

Manuscript Division: Papers of Claude Charles Bloch, George Dyer, Ernest J. King

MARINE CORPS HISTORICAL CENTER (QUANTICO, VA)

Oral history taken by Historical Division, U.S. Marine Corps: Alva B. "Red" Lasswell

NATIONAL CRYPTOLOGIC MUSEUM (FORT MEADE, MD)

Midway CINCPAC message

Museum Library: Papers of David Kahn

Oral histories taken by National Security Agency's Center for Cryptologic History: James B. Capron Jr., Edwin T. Layton, Earl Stone, Durwood G. "Tex" Rorie, Wesley A. "Ham" Wright

NATIONAL MUSEUM OF THE PACIFIC WAR (FREDERICKSBURG, TX)

Museum Archive: Papers of John Costello

Oral History Collection: Donald M. "Mac" Showers

NAVAL CRYPTOLOGIC VETERANS ASSOCIATION (PENSACOLA, FL)

NCVA Library: Oral histories of Elmer Dickey, Tommy Dyer, Bankson T. Holcomb, W. J. "Jasper" Holmes, Carl Jensen, Homer Kisner, Albert J. Pelletier, Laurance Safford, Wesley A. "Ham" Wright

NAVAL WAR COLLEGE (NEWPORT, RI)

Naval Historical Collection: Papers of Edwin T. Layton, Manuscript Register Series, No. 69

NAVY HISTORY AND HERITAGE COMMAND (WASHINGTON, D.C., NAVY YARD)

Navy Department Library: Officer biography files; cryptologic documents, including materials from the SRH, SRMA, SRMN and SRMD and SRNS series

Operational Archives: CINCPAC command files, World War II; CINCPAC *Greybook* (War Plans, CINCPAC files, Captain Steele's "Running Estimate and Summary")

UNIVERSITY OF COLORADO AT BOULDER

Norlin Library (Navy Japanese Language School Collection): William J. Hudson Collection and the Papers of Roger Pineau

UNIVERSITY OF HAWAII (HONOLULU)

Special Collections: Reminiscences of Navy personnel and civilians from 7 December 1941

UNIVERSITY OF MARYLAND (COLLEGE PARK)
    Hornbake Library (Archives and Manuscript Department): Papers of Gordon
    W. Prange (Accession No. 2002-78)

UNIVERSITY OF WYOMING (LARAMIE)
    American Heritage Center: Papers of C. C. Hiles (Accession No. 01448), Laur-
    ance Safford (Accession No. 01357), Harry Elmer Barnes (Accession No.
    00745), Clay Blair (Accession No. 08295), Husband E. Kimmel (Acces-
    sion 03800)

U.S. NAVAL INSTITUTE (ANNAPOLIS, MD)
    Archives and Library: Oral histories of Forrest R. "Tex" Biard, George Dyer,
    Tommy Dyer, Edwin T. Layton, Arthur McCollum, John Redman, Joe
    Rochefort

Oral Histories and Presentations

Biard, Capt. Forrest "Tex," USN (Ret.), presentation, 14 June 2000, "Break-
    ing Japanese Codes and Decisive Results Pre–Pearl Harbor Through
    Midway," Admiral Nimitz National Museum of the Pacific War, Fred-
    ericksburg, TX; oral history, 15, 21 August 1984. Interviews with Cdr.
    Etta-Belle Kitchen, USN (Ret.), U.S. Naval Institute, Annapolis, MD.
Capron, CWO James B. Capron Jr., USN (Ret.), 3 October 1984. NSA
    OH25-84. Interview with Robert D. Farley. National Cryptologic Mu-
    seum, Fort Meade, MD.
Dickey, Ens. Elmer, USN (Ret.), 23 September 1983. Naval Security Group inter-
    view with Cdr. I. G. Newman, USN (Ret.). NCVA Library, Pensacola, FL.
Dyer, Vice Adm. George C., USN (Ret.), 13 November 1969. Interview No. 6
    with John T. Mason Jr., Naval Institute oral history, Annapolis, MD.
Dyer, Capt. Thomas H. "Tommy," USN (Ret.), 15, 22, 29 August 1983; 6,
    14, 20 September 1983. Interviews with Paul Stillwell, Naval Institute
    oral history, Annapolis, MD; interview NSA-OH01-82 with Captain
    Dyer, 29 January 1982, by R. D. Farley and H. F. Schorreck, obtained
    by author through NSA FOIA office (DC321), Fort Meade, MD; Naval
    Cryptologic Veterans Association interview with Captain Dyer, 26 August
    1976, by Griff Chiles, NCVA Library, Pensacola, FL.
Holcomb, Brig. Gen. Bankson T., USMC (Ret.), 14 September 1970. Marine
    Corps Historical Center, Quantico, VA; 8 May 1983 oral history with
    NCVA, NCVA Library, Pensacola, FL.
Holmes, Capt. W. J. "Jasper," USN (Ret.), 13 September 1977. NSA interview
    by H. F. Schorreck and Ray Schmidt, NCVA Library, Pensacola, FL.
Jensen, LCDR Carl, USN (Ret.), 23 September 1983. Naval Cryptologic
    Veterans Association interview by LCDR Kent Wells, USN (Ret.), NCVA
    Library, Pensacola, FL.

Kisner, Capt. Homer L., USN (Ret.), 23 September, 1923. Naval Cryptologic Veterans Association interview with Bob Weller, NCVA Library,
Pensacola, FL.

Lasswell, Col. Alva B. "Red," USMC (Ret.), 1968. Interview with Benis M.
Frank. Marine Corps Historical Center, Quantico, VA.

Layton, Rear Adm. Edwin T. "Eddie," USN (Ret.), 30–31 May 1970. Interview with Cdr. Ette-Belle Kitchen, USN (Ret.). Naval Institute oral history, Annapolis, MD., 7–8 February 1983. NSA OH02-83, interview with
Robert D. Farley, National Cryptologic Museum, Fort Meade, MD; May
1983 interviews with John Costello and Capt. Rogert Pineau, USNR
(Ret.), Layton Papers, Naval Historical Collection, Naval War College,
Newport, RI.

McCollum, Rear Adm. Arthur, USN (Ret.), vols. 1 and 2, nineteen interviews
conducted between 8 December 1970 and 8 September 1971 with John
T. Mason Jr., Naval Institute oral history, Annapolis, MD.

Pelletier, Capt. Albert J., USN (Ret.), 18 September 1982. Naval Cryptologic
Veterans Association interview by Bob Weller, USNR (Ret.), NCVA Library, Pensacola, FL; "The Albert J. Pelletier Jr. Story," by Capt. Albert
J. Pelletier, special publication, U.S. Naval Cryptologic Veterans Association, Spring, 2003, www.usncva.org.

Redman, Vice Adm. John R., USN (Ret.), 5, 6 June 1969. Interview with John
T. Mason Jr., Naval Institute oral history, Annapolis, MD.

Rochefort, Capt. Joseph, USN (Ret.), 14 August 1969, 21 September 1969.
Interview with Cdr. Etta-Belle Kitchen, USN (Ret.), Naval Institute oral
history, Annapolis, MD; Walter Lord interview with Capt. Joe Roche-
fort, 14 April 1966, Operational Archives, Navy Historical and Heritage
Command, Washington Navy Yard; Gordon W. Prange interviews with
Capt. Joe Rochefort, 26 August 1964 and undated September 1964,
Archives and Manuscripts Department, University of Maryland, College
Park, MD; Harry Elmer Barnes correspondence regarding interview with
Capt. Joe Rochefort, 14 May 1962, Papers of C. C. Hiles, American
Heritage Center, University of Wyoming, Laramie.

Rorie, Lt. Cdr. Durwood G. "Tex," USN (Ret.), 5 October 1984. NSA OH27-
84. Interview with Robert D. Farley, National Cryptologic Museum, Fort
Meade, MD.

Safford, Capt. Laurance, USN (Ret.), undated interview with Ray Schmidt,
NCVA Library, Pensacola, FL.

Showers, Rear Adm. Donald M. Mac, USN (Ret.), 13 March 1998. Admiral
Nimitz Museum and University of North Texas Oral History Collection,
No. 1257. Interview with Bill Alexander. National Museum of the Pacific
War Library, Fredericksburg, TX.

Stone, Adm. Earl, USN (Ret.), 9 February 1983. NSA OH03-83. Interview
with R. D. Farley, National Cryptologic Museum, Fort Meade, MD.

Wright, Capt. Wesley A. "Ham," USN (Ret.), 24 May 1982. NSA OH11-82. Interview with R. D. Farley and H. F. Schorreck, National Cryptologic Museum, Fort Meade, MD; interview with Captain Wright by David Kahn, 12 December 1963, Kahn Papers, National Cryptologic Museum, Fort Meade, MD; interview with Captain Wright by John Costello and Capt. Roger Pineau USNR (Ret.), 24 May 1984, Layton Papers, Naval Historical Collection, Naval War College, Newport, RI.

Author's Interviews with Station Hypo and Station Cast Veterans

OFFICERS

Rear Adm. Donald Mac Showers, Capt. Forrest R. "Tex" Biard, Lt. Cdr. Wilvan G. Van Campen (phone conversation, hereafter designated by P).

ENLISTED MEN

Radiomen and intercept operators: Maynard Albertson [P], James B. Capron Jr. [P], Andrew J. Cooper, Joseph C. Howard [P], Philip H. Jacobsen, Harold E. "Hal" Joslin, Roy C. Sholes [P], Duane L. Whitlock [P], Rodney Whitten [P].

Yeomen and petty officers: Warren Hopper [P], Walter H. Jester [P], Ferdinand T. Johnson, Michael "Mike" Palchefsky, John Rutledge [P].

Many of the enlisted men cited here retired as officers. Also, radiomen Albertson, Capron, Joslin, Sholes, Whitlock, and Whitten were graduates of the Navy's legendary On the Roof Gang program that between 1928 and 1941 instructed 176 U.S. Navy radio operators in the art of copying radio messages transmitted in Japan's katakana syllabary.

Personal Papers and Memoirs

Papers of Tommy Dyer, provided courtesy of Ann L. Dyer.

Papers of Joseph Finnegan, provided courtesy of Gregory Finnegan, Cambridge, MA.

Memoirs of Col. Alva Bryan Lasswell, undated, provided courtesy of the Lasswell family.

Papers of Joe Rochefort, provided courtesy of Mrs. Janet Rochefort Elerding, Newport Beach, CA; Rochefort service record (medical history and reports on the fitness of officers), National Personnel Records Center, Military Personnel Records, St. Louis, MO.

Papers of Donald M. Mac Showers, in his personal possession.

Dissertations, Theses, and Special Studies

Barde, Robert Elmer. "The Battle of Midway: A Study in Command." Ph.D. diss., University of Maryland, 1971. University Microfilms, Ann Arbor, MI.

Benson, Robert Louis. *A History of U.S. Communications Intelligence during World War II: Policy and Administration.* Fort Meade, MD: NSA Center for Cryptologic History, 1997.

Falke, Lt. Cdr. Brian G., USN. "Battle of Midway: USS *Hornet* (CV-8) Air Group." Research report. Air Command and Staff College, Air University, Maxwell Air Force Base, AL, April 2000.

Hanyok, Robert J., and David P. Mowry. *West Wind Clear: Cryptology and the Winds Message Controversy—A Documentary History*. Fort Meade, MD: NSA's Center for Cryptologic History, 2008.

Kobayashi, Masahiko. "U.S. Failures in the Pearl Harbor Attack: Lessons for Intelligence." Master's thesis, Fletcher School, Tufts University, May 2005.

Naval War College. "Battle of Midway, Including the Aleutian Phase of June 3 to June 14, 1942: Strategic and Tactical Analysis." Produced by Special Projects Section headed by Commodore Richard W. Bates. Newport, RI, 1948.

Parker, Frederick D. *Pearl Harbor Revisited: United States Communications Intelligence 1924–1941*. Center for Cryptologic History, National Security Agency. CH-E32-94-01, 1994.

———. *A Priceless Advantage: U.S. Navy Communications Intelligence and the Battles of Coral Sea, Midway, and the Aleutians*. Center for Cryptologic History, National Security Agency. CH-E32-93-01, 1993.

Piacine, Lt. Col. Robert F., USAF. "Pearl Harbor: Failure of Intelligence?" Research report. Air War College, Air University. Maxwell Air Force Base, AL, 1997.

U.S. Naval Cryptologic Veterans Association. *Echoes of Our Past*. Pensacola, FL: Special Publication, 2008.

———. *A History of Communications Intelligence in the United States with Emphasis on the U.S. Navy*. Pensacola, FL: Special Publication, fall 2004.

———. *Intercept Station "C": From Olongapo through the Evacuation of Corregidor 1929–1942*. Washington, D.C.: Special Publication, fall 2003.

———. *RIP-5: The Underwood Code Machine*. Pensacola, FL.: Special Publication, spring 2006.

U.S. Office of Naval Intelligence. *The Japanese Story of the Battle of Midway*. Washington, D.C.: GPO, 1947. Translation of parts of First Air Fleet, Detailed Battle Report No. 6, Midway Operations, 27 May–9 June 1942, in *ONI Review*, May 1947.

U.S. Strategic Bombing Survey (Pacific). *The Campaigns of the Pacific War*. Naval Analysis Division. Washington, D.C.: GPO, 1946.

Internet Resources

GENERAL

Cryptologic Documents in the Navy Department Library: www.ibiblio.org/hyperwar/USN/oe/Crypto-NavyLibHW.html

Hyperwar: Pacific Theater of Operations: www.ibiblio.org/hyperwar/PTO/Magic/index.html

National Archives, U.S.: www.archives.gov/

National Cryptologic Museum: www.nsa.gov/about/cryptologic_heritage/
museum

Navy History and Heritage Command: www.history.navy.mil/

Naval Institute, U.S.: www.usni.org/

U.S. Naval Cryptologic Veterans Association: www.usncva.org

PEARL HARBOR

Investigation of the Pearl Harbor Attack: www.ibiblio.org/pha/pha/congress/
part_o.html, www.ibiblio.org/pha/pha/invest.html

The Magic Chronology, with documents: www.ibiblio.org/pha/timeline/
Magic.html

Pearl Harbor Revisited: U.S. Navy Communications Intelligence, 1924–1941:
www.history.navy.mil/books/comint/ComInt-4.html

Pearl Harbor Associates: www.ibiblio.org/phha

MIDWAY

Battle of Midway Roundtable: www.midway42.org

The Imperial Japanese Navy: www.combinedfleet.com/kaigun.htm

A Priceless Advantage: U.S. Navy Communications Intelligence and the Battles of Coral Sea, Midway, and the Aleutians: www.century.net/midway/
priceless

The Role of Comint in the Battle of Midway (SRH-230): www.history.navy
.mil/library/srh230.htm

Published Sources

BOOKS

Allen, Thomas B., and Norman Polmar. *Code-Name Downfall: The Secret Plan to Invade Japan—And Why Truman Dropped the Bomb*. New York: Simon and Schuster, 1995.

Aldrich, Robert J. *Intelligence and the War against the Japanese: Britain, America and the Politics of Secret Service*. Cambridge: Cambridge University Press, 2000.

Alvarez, David. *Secret Messages: Codebreaking and American Diplomacy, 1930–1945*. Lawrence: University of Kansas, 2000.

Andrew, Christopher. *For the President's Eyes Only: Secret Intelligence and the American Presidency from Washington to Bush*. New York: First Harper Perennial, 1996.

Bailey, Beth, and David Farber. *The First Strange Place: Race and Sex in World War II Hawaii*. Baltimore: Johns Hopkins University Press, 1992.

Bath, Alan Harris. *Tracking the Axis Enemy: The Triumph of Anglo-American Naval Intelligence*. Lawrence: University of Kansas, 1988.

Beach, Edward L. *Scapegoats: A Defense of Kimmel and Short at Pearl Harbor*. Annapolis, MD: Naval Institute Press, 1995.

———. *The United States Navy: 200 Years*. New York: Henry Holt, 1986.

Bichino, Hugh. *Midway*. London: Cassell, 2001.

Bix, Herbert P. *Hirohito and the Making of Modern Japan*. New York: HarperCollins, 2000.

Blair, Clay, Jr. *Silent Victory*, vol. 1. Philadelphia: J. B. Lippincott, 1975.

Boone, J. V. *A Brief History of Cryptology*. Annapolis, MD: Naval Institute Press, 2005.

Borch, Fred, and Daniel Martinez. *Kimmel, Short, and Pearl Harbor: The Final Report Revealed*. Annapolis, MD: Naval Institute Press, 2005.

Brinkley, David. *Washington Goes to War*. New York: Ballantine Books, 1988.

Budiansky, Stephen. *Battle of Wits*. New York: Free Press, 2000.

Buel, Thomas B. *Master of Sea Power: A Biography of Fleet Admiral Ernest J. King*. Annapolis, MD: Naval Institute Press, 1980.

———. *The Quiet Warrior: A Biography of Raymond A. Spruance*. Boston: Little, Brown, 1974.

Clark, Ronald. *The Man Who Broke Purple: The Life of Colonel William F. Friedman, Who Deciphered the Japanese Code in World War II*. Boston: Little, Brown, 1977.

Clausen, Henry C., and Bruce Lee. *Pearl Harbor: Final Judgment*. Da Capo Press, 1992.

Cohen, Eliot, and John Gooch. *Military Misfortunes: The Anatomy of Failure in War*. New York: Free Press, 1990.

Conroy, Hilary, and Harry Wray. *Pearl Harbor Reexamined: Prologue to the Pacific War*. Honolulu: University of Hawaii Press, 1990.

Costello, John. *The Pacific War*. New York: Rawson, Wade, 1981.

Cowley, Robert, ed. *What If? The World's Foremost Military Historians Imagine What Might Have Been*. New York: Berkley Books, 1999.

Cressman, Robert J., Steve Ewing, Barrett Tillman, Mark Horan, Clark Reynolds, and Stan Cohen. *"A Glorious Page in Our History": The Battle of Midway, 4–6 June 1942*. Missoula, MO: Pictorial Histories, 1990.

DeBrosse, Jim, and Colin Burke. *The Secret in Building 26: The Untold Story of America's Ultra War against U-Boat Enigma Codes*. New York: Random House, 2004.

Dingman, Roger. *Deciphering the Rising Sun: Navy and Marine Corps Codebreakers, Translators, and Interpreters in the Pacific War*. Annapolis, MD: Naval Institute Press, 2009.

Dixon, Norman F. *On the Psychology of Military Incompetence*. New York: Basic Books, 1976.

Dorwart, Jeffrey M. *Conflict of Duty: The U.S. Navy's Intelligence Dilemma*. Annapolis, MD: Naval Institute Press, 1983.

Drea, Edward J. *MacArthur's Ultra: Codebreaking and the War against Japan, 1942–1945*. Lawrence: University of Kansas Press, 1992.

Dull, Paul S. *A Battle History of the Imperial Japanese Navy (1941–1945)*, Annapolis, MD: Naval Institute Press, 1978.

Evans, David C., ed. *The Japanese Navy in World War II: In the Words of Former Japanese Naval Officers*. Annapolis, MD: Naval Institute Press, 1969.

Evans, David C., and Mark R. Peattie. *Kaigun: Strategies, Tactics, and Technology in the Imperial Japanese Navy, 1887–1941*. Annapolis, MD: Naval Institute Press, 1997.

Farago, Ladislas. *The Broken Seal: The Story of "Operation Magic" and the Pearl Harbor Disaster*. London: Arthur Barker, 1967.

Ferris, John Robert. *Intelligence and Strategy: Selected Essays*. New York: Routledge, Taylor and Francis, 2005.

Frank, Richard. *Downfall: The End of the Imperial Japanese Empire*. New York: Random House, 1999.

———. *Guadalcanal*. New York: Random House, 1990.

Friedman, William F. *Elements of Cryptanalysis*. Laguna Hills, CA: Aegean Press, 1976.

Fuchida, Mitsuo, and Masatake Okumiya. *Midway: The Battle That Doomed Japan, the Japanese Navy's Story*. Annapolis, MD: Naval Institute Press, 1955.

Furer, Julius Augustus. *Administration of the Navy Department in World War II*. Washington, D.C.: Naval History Division, Department of the Navy, 1959.

Gannon, Michael. *Pearl Harbor Betrayed: The True Story of a Man and a Nation under Attack*. New York: Henry Holt, 2001.

Gay, George. *Sole Survivor: A Personal Story about the Battle of Midway*. Midway, 1979.

Goldstein, Donald M., and Katherine V. Dillon, eds. *The Pearl Harbor Papers: Inside the Japanese Plans*. Washington, D.C.: Brassey's, 1993.

Halsey, William F., with J. Bryan III. *Admiral Halsey's Story*. Washington, D.C.: Zenger, 1947.

Haufler, Hervie. *Codebreakers' Victory: How the Allied Cryptographers Won World War II*. New York: New American Library, 2003.

Heinrich, Waldo H., Jr. "The Role of the United States Navy," in *Pearl Harbor as History: Japanese-American Relations, 1931–1941*, Dorothy Borg and Shumpei Okamoto with Dale K. A. Finlayson, eds. New York: Columbia University Press, 1973.

———. *Threshold of War: Franklin D. Roosevelt and American Entry into World War II*. New York: Oxford University Press, 1988.

Hepburn, Richard D. *History of American Naval Dry Docks: An Ingredient to a Maritime Power*. Arlington, VA.: Neosis, 2003.

Hinsley, F. H., and Alan Stripp, eds. *Codebreakers: The Inside Story of Bletchley Park*. Oxford: Oxford University Press, 1993.

Hoehling, A. A. *The Week before Pearl Harbor.* New York: W. W. Norton, 1963.

Holmes, Wilber Jasper. *Double-Edged Secrets: U.S. Naval Intelligence Operations in the Pacific during World War II*. Annapolis, MD: Naval Institute Press, 1979.

Holtwick, Jack S., Jr., ed. *History of the Naval Security Group to World War Two* (SRH-355), vols. 1 and 2. Pensacola, FL: U.S. Naval Cryptologic Veterans Association, Special Publication, fall 2006. (These volumes are also available at the Navy Department Library, Washington Navy Yard.)

Horn, Steve. *The Second Attack on Pearl Harbor: Operation K and Other Japanese Attempts to Bomb America in World War II*. Annapolis, MD: Naval Institute Press, 2005.

Howarth, Stephen. *Morning Glory: A History of the Imperial Japanese Navy*. London: Hamish Hamilton, 1983.

———, ed. *Men of War: Great Naval Leaders of World War II*. New York: St. Martin's Press, 1992.

Howeth, L. S., ed. *History of Communications-Electronics in the United States Navy*. Washington, D.C.: Bureau of Ships and Office of Naval History, 1963.

Hoyt, Edwin P. *How They Won the War in the Pacific: Nimitz and His Admirals*. New York: Lyons Press, 2000.

Iriye, Akira. *Pearl Harbor and the Coming of the Pacific War*. Boston: Bedford/St. Martin's, 1999.

Isom, Dallas Woodbury. *Midway Inquest: Why the Japanese Lost the Battle of Midway*. Bloomington: Indiana University Press, 2007.

Janis, Irving L. *Victims of Groupthink: A Psychological Study of Foreign-Policy Decisions and Fiascoes*. Boston: Houghton Mifflin, 1972.

Kahn, David. *The Codebreakers: The Story of Secret Writing*. New York: Scribner, 1967.

———. *The Reader of Gentlemen's Mail: Herbert O. Yardley and the Birth of American Codebreaking*. New Haven: Yale University Press, 2004.

Karsten, Peter. *The Naval Aristocracy: The Golden Age of Annapolis and the Emergence of Modern American Navalism*. New York: Free Press, 1972.

Keegan, John. *Intelligence in War: Knowledge of the Enemy from Napolean to Al-Qaeda*. New York: Knopf, 2003.

Kennedy, David. *Freedom from Fear: The American People in Depression and War, 1929–1945*. New York: Oxford University Press, 1999.

Kernan, Alvin. *The Unknown Battle of Midway: The Destruction of the American Torpedo Squadrons*. New Haven: Yale University Press, 2005.

Kimmel, Husband E. *Admiral Kimmel's Story*. Chicago: Henry Regnery, 1955.

King, Ernest J., and Walter Muir Whitehill. *Fleet Admiral King: A Naval Record*. New York: W. W. Norton, 1952.

Kirkpatrick, Lyman B., Jr., *Captains Without Eyes: Intelligence Failures in World War II*. London: Collier-Macmillan, 1969.

Komatsu, Keiichiro. *Origins of the Pacific War and the Importance of "Magic."* New York: St. Martin's Press, 1999.

Kotani, Ken. *Japanese Intelligence in World War II*, Chiharu Kotani, trans. Oxford: Osprey, 2009.

Lambert, John W., and Norman Polmar. *Defenseless: Command Failure at Pearl Harbor*. St. Paul, MN: MBI, 2003.

Larrabee, Eric. *Commander in Chief: Franklin Delano Roosevelt, His Lieutenants and Their War*. New York: Harper and Row, 1987.

Layton, Edwin T., with John Costello and Roger Pineau. *"And I Was There": Pearl Harbor and Midway—Breaking the Secrets*. New York: William Morrow, 1985.

Leutze, James. *A Different Kind of Victory: A Biography of Admiral Thomas C. Hart*. Annapolis, MD: Naval Institute Press, 1981.

Levite, Ariel. *Intelligence and Strategic Surprises*. New York: Columbia University Press, 1987.

Lewin, Ronald. *The American Magic: Codes, Ciphers and the Defeat of Japan*. New York: Farrar, Straus and Giroux, 1982.

Lord, Walter. *Day of Infamy*. New York: Henry Holt, 1957.

———. *Incredible Victory*. New York: Harper and Row, 1967.

Love, Robert J., Jr., ed. *The Chiefs of Naval Operations*. Annapolis, MD: Naval Institute Press, 1980.

———, ed. *Pearl Harbor Revisited*. New York: St. Martin's, 1995.

Lundstrom, John B. *Black Shoe Carrier Admiral: Frank Jack Fletcher at Coral Sea, Midway, and Guadalcanal*. Annapolis, MD: Naval Institute Press, 2006.

———. *The First South Pacific Campaign: Pacific Fleet Strategy December 1941–June 1942*. Annapolis, MD: Naval Institute Press, 1976.

———. *The First Team: Pacific Naval Air Combat from Pearl Harbor to Midway*. Annapolis, MD: Naval Institute Press, 1984.

Macksey, Kenneth. *Military Errors of World War Two*. New York: Barnes and Noble, 2003.

Marston, Daniel, ed. *The Pacific War Companion: From Pearl Harbor to Hiroshima*. Oxford: Osprey, 2005.

Miller, Edward S. *Bankrupting the Enemy: The U.S. Financial Siege of Japan before Pearl Harbor*. Annapolis, MD: Naval Institute Press, 2007.

———. *War Plan Orange: The U.S. Strategy to Defeat Japan, 1897–1945*. Annapolis, MD: Naval Institute Press, 1991.

Moore, Jeffrey M. *Spies for Nimitz: Joint Military Intelligence in the Pacific War*. Annapolis, MD: Naval Institute Press, 2004.

Morison, Samuel Eliot. *Coral Sea, Midway and Submarine Actions: May 1942–August 1942*. Edison, NJ: Castle Books, 1949.

———. *The Rising Sun in the Pacific: 1931–April 1942*. Edison, NJ: Castle Books, 1948.

Mrazek, Robert J. *A Dawn Like Thunder: The True Story of Torpedo Squadron Eight*. New York: Back Bay Books, 2008.

Okins, Elliott. *To Spy or Not to Spy*. Chula Vista, CA: Pateo, 1985.

Packard, Wyman H. *A Century of U.S. Naval Intelligence*. Washington, D.C.: Department of the Navy, 1996.

Parshall, Jonathan, and Anthony Tully. *Shattered Sword: The Untold Story of the Battle of Midway*. Washington, D.C.: Potomac Books, 2005.

Potter, E. B. *Nimitz*. Annapolis, MD: Naval Institute Press, 1976.

Prados, John. *Combined Fleet Decoded: The Secret History of American Intelligence and the Japanese Navy in World War II*. New York: Random House, 1995.

Prange, Gordon W., with Donald M. Goldstein and Katherine V. Dillon. *At Dawn We Slept: The Untold Story of Pearl Harbor*. New York: McGraw-Hill, 1981.

———. *December 7: The Day the Japanese Attacked Pearl Harbor*. New York: McGraw-Hill, 1988.

———. *Miracle at Midway*. New York: McGraw-Hill, 1982.

———. *Pearl Harbor: The Verdict of History*. New York: McGraw-Hill, 1986.

Reynolds, David. *From Munich to Pearl Harbor: Roosevelt's America and the Origins of the Second World War*. Chicago: Ivan R. Dee, 2001.

Richardson, James O., with George C. Dyer. *On the Treadmill to Pearl Harbor: The Memoirs of Admiral James O. Richardson*. Washington, D.C.: Department of the Navy, 1973.

Rusbridger, James, and Eric Nave. *Betrayal at Pearl Harbor: How Churchill Lured Roosevelt into World War II*. New York: Summit Books, 1991.

Russell, Francis, and the editors of Time-Life Books. *The Secret War*. New York: Time-Life Books, 1981.

Russell, Ronald W. *No Right to Win: A Continuing Dialogue with Veterans of the Battle of Midway*. New York: iUniverse, Inc., 2006.

Schom, Alan. *The Eagle and the Rising Sun: The Japanese-American War, 1941–1943*. New York: W. W. Norton, 2004.

Slackman, Michael. *Target: Pearl Harbor*. Honolulu: University of Hawaii Press and Arizona Memorial Museum Association, 1990.

Smith, Bradley F. *The Ultra-Magic Deals: And the Most Secret Special Relationship, 1940–1946*. Shrewsbury, England: Airlife, 1993.

Smith, Laurence Dwight. *Cryptography: The Science of Secret Writing*. New York: Dover Publications, 1943.

Smith, Michael. *The Emperor's Codes: The Breaking of Japan's Secret Ciphers.* New York: Penguin Books, 2002.

Smith, Peter C. *Midway: Dauntless Victory.* South Yorkshire, England: Pen and Sword Maritime, 2007.

Spector, Ronald H. *At War at Sea: Sailors and Naval Combat in the Twentieth Century.* New York: Viking, 2001.

———. *Eagle Against the Sun: The American War with Japan.* New York: Free Press, 1985.

———. *Listening to the Enemy: Key Documents in the Role of Communications Intelligence in the War with Japan.* Wilmington, DE: Scholarly Resources, 1988.

Steely, Skipper. *Pearl Harbor Countdown: Admiral James O. Richardson.* Gretna, LA: Pelican, 2008.

Stephan, John J. *Hawaii Under the Rising Sun: Japan's Plans for Conquest after Pearl Harbor.* Honolulu: University of Hawaii Press, 1984.

Stillwell, Paul, ed. *Air Raid, Pearl Harbor! Recollections of a Day of Infamy.* Annapolis, MD: Naval Institute Press, 1981.

Stinnett, Robert B. *Day of Deceit: The Truth about FDR and Pearl Harbor.* New York: Free Press, 2000.

Symonds, Craig L. *Decision at Sea: Five Naval Battles That Shaped American History.* Oxford: Oxford University Press, 2005.

Toland, John. *Infamy: Pearl Harbor and Its Aftermath.* New York: Doubleday, 1982.

Ugaki, Matome. *Fading Victory: The Diary of Admiral Matome Ugaki, 1941–1945*, Masataka Chihaya, trans. Pittsburgh: University of Pittsburgh Press, 1991.

U.S. Bureau of Yards and Docks. *Building the Navy's Bases in World War II*, vol. 1. Washington, D.C.: GPO, 1947.

U.S. Congress. *Pearl Harbor Attack: Hearings before the Joint Committee of Investigations of the Pearl Harbor Attack.* 79th Congress, 39 parts. Washington, D.C.: GPO, 1946.

Van der Rhoer, Edward. *Deadly Magic: A Personal Account of Communications Intelligence in World War II in the Pacific.* New York: Charles Scribner's Sons, 1978.

Victor, George. *The Pearl Harbor Myth: Rethinking the Unthinkable.* Washington, D.C.: Potomac Books, 2007.

Wildenberg, Thomas. *All the Factors of Victory: Admiral Joseph Mason Reeves and the Origins of Carrier Airpower.* Washington, D.C.: Brassey's, 2003.

Willmott, H. P. *The Barrier and the Javelin: Japanese and Allied Strategies February to June 1942.* Annapolis, MD: Naval Institute Press, 1983.

———. *Empires in the Balance: Japanese and Allied Strategies to April 1942.* Annapolis, MD: Naval Institute Press, 1982.

Willmott, H. P., with Tohmatsu Haruo and W. Spencer Johnson. *Pearl Harbor*. London: Cassell, 2001.

Winton, John. *Ultra in the Pacific: How Breaking Japanese Codes and Ciphers Affected Naval Operations against Japan, 1941–1945*. London: Leo Cooper, 1993.

Wohlstetter, Roberta. *Pearl Harbor: Warning and Decision*. Stanford: Stanford University Press, 1962.

Wrixon, Fred B. *Codes, Ciphers, and Other Cryptic and Clandestine Communication*. New York: Black Dog and Leventhal, 2005.

Yardley, Herbert O. *The American Black Chamber*. Indianapolis: Bobbs-Merrill, 1931.

Zacharias, Ellis M. *Secret Missions: The Story of an Intelligence Officer*. Annapolis, MD: Naval Institute Press, 2003.

ARTICLES

Budiansky, Stephan. "Too Late for Pearl Harbor." U.S. Naval Institute *Proceedings* (December 1999): 47–51.

Canfield, Eugene. "All Signs Pointed to Pearl Harbor." U.S. Naval Institute *Proceedings* (December 2004): 42–46.

Cope, Harley. "'Climb Mount Niitaka!'" U.S. Naval Institute *Proceedings* (December 1946): 1515–19.

Costello, John E. "Remember Pearl Harbor." U.S. Naval Institute *Proceedings* (September 1983): 53–62.

Fort, Brian. "Midway Is Our Trafalgar." U.S. Naval Institute *Proceedings* (June 2006): 64–66.

Fuchida, Mitsuo, ed. Roger Pineau. "I Led the Air Attack on Pearl Harbor." U.S. Naval Institute *Proceedings* (September 1952): 939–52.

Fukudome, Shigeru. "Hawaii Operations." U.S. Naval Institute *Proceedings* (December 1955): 1315–31.

Gaillard, Lee. "The Great Midway Crapshoot." U.S. Naval Institute *Proceedings* (June 2004): 64–67.

Gannon, Michael. "Reopen the Kimmel Case." U.S. Naval Institute *Proceedings* (December 1994): 51–56.

Hanyok, Robert J. "How the Japanese Did It." *Naval History* (December 2009): 44–50.

———. "'Catching the Fox Unaware': Japanese Radio Denial and Deception and the Attack on Pearl Harbor." *Naval War College Review* (Autumn, 2008): 99–124.

Hechler, Ted, Jr. "Like Swatting Bees in a Telephone Booth." U.S. Naval Institute *Proceedings* (December 1980): 72–74.

Holmes, W. J. "Rendezvous in Reverse." U.S. Naval Institute *Proceedings* (August 1953): 897–99.

Kahn, David. "Did Roosevelt Know?" *New York Review of Books*, 2 November 2000.

———. "An Historical Theory of Intelligence." *Intelligence and National Security* (fall 2001): 79–92.

———. "The Intelligence Failure of Pearl Harbor." *Foreign Affairs* (winter 1991–92): 138–52.

———. "Pearl Harbor and the Inadequacy of Cryptanalysis." *Cryptologica* (October 1991): 273–89.

———. "The Rise of Intelligence." *Foreign Affairs* (September–October 2006): 125–34.

———. "Roosevelt, Magic, and Ultra." *Cryptologia* (October 1992): 289–319.

Kennedy, David M. "Victory at Sea." *Atlantic* (March 1999).

Layton, Edwin T., trans. "America Deciphered Our Code." U.S. Naval Institute *Proceedings* (June 1979): 98–99 (original is attributed to the War History Room of the Japan Defense Agency, Tokyo).

———. "Rendezvous in Reverse." U.S. Naval Institute *Proceedings* (May 1953): 478–85.

Lundstrom, John B. "A Failure of Radio Intelligence: An Episode in the Battle of the Coral Sea." *Cryptologia* (April 1983): 97–118.

Morton, Louis. "The Japanese Decision for War." U.S. Naval Institute *Proceedings* (December 1954): 1325–35.

———. "Pearl Harbor in Perspective: A Bibliographical Survey." U.S. Naval Institute *Proceedings* (April 1955): 461–68.

Parker, Frederick D. "How Op-20-G Got Rid of Joe Rochefort." *Cryptologia* (July 2000): 212–35.

Slonim, Gilven M. "A Flagship View of Command Decisions." U.S. Naval Institute *Proceedings* (April 1958): 80–89.

Stripp, Alan. "Breaking Japanese Codes." *Intelligence and National Security* (October 1987): 135–50.

Ward, Robert E. "The Inside Story of the Pearl Harbor Plan." U.S. Naval Institute *Proceedings* (December 1951): 1271–83.

Wild, Thomas. "How Japan Fortified the Mandated Islands." U.S. Naval Institute *Proceedings* (April 1955): 401–7.

Index

OP-20-G and, 322, 338–40; training
in intelligence analysis, 262–63; transport of intercepts to, 119, 182, 210,
230–31; wartime footing for, 111;
wives' knowledge about work done by
men of, 195–96, 500n39; workload
of, increase in, 226, 302–3

Imperial Japanese Navy (IJN): capabilities of, understanding of through
codebreaking, 41; capital ships,
tonnage limitations on, 30; central
Pacific activities, intelligence on,
237–39, 241–42, 287–88; communication procedures of, 132–34;
fleet organization of, 128–32, 222;
flying boats, 246, 247, 248–52, 253,
305–6, 360–61, 462, 508n37; intelligence on, 200, 201–2, 268, 292–93;
land-based stations, messages from,
136–37, 160–61, 223; Main Body
and Midway battle, 343–44, 354,
365, 367, 377–78, 519n36; messages
from, percentage read, 204, 501n14;
Midway, force strength for, 353, 360,
362–63, 521n18; Midway assault
plans, intelligence on, ix–x, 1–2, 5;
movement of, prediction of, 232;
Naval Air Force, organization of,
131; naval warfare change by, 222;
radio deception and movement of,
134–37, 160–61, 212–13, 221, 223–
24, 265, 267, 467, 504n32, 538n9;
radio deception to trick, 5, 334–36,
338–39, 518nn3–4; ships, messages
from, 160, 164; strategic warfighting
doctrine, 127; successes of, 225; target in Midway Atoll, identification of,
1, 2, 3, 5; war preparation activities
of, intelligence on, 122–23, 128–32,
133–34, 156–57, 225; war scare and
drive into South China Sea, 110–11,
113. See also kido butai (striking force)
Imperial Japanese Navy (IJN) carriers:
central Pacific activities, 237–38,
287; Coral Sea campaign, 269–72,
276, 280, 290–92; Halsey, pursuit
of by, 247; intelligence on, 111, 129,
136, 139, 150–51, 160, 161, 162,

163–64, 170, 179, 180–82, 192–93,
194–95, 196, 223–24, 236, 237,
499n25; kido butai component, 131;
Midway campaign, 300, 359, 362,
373, 375, 377–79, 380; Operation
K, second, 297, 319; Pearl Harbor,
second attack on, 245–46; radio
sender and radio deception, 196,
373, 467, 538n9; Truk location of,
237–38; Wake Island campaign,
208–9; war preparation activities of,
intelligence on, 122, 129
Indianapolis, 77–78, 84, 89, 104
intelligence: assignment to, attitudes toward, 28–29, 42; intelligence officers
in war zones, policy on, 411; need-
to-know principle, 52; responsibilities
of intelligence organizations, 276–77;
sharing of between Army and Navy,
165, 167–70, 193, 337–38, 493n33,
494n47; sharing of between ONI and
ONC, 41–42, 43, 59–60, 87, 477n47;
tell-all memoirs of operatives, 55–56;
value of Rochefort's work in, ix–x, 4–5
Intelligence Center, Pacific Ocean Area
(ICPOA), 385–91, 394–96, 400, 417–
18, 527n15, 531n3

Japan: declaration of war against, 199;
home islands, attack on, 255–56;
honor, concept of in, 56–57, 190; living and economic conditions in, 429;
Manchuria, seizure of by, 56, 126;
merchant vessels, withdrawal of, 133,
487n27; nationalism in, 56; Navy
plans for conflict with, 33, 59, 68–69,
79, 127; negotiations between U.S.
and, 183–84; rational actions from,
expectation of, 69, 79, 125–26, 127,
180, 190; Red Code, 37–41, 475n57;
surrender of, 429–30; tripartite treaty,
184; U.S., relations with, 90, 123,
152–53, 158–59, 160; war between
U.S. and, expectations about, 125–26;
war options of, analysis of, 79. See
also diplomatic codes and traffic,
Japanese; Imperial Japanese Navy (IJN)
Japanese language: escort of Japanese
midshipmen and language knowl-

About the Author

Elliot Carlson traces his interest in the Pacific War to his first job out of college, writing editorials for the *Honolulu Advertiser*. After winning a Congressional Fellowship that took him to Washington, Carlson began a journalistic career during which he worked as a staff writer for the *Wall Street Journal* and *Newsweek*, later freelancing from Belgrade, Yugoslavia. He served as editor of AARP's monthly newspaper until 2004, when he resumed his interest in the Pacific War, beginning work on the Rochefort biography. A graduate of the University of Oregon and Stanford University, Carlson lives with his wife in Silver Spring, Maryland.